LIBRE PENSÉE ET LITTÉRATURE CLANDESTINE
Collection dirigée par Antony McKenna

31

HISTORIA
ECCLESIASTICA

Dans la même collection

(Suite en fin de volume)

Thomas HOBBES

HISTORIA
ECCLESIASTICA

Critical edition, including text, translation,
introduction, commentary and notes,

by Patricia SPRINGBORG,
Patricia STABLEIN and Paul WILSON

PARIS
HONORÉ CHAMPION ÉDITEUR
2008

www.honorechampion.com

Published with the support of
the Free University of Bozen-Bolzano

Diffusion hors France: Éditions Slatkine, Genève

www.slatkine.com

ACKNOWLEDGEMENTS

This edition represents 15 years of labour on my part and the substantial contribution of many generous scholars. First and foremost I wish to acknowledge the work of Dr. Patricia Stablein, who worked on the project from 1995-2000 as co-translator, especially for her important contribution to the apparatus, which is also acknowledged in her inclusion on the title page. This project was funded under the title 'Hobbes and the Poets', by the Australian Research Council Large Grant Scheme, grant no: A79602887, awarded to me for the calendar years of 1996 to 1998, which also paid Dr. Stablein's salary for this period, during which she was a scholar-in-residence first at the Folger Shakespeare Library and then at La Trobe University. I wish to acknowledge my great debt to the ARC, for without their generous support such a complex project would not have been possible. I wish also to acknowledge the work of Paul Wilson, Australian Latin scholar and now diplomat, whom I commissioned to undertake an independent translation of Hobbes's Latin text against which to cross-check our own. We incorporated many of Paul Wilson's succinct formulations, for which I truly thank him.

Expert scholars also contributed substantially. First among them is Donald Russell, Emeritus Professor of Latin Literature in the University of Oxford, who so generously worked on improving the translation and apparatus during my time as a Senior Visiting Research Fellowship at St. John's College, Oxford, from July 2001 to February 2002. Professor Russell, with customary modesty, refused to allow me to acknowledge his specific contributions, which are to be found on every page. This translation will join a shelf-full of books by scholars who have been similarly assisted over the years by an outstanding scholar who is also known for his kindness.

Dr. Noel Malcolm, Fellow of All Souls' College Oxford, offered generous assistance of another kind, putting at our disposal his immense skill at palaeographic analysis. Dr. Malcolm spent several days in the British Library examining the Harley MS and his analysis of the state of the MSS is summarized in Appendix A of the Introduction, 'A Survey of the MSS and Printed Texts'. To the many scholars who offered assistance on points of detail and for reading drafts of the material, I would like to single out for special thanks Quentin Skinner, Regius Professor of History in the University of Cambridge, Mark Goldie, Vice-Master at Churchill College, Cambridge, John Pocock, Professor Emeritus of the John's Hopkins University, Professor Gianni Paganini, Professore Ordinario di Storia della Filosofia, Università del Piemonte Orientale, and the late Professor Karl Schuhmann, renowned Hobbes scholar at Utrecht University. I would like especially to express my gratitude to the Karl Schuhmann for useful discussions and for going through his *Chronique* with me for relevant items before it was published; and I would also like to thank Professor Franck Lessay, who is preparing the French translation of the *Historia Ecclesiastica* for Vrin, for discussions on several occasions, and for supplying me with the Italian translation of the poem. Professor Gianni Paganini, has a deep knowledge of the *Historia Ecclesiastica*, and I am greatly indebted to him for his papers, some of which I read before publication; for his help with the orthography of the 'ὁμοούσιον/'ὁμοιούσιον terminology in Hobbes's texts; and for his comments on this edition. Dr. Jean Dunbabin, Fellow and Tutor in History, St Anne's College, Oxford, whom I consulted on Medieval Logic, and the late Godfrey Tanner, Professor of Classics at the University of Newcastle, Australia, also provided specific information. To the Trustees of the Chatsworth Estate and the Librarian at Chatsworth, Peter Day, as well as to the librarians of the British Library, the Royal Copenhagen Library, the Bodleian, the Cambridge Library and the Folger Shakespeare Library, Washington DC, where I spent days and weeks, manuscript checking, I wish to extend my grateful thanks for their hospitality and assistance.

I am enormously thankful to those institutions which provided me financial support for full-time research for this and other projects in the years 1993-2003: The University of Sydney and The Folger Institute (1993); The Woodrow Wilson International Center for Scholars (1993-4); the Brookings Institution, Washington, D.C., and the John D.

and Catherine T. MacArthur Foundation for a Research and Writing Grant which the Brookings Institution administered (1994-5). To my program directors at these institutions, Lena Orlin at the Folger Institute; Jim Morris, Michael Lacey, and Ann Sheffield, at the Woodrow Wilson Center; John Steinbruner at Brookings and Kate Early at the MacArthur Foundation; I am truly thankful for support and kind understanding as I juggled my projects. I owe the Wissenschaftskolleg zu Berlin a great debt of gratitude for a Fellowship, 2000-2001, which provided such congenial conditions and excellent library facilities, and I am not less indebted to the Swedish Collegium for Advanced Study in the Social Sciences (SCASSS), in Uppsala, 2002-3, where the work continued. I truly thank Björn Wittrock, Barbro Klein, and Göran Therborn, the directors and their excellent staff for their support. I wish in general to thank the University of Sydney, and particularly the Government Department, my home institution for so many years, for the tolerance it has shown for my projects and its generosity in releasing me from teaching duties to pursue them. And I am also indebted to the School of Economics of the Free University of Bolzano for the excellent facilities extended to me in the final stage of this project. I especially thank Dr. Tanja Mayrguendter at the Free University of Bolzano, for doing the Index with such extraordinary efficiency and good will. To the anonymous publisher's reader for a very detailed report, I am truly grateful; and to Professor Antony McKenna, my editor at Honoré Champion, for showing such faith in this project and undertaking to publish the full edition with this venerable French publishing house, I express my warmest thanks, as I do to Marlyse Baumgartner and Olivier Mottaz, who have so patiently shepherded it through the press. I would also like to thank Peter Momtchiloff of Oxford University Press for his co-operation in ensuring that this edition involves no conflict with my legal obligations under the terms of my contract for the Clarendon Hobbes. Last but not least, I thank my sons, Ziyad Latif and George Daniel Springborg, who have shown remarkable enthusiasm for their mother's writing projects.

DEDICATION

This edition is dedicated to those who have helped in its preparation, especially Donald Russell, Noel Malcolm, Gianni Paganini, Antony

McKenna and the late Karl Schuhmann, without whose generous assistance it would never have appeared. It is also dedicated to the institutions which supported it (some without knowing it), and to those scholars whose unstinting support has so greatly contributed to it, J.G.A. Pocock and Quentin Skinner. Humanist scholarship of this sort does not easily find financial support in an academic world increasingly dominated by commercial interests, and so we are especially grateful to these institutions and to Antony McKenna and Honoré Champion for the generous spirit in which they undertook to publish it.

A NOTE ON TEXTS AND SOURCES

The copy text for this edition is the 1688 printed edition of the *Historia ecclesiastica carmine elegiaco concinnata*, ed. with a preface by Thomas Rymer (London, Andrew Crooke, 1688, STC H2237). The decision to use the printed edition, rather than the MSS, as that form of the text that best represents the intentions of the author, is based on the advice of Professor Donald Russell, who found the printed edition superior to the MSS in terms of the Latin; a finding confirmed by an exhaustive analysis of the sources undertaken in consultation with Dr. Noel Malcolm, in which we systematically compared the MSS, (A) BL Harl. 1844 (Hobbes, *Historia ecclesiastica Romana'*), (B), the Grund MS. (Bibliotheca Thotiana VII, 'Thotts Sml. 4o Nr 213. Hobbes, *Historia ecclesiastica Romana'*), and (C) the Vienna MS (Stiftung Fürst Liechtenstein, Vienna MS N-7-6), with the printed edition. In Appendix A: 'A survey of the MSS and printed texts', a summary of our joint findings, based on the evidence suggested by Professor Russell and on Dr. Malcolm's careful palaeographic analysis, is put forward, along with the evidence for this editorial decision.

The Glossary of Proper Names is selective, its reference point being the poem rather than the apparatus, and contains biographical notes and additional material that would have unduly encumbered the text. In terms of sources, where specialist works were not available, we have resorted to the usual range of encyclopaedias and biographical dictionaries listed in the Bibliography under 'Bibliographic Sources, Grammars and Lexicons', especially: *Pauly-Wissowa*,

The Oxford Classical Dictionary, The Encyclopedia of Philosophy, The Oxford Dictionary of the Christian Church, The Dictionary of Seventeenth Century British Philosophers, Encyclopedia Britannica (11th edn), *The Catholic Encyclopedia,* and the *Dictionary of National Biography,* (*DNB*), the *Dictionary of British and American Writers 1660-1800,* the *New Encyclopaedia Britannica,* the *Routledge Encyclopedia of Philosophy* and online data bases and sources such as such as *European Writers, 1000-1900* and *The Columbia Encyclopedia* (on-line version). Unless otherwise acknowledged, the reader can assume that the biographical information is from some combination of these sources.

In our translation of the *Historia Ecclesiastica,* we have used where possible contemporary dictionaries held in the Hardwick Hall Library to which Hobbes had access (as per the Hardwick Hall Booklist in Hobbes's hand, Chatsworth MS E1A). So, for instance, we have preferred Thomas Cooper's invaluable *Thesaurus Linguae Romanae & Britannicae* (London, 1565), listed at shelf mark R.3.1., over other contemporary dictionaries, such as Robert Estienne's *Dictionariolum puerorum, Tribus Linguis.* (London, 1552), and Thomas's *Dictionarium Linguae Latinae et Anglicanae* (Cambridge, 1587), which are not in fact listed. Establishing nuances and alternative readings has involved us in using the usual modern dictionaries, the *Oxford Latin Dictionary, Lewis & Short,* Chambers Murray's *Latin-English Dictionary* (London, 1933), as well as grammars and specialist books, such as *Gildersleeve's Latin Grammar* (New York, 1990), Maltby's *Lexicon of Ancient Latin Etymologies* (Leeds 1991), Latham's *Revised Medieval Latin Word-list* (Oxford, 1965) and Palmer's *The Latin Language* (London, 1968). For late classical and medieval Latin we have often consulted Alexander Souter's, *Glossary of Later Latin to 600 AD.* (Oxford, 1964). For Greek we have used Liddell and Scott's *Greek-English Lexicon* (Oxford, 1996), for Homeric Greek, Autenreith's *Homeric Dictionary* (Oxford, 1873). and for late Greek, Gingrich's *Greek-English Lexicon of the New Testament and Other Early Christian Literature* (Oxford, 1952).

For ecclesiastical sources we have used the *Patrologiae Graecae Cursus Completus (P.G.),* The *Patrologiae Latinae Cursus Completus (P.L.),* Hefele's *Histoire des conciles d'après les documents originaux* (Paris, 1907-49), and Brunet's *Manuel du Libraire,* a translation of his *Biblioteca veterum Patrum et antiquorum scriptorium ecclesiasticorum* (Paris, 1575), as well as a wide range of secondary literature. Full references for all these works are included in the Bibliography. Finally, to check Hobbes MSS I have used Beal's *Index of English Literary Manuscripts* (London, 1987), the Historical Manuscripts Commission, *H.M.C. Thirteenth Report*, Appendix, Part 1 vol. 2: *The Manuscripts of His Grace the Duke of Portland, preserved at Welbeck Abbey*, (London, 1893), and the various editions of *The Short Title Catalogue* and Wing.

The Introduction is by Patricia Springborg, informed by her collaborators, and incorporates material from her previous essays on the *Historia Ecclesiastica*. She would like to express gratitude to her publishers for permission to reprint passages from: 'Thomas Hobbes on Religion', in the *Cambridge Companion to Hobbes*, ed. Tom Sorell (Cambridge, Cambridge University Press, 1996), pp. 346-80; 'Writing to Redundancy: Hobbes and Cluverius', *The Historical Journal*, vol. 39, no. 4 (December 1996), pp. 1075-78; 'Hobbes and Historiography: Why the future, he says, does not Exist', in *Hobbes and History*, ed. G.A.J. Rogers and Tom Sorell, (London, Routledge, 2000), pp. 44-72; 'Classical Translation and Political Surrogacy: English Renaissance Classical Translations and Imitations as Politically Coded Texts', *Finnish Yearbook of Political Thought*, vol. 5 (2001), pp. 11-33; 'Hobbes's Theory of Civil Religion: the *Historia Ecclesiastica*', in *Pluralismo e religione civile*, ed. Gianni Paganini and Edoardo Tortarolo (Milano, Bruno Mondatori), 2003, pp. 61-98; '*Behemoth* and Hobbes's "Science of *Just* and *Unjust*"', *Filozofski vestnik*, special issue on Hobbes's *Behemoth*, ed. Tomaz Mastnak, vol. 24, no. 2 (2003), pp. 267-89; 'The Enlightenment of Thomas Hobbes: Review Essay on Noel Malcolm's, *Aspects of Hobbes'*, *British Journal for the History of Philosophy*, vol. 12, no. 3 (2004), pp. 513-34; 'Hobbes and Epicurean Religion', in *Der Garten und die Moderne: Epikureische Moral und Politik vom Humanismus bis zur Aufklarung*, ed. by Gianni Paganini and Edoardo Tortarolo, (Stuttgart-Bad Cannstatt, Rommann-holzboog Verlag, 2004), pp. 161-214; 'Classical Modeling and the Circulation of Concepts in Early Modern Britain', Contributions, vol. 1, no 2 (2005), pp. 223-44; and 'The Duck/Rabbit Hobbes: Review Essay of Jeffrey Collins, *The Allegiance of Thomas Hobbes'*, *British Journal for the History of Philosophy*, vol. 14, no. 4 (2006), pp. 765-71.

Hist. Eccl. = *Historia Ecclesiastica*

A =   BL Harl. 1844

uA   indicates the uncorrected text subsequently corrected with marginal insertions A which generally correspond to the 1688 printed edition. (Unless otherwise noted the translation follows 1688 and/or corrected A)

B =   Grund MS. Bibliotheca Thotiana VII, 'Thotts Sml. 4o Nr 213. Hobbes, Historia ecclesiastica Romana'.

uB   indicates an error (that has been corrected)

C =   Vienna MS, Stiftung fürst Liechtenstein, Vienna MS N-7-6

mv   material variant, indicating a change of meaning

sc =   silent corrections to the copy text.

~   indicates cases in **A** where marginal rectifications are incomplete due to material lost in the gutter when uA was too closely cropped and too tightly sewn.

All variations in punctuation are noted because, although in neo-Latin punctuation is no sure guide to syntax, variations may be important in establishing the provenance of the work and its relation to the copy text.

Consistent but grammatically insignificant spelling variants are not normally noted:

• e.g. **A B C** use the form Gothus, 1688 uses Gotthus
• **uA and B** use the form religio, 1688 and A and C use relligio
• **A B** use Theologus, C 1688 Theiologus
• **C** does not capitalize most proper names or epithets, e.g.: metus, relligio or its forms, haereticus, rex, regnum, imperium, divinus, deus and its forms, librus sacrus, sanctus, urbs, chorea hypostatica, patrus, ecclesia, doctor, pontifex, etc. (but does consistently capitalize Papa, for Pope, and tends to write forms of DEUS in full caps), simulachra, serpens, sacerdos, daemon, ecclesia patrum, synodus, clerus, praesulis, schola, does not capitalize the proper names Aeneus and Iris, but does capitalize Circe, Album, Roma, but not veneta.

14 ABBREVIATIONS

ABBREVIATIONS: GENERAL

An asterisk indicates a glossary entry

Beh. = *Behemoth, or The Long Parliament*, ed. Ferdinand Tönnies (London, 1889, facsimile edn, ed. Stephen Holmes, Chicago, University of Chicago, 1990). All citations to *Behemoth* (*Beh.*) are to the Tönnies edn unless otherwise noted.

Brunet = Jacques Charles Brunet's *Manuel du Libraire*, a translation of his *Biblioteca veterum Patrum et antiquorum scriptorium ecclesiasticorum* (Paris, 1575)

Cooper = Thomas Cooper, and Sir Thomas Elyot, *Thesaurus Linguae Romanae & Britannicae* (London, 1565).

Dialogue = *Dialogue Concerning the Common Laws*, 1681 (*EW* VI), in Hobbes, *Writings on Common Law and Hereditary Right*, ed. Alan Cromartie and Quentin Skinner (Oxford, Clarendon Press, 2005), unless otherwise indicated.

DNB = *Dictionary of National Biography*, Oxford, Oxford University Press, 1995.

Elyot = Thomas Elyot, *Dictionary* (London, 1538).

EW = *The English Works of Thomas Hobbes*, ed. Sir William Molesworth (London, Bohn, 1839-45), 11 vols.

Hardwick Hall book list = MS E1A, in Hobbes's hand, divided between general authors and a separately listed 'Theological Library', which catalogues the books that Hobbes collected for his patron, William Cavendish, the first Earl of Devonshire, and to which he had access.

Hist. Narr. = *Historical Narration Concerning Heresy*, 1668 (*EW* IV).

Hobbes, *Correspondence* = Hobbes, *The Correspondence*, ed Noel Malcolm, 2 vols, Clarendon Edition of the Works of Hobbes, vols. 6 and 7 (Oxford, Clarendon Press, 1994).

Invernizzi note = annotations made by G. Invernizzi to the Italian edition of *Th. Hobbes, Storia Ecclesiastica, narrata in forma di carme elegiaca*, in *Th. Hobbes, Scritti teologici*, trans, G. Invernizzi and A. Luppoli (Milan, Franco Angeli, 1988).

Lev., Leviathan = *Leviathan* [1651], with selected variants from the Latin edition of 1668 ed. Edwin Curley (Indianapolis, Ind., Hackett Publishing, 1994), referencing chapter (small Roman numerals), section (§), pagination of the Head edition/and of the Curley edition.

LL = Latin *Leviathan*, 1668 (*OL*, III); cited from the variants included in Curley's English *Leviathan* for the main body of the work; and, for the Appendix (*OL*, III, 564-65), from the translation by George Wright, *Interpretation*, vol. 18, 3 (1991), pp. 324-413, unless otherwise indicated.

MacDonald and Hargreaves = Macdonald, Hugh and Mary Hargreaves, *Thomas Hobbes: A Bibliography* (London, The Bibliogaphical Society, 1952).

Molesworth note = annotations made by Molesworth to the *Historia Ecclesiastica* in *OL* V *(q.v.)*

OCD = Oxford Classical Dictionary Oxford, Oxford University Press, 1983.

ODCC = Oxford *Dictionary of the Christian Church*, ed. F.C. Cross (rev. edn, Oxford 1974)

OL = *Thomae Hobbes... Opera Philosophica quae Latine scrisit omnia.* Sir William Molesworth, ed. (London: Bohn, 1839-45), 5 vols.

PG = *Patrologiae Graecae Cursus Completus (P.G.)*, ed. Jacques-Paul Migne (Paris, Garnier, 1880), many reprintings.

PL = *Patrologiae Latinae Cursus Completus (P.L.)*, ed. Jacques-Paul Migne (Paris, Garnier, 1880), many reprintings.

Thomas = Thomas Thomas, *Dictionarium Linguae Latinae et Anglicanae* (Cambridge, 1587)

HOBBES'S HISTORIA ECCLESIASTICA: INTRODUCTION
HOBBES, HISTORY, HERESY AND THE UNIVERSITIES

BY PATRICIA SPRINGBORG

CHAPTER 1

TEXT AND CONTEXT, TEXT AND RECEPTION

1.1 HOBBES'S ECCLESIOLOGY AND THE SEQUENCE OF TEXTS

Thomas Hobbes (1588-1679) is without doubt the greatest English-language encyclopaedic philosopher, the equal to, perhaps even eclipsing, *Descartes, his archrival, in the boldness of his solutions to major philosophical problems. But his reception has been frustrated by peculiar textual difficulties. At the close of 1651, when Hobbes returned from his exile in France, all his political writings hitherto had been published in England and in English. *The Elements of Law, Natural and Politic*, which had circulated in manuscript as early as 1640, was published in two parts as *Humane Nature: or the Fundamental Elements of Policie* in February 1650 and *De Corpore Politico. Of the Elements of Law, Moral and Politic* in May 1650. The English translation of *De cive* made by Charles Cotton under the title *Philosophicall Rudiments concerning Government and Civill Society*, became available by March 1651; while *Leviathan* was first available in May 1651. But from this point on Hobbes's notoriety was such that no further political works could be licensed in England in his lifetime.

The reception and censorship of Hobbes's texts have recently been addressed in a nuanced way.[1] During the Interregnum his works

---

[1] For the reception of Hobbes in Europe, see Noel Malcolm's excellent 'Hobbes and the European Republic of Letters', in *Aspects of Hobbes* (Oxford, Clarendon Press, 2002), pp. 457-546; and Jeffrey Collins's revisionist *Allegiance of Thomas Hobbes* (Oxford, Clarendon Press, 2005). See also Collins, 'Silencing Thomas Hobbes: The Presbyterians and Leviathan', in Patricia Springborg, ed., *The Cambridge Companion to Hobbes's Leviathan* (New York, Cambridge University Press, 2007), pp. 478-500.

were most 'vendible',[1] recopied and pirated by London booksellers gathered around St. Paul's, close to Hobbes's lodgings on Fetter's Lane, the hub of this industry being Crooke's printery, which circulated also his correspondence. But his Interregnum reception contrasts sharply with the censorship regime of the Restoration, which banned *Leviathan*, on account of its ecclesiology, as 'a most poisonous piece of Atheism'[2] and an affront to the Anglican establishment. Perhaps as a consequence of this Restoration legacy of suppression, there was until the mid-nineteenth century no complete collection of Hobbes's works; while the edition produced by Sir William Molesworth in 1839-45 is comprehensive but unreliable.[3] Only now are critical editions of all of his works slowly becoming available in English,[4] the reason, perhaps, why Anglophone Hobbes scholarship is so peculiarly *Leviathan* focused.

The situation on the Continent, where Hobbes's Latin works were first published, was considerably better. *De cive*, published in France in 1642, and the *Opera Philosophica*, published posthumously in 1688 in Amsterdam, a city so hospitable to the international book trade, circulated freely and were reprinted many times. As a consequence a Continental philosophical tradition of Hobbes scholarship grew up centred on the Latin works. The first vernacular translation of the *Historia Ecclesiastica* is, in fact, in Italian, prepared by G. Invernizzi and A. Luppoli and published in 1988 in the anthology

---

[1] Quentin Skinner, 'Hobbes's Theory of Political Obligation', in *Visions of Politics* (3 vols, Cambridge, Cambridge University Press, 2002), vol. 3, pp. 266-7.
[2] *Diary of Thomas Burton*, ed. J.T. Rutt (4 vols, London 1828), I, p. 349, cited in Philip Milton, 'Hobbes, Heresy and Lord Arlington', *History of Political Thought*, vol. 14, 4 (1993), pp. 542-6, at p. 515.
[3] *The English Works of Thomas Hobbes*, ed. Sir William Molesworth (London, Bohn, 11 vols, 1839-45, referred to as *EW*), and the *Opera Philosophica quae Latine scripsit omnia*. Sir William Molesworth, ed. (London, Bohn, 5 vols, 1839-45, referred to as *OL*). So, for instance, important excisions made by Hobbes to the MS of *Behemoth*, indicative of its purposes in targeting the Laudian bishops as catalysts for the Civil War, are missing both in Crooke's posthumous printed edition of 1682 (presumably by prior arrangement with Hobbes) and Molesworth, but carefully reconstructed in the Tönnies 1889 edition. See Collins, *Allegiance*, p. 86 and notes.
[4] See the *Clarendon Edition of the Works of Thomas Hobbes*, which has so far produced 5 volumes, *De cive* in the Latin and the English translation (the latter mistakenly attributed to Hobbes), 2 volumes of the Hobbes *Correspondence*, and the *Dialogue Between a Philosopher and a Student of the Common Laws of England*. Other volumes are in progress. For *Leviathan*, see the excellent 2 volume critical edition by Karl Schuhmann and G.A.J. Rogers (Bristol, Thoemmes, 2003).

Th. Hobbes, Scritti teologici, introduced by the Milanese Hobbes scholar, Arrigo Pacchi. Although it has a minimal critical apparatus and is not based on archival or manuscript research, it is a good translation and has been cross-referenced in our apparatus on important points. A French translation is also in preparation for the Vrin edition of the complete works of Hobbes, some 12 volumes of which have already appeared, and I have had useful discussions with the editor and translator, Franck Lessay.

This then is the first English translation of Hobbes's *Historia Ecclesiastica*, a Latin poem of 2242 lines and 103 pages in the first printed edition published posthumously in London in 1688, and only available in English up until now in the anonymous 1722 paraphrase, *A True Satirical Ecclesiastical History, from Moses to the Time of Luther*.[1] This witty paraphrase departs far from the text and, because it is cast as a burlesque, over-interprets Hobbes's intentions in a way that is misleading, which might in part account for the poem's neglect. For, until the last decade there was not a single book or article out of the many thousands of items in the secondary literature on Hobbes that addressed his Latin poetry or mentioned the *Historia Ecclesiastica* except in passing.[2] The poem, to the extent that it

---

[1] The 1722 paraphrase, *A True Satirical Ecclesiastical History, from Moses to the Time of Luther* (London, E. Curll), which includes a translation of Rymer's preface to the Latin poem, removes the quotation from Ovid's *Metamorphoses*, I.130-1, 'Fraudesque dolique Insidiaeque et vis et amor sceleratus habendi', to the end of the preface, substituting on the title page a quotation from '*Dr.* Brydges *to the Clergy of* Rochester', i.e., James Brydges, the first Duke of Chandos (1674-1744), since 1694 a Fellow of the Royal Society, for whom Handel composed a couple of anthems, but whose immense fortune only barely survived the South Sea Bubble. He was, it seems, addressing the congregation of Francis Atterbury (1662-1732), the high-flying Bishop of Rochester. Although from a later chapter in Church history, probably concerned with Dissenters, it reads:

> The wicked Policy of *blending Creeds, removing* Ancient Landmarks, *disguising* Truth *for Fear it should give Offence, and throwing down* Walls and Bulwarks, *that the Enemy might not take Umbrage at them, have been the means whereby Falsehoods have succeeded from the Beginning.*

[2] For recent essays on the *Historia Ecclesiastica*, see Franck Lessay's 'Hobbes and Sacred History', and Johann P. Sommerville, 'Hobbes, Selden, Erastianism, and the History of the Jews', both published in G. A. J. Rogers and Tom Sorell, eds., *Hobbes and History* (London, Routledge, 2000), pp. 147-59 and 160-187. See also my 'Hobbes, Heresy and the *Historia Ecclesiastica*', *Journal of the History of Ideas*, 55, 4 (1994), 553-571 (Reprinted in *Great Political Thinkers*, ed. John Dunn and Ian Harris, Cheltenham, Elgar, 1997, vol. 3, pp. 599-617), which was, I think, the first article on the poem in English; and Springborg, 'Hobbes's Theory of Civil

has been noticed at all, seems not to be regarded among Hobbes's serious works. But Thomas Rymer's claim in his Preface to the 1688 printed edition that the poem is the summation of a life-time's reflection on church history by an old man who decided finally, like Pythagoras and the oracles of Apollo, to fix his system in verse, tells against such a *prima facie* judgment;[1] as does Hobbes's own valuation of his poem, judging by his efforts to recover the manuscript and get it licensed for printing; while, in the reception of Hobbes's work, his ecclesiology was regarded as of utmost importance. The *Historia Ecclesiastica* fits into the schema of Hobbes's works in a hitherto unexplained way, as a missing link between the English and the Latin *Leviathans*, as we shall see.

The twentieth century revival of Hobbes scholarship has focused on establishing the integrity of *Leviathan* by restoring the last two books on religion, missing from earlier modern editions and largely ignored. Recent revisionist Hobbes scholarship has shown that it was precisely his religious doctrine, and specifically his Erastianism, the doctrine that the state is supreme over the church in ecclesiastical matters,[2] that flouted the religious sensibilities of his contemporaries, causing wave after wave of hostile reaction and concerted efforts at censorship of his heretical views, first from Presbyterians and then by Anglicans at home;[3] and on the Continent, to the point where the Elector of Saxony, Friedrich Augustus, stepped in to prevent the republication of the *Opera Philosophica*.[4] Hobbes's Erastianism followed ineluctably from his philosophical theory, his

---

Religion: the *Historia Ecclesiastica'*, in *Pluralismo e religione civile*, ed. Gianni Paganini and Edoardo Tortarolo (Milano, Bruno Mondadori, 2003), pp. 61-98. For Gianni Paganini's numerous recent essays, which cast important light on the philosophy and theology of the *Historia Ecclesiastica*, see below.

[1] See Thomas Hobbes, *Historia ecclesiastica carmine elegiaco concinnata* (London, Andrew Crooke, 1688), ed. with a preface by *Thomas Rymer 1641?-1713, English literary critic and Historiographer Royal. See the opening to Rymer's preface, lines 1-20.

[2] Erastus, a follower of Zwingli whose real name was Thomas Liebr (1524-83), advocated subordination of the Church to the State on the basis of an analogy between the Christian and Jewish dispensations in which civil rulers had supremacy in matters of religion.

[3] Collins's *Allegiance* provides the first systematic analysis of Hobbes's ecclesiology in terms of the Interregnum and post-Interregnum struggles in which he was engaged.

[4] See Noel Malcolm, 'Hobbes and the European Republic of Letters', p. 461.

Laws of Natural Reason and his defense of sovereignty, and it was the rigorousness of his position that made it so dangerous in the eyes of his contemporaries. The Latin *Leviathan* took back some of the most controversial doctrines and inflammatory rhetoric of the English, especially the doctrine of the Trinity, as well as material that might be read as endorsing Cromwellian Independency; but it added more, in particular the rehearsal of Hobbes's credo of disbelief, his analysis of the Nicene Creed. The *Historia Ecclesiastica* not only anticipates, but more fully develops some of this new material, known to us hitherto – and then not widely known – only from the Appendix to the Latin *Leviathan*, and incidental material in *Behemoth* and the *Dialogue Concerning the Common Laws*, works roughly contemporaneous.

Context problematizes Hobbes's *Ecclesiastical History* in a way that cannot be ignored, demonstration, if such were needed, that we are not justified in excluding a substantial work by a major thinker on *prima facie* grounds. Contextualizing the *Historia Ecclesiastica* casts important light on the circumstances in which Hobbes found himself in the early 1660s, as I try to show, interweaving analysis of the content of the poem and its arguments with an account of institutional structures and practices, fields of reference often neglected in Hobbes studies, even by those claiming to provide a contextual account.[1] This is necessarily a work of synthesis and I am greatly indebted to the work of many different scholars on the contexts for Hobbes's thought, as I gratefully acknowledge. In terms of primary research, the main contribution to Hobbes scholarship presented

---

[1] For a mild critique of the Cambridge contextual historians, to whom I am otherwise greatly indebted, for the thinness of their institutional accounts, see my 'Republicanism, Freedom from Domination and the Cambridge Contextual Historians', *Political Studies,* 49, 5 (2001), 851-76. Jeffrey Collins, in the Introduction to *The Allegiance of Thomas Hobbes*, p. 9, makes a similar claim, that the focus of the Cambridge School on linguistic paradigms, 'often leaves other, more material aspects of a subject's context relatively unexplored'. Wittgenstein cast a long shadow at Cambridge and the Wittgensteinian focus on solipcism and the problem of other minds, I would add, perhaps unduly complicates the problem of the epistemology of the text. See for instance J.G.A. Pocock, 'The Concept of Language', in Anthony Pagden (ed.), *The Languages of Political Theory in Early Modern Europe* (Cambridge, Cambridge University Press, 1987), pp. 19-38; and Quentin Skinner, Interpretation and the Understanding of Speech Acts', in *Visions of Politics*, vol. 1, pp. 117-20.

here is archival work on Hobbes's book list and the range of sources, Patristic, ecclesiological, theological and occult, to which he had access; as well as an introduction to Hobbes's poetics, his literary sources and aesthetics; the latter a vast subject yet to be examined by scholars in any detail.[1]

The *Historia Ecclesiastica* belongs to a stream of Hobbes's works on heresy that gathers force around the years 1666 to 1670. The dating and significance of these works is still for the most part imprecise. It is generally established that Hobbes had heterodox and firmly held theological views; that these predate the storm of controversy which greeted the publication of *Leviathan* in 1651, and were indeed set out against Bramhall as early as 1645; but that Hobbes's desire to vindicate himself against heresy charges in

---

[1] The first systematic work on Hobbes's aesthetics is Horst Bredekamp's *Thomas Hobbes Visuelle Strategien* (Berlin, Akademie Verlag, 1999), reissued as *Thomas Hobbes der Leviathan: Das Urbild des modernen Staates und seine Gegenbilder 1651-2001* (Berlin, Akademie Verlag, 2003). See also Bredekamp, 'Thomas Hobbes's Visual Strategies', in Patricia Springborg, ed., *The Cambridge Companion to Hobbes's Leviathan* (New York, Cambridge University Press, 2007) pp. 29-60. The most exhaustive study of the Leviathan image is still Carl Schmitt's *The Leviathan in the State Theory of Thomas Hobbes* (1938. Trans. George Schwab. Westport, Connecticut, Greenwood Press, 1996). For an essay that addresses Carl Schmitt on the shock value of Leviathan imagery, see Johan Tralau, 'Leviathan, the Best of Myth: Medusa, Dionsos, and the Riddle of Hobbes's Sovereign Monster', in Springborg, ed., *The Cambridge Companion to Hobbes's Leviathan*, pp. 61-80. Quentin Skinner's magisterial *Reason and Rhetoric in the Philosophy of Hobbes*. (Cambridge, Cambridge University Press, 1996) provides a survey of Renaissance humanist culture in which he sees Hobbes situated, necessary to an examination of Hobbes's poetics and aesthetics. Essential to the task are also the techniques of iconographic analysis Skinner employs in his essays, 'Ambrogio Lorenzetti and the portrayal of virtuous government', and 'Ambrogio Lorenzetti on the power and glory of republics', essays 3 and 4 in *Visions of Politics*, vol. 2. See also the pioneering essays by Maurice Goldsmith, 'Picturing Hobbes's Politics: the Illustrations to the *Philosophicall Rudiments*', in *Journal of the Warburg and Courtauld Institutes*, vol. 44 (1981), pp. 231-7; 'Hobbes's Ambiguous Politics', *History of Political Thought*, vol. 11 (1990), pp. 639-73; and on the iconography of Leviathan see Patricia Springborg, 'Hobbes's Biblical Beasts: Leviathan and Behemoth', *Political Theory*, vol. 23, 2 (1995), pp. 353-75. For the Cavendish circle and its literary, dramatic and scientific projects, see the special issue of *The Seventeenth Century*, vol. 9, no. 2 (1994), edited by Timothy Raylor. See also Raylor's pathbreaking '"Pleasure Reconciled to Virtue": William Cavendish, Ben Jonson and the Decorative Scheme of Bolsover Castle', *Renaissance Quarterly*, vol. 52, no. 2 (1999), pp. 402-39, which explores a Cavendish project of iconographic imitation that transports to Bolsover Castle images from the Palazzo del Te in Mantua.

general and the atheism charges that the parliament was prepared to lay against him in 1666-7, in particular, precipitated a flood of works in those years, abating around 1670. Of these works, seven, including the *Historia Ecclesiastica*, deal with heresy: Hobbes's *Response to Bramhall's 'The Catching of Leviathan'*, written in 1666-7; the Chatsworth MS on Heresy of 1673; his *Historical Narration Concerning Heresy* of 1668; *De Haeresi*, his Appendix to the Latin *Leviathan* of the same year; the *Dialogue Concerning the Common Laws*, written after 1668, the section on heresy relating to the Scargill affair of 1669; and *Behemoth*, written between 1668 and 1670. In what follows I will show that the *Historia Ecclesiastica*, although recorded as completed only in 1671, may stand earlier in this series. There are several clues in its preoccupations. So, for instance, Hobbes casts the central power struggle between *Arius and *Alexander as that between an Elder (*Presbyter*) and a Bishop (*Ephor*), playing on terms that are never innocent, Presbyterians and Bishops being his nemeses in the 1650s and 1660s. It demonstrates a level of interest in the early Church Councils and subtleties of scholastic doctrine also to be found in the companion works, the *Historical Narration Concerning Heresy* and the 1668 Appendix to the Latin *Leviathan*, but missing from the English *Leviathan*; while Hobbes's engagement with Bellarmine and seventeenth century scholastics, so evident in the English *Leviathan*, is missing from the *Historia Ecclesiastica* and his other works of the 1660s.[1]

Of the many ways in which the Historia Ecclesiastica differs from its companion pieces, the first is in being cast in verse, for reasons that Thomas Rymer has already speculated upon in his

---

[1] *Hist. Eccl.*, lines 550-5. On *Leviathan* and Bellarmine, see Patricia Springborg, 'Thomas Hobbes and Cardinal Bellarmine: *Leviathan* and the Ghost of the Roman Empire', *History of Political Thought*, vol 16, 4, (1995), pp. 503-31; and Springborg, 'Hobbes on Religion', in *The Cambridge Companion to Hobbes*, ed. Tom Sorrell (Cambridge, Cambridge University Press, 1995) pp. 346-80. For the most recent attempt to date the works of the 1660s, see the Appendix to P. Milton, 'Hobbes, Heresy and Lord Arlington'; and Samuel Mintz, 'Hobbes on the Law of Heresy: A New Manuscript, *Journal of the History of Ideas*, vol. 29, no 3 (1968), pp. 409-14. Alan Cromartie and Quentin Skinner, in *Hobbes, Writings on Common Law and Hereditary Right: A dialogue between a philosopher and a student, of the common Laws of England. Questions relative to Hereditary right*, (Oxford, Clarendon Press, 2005), which reached me late, do not differ significantly from my conclusions based on the same sources.

learned preface. As an epitome of Hobbes's philosophical system, as
Rymer claims, it is also an aid to understanding those works that surround it. The poem is not unambiguous, however. Nor are the purposes for which it was written entirely clear; it has no epistle dedicatory from which we can infer them; and in fact no presentation
copy survives. Two not unrelated possibilities present themselves:
the first being to impress his antiquarian friends both at home and on
the Continent; the second, to deflect criticism of his own heterodoxy
by reframing the whole question of heresy as a way of absolving
himself; a policy that Hobbes was also to adopt in his later works on
heresy. Regarding the first, as Rymer suggests, this poem is a work
of self-promotion, a piece of self-celebration that is also a fitting
humanist final flourish. Latin verse as a form of Renaissance display
on the part of amateur poets put him in the company of humanists
from Erasmus to William Petty, and there were very few members of
the European Republic of Letters who could not turn their hand to it.
In the same decade blind Milton, self-consciously presenting
himself in the tradition of blind *Homer, published the greatest epic
poem of the English language, *Paradise Lost* of 1667, also written
between 1650 and 1660.[1]

   Regarding the second possibility, if most of the items produced
during Hobbes's burst of creative activity in the 1660s are exercises
in public relations to deflect the heresy charges laid against him,[2] the
Historia Ecclesiastica, may predate them, and might even have
started out as something else. *Aubrey reports some 500 lines of it
already in existence by 1659, whereas his first report of a motion by
the bishops against Hobbes dates to 1661, the Bill on Heresy dating
to 1666. Written both in Latin and in verse to filter the audiences that
might receive it, the poem presented two shields against the general
public behind which Hobbes could develop the private exposition of
some of his more controversial views. But the poem seems to
undergo certain transformations, suffering vicissitudes of various
kinds, as we shall see, and the fair copy by Wheldon, Hobbes's

---

[1] See the reference to 'Blind Thamyris and blind Maeonides' in Milton, *Paradise Lost* (1667), book 3, line 35; c.f. *Hist. Eccl.*, line 1699, where Hobbes refers
to Homer as Maeonides. I thank Professor Donald Russell for this note.
   [2] On this burst of creative activity, see Richard Tuck, *Philosophy and Government 1572-1651* (Cambridge, Cambridge University Press, 1993), pp. 340-5.

amanuensis, is only paid for in 1671. In final form the *Historia Ecclesiastica*, can be read, perhaps after some emendation, as a reflection of the tumultuous events of the early 1660s when, with the Restoration, the vilification campaign against Hobbes recommenced in earnest. For Hobbes the best defense was always offense and in this respect the poem does not differ from the other works of the 1660s in presenting an exposition of his Erastian ecclesiology, but this time in light of a history of civil religion that extends into remote Antiquity, for which he mobilizes impressive humanist sources.[1]

The poem's triumphal air might not only be the reflections of a man confident of his reputation, expounding his now celebrated philosophical system in epic verse.[2] If, as the evidence suggests, Hobbes's poem was well under way by 1659, his triumphalism may also reflect his Interregnum success as a public figure under Cromwell, the new Erastian Godly Prince. *Leviathan* was widely received as a legitimation of the Commonwealth on the grounds of the pact between sovereign and citizens for the exchange of protection and obedience that Hobbes laid out. In the very last paragraph of the 'Review and Conclusion' he declared his intentions:[3]

> And thus I have brought to an end my Discourse of Civil and Ecclesiastical Government, occasioned by the disorders of the present time, without application [= obsequiousness], and without other design than to set before men's eyes the mutual relation between protection and obedience, of which the condition of human nature and the laws divine (both natural and positive) require an inviolable observation [= observance].

The burning question raised by the regicide, to whom political obligation is now owed, was one that Hobbes, like Locke, set himself to answer. Both authors framed the question in terms of the conflicting rights and obligations with which citizens, who had taken oaths of allegiance to the Stuart Crown, were faced. And both

---

[1] See Richard Tuck, 'The Civil Religion of Thomas Hobbes', in Nicholas Phillipson and Quentin Skinner, eds, *Political Discourse in Early Modern Europe* (Cambridge, Cambridge University Press, 1993), pp. 120-38; and Patricia Springborg, 'Hobbes's Theory of Civil Religion'.

[2] Rymer's preface to the *Hist. Eccl.*, lines 1-20.

[3] *Lev.*, Review and Conclusion §17, 396/496-7.

answered it in terms of the right to self-preservation and the formula for legitimacy expressed as an exchange of protection for obedience. Both, moreover, saw religion as the cause of civil war and, looking at their own recent history and across the Channel to continental Europe, it is not hard to see why. That both resolved the issue prudentially according to the Erastian formula laid down by the Treaty of Westphalia, *cuius regio eius religio*, is also easy to understand. So, Hobbes's long review of the question 'when it is that men may be said to be conquered, and in what the nature of conquest and the right of the conqueror consisteth',[1] prompted him to declare that:[2]

> for him that hath no obligation to his former sovereign but that of an ordinary subject, it is then when the means of this life is within the guards and garrisons of the enemy; for it is then that he hath no protection from him [his former sovereign], but is protected by the adverse party for his contribution.

With characteristic prescience Hobbes predicted the high risk outcome to an author who condoned regime change:[3]

> And though in the revolution of states there can be no very good constellation for truths of this nature to be born under (as having an angry aspect from the dissolvers of an old government, and seeing but the backs of them that erect a new), yet I cannot think it will be condemned at this time, either by the public judge of doctrine, or by any that desires the continuance of public peace.

That Hobbes wrote *Leviathan* in defense of obligation to the new regime we have plenty of evidence to confirm. At the time of writing, in September 1649, he had reported to *Gassendi, as Cromwell was brutally subduing Ireland: 'I am certainly looking after myself for my return to England, should it happen by any chance'.[4] And when, in the spring of 1651, his long-time associate Edward Hyde, Earl of Clarendon, who was deeply offended by *Leviathan*, sought his reasons for writing it, Hobbes confessed 'The

---

[1] *Lev.*, Review and Conclusion §7, 391/491.
[2] *Lev.*, Review and Conclusion §6, 390-391/490.
[3] *Lev.*, Review and Conclusion §17, 396/497.
[4] Hobbes to Gassendi, 12 Sept. 1649, Hobbes *Correspondence*, ed. Malcolm (Oxford, Clarendon Press, 1994, 2 vols), p. 179; see Collins, *Allegiance,* p. 117.

truth is, I have a mind to go home'.[1] Walter Pope later recalled that
Hobbes 'had returned from Paris in order to print his Leviathan at
London, to curry favour with the Government'.[2] Once home Hobbes
submitted himself to the Cromwellian Council of State, but as White
Kennett reports, he 'was call'd to no question by Oliver, who had no
Reason to dislike his Tenets'.[3] Within weeks, Edward Nicholas was
able to report of Hobbes and the Cromwellians that 'Mr. Hobbes is at
London much caressed, as one that hath by his writings justified the
Reasonableness of their Arms and Actions'.[4] If Lord Saye and Sele
assessed Cromwell's Erastian church settlement as 'fitter for hobbs
and atheists then good men and christians',[5] John Milton referred to
it as an English 'civil papacie', noting that whereas in the 1640s he
had fought 'regal tyranie over the State', now his concern was with
'Erastus and state tyranie over the church'.[6] *Leviathan* was reported
in some quarters as enjoying success as a textbook among university
'Tutors',[7] but was reviled by the Platonist Henry More, who declared
of the Interregnum that 'a plague of Hobbesian Errors at that time
began to spread most dreadfully'.[8] Hobbes himself, by now a familiar London figure, was praised by many and notorious among some
as having a 'supercilious Saturnine Opiniarety'.[9] His flirtation with

---

[1] Reported by Edward Hyde, Lord Clarendon, *A Brief View and Survey of the
Dangerous and Pernicious Errors to Church and State in Mr. Hobbes's Book entitled Leviathan* (Oxford, 1676), p. 8; see Collins, *Allegiance*, p. 119.

[2] Walter Pope, The *Life of the Right Reverend Father in God, Seth, Lord Bishop
of Salisbury* (London, 1697), p. 117; see Collins, *Allegiance*, p. 165.

[3] White Kennett, *A Sermon Preach'd at the Funeral of the Right Noble William
Duke of Devonshire . . . with some Memoirs of the Family of Cavendish* (London,
1708), p. 16; cited by Collins, *Allegiance*, p. 165.

[4] Nicholas to Hatton, 22 Feb. 1652, BL Birch MS 4180, fol. 55; cited by
Collins, *Allegiance*, p. 165.

[5] Lord Saye and Sele to Lord Wharton, 22 Dec. 1657, *English Historical
Review*, vol. 10 (1895), pp. 106-7; cited by Collins, *Allegiance*, p. 165.

[6] John Milton, *A Treatise of Civil Power in Ecclesiastical Causes: shewing that
it is not lawfull for any power on earth to compel in matters of Religion* (London,
1659), pp. 7, 31, 49; cited by Collins, *Allegiance*, p. 171.

[7] Hyde to Barwick, 25 July 1659, in Karl Schuhmann, *Hobbes. Une chronique*
(Paris, Vrin, 1998), p. 167; see Collins, *Allegiance*, p. 163.

[8] Henry More, 'Animadversions on Hobbs, concerning Thoughts of Man', in
Letters on Several Subjects . . . (London, 1694), p. 94; cited by Collins, *Allegiance*,
p. 163.

[9] Hooke to Boyle, 1664, BL Add. MS 6193, fol. 68; cited by Collins, *Allegiance*, p. 163.

the Commonwealth was an action for which under the Restoration
he was endlessly to atone; and these facts provide the background to
the poem.

Announced in the 1688 edition as *A Church History in the form
of an Elegiac Poem*, the *Historia Ecclesiastica*, is in fact a discourse
between two interlocutors, a format it shares in common with three
of its companion pieces, the *Dialogue Concerning the Common
Laws*, the Appendix to the Latin *Leviathan*, and *Behemoth*.[1] In the
Historia Ecclesiastica, unlike the other works, the interlocutors
require some dramatic introduction and engage in some pastoral pre-
liminaries.[2] Set while the Civil War is still in progress, the interlocutors begin by reflecting upon the pleasures of the countryside, compared with the perils of the city in time of war – perhaps a reference
to Hobbes's withdrawal to France in 1640, and later to distant Derbyshire. The topic then turns to the question of the causes of war and
especially civil war, taking up the principal theme of *Behemoth*, that
religion is the primary cause of civil conflict; followed in this case
by an account of religion as a palliative for fear of death; an Epicurean account heavily indebted to Lucretius and Diodorus Siculus,
and reminiscent of chapter 12 of *Leviathan*, as we shall see. He por-
trays primitive Christianity as a simple and pacific religion satisfying the requirements of a civil religion, up to its encounter with, and
contamination by, the Greek philosophical sects and the rise of Arianism.[3] At lines 643-4, Secundus remarks, 'I really want to know
what happened because it is relevant to the history of heresies',
which more or less sums Hobbes's history up. What follows, the
bulk of the poem in fact, concerns doctrinal developments that permitted the rise of clericalism and its most extreme form, the Papal
ascendancy. From the Council of Nicaea, convened by Constantine
in 325, up to thirteenth century,[4] the two interlocutors trace an

---

[1] It is not impossible that the two interlocutors, A and B, in the *Historia Ecclesiastica*, *Behemoth* and the 1668 Appendix, and the Philosopher and the Lawyer in
the *Dialogue*, represent real people; and, in the case of the *Ecclesiastical History*,
Professor Donald Russell has made the inspired guess that they might be Hobbes
and Daniel Scargill. But an answer to these questions would require an exhaustive
content analysis of the texts for which, it seems from a preliminary survey, Hobbes
gives us few real pointers.
[2] *Hist. Eccl.*, to line 70.
[3] *Hist. Eccl.*, lines 70-870.
[4] *Hist. Eccl.*, lines 870-1231.

ineluctable rise in the ideological, political and economic power of the papacy.[1] Only as a coda does Hobbes address papal decline under the challenge to the Church presented by the reformers, from the Valdensians and Lollards, down to *Martin Luther, upon which the poem rather abruptly breaks off.[2]

Franck Lessay in his excellent essay on the *Historia Ecclesiastica*, 'Hobbes and Sacred History', has analyzed the structure of the poem in similar terms.[3] But to speak of structure risks over schematizing a work that is shaped untidily, giving the impression of having been picked up and put down many times, themes breaking off, only to be picked up again later, for no obvious reason – perhaps it had even been reconstructed or at least partially rewritten.[4] The haphazard structure of the poem suggests a work of private reflection, his Epicurean garden, to which Hobbes could retreat under duress. In order to establish the immediate context for the poem, then, it is necessary to look in some detail at the campaigns waged against him, first by the Presbyterians, and then by the Bishops, to which in final form it may be read as some sort of response.

1.2 HOBBES, DEIST, ATHEIST, OR EPICUREAN?

Hobbes's *Rezeptionsgeschichte*, particularly on the Continent, suggests that from the 1642 publication of *De cive*, he was considered a Deist, if not indeed an atheist, and that it was for this reason that he was so avidly read and debated. Edward Nicholas, referring to Hobbes's exile, observed to Edward Hyde, Lord Clarendon, in 1652 that 'Papists (to the shame of the true Protestants) were the chief cause that that grand Atheist was sent away'[5] – the remark may be read as referring to the machinations of the Catholic Erastians, the Blackloists, to whom Hobbes became closely bonded in exile, where

---

[1] *Hist. Eccl.*, lines 1232-2094.
[2] *Hist. Eccl.*, lines 2095 to 2232.
[3] Franck Lessay, 'Hobbes and Sacred History'.
[4] I thank Professor Donald Russell especially for his remarks to this effect.
[5] Nicholas to Hyde, 18 Jan. 1652, BL Birch MS 4180, fol. 54; see Collins, *Allegiance*, p. 146.

they too joined the Louvre faction in Paris centred round Queen
Henrietta Maria.[1] The epistle dedicatory to *De cive*, addressed to the
Marquis of Newcastle, was indeed programmatic, targeting religion
in a striking way:[2]

> From the two principall parts of our nature, Reason and Passion,
> have proceeded two kinds of Learning Mathematicall and Dogmati-
> call. The former is free from controversies and disputes because it
> consisteth in comparing Figures and Motions only; in such things
> Truth and the Interests of men oppose not each other.

Pierre Gassendi, Hobbes's great friend in Paris, in his commendatory
letter on *De cive*, addressed to Samuel Sorbière, and dated April 28,
1646, had already expressed reservations on the religious doctrine,
remarking:[3]

> The book is truly uncommon, and worthy of being handled by all
> who are sensible of higher things; nor (if I set aside those parts
> which pertain to religion, in which we are ἑτερόδοξοι [of different
> beliefs]), do I know of any writer who examines an argument more
> deeply than he.

A possible reading of Gassendi's remark would be to the effect that
both Hobbes and he are heterodox, as Epicureans, and perhaps this
was intimated. As already noted, the 1688 printed edition of the *Historia Ecclesiastica* has a prefatory epigram from Ovid's *Metamorphoses* I.130-1 on the title page, which reads: 'there emerged
deceits and tricks and betrayals and violence and wicked lust of
ownership'. This epigram flags an Epicurean or Deist position
which treats religion as superstition and the source of all our ills and,
although we have no evidence that Hobbes placed it, long passages

---

[1] See Jeffrey Collins, 'Thomas Hobbes and the Blackloist Conspiracy of 1649',
the *Historical Journal*, vol. 45 (2002), pp. 305-331.
[2] *De cive*, BL Harley MS 4235.
[3] MSS : Bibliothèque Nationale, MS Fonds Latin 10352, vol. 2, ff. 78v-79r. The
original Latin version of the letter, which was not published until the 3rd edition of
De cive (sigs. 10-11), is printed immediately following Hobbes's Preface in *De
Cive: the Latin Version*, edited by Howard Warrender (Oxford, Clarendon Edition
of the Works of Thomas Hobbes, vol. 2, 1983), pp. 85-6; the translation quoted here
is printed in *De Cive: the English Version*, edited by Howard Warrender (Oxford,
Clarendon Edition of the Works of Thomas Hobbes, vol. 3, 1983), p. 297.

of the *Historia Ecclesiastica* are Ovidian,[1] while the very trope of fear, on which Hobbes so strongly plays, signals a commitment to Epicureanism, which postulates fear, and in particular fear of death, as a wellspring of religion.[2]

When in the poem Hobbes attributes the power of priests to their exploitation of human vulnerability to superstition, by inventing nightmares and fears of eternal torments, his account is Epicurean. 'If we were not troubled by our suspicions of the phenomena of the sky and about death, fearing that it concerns us, and also by our failure to grasp the limits of pains and desires, we should have no need of natural science', *Epicurus had maintained (Κγριαι Δοχαι, XI). 'A man cannot dispel his fear about the most important matters if he does not know what is the nature of the universe, but suspects the truth of some mythical story. So that without natural science it is not possible to attain our pleasures unalloyed', (Κγριαι Δοχαι, XII).[3] Hobbes had opened *Leviathan* by attributing to 'ignorance of how to distinguish dreams, and other strong fancies, from vision and sense', the rise of 'the greatest part of the religion of the gentiles in time past, that worshipped satyrs, fawns, nymphs, and the like; and now-a-days the opinion that rude people have of fairies, ghosts, and goblins and the power of witches',[4] signaling book 4 'On the Kingdom of Darkness' devoted to this topic. But Virgilian although book 4 of *Leviathan* is, with a panoply of underworld ghosts and

---

[1] *Hist. Eccl.*, lines 109-20 recall Ovid's characterization in *Metamorphoses* I.130-1 of the Iron Age, a period of brutal war; especially line 120, echoing Ovid, *Met.* 1.100: 'mollia per agebant otia'. See also *Lev.*, xlvi, $6, 368/455 ff., which gives an Ovidian/Epicurean account of the rise of the arts, beginning: '*Leisure* is the mother of *philosophy*; and *Commonwealth*, the mother of *peace* and *leisure*'.

[2] In this brief survey I draw on my essay, Springborg, 'Hobbes and Epicurean Religion', in *Der Garten und die Moderne: Epikureische Moral und Politik vom Humanismus bis zur Aufklarung*, ed. by Gianni Paganini and Edoardo Tortarolo (Stuttgart, Rommann-holzboog Verlag 2004), pp. 161-214. Without rehearsing the full extent of Hobbes's Epicureanism here, where it becomes an issue in the text, I do discuss it, as in the notes to lines 80-100, 270-300, 1410-30, 1644-60, 2130-40, etc.

[3] See Cyril Bailey, *Epicurus: the Extant Remains* (Oxford, Clarendon Press, 1926), p. 97. See also *Lev.*, xii, §§5-24, on the origins of religion in native curiosity and fear.

[4] Hobbes *Lev.*, ii, §8, 8/11. (c.f., Lat. Appendix, iii, 3-4; *OL* III, 560).

spirits, the poem is more ostentatiously a display of his classical knowledge, and more deliberately Epicurean.

Following Lucretius, *De Rerum Natura* 1.102-3, 1.130-5, Hobbes claims early in *Leviathan* that the power of priests was deliberately based on the exploitation of superstition.[1] Lucretius had therefore proclaimed as his task 'to loose the mind from the close knots of superstition', connecting *religio* with *religare*, 'to bind fast', a text that strikingly summarizes Hobbes's purpose, emphasizing the therapeutic function of science and natural philosophy as a palliative for fear.[2] Untying the knots of fear and superstition is precisely the idiom that Hobbes uses in the famous chapter 47, §19, of *Leviathan*, where he epitomizes the history of religion, later to be more fully developed in the poem, as a 'web of power' spun by priests and presbyters, that must be unraveled as it was constructed, the knots on people's liberty untied as they were tied. 'The web begins at the first elements of power, which are wisdom, humility, sincerity, and other virtues of the Apostles, whom the people, [having been] converted, obeyed out of reverence, not obligation'. Hobbes notes, 'Their consciences were free, and their words and actions subject to none but the civil power':[3]

> Afterwards, the presbyters (as the flocks of Christ increased), assembling to consider what they should teach, and thereby obliging themselves to teach nothing against the decrees of their assemblies, made it to be thought the people were thereby obliged to follow their doctrine, and when they refused, refused to keep them company (that was then called excommunication) . . . . And this was the first knot upon their liberty. And the number of presbyters increasing, the presbyters of the chief city or province got themselves an authority

---

[1] Hobbes *Lev.*, ii, §8, 8/11, following Lucretius, *De Rerum Natura* 1.102-3, 1.130-5. Hobbes went on to claim:
> And for fairies, and walking ghosts, the opinion of them has I think been on purpose, either taught, or not confuted to keep in credit the use of exorcisme, of crosses, of holy water, and other such inventions of ghostly men.

[2] Lucretius, *De Rerum Natura* 1.932, tr. W. H. D. Rouse, commentary by M. F. Smith, Loeb edn. (London, Heinemann, 1975), p. 78. On Epicurean philosophy as a palliative for fear of death, see Jean Salem, *Tel un dieu parmi les hommes: l'ethique d'Epicurus* (Paris, Vrin, 1989); and M. Guyau, *La Morale d'Épicure et ses Rapports avec les Doctrines Contemporaines* (Paris, Ancienne Librairie Germer Baillière, 1886).

[3] *Lev.*, xlvii, §19, 385/481.

over the parochial presbyters, and appropriated to themselves the names of bishops. And this was a second knot on Christian liberty. Lastly the Bishop of Rome, in regard of the imperial city, took upon him an authority (partly by the wills of the emperors themselves and by the title of Pontifex Maximus, and at last, when the emperors were grown weak, by the privileges of St Peter) over all other bishops of the empire. Which was the third and last knot, and the whole synthesis and construction of the pontifical power.

It is an account that Hobbes retained in the Latin *Leviathan*, where much of his invective against the Presbyterians is dropped, but in modified form, for there blame for departure from the simple religion of primitive Christianity is laid at the door of philosophers and bishops more generally.[1] Faithful to the principle that 'as the invention of men are woven, so also are they ravelled out; the way is the same, but the order is inverted',[2] shows in the English *Leviathan* how the first knot was untied: 'First the power of the Popes was dissolved totally by Queen Elisabeth', who made the bishops accountable to her.[3]

Afterwards the Presbyterians lately in England obtained the putting down of the episcopacy. And so was the second knot dissolved. And almost at the same time the power was taken also from the Presbyterians. And so, we are reduced to the independency of the primitive Christians, to follow Paul, or Cephas, or Apollos, every man as he liketh best.

Independency returned men to the religious simplicity of early Christianity, where doctrinal belief did not stand in the way of 'Render[ing] unto Caesar the things that are Caesars and unto God

---

[1] See §122 of the 1668 Appendix to the *LL* (Wright's translation, my emphases):

[122]B. It was the pride of the philosophers of whom I have just spoken, ignorant men living at the time of the apostles, who had learned to dispute more subtly and orate more powerfully than other men. These men, in entering upon the way of Christ, were almost *of necessity chosen as bishops and elders* to defend and propagate the faith, and, as much as in them lay, even as Christian converts, they held fast to the teachings of their pagan masters. Accordingly, they sought to interpret the Holy Scriptures so as to preserve at once their own philosophy and the Christian faith, as though they were the same thing.

[2] *Ibid.*

[3] *Lev.*, xlvii, §20, 385/481-2.

the things that are God's', Hobbes implied.[1] His emphasis on Presbyters and Presbyterians as religious power-mongers, who tied knots
in the liberty of subjects equal to those of the papacy, is not incidental, as we shall see. The theme of unraveling the history of the church
in the Epicurean manner is resumed in the *Historia Ecclesiastica*.
Noting, perhaps with allusion to the spurious *Donation of Constantine*, how 'the power of the Pope (power that was stolen), secretly
increased, until he was more powerful than the Roman Emperor',[2]
Primus prompts Secundus to ask: 'How from being a poor pseudo-
philosopher did he succeed in becoming second to God on earth?'[3]
To which Primus replies, 'The delicate thread of history I am now
unraveling will reveal an answer concisely and clearly enough'.[4]

Opinion differs on Hobbes's response to the consequences of his
own boldness. Charles II characterized him as 'the beare', declaring
'"Here comes the beare to be bayted"'.[5] But the Whig Bishop White
Kennett describes him as a fearful old man, painting an altogether
unattractive picture of him in his last days, afraid to be alone in the
house, transported like a baby with his patron, Devonshire, from
house to house.[6] Hobbes's fearfulness, so exploited by Kennett, has
a surface explanation in his anxiety that even if he were not burned
for heresy, his works might be. But fear of death, as we have noted,
is also a marker for Epicureanism. At least twelve sermons were
preached in Hobbes's lifetime, or shortly thereafter, by prominent
clergymen, all of whom convicted him of Epicureanism.[7] And while
such a chorus might be dismissed with the observation that 'Epicurean' was a smear equal to the charge of atheism, in fact, this is to
underestimate the sophistication with which Epicureanism – and for
that matter atheism – was understood at the time.

---

[1] Mark 12:17.
[2] *Hist. Eccl.*, lines 871-2.
[3] *Hist. Eccl.*, lines 881-2.
[4] *Hist. Eccl.*, lines 883-4.
[5] As reported by Aubrey, *Brief Lives*, 1898, 1.335, who notes that Charles II
came to have a good opinion of Hobbes.
[6] White Kennett, White, *A Sermon Preach'd at the Funeral of the Right Noble
William Duke of Devonshire . . . with some Memoirs of the Family of Cavendish*
(London, 1708), p. 113.
[7] See Charles T. Harrison, 'Bacon, Hobbes, Boyle, and the Ancient Atomists', in
Harvard Studies and Notes in Philology and Literature, 15 (1933), pp. 191-218. Harrison, who takes seriously the charge that Hobbes was an Epicurean, lists the preachers.

Epicureanism, like its Hellenistic kin, Stoicism and Scepticism, was a house with many mansions. It is impossible to capture in the term 'Epicurean' the rich range of theories that coalesced in this particular tradition, much less the wide range of thinkers who participated in it. To say that Hobbes was an Epicurean at all is to make a claim that must be hedged about with caveats. He could not be an Epicurean *tout court*. We are necessarily speaking of the sort of synthesis involved in the *Rezeptzionsgeschichte* of any philosopher long dead. This does not rule out, however, the self-conscious adoption of antique philosophical positions; and those who adopted Epicurean postures in the later ages had many reasons for doing so. Hobbes was thus an Epicurean many times removed, and this is no small point. For Hobbes, like most of us, was primarily engaged by contemporary debates and, while positions in these debates were often flagged by the banners of the classical philosophical schools, these were often surrogates for new or modified theories that the world was not yet ready to accept in their own right. The revival of ancient philosophical positions was a way of characterizing a certain set of doctrines or, as in Hobbes's case of characterizing a mind-set that was anti-doctrine. Epicureanism permitted one to be sceptical about the gods without being technically an atheist. To hold to this profile and qualify for membership in coteries which identified themselves as Epicurean, Hobbes went to considerable lengths to flag a generally Epicurean point of view.

The ebb and flow in the reception of Epicureans ideas sometimes produced a flood, as with the rediscovery by Poggio Bracciolini of the writings of Lucretius in 1418, and at others reduced to a trickle. Neo-Epicureanism was in fact rather widespread in England following the translation of the first book of Lucretius' *De rerum natura* by John Evelyn in the 1650s, and particularly after the publication of the excellent full edition by Thomas Creech in 1682, which was to run through many printings. In its proto-Enlightenment resurrection Epicureanism provided the space of reflection for new scientists and humanists, personally sceptical, but who nevertheless saw in religion an answer to the deep well-springs of cosmic anxiety that created a restless instability among the multitude.[1] This anxiety was

---

[1] *Lev.*, ii, §7-10, 6-8/10-11, and xii, §5-12, 52-5/63-67; *Hist, Eccl.* lines 79-110.

deemed to open the door to the religious charlatans, soothsayers and snake-oil salesmen, of whom Hobbes gives such a rich catalogue in the poem, including 'those deceivers we've called Astrologers', and particularly the Chaldean augurer, variously described as 'Astrologer, pimp, Chaldean, Philosopher and lying Jew; as well as Mathematician, Soothsayer, good-for-nothing, cheat and poisoner'.[1] These were not idle smears; for to Hobbes, in the tradition of the Democritean and Epicurean *Kulturgeschichte*, the origins of astrology and religion were the same.[2] His scorn for the priests parallels that of Lucretius in *De rerum natura* 1.102-3, and 109 where he excoriates the *vates*, his term for 'all professional supporters of traditional religion and mythology, both priests and poets'.[3] Lucretius, having uttered the fateful lines (1.100-1) that Voltaire believed would last as long as history: 'So potent was Superstition (*religio*) in persuading to evil deeds', had gone on to warn Memmius (1.102-3), the aristocratic backslider to whom the poem is addressed: 'You will yourself some day or other seek to fall away from us [i.e., the Epicureans], overborne by the terrifying utterances of priests (*vatum*)'. At lines 108-11, Lucretius pointed out that if men understood the finitude of their suffering, that is to say, that the soul dies with the body, 'somehow they would have strength to defy the superstitions and threatening of the priests (*vatum*); but as it is, there is no way of resistance and no power, because everlasting punishment is to be

---

[1] Hobbes, *Hist. Eccl.*, lines 192, 300-1.

[2] *Kulturgeschichte* is the term used by Thomas Cole and a long line of German classicists to characterize the account of the origins of civilization by Stoics, Sceptics and Epicureans, who postulated the interlocking developments of needs-driven technology and constantly expanding mental horizons involved in satisfying them. See Thomas Cole, *Democritus and the Sources of Greek Anthropology*, (Oxford, Oxford University Press, 1990). See also Woldemar Graf Uxkull-Gyllenband, *Griechische Kulture-Entstehungslehren* (Berlin, Leonhard Simion, 1924); Gustav Jelenko, 'Die Komposition der Kulturgeschichte des Lucretius', *Wiener Studien*, vol 54 (1936), pp. 59-69; and Walter von Spoerri's important works, 'Über die Quellen des Kulturentstehung des Tzetzes', *Museum Helveticum*, vol. 14 (1957), pp. 183-8; and *Späthellenistische Berichte über Welt, Kultur und Götter* (Basel, Friedrich Rienhardt, 1959). After his Lucretian account of the 'origin of the state', Hobbes follows with the 'origin of astrology' and the 'origin of the arts', *Hist. Eccl.*, lines 116-60, indicated by marginal headings in the MSS.

[3] See M. F. Smith's introduction to Lucretius, *De Rerum Natura*, Loeb edn, pp. 10-13 and notes.

feared after death'.[1] And yet, in a telling phrase, Lucretius (6.75) was willing to allow that it is right to approach the shrines of the gods with placid hearts, and 'to receive with tranquil peace of spirit the images (*simulacra*) which are carried to men's minds from their holy bodies', as if condoning popular or state-sanctioned religion.[2] These ambivalences in the Epicurean sources are faithfully replicated by Hobbes and, as we shall see, a mark of his Epicureanism so far unexplored by commentators.

In point of fact Hobbes had an important contemporary source for the Epicurean tradition as a rich and syncretistic movement, in the person of Pierre Gassendi, with whose work he became acquainted as early as 1634-6, through conversations with Marin Mersenne. In a letter to Rivet of 17 September 1632,[3] Mersenne reported: 'Monsieur Gassendi poursuit tousjours sa philosophie épicurienne. J'en ay deja leu 28 cayers, chacun de 8 feuilles de grand papier'. Gassendi's *De vita et doctrina Epicuri* was completed in draft by 1633. A letter dated 10 October 1644 from Charles Cavendish to John Pell, reports: 'Mr Hobbes writes Gassendes his philosophie is not yet printed but he hath reade it, and that it is big as Aristotele's philosophie, but much truer and excellent Latin'.[4] Cavendish refers to Gassendi's *Life of Epicurus and Animadversions on the Ten Books of Diogenes Laertius* published in 1649. The two men were working alongside one another in Paris at the time. But as Gianni Paganini demonstrates, the Hobbes-Gassendi dialogue was not all one way, and Gassendi, in his comment to Epicurus *Ratae sententiae* 33 late in

---

[1] *Ibid.*
[2] See Bailey's commentary to line 6.75 in his critical edition of Lucretius' *De Rerum Natura* (Oxford, Clarendon, 1947), pp. 1554-5, who notes that 'although there is abundant testimony in Diog[enes] Laert[ius] and Philodemus to Epicurus' attendance at religious ceremonies in the temples, this is the only place where Lucr[etius], who denounced the ordinary ceremonies in V. 1198-1202, speaks of the possibility of such observance on the part of an Epicurean'. Bailey adds, 'We may perhaps guess that Lucr[etius] himself did not show the same devotion as his master.'
[3] *Correspondance du P. Marin Mersenne*, Paul Tannery, Cornelis de Waard and Armand Beaulieu, eds. (Paris, 1932-1986, 16 vols), vol. 11, pp. 229-231.
[4] Published in J. O. Halliwell, *A Collection of Letters Illustrative of the Progress of Science in England from the Reign of Queen Elisabeth to that of Charles the Second*, (London, Historical Society of Science, 1941), p. 85, and cited in Paganini, 'Hobbes, Gassendi et Pyschologie', n. 12.

the *Animadversions*, to illustrate human aggressivity in the state of
nature, made an important concession to Hobbes by including his
famous aphorism, 'homo homini lupus'.[1] Later, in the ethical part of
the *Syntagma*, dating to the years 1645-6, after the publication of the
first edition of *De cive* in 1642, and before the second (which
Gassendi helped his friend Samuel Sorbière promote), he made
transparent reference to Hobbes on freedom in the state of nature.[2]
    Hobbes's Epicurean affiliations were not merely academic. This
was a philosophy admirably suited to the life of the courtier's client,
intellectually demanding and politically hazardous as it was. Steering a path between the Scylla of chance and the Charybdis of necessity was not easy. Hobbes belonged to the Cavendish and Great Tew
circles, coteries of atomists, poets and dramatists who, not without
reason, emulated the philosophers of the Garden.[3] Epicurus' dictum
that the wise man loved his friends as himself,[4] was a rule they practiced. The legendary interest of the Epicureans in natural science
found its parallel among these circles of New Scientists, as we have
evidence from the Hobbes *Correspondence*, which includes a letter
from Sorbière to Hobbes, written in Epicurean code and referring in

---

[1] Paganini, 'Hobbes, Gassendi e la psicologia del meccanicismo', in *Hobbes
Oggi*, ed. Arrigo Pacchi (Milan, Franco Angeli, 1990), pp. 351-446, at p. 438; a discovery made simultaneously by Olivier Bloch in his 'Gassendi et la théorie politique
de Hobbes'; in *Thomas Hobbes, Philosophie première, théorie de la science et politique*, ed. Yves Charles Zarka and Jean Bernhardt (Paris, P.U.F., 1990), p. 345. See
also the seminal piece by François Tricaud, '"Homo homini Deus", "Homo homini
Lupus": Recherche des Sources des deux formules de Hobbes', in *Hobbes-Forschungen*, ed. R. Koselleck, and R. Schnur, (Berlin, Duncker & Humblot, 1969), pp. 61-70.
[2] Gassendi, *Syntagma*, vol. 2, p. 755a-b, cited in Paganini, 'Hobbes, Gassendi
and the Tradition of Political Epicureanism', *Hobbes Studies*, vol 14, 2001, pp. 3-
24; reprinted in *Der Garten und die Moderne. Epikureische Moral und Politik vom
Humanismus bis zur Aufklärung*, (Stuttgart, Frommann-Holzboog 2004), pp. 113-
137, at p. 128.
[3] Among members of the Great Tew circle Chillingworth was a known Epicurean, but the model of the sage in 17th century scientific circles is a largely neglected
subject. See however, Charles T. Harrison, 'The Ancient Atomists and English Literature of the Seventeenth Century', *Harvard Studies in Classical Philology*, vol. 45
(1934), pp. 1-79; W. B. Fleischmann, *Lucretius and English Literature* (Paris, A. G.
Nizet, 1964); R. H. Kargon, *Atomism in England from Hariot to Newton* (Oxford,
Clarendon Press, 1966); and Stephen Clucas, 'The Atomism of the Cavendish Circle:
A Reappraisal', *The Seventeenth Century*, vol. 9, no. 2 (1994), pp. 247-73.
[4] Epicurus, *Sent. Vat.* 23, 52, 78, and *Sent.* 27. See M. F. Smith's introduction to
De Rerum Natura, p. xliii.

strikingly Lucretian terms to the 'undivided friendship' between them. Proffering his letter as 'evidence of the worship with which I honour you and heroes like you', Sorbière goes on to eulogize the superiority of savants, among whose company he and Hobbes are included, compared with the common mob, quoting famous lines from Lucretius, *De rerum natura* book one: [1]

> So I think I too am blessed with the title 'hero', since while I was considering the grovelling baseness of human life, while I was contemplating the stupidity of most mortals, often thinking that man differed by next to nothing from brute animals, you appeared: 'the quick vigour of your mind ventured far beyond the flaming ramparts of the world, and voyaged in mind and spirit through the immeasurable universe'.

Malcolm is surely right to comment: 'reading (literally) between these lines we find that Sorbière is implying that Hobbes has overthrown religious superstition'.[2]

The suggestion of an Epicurean coterie of like-minded savants and bon vivants is borne out by further correspondence between Hobbes and Sorbière. The letter Sorbière to Hobbes, January/February 1657,[3] introduces a number of Epicurean tropes, including the Epicurean laugh:[4]

> After receiving your latest letter, the excellent M. du Bosc entertained us sumptuously in his mansion, together with du Prat and de

---

[1] Sorbière to Hobbes Jul. 11, 1645, Hobbes *Correspondence,* pp. 122-3. Malcolm notes (p. 123, n.2) that Sorbière is quoting from Lucretius *De rerum natura,* I, lines 72-4, 62-3, 66-7 and 72-4. The passage in Malcolm's translation is as follows:
> While human life could be seen grovelling, crushed to the earth by the weight of superstition [religion] a Greek was the first mortal who dared to raise his eyes in defiance so the quick vigour of his mind prevailed, and he ventured far beyond the flaming ramparts of the world, and voyaged in mind and spirit through the immeasurable universe.

[2] Hobbes *Correspondence,* p. 123, note 2.
[3] Hobbes to Sorbière, Feb. 1657, Hobbes *Correspondence*, pp. 444-5, trans. Malcolm.
[4] Jean Salem, *Tel un dieu parmi les hommes,* pp. 167-72, comments at length on Epicurus' injunction to his disciple 'to laugh while philosophizing' (*Vatican Sentence* 41). The 'Epicurean laugh' was both provocative and seditious, a 'deliberate polemical strategy' to mock the stupidity of the common herd, on the one hand, and to counter the gravity and arrogance of the Platonist philosopher, on the other. In a section on the 'Epicurean laugh and the critique of language' pp. 172-4, Salem notes

Martel; that very learned old man de La Mothe le Vayer[1] was also there. Our conversation lasted until nightfall; we talked mainly about you and philosophical matters – not about other people's houses and estates. I salted our banquet with wit and erudition, and there was laughter too; but we also meditated deeply on difficult problems. You know what our host is like and what an irreverent scoffer I am.[2] Du Prat has the same tendency; and when some knotty problem was tormenting us like a torturer's noose, de Martel did not hesitate to turn his mind to lighter things. For it is well known that nothing is more conducive to good health, both in body and in mind, than wise laughter and well-tempered mirth in the company of our closest friends.[3] Jests are stronger than bitter arguments, and they often provide a more acute analysis of important matters. To show you what the discussion was about, here is an extract from my criticism, which I read out there and now submit to your judgement. For it helps me if I sometimes tell you, or du Prat and the others, about the doubts which occur to me during my reading. I have commented on a great many things in your Physics; but there would have been no need for my scribbling about them if you had been present to dispel our uncertainties.

Sorbière proceeds to discuss the opinion of his French colleagues on what differentiates Hobbes's physics from that of Epicurus: 'The

---

the self-mockery of the Epicureans, their deflationary critique of language, and their nominalism. Cicero's refusal to define words empty of sense ('voce inani sonare', De fin. 2.14.48), and his deflationary definition of good as what benefits us and bad as what harms us (Tusc. Disp., 5.26.73), was typical. See also Quentin Skinner, 'Hobbes and the Classical Theory of Laughter' in Tom Sorell and Luc Foisneau, eds., Leviathan after 350 Years (Oxford, Clarendon Press, 2004).

[1] Malcolm, Hobbes Correspondence, p. 435, notes: 'François de La Mothe le Vayer (1588-17672), a scholar and littérateur, was a protégé of Richelieu in the 1630s and was appointed tutor to the duc d'Orléans (1649) and to Louis XIV (1652). A friend of Mersenne, he was the author of numerous works, strongly influenced by classical and Montaignian scepticism.'

[2] Malcolm notes, p. 435: 'Sorbière is adapting a phrase from Persius, Saturae, 1.12'.

[3] Note how Sorbière nicely captures the Epicurean ethos, a hygienic notion of happiness promoted by the sage and his circle, who venerate friendship and the fellowship of an elite and disdain the stupidity of the masses. Jean Salem, Tel un dieu parmi les hommes, pp. 140-1, notes that if the Stoics enlarged the polis to the level of the oikoumene, the Epicureans narrowed it to a circle of friends. Numenius of Apamea, a 2nd century Neoplatonist, had declared that 'the harmony of the Epicureans among themselves resembled that which reigned in a true republic, without the least sedition, animated by the spirit of a single will'. Salem, p. 133, citing Numenius Fragments, fr. 24.

main difference between your philosophy and that of Epicurus is on the existence of a vacuum, which you deny, and which you try hard to disprove'. Hobbes responds in a letter dated February 1657, noting that his 'argument against the existence of a vacuum was drawn from an experiment', but that: 'I did not think that Epicurus' theory was absurd, in the sense in which I think he understood the vacuum. For I believe that he called "vacuum" what Descartes calls "subtle matter", and what I call "extremely pure ethereal substance", of which no part is an atom, and each part is divisible (as quantity is said to be) into further divisible parts'.[1]

Lucretius' choice of subject, reflected in his title *On the Nature of Things*, which was a translation of Epicurus' title, Περί Φύσεως, affirmed his interest in natural science as a prophylactic against superstition.[2] In the Epicurean proselytizing tradition, the aim of which was to win adherents to the philosophy of the Garden, Lucretius was frank about using poetry as a bait, and the need to sweeten the pill for the masses. Because his task was great, 'to loose the mind from the close knots of superstition', and 'because the subject is so obscure', as a healer of the mind, like the doctor administering unwelcome medication to a child, he has to coat the rim of the medicinal cup with the honey of the Muses, that is to say, poetry.[3] Sweetening the pill is an exercise which the *Historia Ecclesiastica* may well have been intended to demonstrate.

To what central doctrines Hobbes was, even for therapeutic reasons, prepared to subscribe, and with what degree of sincerity, opinion again differs.[4] Hobbes himself, in his response to Bramhall's *Of Libertie and Necessitie*, claimed to subscribe to predestination,

---

[1] Hobbes to Sorbière, Feb. 1657, Hobbes *Correspondence*, pp. 444-5, Malcolm trans.

[2] M. F. Smith's introduction to Lucretius, *De Rerum Natura*, p. lii.

[3] *De Rerum Natura* 1.932-50, editor's introduction, pp. l-li.

[4] See most recently the debate between Edwin Curley and A. P. Martinich, beginning with Curley's '"I durst not write so boldly", or How to read Hobbes' theological-political Treatise', in E. Giancotti, *Hobbes e Spinoza. Scienza e politica* (Napoli, Bibliopolis, 1992), pp. 497-594, and 'Calvin and Hobbes, or Hobbes as an Orthodox Christian', *Journal of the History of Philosophy*, vol. 34 (1996), pp. 257-71; to which Martinich replies with 'On the Proper Interpretation of Hobbes's Philosophy', *Journal of the History of Philosophy*, vol. 34 (1996), pp. 273-83; to which Curley again responds with his 'Reply to Professor Martinich', *Journal of the History of Philosophy*, vol. 34 (1996), pp. 285-7.

which, once converted into determinism, again puts him with the
Epicureans. A. P. Martinich claims to the contrary, that Hobbes's definition of religious orthodoxy is in fact that of Elizabeth I's High
Commission on Christian Doctrine, which endorsed the religious
decrees of the first four councils of the early church', including the
Nicene Creed.[1] But only as a prudential rule, I would add, and not
because he necessarily believed their content. In both the *Historia
Ecclesiastica* and the 1668 Appendix to the Latin *Leviathan*, *De
haeresi*, Hobbes makes much of the fact that the Council of Nicaea
was originally called without authority to settle a dispute between a
church Elder (Arius) and a Bishop (Alexander), and that its doctrinal
pronouncements were only possible because of a lax censorship
regime on the part of Constantine.[2] In his analysis of the Nicene
Creed in the Latin Appendix, as we will see (see chapter 6.3),
Hobbes gives such a blatantly contradictory account of its provisions
as to call into serious question any pretense to Christian belief.[3]

Martinich claims that Hobbes's deep pessimism about human
nature, as a product of his Calvinist education at Magdalen Hall in
Oxford, and his rejection of Platonic Augustinianism and Aristotelian Thomism for the Baconian 'new science', favoured a secular
account of human nature and theism.[4] But I would add that Calvinist
predestinarianism, once converted into determinism, trivializes religious belief, as no more than a product of 'train[s] of imagination'[5]
produced by sensation, and no less, and therefore non-culpable: 'For

---

[1] A. P. Martinich, *The Two Gods of Leviathan* (Cambridge, Cambridge University Press, 1992), p. 2.
[2] See *Hist. Eccl.*, lines 545-6 ff. and commentary, and the 1668 Appendix to the
LL §124 (tr. Wright, p. 370).
[3] Hobbes's rejoinder to such a charge would of course be that the paradoxes lie
within Christian belief itself. So in the 1668 Appendix to the *LL*, §214 (tr. Wright),
Interlocutor A concludes of the Bible:
> [213]A. There are many other paradoxical arguments in the same book, but,
> because they are of too little importance for us to linger over now, I shall not
> bring them up.

To which B replies:
> [214]B. As you wish. But, in these instances you have brought up, I find
> nothing against the faith of our church, although there are several which defeat
> the teaching of private theologians.

[4] Martinich, *The Two Gods of Leviathan*, pp. 4, 7.
[5] Hobbes's term for this process in the title to *Leviathan*, chapter 3.

there is no conception in a man's mind which hath not at first, totally or by parts, been begotten upon the organs of sense'.[1] It is for this reason that Hobbes insists that the internal court of private opinion, *in foro interno*, is a non-culpable realm that escapes the scrutiny of *in foro externo*, the public court.[2] It is also worth noting that whatever residues of a Calvinist education might have remained in Hobbes general orientation to human nature were not sufficient to impress the Calvinist synods of the Low Countries. Gisbertus Cocquius, an Hebraist and one of Hobbes's most percipient critics, who systematically examines Hobbes's biblical exegesis, fundamental articles of faith and his doctrine of the Trinity,[3] notes in his dedication that *Leviathan* was banned by the Synod of Utrecht.[4]

Most likely Hobbes's theology could be summed up in the words of his fellow friend, natural scientist and humanist, Sir Thomas Browne (1605-82), who claimed that he submitted to the articles of the Church of England, following neither the rule of Luther or Calvin, nor fully condemning the Council of Trent or wholly endorsing the Synod of Dort, but using his own conscience as his guide:[5] 'As there were many Reformers, so likewise there were many reformations', he observed, 'every Country proceeding in a particular way and Method according to their nationall interest'. In fact, Browne observed, Henry VIII himself was no reformer, simply a Prince who perpetuated the faith of Rome in his own way;[6] whereas

---

[1] *Lev.*, i, §2, 3/6.

[2] *Lev.*, xv, §36, 79/99, 'The laws of nature oblige *in foro interno*, that is to say, they bind to a desire they should take place; but *in foro externo*, that is, to the putting them in act, not always'. In the *LL*, as Curley notes, Hobbes states the distinction more clearly: 'The laws of nature oblige *in foro interno*, i.e., their transgression is not properly to be called a crime, but a vice. But they do not always oblige *in foro externo*'.

[3] Gisbertus Cocquius, *Hobbesianismi Anatome, Qua innumeris Assertionibus ex Tractatibus de Homine, Cive, Leviathan Juxta seriem locorum Theologiae Christiane Philosophi illius a Religione Christiana Apostasia demonstratur, & refutatur* (Utrecht, Franciscum Halma, 1680), chs, 3-7, 8-15. Lecoq, in the vernacular, may well have been the butt of Hobbes's 'Ducocalanus' jokes, see *Hist. Eccl.*, lines 1882-4, and Rymer's Glossary.

[4] Gisbertus Cocquius, *Hobbesianismi Anatome*, p. iv. I thank Johann Sommerville for pointing this out to me, a piece of information corroborated by Noel Malcolm, 'The Printing of the "Bear"', p. 381, n 163.

[5] *Religio Medici*, §5, in *The Major Works of Sir Thomas Browne*, ed. C. A. Patrides (Harmondsworth, Penguin, 1977) pp. 64-5.

[6] *Religio Medici*, §4, §5, *loc. cit.*, pp. 64-5.

Hobbes, by his own admission, as Aubrey recounts, liked the Church of England 'best of all other'.[1] A deathbed declaration (as he thought) made to his confessor Dr. John Cosins, this was an extraordinary about face if we can believe it, for Cosins, prebend at Durham Cathedral and Vice-Chancellor of Cambridge was the enthusiastic promoter of Laudean Anglo-Catholic ceremonies, and the 'dual spheres' policy that had so polarized the realm, and to which Hobbes was so vehemently opposed.[2] But at this very time, Hobbes had also sounded a more characteristic note. Plagued by the attempted ministrations of Catholic, Anglican and Genevan divines, Aubrey tells us, he dispatched them with the threat, 'Let me alone, or els I will detect all your cheates from Aaron to yourselves'.[3] Aubrey comments in his anodyne way, 'I thinke I have heard him speake something to this purpose'. Hobbes's threat could be read as a brief for the *Historia Ecclesiastica* regarding the credibility of priests and prophets, where Primus lists first Moses, whose credibility rests on his miracles in Egypt and 'turning back the sea'; then Aaron and his brother the High Priest, each to whom God spoke in turn; then the Prophets of the Old Testament, and 'Christ who was God'; finally 'the Paraclete, that is the Church of Christ', each of whom is equally credible (or incredible) in his claim to speak the word of God. At which point Secundus adds 'the Fanatics, the new lights of this age, and, if you wish, throw in the Pontiff of Rome' for good measure.[4]

On the face of it Hobbes by adopting minimalist Christian beliefs, seemed to join the ranks of those Latitudinarians who hoped to preserve in Anglicanism one of the most ancient marks of the Christian Church: its catholicity in the face of heresy and schism; and who were later accused of being Hobbist.[5] But the way that he drops paradoxes into otherwise non-paradoxical writings, and his indulgence in outrageous contradiction have prompted David

---

[1] Aubrey, *Brief Lives*, vol. 1, p. 353.

[2] See Collins, *Allegiance*, pp. 77-8. Cosins was no stranger to politics. See his *Account of the Proceedings in Parliament (1666, 67, and 68), between Dr. Cosins, Bishop of Durham, and the Gentlemen Freeholders of the County Palatine.*

[3] Aubrey, *Brief Lives*, vol. 1, p. 353.

[4] *Hist. Eccl.*, lines 39-50.

[5] See Collins, *Allegiance,* pp. 273-4. Collin's observes how hard Thomas Tenison – who had been Scargill's Cambridge tutor – Tillotson, Stillingfleet and Samuel Parker had to pedal to distance themselves from Hobbes.

Berman to accuse him of 'theological lying'.[1] As Berman defines the term, deists who 'say they believe in a future life', but whose statements 'constitute a subversion' of that belief, are indulging in more than simply irony, and are rather practicing 'the Art of theological lying'.[2] Curley puts it more mildly, attributing to Hobbes a particular form of irony which he calls 'suggestion by disavowal': 'In this rhetorical device a writer presents a series of considerations which might reasonably lead his reader to draw a certain conclusion, but then denies that that conclusion follows.'[3] While not as strong a charge as that of 'theological lying', Curley's accusation is to the same effect. Hobbes was a much more radical religious thinker than it was prudent to appear in public. In a period of state censorship in which heterodoxy commanded Draconian punishments, Hobbes, who was personally under indictment for atheism, could not afford to risk stating his views directly. Was it not also, I might add, that by leading his reader through the intricacies of orthodox doctrine, and then undermining them as a tissue of contradictions, he created a more compelling case for his own Erastian doctrine?

About his Erastianism and his hatred of priestcraft we can be certain. And if it was from the vantage point of state security that Hobbes viewed the long history of radical sectarianism going back to the Greeks, he was by no means alone. The maxim *cuius regio eius religio*, which allowed the Prince to decide the religious denomination of his people, was the principle on which the Treaty of Westphalia of 1648, that concluded the Thirty Year's War and gave rise to the modern European system of states, had been founded. It was a prudential rule that Hobbes also endorsed in the name of peace. The separation of the public and private spheres, on which the modern state system is predicated, was already anticipated in Hobbes's distinction between the internal court of conscience, *in foro externo*,

---

[1] On 'theological lying', see David Berman, 'Deism, Immortality, and the Art of Theological Lying', in J. Leo Lemay, ed., *Deism, Masonry and the Enlightenment* (Newark, N.J., University of Delaware Press, 1987), pp. 61-78; David Berman, 'Disclaimers as Offence Mechanisms in Charles Blount and John Toland', in M. Hunter and D. Wootton, eds, *Atheism from the Reformation to the Enlightenment* (Oxford, Clarendon Press, 1992), pp. 255-72.

[2] Berman, 'Deism, Immortality, and the Art of Theological Lying', pp. 62, 76.

[3] Curley, 'Calvin and Hobbes', pp. 261-2,

and the external court of public obedience, *in foro interno*; but it had yet to be realized in official decrees of religious toleration. Hobbes, moreover, was himself no tolerationist. In the 1668 Appendix to the Latin *Leviathan*, summing up the conclusion to be drawn from the ecclesiastical history just narrated, consistent with the *Historia Ecclesiatica* and *Behemoth*, his last words on matter, he clearly stated:[1]

> [134]B. [I]t is altogether necessary that precaution be taken in king-doms and commonwealths lest sedition and civil wars arise. And, since these very frequently arise out of doctrinal differences and battles of intellect, those must certainly be coerced by some punish-ment who, in public meetings or in books, teach things contrary to what the laws of princes and commonwealths have ordained.

It was a view anticipated in the English *Leviathan*, where Hobbes, taking a self-consciously anti-Socratic line, made bold to argue that even those who teach the truth should sometime be banned in the interests of the state: 'For disobedience may lawfully be punished in them that against the laws teach even true philosophy'.[2]

1.3 HOBBES AND THE PRESBYTERIANS

Meaning cannot simply be inferred from context. Correspond-ingly, the reception of a work is only one indicator of its sense, pre-cisely because it is so heavily biased towards immediate context. But context is always important, supplying the deep structures of meaning in the same way that grammatical structure frames the meaning of words in a sentence. The flow of events and institutional changes from absolute monarchy to revolution and regicide and back to Restoration, is essential to an understanding of Hobbes's texts and their sequencing. If *The Elements of Law* of 1640 was

---

[1] 1668 Appendix to the *LL*, §134 (tr. Wright); see also Wright, 'The 1668 Appendix and Hobbes's Theological Project', in Patricia Springborg, ed., *The Cambridge Companion to Hobbes's Leviathan*, pp. 392-411, at p. 402, where this passage is particularly noted.

[2] *Lev.*, xlvi, §42, 379/468.

designed, at Newcastle's instigation, for Charles I against the Anglo-Catholic revival under Laud;[1] and *De cive* of 1642 responded to the Long Parliament;[2] *Leviathan* of 1651, by the same inescapable logic, addressed the Commonwealth of Cromwell and his Independents. All this follows if we take Hobbes's Erastianism seriously, as Jeffrey Collins has so persuasively argued. So while *De cive* challenged the supporters of Laudian ecclesiastical dualism and the separate but equal spiritual and temporal spheres, seeking to recover the English Erastian Reformation of the Tudors, *Leviathan* attacked a new phenomenon, the Covenanted sectarians, specifically the Scottish National Covenant and the Presbyterian-oriented Westminster Assembly of Divines – the latter first convened in July 1643 – who threatened that Erastian settlement.[3]

Collins has made a compelling revisionist case for the causes of the general hostility with which Hobbes's works were received being due to his growing support in the 1650s for Cromwellian Independency and his life-long antipathy to government by bishops, whether Laudian or Presbyterian. *Leviathan*, as Collins argues, sought an accommodation with a new Erastian godly prince, the Lord Protector Cromwell and his Independents in their loosely gathered, bishopless congregations. So in chapter 42, commenting on the decisive issue of excommunication with reference to Paul's first *Letter to the Corinthians*, Hobbes defended the authority of gathered congregations in 'the assembly of the Christians dwelling in the same city (as in Corinth, in the assembly of the Christians of Corinth)', as the norm 'before the conversion of Kings, and men that had sovereign authority in the commonwealth'.[4]

Beginning with *The Elements of Law* and *De cive* and through the Interregnum, hostility to Hobbes went in waves, the first being the campaign, only very recently examined, waged by Presbyterians through members of the Stationer's Company, that guild of English

---

[1] Hobbes, *The Elements of Law Natural and Politic*, including 'A Short Tract on First Principles', ed. Ferdinand Tönnies (1889), reissued with a new Introduction by M. M. Goldsmith (London, Cass, 1969); see Collins, *Allegiance,* pp. 60-1.

[2] Collins, *Allegiance,* p. 63.

[3] *Ibid.,* p. 64.

[4] *Lev.,* xli, §19, 276/344, referring to Paul 1 Cor. 5:11-12 on excommunication; see Collins, *Allegiance,* p. 125.

booksellers and printers authorized to license books.[1] In 1652 five
printers and booksellers were signatories to the tract *A Beacon Set on
Fire*, that listed 23 'Popish and Blasphemous Books' including
Hobbes's *Leviathan*, protesting not only the books themselves, but
the laxness of the licensing regime that allowed them to be printed.[2]
The association of Hobbes with Catholic writers is not as strange as
it may seem, for the tracts listed promulgated the views of those who
also pressed for moderation, including Thomas White (1593-1676),
whose *De Mundo* was the vehicle for Hobbes's early exposition of
his *philosophia prima*.[3] The *Beacon* targeted one notable Catholic
tract, *The Christian Moderator*, written by John Austin (1613-69),[4] a
priest who makes the first known print reference to *Leviathan*, from
which it borrows significantly, and precisely the Erastian arguments
that made Hobbes so infamous with the Presbyterians and the
bishops. Like Hobbes, these moderate Catholics were beginning to
look with favour upon Oliver Cromwell as a new Erastian prince
who would permit a degree of religious toleration.[5]

Austin belonged in fact to a circle of Erastian Catholics known as
the Blackloists, who were followers of the Thomas White, the
philosopher priest with whom Hobbes was associated, and who
wrote under the pseudonym 'Blacklo'.[6] The Blackloists were almost

---

[1] For the account of this campaign, I am indebted to Collins's 'Silencing
Thomas Hobbes'.

[2] *A Beacon Set on Fire: or the Humble Information of Certain Stations and
Citizens of London to the Parliament and Commonwealth of England. Concerning
the Vigilancy of Jesuits, Papists, and Apostates . . . to Corrupt the pure Doctrine of
the Scriptures . . .* (London, 1652), pp. 3-4, 7-8. See Collins, 'Silencing Thomas
Hobbes', p. 483.

[3] Thomas Hobbes [1642] (1973), *Critique du De Mundo de Thomas White*, ed.
Jean Jacquot and H. W. Jones (Paris, Vrin, 1973).

[4] *The Christian Moderator; or Persecution for Religion condemned by the
Light of Nature, by the Law of God, the Evidence of our Principles, but not by the
Practice of our Commissioners for Sequestrations – In Four Parts* (London, 1652,
4to.). Published under the pseudonym of William Birchley, it disclaims the pope's
deposing power. See Collins, 'Silencing Thomas Hobbes', pp. 492-4.

[5] Jeffrey Collins discusses these connections in light of Hobbes's ecclesiology
in 'Thomas Hobbes and the Blackloist Conspiracy'.

[6] Educated at Douai and President of the English College in Lisbon for 1630 to
1633, when he and returned to England, White wrote about 40 theological works,
several of which were censured by the Inquisition for unorthodox views about purgatory, hell and the infallibility of the pope, in decrees dated 14 May, 1655, and 7
Sept., 1657. He was chiefly opposed by George Leyburn, the president of Douai and

as wedded to the excoriation of the Jesuits and the Tridentine papacy as the Erastians, and like them appealed to the new science, although committed to an eclectic Aristotelianism.[1] After the flight of White to Paris in 1643, some elements of the Blackloists became embedded in the Louvre faction centred round Henrietta Maria, to which Edmund Waller (1606-1687) and Kenelm Digby (1603-65), the Queen's emissary in Rome whom Hobbes met in Paris, also belonged.[2] It was a wide and shifting circle, including many of Hobbes's literary acquaintances of the 1640s such as Abraham Cowley (1618-1667) and William Davenant (1606-1668), and it had strong Catholic currents. This shadowy court faction provided the background threat of French hostility and an ultramondane papacy, on which Parliamentarians and Presbyterians for decades played.

The Beacon responded to the amorphous threat that such a coalition posed; it claimed that the works against which it petitioned, threatened the 'Salvation and Damnation of millions of Souls' who had been placed on the 'High-way to eternal Perdition', calling on Parliament to 'suppress them'.[3] *A Beacon Set on Fire* set off a chain reaction, and a supportive *Second Beacon Fired by Scintilla* quickly followed. The Levellers answered with *Beacons Quenched,* composed by members of the New Model army who opposed the proposal for greater censorship as a form of 'Presbyterian slavery'.[4]

Robert Pugh, who wrote a life of him no longer extant, and a work called *Blacklo's Cabal*, in which he accuses White of opposition to episcopal authority, and disloyalty to the pope. On Thomas White and the Blackloists, see Beverly Southgate, *Covetous of Truth: the Life and Works of Thomas White, 1593-1676* (Dordrecht, Reidel, 1993), pp. 35-9; and Robert Bradley, 'Blacklo and the Counter-Reformation: An Enquiry into the Strange Death of Catholic England', in Charles Howard Carter, ed., *From Renaissance to the Counter Reformation* (New York, 1965), pp. 355-8. See also Collins, *Allegiance,* pp. 90-1.

[1] Beverly Southgate, '"A Medley of Both": Old and new in the Thought of Thomas White', *History of European Ideas*, vol. 18 (1994) pp. 53-9, at p. 53, and Southgate, '"To Speak the Truth": Blackloism, Scepticism and Language', *Seventeenth Century*, vol. 10 (1995), pp. 237-54.

[2] Digby to Hobbes, 1 Oct. 1636, 17 Jan. 1637, 11 Sept 1637, Hobbes *Correspondence*, Noel Malcolm, ed., pp. 36, 242-50.

[3] *A Beacon Set on Fire*, pp. 3-4, 7-8, cited by Collins, 'Silencing Thomas Hobbes', p. 483.

[4] Thomas Pride, et al., *The Beacon's Quenched: or the Humble Information of divers Officers of the Army . . . Concerning the Machivilian design of the Presbyterians, now carrying on by the Stationers of London* (London, 1652), p. 9.

Another *Beacon* followed, *The Beacon Flameing with a Non Obstante*. The signatories to the first *Beacon*, Luke Fawne, Samuel Gellibrand, Joshua Kirton, John Rothwell, Thomas Underhill and Nathaniel Webb, were notable for their tight web of Presbyterian connections, most of them having printed works for the Presbyterian Westminster Assembly of Divines of the 1640s and its leaders, Edmund Calamy (1600-1666), Thomas Edwards (1599-1647), Daniel Cawdrey (1588-1664), and Richard Baxter (1615-91). Underhill had published the Presbyterians Richard Vines, Anthony Burgess, Daniel Cawdrey, as well as John Wallis's *Brief and Easie Explanation of the Shorter Catechism, presented by the Assembly of Divines* (1653); while Gellibrand had published Psalters for the Assembly, as well as the works of prominent Presbyterian leaders such as Calamy and the Scottish Presbyterian commissioner Robert Baillie. Luke Fawne published many Presbyterians authors as well as a 1648 *Exhortation of Lancaster Presbyterians for discipline*; while Rothwell published for the Westminster Assembly and a 'catalogue' of 'orthodox' books approved by Calamy, as well as the writings of the Presbyterian executed for plotting against the Commonwealth in 1650, Christopher Love.[1]

If the signatories to the first *Beacon* were all petitioners, the third and fourth *Beacon*s defending the Presbyterian position appear to have come from Underhill's press, judging by the sign of the anchor on their title page, which was also the sign for his shop. Both Underhill and Rothwell had been personally involved in the printing and sale of Baxter's books.[2] Baxter's networks were wide, and in February 1652 his fellow Presbyterian Thomas Hill, master of Trinity College, Cambridge, had confessed to him: 'Your deep detestation of Hobbs his Leviathan hath awakened some of us to consider what is fitt to be done therein',[3] to which Baxter responded by speculating further about the 'horrid consequences in Hobb'es Booke'.[4] The campaign waged against the dissemination of Hobbes's works by the

---

[1] Jeffrey Collins, 'Silencing Thomas Hobbes', pp. 484, and 497, n. 32.
[2] *Ibid.*, pp. 485, and 497 n. 36.
[3] Hill to Baxter, 13 Feb. 1652. Dr. William's Library, Baxter Correspondence, iii, fo. 266; see Collins, 'Silencing Thomas Hobbes', p. 486, n. 38.
[4] Baxter to Hill, 8 Mar. 1652, Dr. William's Library, Baxter Correspondence, iii, fos. 272-3; see Collins, 'Silencing Thomas Hobbes', p. 486, n. 38.

Presbyterian printers focused precisely on his interpretation of Christianity as a civil religion that undermined established churches and could play into the hands equally of Independents and Catholics, whom they thus lumped together.

John Wallis, Savillian Professor of Mathematics at Oxford, and Parliamentarian, although at one time Cromwell's man, also had close ties with this group having served as a secretary to the Westminster Assembly of Divines, and allied himself to the dominant Presbyterian faction, composing the guide to their *Shorter Catechism* of 1653, already mentioned. At Oxford he defended an essentially Presbyterian church settlement against the rising tide of Independency represented by his foe John Owen (1616-1683). His campaign against Hobbes waged in the 1650s is too well known to bear rehearsing.[1] Ostensibly about Hobbes's mathematics, it was in fact more widely focused, targeting his theology and ecclesiology. Wallis was especially close to two signatories to the *Beacon* petition, Gellibrand and Underhill, both of whom had handled works by him during the Interregnum.[2] The writings of these Presbyterian leaders must have been known to Hobbes, for the Hardwick Hall Library lists many, including Daniel Cawdrey's *Independency a Great Schism* (1630); Samuel Rutherford's *Free Disputation against Pretended Liberty of Conscience* (1649); and Thomas Edwards's (1646) *Gangraena; or a Catalogue and Discovery of many Errours, Heresies, Blasphemies, and pernicious Practices of the Sectaries of this Time, vented and acted in England in these four last Years* (1646).

If the campaign against Hobbes by the Presbyterian Printers represented 'the first printed attack on Hobbes's *Leviathan* in England',[3] this was the opening shot in a long war at each stage of which Hobbes's person as well as his works were under threat, involving

---

[1] See D. M. Jesseph, *Squaring the circle: the war between Hobbes and Wallis* (Chicago, University of Chicago Press, 1999). Jesseph, who is an historian of mathematics and is editing Hobbes's mathematical works for the *Clarendon Edition of the Works of Thomas Hobbes*, is nevertheless attentive to the wider debate in which Hobbes's disagreements with Wallis are situated, whereas most other treatments of the Hobbes-Wallis controversy have confined themselves to the mathematical problems.

[2] See Collins, 'Silencing Thomas Hobbes', p. 488, n. 50.

[3] Collins, 'Silencing Thomas Hobbes', p. 491.

subsequent confiscations and burnings. The second important wave
of his reception in England was the campaign waged against him by
the Bishops, which I will investigate in some detail as the immediate
context for his works on heresy. The Scargill episode was a last
sortie and one that led to another round of paper burning. Hobbes
came perilously close to the heresies of Arianism,[1] and Socinianism[2]
but his Erastianism was the greatest cause for his vilification.[3] When
his acolyte, Daniel Scargill, declared himself to be a Hobbist pro-
fessing no belief but what the sovereign had commanded, this bald
statement of the Erastian position was received as a version of the
liar paradox, inviting disbelief in anything the utterer spoke. It was a
disbelief that was transferred to Hobbes himself; and the international prohibitions against his texts by the papacy and Presbyterian
synods might be considered the third wave in his hostile reception.

Hobbes had closed the famous chapter 12 of *Leviathan*, 'Of Religion', with a characteristic barb: 'I may attribute all the changes of
religion in the world to one and the same cause, and that is, unpleas-
ing priests, and those not only amongst Catholics, but even in the
church that hath presumed most of reformation'.[4] It was a remark
that was silently dropped from the 1668 Latin *Leviathan*.[5] That it
may be read as endorsement of bishopless congregations and an
attack on the Presbyterians, we know from *Behemoth*, where Hobbes
made it clear that it was they who 'presumed most of reformation',
outdoing both Luther and Calvin in their reforming zeal, yet reinstating ecclesiastical hierarchy.[6] In Book 4 of the Latin *Leviathan*,

---

[1] The heresy propagated by *Arius (AD 260-336), denying the Divinity of
Jesus Christ.

[2] Socinianism, named after Socinus, the Latinized name of Lelio Francesco
Maria Sozzini (1525-1562), an Italian Protestant theologian, is a heresy prominent
in the 17th century that rejects traditional doctrines such as the Trinity and original
sin. See Gianni Paganini's forthcoming essay, 'Hobbes e il socinianesimo',
Relazione presentata al Congresso: *Fausto Sozzini e la filosofia in Europa*, Università di Siena, 25-27 novembre 2004.

[3] Pacchi in the Introduction to his edition of Hobbes's *Scritti teologici*, pp. 11-
23 has drawn attention to Hobbes's Arian sympathies.

[4] *Lev.*, xii, §32, 60-1/74.

[5] See Collins, *Allegiance*, p. 274.

[6] See Curley's note, referring to *Behemoth, or The Long Parliament*, ed. Ferdinand Tönnies (London, 1889, facsimile edn, ed. Stephen Holmes, Chicago, University of Chicago, 1990), p. 136.

'Of the Kingdome of Darkness', chapter 47, 'Of the Benefit that proceedeth from such Darkness', whole sections of the original addressing 'the authors, therefore, of this darkness in religion . . . the Roman and the Presbyterian clergy', and endorsing the abolition of Bishops and Independency, were also silently dropped;[1] an indication of the changing circumstances in which Hobbes found himself. By 1668 the Restoration was securely established and there was no need to bait the now defeated sectaries. Moreover, the Latin *Leviathan* was directed at a European audience and, as Hobbes himself remarked, for this reason he had omitted from the 1668 volume 'some such passages as strangers are not concerned in'.[2]

The sheer space devoted to ecclesiology in *Leviathan* as opposed to *De cive* is a measure of the relative seriousness with which Hobbes viewed sectarian threats to the Commonwealth at that time. If sectarianism was a major cause for the English Civil War of the 1640s, by the time of writing the *Historia Ecclesiastica* it had raised its head again to threaten the Cromwellian settlement. In 1657 Puritan sectaries in the city and army, largely Baptists, put up opposition to the proposal to crown Oliver King, and allow him to create a second chamber of men chosen as 'Lords'.[3] And in 1658 Baptists were heavily involved in two significant events. The first was the preparation of a petition by City Sectaries and Commonwealth men for presentation to parliament demanding that it guarantee rights and freedoms assured by successive parliaments as the 'Supreme Power'. The second was army disaffection against Oliver instigated by six Baptist officers in his own regiment, who were sacked when they could not satisfy him as to 'what they meant by the Good Old Cause' that they claimed he had abandoned.[4]

The death of Oliver in 1658, and Sir Henry Vane's rallying cry in his *Healing Question*, urging friends to the Good Old Cause to lay

---

[1] *Lev.*, xlvii, §§4-34, 381-7/478-84, compare with xlvii (*OL*) 323-7/485-8; see Collins, *Allegiance*, p. 275.

[2] See *Answer to Bishop Bramhall*, *EW* IV, p. 317, noted in George Wright, 'The 1668 Appendix and Hobbes's Theological Project', p. 392.

[3] See the 'Address of the Anabaptist Ministers in London', 3 April, 1657, in *Original Letters and Papers of State Addressed to Oliver Cromwell*, ed. John Nickolls (London, 1743), pp. 142-3, cited by Barbara Taft in 'That Lusty Puss, the Good Old Cause', *History of Political Thought*, vol. 5, no. 3 (1984), pp. 447-68, at p. 455.

[4] Barbara Taft, 'That Lusty Puss, the Good Old Cause', p. 455.

aside their differences and advance the principles of the old
Parliament and army, prompted a revival of the petition that had
caused the dissolution of Oliver's last parliament, this time presented
to the Commons by leading Baptists with thousands of additional
signatures. Preachers and pamphlets generated a flurry of sectarian
and millenarian rhetoric 'recalling "those virgin daies" when all was
"lovely harmony" between Parliament and the "honest unbias'd
people"'.[1] The upshot was a General Council which produced a man-
ifesto advanced in support of the Good Old Cause by three Baptist
colonels.[2] Of Sir Henry Vane, the most impressive of the Parliament
men, Barbara Taft observes: 'Vane's dedication to religious liberty
never wavered, though his own mysticism had deepened steadily.
His religious writings meant little beyond circles of fanatical Fifth
Monarchists dreaming of an earthly Kingdom of Heaven'.[3] By the
time he wrote the *Historia Ecclesiastica* these events may have
caused Hobbes to harden his position against the Independents and
those sects that resisted the established church and organized themselves in loose confederations of 'gathered congregations'. For there
he lumps together '*Independents,* Quakers, *Presbyterians, *Fifth
Monarchy Men, *Episcopalians, *Anabaptists', as a motley crowd
of enemies of the state.[4]

It is not difficult to see Hobbes's account of the doctrinal struggles between the Emperor and Church Councils in the *Historia
Ecclesiatica* as an analogue for the struggle for supremacy between
the Crown and the sects in England in the revolutionary period. If he
had attacked Presbyterianism for 'erecting a power beyond the
Papall in jurisdiction' as early as 1656,[5] his long disquisitions on the
papacy and his battle with Bellarmine in *Leviathan* could also be
read as surrogates for his attack on the Laudians and Presbyterians,
wedded like Catholicism to government by bishops. For, to Hobbes
the pope was an anti-*Leviathan*, much in the tradition of Paolo Sarpi,
who saw both pope and emperor as dual Leviathans, challenging one

---

[1] *Ibid.*, p. 457.
[2] *Ibid.*, pp. 457-8.
[3] *Ibid.*, p. 463.
[4] *Hist. Eccl.*, line 1560 and Rymer's Glossary, *q.v.*
[5] Stubbe to Hobbes, 25 Oct. 1656, Hobbes *Correspondence*, pp. 334-7; see
Collins, *Allegiance,* p. 221n.

another to further their private interests.[1] Papal posturing of this sort is vividly recounted in the *Historia Ecclesiastica*, where the popes at the peak of their ascendancy, were arrayed like the sun,[2] hurled thunderbolts like Jupiter, trampled the necks of kings;[3] and like distant nodding oriental potentates commanded a whole world of riches, blown to them by 'the chill East wind, the African wind, the West wind and the North'.[4] Hobbes's pope is the mirror of the Caesaropapist Byzantine Emperor, and his description evokes Plutarch's ridicule of the pretensions to divinity of Roman emperors who allowed themselves to be bowed down to 'like a barbaric idol'.[5]

1.4 HOBBES, THE UNIVERSITIES AND CROMWELL

If the *Elements* responded to the Laudian Anglo-Catholic revival then, *De cive* to the ecclesiastical disputes of the Long Parliament, and *Leviathan*, like *Behemoth* to the sectarian causes of the Civil War, to what immediate environment did the *Historia Ecclesiastica* respond? Almost certainly begun before Cromwell's death, if we look at those works published around the time of writing, it is not hard to see it as yet another of Hobbes's replies to his critics, targeting the universities, and particularly Oxford, for the concerted attack on his doctrines by Presbyterian as well as High Church divines. Written in Latin, like many of his works targeting academics, and in verse, perhaps better to impress them, the *Historia Ecclesiastica*, if it is a question of volume, addresses more lines to the foundation, function, growth, and systematic error of the universities, which are seen as outposts of papal and ecclesiastical power, than to any other topic.[6] The debates immediately surrounding the composition of the

---

[1] Paolo Sarpi, *The Historie of the Council of Trent Conteining Eight Bookes . . .* , trans. Nathaniel Brent (1620), 23-4, 28-9. See Collins, *Allegiance,* p. 56.

[2] *Hist. Eccl.*, lines 1530-5.

[3] *Hist. Eccl.*, 2185-97.

[4] *Hist. Eccl.*, lines 2191-2.

[5] *Hist. Eccl.*, lines 2193-4. See Plutarch, *How to tell a Flatterer* 65d, and *On the Fortune or the Virtue of Alexander* 331a. See Glenn F. Chestnut, *The First Christian Histories: Eusebius, Socrates, Sozomen, Theodoret and Evagrius* (Paris, Editions Beauchesne, 1986) p. 142.

[6] *Hist. Eccl.*, especially lines 1600 to 1974.

Historia Ecclesiastica were precisely on the subject of ecclesiastical government and schism, for the most part conducted by University divines, and the poem also represents a response to the challenge of specific divines, like John Bramhall (1594-1663), whose *Catching of the Leviathan*, was published in 1658.

The universities were thus the target of Hobbes's doctrines to a degree that is not commonly understood. It was as a project for the universities that Hobbes presented his 'science of *just* and *unjust*' in *Leviathan*; language that he does not use in that work, however, but only when he later comes to reflect upon it in *Behemoth*.[1] There he demands: 'Why may not men be taught their duty, that is, the science of just and unjust, as divers other sciences have been taught, from true principles, and evident demonstration; and much more easily than any of those preachers and democratical gentlemen could teach rebellion and treason?'[2] Much of *Behemoth* is devoted to showing how preachers and educators produced by the universities, together with 'democratical gentlemen' and classical republicans dominating parliament, impeded the reception of his 'demonstrable science' of justice in *Leviathan*, designed to appeal to those very universities. *Behemoth* (*c.* 1668) was a tract surreptitiously printed in faulty copies, and 'no book being more commonly sold by booksellers', according to William Crooke, the printer of the 1682 edition. There Hobbes bemoaned the fact that the universities encourage speculation concerning politics, government and divinity, and so become hotbeds of civil discord and rebellion:[3]

> I despair of any lasting peace till the universities here shall bend and direct their studies . . . to the teaching of absolute obedience to the laws of the king and to his public edicts under the Great Seal of England. For Latin, Greek and Hebrew, it would be better to substitute French, Dutch and Italian; philosophy and divinity advantage their professors but make mischief and faction in the state; natural philosophy may be studied in the gazettes of Gresham college.

---

[1] See Patricia Springborg, '*Behemoth* and Hobbes's "Science of *Just* and *Unjust*"', *Filozofski vestnik*, special issue on Hobbes's *Behemoth*, ed. Tomaz Mastnak, vol. 24, no. 2, 2003, pp. 267-89.

[2] *Beh.*, p. 39.

[3] *Ibid.*

Hobbes's reference to Gresham College, London, established in 1597 by Sir Thomas Gresham, founder of the Royal Exchange modeled on the Antwerp Bourse, is telling. Here during the Interregnum the Royal Society conducted weekly meetings. Such a 'modern' pragmatic institution was in direct contrast to the universities, initially developed as papal foundations intended for religious indoctrination, as he argues in the *Behemoth* and the *Historia Ecclesiastica*.[1] In the Latin *Leviathan*, in a passage paralleling those in the companion works, but missing from the English *Leviathan*, Hobbes forcibly makes this case – perhaps an indication of his greater interest in the universities in the 1660s, and a clue to the dating of the passage in the poem.[2]

> So by the sermons of the ecclesiastics sent from the universities into almost all the cities, towns and parishes of the Christian world, and by the published writings, it was fixed indelibly in the minds of all Christians *that there is no other rule of just and unjust except the dictates of the Roman Church, that kings are not to be obeyed further than is permitted by the Roman Church, and kings themselves ought to obey the Roman pontiff like sheep.* And they accomplished what they set out to accomplish.

But even in the English *Leviathan* Hobbes makes an implicit call for university reform, noting in the opening chapter his intention to address 'the use of universities . . . in a Commonwealth'.[3] It is not difficult to see his entire project of civil science, of which he immodestly and inaccurately claims to be the founder, as an exercise in civic education.

His call was not heeded, as he notes in *Behemoth*, and when men had 'grown weary at last of the insolence of the priests', they turned instead to 'the democratical principles of Aristotle and Cicero, and from the love of their eloquence fell in love with their politics, and that more and more, until it grew into the rebellion we now talk of'.[4]

---

[1] *Hist. Eccl.*, lines 1847-82 closely parallel the account in *Beh.*, pp. 40-1 of the rise of the universities, beginning with Paris and followed by Oxford, as papal instruments and seats of theology.

[2] *LL* xlvi (*OL*) §14, 320/473 (Curley edn), Hobbes's emphases.

[3] *Lev.*, i, §5, 4/7.

[4] *Beh.*, p. 43.

Hobbes rails against the delinquency of the universities that have suppressed his doctrines (as set out in *De cive* and *Leviathan*), which 'notwithstanding the obscurity of their author, have shined, not only in this, but also in foreign countries, to men of good education', but were systematically excluded from the university curricula by preachers who taught the contrary:[1]

> And, therefore, the light of that doctrine has been hitherto covered and kept under here by a cloud of adversaries, which no private man's reputation can break through, without the authority of the Universities. But out of the Universities, came all those preachers that taught the contrary. The Universities have been to this nation, as the wooden horse was to the Trojans.

The universities, not surprisingly, resented Hobbes's slander; just as they resented the Cromwellian Visitations, of which he approved. John Wallis (1616-1703), Savillian Professor of Mathematics in the University of Oxford, confided to his correspondent Christian Huygens in 1659, 'Our Leviathan is furiously attacking and destroying our Universities (and not only ours but all) and especially ministers and the clergy and all religion, as though the Christian world had not sound knowledge'.[2] When challenged by Seth Ward (1617-89), Savillian Professor of Astronomy at Oxford, that he wished the state to impose *Leviathan* on the universities, Hobbes, in his *Six Lessons to the Professors of the Mathematiques* of 1656, did not disagree: 'I would have the State make use of [the universities] to uphold the civill Power, as the Pope did to uphold the Ecclesiasticall. Is it not absurdly done to call this an Injury?'[3] Dedicated to Henry Pierrepont, an intimate who 'very much honour[ed] [the] Lord Protector',[4] the *Six Letters* not only defended Hobbes's sometimes indefensible

---

[1] *Beh.*, p. 40.

[2] Wallis to Christian Huygens, 1659, quoted in James Jacob, *Henry Stubbe: Radical Protestantism and the Early Enlightenment* (Cambridge, Cambridge University Press, 1983), p. 14; see Collins, *Allegiance,* p. 216.

[3] Hobbes, *Six Lessons to the Professors of the Mathematiques. One of Geometry, the other of Astronomy: In the Chaires set up by the Noble and Learned Sir Henry Savile, in the University of Oxford* (London 1656), pp. 61-2; see Collins, *Allegiance,* p. 219.

[4] See Collins, *Allegiance,* p. 217, citing the *Clarendon State Papers,* vol. iii, p. 412, and Marchemont Nedham's *Mercurius Politicus,* 22-29 July 1658.

mathematical theories, but explicitly upheld Cromwell's Erastian Church settlement. There Hobbes openly accepted Ward's charge that he wrote *Leviathan* to impose his doctrines on the universities, concluding with the extraordinary claim that these very doctrines had reconciled some thousand men to the Commonwealth. 'The cause of my writing that Book', he confessed,[1]

> was the consideration of what the Ministers before, and in the beginning of the Civill War, by their preaching and writing did contribute thereunto. Which I saw not onely to tend to the Abatement of the then Civill Power, but also to the gaining of as much thereof as they could (as did afterwards more plainly appear) unto themselves. I saw also that those Ministers, and many other Gentlemen who were of their Opinion, brought their Doctrines against the Civill Power from their Studies in the Universities. Seeing therefore that so much as could be attributed to the Peace of our Country and the settlement of Soveraign Powers without an Army, must proceed from Teaching; I had reason to wish, that Civill Doctrine were truly taught in the Universities. And if I had not thought that mine was such, I had never written it. And having written it, if I had not recommended it to such as had the Power to cause it to be taught, I had written it to no purpose. To me therefore . . . it was very necessary to commend my Doctrine to such men as should have the Power and Right to Regulate the Universities. I say *my Doctrine*; I say not my *Leviathan*. For wise men may so digest the same Doctrine as to fit it better for a publique teaching. But as it is, I believe that it hath framed the minds of a thousand Gentlemen to a consciencious obedience to present Government, which otherwise would have wavered in that Point.

'Take heed of calling them all Atheists that have read and approved my Leviathan', Hobbes admonished Ward (without in fact protesting the charge against himself).[2] 'See therefore how much you have been transported by your malice towards me, to injure the Civil Power by which you live'.[3] Cromwell had been personally installed as Chancellor of Oxford in 1650 and John Owen, his Vice-Chancellor dominated the new board of Visitors which virtually

---

[1] Hobbes, *Six Lessons*, pp. 56-7; see Collins, *Allegiance,* p. 218.
[2] Hobbes, *Six Lessons*, pp. 61-2; see Collins, *Allegiance,* p. 219.
[3] *Ibid.*

governed the university on behalf of the Independents from 1652.[1] That Hobbes endorsed parliamentary Visitations, both in the Interregnum and under the Restoration, he makes clear in both *Behemoth* and in the *Six Letters* because, as he charges in the latter, the universities were hotbeds of sedition *'both against the former and the present government'*.[2] He even contemplates a 'Lay-University' purged of such men, just as earlier, in 1641, in a letter to his patron the Earl of Devonshire, he had considered with favour a Nottingham petition calling for lay commissioners to replace bishops, as appropriate to the rising power of Independency and the Long Parliament's project of dismantling the Laudian Church:[3]

> I have seene the Nottinghamshire petition against the B[ishop]s. In it there are reckoned up abondance of abuses committed by Ecclesiasticall persons and their Officers, which can neyther be denyed nor excused. But that they proceed from the Episcopacy it selfe, is not so evidently proved. Howsoever since the Covetousnesse and supercilious behaviour of the persons, have made the people weary of that forme, I see nothing to be misliked in the new way propounded. If it please any that there are to be so many Lay Commissioners for church matters and so few ministers, I thinke it will be those that have most desired the change and made account to have the Episcopall authority divided amongst them. I am of the opinion that Ministers ought to minister rather then governe; at least that all Church government depend on the state, and authority of the Kingdome, without which there can be no unity in the church. Your Lordship may perhaps thinke this opinion but a fancy of Philosophy. But I am sure that Experience teaches, thus much, that the dispute for [precedence] between the spirituall and civill power, has of late more then any other thing in the world, bene the cause of civill warres, in all places of Christendome.

Henry Stubbe (1632-76), an early Enlightenment figure schooled in the Erastian writings of Machiavelli, Grotius and Selden, who had laboured at a Latin translation of *Leviathan*, until called off it as impolitic, was one of Hobbes's greatest allies at Oxford and an

---

[1] See Collins, *Allegiance*, p. 208.
[2] *Beh.*, pp. 147-8; and *Six Letters*, p. 60 (my emphases); see Collins, *Allegiance*, p. 219.
[3] Hobbes to Devonshire, 23 Jul. 1641, Hobbes *Correspondence*, p. 120, cited by Collins, *Allegiance*, p. 80.

important correspondent. Commenting on Hobbes's response to John Wallis's attack on the Independents in his *Mens Sobria* of 1656 in a letter now lost, Stubbe summed up his views as well as Hobbes's, when he claimed that Wallis's principles 'will carry us on with a farre greater apparence to a Pope, than a Presbitery; and the title of *Minister u[niversa]lis Ecclesiae* is the very cosen germane to that old mystery of iniquity, *Episcopus Ecclesiae catholicae*'.[1] But by 1656 the climate of opinion in Oxford had already changed, due in no small measure to the machinations of Cromwell and his men. In October of that year Stubbe reported to Hobbes the good news that John Owen and Du Moulin had defended Independency against Wallis's *Mens Sobria*. When Hobbes apparently expressed optimism at the news, Stubbe replied: 'Your reconcilement to the University pleaseth, and so I give out that Du Moulin's book and the Vice-Chancellor's [Owen's] are the pieces that have gained your good esteeme'.[2]

If Cromwell's Vice-Chancellor John Owen was the principal cause of Hobbes's mollification towards the university, Louis Du Moulin, well represented in the Hardwick Hall booklist (*q.v.*), was another. Born into the famous French theological family, Du Moulin was appointed Camden Professor of Ancient History as a result of the Oxford Visitation of 1648, a man remembered by Wood as a 'fiery violent and hot-headed Independent'.[3] The work by Owen that Hobbes commended so highly was undoubtedly his *Of Schism: the True Nature of it Discovered and Considered with Reference to the Present Differences in Religion*, of 1657, an important defense of Independency by one of the architects of the Interregnum Church settlement. Owen argued an unusual definition of schism, defending 'gathered communities' and insisting that a scriptural definition of schism could not be equated with institutional separation, which Paul's first letter to the Corinthians explicitly sanctioned. The Pauline notion of separation was far removed from that priestly caste

---

[1] Stubbe to Hobbes, 9 Nov. 1656, Hobbes *Correspondence*, pp. 338-9, quoted by Collins, *Allegiance*, p. 221.

[2] Stubbe to Hobbes, 14 Feb. 1657, Hobbes *Correspondence*, p. 449; see Collins, *Allegiance*, p. 225.

[3] Anthony Wood, *Athenae Oxonienses* (2 vols. London, 1691-2), vol. 2, p. 754; see Collins, *Allegiance*, p. 224.

of the 'old imperial government', which was Roman Catholicism, he insisted.[1] Of the many rejoinders Owen's work attracted, that of Daniel Cawdrey, a member of the Westminster Assembly of Divines allied with the Oxford Presbyterian faction, was the most vocal. In *Independencie a Great Schism proved against Dr. Owen*, of the same year, Cawdrey reinstated the conventional view of schism as 'causeless Separation from a true church', arguing that Paul's church at Corinth, far from being a separate congregation, belonged to a group of assemblies organized into a 'collectively' unified church, and declaring that 'All the present Schisms strike principally at the Ministers of the Gospel'.[2] Schism was the principal topos of the *Historia Ecclesiastica*, already in the making as these debates raged.

Du Moulin was a powerful spokesman for Erastian ecclesiology and Grotian natural rights theory, also writing about the time Hobbes began the poem; and the work to which Stubbe refers is likely his *Paraenesis ad aedificatores imperii in imperio*, of 1656. Du Moulin invoked Hobbesian arguments, but the compliments he paid the philosopher were mostly backhanded. So, praising Erastus for exposing 'ecclesiastical jurisdiction and excommunication as frauds', Du Moulin observed to Baxter that God 'hath permitted that men as ill principled as Grotius and Selden, yea Hobbes, as bad as can be, should come nearer the truth than many good men'.[3] Collins notes that by 1669 Hobbes's name was a 'virtual by-word for atheism', and Richard Baxter was one of his more prominent and implacable enemies.[4] Du Moulin did not shirk the language of *Leviathan*, however, claiming, 'It were to be wished that all Christian Magistrates would govern without that distinction of Powers, Ecclesiastical and Civil', and insisting that a church synod had no more power than 'a company of merchants or sea-men called by the Parliament to give them advice about trade and navigation'.[5]

---

[1] Owen, *Of Schism*, in *The Works of John Owen*, ed William Goold (28 vols. Edinburgh, 1826) vol. 13, pp. 100-1; see Collins, *Allegiance,* p. 234.

[2] Cawdrey, *Independencie a Great Schism*, pp. 7-8, 10-12 and 55; see Collins, *Allegiance,* p. 233.

[3] Du Moulin to Baxter, late 1669, Dr William's Library, Baxter Correspondence, vi, fos. 191-2; see Collins, *Allegiance,* p. 230.

[4] See Collins, *Allegiance,* p. 230.

[5] Du Moulin, *Paraenesis ad aedificatores imperii in imperio* (1656), pp. 12-13, 114; see Collins, *Allegiance,* p. 226.

Defending Erastus and the Erastians of the Westminster Assembly, including* John Selden, he, like Hobbes, attacked the Presbyterian notion of excommunication as the instrument with which the Pope 'hath built up his mystery of iniquity and founded an empire within the empire of Emperours'.[1] Independents, by contrast, achieved the 'strength'ning of Empires, especially of Monarchies',[2] he claimed, precisely because they were governed by the state, preventing 'ten thousand National Churches' from overrunning the land like 'a confusion of empires'.[3] But Du Moulin was also a trimmer, and close to death in 1680 he published *An Appeal to all Non-conformists in England to God* . . . in which, now vying for the King's favour and that of the Latitudinarians against the high-churchmen, he tried to distance Independency from the person of Cromwell, declaring: 'Oliver Cromwell's army, like that of King David's in the Wilderness, was a Medley or a Collection of all Parties that were discontented, as some Courtiers, some Episcopalians, few of any Sect, but most of none, or else of the religion of Thomas Hobbes'.[4]

Hobbes's critics were capable of a subtle reading of his religious project. Bramhall, like his peers, targeted Hobbes's Erastianism, his denial of the sacraments, rejection of the apostolic succession, the divine right of bishops, and the right of the church to decide doctrine. 'We are taught in the Creed to believe the Catholick or Universal church', Bramhall opined, 'But T.H. teacheth us the contrary'.[5] With allusion to Hobbes's Arianism, he declared: 'He might have been

---

[1] Du Moulin, *Of the Right of Churches and the Magistrate's Power over Them* (1658), pp. 194, 193, 326-9; see Collins, *Allegiance*, p. 226.

[2] Du Moulin, *The Conformity of the Discipline and Government of those who are commonly called Independents to that of the Ancient, Primitive Christians* (1680), pp. 16-17; see Collins, *Allegiance*, p. 229.

[3] Du Moulin, *The Power of the Christian Magistrate in Sacred Things* (1650), pp. 117-22; see Collins, *Allegiance*, p. 228 Moulin's phraseology finds an echo in lines 1061-2 of the *Hist. Eccl.*, about heresies 'changing into more forms than Proteus of old', and lines 2020-30, describing the mendicant orders swarming into the land like locusts.

[4] Du Moulin, *An Appeal of all the Non-conformists in England to God and all the Protestants of Europe* . . . (1681), pp. 20-1; see Collins, *Allegiance*, p. 230.

[5] Bramhall, *The Catching of the Leviathan, or the Great Whale* (1658), printed in Bramhall *Castigations of Mr. Hobbes his last animadversions, in the case concerning liberty and universal necessity* . . . . (London, 1658), pp. 480-5; see Collins, *Allegiance*, p. 267.

one of Tiberius his Council, when it was proposed to the Senate, Whether they should admit Christ to be God or not'.[1]

Herbert Thorndike, a Cambridge educated High Churchman, who upheld the doctrine of ecclesiastical dualism in his *Epilogue to the Tragedy of the Church of England* of 1659, which was an elaborate rejoinder to *Leviathan*, also charged Hobbes with Arianism in denying the divinity of Christ. He decried the monstrous 'conceit' of *Leviathan* that Christ came merely 'to restore the kingdome of God which the Jewes cast off when they rejected Samuel', which accounted him no more than a second Moses[2] – one of the many references to the 'philo-Semitic *Leviathan*'.[3] Among Hobbes's most astute readers, Thorndike explicitly connected Hobbes's Erastianism to Machiavelli, noting of his 'dissolution of Ecclesiastical power into the Secular' that it made of Christianity a mere civil religion.[4] Writing before the Scargill affair, Thorndike already accused Hobbes of the liar paradox:[5]

> a Religion taken up as a means to govern people in civil peace, (which is not onely the opinion of Machiavellians . . . but also those Philosophers, if any such there be, who do admit a Religion of all maxims which nature and reason hath taught men to agree in, but, that which supposeth revelation from above, onely as the Religion of their Countrey, not as true). I say, hee that should believe this, must necessarily believe nothing of the Church, more than the sovereign shall make it.

Thorndike, as early as 1649, in his *Discourse of the Right of the Church in a Christian State*, written in the wake of the regicide and the deliberations of the Westminster Assembly, had diagnosed Machiavellian statism and the anti-clericalism of the Venetian Paolo

---

[1] Bramhall, *The Catching of the Leviathan*, p. 493; see Collins, *Allegiance*, p. 267.

[2] Thorndike, *Epilogue*, 'to the reader', pp. 101, 81, cited by Collins, *Allegiance*, p. 251.

[3] See Collins, *Allegiance*, p. 238. On this topic see my 'Hobbes, Heresy and the *Historia Ecclesiastica*'; and Johann P. Sommerville, 'Hobbes, Selden, Erastianism, and the History of the Jews', in G.A.J. Rogers and Tom Sorell, eds., *Hobbes and History* (London, Routledge, 2000), pp. 160-187.

[4] Thorndike, *Epilogue*, 'to the reader', p. 146, cited by Collins, *Allegiance*, p. 252.

[5] *Ibid.*

Sarpi as sources of English Erastian Independency and schism. In a declaration that also included rivers as a tag for surrogacy, he observed of these twin influences: 'if we consider the ground on which both stand, they will appear to be as the Rivers that rise out of Apennius, which empty themselves, some into the sea of Tuscany, others into the gulf of Venice'.[1]

The claim was not without precedent. John Hall of Durham, a member of Hobbes's Independence-inclined interregnum circle, had openly referred to 'the famous father Paul of Venice, whose excellent endeavours of asserting the Civil Right against the Ecclesiastick usurpation will scarcely bee forgotten';[2] while from 1648 on, Jeffrey Collins has argued, Cromwell 'was relentlessly characterized as a "Machiavellian"', his greatest 'Machiavellian treacheries', deemed to be his manipulation of religion.[3] Marchamont Nedham, the ubiquitous pamphleteer who was allied to Cromwellian Magisterial Independents, declaimed in one issue of *Mercurius Politicus* that 'Treason never walks so secure as under the cloak of religion',[4] the unmasking of which was the journal's mission. Marshalling Lipsius, Guiccardini and Tacitus to demonstrate the demonism of priestcraft, Nedham dared to cite Machiavelli on the danger of prophets armed, as demonstrated by Savonarola.[5] In the Introduction to his *Excellency of a Free Nation*, he referred both to Sallust and Machiavellian republican arguments.[6] In the case of Nedham we have a classical republican who was in fact a convinced Hobbist and an overt

---

[1] Thorndike, 'A Review', in *Right of the Church*, pp. iii-iv, cited by Collins, *Allegiance*, p. 253.

[2] John Hall *A Gagg to Love's Advocate* (1651), p. 10, cited by Collins, *Allegiance*, p. 197.

[3] See Collins, *Allegiance*, p. 156-7, citing the tract *A Hue and Cry After Cromwell* (1649), pp. 1-2.

[4] *Mercurius Politicus*, issue 55 (19-26 June 1651), p. 879; see Collins, *Allegiance*, p. 200.

[5] Nedham, *The Case of the Common-wealth of England Stated: the Equity, Utility, and Necessity of a Submission to the Present Government Cleared out of Monuments both Sacred and Civill all the scruples and pretenses of the opposite parties: Royalists, Presbyterians, Scots, Levellers* ... (London, 1650), pp. 20, 98-9; see Collins, *Allegiance*, p. 200.

[6] Marchamont Nedham, *The Excellency of a Free State* (1656 edn), ed. Richard Baron, London, p. xxvi, cited in Quentin Skinner, *Liberty Before Liberalism* (Cambridge, Cambridge University Press, 1998), pp. 63-4.

Cromwellian. His defense of Cromwell and the Protectorate in *The Case of the Commonwealth of England* simply states the main tenets of the Cromwellian regime, while we have a plethora of examples for his Hobbism, mostly unacknowledged, however. In *The Excellencie of a Free State* Nedham uses the term compact like Hobbes, but without citing him, to designate an agreement between the people that creates a society, as opposed to an agreement between a ruler and the people, contemplated in the sectarian covenant model advanced by Johannes Althusius in *Politica* (1614) and Samuel Rutherford in *Lex, Rex* (1644).[1]

Hobbes in *Behemoth* struck a Machiavellian tone himself when he noted that the sects 'were Cromwell's best cards, whereof he had a very great number in the army, and some in the House, whereof he himself was thought one; though he were nothing certain, but applying himself always to the faction which was strongest, and was of a color like it'.[2] His assessment matches that of the anonymous tract, *Perfect Politician: Or the . . . Life and Actions (Military and Civil) of Oliver Cromwell* (1681), where Cromwell's attachment to toleration is explained as a 'masterpiece in politics', which 'procured him a party'.[3] And this is precisely how Hobbes's Cromwell was read by Adam Ebert, a Frankfurt law professor in the employ of Frederick I, who undertook to translate *Behemoth*, believing that in Cromwell Hobbes had portrayed 'the ideal of the Tacitean prince'.[4] In this respect Hobbes returns to the humanist models of his early career, his 'Cromwell recall[ing] the Augustus of the *Horae Subsecivae*, who had seized the "Supremacy in matters Ecclesiastical, which is one of the chiefest guides of a Commonwealth"'.[5] Thucydides, Cicero, Tacitus, Varro and Polybius, Epicurus, Lucretius, Diodorus, Machiavelli, Paolo Sarpi, Montaigne and Lipsius, are the thinkers to

---

[1] Skinner, *Liberty before Liberalism*, pp. 63-4.

[2] *Beh.*, p. 136; Collins, *Allegiance*, p. 156.

[3] See Collins, *Allegiance*, p. 156.

[4] See Collins, *Allegiance*, p. 156n, citing Noel Malcolm, 'Behemoth Latinus: Adam Ebert, Tacitism and Hobbes', *Filozofski vestnik*, vol. 24 (2003), pp. 85-120, at pp. 106-19.

[5] See Collins, *Allegiance*, p. 156, citing *Horae Subsecivae* [1620], in *Three Discourses: A Critical Modern Edition of Newly Identified Work of the Young Thomas Hobbes*, ed. N. B. Reynolds and A. W. Saxonhouse (Chicago, Il., University of Chicago Press, 1995), p. 50.

whom we must look for the provenance of Hobbes's religious views, so sceptical that they take him into uncharted waters, at one time even a supporter of Cromwell, because he played the sects off against one another and promised a bishopless regime, a departure that Hobbes lived to regret under the Restoration.

1.5 HOBBES'S CONTINENTAL RECEPTION

If we cannot infer meaning directly from context, inferring meaning from a work's reception is an even more doubtful enterprise, particularly in the case of polemical and adversarial writings. But reception is another set of facts. Latin, the language of the European Republic of Letters, made Hobbes's works almost immediately accessible on the Continent. As a consequence, by sheer volume his Continental reception was at least equal to his reception at home,[1] his audience understandably greater in the Protestant north – to which the presentation of his prose works in Latin was principally directed – than in the Catholic south. *De cive* continued to be the most influential of his writings abroad precisely because of its continuing availability in Latin, for, until 1668 *Leviathan* was available only in English, a language which, with a few notable exceptions like Pufendorf (who in fact owned the 1667 Dutch edition of *Leviathan*) and Voltaire, the Continental public could not read.[2] The publication of the *Opera Philosophica* in Amsterdam in 1688 introduced Hobbes's *philosophia prima* as well as his scientific works to the European Republic of letters, prominent members of whom became interested in him for a range of reasons, in particular for his ecclesiology and Erastianism. As Noel Malcolm notes:

> Before the standard line on Hobbes had . . . begun to incorporate him in to a tradition of philosophical atheism, a very different

---

[1] For the reception of Hobbes in Europe, see Noel Malcolm's excellent, 'Hobbes and the European Republic of Letters', in *Aspects of Hobbes*, pp. 457-546. This chapter draws on my review of Malcolm: see Springborg, 'The Enlightenment of Thomas Hobbes: Review Essay on Noel Malcolm's, *Aspects of Hobbes*', *British Journal for the History of Philosophy*, 12 (3) 2004, pp. 513-34. I thank the publishers for the right to reprint some of the material.

[2] Malcolm, 'Hobbes and the European Republic of Letters', p. 462.

accusation had exercised the minds of many of his critics: 'indif-
ferentism' . . . a general term used by defenders of confessional
orthodoxy (especially Lutherans and Calvinists) to stigmatize a
variety of thinkers – Erastian political theorists, rationalist
philosophers, ecumenist and irenicist theologians – who down-
played the differences between the denominations and suggested
that practices or doctrines could legitimately vary from Church to
Church or from state to state, so long as the few fundamentals of
Christian belief were maintained by all.[1]

The statesman and polymath, Freiherr Johann Christian von
Boineburg (1622-52), who had read *De cive* by October 1650 and
reported on *Leviathan* in December 1656, which, as Malcolm
remarks, appears to qualify him as 'the first person in Germany to
take notice of [it]',[2] fits the profile of the politically engaged Northern intellectual most likely to read Hobbes. Brought up a Lutheran,
he had studied at Jena (1638-43), and then at Helmstedt University
(1643-4), After serving the Landgraves of Hesse-Darmstadt and
Hesse-Braubach, von Boineburg accepted the offer in 1653 from
Johann Philipp von Schönborn, archbishop-elector of Mainz, to
become marshal of the court of Mainz and prime minister, on condition that he convert to Catholicism. Proving himself to be an Erastian he accepted, working in this capacity for a balance of power
between the Habsburg emperor and the German princes and a solution to the Roman Catholic-Lutheran-Calvinist conflict; but unsuc-
cessfully. The victim of political intrigue, he retired from politics and
devoted himself to research, leaving a voluminous correspondence
(still extant) with literary figures and scientists. For von Boineburg
Hobbes headed the list of a veritable Who's Who of *libertins* that
included Vossius, Caspar Barlaeus, Marc'Antonio de Dominis,
Georg Calixtus, Conrad Berg, Grotius, Thomas Browne, Acontius,
Scioppius, Casaubon, and La Peyrère, whom he characterized as
the type to 'adhere to no confession, preferring his own beliefs'.[3]
The Freiherr at one point referred to Hobbes along with his old
friend Edward Herbert, among the 'teachers of self-love, licence,
and religious indifference'.[4]

---

[1] *Ibid.*, p. 478.
[2] *Ibid.*, p. 518.
[3] *Ibid.*, p. 478.
[4] *Ibid.*

Once Hobbes acquired a Deist profile, demand for *De cive* gathered apace. A second enlarged edition arranged by Samuel Sorbière was published by Elsevier in Amsterdam in 1647, but immediately sold out, being reset and republished in the same year. Further printings in 1657 (Amsterdam), 1760 (Amsterdam), 1696 (Amsterdam), c.1704 (Halle), 1742 (Amsterdam?), 1760 (Lausanne) and 1782 (Basel), kept the work in circulation.[1] Next most important on the Continent after *De cive*, was the Latin collection of Hobbes's works, the *Opera philosophica*, published in 1668 at Amsterdam by Johan Blaeu with Sorbière's assistance, which included *De cive*, along with works on metaphysics, physics and optics (*De corpore*, *Dialogus physicus*, *Problemata physica*, *De homine*), and the Latin *Leviathan*, especially prepared by Hobbes for this edition.

The *Historia Ecclesiastica* eventually found its European public too and was substantially excerpted in S. J. Baumgarten's 12 volume *Nachrichten von merkwürdigen Bücher* of 1752-8.[2] Indeed, some forty years previous, the early German Enlightenment figure, Christian Thomasius (1655-1728), who equaled Leibniz in his enthusiasm for Hobbes and who, as a founder of the new university at Halle, had a significant student following, had already made an extensive German summary of the poem. Thomasius was a Deist, which makes him representative of the other type of Northern European intellectual to whom Hobbes appealed. The son of the philosopher Jakob Thomasius, Leibniz's teacher, he began his career at the University of Leipzig studying Physics, Mathematics, History and Philosophy, graduating Magister in 1672. Taking an early interest in Pufendorf's theories of Natural Law, jurisprudence became his vocation at successive universities: Frankfurter Universität Viadrina (1675), Frankfurt Oder (1679), back to Leipzig, then Halle (1690). Famous for his application of Pufendorf's theories of natural law to specific cases, beginning with his dissertation on bigamy in 1684, Thomasius was constantly involved in legal controversy. In 1687 his *Lehrbuch des Naturrechtes* appeared, and in 1699 his legal anthology, *Summarischer Entwurf der Grundregeln, die einem studioso juris zu wissen nöthig*. In 1701 his *De crimine magiae* was published,

---

[1] *Ibid.*, p. 459.
[2] *Ibid.*, p. 460, n. 9.

'to which the gradual abolition of witch-trials in Brandenburg-Prussia in the period 1714-28' is largely attributed.[1] Emphasizing at the outset Hobbes's theme of priestcraft, metaphysics and theology as instruments of clerical control, Thomasius read the *Historia Ecclesiastica* as a gloss on *Leviathan*, referring readers to Chapter 45 of that work, which addresses the relics of pagan demonology in the Christian Church.[2] He had no quarrel with Hobbes's account of the theology of the early Church in the poem,[3] disagreeing only on the doctrine of mortalism and a citizen's obligation to obey the sovereign in religious matters, his reading of Hobbes otherwise representative of Enlightenment Deists:[4]

> Leaving those points aside, I say, this is certainly no trifling work that Hobbes has written; with it, he has thrust his hand, so to speak, into the heart and bowels of the Pope, and has found out his hiding-place better than anyone before him.

Negative publicity tends to whet the public appetite better than positive, as Thomasius clearly understood, when at the opening of his published synthesis of Hobbes's *Vita* and the Aubrey-Blackburne 'Vitae auctarium', he observed:[5]

> Most people are so constituted that when they read the writings of someone whose name is in the black book . . . they are immediately gripped by their prejudices, and try to find the most harmful poison and most dreadful heresies in every word and syllable . . . . Now, even though Hobbes has written much that most orthodox people would not be happy to repeat, nevertheless he has also written and discovered much that we should accept from him with thanks.

---

[1] See Malcolm, 'Hobbes and the European Republic of Letters', pp. 531-2, and Wikipedia, de.wikipedia.org/wiki/Christian_Thomasius.
[2] Christian Thomasius, *Summarischer Nachrichten von auserlesenen, mehrentheils alten, in der Thomasischen Bibliotheque verhandelnen Büchern*, 24 parts, part 4 (Halle and Leipzig, 1715-1718), pp. 315-17, discussed by Malcolm in 'Hobbes and the European Republic of Letters', p. 532 and notes.
[3] Thomasius, *Summarischere Nachrichten*, part 4 (1715), pp. 315-17, Malcolm, *loc. cit.*, p. 532.
[4] Thomasius, *Summarischere Nachrichten*, part 4 (1715), p. 357, Malcolm, *loc. cit.*, p. 532.
[5] Thomasius, *Summarischere Nachrichten*, part 2 (1715), p. 166, Malcolm, *loc. cit.*, p. 532.

The rhetorical question with which Thomasius closed the work is marked by the ingenuousness that often disguised deviant views: 'So what should we think of Hobbes? Does he belong to the list of atheists?', he asked, replying, 'I do not want to, indeed I cannot, say so'.[1]

By 1711, due in no small part to the interest generated by Thomasius in Halle, demand for a new edition of Hobbes's works had grown sufficiently for the German publisher Thomas Fritsch, in nearby Leipzig, to take on the project with his brother Caspar;[2] a project that was thwarted when the Elector of Saxony, Friedrich Augustus, personally intervened with the book-licensing authorities to prevent it.[3] But this did not staunch a steady flow of dissertations, books, sermons, tracts and clandestine pamphlets addressing Hobbes and his works, sometimes hot on the heels of their publication, in small cities that we do not think of as particularly cosmopolitan, like Kiel, Rostock, Dittmarschen, in Schlieswig Holstein, as well as in Berlin, Bremen, Cologne, Hamburg, and major university cities like Greifswald, Leipzig, Dresden, Tübingen, Halle and Jena. A guide to the second hand book market from the mid-eighteenth century described Hobbes's 1668 *Opera philosophica* as a 'Highly sought after collection, copies of which have become quite rare in the trade – which has raised their value'.[4]

One of the most bizarre episodes in Hobbes's Continental *Rezeptionsgeschichte* was the 'the three imposters' phenomenon, linking Hobbes, Spinoza and Descartes 'to construct a genealogy of modern atheism'.[5] The 'three imposters' were in fact a movable feast and sometimes comprised Edward Herbert, Hobbes and Spinoza, sometimes Hobbes, Spinoza and Balthsar Dekker. As a genre, the work known as *De tribus impostoribus*, or *De imposturis religionum*, was a version of manuscripts circulated clandestinely, claiming to expose Moses, Mohammed and Jesus as imposters, and rumoured to date from the sixteenth century. In fact this work was written in 1688 by

---

[1] Thomasius, *Summarischere Nachrichten*, part 2 (1715), p. 182, Malcolm, *loc. cit.*, p. 532.

[2] Malcolm, 'Hobbes and the European Republic of Letters', p. 533.

[3] *Ibid.*, pp. 461-3.

[4] *Ibid.*, p. 469.

[5] *Ibid.*, p. 481.

Johann Joachim Müller, an obscure Hamburg intellectual who 'displayed an unusually detailed knowledge of Hobbes's writings'.[1] It achieved extraordinary circulation figures: 'more than seventy copies have been recorded in collections in Germany, Austria, Italy, France, England, Holland, Denmark, and Russia'.[2] A later addition to the genre, which appeared between 1700 and 1704, is even more bizarre, for although 'presented as the long sought-after treatise on the "three imposters"', it was not that at all, in fact, but a slightly altered version of a different text, the 'Esprit de Monsieur de Spinoza', written probably in the 1680s. In the various versions in which it circulated – and at least 169 manuscript copies are recorded – including two printed versions, *La Vie et l'Esprit de Mr Benoît de Spinosa*, and *Traité des trois imposteurs*, the work although ostensibly inspired by Spinoza, 'borrowed directly and extensively from Hobbes' on the origins of religion in fear and superstition, the machinations of priests, contamination of Christianity by pagan demonology, quoting directly from the Latin *Leviathan* and its important 1668 Appendix.[3]

The 'three great imposters' became the target of a series of attacks by such Lutheran professors or divines, as Jakob Thomasius, father of Christian, as early as May 1670 at Leipzig; by Christian Kortholt at the University of Kiel; by Michael Berns at Dittmarschen; and by Ernst Kettner at the University of Leipzig. So, 'by the first decade of the eighteenth century, an entire canon of unorthodoxy had thus been established that, according to writers such as Valentin Ernst Löscher in Dresden and Zacharias Grapius in Rostock, ran from Pomponazzi, the early Socinians and Vanini, via Herbert, Descartes, Hobbes and Spinoza, to Bekker, Locke, and Toland'.[4] Nor was Hobbes's reception confined to professors and divines. His doctrines were also discussed and

---

[1] *Ibid.*, p. 491.

[2] See Malcolm, 'Hobbes and the European Republic of Letters', p. 491, citing J. J. Müller, *De imposturis religionum (De tribus impostoribus)*, ed. W. Schröder (Stuttgart, 1999), pp. 40-66, at p. 58.

[3] See Malcolm, 'Hobbes and the European Republic of Letters', pp. 492-3, citing the Introduction to Françoise Charles-Daubert's edition of *Le 'Traité des trois imposteurs' et 'La Vie et l'Esprit de Spinosa': philosophie clandestine entre 1678 and 1768* (Oxford, 1999), pp. 5-7, 102-6, 449-55.

[4] Malcolm, 'Hobbes and the European Republic of Letters', pp. 492-3.

disputed in dissertations by conservative, and sometimes Aristotelian, jurists in the Netherlands, Tübingen, Kiel, and Copenhagen, from 1659 on, most famously by Pufendorf, who openly acknowledged his debt to Hobbes.[1]

If Hobbes's European reception by sheer volume appears to be greatest in the Protestant north, particularly Germany, Holland, Denmark and Sweden, it would be a mistake to underestimate his French readership. Malcolm reports the findings of a bibliographic survey of library catalogues in France for their holdings of Hobbes's works:[2]

> Yves Glaziou's analysis of thirty-eight catalogues of French eighteenth century private libraries yields the following results: ten had *De cive* in Latin and fourteen had it in French, thirteen possessed the *Opera philosophica*, three had the Latin *Leviathan*, one had *De corpore* and one *De homine*. A fairly similar pattern emerges from the 'Catalogue collectif de la France', which lists the holdings of fifty-five public libraries: thirty-six copies of *De cive* in Latin and thirty-seven in French, fourteen copies of the *Opera philosophica*, five of the Latin *Leviathan*, five of *De corpore*, and five of *De homine*.

Notoriety enhanced reception. None of Hobbes's works of the 1660s had been passed by the English Stationer's Register, and all were early listed in the Papal Index of Prohibited Books.[3] *De cive* had been placed on the Index in 1654, although four editions had previously been issued; and Oxford University Press was ordered to burn it in 1683, after six editions had been published, while the rest of Hobbes's works were added to the Papal Index in 1709. *De cive* was formally banned by the Court of Holland, which in 1674 extended the ban to *Leviathan*, and by the Swiss canton of Bern which banned 'the atheistical and deistic writings of Hobbes together with those of Aretino, Machiavelli, Herbert, Spinoza, and [Richard] Simon'.[4]

---

[1] *Ibid.*, pp. 520-1.
[2] Malcolm, 'Hobbes and the European Republic of Letters', p. 460, citing Yves Glaziou, *Hobbes en France au XVIIIe siècle* (Paris, P.U.F., 1995), pp. 222-35.
[3] See Malcolm, 'Hobbes and the European Republic of Letters', p. 470.
[4] See Malcolm, 'Hobbes and the European Republic of Letters', p. 470.

CHAPTER 2

TEXT AND TIME FRAME:
MATERIAL EVIDENCE

2.1 MATERIAL EVIDENCE, PRELIMINARY

It is worth reviewing the external evidence and the time-frame of the *Historia Ecclesiastica* for the light it sheds on Hobbes's intentions and his intended audience. More important still is the hitherto neglected task of reviewing the internal evidence and examining the relationship between his various works on those crucial issues on which the heresy charges turned: the nature of the Trinity, the divinity of Christ, and the authority of the Scriptures. Heterodox views on any one of these issues had been made hanging offences by the Parliament in 1648 and 1650 (see chapter 3.1).

Let us turn first to the material evidence for the poem, to be examined in detail in chapter 3. We have a printed book in Latin, a printed paraphrase of the book in English, and three manuscripts of the poem: two more or less contemporaneous and one later, and two of Continental provenance and one English. We also have a number of conflicting reports about the poem from contemporaries, the bulk of them from Hobbes's biographer John Aubrey. Then we have a fair amount of circumstantial evidence in the form of atheism charges against Hobbes and the changing laws in terms of which they were framed, to which the poem might be a response, as well as a limited range of influential statesmen to whom it might be addressed by way of an appeal for support or protection.

The *Historia Ecclesiastica,* was printed by Crooke, the printing house of all Hobbes's English works with the exception of his 'Answer' to Davenant's Preface to *Gondibert,* printed with it. In the

case of the *Ecclesiastical History*, the printer was not the intrepid
Andrew Crooke, publisher of the *Elements of Law* and *Leviathan*,
who had also issued two surreptitious editions of Sir Thomas
Browne's *Religio Medici* in 1642, but the more cautious William
Crooke, who did not permit the company name to appear on the title
page. The poem is simply announced as *A Church History in the
form of an Elegiac Poem: Historia Ecclesiastica Carmine Elegiaco
Concinnata. Authore Thoma Hobbio Malmesburiensi. Opus Posthu-
mum, Augustae Tinobantus: Anno Salutis MDCLXXXVIII.* But the
title page includes the epigram from Ovid's *Metamorphoses* I.130-1,
already mentioned, a comment on religion that became a Deist bye
word, and probably selected by Thomas Rymer, who supplied the
long and interpretive preface that is very useful in situating the work.
Rymer, a Royalist with ties to literary circles we know Hobbes frequented, who had worked with Waller and Dryden, had himself participated in the translation of Ovid's *Tristia*. As one sees immediately, the title page reads very differently from that of the eighteenth
century English paraphrase, *A True Ecclesiastical History From
Moses to the Time of Martin Luther*, about which we know so little.

In addition to the 1688 printed edition and the 1722 paraphrase,
we have three manuscripts. The first MS, (A), although undated,
must have been transcribed some time before the printed edition
appeared in 1688, because it is corrected in heavy black ink to that
edition. It is held in the British Library as BL Harl. 1844, its title
page reading, *Historia Ecclesiastica Romana. Autore Pereximio
Viro THOMA. HOBBESIO Malmesburiensi (History of the Roman
Church by that very esteemed author, Thomas Hobbes of Malmesbury)*. The other two MSS are of Continental provenance, the second
MS, (B), is the Royal Copenhagen Library MS Thotts Sml., 4o Nr.
213. Its title page reads: *HISTORIA ECCLESIASTICA ROMANA.
consignata à THOMA HOBBESIO. Ex Bibliotheca My Lord
Vaugan.exscripsit Londini, Georgius Grund Ad 1685 (HISTORY OF
THE ROMAN CHURCH, signed by Thomas Hobbes. From My Lord
Vaughan's Library, copied in London by George Grund, AD 1685)*.
It appears to be a better copy of the same original as MS A before it
was corrected to the 1688 edition, thus allowing us to date both MSS
as contemporaneous and prior to the printed book. The third MS,
(C), the Vienna MS, simply replicates the 1688 printed edition, but
gives the date as 1678.

This was an age in which books were expensive and scarce and it was not uncommon for a bibliophile to make scribal copies, which would account for MSS B and C.[1] But Hobbes's manuscripts were a special case. Some, particularly the *Elements of Law*, seem to have been designed for scribal publication, to be circulated only among Gentlemen of a certain persuasion, and we have Hobbes's own testimony on that work's wide exposure. Other works remained in manuscript due to their failure to pass the Stationer's Register and Hobbes's printer undertook to circulate them. William Crooke circulated manuscripts of *Behemoth, Dialogue of the Common Laws*, and the *Historical Narration Concerning Heresy*.[2] And in June 1675, he published *A Supplement of Mr Hobbes his Workes printed by Blaeu at Amsterdam*, advertising a catalogue of the author's various manuscripts, including the *Historia Ecclesiastica Romana*, which presumably he also had in his possession. This undoubtedly accounts in part for the variances between the MSS that have survived, for so much copying was bound to produce corrupted texts. The variants between MSS A, B and C tell us a great deal about their dating and their relation to the 1688 printed edition (see Appendix A, 'A Survey of the MSS and printed texts').

Apart from the printed book, the manuscripts and the eighteenth century paraphrase, we have at least four important pieces of circumstantial evidence for the dating of Hobbes's poem, and more complex evidence that I will later discuss in chapter 3. Of these four facts, three are well known. They are that:

1. Aubrey records that in 1659 Hobbes had written some 500 lines of the poem while he was staying at 'Little Salisbury House (now turned to the Middle Exchange)' in London;[3]

2. the account book of James Wheldon's personal finances, dated Sept-Oct 1671, 'At Chatsworth', records: 'Given me by Mr. Hobbes

---

[1] I am grateful to Noel Malcolm for this observation, Personal Communication, Malcolm to Springborg, 27/1/2005.

[2] See Mark Goldie, 'Andrew Crooke', in the new *DNB*.

[3] John Aubrey, *Brief Lives*, vol. 1, pp. 338-9:

> In 1659, his lord was and some years before-at Little Salisbury House (now turned to the Middle Exchange), where he wrote, among other things, a poem in Latin hexameter and pentameter, of the encroachment of the clergy (both Roman and reformed) on the civil power. I remember I saw then over five hundred verses (for he numbered every tenth as he wrote). I remember he did read Cluverius's Historia universalis, and made up his poem from this.

for writing a book, *Historia Ecclesiastica Romana*, one pound';[1] and

3. William Crooke's catalogue of Hobbes's various manuscripts, including the *Historia Ecclesiastica Romana*, published in June 1675 as *A Supplement of Mr Hobbes his Workes printed by Blaeu at Amsterdam.*[2]

A fourth fact has not been previously taken into account and may cast some light on the nature of the poem and why Hobbes wrote it:

4. A letter from François du Verdus to Hobbes, dated [24 July] 3 August 1664, reported to Hobbes news from M. du Prat, that 'you were putting your entire philosophical system into Latin verse, in a style somewhat similar to that of Hesiod, with whose works you had closely familiarized yourself for that purpose'.[3]

This fourth fact is not so decisive and has been dismissed by Noel Malcolm,[4] but in what follows I shall make the case for this also being a reference to the *Historia Ecclesiastica*.

In terms of sources we have an invaluable archive in the Hardwick Hall library that Hobbes helped assemble for his patron, William Cavendish, 2nd Earl of Devonshire (c. 1590-1628), as he proudly notes in his Latin verse autobiography.[5] There are two Cavendish book lists extant, which should not be confused,

---

[1] Miriam Reik, *The Golden Lands of Thomas Hobbes* (Detroit, Wayne State University Press, 1977), p. 225, n.3.

[2] K. Schuhmann, *Hobbes. Une chronique.* I thank Professor Lessay for pointing this out to me.

[3] Du Verdus to Hobbes, [24 July] 3 August 1664, Hobbes *Correspondence*, p. 625.

[4] Malcolm's note to du Verdus' letter, Hobbes *Correspondence*, p. 625.

[5] Hobbes's *Vita*, lines 77-84 *OL* I, p. xvii, where he in fact claims the library to have been his, but purchased by his patron William Cavendish Earl of Devonshire: 'Thus I at ease did live, of books, whist he [Cavendish]/ Did with all sorts supply my library'; a report corroborated by Aubrey in *Brief Lives*, vol. 1, p. 338: 'I have heard [Hobbes] say, that at his lord's house in the country there was a good library, and that his lordship stored the library with what books he thought fit to be bought'. A free translation of Hobbes's Latin verse *Vita* is published in the prefatory materials to by Edwin Curley's edition of *Leviathan* (Indianapolis, Ind., Hackett Publishing, 1994), pp. liv to lxiv, see at p. lv, lines 77-8. Hobbes proceeds briefly to discuss the library's contents at lines 80-5.

Chatsworth MS E1A, which is in Hobbes's own hand, and was
drawn up in the 1620s to record the contents of the Hardwick Hall
Library, but also includes additions made by Hobbes in the 1630s
after he returned to the Cavendish household; and MS E2, which has
been established by Noel Malcolm as in the hand of Robert Payne,
Oxford don, chaplain to the Earl of Newcastle and collaborator on
scientific pursuits.[1] MS E1A, the Hardwick Hall book list (as I refer
to it) is divided between general authors and a separately listed 'Theological Library', which catalogues the books that Hobbes collected
and to which he had access. Although not yet published in full, or
systematically analyzed, it is invaluable in disclosing the range of
Hobbes's possible ecclesiastical sources, and I analyze its contents
in Appendix B.

MS E2, which is not in Hobbes's hand, is also not a catalogue of
the Cavendish library. It in fact corresponds to the Bodleian Library
catalogues for this period, the reason being that most of the books it
comprises were those Kenelm Digby had inherited from his tutor at
Gloucester Hall, Oxford, Thomas Allen (1542-1632), mathematician and practitioner of the occult sciences, which, in consultation
with Sir Robert Cotton and Archbishop Laud, Digby deposited in the
Bodleian Library (while a further collection of the Arabic MSS was
transferred through Laud to St. John's College library, Oxford). MS
E2 has been taken by some Hobbes scholars, following Pacchi, who
published it, to represent Hobbes's 'ideal library', which might have
been the case were it, as Pacchi assumed, in Hobbes's hand.[2] But it is
interesting to speculate why Payne might have copied it, presumably
at the request of his patron, and it records an archive to which
Hobbes may well have had access, as being in the possession of one
of his associates whom Hobbes knew in Paris. Sir Kenelm Digby,
author, naval commander, diplomat and alchemist, who underwrote

---

[1] See the *Index of English Literary Manuscripts*, vols. I (1450-1625) and 11
(1625-1700) compiled by Dr. Peter Beal (London, 1980), at vol. 2. part 1, pp. 576-
86. MS E2 in the Chatsworth archive has been established by Noel Malcolm as in
the hand of Robert Payne, and not Hobbes. See Malcolm, 'Robert Payne, the
Hobbes Manuscripts, and the "Short Tract"', in *Aspects of Hobbes*, p. 82, n. 7.
[2] See Arrigo Pacchi, 'Una "biblioteca ideale" di Thomas Hobbes: il MS E2 del-
l'archivio di Chatsworth', *Acme, Annali della Facoltà di Lettere e Filosofia dell'
Università degli Studi di Milano*, vol. 21, no. 1, 1968, pp. 5-42.

the publication of *De cive*, was an intimate of the Mersenne circle, a member of the Blackloist group and a mastermind of the Louvre faction in Paris.[1] He is the probable conduit for Hobbes's interest in Renaissance esoterica, alchemy and magic.

MS E2 is heavily weighted in favour of science and mathematics, comprising sections on 'Science', 'Arithmetic and Numbers', 'Geometry and Measurement', 'Astronomy', and 'Perspective'. But more than half the items reflect Digby's interest in alchemy and the occult, including works by John Dee (item 622), Ficino (item 637), Proclus (items 760 and 761), Psellus (item 762), the Hermes Trismegistus (item 706), and Rosselius' Commentary on it (item 772), Reuchlin's and other works on the Cabala (items, 56, 57, 58), as well as various books on witchcraft (items 766, 787, 842, 843), angels (item 777), and general books on magic and the occult (items 625, 681, 687, 688, 710, 718, 739, 747, 752, 781, 817), even a book on Egyptian hieroglyphics (item 852) and Arabic grammar (item 47). The question of Hobbes's interest in Orientalia and the occult is provoked by the *Historia Ecclesiastica* in particular, but relatively unexplored (see chapter 5.2).

2.2 TEXT AND TIME FRAME: MANUSCRIPTS AND REPORTS

The *Historia Ecclesiastica* has a textual history so complex that it cannot be established with certainty. The four pieces of material evidence for its existence, set out in chapter 2.1, are complicated by a series of apparently discrepant and conflicting reports, which I will treat together as items 1 through 9. A work too controversial to be printed in England in Hobbes's life-time, and circulated first in manuscript, its later entry into the networks of clandestine Continental Deist literature probably accounts for two out of the three extant MSS, both of which have Continental provenance: the Thott MS.213 of 1685 (B), copied by Georg Grund and now housed in the Royal Copenhagen Library, and the eighteenth century Vienna MS (C), about which we have no information.

---

[1] See Collins, *Allegiance,* pp. 89, 91, 113, 136-9, 147.

The third manuscript, Harley MS 1844 (A), held in the British Library, and presumably of local provenance, is puzzling. When the loose leaves onto which it was transcribed were subsequently bound too tightly, somebody took the trouble to rectify the material lost in the gutter, as well as making significant changes to the text and the versification. The corrector, whoever he may have been, appears to have corrected the MS to the 1688 printed edition. The uncorrected Harley MS (A), visible beneath the corrections in heavy black ink, in fact corresponds closely to the Thott MS. (B), copied by Grund, as he acknowledges, from a manuscript lodged in 'My Lord Vaughan's Library' and 'signed by Hobbes', which was probably a copy of Wheldon's fair copy. For the copy from which both the Harley, in its corrected and uncorrected forms, and the Grund copies were made seems to be inferior to that from which the 1688 printed edition was made.[1] The MS from which Thott 213 (B) was copied, in any event, fell short of a formal presentation copy, judged by the standards of the presentation copies of *Leviathan* and Hobbes's *Thucydides*, and given that it lacks a dedicatory preface and any indication of whom the intended recipient might be.

It is plausible that Hobbes presented the original MS to Lord Vaughan, as Grund's attribution and remarks by Hobbes's amanuensis, Wheldon, suggest. *John Vaughan (1603-74), judge and legal theorist, was known to have similar political views to Hobbes, and Aubrey lists him among his London acquaintances, reporting that Hobbes 'was much in London till the restoration of his majesty, having here convenience not only of books, but of learned conversation, as Mr John Selden, Dr William Harvey, John Vaughan etc.'.[2] Judge Vaughan, friend, and executor of Hobbes's friend John Selden's estate, had been appointed Chief Justice of the Common Pleas in 1668, and was said in fact by Aubrey to have been Hobbes's

---

[1] For the provenance of the Thott MS. see Noel Malcolm's fine piece of archaeological work on Georg Grund, incorporated as Appendix C, below. And for the relationship between the MSS I am indebted to Malcolm for a long memorandum dated 1/10/2000, the basis for Appendix B.

[2] Aubrey, *Brief Lives*, vol. 1, p. 338. Judge *John Vaughan (1603-74) is the most likely candidate, given Aubrey's evidence, although John Vaughan (1640-1713), the fourth Earl of Carbury, an amateur mathematician and Fellow of the Royal Society, is just possible. See Malcolm, Hobbes *Correspondence* p. 396 n. 1.

'greatest acquaintance'.[1] He is referred to twice by Aubrey in connection with another of Hobbes's works on heresy, the *Dialogue of the Common Laws*, as someone 'who haz read it and much commends it', 'haz perused it and very much commends it, but is afrayd to license for feare of giving displeasure'.[2] Vaughan's death in 1674 would then supply a *terminus ad quem* for the dating of the poem. We have five different reports by Aubrey (items 1, 2, 3, 5, and 8 below) as well as important material evidence (items 4, 6, 7, and 9), from which to piece together a *terminus a quo* and chart the progress of the work.

(1) The first is Aubrey's report in his biography of Hobbes that:[3]

> In 1659 [Hobbes] wrot, among other things, a poeme in Latin Hexameter and Pentameter, of the encroachment of the clergie (both Roman and reformed) on the civil power. I remember I saw there 500+ verses for he numbred every tenth as he wrote.

Aubrey adds: 'His amanuensis remembers this poeme, for he wrote them out, but knows [not what became of it]'. Aubrey speaks as if the copy he sighted was written by Hobbes, 'for he numbred every tenth as he wrote', and recopied by Wheldon. But we have his own testimony that Hobbes's hand was palsied by 1650 and illegible by 1665-6.[4] Was it Hobbes's or his amanuensis, James Wheldon's copy that he sighted in 1659? And what happened to these manuscripts? The contemporary manuscripts extant, Harley 1844 (A), and Royal Copenhagen Thott MS (B), do not number the lines, which are however numbered in the Vienna MSS (C), but copied from the 1688 printed edition. Aubrey's report goes on to

---

[1] Aubrey *Brief Lives*, vol 1, p. 369. On Vaughan, see Noel Malcolm, Hobbes *Correspondence*, p. 396: comments to letter 107 from Henry Stubbe to Hobbes, Oxford Dec. 16 1656; Malcolm cites a work on Vaughan that I have not been able to trace: Williams, 'Sir John Vaughan [of Trawscoed, *The National Library of Wales Journal*, vol. 8, 1953-4, pp. 33-48, 121-46, 225-41], at p. 228. For Judge Vaughan's political views, and their similarities to those of Hobbes, see Richard Tuck, *Natural Rights Theories* (Cambridge, Cambridge University Press, 1979), pp. 125, 138.

[2] Aubrey to Wood, 3 February 1672/3, and Aubrey to John Locke, 11 February 1673, cited by P. Milton, in 'Hobbes, Heresy and Lord Arlington', pp. 517-18.

[3] Aubrey *Brief Lives*, I, p. 338.

[4] *Ibid.*, I, p. 165.

speculate about the fate of the verses, suggesting that Hobbes may have burned them:[1]

> There was a report, (and surely true) that in Parliament, not long after the king was setled, some of the bishops made a motion, to have the good old gentleman burn't for a Heretique; which he hearing, feared that his papers might be search't by their order, and he told me he had burn't part of them.

(2) We have a second, and slightly different, report from Aubrey, this time in an undated antiquarian work mostly compiled between 1659 and 1670, although this item probably dates to 1674, where he records:[2]

> About the time of the Kings Returne, he [Hobbes] was makeing of a very good Poëme in Latin hexameters: it was the *History of the Encroachment of the clergie (both Roman and Reformed) on the Civil Power*. I sawe at least 300 verses (they were mark't). At what time there was a report the Bishops would have him burn't for a Heretique. So he then feared the search of his papers, and burned the greatest part of these verses.

Aubrey sets the possibility of Hobbes's indictment by the bishops, and the subsequent burning of his papers, very early: 'not long after the king was setled, some of the bishops made a motion, to have the good old gentleman burn't for a Heretique' according to item (1); and 'about the time of the Kings Returne [in 1660]' according to item (2). Aubrey consistently argues that the bishops proposed a motion against Hobbes in the Lords shortly after the Restoration, which if true could not have been before November 20, 1661, as I shall later argue. Aubrey promises to check his facts, but never does. It is most likely that if Hobbes had burned his papers, it would have been in the early 1660s at the time at which he was threatened with legal process for atheism. We have testimony from the *Historical*

---

[1] Bodl. Ms Aubr. 9, f. 42 (Aubrey *Brief Lives*, I, p. 339).
[2] Aubrey, *An Essay towards a Description of the North Division of Wiltshire*, cited by Milton, 'Hobbes, Heresy and Lord Arlington', p. 510. Milton speculates on the basis of interpolations in this part of Aubrey's text, which mention the composition of Hobbes's 'life [*Vita*] last year viz 1673 in Latin-verse', that this particular entry was made around 1674.

Narration concerning Heresie, that Hobbes felt soon after 1660 that the bishops, possibly in league with the Presbyterians, were teamed up against him. But if the Presbyterian party was strongest in the Convention parliament of 1660, the Bishops did not sit in that assembly, so Hobbes must be speaking of an extended period of hostility:[1]

> It pleas'd God . . . to restore His most Gracious Majesty that now is, to his Fathers Throne, and presently [= at once] His Majesty restored the Bishops, and pardoned the Presbyterians; but then both the one and the other accused in Parliament this Book of Heresie, when neither [*sic.*] the Bishops before the War had declared what was Heresie, when if they had, it had been made void by putting down of the High Commission at the importunity of the Presbyterians.

(3) The first piece of material evidence we have for the *Historia Ecclesiastica*, as previously noted, is to be found in the account book of James Wheldon's personal finances, which records payment for copying the poem, dated Sept-Oct 1671: 'At Chatsworth. Given me by Mr. Hobbes for writing a book, *Historia Ecclesiastica Romana*, one pound'.[2]

(4) We have further evidence in Hobbes's Latin prose autobiography, *Vitae Hobbinae Auctorum*, of 1672, which refers to both *Behemoth* and some two thousand verses having been written in about his eightieth year, but that the time was not right to publish them.[3] The syntax for the latter remark is ambiguous, however, and could refer to either the poem or *Behemoth*, or both.[4]

---

[1] *Hist. Narr.*, p. 160 (*EW* IV, p. 407), cited in Cromartie, introduction to Hobbes's *Dialogue Between a Philosopher and A Student of the Common Laws of England*, p. li.

[2] Chatsworth, MS Hardwick 19, entries for Sept. and Oct. 1671. Noted in Miriam Reik, *The Golden Lands of Thomas Hobbes*, p. 225, n. 3. Linda Levy Peck has also used the Chatsworth account books as important material evidence to establish Hobbes's movements, and in particular his London presence, see her 'Constructing A New Context for Hobbes Studies', in *Politics and the Political Imagination in Later Stuart Britain, Essays Presented to Lois Green Schwoerer*, Howard Nenner, ed., (Rochester, N.Y., University of Rochester Press, 1998), pp. 161-79.

[3] *Vitae Hobbinae Auctarium*, in *OL* I, p. xvii.

[4] I am grateful to Noel Malcolm for pointing out this syntactical ambiguity.

(5) We have another, but not necessarily inconsistent, report from Aubrey to Wood in 1673, that suggests the poem had been completed by then: 'He haz also another Poëm about 4000 Latin Hex[ameters] & Pent[ameters] viz *Historia Ecclesiastica Romana* [which] shews the Encroachments of the Church on the Secular Power: it will not be licensed, but may be printed hereafter'.[1]

(6) Shortly after Hobbes's death in 1679, when Aubrey set about to execute his promise to write Hobbes's biography, he interrogated James Wheldon, Hobbes's amanuensis who was responsible for the fair copy of the verses. Wheldon told him: 'For those Latine verses you mention about Ecclesiasticall Power, I remember them, for I writ them out, but know not what became of them, unlesse he presented them to judge Vaughan, or burned them as you seemed to intimate'.[2] Wheldon also told Aubrey that Hobbes had burned some Latin verses which he had been sent by Crooke, his publisher.[3]

(7) Later in Aubrey's biography of Hobbes, he records his efforts, including a letter to Hobbes's printer, William Crooke, to track the poem down; efforts which were eventually rewarded with the discovery of a MS, referred to by Aubrey and Wheldon by the title *Historia Ecclesiastica Romana*.[4]

(8) That the manuscript was indeed in existence by 1675 is confirmed by the catalog printed by William Crooke in June of that year and appended to *A Supplement of Mr Hobbes his Workes printed by Blaeu at Amsterdam*, to advertise various Hobbes manuscripts in Crooke's possession, among which the *Historia Ecclesiastica Romana* is listed. The *Supplement*, which MacDonald and Hargreave describe as a 'symposium', comprised six smaller works, including Hobbes's Latin poem, *De Mirabilibus Pecci*, works in response to Wallis, as well as works on Geometry, and a catalogue

[1] Aubrey to Wood, 5 July 1673, Bodl., Ms. Wood F. 39, f. 219, cited by Milton, 'Hobbes, Heresy and Lord Arlington', p. 545.
[2] Wheldon to Aubrey, 16 January 1679/80, Aubrey in *Brief Lives*, I, P. 382, cited by Milton, 'Hobbes, Heresy and Lord Arlington', p. 511.
[3] Wheldon to Aubrey, 16 January 1679/80.
[4] Aubrey, *Brief Lives*, I, p. 364.

of the author's works, including the MSS. As MacDonald and Hargreave note, 'the title page, *De Mirabilibus Pecci*, and the catalogue at the end, were printed together (forming A-C4) and are the only parts of this work printed especially for it'.[1]

These pieces of evidence are corroborative to a certain extent, but also raise important questions. All the evidence points to 300 to 500 lines of the poem having been completed in 1659, if we are to believe Aubrey, some 2000 having been completed by 1669, if we are to believe Hobbes, and the work completed in more or less final form by 1673 or even 1671 – to the extent of some 4000 lines if we are to believe Aubrey. It is a curious and unremarked fact that Aubrey virtually doubles the length of the poem of 2242 lines that has survived – to make it 4000 lines – were the missing 1500 lines burned?[2] Or is there a simpler explanation? Aubrey is inconsistent in his references to lines and verses. It is noteworthy that his first mention of the *Historia Ecclesiastica* is of 'a poeme in Latin Hexameter and Pentameter' of which he saw '500+ verses', adding that Hobbes 'numbred every tenth as he wrote';[3] but it is every tenth line, not verse, of the 1688 printed edition that is numbered, in fact, and the Harley and Thott MSS are numbered not at all. Aubrey's mention in his communication to Wood of a 'Poëm about 4000 Latin Hex[ameters] & Pent[ameters] viz *Historia Ecclesiastica Romana*', is more plausibly read as referring to lines than to verses, however.[4]

---

[1] See item 106, pp. 78-9 in MacDonald and Hargreaves, *Thomas Hobbes: A Bibliography* (London, The Bibliographical Society, 1952), where it is listed as *A Supplement to Mr. Hobbes His Works Printed by Blaeu at Amsterdam, 1661, Being a third Volume*, London, Printed by J.C. for W. Crooke 1675. (See also Karl Schuhmann, *Hobbes: Une chronique*, p. 218.) It is not clear whether this MS survives. Hobbes, *De Mirabilibus Pecci*, BL Egerton MS 669 (HbT2, *Index of Literary Manuscripts*, vol. 2, part 1, p. 576), described by Peter Beal, the compiler as a copy subscribed 'mihi' in a late 17c. miscellany, matches the description to some extent. Not only does the miscellany include works by Wallis, Southy and others, but Waller's *Panegyrick to Oliver*, and Dryden's *Upon Oliver*, also included, are listed in the table of contents as 'printed mihi', as if to say, by Crooke, followed by a note in another hand: 'Mr. Matthews, the Binder, London Mar. 1667'. Hobbes's *De Mirabilibus Pecci: Being the Wonders of the Peak in Darbyshire*, was first printed by William Crooke in 1678.

[2] Aubrey to Wood, 5 July 1673, Bodl., Ms. Wood F. 39, f. 219.

[3] Aubrey *Brief Lives*, I, p. 338.

[4] Aubrey to Wood, 5 July 1673, Bodl., Ms. Wood F. 39, f. 219, cited in Milton, 'Hobbes, Heresy and Lord Arlington', p. 545.

Noel Malcolm's suggestion to me that Wood may have understood Aubrey to have mentioned 2000 verses (each comprising a hexameter and a pentameter line), and then doubled them to get 4000 lines, is a plausible one.[1]

Note that while Aubrey's reports (1), (2), read as if the poem is still missing, (5) and (7) read as if it has been found. In (5) Aubrey suggests that Hobbes intended to publish it but, aware of the King's refusal to have his other works on heresy licensed, knew that publication would be delayed; (7) confirms the existence of such a MS; and (8) establishes that a manuscript reported as *Historia ecclesiastica romana* (presumably that later printed as *Ecclesiastica historia carmine elegiaco conscripta*) is in the possession of Hobbes's English printer, William Crooke. Quite what is the provenance of this MS we cannot be sure. If it was Wheldon's fair copy, then this may have served as the publisher's copy text, for, shortly before his death Hobbes had promised his printer Crooke, 'If I leave any Mss worth printing, I shall leave word you shall have them . . .'[2].

The Folger Shakespeare Library Catalogue indicates Crooke as the publisher of the *Historia Ecclesiastica*, but the wrong Crooke, Andrew, William Crooke's older cousin, an active bookseller, first listed in the Stationers' Register in 1630, and publisher in 1637 of Ben Jonson's *The Staple of News* and *Bartholomew Fair*.[3] Malcolm speculates that 'since the first work by Hobbes which is known to have been printed by Crooke [also] appeared in 1637 (*A Briefe of the Art of Rhetorique*), it is conceivable that Jonson, in the final year of his life, had recommended the printer to Hobbes'.[4] Andrew Crooke died in 1674,[5] the *terminus ad quem* for the poem on the assumption that it was presented to Vaughan, but it was not published until 1688. It is not impossible that Andrew Crooke could have had the manuscript in his possession before he died, and that William Crooke, who took over the business, then published it.

---

[1] Personal Communication, Malcolm to Springborg, 27/1/2005. Note that the 1668 Glossary (*q.v.* pp. 604-9) also confuses lines and verses.

[2] Hobbes *Correspondence*, p. 772.

[3] See Malcolm's entry on William Crooke in the Biographical Register of his Hobbes *Correspondence*, p. 823.

[4] *Ibid.*

[5] Noted by Macdonald and Hargreaves, *Bibliography of Hobbes*, p. 28.

At first glance it seems strange that Crooke did not put his name on the title page of the *Historia Ecclesiastica*, especially given that every work of Hobbes published in England, except his 'Answer' to the Preface to Davenant's *Gondibert*, bore a Crooke imprint.[1] But this was a period in which the very contentiousness of Hobbes's views caused a great deal of confusion and dissembling, as we know from Noel Malcolm's clever detective work on the printing of 'the Bear', the second edition of *Leviathan*.[2] Circumstances surrounding the passage of the Bill against Atheism and Profaneness through the two Houses of Parliament in 1666 and 1667, and the possible indictment of Hobbes under its terms, taken together with raids on printing presses clandestinely publishing Hobbes's works, created an atmosphere of great fear and uncertainty. Hobbes's poem did not suffer the same vicissitudes as *Leviathan*, the second edition of which, Malcolm persuasively argues, was literally stitched together out of the leavings of an attempted printing by John Redmayne, put out to him by William Crooke, and confiscated in the course of a raid on his printery by the Stationers' Company in 1670, which somehow made their way to Amsterdam, where they were cobbled together in a printing hurriedly prepared by Christoffel Cunradus. But the recorded appearances and disappearance of the poem suggest that it was just as hot to handle.

In this environment of suspicion, William Crooke's reluctance to put his name to the work is explicable, although admittedly this is now eighteen years later and circumstances had improved somewhat. In June 1679, a Whig controlled Parliament had allowed the Licensing Act to lapse, and the crown's only recourse to control printing was by means of the royal prerogative.[3] On May 12 1680, a decree forbade the publication of 'any news – whether true or false'. But it was whistling in the wind. As in 1640, when the Licensing Act

---

[1] *Ibid.*

[2] Noel Malcolm, 'The Printing of the "Bear": New Light on the Second Edition of Hobbes's Leviathan', in Malcolm, *Aspects of Hobbes*, pp. 336-82.

[3] See Lois Schwoerer, 'Liberty of the Press and Public Opinion 1660-95', in J. R. Jones, *Liberty Secured: Britain Before and After 1688* (Stanford, Ca., Stanford University Press, 1992) pp. 213-14; and Timothy Crist, 'Government Control of the Press after the Expiration of the Printing Act in 1679', *Printing History*, vol. 5 (1979), pp. 48-77.

lapsed, a spate of pamphlet and newspaper publication followed. Perhaps Crooke, having bided his time since at least 1675, and tested the water, finally took his moment in 1688, a not insignificant year.

This preliminary survey of the textual history of the *Historia Ecclesiastica* would not be complete without the afore-mentioned piece of startling evidence that has so far not been noticed or has been discounted:

(9) In the summer of 1664, François du Verdus, writing to Hobbes from Bordeaux,[1] reports to him news from M. du Prat, that 'you were putting your entire philosophical system into Latin verse, in a style somewhat similar to that of Hesiod, with whose works you had closely familiarized yourself for that purpose'. Verdus enthuses: 'As soon as I heard mention of a philosophical poem, I conceived the plan of translating it, as soon as it appeared, into Italian *versi sciolti*, like the ones Annibale Caro used in his translation of the *Aeneid*.'[2] Verdus then proceeds to give Hobbes a sample of his style in the form of his own English translation of an opera he wrote in Italian called 'Iris in Love with Phoenix'. After giving his sample translation, du Verdus informs Hobbes of his plan to have his own translation of all Hobbes's works printed ('translated, that is, from the new edition of which M. Blaeu has promised to send me a copy as soon as he has done it'). Although he did not live to see the completion of his project, Du Verdus did in fact publish a French translation of *De cive*, and made an astonishing suggestion regarding his proposed translation of *Leviathan* that is an important pointer to Hobbes's purposes in publishing that work.

Personally engaged in property disputes with the Church in Bordeaux, Du Verdus was as ardent an Erastian and anti-clericalist as Hobbes.[3] He read *Leviathan* as a bible for the Cromwellian Commonwealth, marveling that, as the very model of a bishopless Erastian state, it was surprising that the Commonwealth had not 'heaped the highest rewards' on Hobbes for showing 'that the authority of the

---

[1] Du Verdus to Hobbes, [24 July] 3 August 1664, Hobbes *Correspondence*, p. 625.

[2] *Ibid.*

[3] Du Verdus to Hobbes, 17 Aug. 1656, 23 Nov. 1656, and 12 Mar. 1657, Hobbes *Correspondence*, pp. 299, 325, 367-74 and 454.

state is absolute and indivisible'.[1] Du Verdus even proposed in 1654 removing himself to England as a 'safe haven' in which he could pursue his study of Bacon and Hobbes in peace;[2] whereupon Hobbes offered advice on how to ingratiate himself with the Protectorate,[3] extending to him repeated invitations to come, in response to which Du Verdus divulged:[4]

> What a pleasure it would give me, Sir, to be supported by Protestants; to try to become known to the Lord Protector; to dedicate my translation of your book to him; and to beg him, in my dedication, to send a copy to the [French] King and invite him to read it, to learn from it about the rights of the sovereign which were stolen from him by the priests!

Du Verdus was not singular among Hobbes's French associates in his estimate that *Leviathan* was targeted at Cromwell, as a sovereign who was not shackled by Bishops and priests. Thomas de Martel, the French lawyer Hobbes met in exile, described the *Humble Petition and Advice*, that constitutional document drawn up by MPs in 1657 under which the Lord Protector Cromwell was offered the Crown, as the 'last act' of the English 'Revolution', corresponding 'exactly' to Hobbes's 'demonstrations on the subject of sovereign authority'.[5] Samuel Sorbière, who not only helped shepherd the second edition of *De cive* through the press but, like Du Verdus, made a French translation, and also hoped to visit Hobbes in London, was, according to John Evelyn, who knew him, both a devotee of the 'heterodox pieces of Mr. Hobbes' and a 'Great favorite of our late Rep[ublic] . . . or rather the villainy of Cromwell'.[6]

It is in this context that we should read Du Verdus' remark in his letter of 1664 requesting permission to translate Hobbes's poem that,

---

[1] Du Verdus to Hobbes, 13 Dec. 1655, Hobbes *Correspondence*, p. 228, cited by Collins in *Allegiance,* p. 174, to whom I am indebted for this important account of du Verdus' relation to Hobbes.

[2] Du Verdus to Hobbes, 10 Aug. 1654, Hobbes *Correspondence*, pp. 196-7.

[3] Du Verdus to Hobbes, 26 Mar. 1656 and 14 May 1656, Hobbes *Correspondence*, pp. 263 and 285.

[4] Du Verdus to Hobbes, 22 Dec. 1656, Hobbes *Correspondence*, p. 414.

[5] Martel to Hobbes, 15 Apr. 1657, Hobbes *Correspondence*, p. 464.

[6] Evelyn to Sprat, 31 Oct. 1664, BL Evelyn MS 39a, fol. 128.

in the meantime, he is 'waiting to descover how exactly I can live with our druids of the Kingdom of Darkness' – a reference to the extravagant imagery of Hobbes's 'Kingdom of Darkness' in book four of *Leviathan* as excoriating Jesuits.[1] Malcolm notes, that 'druids' was an appellation Hobbes never in fact applied to Jesuits himself.[2] But, I would add, Du Verdus' reference to Druids may also be read as a coterie reference, signaling his knowledge of the treatises on gentile religions by the Antiquarians, Vossius, *Cluverius, Aubrey, *Herbert of Cherbury and, of course, Hobbes. Philip Cluverius in his *Germaniae Antiquae Libri Tres* quotes Diodurus Siculus on Druids, as Hobbes was later to do in *Behemoth*, just as they both quote Diodorus on the Egyptians;[3] and Cluverius was a major source for Hobbes's *Historia Ecclesiastica*, as we shall see.[4] Aubrey had been the first to claim that Stonehenge might have been a Druid temple, a suggestion he developed in correspondence with friends.[5]

Du Verdus' mention of Annibale Caro (1507-66), raises an entirely different set of considerations. Caro, a writer of burlesques and satires in blank verse (*versi sciolti*), beginning with his *Ecloga* (1534) and including *Eneide di Virgilio, tradotta in versi sciolti* (1581), may be taken as a clue to the style of Hobbes's own poem, and the reason why Rymer gave it the subtitle: *carmine elegiaco concinnata*, if in fact it was Rymer who gave it. There can be no doubt in my mind that du Verdus' reference is to the *Historia*

---

[1] Du Verdus to Hobbes, [24 July] 3 August 1664, Hobbes *Correspondence*, p. 627.

[2] Malcolm, Hobbes *Correspondence*, p. 628 n. 9.

[3] Philip Cluverius *Germaniae Antiquae Libri Tres* (Amsterdam 1626), pp. 198 and 201, and Hobbes, *Beh.*, pp. 91 and 91-2, respectively; see Collins, *Allegiance*, p. 50 ns 241 and 242.

[4] On Hobbes and Cluverius see my 'Writing to Redundancy: Hobbes and Cluverius', *The Historical Journal*, vol. 39 (1996) pp. 1075-8 and the discussion to follow.

[5] Aubrey's *Monumenta Britannica*, based on field-work at Avebury and Stonehenge and notes on many other ancient sites, remains largely in manuscript, but its original title is said to have been 'Templa Druidum'. A scheme was afoot in 1692 to publish the manuscript and a prospectus and a specimen page were issued in 1693, but nothing more came of the project. In 1694, the deist John Toland entered into correspondence about Aubrey's thesis and in 1695 excerpts of Aubrey's book were published, giving the theory wider circulation.

Ecclesiastica, this despite the fact that Malcolm dismisses the possibility with the following remarks:[1]

> The only surviving work to which this could possibly refer is the poem 'De motibus solis, aetheris et telluris' (Toronto MS 3064, printed in *Anti-White*, pp. 441-7); but its editors have argued that this poem was written before the completion of *De corpore* (*ibid.*, pp. 75-7). The Latin verse *Historia Ecclesiastica* was not written until Sept.-Oct. 1671, when James Wheldon received payment for writing it out (Chatsworth, MS Hardwick 19, entry for that date).

Du Verdus is not lightly dismissed. One of Hobbes's most devoted disciples and correspondents, who shared his mindset, he is likely to have understood Hobbes's purposes in writing the *Historia Ecclesiastica* very well, and this major poem can be seen to fit his description, while the brief astronomical poem *De motibus solis, aetheris et telluris* does not. Regarding the dating, it is true that the Chatsworth account book corroborates a date of 1671 for the copying of the *Historia Ecclesiastica* by Wheldon, but this does not mean that it was only completed in 1671. Du Verdus' 1664 description of the poem as a translation of Hobbes's entire philosophical system into Latin verse suggests a work already substantially completed and corroborates Rymer's assessment of the poem's purpose. On this assumption, what could account for the gap of almost seven years between the poem's substantial completion, in 1664, and the making of a fair copy, in 1671? In fact, if one set of verses went missing or was burned, as we now have four pieces of evidence to suggest (items 1, 2, 6, and 7), du Verdus' account might refer to an earlier version of the poem, for which we have evidence as early as 1659, as being between 300 and 500+ verses that were later burned.

As already noted, Aubrey's report suggests two copies, Hobbes's which he saw, and Wheldon's which he heard about (from Wheldon). The poem that Wheldon remembers copying might have been a later and longer reconstruction, made by Hobbes when he felt the coast was clear. Possibly the shorter poem was more Hesiodic in tone than the version that was ultimately printed. This is not impossible. The *Historia Ecclesiastica* fits du Verdus' description as an epitome of

---

[1] Malcolm, Hobbes *Correspondence*, p. 628 n.

Hobbes's entire philosophical system in Latin verse. That it was seen, at least in its early version, to be in a Hesiodic style and at the same time a fit candidate for translation by someone who specialized in burlesques and satires, is also plausible. Although the theogony with which Hobbes begins his poem is clearly taken from Diodorus Siculus, it parodies Hesiod's own *Theogony*, its story of the creation of the world, and genealogies of the gods and heroes from the pagan cosmologies.[1] It is also possible to see remnants of Hesiodic themes from *Works and Days* in Hobbes's account of the calendar of Christian feasts as a co-optation of earlier pagan festivals, such as the feast of Chronos, or Saturnalia, which becomes Carnivale, the celebration of *Priapus and the May pole, the feasts of Ceres Bacchus and the *Ambarvalia.[2] The poem even contains a relic of the myth of Iris as a rainbow,[3] the subject of du Verdus' sample of poetry from his opera, 'Iris in love with Phoenix', that he presents as evidence of his translation skills.

In sum, since Hobbes's poem, as we have it in final printed form, begins as an imitation of a classical Greek or Latin poem in the tradition of the idylls of Theocritus and Horace's epodes,[4] it is not at all implausible that, seen in progress in 1664, it could be characterized as Hesiodic. That it was material for burlesque, we know from the English paraphrase, *A True Ecclesiastical History From Moses to the Time of Martin Luther*, which is in the tradition of Scarron's *Le Virgile Travestie*, a notorious work and much imitated in Hobbes's day. Paul Scarron (1610-1660), who frequented *Libertin* circles in Paris to which some of Hobbes's friends, including du Verdus,[5] belonged, had written *Le Virgile Travestie* from 1648-52, using Virgil's *Aeneid* as a vehicle for contemporary comment.[6] In 1656 G. de Brebeuf had published *Lucain Travestie*. In 1664 Charles Cotton, Hobbes's acquaintance, had published *Scarronides, or Virgil*

---

[1] *Hist. Eccl.*, lines 80-350.

[2] *Hist. Eccl.*, lines 1338-54.

[3] *Hist. Eccl.*, line 1403.

[4] *Hist. Eccl.*, lines 1-10 and notes.

[5] See Noel Malcolm, Hobbes *Correspondence*, Biographical Register, pp. 908-9, for du Verdus' connections to de Martel, Roberval and the Mersenne circle.

[6] See the modern edition of Scarron's *Le Virgile Travestie*, ed. Jean Serroy (Paris, Garnier, 1988).

Travestie, a mock-poem on the first book of the *Aeneid* in imitation of Scarron; and in 1674 Cotton's translation of *Lucain travestie* entitled *Burlesque upon Burlesque: or the Scoffer Scoff'd,* appeared. This was not the end of it: in 1675 Monsey of Pembroke hall, Cambridge, produced his own *Scarronides, a mock-poem, being the second and seventh books of Vergil's Aeneid*; while John Phillips's *Maronides,* in imitation of the fifth and sixth books of the *Aeneid,* took parody to new lows; only to be outdone by James Farewell, author of *The Irish Hudibras, or Fingallian Prince, Taken from the Sixth Book of Virgil's Aenaeids, and Adapted to the Present Times,* an adaptation written in 1689 that served as an encomium of William III. In 1664, James Scudamore's *Homer à la Mode, A Mock Poem upon the first and second Books of Homer's Iliads* appeared; and in 1680, Alexander Radcliffe had produced an *Ovide Travestie.*

This was a tradition with many layers, for Lucian himself, a poet much celebrated by Hobbes, in his *Satires,* especially in his *Dialogues of the Gods,* had lampooned Hesiod's *Theogony* and Ovid's *Metamorphoses.*[1] But none of the seventeenth century Scarronesque Travesties referred much to Virgil or Ovid. They were rather irreverent works of political and social comment, or simply vulgar humour, the classical tag designed to get past the censor – a strategy much like that of the Aristotelian commentaries, so-called, another entire genre of philosophical, theological and political thought, that pretended to be commentaries on Aristotle for ease of circulation.[2] The participation in this burlesque tradition of Charles Cotton, member of the Cavendish circle and almost certainly the translator of Hobbes's *De cive,* is particularly noteworthy.[3] And if Hobbes's *De*

---

[1] See *Lucian, *Works,* vol. 7, ed. M.D. Macleod, London, Heinemann, 1961, pp. 262-49.
[2] See Cees Leijenhorst on Hobbes and the Aristotelian commentaries in his *Hobbes and the Aristotelians: The Aristotelian Setting of Thomas Hobbes's Natural Philosophy* (Utrecht, Zeno Institute for Philosophy, 1998); republished as *The Mechanization of Aristotelianism: The Late Aristotelian Setting of Thomas Hobbes's Natural Philosophy* (Leiden, Brill, 2002).
[3] See Timothy Raylor, *Cavaliers, Clubs and Literary Culture: Sir John Mennes, James Smith and the Order of the Fancy* (Wilmington, Del., University of Delaware Press, 1994); and Noel Malcolm, 'Charles Cotton, 'Translator of Hobbes's *De cive*', *Huntington Library Quarterly,* vol. 61 (1998), pp. 259-87, reprinted in *Aspects of Hobbes,* pp. 234-58.

mirabilibus pecci of 1627/8 is the only straight burlesque from the master's hand, Cotton's *The Wonders of the Peake* of 1681, is remarkably derivative of it. Burlesque was a way to get around the censor and that may have been what Du Verdus had in mind.

To summarize then, some of the confusion surrounding the textual and publication history of the *Historia Ecclesiastica* might be resolved if the different reports listed in items (1) through (9) are understood as referring to different versions of the poem. Professor Donald Russell has noted of the poem that it gives the impression of being picked up and put down, themes break off and are only resumed much later, if at all, whereas some lines are repetitious.[1] This could be explained if the final form were in fact a reconstruction of an earlier version that was burned. Aubrey's report of 1659 (item 1), which mentions the verses being numbered in tens, is also the report in which he suggests that Hobbes may have burned them.[2] Perhaps it was this early poem of 500+ lines that was put to the torch in the 1660s (after 1664 if du Verdus' letter, item 9, in fact refers to it); but Hobbes later reconstructed it, completing it by 1671 – the year in which Wheldon was paid for the fair copy (item 2). In the reconstruction, one supposes, he brought the curtain down at the Reformation for prudential reasons, so that the earlier promise of a poem addressing the *Encroachment of the clergie (both Roman and Reformed) on the Civil Power* is not fulfilled.

As Noel Malcolm has suggested, either of Wheldon's propositions of 1679/80 might be true about the fate of the verses he copied and '[knew] not what became of them, unlesse he [Hobbes] presented them to judge Vaughan, or burned them as you [Aubrey] seemed to intimate' (item 6).[3] For, it is Aubrey on whom we rely for the claim that they were burned. In other words, they were indeed presented to Vaughan (and copied again by someone much less careful than Wheldon), or they were burned. Or, as seems more likely, given that the verses are reported as turning up again, they were not burned at all, but temporarily disappeared, so that (item 3), the entry in Wheldon's account book referring to his fair copy of the

---

[1] Donald Russell to Springborg, personal communication.
[2] Bodl. Ms Aubr. 9, f. 42 (Aubrey *Brief Lives*, I, p. 339).
[3] Letter Malcolm to Springborg, 1/10/2000.

poem *Historia Ecclesiastica Romana* completed by 1671, refers to
the MS of the poem of this name listed in Crooke's catalogue (item 8),
and incorporated in his *'Supplement* to Blaeu's *Hobbes his Workes'*
of 1675. The absence of line numbering in the Harley and Grund
manuscripts, and the high level of variants, taken together with the
fact, as Noel Malcolm has pointed out to me, that Wheldon's beautiful hand is not easily miscopied, are evidence for the view that
Wheldon's copy may have (temporarily) disappeared, and that
Grund and Harley 1844 were made from an inferior, and possibly
hastily written, copy that somehow survived.[1]

Possibly Hobbes had indeed given a signed copy of the MS to
Vaughan (although not Wheldon's fair copy), knowing that it would
not be licensed for printing in the foreseeable future. This would
follow a pattern of scribal publication familiar from the textual
history of *Behemoth*.[2] Aubrey tells us in letters from the 1670s that,
having failed to get permission to print his *History of the Civil War*,
Hobbes gave it to Crooke, allowing him to make a copy, and then
gave the fair copy to a 'learned gentleman' – an indication of how
printers could circulate unlicensed MSS. Along similar lines Aubrey
informed Locke in the 1670s about Hobbes's *Dialogue of the
Common Law*, that if he paid 50 shillings he could get a copy. On
February 11, 1673, Aubrey writes Locke about:[3]

> A MSS or two (worthy of your perusall) of my old friend Mr Th:
> Hobbes. One is a Treatise concerning the Lawe, which I importun'd
> him to under take about 8 yeares since . . . Mr. H. seem'd then some-
> thing doubtfull he should not have dayes enough left to goe about
> such a work. In this treatise he is highly for the Kings Prerogative:
> Ch: Just: Hales haz read it and very much mislikes it; is his enemy
> and will not license it. Judge Vaughan has perusd it and very much
> commends it, but is afrayed to license for feare of giving displea-
> sure. 'Tis a pitty fire should consume it, or that it should miscarry as
> I have known some excellent things. I never expect to see it printed,
> and intended to have a copy, which the bookeseller will let me have

---

[1] *Ibid.*
[2] *Ibid.* See also Harold Love, *Scribal Publication in Seventeenth-century England* (Oxford, Clarendon Press, 1993; repr. 1997).
[3] Aubrey to Wood, 11 February 1673, in *The Correspondence of John Locke*, ed. E. S. De Beer (Oxford, 1976 –), vol. 1, pp. 375-6.

for 50s . . . I have a conceit that if your Lord [Shaftesbury] sawe it he would like it.

Wheldon's notice of the completion date of the poem and its possible presentation to Judge Vaughan are important considerations that commentators have largely ignored. If Philip Milton's excellent textual archaeology has succeeded in disqualifying Tuck's case for *Henry Bennet, Lord Arlington as the intended recipient of Hobbes's work,[1] it has not disqualified Arlington's associate, Judge Vaughan, whom Wheldon suggests as the recipient – this is if we read the emphases of Wheldon's letter correctly.[2] That a MS copy of the *Historia Ecclesiastica*, signed by Hobbes, remained in the same Judge Vaughan's London library as late as 1685, some 11 years after Vaughan's death, to provide the text from which Grund made his copy, is noteworthy. The library must have passed intact to Vaughan's heir, and Hobbes's MS was still there, so it clearly was not the copy that Crooke was advertising in his catalogue in June 1675. That the inferior Harley and Grund MSS both have the same provenance, a copy in Vaughan's library signed, although not necessarily dedicated, by Hobbes (Grund does not indicate a dedication to Vaughan), may indicate a copy either given by Hobbes, or obtained from Crooke. The fact that it was a corrupted copy would in this case simply be due to the exigencies of manuscript circulation from Crooke's shop, for surely he would not have circulated Wheldon's fair copy, but rather copies made from it. It was from such a copy that the defective Harley copy was then made; and it was still in Vaughan's library in 1685 when Grund, who was a far better Latinist than the Harley copyist, made his less defective copy.

The odds that the verses may never have been burned increase. There seems to be a great deal of confusion about what was circulated in and out of Crooke's shop and what was burned and not burned. There is parallel (and perhaps overlapping) confusion concerning

---

[1] Milton, 'Hobbes, Heresy and Lord Arlington', responding to Richard Tuck, *Hobbes* (Oxford, 1989), pp. 32-7; Tuck, 'Hobbes and Locke on Toleration', in *Thomas Hobbes and Political Theory*, ed. Mary G. Dietz (Lawrence, KA, University of Kanzas Press, 1990), pp. 153-71; and Tuck, *Philosophy and Government 1572-1651* (Cambridge, Cambridge University Press, 1993), pp. 335-45.

[2] Wheldon to Aubrey, 16 Jan. 1679/80, as raised in Malcolm's letter to Springborg, 1/10/2000.

the various versions of Hobbes's autobiographies, verse and prose, and whether they were burned or not. So, for instance, Hobbes wrote the first draft of his verse autobiography, *Vita Carmen Expressa*, in 1672, sent it to Crooke, later asked for it back and, at the time of his death it was believed he had burned it, only for it to turn up in the Devonshire Collection of Hobbes manuscripts. Wheldon's report to Aubrey of 16 January, 1679/80, concerning Hobbes's *prose* autobiography (which had a different but similarly confusing history, as having been given by Hobbes to Aubrey and then requested back a couple of years before his death), may, when speaking of Hobbes's 'Latin Verses', in fact be referring to the Latin verse autobiography, and not to the *Historia Ecclesiastica* at all. So we can read the reference to Latin verses in item 7, Wheldon to Aubrey, 16 January, 1680, differently, as referring rather to the verse *Vita*:[1]

> I am glad Mr Crooke has received his life in Prose, which was the only thing Mr. Halleley got possession of, and sent it to him by my hand. Mr. Halleley tells me that Mr Hobbes (in the time of his sickenesse) told him he had promised it to Mr. Crooke, but said he was unwilling that it should ever be published as written by himself; and I believe it was some such motive, which made him burne those Latin verses, Mr Crooke sent him about that time.

In sum, that Wheldon's fair copy, with the numbered verses, resurfaced to provide the copy text for the 1688 printed edition, where the verses are also numbered, or was in Crooke's hands all along, is highly likely. The final piece of evidence (8) suggests as much; while reports (6), (7) and (8) seem to refer to the same MS, *Historia Ecclesiastica Romana*, now in the possession of William Crooke, but which was printed with the amended title, *Ecclesiastica historia carmine elegiaco conscripta*, an issue to which I will return.

---

[1] Wheldon to Aubrey, 16 Jan. 1679/80, Aubrey in *Brief Lives*, vol. I, p. 382, cited in the anonymous note on 'The Autobiographies of Thomas Hobbes', in *Mind*, New Series, vol, 48, no 191 (1939), pp. 403-7, at p. 403, to which I am indebted for this short account.

CHAPTER 3

HOBBES AND HERESY

3.1 Heresy and the *Historia Ecclesiastica*:

If we take the bulk of Hobbes's poem as we have it in final printed form, the *Historia Ecclesiastica* differs by genre, but not necessarily by substance, from the cluster of works on heresy of the mid 1660s, where Hobbes was seeking not only to exonerate himself, but also to recast the whole issue. In 1658, Bramhall had published *The Catching of Leviathan*, fulfilling an intention announced already in 1655 to refute *Leviathan*, 'this work pernisiouc to piety as politics and destructive of all social bonds between prince and subject, father and son, master and servant, husband and wife'. Bramhall was motivated, at least in part, by his annoyance at the publication without permission in the previous year of his debate with Hobbes that had taken place some ten years earlier.[1]

But the encounter with Bramhall was only the beginning of Hobbes's problems, which became seriously worrying by 1666, when a Commons' Committee considering a Bill against atheism and profaneness targeted him. Hobbes's strategy seemed to be to recast the question of heresy, deflecting back onto the authorities the onus to prove that someone like a Thomas Hobbes (or a Daniel Scargill), who maintained no doctrines but the minimalist faith in Christ and obedience to the sovereign power, could be guilty of sectarianism – the true meaning of heresy – and its seditious consequences. So he begins

---

[1] See Franck Lessay, ed. *De la Liberté et de la Nécessité,* Paris, Vrin, 1993, *Œuvres de Thomas Hobbes*, 11.1, p. 122.

An Historical Narration Concerning Heresy[1] by defining heresy
after the manner of Diogenes Laertius, as a Greek word meaning
the taking of an opinion.[2] The chief opinionated philosophers were
Pythagoras, Plato, Aristotle, Epicurus, Zeno and their disciples,
he claims, 'in love with great names, though by their impertinent
discourse, sordid and ridiculous manners they were generally
dispised'.[3]

This was a strategy of redefinition that Hobbes steadfastly
maintained in all the works on heresy, including the *Historia
Ecclesiastica*. There heresy is introduced in a curious way, suggesting that one can virtually be a heretic without knowing it, as if it was
simply a matter of the kind of difference of opinion that the internal
court (*in foro interno*) is designed to accommodate. Primus's
mention of 'the Stoa, the Peripatetic and the names of many sects
[that] are encountered in ancient history', prompts Secundus to ask:[4]

> *Se.*   A sect? What's that pray? For to me the mere invective
> makes me think it is a great crime.
>
> *Pr.*   The fighting of learned men against learned men, doctrine
> against doctrine, was called 'sect' by the Greeks.
>
> *Se.*   Of what law, I ask you, was a 'sect' a violation? Of a native-
> born law or one imposed, so that I can know it to be a crime?
>
> *Pr.*   Neither. Because no man errs deliberately, and among the
> Greeks all philosophy was free.

---

[1] *EW* IV, pp. 387-408.

[2] Diogenes Laertius, *Lives and Opinions of the Eminent Philosophers* 1.20,
defined the term sect (*hairesis*) in terms of adherence to a fixed set of doctrines,
referring at 1.19 to the nine Greek philosophical schools cited in Hippobotus' work
On Philosophical Sects. Richard Tuck in 'The Civil Religion of Thomas Hobbes',
pp. 133-4, suggests *Denis Petau's ('Petavius'), *Theologicorum Deorum* (Paris,
1644 –), *Prolegomena* ch. 3, as a source for the same argument in *Lev., xlii, §130,
318/395*; an argument repeated in the 1668 Appendix to the *LL* (§6, Curley edn,
p. 521). Petau was also read by Grotius, Gassendi and Mersenne; and his *Theologicorum Deorum* appears in the Hardwick Hall book list at shelf mark X.3.1 (see App-
pendix A). For Petau's importance as a model for Hobbes, representative of historically and philologically sensitive Jesuit Patristic scholarship, see the expanded
English-language version of Paganini's essay, 'Hobbes, Valla and the Trinity',
British Journal for the History of Philosophy, vol. 40, no 2 (2003), pp. 183-218, at
p. 198 ff.

[3] *EW* IV, p. 387.

[4] *Hist. Eccl.*, lines 19-28.

As we will see, the less abrasive tone in the poem may signal that the greatest danger to Hobbes from heresy charges was now over. In order to understand how events may have conspired to change the focus of Hobbes's poem from a classical imitation in the elegiac style, to yet another reflection on heresy – although by now a milder one – it is worth reviewing the evidence for threats of a heresy charge against Hobbes himself. Here the evidence is almost as confusing as the textual evidence for the poem. First we have the report of Aubrey, already quoted, that bishops proposed a motion against Hobbes in the Lords shortly after the Restoration, which if true could not have been before November 20, 1661. Aubrey made three notes to remind himself to check the facts with Seth Ward, Bishop of Salisbury, but records no result.[1] Second we have the report of the hostile Whig Bishop, White Kennett, who, writing some forty years after the event, and depending probably on Cavendish testimony, claims of Hobbes that:[2]

> In October 1666, when Complaint was made in Parliament against his Books, and some Proceedings against him were depending, with a *Bill against Atheism and Prophaneness*, he was then at Chatsworth, and appear'd extreamly disturb'd at the News of it; fearing that Messengers would come for him, and the Earl would deliver him up, and the Two Houses commit him to the Bishops, and they decree him a Heretick, and return him to the Civil Magistrate for a Writ *de Heretico comburendo*. This terror upon his Spirits made them sink very much: He would be often confessing to those about him, that he meant no Harm, and was no obstinate Man, and was ready to make any proper Satisfaction. For his prevailing Principle, and his Resolution upon it, was to suffer for no Cause whatever. Under these Apprehensions of Danger he drew up *An Historical Narration of Heresie, and the Punishment thereof*, labouring to prove that there was no Authority to determine Heresie, or to punish it, when he wrote the *Leviathan*; and that since the dissolving of the High Commission Court, no other Courts have any Power to decree any Opinion to be heretical; and wonders, that since His Majesty had Restored the Bishops, and pardon'd the Presbyterians, both the

---

[1] Bodl ms. Aubr. 9, ff. 7, 7v, 41v (Aubrey, *Brief Lives*, I, p. 339), cited in Milton, 'Hobbes, Heresy and Lord Arlington', p. 511.

[2] White Kennett, *A Sermon Preach'd at the Funeral of the Right Noble William Duke of Devonshire* (London, 1708), p. 113, cited by Milton, 'Hobbes, Heresy and Lord Arlington', p. 511.

one and the other should accuse in Parliament his Book of Heresie; and so runs away into a complaint of the Fierceness of Divines.

It is noteworthy that Kennett corroborates the immediate context of the *Historical Narration* as a work specifically designed to address the legal case against heresy and the dual campaigns against Hobbes by the Presbyterians and the bishops. The wide discrepancies between the accounts of Aubrey and Kennett on the dating and nature of the proceedings against Hobbes can perhaps be resolved in the following way. While Kennett's report would be likely to reflect the Cavendish view of the matter, Aubrey's testimony was that of one closest to the subject. As Robert Willman has suggested, Aubrey often reports word of mouth testimony, which may account for some of his inaccuracies. His intelligence that there were to be proceedings against Hobbes by Bishops in the 'Upper House', about which he seems unsure in any event and apparently failed to check with the Bishop of Salisbury, may well have referred to an action in the Upper House of Convocation, rather than the Lords.[1] As Willman notes, the Lords did not in any event have jurisdiction in the matter of heresy, which was a matter for the ecclesiastical courts, and Kennett was right, in fact, that after 'the dissolving of the High Commission Court no other Courts [had] any power to decree an opinion to be heretical'. This was established in a later, but not entirely unrelated case, when there was an attempt to censure William Whiston, whose position on primitive Christianity was rather close to that of Hobbes, for Arianism. 'Archbishop Tenison (an old opponent of Hobbes) looked into the question and reported back that "there does not seem to have been any exercise of such a judicature for this last hundred years or thereabouts"'.[2] The Registers of the Upper House of Convocation in fact contain no reference to a motion on Hobbes,[3] nor does he himself mention that body as being

---

[1] Robert Willman, 'Hobbes on the Law of Heresy', *Journal of the History of Ideas,* vol. 31 (1970), pp. 607-13, at p. 609.

[2] As Milton, 'Hobbes, Heresy and Lord Arlington' notes, p. 513, n. 48. See David Wilkins, *Concilia Magna Britanniae et Hiberniae* (4 vols, London, 1737), IV, p. 646; and for a full account see Eamon Duffy, '"Whiston's Affair": the Trials of a Primitive Christian 1709-24', *Journal of Ecclesiastical History*, vol. 27 (1976), pp. 129-50.

[3] See Edmund Wilson, *Synodus Anglicana,* Appendix III (London, 1702) cited by Milton, 'Hobbes, Heresy and Lord Arlington', p. 513 n. 49.

implicated. It is possible that Aubrey is reporting vaguely mentioned 'proceedings' of which Kennett too got wind, but locates in 1666 (in fact Convocation did not meet between 1664 and 1689) instead of 1661, and which came to nothing.[1] It may be these unsubstantiated reports which have caused various scholars to claim that the bishops instituted heresy proceedings against Hobbes.[2]

If the threat to Hobbes from the Bishops was vague and based on hearsay, the threat from the Commons was more palpable. Reports suggest that at two different times Hobbes may have been under indictment. The first, January 1657, records *Leviathan* having been presented to a committee of the House of Commons as 'a most poisonous piece of atheism'.[3] And it was from laws against atheism, rather than heresy, that Hobbes had the most to fear. The second report by a Commons' Committee considering a Bill against atheism and profaneness, dated 17 October 1666, follows the Great Fire of London and is evidence of the hysteria it provoked:[4]

> *[It] Ordered,* That the Committee to which the Bill against Atheism and Profaneness is committed, be impowered to receive Information touching such Books as tend to Atheism, Blasphemy or Profaneness, or against the Essence or Attributes of God; and in particular the Book published in the Name of one *White*; and the Book of Mr. *Hobbs*, called *The Leviathan*; and to report the Matter, with their Opinions, to the House.

The MP for Derbyshire, and a Cavendish client, John Milward, a day after being appointed to this committee, in fact recorded that it had rapidly concluded deliberations and that it 'was moved in the House that certain atheistical books should be burned, among which Mr. Hobbes's *Leviathan* was one'.[5] It was probably Milward, as Milton speculates, who relayed the information to Hobbes, and it is

---

[1] Milton, 'Hobbes, Heresy and Lord Arlington', p. 514.

[2] See Steven Shapin and Simon Schaffer, *Leviathan and the Air-Pump* (Princeton, Princeton University Press, 1985), p. 294, and Johann P. Sommerville, *Thomas Hobbes: Political Ideas in Historical Context* (London, Macmillan, 1992), p. 166.

[3] *Diary of Thomas Burton*, I, p. 349, cited in Milton, 'Hobbes, Heresy and Lord Arlington', p. 515.

[4] *The Journals of the House of Commons* (London, 1742 –) vol. 8, p. 636.

[5] *The Diary of John Milward*, ed. Caroline Robbins (Cambridge, Cambridge University Press, 1938), p. 25, cited in Milton, 'Hobbes, Heresy and Lord Arlington', p. 515.

to this action of 1666, and Hobbes's frightened response, that Bishop Kennett's report doubtless refers. Once again the White mentioned was Thomas White, the Catholic priest, leader of the Blackloists, on whose *De Mundo* Hobbes had written his commentary in Paris.[1] Although no record of a motion is to be found in the Commons' Journal, news of the impending action got around and, in Oxford, Anthony Wood made a note in his diary that somewhat embroidered the truth:[2]

> At length after the Parliament had censur'd it, (as also the book of *Purgatory* written by *Tho. De Albiis*) [i.e., Thomas White] in the month of *Oct.* 1666 (in which month a Bill was brought into the House against Atheism and Profaneness) and some of the principal Heads of this University had found therein, as in that *De Cive*, several positions destructive to the sacred persons of Princes, their state and government, and all humane society, the venerable Convocation did, by their judgment and decree past among them on the 21 of *July* 1683, condemn them as pernitious and damnable and thereupon caused the said two books to be publickly burnt.

Unsuccessful attempts to legislate against profanity had been initiated by the Commons in 1624, 1650, 1660, 1663, and 1665.[3] However, the 1666 Bill against atheism, the first of its kind, was altogether another matter. In the form in which it was sent up to the Lords in January 1667 its ambit included:[4]

> Any person who shall by word, writing or printing deride or deny, scoff at or dispute against the Essence, Person, or Attributes of God the Father, Son or Holy Ghost given unto them in the Sacred Scriptures, or the Omnipotency, Wisdom, Justice, Mercy, Goodness, or Providence of God in the Creation, Redemption, or Governance of the World, or denys the Divine Authoritie of any of the bookes of Canonical Scripture contained in the Old and New Testament, received and established in the Church of England.

---

[1] See Hobbes, *Critique du De Mundo de Thomas White.*

[2] Anthony Wood, *Athenae Oxonienses,* vol. 2, p. 91. White's work under censure was *The Middle State of Souls. From the hour of Death to the day of Judgment* (London, 1659), a work on purgatory which inspired perhaps *Hist. Eccl.,* lines 2006-18.

[3] See Milton, 'Hobbes, Heresy and Lord Arlington', pp. 516-17.

[4] *HLRO,* Parchment Coll., HL, 31 Jan. 1667, cited in Milton, 'Hobbes, Heresy and Lord Arlington', p. 519.

Hobbes's unorthodox doctrine of the Trinity in the English *Leviathan* could certainly be read as in violation of these provisions. Moreover, when in October 1667 the Bill was reintroduced into the Lords, its ambit was expanded to include the words 'and the Immortality of mens soules and the resurrection of the body and the eternal rewards in Heaven, and eternal torments in Hell'.[1] Hobbes's denial in *Leviathan* of the immortality of the soul and the eternal torments of Hell were clearly in violation of the later provisions. The Bill's other provisions were frightening enough. It shifted litigation from the ecclesiastical to the criminal courts, imposing a fine for first offenders, but banishment for second offenders, and the possibility of hanging – although never burning – for those unwise enough to return from exile. Its radical constitutional departures caused opposition and in March 1668 the judiciary was consulted about the Bill, replying that in its opinion 'the offences in it were not of temporal cognizance'.[2] The Bill then made no further progress.

It is in this context that Richard Tuck, drawing on two different reports of Aubrey, makes the case that Hobbes's *Dialogue of the Common Laws* may have influenced the judges' objections to the Bill. On February 3, 1673 Aubrey informed Wood:[3]

> [Hobbes] haz writt a treatise concerning Lawe which 8 or 9 years since I much importuned him to doe & in order to it gave him the L: Ch: Bacons *Maxims of the Lawe* . . . He drives on in this the K's Prerogative high. Judge Hales (who is no great courtier) haz read it and much mislikes it, & his enemy, Judge Vaughan haz read it and much commends it. I have lately desired Dr Lock to get a transcript of it, and I doubt not that the present Lord Chancellor (being much for the king's prerogative) will have it printed.

Locke is John Locke, the philosopher and statesman, and the Lord Chancellor is his patron, once again Anthony Ashley Cooper (1621-1683), first Earl of Shaftesbury.

---

[1] *HLRO*, Main Papers, HL, 14 Oct. 1667, cited in Milton, 'Hobbes, Heresy and Lord Arlington', p. 519.

[2] Milton, 'Hobbes, Heresy and Lord Arlington', p. 517, citing *HLRO*, Com. Book, HL, 16 April 1668.

[3] Aubrey to Wood, 3 February 1673, Bodl. Ms. Wood F. 39, f. 196v., cited by Milton, 'Hobbes, Heresy and Lord Arlington', p. 518.

On the basis of this evidence Richard Tuck claims of Hobbes's works on heresy written between 1666 and 1670: 'These works were not written simply as a defence of himself against Parliament, as his relationship with Arlington illustrates. Hobbes clearly intended his views to be used in the political debates of 1666-70 about toleration'.[1] But Philip Milton has shown that the textual basis for such a claim is flawed, while what Tuck takes for toleration I would argue as Hobbes's Erastianism, as earlier discussed. The suggestion that Hobbes's counsel might be listened to by senior judges of the realm on the question of religious toleration is in any event far-fetched. Moreover, Tuck's case that the judges' reading of Hobbes's *Dialogue* reported in 1673 influenced their objections to the heresy Bill in April 1668 assumes that the sections of the *Dialogue* on heresy had been written at that time, which is unlikely. This does not rule out the possibility, however, that Hobbes may have been seeking to enlist the judiciary in his own case, and particularly Vaughan, whom we know to have had some sympathy for his views.

In 1666 Hobbes, who since 1662 had been having difficulty getting his works printed, had dedicated to Arlington *De Principiis et Ratiocinatione Geometrarum*, perhaps to improve its chances of being licensed.[2] White Kennett had vaguely reported that Hobbes 'retain'd a Friend or two at Court, and especially the Lord *Ar——-n*, to protect him if Occasion should require'.[3] The principal instance of this vague attribution of patronage, on which Tuck leans for his thesis, is Hobbes's letter to Arlington's Under Secretary, Joseph Williamson, expressing thanks for 'my Lord Arlingtons mediation either by himselfe, or by you'.[4] The favour Arlington granted, Milton concludes on the basis of further evidence, concerned the pension of one hundred pounds a year promised by the King.[5] A year or so later Hobbes had appended to the manuscript of *Behemoth* a dedication to Arlington with the words: 'Your Lordship may do

---

[1] Tuck, *Philosophy and Government 1572-1651*, p. 342.

[2] Milton, 'Hobbes, Heresy and Lord Arlington', p. 508.

[3] Kennett, *Memoir*, p. 108, cited in Milton, 'Hobbes, Heresy and Lord Arlington', p. 525.

[4] *PRO*, SP 29/204/1, as cited by Milton, 'Hobbes, Heresy and Lord Arlington', p. 526.

[5] Milton, 'Hobbes, Heresy and Lord Arlington', p. 528-31.

with it what you please. I petition not to have it published. But I pray your Lordship not to desist to be as favourable as you have been to me that am [etc.]'.[1] Hobbes called Arlington's Under Secretary, Joseph Williamson's good offices into service again on June 30, 1668, when he wrote him specifically concerning a passage in the *Historical Narration Concerning Heresy*, which he was presumably petitioning Arlington to license:[2]

> I haue sent you sealed here the book I spake to you of. The words which you mislike are in the last page but one, which is the 12th page of the tract concerning Heresie, and they are these

>> Some man may perhaps ask whether no body was condemned and burnt for Heresie during the time of the High Commission. I haue heard there were. But they who approue such executions may peradventure know better grounds for them then I doe. But those grounds are very well worthy to be enquired after.

> They may be left out without trouble to the rest that goes before and after. I see no cause of exception against them, and desire to have them stand, but if the rest cannot be licensed whilst these words are in, you may put them out.

In this case Arlington, if indeed he was ever consulted, showed no favour and the *Narration* was not licensed. As Milton suggests, far from being in a position to influence Arlington or the judges on legislation that involved the issues of heresy and toleration, Hobbes if anything 'needed protection *against* Arlington, who (it may be noted) was instrumental in committing William Penn to the Tower for some eight months in 1668-9 for having written against the Trinity.'[3] *Behemoth* was refused on the objections of the bishops, who also prevented the reprinting of *Leviathan*, according to Aubrey. Not even the Latin *Leviathan* could be printed. In fact none

---

[1] Hobbes, *Beh.*, p. v., cited in Milton, 'Hobbes, Heresy and Lord Arlington', p. 526.

[2] *PRO*; SP 29/242/79. Reproduced Hobbes, *Correspondence*, ed. Malcolm, p. 699.

[3] Milton, 'Hobbes, Heresy and Lord Arlington', p. 527, citing *CSPD* 1668-9, pp. 98, 116, 146, 372, and *The Papers of William Penn*, ed. Mary Maples Dunn and Richard S. Dunn (5 vols, Philadelphia, PA, University of Pennsylvania Press, 1981-6) I, pp. 81-97.

of Hobbes's works on heresy was licensed. Arlington, so far from extending any favours in this way, directed his agents to confiscate a clandestine edition of *Leviathan* and close down the printer, as recorded by one of them in a letter to Williamson of 1670. It was this very edition, seized from Redmayne's printery, which was resurrected as the 'Bear' with the false imprint of London 1651, probably under the auspices of Andrew Crooke, Hobbes's publisher.[1] Quite what Hobbes's role was in this extraordinary clandestine printing, we do not know, but as Milton remarks,[2] he must have been consulted, which suggests that by 1670 he was less fearful for his neck than is commonly supposed.

Indeed Hobbes was technically protected from the specific provisions of the 1666-68 Bill on heresy – which in any event miscarried – as far as his unorthodox opinions in his *Leviathan* of 1651 were concerned, by the Act of Oblivion of 1660.[3] By the provisions of that Act the King at the Restoration had granted a general amnesty for crimes committed under the Commonwealth; and it is to this act that Hobbes refers in the claim reported by White Kennett that he was not technically liable, because 'there was no Authority to determine Heresie, or to punish it, when he wrote the *Leviathan*'.[4] But fear of being burned at the stake for heresy in this period, was certainly not groundless. In fact the laws against heresy were late in England, dating from the rise of the Lollard movement. In 1401 heresy was first made a capital offence and the common law writ *de haeretico comburendo* was devised and used to authorize the execution of William Sautre, the first heretic to be burned in England.[5] As Philip Milton points out, this created 'a unique offence, a spiritual offence with a temporal punishment and, as such, it lay outside the common law division of offences into treasons, felonies and misdemeanours'.[6]

---

[1] See Noel Malcolm `The Printing of the "Bear": New Light on the Second Edition of Hobbes's Leviathan', in *Aspects of Hobbes*, pp. 336-382.

[2] Milton, 'Hobbes, Heresy and Lord Arlington', pp. 537-8.

[3] 12 Car. II, c. 11, cited Milton, 'Hobbes, Heresy and Lord Arlington', p. 519 n. 74.

[4] White Kennett, *A Sermon Preach'd at the Funeral of the Right Noble William Duke of Devonshire*, p. 113, cited above.

[5] 2 Hen. IV, c.15. See also Wilkins, *Concilia*, III, p. 255-63, cited in Milton, 'Hobbes, Heresy and Lord Arlington', p. 521, n. 83.

[6] Milton, 'Hobbes, Heresy and Lord Arlington', p. 521.

The inter-jurisdictional nature of the crime meant that secular authorities might apprehend suspects, but that it was left to ecclesiastical courts to try them.

At the Reformation, when heresy became a real issue, Parliament had ventured into the fray and medieval provisions were rapidly reversed and reinstated in a confusing series of Acts under different sovereigns. So what Henry VIII retained of the medieval law, Edward VI repealed, whereas Mary reversed Edward VI's legislation, reinstating the pre-1533 law in full, which was repealed in turn under Elizabeth by the Act of Supremacy of 1559.[1] The Elizabethan Act remained in force until the Long Parliament, and included the following provisions: §VI repealed the medieval statutes for the last time; §VIII empowered the Crown to appoint commissioners charged with correcting heresies and related abuses; §XX defined heresy as a justiciable offence in terms of violation of Scripture, the first four General Councils, or the provisions of Parliament. Most importantly the Elizabethan Act did not repeal *De haeretico comburendo*. Sir Matthew Hale, summarizing the effects of the Act of 1559 after the Restoration, declared:[2]

> I think that at common law, and so at this day, (all former statutes being now repeald by 1 *Eliz. Cap. 1*.) if the diocesan convict a man of heresy, and either upon his refusal to abjure, or upon a relapse decree him to be deliverd over to the secular power, and this be signified under the seal of the ordinary into the chancery, the king might thereupon by special warrant command a writ *de haeretico comburendo* to issue, tho this were a matter that lay in his discretion to grant, suspend, or refuse, as the case might be circumstantiated.

The power *de haeretico comburendo* was rarely invoked, Papists being rather hanged as felons or beheaded as traitors. But the fact that the writ for burning was reserved for 'deviant Protestants – *Anabaptists, Arians and the like'[3] – would have given Hobbes

---

[1] 1 Eliz.c.1, cited by Milton, 'Hobbes, Heresy and Lord Arlington', p. 522, whose summary of the provisions I repeat.

[2] Sir Matthew Hale, *Historia Placitorum Coronae* (2 vols, London, 1736), I, p. 392, cited by Milton, 'Hobbes, Heresy and Lord Arlington', 'Hobbes, Heresy and Lord Arlington', p. 522.

[3] Milton, 'Hobbes, Heresy and Lord Arlington', p. 522.

cold comfort. He shows a perhaps understandable confusion about the legislation in general, claiming, as Milton points out, in the Chatsworth MS on Heresy that the power *de haeretico comburendo* was founded on 25 Hen. VIII, c. 14.[1] In the *Dialogue Between a Philosopher and a Student of the Common Laws of England*, however, the interlocutor designated as the Lawyer claims that it was 'grounded upon' 2 Hen. IV c. 15 and 2 Hen. V. c.7; while in the same work the interlocutor designated as the Philosopher claims that it was put into the register after 25 Hen.VIII, c. 14 repealed those provisions.[2] In fact 25 Hen.VIII c. 14 had repealed 2 Hen. IV, c. 15, but left in force 5 Ric. II, c. 5 and 2 Hen. V, c. 7.[3]

In the *Historia Ecclesiastica,* lines 2170-5, Hobbes not only claims that Henry IV 'was the first to make a legal holiday – "Live-Burning Day" – out of roasting heretics', but supplies a motivation for the move: to ingratiate himself with the clergy and spite his anti-clerical father. The last, and unsuccessful, attempt to have a heretic burned was in 1639, although as recently as 1622 two Arians had been burned for doubting the proof of Christ's divinity – a fact that may have given Hobbes cause for concern. By 1639 the High Commission had been unwilling to act in the matter and the law that under Mary Tudor had claimed more than 300 victims, including the famous Oxford martyrs, Bishops, Cranmer, in 1556 and Latimer and Ridley in 1555, was subsequently abolished by the Long Parliament 17 Car. I, c. 11. This act deprived ecclesiastical judges of their powers to impose temporal sanctions, effectively depriving clergy of all secular jurisdictions (17 Car. I, c. 27), within which heresy now fell. It did not abolish *de haeretico comburendo*, however, which awaited 29 Car. II, c. 9 of 1677, two years before Hobbes's death.

Hobbes's fears were not groundless, therefore. However, the bishops had no power to convict under *de haeretico comburendo*,

---

[1] Milton, 'Hobbes, Heresy and Lord Arlington', p. 521, citing the Chatsworth MS on Heresy of 1673, published by Mintz, 'Hobbes on the Law of Heresy', p. 414.

[2] See Hobbes, *A Dialogue Between a Philosopher and a Student of the Common Laws of England,* ed. Joseph Cropsey (Chicago, University of Chicago Press, 1971), pp. 131, 145, cited by Milton, 'Hobbes, Heresy and Lord Arlington', p. 521 n. 83.

[3] Milton, 'Hobbes, Heresy and Lord Arlington', p. 521 n. 84.

and Vaughan was a judge with some power to influence a decision, which could only be issued by the Chancellor on the specific instructions of the King in Council.[1] Although Hobbes constantly insisted that he could not be punished for *Leviathan* because it violated no laws in force when it was published,[2] and that he was later protected by the Act of Indemnity and Oblivion of 1660,[3] this was not quite true. Parliament may have abolished the episcopate and the ecclesiastical courts, but it did not abrogate its own powers to punish heretics. Two ordinances passed before *Leviathan* was written, the Ordinance for the punishing of Blasphemies and Heresies of 1648 and the *Act against several Atheistical Blasphemous and Execrable Opinions* of 1650, implicated Hobbes. By the provisions of the first, denial of the divinity of Christ or unorthodox views on the Trinity, by both of which terms he could be construed guilty, were 'felonies without benefit of clergy . . . punishable by hanging on the first conviction'.[4] That Hobbes did not in fact believe that the Act of Oblivion simply exculpated him is evident from his elaborate pleading to the king against its terms in the *Apology for himself and his Writings*, which was read to the Royal Society on March 19, 1662, and addressed to Charles II as follows:[5]

> I will not break the custom of joyning to my Offering a Prayer; And it is, That Your Majesty will be pleased to pardon this following short Apology for my Leviathan. Not that I rely upon apologies, but upon your Majesties most Gracious General Pardon.
>
> That which is put in it of Theology, contrary to the general Current of Divines, is not put there as my Opinion, but propounded with submission to those that have the Power Ecclesiastical.
>
> I never did after, either in Writing or Discourse, maintain it.
>
> There is nothing in it against Episcopy; I cannot therefore imagine what reason any Episcopal-man can have to speak of me (as

---

[1] Milton, 'Hobbes, Heresy and Lord Arlington', p. 524.

[2] See *EW* IV, pp. 355, 366, 407; *OL* I, p. 560, *OL* IV, p. 301, cited by Milton, 'Hobbes, Heresy and Lord Arlington', p. 523, n. 91.

[3] 2. Car. II, c. 11.

[4] C.H. Firth and R.S. Rait, *Acts and Ordinances of the Interregnum* (3 vols, London, 1911), I, pp. 1133-6, II, pp. 409-12, cited in Milton, 'Hobbes, Heresy and Lord Arlington', p. 523, n. 93.

[5] Published in Hobbes, *Seven Philosophical Problems* (London, 1682), sigs. A2v. – A3v., *EW* VII, pp. 4-6. See Milton, 'Hobbes, Heresy and Lord Arlington', p. 507 n. 24.

I hear some of them do) as an Atheist, or a man of no Religion, unless it be for making the Authority of the Church wholly upon the Regal Power; which I hope your Majesty will think is neither Atheism nor Heresie.

But what had I to do to meddle with matters of that nature, seeing Religion is not *Philosophy*, but *Law*.

It was written at a time, when the pretence of Christs Kingdom was made use for the most horrid Actions that can be imagined; And it was in just indignation of that, that I desired to see the bottom of that Doctrine of the Kingdom of Christ, which divers Ministers then Preached for a Pretence to their Rebellion; which may reasonably extenuate, though not excuse the writing of it.

There is therefore no ground for so great a Calamny in my writing. There is no sign of it in my Life; and for my Religion, when I was at the point of death at *St. Germains*, the Bishop of *Durham* can bear witness of it, if he be asked. Therefore, I a most humbly beseech Your Sacred Majesty not to believe so ill of me, if snatching up all the Weapons to fight Your Enemies, I lighte upon one that had a double edge.

There are several things to be noted about this extraordinary piece of pleading. In the first case, the specious ingenuousness invites comment. Hobbes could very well imagine what the bishops had in mind when they objected to his doctrine of 'making the Authority of the Church wholly upon the Regal Power', the whole tenor of which was to undermine the episcopacy as an institution. Not only that, but he had personally attacked specific bishops, Bramhall, who by 1662 was safely in Ireland, and Seth Ward, whom he compared with a little barking dog.[1] In *Six Lessons to the Professors of Mathematicks* Hobbes had addressed Ward together with Wallis as '*uncivill Ecclesiastiques, Inhumane Divines, Dedoctors of Morality, Unasinous Colleagues, [an] Egregious pair of* Issachars, *most wretched Vindices* and *Indices Academarium*'.[2] It must finally be noted that Hobbes's 1662 *Apology*, read to the Royal Society and presented to the King, was published in 1662 as *Problemata Physica* – a typical resort to innocuous titles and the use of Latin to cloak controversial matters.[3] It was published in English only posthumously in 1682 in

[1] *EW* V, p. 455.
[2] *Six Lessons*, p. 64 (*EW* VII, p. 356), cited in Milton, p. 505, n. 20.
[3] *OL* IV, pp. 301-30.

Hobbes's work *Seven Philosophical Problems* and William Crooke claims that Hobbes had made the English translation himself.[1]

Nor was Hobbes quite the consistent Royalist he claimed to be, as we have seen. Clandestine printings of *Leviathan* suggested that he was probably read as supporting the sovereignty of Parliament. The `Review and Conclusion' make important concessions in that direction, as we have seen; while Wallis had made the accusation that Hobbes had in fact supported Cromwell, and in the *Six Lessons* Hobbes not only did not deny it, but made bold to boast that *Leviathan* had 'framed the minds of a thousand Gentlemen to a conscientious obedience to present Government, which otherwise would have wavered in that point'.[2] If Hobbes sounds uncharacteristically contrite in the *Apology*, he has reason to be sorry then. Not only did he have to scramble to mend fences with the king, but associates had recorded an outbreak of uncharacteristic piety on his part. It is with some scepticism, then, that we must read Hobbes's account in the *Apology* of what transpired when he was near death in France; an account which he repeats in his prose autobiography along the same lines, but which was subject to rather different interpretations at the time.

By 1668 Hobbes's fabled timorousness was evident in a certain justified paranoia that he was effectively under attack by everyone: 'Many politicians and clergy dispute with me about the right of the King. Mathematicians of a new kind dispute with me about geometry ... Those Fellows of Gresham [the Royal Society] who are most believed and are like masters of the rest dispute with me about physics .... They are all hostile to me .... The algebraists revile me', he wailed, once more in Latin.[3] This was a lament he managed to insert into the preface of *Dialogus Physicus* prepared for an edition of his Latin writings planned during Samuel Sorbière's visit of 1663, but published in Amsterdam as the *Opera Philosophica* only in 1668. Most significant among the lamentations is the claim that 'One part of the clergy forced me to flee from England to

---

[1] *EW* VI, p. 164. See Thomas Birch, *The History of the Royal Society of London* (4 vols, London, 1756-7), I, p. 78.

[2] *Six Lessons*, p. 57 (*EW* VII, p. 336), see Collins, *Allegiance,* p. 218.

[3] *OL* IV, p.p. 236-7, cited by Milton, 'Hobbes, Heresy and Lord Arlington', p. 508.

France; and another part of the clergy forced me to flee back from France to England'.[1]

Hobbes as usual was putting his own construction on events. By this time he has given several different accounts of his reasons to flee England in 1640. 'The reason I came away', he told Lord Scudamore closer to the event in 1641, 'was that I saw words that tended to advance the prerogative of kings began to be examined in Parliament'.[2] Perez Zagorin, who has published the letter to Scudamore, believes it related to the impeachment of Strafford, in fact.[3] However, some years later Hobbes accounted his actions to Aubrey differently. 'He told me', Aubrey reports, 'that bp Manwaring (of St. David's) preach'd *his doctrine*; for which, among others, he was sent to the Tower. Then thought Mr. Hobbes, 'tis time now for me to shift my selfe, and so withdrew into France, and resided at Paris'.[4] By 1670, however, most of Hobbes's fears for his person had been allayed and he need worry only about keeping his works from the fire.

In the light of very justified fears, Tuck's case for the centrality of Lord Arlington, Secretary of State, to Hobbes's concern with heresy may perhaps be recast. We may suppose that Hobbes's reasons for getting the judiciary, and particularly Judge Vaughan, on side are the same reasons for which he might want the favour of the Secretary of State. Hobbes had sailed perilously close to the wind, as the *Historia Ecclesiastica*, which might be read as a private running commentary on his state of mind throughout this period, suggests. He needed

---

[1] *Ibid.*

[2] Hobbes to Lord Scudamore, 12 April, 1641, in Perez Zagorin, 'Thomas Hobbes's Departure from England in 1640: An Unpublished Letter', *Historical Journal*, vol. 21 (1978), pp. 157-60, cited by Milton, 'Hobbes, Heresy and Lord Arlington', p. 501.

[3] Zagorin, *loc. cit.,* p. 159.

[4] Aubrey, *Brief Lives,* I, p. 334, see Milton, 'Hobbes, Heresy and Lord Arlington', p. 501; and Sommerville, *Hobbes in Context*, pp. 80-9. Collins, in *The Allegiance of Thomas Hobbes* pp, 81-2, argues the revisionist case, that Hobbes's nervousness about being associated with clergymen like Maynwairing and Sibthrop is because, at this point, he was inclined more to the Erastianism of the Independents and was therefore 'displeased that high-churchmen had discredited his own absolutist political theory by associating it with their own heavy-handed rule of the church'.

protection. As Franck Lessay has noted, the poem ends abruptly, with passing reference to Luther, Wycliff and the Lollards, but no mention of Calvin or the English Reformation.[1] Lessay speculates on this basis that, perhaps for reasons of security, Hobbes's poem remains unfinished. It is quite possible that Hobbes burned concluding verses that dealt with the Reformation and the post-Reformation English Church that might have existed in an earlier version. We have a possible piece of evidence in the fact that the last four lines of MS Harley 1844 (A) are in the corrector's hand, while the catchword *Et* on the previous page is in the first hand, as if a page or pages had been lost or removed. And while the Thott MS B is all in the same hand and it breaks off at the same point, it does not conclude with *Finis*, and it is just possible that the copyist realized that the poem had not originally ended here.

It is certainly odd that a history of the Church written in the mid-seventeenth century does not include reference to the Council of Trent, of 1545-63, surely the most important Church Council of the early modern age. Initially convened to heal the schism between Catholics and Protestants, it was of enormous significance for the history of the Counter-reformation, defining best practice in many doctrinal areas, including Patristics. Moreover the Hardwick Hall book list in Hobbes's hand indicates that important sources on the Council were collected. They include a *Historia Concilii Tridentini*, possibly a Latin version of Paolo Sarpi's famous *Historio del Concilio Tridentino* of 1619, translated by N. Bent as, *The History of the Council of Trent*, 1620 on which John Milton also drew heavily in the *Areopagitica;*[2] along with Martin Chemnitz's *Examinis Concilii Tridentini*.[3] Among the topics Sarpi discussed was the Venice Interdict of 1606, on which he had strong views and the Council of Trent had important bearing. Sarpi was personally

---

[1] Note that although ending his account of the heresy laws with Henry V in the *Historia Ecclesiastica*, Hobbes in the *Narration Concerning Heresy* (*EW* IV, pp. 404-5) extends the account into the reigns of Henry VIII, Edward VI, Elizabeth I and Mary I.

[2] See David Norbrook, *Writing the English Republic: Poetry, Rhetoric and Politics, 1627-1660* (Cambridge, Cambridge University Press, 1999), p. 65.

[3] For Hobbes's book list, which contains three entries for Chemnitz at shelf marks M.4.15, M.4.14, and H.1.7, see Appendix A below.

known to Hobbes through his associate, Fulgenzio Micanzio, whose correspondence with William Cavendish Hobbes translated for his patron.[1]

3.2 HOBBES AND SCARGILL

Perhaps as events changed, Hobbes found in the *Historia Ecclesiastica* the vehicle by which he hoped to re-enter public debate in England, to comment on controversies that he had initially helped catalyze, but which were now closed off to him. The scandal surrounding the notorious Daniel Scargill is a case in point and illustrates a constellation of ideas, initially associated with Hobbes, which came to characterize an interlocking circle of scholars and divines of a Latitudinarian persuasion.[2] It also demonstrates the way in which the views of a proscribed thinker could be propagated in his virtual absence by negative, as much as by positive, publicity, a thesis that Noel Malcolm nicely develops with respect to Hobbes's Continental reception.[3]

Scargill's bold boast that he had 'gloried to be a Hobbist and an Atheist', and his subsequent recantation, at the demand of the King and the Archbishop of Canterbury, Gilbert Sheldon, to a packed congregation at St. Great Mary's, Cambridge, on July 25, 1669, are

---

[1] The correspondence between William Cavendish and Fra Fulgenzio Micanzio has been published, along with Hobbes's translation, as *Lettere a William Cavendish (1615-1628), nella versione inglese di Thomas Hobbes*, ed. Robero Ferrini and Enrico de Mas (Rome, Instituto Storico O.S.M., 1987).

[2] Sources for an overview of these currents in the Restoration Church include, Justin Champion, *The Pillars of Priestcraft Shaken* (Cambridge, Cambridge University Press, 1992); John Spurr, who in '"Latitudinarianism" and the Restoration Church', *The Historical Journal*, vol. 31, no. 1 (1988), pp. 61-82, cautions against treating Latitudinarianism as a social movement; Spurr, '"Rational Religion" in Restoration England', *Journal of the History of Ideas*, vol. 49, no. 4 (1988), pp. 563-85; and Spurr, 'The Church of England, Comprehension and the Toleration Act of 1689', *English Historical Review*, vol. 104, no. 413 (1989), pp. 927-46. For the contest between Cambridge Platonism and Arminianism see the excellent Ph. D. dissertation by William Craig Diamond, *Public Identity in Restoration England: From Prophetic to Economic*, Johns Hopkins University (Ann Arbor Microfilms), 1982.

[3] Noel Malcolm, 'Hobbes and the European Republic of Letters', especially sections 3 and 4, pp. 469-84.

well known.[1] But the extent to which Scargill contributed to the
propagation and systematic examination of Hobbes's views, is not.
The 'bizarre codicil' to Scargill's *Recantation*, that succeeded in
'destabiliz[ing] the whole text',[2] by disavowing as opportunism and
hypocrisy his earlier Hobbist commitment to believe whatever the
sovereign demanded of him, drew attention to the likelihood that
Scargill's recantation was simply another exercise in dissimulation
along classic Hobbesian lines. The longer term consequences of
Scargill's extraordinary behaviour are more surprising, however,
for he had arrived at a formulation of Hobbism that, by its very suc-
cinctness, insinuated itself into the public discourse, challenging
a number of moderate Anglicans to reconsider their positions,
especially when faced with the problem of religious dissent.

It seems that Hobbes had no objection to the inflammatory
reading Scargill gave of his position, and rather preferred to capitalize on it, inserting himself into the debate in the hope of turning it
against the independence of the universities, to which he was so
opposed. But to no avail. Aubrey relates the frustrating incident:[3]

> Mr. Hobbes wrote a letter to . . . (a colonell, as I remember) con-
> cerning Dr. Scargill's recantation sermon, preached at Cambridge,
> about 1670, which he putt into Sir John Birkenhead's hands to be
> licensed, which he refused (to collogue and flatter the bishops), and
> would not returne it, nor give a copie. Mr Hobbes kept no copie, for
> which he was sorry. He told me he liked it well enough himselfe.

Hobbes did not succeed in retrieving his letter but we now have
evidence that Scargill had received from Hobbes a copy, that he too

---

[1] See the *Recantation of Daniel Scargill* (Cambridge, 1669), and the accounts
given of the affair by Samuel Mintz, *The Hunting of Leviathan: Seventeenth-
Century Reactions to the Materialism and Moral Philosophy of Thomas Hobbes*
(Cambridge, Cambridge University Press, 1969), pp. 50-2; and the more substantial
accounts of J. Axtell, 'The Mechanics of Opposition: Restoration Cambridge
v. Daniel Scargill', Bulletin of the *Institute of Historical Research*, vol. 38 (1965),
pp. 102-11; and Jon Parkin, 'Hobbism in the Later 1660s: Daniel Scargill and
Samuel Parker', *The Historical Journal*, vol 42, 1 (1999), pp. 85-108, to whom I am
indebted for the account that follows.
[2] As Parkin notes, 'Hobbism in the Later 1660s', p. 95.
[3] Aubrey, *Brief Lives*, I pp. 360-1. For a discussion of the missing letter, see
Noel Malcolm, Hobbes *Correspondence*, p. lvi; and Parkin, 'Hobbism in the Later
1660s', pp. 85-108.

tried to get it published, and that Birkenhead once again succeeded
in confiscating it. In a letter dated December 1680 to Thomas
Tenison (later Archbishop of Canterbury), a fellow of Corpus Christi,
Scargill's Cambridge College, and sometime mentor to him, Scargill
claims that Hobbes's letter 'made a mighty quoting out of his
Leviathan', and was once again confiscated by John Birkenhead.[1]
He tried to recall the drift of Hobbes's defence:[2]

> I wish I could retrieve a copy of Mr Hobbes his papers writ agt ye
> University of Cambridges proceedings in my Business. He writt
> about 3 or 4 sheets of paper, but I remember little of ym but yt *he
> pleaded ye University had forfeited her Charter by exceeding her
> commission or delegated authority and he made a mighty quoting of
> his Leviathan in defence of himself* yt I remember Sir John Birken-
> head fell a Swearing this man's starved yt takes his own flesh.

Hobbes's intervention in the Scargill affair does not sound like the
pleading of a timorous man. His argument that the University had
exceeded its authority in sending Scargill down resumes the campaign against the universities Hobbes had waged throughout the
Interregnum, as we have seen. For the whole question turned, once
again, on the question of outward conformity to sovereign authority
in matters of religion. And we may guess that Hobbes's 'mighty
quoting of his Leviathan' was designed to kill two birds with one
stone: to remind the authorities of his steadfastness in maintaining
this principle, and thereby exonerate him.[3]

Scargill's version of Hobbism emphasized legal positivism and
moral relativism, a possible but extreme reading of his position that
has nevertheless succeeded in becoming standard. The formulation
was persuasively neat: (1) if lawful dominion is determined by power,
i.e., might is right; and (2) moral right is founded on the law of the
civil magistrate; then (3) even the Scriptures are 'made law onely by
the civil authority'; and (4) 'whatsoever the magistrate commands is

---

[1] Scargill to Tenison, 3 Dec. 1680, BL Add. MS 38, 693, fol. 131; John Aubrey, *Brief Lives,* vol. 1, pp. 360-1.
[2] Scargill to Tenison, fol. 130, emphases added.
[3] Parkin, 'Hobbism in the Later 1660s', p. 105 n. 68. Parkin notes that Hobbes had 'an eye to his own fate', and that 'the incident gave him an opportunity to attack the autonomy of the clerically-dominated universities, whose reform Hobbes saw as essential in his ongoing struggle against priestcraft'.

to be obeyed notwithstanding contrary to divine moral laws'.[1] This
set of arguments fell into the lap of Latitudinarians who, desperate to
stem the tide of sectarian disobedience, interpreted the whole issue
of freedom of conscience as potentially treasonous. Anxiety created
strange bedfellows. So Samuel Parker, chaplain to Archbishop
Sheldon, who had ordered Scargill's public recantation, in his *Discourse of Ecclesiastical Polity* of 1669, 'found himself defending
positions very close to the propositions of which Scargill was repent-
ing in July of the same year'.[2]

But one should not over-dramatize Scargill's impact either. The
problem of Dissent had provoked proto-Hobbesian responses, even on
the part of the establishment, and before the Scargill affair took place.
Religious dissent in any form could be considered a threat to national
security in a realm in which there was no separation of church and
state. Dissenters comprised Protestants, ranging from Presbyterians,
who had no objection in principle to being members of the established
church but were kept out by scruples of conscience, to separatists, in
turn comprising Independents, Baptists and Quakers, as well as those
smaller sects which objected in principle to an established church and
organized themselves in 'loose confederations of "gathered congregations"', as we have seen.[3] Dissent, as a challenge to the national church
on doctrinal grounds, thus raised the old question of sect and schism,
which Hobbes's political works were dedicated life-long to solving.

Not surprisingly, perhaps, the argument against Dissenters to which
Latitudinarians such as Edward Stillingfleet[4] and Simon Patrick[5]
typically appealed even after the Civil War, and before the Scargill

---

[1] Parkin, 'Hobbism in the Later 1660s', p. 95, citing Scargill, *Recantation*,
pp. 1, 4.

[2] Parkin, 'Hobbism in the Later 1660s', p. 97.

[3] See Gordon Schochet, 'John Locke and Religious Toleration', in Lois
G. Schwoerer, ed., *The Revolution of 1688-1689, Changing Perspectives* (Cambridge, Cambridge University Press, 1992), p. 154.

[4] Edward Stillingfleet (1635-1699), Bishop of Worcester, famous for his correspondence with John Locke, defended intolerance in his works the *Unreasonable-
ness of Separation* (1680) and *The Mischief of Separation* (1680).

[5] Simon Patrick (1626-1707), Bishop of Ely and Cambridge Platonist.
Although generally considered a Latitudinarian, Patrick thought of the love of God
like the Platonists, as a medium between the soul and God; inflamed passions,
having the power to close the distance between them, representing the heat generated by the soul's motion.

scandal during the 1660s, could be read as proto-Hobbesian. It was the argument concerning 'indifferency' that we have already noted as voiced by moderate German Lutherans and Calvinists.[1] Since Scripture did not detail the manner of true worship, as Hobbes put it,[2] Natural Law (or the Law of Natural Reasoning) dictated that the Sovereign should determine the outward form of worship in matters indifferent (*adiaphora*).[3] Even what we take to be a classically Hobbesian distinction between the court of internal conscience (*in foro interno*) and the external court of public observance (*in foro externo*),[4] is to be found in the works of these Latitudinarians. So Parker, Stillingfleet and Patrick conceded that men have *de facto* freedom of conscience because in the internal court the dictates of the sovereign cannot reach, compared with the external realm of public worship, which is subject to civil authority.[5] This set of arguments had only to be tweaked a little to satisfy Latitudinarians like Richard Cumberland[6] and John Locke, who, by introducing notions of natural sociability dating back to Cicero and promoted by Hugo Grotius, believed that they rescued their doctrines from the anarchism of Hobbes's state of nature. Locke, in his *Two Tracts on Government*, written in the 1660s but unpublished, had opposed toleration using the very arguments which Parker had proposed in his *Discourse*, and in 1670 had actually made manuscript comments on that work.[7]

---

[1] Malcolm, 'Hobbes and the European Republic of Letters', p. 478.

[2] *Hist. Eccl.*, lines 35-6.

[3] Parkin, 'Hobbism in the Later 1660s', p. 98, referring to Edward Stillingfleet's *Irenicum* of 1661, and Simon Patrick's *Friendly Debate* series, dialogues beginning in 1668. See *Leviathan*, bk 1, ch. 31, §9 ff. and *Hist. Eccl.*, lines 35-6 for Hobbes on liturgical 'matters indifferent'.

[4] *Lev.*, xv, §36, 79/99.

[5] Parkin, 'Hobbism in the Later 1660s', p. 99.

[6] Richard Cumberland (1631-1718), English philosopher, was bishop of Peterborough from 1691. In his *De legibus naturae* [on natural laws] (1672) he both propounded the doctrine of utilitarianism and opposed Hobbes's egoistic ethics.

[7] Parkin, 'Hobbism in the Later 1660s', pp. 103-4, comments:

> It was perhaps queasiness about the Hobbesian implications of the Tracts which had led Locke to his own discussion of natural law and sociability in his (also unpublished) Essays on the law of nature a few years later, in which he partially confronted the Hobbesian problem. One senses that his fundamental uneasiness was not resolved during the mid-1660s as he reworked drafts of his work recommending degrees of toleration, attempting to reconcile viable political authority and potentially dangerous religious liberty. The Parker incident brought both of these issues into sharper focus.

Appeal to Natural Law, as the basis upon which to consign liturgical matters of indifference to the Sovereign, taken together with Ciceronian-Grotian appeals to 'natural sociability', represented ways in which the Latitudinarians tried to put distance between themselves and Hobbes, but without much success. Challenged by a howl of protest from the Dissenters that he was a 'Young Leviathan', Parker, for instance, confessed, 'this is somewhat rank doctrine, and favours not a little of the Leviathan. But yet how can I avoid it? Are these not my own words? .... I am content to confess that I have said something not unlike them'.[1] The charge of Hobbism prompted some exaggerated backpedaling. So, Tenison, Scargill's mortified tutor, wrote a treatise against the 'Monster of Malmesbury', in *The Creed of Mr Hobbes Examined*; while Stillingfleet, whose *Irenicum* was read as Hobbist, reissued the work with an appendix denouncing Hobbes for having 'melted down all Spiritual power into the Civil state, and dissolved the Church into the Commonwealth'.[2]

The influence of the scandalous Mr. Hobbes was not confined to his Erastianism, however, and what is perhaps most surprising is the degree to which Scargill, and Latitudinarian circles in the 1660s to which he belonged, had been infected by a range of arguments that we have come to think of as Hobbesian, including Epicurean notions that we associate also with Gassendi,[3] for which Hobbes was not necessarily the source. As early as 1654, Walter Charleton in his *Physiologia*, had provided a popular account of Gassendi's natural philosophy, while S. P., usually taken to be Simon Patrick, in his *Brief Account of the New Sect of Latitude Men* of 1662, had singled out an interest in natural philosophy, as well as moderate Anglicanism, as characteristic Latitudinarian traits. Latitudinarianism, he claimed, 'which resisted the Laudian or High Church insistence on conformity in nonessentials such as church order and liturgy, [was] "that vertuous mediocrity which our Church observes

---

[1] Parkin, 'Hobbism in the Later 1660s', p. 101, citing Parker's *Defence and Continuation* of the *Discourse* of 1671 (p. 279), which replied to John Owen's attack on him in *Truth and Innocence Vindicated* (London, 1669).

[2] As Collins notes, *Allegiance*, pp. 273-4.

[3] See Parkin, 'Hobbism in the Later 1660s', p. 88.

between the meretricious gaudiness of the Church of Rome, and the squalid sluttery of Fanatick conventicles"'.[1]

Scargill too had first came to public notice for defending a mechanistic account of the origins of the world in Cartesian and Gassendist-Epicurean terms,[2] while John Spencer, Master of Corpus Christi in Scargill's time, believed that natural philosophy along Baconian lines would put paid to astrologers, soothsayers and quacks.[3] It was a thesis that Spencer continued to develop in a startling way, demonstrating an interest in Hebrew divination, and producing two works, the *Dissertatio de Urim et Thummim*, of 1669, and *De Legibus Hebraeorum*, of 1685, which accused the Hebrew priesthood of superstitious and idolatrous practices that they had derived from the Egyptians.[4] Hobbes had made passing reference to this highly inflammatory topic in *Leviathan*, ch. 42 §93, citing *Exodus* 28:30, "'Thou shalt put on the breastplate of judgment, the Urim and Thummim", which he saith is interpreted by the Septuagint *delosin kai aletheian* (that is, as *evidence* and *truth*), and thence concludeth, God had given evidence and truth (which is almost infallibility) to the high priest'.[5] It was a topic that he developed at much greater length in *Behemoth* and the *Historia Ecclesiastica*, as the fable of the 'collar of truth'. Having first established that Hebrew wisdom was derived from Egyptian, Hobbes melded to the mention of Urim and Thummum in *Exodus* the account of the 'collar of truth' given in Diodorus, to show how the Egyptians

[1] See D. F. Wright, *Elwell Evangelical Dictionary* (http://64.233.183.104/ search?q=cache:OBEBaD816n0J:mb-soft.com/believe/txn/latitudi.htm+Simon+ Patrick,+Bishop+of+Ely&hl=en).

[2] Parkin, 'Hobbism in the Later 1660s', p. 88, citing Henry Gosling, a Corpus Fellow, who testified that Scargill had openly defended the thesis that 'Origo mundi petest explicari mechanice' ['The origin of the world can be explained mechanically'] (Lambeth Palace MS 941, fol. 108).

[3] Parkin, 'Hobbism in the Later 1660s', p. 87, citing John Spencer's *Discourse Concerning Prodigies* (1663) which was a specific response to *Mirabilis Annus or the Year of Prodigies and Wonders, being a Faithful and Impartial Collection of Several Signs that hath been seen in the Heavens, in the Earth, and in the Water* (London, 1660).

[4] Parkin, 'Hobbism in the Later 1660s', p. 92.

[5] *Lev.*, xlii, §93, 305/380; For a discussion of Spencer's thesis, see Justin Champion, *The Pillars of Priestcraft Shaken*, pp. 155-7. For Hobbes's references to Urim and Thummin, see also *Beh.*, EW VI, p. 279, and *Hist. Eccl.*, lines 228-274.

converted the question of justice into a question of dominion. He left it to the reader to draw the obvious conclusion that this was a paradigm for Erastianism against the power of priestcraft, and especially against the pope, whose claims to infallibility, although coming rather late in the history of the church, put the entire realm of ethics and morals under the papal hand.

With regard to Spencer, Parkin points to another possible connection between Hobbes and Scargill, specifically through Lord Arlington. When, in March 1669, Scargill was expelled from Cambridge, he left threatening to be 'revenged of Dr. Spencer and his complices' and went to London to get assistance, returning surprisingly, with letters from the king ordering that he be restored to his Fellowship at Corpus.[1] These letters, Parkin surmises, 'must have originated from the office of Arlington and, more specifically from that of his secretary, Joseph Williamson, which was a clearing house for this sort of patronage'. As Parkin notes, 'It should also be borne in mind that another client of Arlington at this time was Thomas Hobbes'.[2] However Scargill seems to have succeeded in gaining Arlington's protection where Hobbes failed.

As a parenthesis, and an example of the wide circulation of Hobbes's texts, even the Latin poetry, it is worth noting that the same Thomas Tenison to whom Scargill wrote in 1680 trying to recall the details of Hobbes's letter in support of his case, in his 1670 critique, *The Creed of Mr Hobbes Examin'd; In a feigned Conference Between Him and a Student in Divinity*, not only mimicked the title of Hobbes's *Dialogue between a Philosopher and a Student of the Common Laws of England,* but also his *De Mirabilibus Pecci* (1627/28). Tenison's work, as Parkin notes, concerns his:[3]

> alter-ego, 'a student in divinity', [who] travels to the Peak District and comes across Hobbes at an inn in Buxton. The encounter is perhaps surprisingly, good-humoured. The student and Hobbes even go bathing together. Thomas de Quincey, recounting the incident in

---

[1] Parkin, 'Hobbism in the Later 1660s', p. 93, n.21, citing Lambeth MS 941, fol. 108.

[2] *Ibid.*

[3] Parkin, 'Hobbism in the Later 1660s', p. 106, citing Thomas de Quincey, *On Murder Considered as One of the Fine Arts* (London, 1980, pp. 16-19), p. 93.

one of his essays, was at a loss to explain how Tenison could 'venture to gambol in the same water with the *Leviathan*'.

What both de Quincey and Parkin miss is the fact that this is an obvious parody of Hobbes's other notable Latin poem, the Scarronesque account of a journey through the Peak District of Derbyshire, in which Dudley is to be found cavorting in the waters of Buxton spring with Elizabeth I. Commentators have generally overlooked this piece of evidence for the circulation of Hobbes's journey poem, whose reception was if anything greater at home than that of the *Ecclesiastical History*, no doubt because of its topicality, and its bawdy and scurrilous content, being wisely treated as a piece of pornography, which undoubtedly assisted its promotion.

CHAPTER 4

HOBBES
AND ECCLESIASTICAL HISTORY

4.1 THE PAPACY, INSTITUTIONALIZATION AND STATE POWER

In *Leviathan* book 2, chapter 28, referring to Job 41:33-4, Hobbes had described the sovereign as 'King of the Proud' and lord of fear, terms that applied equally to the pope in his earthly domain;[1] and in book 4, chapter 47, 'The Kingdom of Darkness', he attributes the imperium of the Bishop of Rome to pagan sources.[2] If the papacy synecdotized the episcopacy, it also metonymized *imperium*. Heresy is the obverse of orthodoxy and orthodoxy is a question of authority. As a history of civil religion, the *Historia Ecclesiastica* is particularly noteworthy for the way that it demonstrates the institutional

---

[1] See *Lev.*, xxviii, §27 166/210:

'There is nothing', saith he, 'on earth to be compared with him. He is made so as not to be afraid. He seeth every high thing below him, and is king of all the children of pride.' [Job 41:33-34] But because he is mortal and subject to decay, as all other earthly creatures are, and because there is that in heaven (though not on earth) that he should stand in fear of, and whose laws he ought to obey, I shall in the next following chapters speak of his diseases and the causes of his mortality, and of what laws of nature he is bound to obey.

[2] See *Lev.*, xlvii, §21 387/482-3:

For from the time that the Bishop of Rome had gotten to be acknowledged for bishop universal, by pretence of succession to St. Peter, their whole hierarchy (or kingdom of darkness) may be compared not unfitly to the kingdom of fairies (that is, to the old wives' fables in England concerning ghosts and spirits and the feats they play in the night). And if a man consider the original of this great ecclesiastical dominion, he will easily perceive that the Papacy is no other than the ghost of the deceased Roman Empire, sitting crowned upon the grave thereof. For so did the papacy start up on a sudden out of the ruins of that heathen power.

ramifications of sectarianism, to which the story of heresy belongs. For, heresy did not become an issue until the Church claimed the powers of excommunication and the interdict. And that was late. Sectarianism, however, is the occupational hazard of philosophers, dating back to the Greeks and the 'Greekification' of Christianity. Hobbes defends throughout the definition of heresy given in Diogenes Laertius 1.20, as contamination by sects[1] – a theme made famous by pre-Reformation humanists *Lorenzo Valla and *Erasmus of Rotterdam. But such elaborate and exhaustive effort was not expended by Hobbes simply to establish that religious matters were to be decided by the Prince (as he pointedly refers to the sovereign throughout the poem). He looks beyond the famous principle of the Reformation state, *cuius regio eius religio*, to see why this claim was in fact necessary. The answer lay not only in the efforts of fledgling nation states to extricate themselves from the catholic Empire, but in the imperial structures of the Catholic Church itself that go back at least until the eleventh century and the Hildebrand reforms, when the Papacy embarked on a series of centralizing measures that pioneered modern state-building.[2]

Christianity was originally a simple religion, such as would appeal to fishermen, Hobbes insists, as his editor Rymer stresses,[3] a view that he shares with Aubrey, Herbert and Vossius, Newton, William Whiston and John Locke,[4] writers of a Latitudinarian persuasion, who were later attacked as Hobbists, as we have seen. Open in structure, simple in doctrine, and concentrated on its crusading

---

[1] *Hist. Eccl.*, lines 1057-1214, see also lines 323-336, 400-450.

[2] Harold Berman, *Law and Revolution, The Formation of the Western Legal Tradition* (Cambridge, Harvard University Press, 1983).

[3] See Rymer Preface, lines 25-7, which reflect the spirit of the poem, where at lines 873-5 Hobbes notes of the pope: 'Of course he was a fisherman and he looked for fish; and the Council was an assembly of fishermen. But instead of fish, power was his most important concern.' Hobbes dwells for long passages on the baits and lures used by the 'fisher of men' to snare his catch, in particular a long passage, lines 1245-84, on the 'shrewd fisherman' that seems to echo Izaak Walton and Charles Cotton Jr.'s *Compleat Angler*. At lines 184-8 Rymer concludes: 'Our author preferred on this matter to learn Christian simplicity among the first Apostles and fishermen rather than to lose his little brain, bewildered, among the Nicene Fathers and Greekling Theosophists.'

[4] See, for instance, Locke's *Reasonableness of Christianity* (1695) and Whiston's, *Primitive Christianity Revived* (1711).

mission of salvation, the early Church eschewed governmental structures according to the directives of the New Testament.[1] Doctrinal complexity was only introduced when out-of-work Greek philosophers expelled from Rome joined the Christian faith and, facilitating the imperialization of the church, corrupted it. Hobbes's withering contempt for the 'Greeklings',[2] in the spirit of Juvenal and the Roman satirists, has its roots in the dissensions of the Eastern Councils; while his apparently inconsistent hostility to the ancient tongues is also probably targeted at the foundation of the Greek chairs at Oxford and Cambridge, responsible for the revival of Platonism, as we shall see. In the form of Christian or Cambridge Platonism, its metaphysics and infectious 'Enthusiasm', in particular the doctrine of essences, stood for everything to which Hobbes's epistemology and ontology were opposed.

Hobbes's long disquisition on the papacy in the *Historia Ecclesiastica* has other targets, as a particularly telling passage in *Leviathan* alerts us. Invoking a renowned trope from Plutarch on Fortuna, who having flitted through the 'dry places' of Asia, enters Rome prepared to take up her abode,[3] Hobbes relates how, the papacy, now beguiled by China, Japan and the Indies, has ceded power in England to the Presbyterian Assembly of Divines who, as the new broom that sweeps everything clean, may well prove worse:[4]

> But who knows that this spirit of Rome, now gone out, and walking by missions through the dry places of China, Japan, and the Indies,

---

[1] *Hist. Eccl.*, lines 400-450.

[2] *Hist. Eccl.*, lines 325-30. See Rymer's use of the term 'Greekling' (*Graeculus*), also used by Valla and Erasmus, Preface, line 135.

[3] See Plutarch, *De Fortuna Romanorum*, (Loeb Classical Library, 1936 edn), p. 331:

> Fortune, when she had deserted the Persians and Assyrians, had flitted lightly over Macedonia, and had quickly shaken off Alexander, made her way through Egypt and Syria, conveying kingships here and there; and turning about . . . . But when she was approaching the Palatine and crossing the Tiber, it appears that she took off her wings, stepped out of her sandals, and abandoned her untrustworthy and unstable globe. Thus did she enter Rome, as with intent to abide, and in such guise is she present today, as though ready to meet her trial.

[4] See *Lev.,* xlvii, 34, 323-4/484, my emphases. George Wright in his essay 'The 1668 Appendix and Hobbes's Theological Project', p. 403, already noted the reference to the Presbyterian Assembly of Divines, and that Hobbes was probably also referring to the efforts of Catholic missionaries such as Francis Xavier, Matteo Ricci, Luis Frois and Alessandro Valignano.

that yield him little fruit, may not return, or rather an assembly of spirits worse than he, enter, and inhabit this clean swept house, and make the end thereof worse than the beginning? *For it is not the Roman clergy only, that pretends the kingdom of God to be of this world, and thereby to have a power therein, distinct from that of the civil state.* And this is all I had a design to say concerning the doctrine of my POLITICS. Which when I have reviewed, I shall willingly expose it to the censure of my country.

This is a strong summary statement of intent, resumed in the 'Review and Conclusion' of the English *Leviathan*, which also directs attention to the nature of the work, as 'occasioned by the disorders of the present time' and the 'revolution' they called forth. From Aubrey's account, it seems that Hobbes planned to address the Protestant sects, and even the national churches, as destabilizing countervailing powers in his *History of the Encroachment of the clergie (both Roman and Reformed) on the Civil Power*, but maybe later thought the better of it, as I have speculated.[1] In 1647, when he was preparing his new edition of *De cive*, Hobbes already signaled a reading of his attack on the papacy as a surrogate for an attack on episcopacy in general, and specifically the Laudeans and Presbyterians. 'I found my book very sharply criticized', he complained, 'on the ground that I have immoderately enhanced the civil power, but by Churchmen; on the ground that I have taken away liberty of conscience, but by Sectarians'.[2] He went on to confess:[3]

> I do not conceal, that this applies to the authority in foreign countries which may attribute to the Head of the Roman Church, *and also to the power which bishops elsewhere, outside the Roman Church, demand for themselves in their own commonwealth*, and finally to the liberty which even the lowest citizens claim for themselves on the pretext of religion. What war ever broke out in the Christian world that did not spring from this root or was fed by it?

---

[1] Included in Aubrey's, *An Essay towards a Description of the North Division of Wiltshire*, under the heading 'Westport juxta Malmesbury', Bodl. Ms. Aubr. 3, f. 28 (Aubrey, *Brief Lives*, I, p. 394), cited by P. Milton, 'Hobbes, Heresy and Lord Arlington', p. 510.

[2] Hobbes, *De cive, On the Citizen*, ed. and trans. Richard Tuck and Michael Silverthorpe (Cambridge, Cambridge University Press, 1998), p. 15; see Collins, *Allegiance*, p. 93.

[3] *De cive*, p. 81, my emphases; see Collins, *Allegiance*, p. 93.

Behemoth later continues the strategy, the first of the four dialogues attacking papal claims to determine Christian doctrine under the twin rubrics of papal infallibility and the right of excommunication: 'And this power not only the Pope pretends to in all Christendom; *but most bishops also, in their several dioceses, jure divino, that is, immediately from Christ, without deriving it from the Pope*'.[1] It was because of the implicit attack on the episcopacy of the Reformed church that John Aubrey, in a letter to John Locke of 1673, reported that 'the king read [*Behemoth*] and likes [it] extreamly, but tells [Hobbes] there is so much truth in it he dares not license it for feare of displeasing the Bishops'.[2] Hobbes severely censured his own manuscript of *Behemoth* at some point, so much so that the printed edition published in 1682 does not contain the suppressed passages, and only the painstaking reconstruction by Ferdinand Tönnies, working from Hobbes's annotated MS, reproduces them in the 1889 edition. As Collins notes, 'the suppressed pages are those portions of *Behemoth* in which Hobbes most daringly attacked the Laudian church'.[3]

The bulk of Hobbes's *Ecclesiastical History* concerns the rise of the papacy, credited to the capital it makes of Greek philosophy in its contest with the secular state. And here Hobbes draws on a wide range of Patristic sources, in particular the famous fourth century *Historiae Ecclesiasticae*, works of the Greek and Latin Fathers and sixteenth and seventeenth century Jesuit commentaries. For, the question of the relation of religion to civil conflict was one also posed by the ecclesiastical historians, responding to charges that Christianity was the cause of rupture in the state. Hobbes is acutely aware of the political purchase yielded to the papacy by the codifications of successive Church Councils, and this becomes the focus of his work. In the plethora of synods and general ecumenical councils that Hobbes catalogues, the early Church created the problem

---

[1] *Beh.*, p. 6, my emphases; see Collins, *Allegiance,* p. 83.
[2] Aubrey to Locke, 1673 in Maurice Cranston, 'John Locke and John Aubrey', *Notes and Queries,* vol. 197 (1952) pp. 383-4; see Collins, *Allegiance,* p. 86. Anthony Wood also wrote that *Behemoth* contained 'several things against religion, antient learning, universities, etc.', Wood *Athenae Oxoniensis*, vol. 2, p. 481.
[3] See Collins, *Allegiance,* p. 86.

of heresy by developing doctrinal orthodoxy. Armed with the metaphysics of the Greek and Hellenistic age, doctors from the Eastern and Western empires traveled from all corners of Christendom to councils and synods on a regular basis to debate the nature of God, the persons of the Trinity, and what it could mean to say that the Son and Holy Ghost 'proceeded from the Father' or that the 'Holy Ghost proceeded from the Father'.[1]

In this period the Eastern Church was in the ascendancy and most of the councils took place in Eastern cities under the aegis of the Patriarch of Alexandria, of Antioch or of Constantinople.[2] Only later did the sites move West,[3] to Italy at Ferrara-Florence and Trent, as the power of the Bishop of Rome rose. But once under way, the rapid institutionalization of the Papacy and corporatization of the Church following the Gregorian Reforms of AD 1075 challenged the Empire to follow suit. If the revival of Aristotle in the thirteenth century, on the basis of texts reintroduced through the Caliphate at Cordoba, was a triumph of scholasticism, so was the thirteenth century reception of Roman Law. The codification of Canon Law, which co-opted Roman Law principles in the form of Natural Law, prompted the formalization of common law, commercial law, burgher's law, city law, and so on.

Hobbes, writing post-Valla, does not bother to raise the issue of *The [Supposed] Donation of Contantine*, the document in which the Emperor was long believed to have ceded Western Christendom to the pope, and what it might have contributed to this centralizing process. Indeed in the poem Hobbes locates the critical moment in papal ascendancy not with the supposed Donation of Constantine to Pope Sylvester, but rather with Charlemagne's subservience to *Pope Leo III (795 to 816). Even so, the role of Constantine, a much debated figure in Hobbes's day, is pivotal. Like the famous fourth century histories after which it is named, the *Ecclesiastical Histories* by *Eusebius, *Evagrius, *Rufinus, *Socrates Scholasticus,

---

[1] *Hist. Eccl.*, lines 705-800.
[2] *Hist. Eccl.*, lines 1057-1214. See Walter Ullmann, *Medieval Papalism: The Political Theories of the Medieval Canonists* (London, 1949), and Ullmann, *The Origins of the Great Schism* (London, 1948).
[3] *Hist. Eccl.*, lines 705-800.

*Sozomen, and *Theodoret, Hobbes's *Historia Ecclesiastica* is overwhelmingly concerned with the heresies dealt with by Constantine at the Council of Nicaea in AD 325.[1]

Hobbes follows John Milton in making Constantine a figure for Charles I, as protector of the Church and realm, although for Milton it was a negative identification. For Hobbes there is some ambiguity. Constantine is at once the Emperor who bathed his realm in the blood of unbelievers as a consequence of his monotheism.[2] At the same time, as the first Christian emperor he convened in person the first general ecumenical council and, by his prudence guided its deliberations, steering a middle path between claimants. As doctrinal positions solidified in the early Church and orthodoxy was consolidated, the Arians were cast in the role of chief heresiarch, and in debate after debate, council after council, Arianism in some form reared its head. The issues, too complex to detail in their minutiae, turned on the relationship of Christ to the Godhead. Were the three persons of God, Father, Son and Holy Ghost, of the same substance, or only of like substance? If the former, what then of the claim that Christ was God made flesh? And if the latter, did this mean a hierarchy of divine natures, Father, Son and Holy Ghost, in descending order and of diminishing power?[3]

From the fourth century Council of Nicaea to the sixteenth century Council of Trent these issues were debated. The outcome was, in Hobbes's view, the construction of a grand cultural edifice that made of the papacy itself a great Leviathan. The more intense and frequent the councils, the more polarized the parties, the more the power of the papacy grew on the crest of the wave.[4] As church historians acknowledge, this growth in papal power was accompanied by expressly articulated imperial claims and appeal to concepts

---

[1] See Norbrook, *Writing the English Republic,* p. 111. Milton used Constantine as a surrogate for Charles I, attacking him ferociously, as defended by the clergy because he defended them, and as having begun the marriage of church and emperor. See Milton's *Apology against a Pamphlet,* and *Of Reformation,* in *The Prose Works of John Milton,* ed. R. W. Griswold, 2 vols (Philadelphia, PA, John W. Moore, 1847), vol. 1, pp. 943-4 and 554, respectively.

[2] *Hist. Eccl.,* lines 555-6.

[3] For Hobbes on the 'homoousion' question, see *Hist. Eccl.,* lines 617-20, 663-4, 674, and 751-2.

[4] *Hist. Eccl.,* lines 557-70.

of 'universal empire',[1] claims representing papal self-consciousness of the capacity to build a powerful state edifice, not on the basis of an *ethne* or a territory initially, but on the crusading force of ideology. An ideology generated out of sacred texts, it gradually gathered to itself armies and territories, philosophers and kingships, to become as Roman and Catholic as it claimed itself to be.[2] So when, in *Leviathan*, Hobbes declared the Pope to be 'the Ghost of the Roman Empire sitting enthroned upon the grave thereof', this was no idle boast. To Hobbes the papacy represented the first and greatest example of Machiavelli's 'prophet armed'.[3]

The imperialization of western European kingship may have awaited the 'Papal Revolution' of the eleventh century, but the institutionalization of the papacy itself had responded to external and Eastern threats. The Church had assisted in the work of rural reconstruction, for which the manorial system of feudalism was so appropriately adapted, to bring land back into cultivation after the devastating and depopulating wars of the late Roman Empire. Christianity allowed the pacification of the countryside, in the hope of banishing rural superstitions as well as increasing productivity; and monasteries led the way.[4] Monks introduced literacy, developing as a priestly scribal caste with a monopoly on the Book,[5] much after the style of the Egyptian priestly caste, as Hobbes suggests.[6]

In AD 1100 Western Europe was still bereft of political legal and ecclesiastical institutions, however, apart from occasional

---

[1] See Brian Tierney, *Origins of Papal Infallibility 1150-1350: a Study on the Concepts of Infallibility, Sovereignty and Tradition in the Middle Ages* (Leiden, E. J. Brill, 1972); Uta-Renate Blumenthal, *The Investiture Controversy. Church and Monarchy from the Ninth to the Eleventh Century* (Philadelphia, University of Pennsylvania Press, 1988); Colin Morris, *The Papal Monarchy: The Western Church from 1050-1250* (Oxford, Clarendon, 1989); Harold J. Berman, 'The Papal Revolution', in *The Middle Ages*, Vol. II, *Readings in Medieval History*, ed. Brian Tierney, 4th edn. (New York, McGraw Hill, 1992), pp. 217-23; Walter Ullmann, *The Growth of Papal Government in the Middle Ages*, 3rd ed. (Cambridge, 1970); and Ullmann, *Medieval Papalism: The Political Theories of the Medieval Canonists* (London, 1949).

[2] *Hist. Eccl.*, lines 1755-8.

[3] See Machiavelli, *The Prince*, chapter 6, on the prophet armed versus the prophet unarmed.

[4] Harold Berman, *Law and Revolution*, pp. 62-3.

[5] *Ibid.*, pp. 64-5.

[6] *Hist. Eccl.*, lines 2020-2050.

royal proclamations of customary law, edicts of Church Councils, and codices, as well as '"magical-mechanical" modes of proof by ordeal and compurgation'.[1] Church structures reflected the practices of the conquering 'barbarians' to a greater extent than we normally assume, and Hobbes makes references to *codices*, with an apparently clear sense of their primitive Germanic force.[2] As Henry Sumner Maine remarked so long ago, Germanic law bore remarkable similarities to non-Western cosmically integrated customary law;[3] and even Christian Penitentials were in the tradition of Germanic group atonement. The sacraments were as yet unsystematized and the clergy did not yet have the power to release the faithful from their sins.

So, for instance, the Penitential of Burchard of Worms, AD 1010 begins: 'This book is called "the Corrector" and "the Physician", since it contains ample corrections for bodies and medicines for souls and teaches every priest, even the uneducated, how he shall be able to bring help to each person . . .'.[4] Hobbes mocks the language of these Penitentials with his satirical references to the spells and potions (*pharmaka*) with which the early Church plied its trade. *Pharmakon*, a typically Epicurean term for poison, magic potion, charm; medicine, remedy, or drug, in the Christian era had a special reference to the Eucharist as *pharmakon Athanasias*, the medicine of (i.e. means of attaining) immortality.[5] Hobbes employs this use at line 1091 of the *Historia Ecclesiastica*, referring to the Eucharist, as the remedy of sin, but not without implying sorcery.[6]

---

[1] Berman, *Law and Revolution*, p. 76, pp. 81-3.

[2] *Hist. Eccl.,* lines 710, 975, 1451, and 1510.

[3] Berman, *Law and Revolution*, pp. 81-3, citing Henry Sumner Maine, *Ancient Law: Its Connection With the Early History of Society, and Its Relation to Modern Ideas* (London, John Murray, 1861).

[4] Berman, *Law and Revolution*, p. 71.

[5] See the Arndt & Gingrich Greek dictionary. *Pharmacus*, according to Lewis & Short, from Gr. *pharmakos*, referred to a poisoner, or sorcerer in post-Augustan Latin (see Petronius, *Satyricon*, 107.15).

[6] *Hist. Eccl.,* line 1252, Hobbes employs a different use of the term *pharmaca* when referring to the lures and potions used by the fisherman, mimicking the language of Izaak Walton and Charles Cotton, *The Compleat Angler* (1653), ed. Jonquil Bevan (Everyman edn, 1993), pp. 137-9, where they discuss the making of pastes to catch carp; and on p. 185 note strong-smelling oils are 'excellent to tempt fish to bite'.

One might argue that prior to the Gregorian reforms the Western empire differed little from the Caesaropapism of the Eastern Empire.[1] Kings exercised a sacral function as 'deputies of Christ',[2] as faithfully represented in Hobbes's account. Disputes over the jurisdiction by bishops were settled in regional synods, in Rome or, equally, in royal courts. Only in the twelfth century did Emperors relinquish the title 'Deputy of Christ' to the Pope, formerly known as the 'Deputy of St. Peter'; and up to this point the clergy were married, appointed by, and intermarried with, the secular authorities.[3] 'The Empire was not a geographical entity but a military and religious authority'.[4] Unlike the Roman Empire it was not ruled by an imperial bureaucracy and, 'in sharp contrast to Caesar's city-studded empire, Charlemagne and his successors had hardly any cities at all'.[5] The empire, neither Roman until 1034 nor Holy Roman until 1254, simply involved a peripatetic emperor moving between France, Burgundy, Italy, Hungary and the Frankish-German homeland. Institutionalization awaited the development of monasticism which provided both Church and Empire with elite cadres capable of carrying it through. The Benedictines of Cluny, founded 910, by AD 1000 controlled 1000 monasteries. The Cluniac Reforms and ensuing centralization created 'the first translocal corporation' and ultimate model for church and empire as a whole.[6] So, for instance, the Cluniac monasteries, with the assistance of the Emperor, initiated the peace movement which concluded the Council of Bourges of 1038. Under the 'Truce of God', as it was called, warfare was suspended, but clerical marriage, sale of offices (simony) and clerical concubinage (nicolaism) which had feudalized the church, were also abolished.[7]

In AD 800, *ecclesia* truly meant the ruling *populus Christianus regnum et sacerdotium*, not quite the *ecclesia* in the Greek sense as a

---

[1] Berman, *Law and Revolution*, p. 88.
[2] *Ibid.*, pp. 92-3.
[3] See *Hist. Eccl.*, lines 1791ff. on married clergy.
[4] Berman, *Law and Revolution*, p. 89.
[5] *Ibid.*
[6] *Ibid.*, p. 89, citing Eugen Rosenstock-Heussy, *Out of Revolution: Autobiography of Western Man*, (New York, 1938). p. 506.
[7] Berman, *Law and Revolution*, p. 91.

popular assembly, of Hobbes's depiction.[1] Charlemagne's English ecclesiastical secretary, Alcuin, had referred already to the *imperium Christianum*. Berman notes that while 'Some historians argue that Pope Leo III made Charlemagne emperor . . . it is closer to the truth to say that Charlemagne made Leo pope'; and as proof of his ecclesiastical power, 'in 813 Charlemagne crowned his own son emperor without benefit of clergy'.[2] In 1067 William the Conqueror had claimed the power to determine whether a pope could rule in England or Normandy. The accession of Henry III in 1046 saw the emperor involved in a scandalous subordination of the papacy, by deposing three rivals and electing his own man. The Saxon Henry III (1017-1056), Duke of Bavaria (which he ruled as Henry IV from 1027-41), Duke of Swabia (which he ruled as Henry I, 1038-45), German king (from 1039) and Holy Roman Emperor (from 1046-56), was a member of the Salian dynasty. A powerful advocate of the Cluniac reforms that tried to purify the Church in the eleventh century, he was the last emperor able to dominate the papacy and was subsequently poisoned by hostile Romans.[3] His third candidate, *Pope Leo IX, who reigned from 1049-54, although a kinsman of Henry III, insisted on the independence of the papacy. The papal party gathered strength in his reign and a pamphlet war ensued, leading to the accession of its leader, Pope *Gregory VII, formerly the monk Hildebrand, who reigned from 1073-85, deposing the Emperor, Henry IV.

The Gregorian, or Hildebrand, Reforms – also known as the Investiture Struggle – concerned the contest between pope and emperor over the power to 'invest' bishops.[4] After 25 years of agitation by the papal party, its leader, Hildebrand, in 1075 declared the political and legal supremacy of the papacy over the entire church, the independence of the clergy from secular authority, as well as the ultimate supremacy of the pope even in secular matters, with the right to depose kings and emperors.[5] While Hobbes does

---

[1] See *Lev.*, xxxix, §2, 248/315.

[2] Berman, *Law and Revolution*, p. 91, citing François L. Ganshof, *The Imperial Coronation of Charlemagne* (Glasgow, Jackson, 1949).

[3] Berman, *Law and Revolution*, pp. 93-5.

[4] *Ibid.*, p. 87.

[5] *Ibid.*, ch. 2, 'The Papal Revolution'. See pp. 576-7 for documentation.

not mention Gregory VII by name, he refers tacitly to his programme, emphasizing the importance of clerical celibacy, on which Gregory campaigned.[1] The emperor, Henry IV of Saxony, had responded militarily and civil war broke out, which was settled in Germany with the Concordat of Worms in 1122, with a temporary settlement in England and Normandy at the Concordat of Bec in 1107, being only finally resolved with the martyrdom of *Thomas Becket in 1170, to which Hobbes makes reference.[2]

The developmental path by which the spread of Christianity gave rise to the institution of 'translocal kingship', the institutionalization of the papacy, and consolidation of the empire as a secular power, led also to the codification of a plurality of orders of law, secular, royal, mercantile, urban, as well as canon law. Church Councils had begun the transmission of Roman Law concepts, but Canon Law, divided into *ius antiquum* and *ius novum*, terms to which Hobbes makes reference, emerges only as a consequence of the Gregorian Reforms.[3] The search for legal texts to support Gregory's reforms accounts for the beginning of the science of canon law.[4] To these institutional features Hobbes was attuned. The institutional avarice of the papacy as a quasi-imperial institution, depicted in the *Historia Ecclesiastica* as scouring the Old World and the New for riches to line its coffers, comes, we may note, relatively late. For, the institutional benefits which the Gregorian Reforms enabled the Church to consolidate, were those accrued largely through mass mobilization against the Moslems in the Crusades from the tenth to the thirteenth centuries. Hobbes's depiction of the Church militant captures both the spirit and the idiom of the *'Divine Aurelius Prudentius', Christian poet but in the Virgilian tradition, who celebrated the Church triumphant, and to whom Rymer alerts us as a source for Hobbes in his learned Preface.[5]

[1] See *Hist. Eccl.*, lines 1787-90.
[2] See *Hist. Eccl.*, lines 1445-6.
[3] Berman, *Law and Revolution,* p. 85. Hobbes uses the terms 'lex Vetus atque Nova' at *Hist. Eccl.*, line 54.
[4] Berman, *Law and Revolution*, p. 576.
[5] Rymer, Preface, line 149.

4.2 HOBBES, THE ANTIQUARIANS AND UNIVERSAL HISTORY

Hobbes's *Historia Ecclesiastica* is a poem with great expectations. It is a mixed genre piece that also aspires to universal history, its account of the creation of the earth, the birth of humankind, the rise of civilization, religion, superstition and the birth of the sciences, paying lip service to the great theogonies of Hesiod, Homer, Virgil, Lucretius, and the more recent universal histories of Hobbes's contemporaries, Walter Raleigh, Alexander Ross, Gerhard Vossius and Johan Clüver. Universal history was also the métier of the ecclesiastical historians from Eusebius on, for whom the historical sweep of Scripture set the agenda for an account stretching from the creation, through the Old Testament prophets, to Christ, Augustus and the founding of Church and Empire, and finally the Christian era from Constantine to the end of the world. Broad outlines of this structure, to which Hobbes's poem pays deference, had been laid out as early as Justin Martyr, Irenaeus, Clement of Alexandria and Origen, and it was an historical schema refined by ecclesiastical historians up to Hobbes's day.[1] Thus his poem covers much the same terrain as his friend Edward Herbert's *De religione gentilium*, his biographer, Aubrey's *Remaines of Gentilisme*,[2] and the universal histories of Ralegh, Ross and Vossius, particularly the latter's great *De theologia gentili, et physiologia Christiana*.

Not coincidentally the dating of Herbert's, Aubrey's and Vossius's histories is contemporaneous with the writing of the *Historia Ecclesiastica*. Herbert's *De religione gentilium, errorumque apud eos causis* was published in Amsterdam in 1663; Aubrey's, *Remaines of Gentilisme and Judaisme*, was published in London in 1666; and Gerardus Johannes Vossius's *De theologia gentili, et pysiologia christiana, sive de Origine ac progressu idololatriae*, was published first in Amsterdam in 1641, later to be republished in 1668. Walter

---

[1] See Chestnut, *The First Christian Histories*, ch 4, pp. 91ff., on Eusebius as a universal historian.

[2] See Edward Herbert, *De religione gentilium, errorumque apud eos causis* (Amsterdam, 1663) translated as The *Ancient Religion of the Gentiles* (London, 1705); Aubrey, *Remaines of Gentilisme and Judaisme* (London, 1666), republished in John Aubrey, *Three Prose Works*, ed John Buchanan-Brown (Fontwell, Sussex, Centaur Press, 1972).

Ralegh's boldly entitled *History of the World*, had been composed earlier, between 1607 and 1614 during his imprisonment in the Tower of London, and the Hardwick Hall Library held a folio edition at the shelf mark P.2.3., according MS E1A. The first two books of Ralegh's *History*, comprising 28 chapters, give a history of the Creation and of the Jews, with parallel accounts of contemporary events in Greek mythology and Egyptian history strikingly similar to Hobbes's *History*.[1] Alexander Ross, author of the catalogue of heresies, *Pansebeia: or A View of All the Religions of the World* (London, 1653), again in the genre of Hobbes's *History*, had undertaken the continuation of Ralegh's project with his *The History of the World, the Second Part, in six books, being a Continuation of Sir Walter Raleigh's*, published in 1652, and his *Animadversions and Observations upon Sir Walter Raleigh's History of the World, wherein his Mistakes are noted, and some doubtful Passages noted*, published in 1653.

The timing and family resemblance between these universal histories are noteworthy. For instance, Vossius's *De theologia gentili*, written in three books and published, not coincidentally, by Hobbes's Dutch publisher, J. & C. Blaeu, had been cited already by Herbert in his *De religione gentilium*. Vossius, born in Heidelberg, and holding chairs of Eloquence and Chronology at Leiden University, from 1622, and later the Chair of Greek, was one of the greatest antiquarians of the seventeenth century. Referred to as 'the greatest Polyhistor of his age', he had a significant following in England. The Hardwick Hall library according to the General List A of MS E1A in Hobbes's hand, lists at shelf mark S.1.1. 'Vossius de Historicis, 2 vol.', presumably Vossius's *De Historicis Graecis Libri IV, Editio altera, priori emendatior, & multis partibus auctior*, and his *De Historicis Latinis*, in the Leiden editions of 1623 and 1627.

Hobbes's poem confronts the contemporary works it so closely resembles, the antiquarian's view of the history of religion, and is itself a display, or perhaps better, a burlesque, of humanist erudition. Beginning with the pagan cosmologies of Homer, Hesiod, Diodorus and Lucretius, and Epicurean speculation on the psychic wellsprings

---

[1] Sir Walter Ralegh's *History of the World*, was noticed in the Stationers' Register in 1611 and according to Camden, published in 1614, but anonymously, and from 1614 to 1678, ten separate folio editions of it appeared.

of religion and superstition, it traverses the history of the earliest civil
religions, those of the Egyptians and Jews, noting the way Christianity became melded to ancient sectarianism through the efforts of
Greek philosophers. The 'Greekification' of primitive Christianity is
one with the rise of sectarianism and heresy, interchangeable terms
for Hobbes, and was an important trope in the works of Lorenzo
Valla and Erasmus of Rotterdam, Hobbes's intellectual forbears.

A series of observations made by Franck Lessay are indicative of
the reasons for Hobbes's initial historiographic focus:[1]

> Christian hagiography was far from being obsolete at the time when
> Hobbes was writing his late books. It might even be said that it served
> as an instrument of cultural transformation. James Ussher, arch-
> bishop of Armagh (and Bramhall's patron in Ireland), established the
> famous chronology of the Bible which dated the Creation in 4004 BC
> – a chronology which remained in use until the 19th century. It was
> also Ussher who, out of a desire to affirm the antiquity of the Church
> of England, decided to promote Anglo-Saxon scholarship on the
> subject and, in 1640, persuaded Sir Henry Spelman to endow a lec-
> tureship at Cambridge for the study of 'domestic antiquities touching
> our Church and reviving the Saxon tongues'.

Ussher's *Chronologia Sacra* appeared in 1660 and represents the
type of work that is Hobbes's target. World history was the particular
métier of reformists, Walter Ralegh, Vossius, and Cluverius, who like
Hobbes himself, sought legitimacy in redescription.[2] But Hobbes
mobilizes impressive classical sources to undercut the historiography of Ussher and those who would give primacy to Hebrew wisdom
as the bulwark of the Reformation. As Lessay has noted, the title
given the English paraphrase of the *Historia Ecclesiastica* published
in 1722, *A True Ecclesiastical History From Moses to the Time of
Martin Luther*, is misleading on all counts.[3] It may be deliberately so,

---

[1] See Franck Lessay, 'Hobbes and Sacred History', p. 151, citing Ussher's
Chronologia Sacra of 1660. See also J. Kenyon, *The History Men: The Historical
Profession in England since the Renaissance* (London, Weidenfeld and Nicolson,
1983).

[2] For *Vossius and Cluverius, in particular, see Patricia Springborg, 'Hobbes,
Heresy and the *Historia Ecclesiastica*', and Springborg, 'Writing to Redundancy:
Hobbes and Cluverius'. I draw on the latter for the following account.

[3] Franck Lessay, 'Hobbes and Sacred History', p. 150. The composition of the
1722 paraphrase may well have been earlier.

to call attention to the fact that, not only does Hobbes deal with the Reformation only in passing, but that his history begins long before Moses and features him hardly at all. For in the long debate over the respective pedigrees of Hebrew and Egyptian wisdom, Hobbes comes down on the side of the Egyptians. He turns to Africa, and in particular Ethiopia, as the cradle of civilization, moving successively to Egypt, Assyria, Chaldaea, Palestine, Greece and Rome.[1] In terms of religious history, the poem is a saga of superstition and snake-oil salesmen, in which, as Lessay rightly points out, 'Moses, Aaron and Abraham are treated in the same allusive way as Plato, Pythagoras and Aristotle'.[2]

Molesworth, on the good authority of Aubrey, believes Cluverius to have been a major source for Hobbes's *Historia Ecclesiastica*, thus placing it primarily in the category of universal history.[3] Aubrey tells us that Hobbes 'did read Cluverius's *Historia Universalis*, and made up his poeme from thence'.[4] But this must be a case of hearsay. There is no such title by Cluverius. Aubrey must have heard it said that Hobbes owed much to a universal history by Cluverius and translated this into a title. Philipp Clüver, the Geographer, had written an *Introductio in Universam Geographicam* (1629), translated into English as *An Introduction to Geography both Ancient and Modern*.[5] Maybe it is the title of this work of which Aubrey gives such a free rendition, taking his cue perhaps from Hobbes's mention of Philip Cluverius as the source for the map to illustrate his translation of Thucydides.[6] But once again Aubrey has not gotten it quite right: not the Cluverius, not the title, and not the content. On his good authority, however, subsequent editors, including Molesworth, have assumed Philipp Clüver to be Hobbes's source, conflating two different Cluverii. So, for instance, Richard Tuck in his biographical

---

[1] *Hist. Eccl.*, lines 1-470.
[2] Lessay, 'Hobbes and Sacred History', p. 150.
[3] Molesworth's descriptive note to the *Hist. Eccl.*, *OL*, vol. V, p. 342.
[4] John Aubrey, in *Brief Lives*, vol. 1, pp. 338-9. 1659.
[5] Ph. Clüver, alias Philip Cluverius, *An Introduction to Geography both Ancient and Modern, comprised in Six Books* (Oxford, Leonard Lichfield, 1657).
[6] Hobbes, *EW* VIII, p. x in his Preface to his translation of Thucydides admits to using a map of Philip Cluverius and descriptions by 'Strabo, Pausanias, Herodotus and some other good authors'.

notes to the Cambridge edition of Hobbes's *Leviathan*, gives Philip Cluverius as Hobbes reference in *Leviathan*,[1] listing his *Germaniae Antiquae Libri Tres* (1616),[2] as the work of the famous geographer to which Hobbes refers.

It is true that the writer commonly known as Cluverius was one Philipp Clüver (1580-1622), a geographer and historian. Born in Danzig, he studied law in Leiden under Joseph Scaliger, became a member of the Leiden academy and visited England. He is the author, among other works, of the aforementioned *Introductio in Universam Geographicam* (1629). As noted, among the more surprising features of Hobbes's *Historia Ecclesiastica*, is the detailed exposition of the ancient Egyptian theogony and its legacy in classical Greece, anticipating speculation on the origins of Greek wisdom, whether it is Egyptian or Hebrew, which was to become a torrent in the age of Newton. Hobbes comes down on the side of the Egyptians. Clüver's work, with a strong focus on the Asia and the Orient, also contains material on the Egyptian origins of Greek wisdom and a curious combination of mythological and aetiological explanation, the new science and the occult, in which Hobbes displays such an interest. It intersperses reflections on Asia as the birthplace of man and religion – the land of the nymph Asia, daughter of Oceanus and Tethys;[3] on the Noachite genealogies and the peopling of Asia by Shem, Africa by Ham and Europe by Japhet;[4] and on the circumnavigation of Asia and Africa 'from Cadiz to the pillars of Hercules' by the Egyptian pharaoh Lothynes and by the Greeks, both of whom are said to have discovered America.[5] For this piece of information he cites Plato's Atlantis story of the Timaeus, Strabo and Diodorus Siculus;[6] venturing the opinion that Egypt was the next civilization after the Assyrian in antiquity; reporting from Homer on her two thousand cities, which included Bubastis and Abydon; and making

---

[1] Richard Tuck, ed., notes to Hobbes's *Leviathan*, p. 58 (Cambridge, Cambridge University Press, 1991), p. lii.

[2] cited in Tuck, notes to Hobbes's *Leviathan*, p. lii.

[3] Philipp Clüver, *Geography both Ancient and Modern*, 1657, pp. 287-8.

[4] *Ibid.*, p. 38.

[5] *Ibid.*, p. 36.

[6] *Ibid.*, pp. 334-5.

mention of Apis and the Egyptian labyrinth.[1] All this material, strange to our ears, is more or less standard in the seventeenth century, a revival of foundation myths that go back to the Greeks. But despite its pseudo-historical digressions, Philipp Clüver's work is indeed a universal geography, and not a world history.

The more likely source for Hobbes is the more obscure Johann Clüver (1593-1633), author of the voluminous *Historiam Totius Mundi Epitome A prima rerum Origine usque ad annum Christi MXDCXXX*, published in 1645. Johann Clüver's epitome and Hobbes's religious history have a common focus 'on how heresy and false traditions have corrupted the church'; on the periodization of sacred history, to show how 'dissident chronologies' threaten the stability of commonwealths;[2] and on the formulation of Christian canonical doctrine in the early councils. Clüver, like Hobbes, begins with the Long Ages of the Biblical patriarchs and the Noachite genealogies up to and including the Jewish diaspora, followed by the Ages of Heroes, of Prophets and Poets, and then of Philosophers and Scribes. He comments on the degeneration of the Jews in the Diaspora, noting that the family of Abraham practiced idolatry, reverting to the worship of Saturn; and he gives the Noachite genealogy according to Josephus, which tells how the eponymous sons of Noah, Shem, Japhet and Cham, populated Asia, Europe and Africa, respectively.[3]

On the crucial question, whether the ancient wisdom was originally Israelite or Egyptian,[4] Clüver plumps for the Israelites, attributing to Abraham the transmission to Egypt of the arts of arithmetic and astronomy, which Pythagoras, Thales, Democritus and other Greeks went to Egypt to learn.[5] But Hobbes came down on the other side, giving a surprising account of the origins of philosophy in the

---

[1] *Ibid.*, pp. 316.

[2] Johann Clüver, *Historiam Totius Mundi*, Preface, p. ii.

[3] *Ibid.*, p. 4.

[4] On the competing claims to ancient wisdom of the Egyptians and the Israelites, see Paolo Rossi's *The Dark Abyss of Time*, Lydia G. Cochrane, trans. (Chicago, University of Chicago Press, 1984); John Gascoigne, '"The Wisdom of the Egyptians" and the Secularisation of History in the Age of Newton', and Garry W. Trompf, 'On Newtonian History', both in Stephen Gaukroger, ed., *The Uses of Antiquity* (Dordrecht, 1992), pp., 171-212, and 213-249, respectively.

[5] Clüver, *Historiam Totius Mundi*, p. 78.

Orient.[1] Clüver cites Josephus on Cadmus the Phoenician (a descendent of Semus or Shem, a Semite) as the founder of history, introducing the age of poets and prophets, and transmitter of the ancient wisdom to Daniel, the Chaldeans, Egyptians, Greeks, Assyrians, Babylonian and Persian monarchies, in that order – a different order from Hobbes, who, following Herodotus perhaps (although without citing him), begins with the Egyptians.[2] Clüver relies on Josephus, the Jewish historian, to refute Manetho on the Egyptian origins of Cecrops and the fabulous stories of the birth of the Erichthoniii, Nilotic-centred accounts.[3] Josephus and Diodorus Siculus are among a number of sources he acknowledges to affirm the story of Cadmus and Europa, Cadmus' arrival in Thebes, his propagation of the art of writing, and the line of Cadmeans, which includes Semele, his daughter and mother of Bacchus, or Jove, and the Greek Heracles.[4] Clüver further draws on Herodotus book 1, Diodorus Siculus, Strabo, Pausanias, Pliny, Justin, Tacitus, Appian, and others for different aspects of his account of the ancient Egyptians, the colonization of Greece by Danaus the Egyptian, Cadmus' counterpart;[5] and the debatable 3,600 year regime of the Assyrians in Asia, founded by Belus in Assur.[6] Some of this strange mixture, typical of the mythographers, finds its way into Hobbes's poem.

---

[1] *Lev.*, xlvi, $6, 369/455. Having adumbrated the principle that '*Leisure* is the mother of *philosophy*; and *Commonwealth*, the mother of *peace* and *leisure*', Hobbes goes on to assert:

> Where first were great and flourishing *cities*, there was first the study of *philosophy*. The *Gymnosophists* of *India*, the *Magi* of *Persia*, and the Priests of *Chaldea* and *Egypt* are counted the most ancient philosophers, and those countries were the most ancient of kingdoms. *Philosophy* was not risen to the *Grecians*, and other people of the west, whose *commonwealths* (no greater perhaps than *Lucca* or *Geneva*) had never peace, but when their fears of one another were equal, nor the *leisure* to observe anything but one another. At length, when war had united many of these *Grecian* lesser cities into fewer and greater, then began *seven men*, of several parts of *Greece*, to get the reputation of being *wise*, some of them for *moral* and *politic* sentences, and others for the learning of the *Chaldeans* and *Egyptians*, which was *astronomy* and geometry. But we hear not yet of any *schools* of *philosophy*.

[2] Clüver, *Historiam Totius Mundi*, Preface, p. iii; c.f., Hobbes, *Hist. Eccl.*, lines 147-90.

[3] Clüver, *Historiam Totius Mundi*, p. 14.

[4] *Ibid.*, p. 17.

[5] *Ibid.*, p. 16.

[6] *Ibid.*, p. 6.

Clüver's project is framed by the periodization of sacred history into seven periods, three 'involving a new heavenly regime', and ten revolutions in world government that constitute his version of history up to and including the reign of Constantine, marking 'a Christian imperial reign, the longest and most felicitous since the flood, ended only by the Ottoman Magog, the Turks, nomads, Scythians and Tartars, who broke the imperial power so that the great eagle of the church vigilant flew to others in this period, as St. John taught us'.[1] The periodization of history is an interest which Hobbes shares, but Clüver's account of the early church[2] is quite perfunctory by comparison with Hobbes's, given the 800 and some pages that Clüver's history runs, sandwiching Jesus Christ into a catalogue of Roman emperors. He charts the doctrinal struggles of the Church Councils with nothing like the same attention to detail as Hobbes, mentioning briefly the central problem of the Trinity and the problematic concept *homoousion*.[3] Having chronicled the history of the Turkish empire from 324 to 1314 AD, coinciding, he claims, with the captivity of Satan for 1000 years,[4] he concludes his epitome with the tenth and last age in the series, the church in waiting for the Second Coming of the Lord, which must patiently observe the dictum 'have faith in Jesus and follow God's commands'.[5] Whatever other differences of detail might distance Hobbes from Johann Cluverius, are compensated by a common focus on two themes: ecclesiology as a story of heresy and superstition; and true Christianity as 'faith in Christ' and obedience to the sovereign.

We are now in a better position to reassess Molesworth's claim that *Leviathan* is more clearly the source for Hobbes's *Historia Ecclesiastica*, than Cluverius – even the right Clüver. And in any event it is not the English, but the Latin, *Leviathan*, to which the poem is so closely related both in time and substance. The careful

---

[1] *Ibid.*, Preface, p. v.

[2] *Ibid.*, bk 7, pp. 164ff.

[3] *Ibid.*, p. 353. The term *homoousion*, 'one substance', was used by the Council of Nicaea, A.D. 325, to define the doctrine of the Trinity, as opposed to the term *homoiousion*, 'like substance', favoured by the Arians. See *Hist. Eccl.*, line 674 and notes.

[4] Clüver, *Historiam Totius Mundi*, bk 9, pp. 351ff.

[5] *Ibid.*, Preface, p. v.

chronology of the history of religion, properly sourced in the marginalia, which Johann Clüver gives, more or less corresponds to the structure of Hobbes's *Ecclesiastical History*, except that much of the occult wisdom which Hobbes's account includes is missing, and where it is included, it is argued somewhat differently. Did Hobbes read both Cluverii, or did he resort to the originals for his Egyptian theogony,[1] for instance, and the strange story, of the ancient Egyptian judicial system and the 'collar of truth'?[2] Hobbes's version, which conflates the account of Urim and Thummum in Exodus, and an account in Diodorus Siculus, is repeated in *Behemoth*.[3]

Rymer makes his own suggestions as to Hobbes's sources for the Oriental material:[4]

> If historians should seek the source for those things about the Ethiopians, Neptune, Jove, and the other gods feasting 'with the excellent Ethiopians', they may consider Homer a sufficiently illuminating witness. Concerning King Ergamenes and that famous massacre of the priesthood, they should consult Diodorus Siculus, book 4. Concerning the well-known Egyptian custom of settling disputes by means of the 'Collar' and the Gem as the 'touchstone of truth', Diodorus Siculus and Aelianus, from whom the very famous Selden, Marsham and several others have excerpted in their works, have the same.

But Rymer misses an obvious source, known to Hobbes through Scargill circles, in John Spencer's *Dissertatio de Urim et Thummim*. It is certainly true to say that in the English *Leviathan* Hobbes had already broached most of the topics he treats in the poem, even the curious case of Urim and Thummim, and this well before Spencer's *Dissertatio* on the subject. John Marsham's *Canon Chronicus Aegyptiacus, Ebraicus, Graecus* (Oxford, 1672), to which Rymer's mention of him must refer, mentions both Athanasius Kirchner

---

[1] *Hist. Eccl.*, lines 1680-2000, 1688 edn, pp. 9-10; 1722 paraphrase, pp. 12-15.

[2] *Hist. Eccl.*, lines 240-80, 1688 edn pp. 12-14; 1722 paraphrase pp. 17-19.

[3] *EW* VI, pp. 278-9. MS E1A, the Hardwick Hall booklist, does not list Spencer's work, but Hobbes had access to libraries in London that might have held it, as Aubrey, *Brief Lives*, vol. 1, p. 338, informs us.

[4] *Hist. Eccl.*, Rymer's Preface, lines 75-88, 1688 edn, p. v; 1722 paraphrase, p. iii.

and John Spenser's *Dissertatio de Urim et Thummim* in the Reader's Preface. But if the publication date of Spencer's work, in 1669, would suggest that it was rather late to be Hobbes's source for the poem (assuming its completion at least by 1671), and far too late for the mention of Urim and Thummim in the English *Leviathan*, the publication of Marsham's work is even later. In *Leviathan*, it is true, 'Urim and Thummum' are mentioned only in passing, and it is difficult to say how far Hobbes had developed his ideas on the subject by 1650. He would have come to know of Spencer later, if only through the Arlington connection, and Scargill's appeal to the Secretary of State in March 1669 (the year in which Spencer's *Dissertatio* was published), to get back his Corpus Fellowship and thus be 'revenged of Dr. Spencer and his complices'.[1] A final judgment on the aetiology of Hobbes's ideas on this subject awaits more work on possible sources, particularly the antiquarians, Marsham, Selden, Vossius and perhaps Joseph Scaliger. Let us just say that the convergence of interests between Hobbes and Spencer must be more than coincidental, and reflects a community of scholars preoccupied with these issues, leaving aside the more difficult question of who influenced whom.

4.3 HOBBES AND THE ECCLESIASTICAL HISTORIANS

The *Historia Ecclesiastica* takes the name of the great ecclesiastical histories by Eusebius Pamphili (c. 260-c. 340), Bishop of Caesarea and 'the father of Church History'; by Rufinus of Aquilea (c. 345-410), 'the Continuator'; by Socrates Scholasticus (c. 380-450), the lawyer from Constantinople; by Sozomen Salaminius (c. 400-450), likewise; by *Evagrius Ponticus (345-399); by the Arian Philostorgius (c. 364-425) of Cappadocia; and by the Nestorian Theodoret of Cyrrhus (c. 393-458). Hobbes's choice of the venerable epithet, *Historia ecclesiastica*, could not have been accidental, and we know from the Hardwick Hall book list that he had access to a wide range of Patristic sources, including most of the

---

[1] Parkin, 'Hobbism in the Later 1660s', p. 93, n.21, citing Lambeth MS 941, fol. 108.

Greek Fathers in Latin translation, as well a considerable range of
Jesuit and Protestant commentaries.

Rymer mentions only Eusebius' *Life of Constantine* and the writings of the Blessed Hilary as among Hobbes's patristic sources, but,
by this mention, gives us a possible clue to the editions of patristic
Historiae Ecclesiasticae Hobbes might have consulted. For, just as he
probably used Valla as a Latin crib for his translation of Thucydides,
so he likely used the Latin translations as a crib for the Greek Fathers.
Valla's Greek to Latin translation of Thucydides was held in the
Hardwick Hall Library at shelf mark Q.2.6, according to Hobbes's
book list (Part B), and the library included a surprising number of
Latin translations of the Greek Fathers in its holdings. The early
Greek *Church Histories* had been accessible in Latin since *Epiphanius Scholasticus, at the suggestion of Cassiodorus, undertook the
translation of Theodoret, Socrates, and Sozomen, which Cassiodorus
edited and selected for his *Historia Ecclesiastica Tripartita*. A work
frequently reprinted, the first edition, published in Paris and Basle
1523, became the basis for subsequent and enlarged anthologies.

In the Hardwick Hall book list we have two possible Latin can-
didates for Hobbes's source for the patristic *Historiae Ecclesiasticae*, one of which we can be almost certain about because it contains
the work by that title of St. Dorotheus of Tyre, cross-referenced on
Hobbes's list. This is the *Eusebii. Pamph. Historia Ecclesiastica
cum Sozomeno et Socrate, Theod. Lect., Evag., et Dorothei Tyri vitis
Prophetarum et Apostolorum ex ejusdem Musculi interpretatione et
Theodoreti H. E. ex versione Joach. Camerarii,* (Basle, 1544, 1549;
2nd edn. Basle, 1557, frequently reprinted). The second candidate,
the *Historiae ecclesiasticae scriptores Graeci*, edited by John
Christopherson, Bishop of Chicester, (Cologne, 1570, also frequently reprinted) includes the *Historiae Ecclesiasticae* of Eusebius
(10 bks), Evagrius (6 bks), Socrates of Constantinople (7 bks),
Theodoret (5 bks) and Sozomen (9 bks), as well as Eusebius's *De
vita Constantini Magni* (3 bks), and the Blessed *Hilary's *De Trinitate*, both mentioned in Rymer's Preface. Eusebius' *Life of Constantine* is not separately listed, although the works of Hilary are, which
suggests that the library may well have had the Christopherson
edition, which includes it, or that Hobbes found a copy elsewhere.
But the Christopherson edition does not include Dorotheus of Tyre's
Historia Ecclesiastica, which means that the anthology listed in

the Hardwick Hall collection with the shelf-mark W.3.19 must have
been another which did, probably the Basel anthology.[1]

I have suggested that Hobbes's preoccupation with heresy was a
principal motivation for his burst of creative activity of the 1660s,
which includes his own *Ecclesiastical History*, and it is true that
from Eusebius on, Christian historiographers were obsessed with
heresy. Hobbes, who condoned Independency and was probably a
Cromwellian Erastian at heart, was perhaps also appealing to the relative tolerance of the humanist historiographers[2] against the rabid
sectarianism of the 1640s and heresiographers such as Ephraim
Pagitt, Thomas Edwards and Alexander Ross. The Restoration
Hobbes might have wanted to establish the credentials of a more Latitudinarian Anglicanism as a civil religion, appealing to its catholicity as a panacea for schism and dissent, in the same way that the
ecclesiastical historians had appealed to catholicity as one of the
marks of early Christian orthodoxy, a feature of Hobbes's strategy
that some readers have mistaken for toleration.

Before making such a judgment it is necessary briefly to review
the Christian historiographic tradition pioneered by the ecclesiastical historians. For, it took some time for the Christian tradition of
universal history to develop. If Luke the evangelist had exhibited a
strong historiograhic sense, there was nevertheless a long gap in the
Judeo-Christian historigraphical tradition between the gospels and
the first Church Histories, a gap that was mostly filled with extra-
canonical *Acta Apostolorum* and other apocryphal New Testament
material. Christian historiography as such first arose in response to
the challenge of Greek and Roman historians who claimed that the
decline of the Roman Empire was due to the vengeance of the gods
against Christianization – a thesis revived in modified form by
Edward Gibbon, for which Hobbes's claims about the sectarian
causes of the English civil war might be seen as an anticipation. It

---

[1] Hobbes may even have used Meredith Hanmer's English translation: *Ancient
Ecclesiastical Histories of the first six hundred years after Christ, written in the Greek
tongue by three learned Historiographers, Eusebius, Socrates and Evagrius* (London,
1577, reprinted 1585 and 1650), which contains Dorotheus' *Lives of the Prophets,
Apostles and Seventy Disciples* also, but is not included in Hobbes's book list.

[2] See Chestnut, *The First Christian Histories*, on the humanism and tolerance
of Socrates Scholasticus.

was this provocative hypothesis of Christianity as a destructive force that the North African lawyer, Quintus Tertullian (c.160-225), and the North African Church Fathers, Bishop Cyprian (d.258), Arnobius of Sicca (from 303), Origen of Alexandria (c. 185-c. 254) and Firmianus Lactantius (c. 240-c. 320) were intent on overturning; a challenge which the universal historians Orosius (c. 385-420), and Augustine of Hippo (354-430) sought again to meet. Lactantius (c. 250-c. 325), also an African, but one of the Western Fathers of the Church, in his *Divine Institutes* and *On the Wrath of God*, although largely ignorant of the Scriptures, melded Stoic notions of justice and the prophecies of the Sibylline books to call down vengeance on persecutors of Christians.[1] Augustine's *City of God*, a towering edifice, paid tribute to the parallels between Church and Empire.

When universal history, the epitome of antique high culture and its values, came to be written again, now in the form of Church History, it was the Greek Fathers, challenged by the resurgence of paganism and its infection of the Church in the form of heresy, who undertook to write it. The striking feature of *koine historia*, or universal history, at the hands of its greatest exemplars, the Hellenistic Polybius and Diodorus, had been its capacity to domesticate the foreign. Catholicity and continuity were its trade marks in the pre-Christian era and, not surprisingly, at the hands of its Christian practitioners. Lucian, *On How to Write History*, and Polybius in his history of the rise of Rome, had pioneered a didactic history in response to the sensationalism of the 'tragic history' school.[2] Aristotle and the Peripatetics, particularly Theophrastus, had played an important role in the conceptualization of universality, transforming Plato's forms into universals or wholes.[3] Aristotle's intuition in the *Poetics* that, while history remains fragmented, poetry universalizes because it reproduces the pathos of the human condition, had become axiomatic. But Aristotle's defence of poetics as the bearer of

---

[1] Garry Trompf, *Early Christian Historiography: Narratives of Retributive Historiography* (London, Continuum, 2000), p. 119.
[2] See Raoul Mortley, *The Idea of Universal History from Hellenistic Philosophy to Early Christian Historiography* (Lewiston, New York, Edwin Mellen Press, 1996), p. 9. I am indebted to Professor Mortley for the interpretive account that immediately follows.
[3] *Ibid.*, pp. 19-20.

universal truths, and history, as particularizing, was reversed by the universal historians, and the long centuries of their labour succeeded in reversing it for posterity as well.[1] Much ink has been spilt on this important reversal, but it is now generally agreed that a change in way of life produced a change in emphasis, registered in terminological change.[2] The multi-ethnic Hellenistic *oekoumene* encouraged emphasis on catholicity (*kathalon*), rather than pathos. Awareness of the multiplicity of history prompted Diodorus to undertake the separation in narrative of events that happened simultaneously.[3] Both Diodorus and Euphorus wrote history *kata genos*, by subject. This in itself registered a terminological shift, for to Aristotle *genos* was what is common, i.e. generic, ultimate entities that defied further subdivision, while for Diodorus and Euphorus *genos* represented a broad grouping suited to the method of universal history.[4] Polybius's hostility to micro history, the 'small things' (*kata meros*) approach, promoted the view that universal history was a happy coincidence of methodology and state of affairs, a realism that united *oukoumene* and *katholon*.[5]

The concept of universal history did not go unchallenged. Plutarch, for example, insisted that he was not writing about *histories* but about *lives*, and that this was an advance, for *life* was more important than *praxis*, or deeds, battles, great events.[6] Perhaps the

---

[1] It was, however, only late in the 18th century, that it became possible to speak of history itself as a universal subject, with the terminological shift from *historia* to *Geschichte*. See Reinhard Koselleck's article on 'Geschichte' in the *Geschichtliche Grundbegriffe: Historisches Lexikon zur politisch-sozialen Sprache in Deutschland*, ed. Otto Brunner, Werner Conze, Reinhart Koselleck, (Stuttgart, Ernst Klett Verlag, 1975, 8 vols) vol. 2, at pp. 647-8. For a discussion of this issue see Patricia Springborg, 'What can we say about History? Reinhart Koselleck and *Begriffsgeschichte*', in *Zeit, Geschichte und Politik: zum achtzigsten Geburtstag von Reinhart Koselleck*, ed. Jussi Kurunmäki and Kari Palonen (Jyväskylä, Finland, Jyväskylä University of Press), pp. 55-84.

[2] Mortley, *The Idea of Universal History*, pp. 10-15.

[3] *Ibid.*, p. 21.

[4] *Ibid.*, pp. 26-7.

[5] *Ibid.*, 28-9.

[6] See Donald Russell, *Plutarch: Selected Essays and Dialogues* (Oxford, Oxford University Press, 1993). See also Russell's celebrated study, *Plutarch* (Oxford, Oxford University Press, 1st edn 1972, 2nd edn 2001), which also treats his humanist legacy, addressing Plutarch's ethics (p. 51 ff.); Plutarch on Thucydides and canons of chronology (p. 58 ff.); Plutarch's moralistic history (pp. 60-1) and Plutarch and Platonism (p. 63 ff.).

greater availability of travel literature and generalized social data encouraged a reaction against the *ergon*,[1] or great deed, the monumental event, underpinned in Herodotus by Homer's concept of fame (to which Hobbes makes mocking reference in the *Historia Ecclesiastica*, line 1871). *Praxis* was a key Hellenistic concept, employed by Callisthenes, Alexander's philosopher, by Posidonius, the first century Stoic, and by Plutarch. For the difference between Plutarch and the universal historians was not as great as he tried to suggest. In his *Lives* characters were typed, in the belief that history was moral and that the external *persona* was a symptom of the soul.[2] Characterology, derived from fragments of the Peripatetics,[3] was critical for holistic history and its focus on behaviour. Aristotle himself had discerned two causes of praxis, thought (*dianoia*) and character (*ethos*). Diogenes Laertius and Posidonius advanced the Peripatetic theory of history by seeing the study of *praxeis* as a branch of ethics and acts as representing the symptomology of the soul. *Praxeis* to Theopompus comprehended the acts of Barbarians as well as of Greeks,[4] and both he and Dionysius of Hallicarnassus understood the study of *praxeis* in terms of discerning motives, feelings, apparent virtues and unsuspected vices;[5] a methodology paradigmatic for Hobbes.

Diodorus, Ephorus and Theopompus were considered by the Church Fathers major philosophers of the Hellenistic world, to which Christianity belonged.[6] Like Polybius, Josephus and Plutarch, they practiced *pragmatike historia*, assuming that acts or deeds, *koinas praxeis*, or *res gestae*, were the appropriate subject of history.[7] *Res gestae* comprised the *Acts of Divine Augustus*, but also the *Acts of the Apostles*.[8] In the grand tradition of the Roman exemplary historians, Lucian, Appian and Dio Cassius, who wrote in the service of old virtues and old gods, the Christian historiographers

---

[1] Mortley, *The Idea of Universal History*, pp. 31-3.
[2] *Ibid.*, p. 60.
[3] *Ibid.*, pp. 54-5.
[4] *Ibid.*, 36-7.
[5] *Ibid.*, p. 39.
[6] *Ibid.*, p. 40.
[7] *Ibid.*, pp. 41-2.
[8] *Ibid.*, p. 42.

wrote in the service of new virtues and a new God, exhibiting a
strong sense of the Church's institutional strength, its new and powerful *ethos*, and melded these to the tropes of ancient historiography.[1]
Among the most important of these was the notion of 'the critical
moment' or *kairos*, the preoccupation of pagan Graeco-Roman historiography, which sought in the decision of a singular individual, or
a single event, the small beginnings of a momentous historical
departure, the Stoic Fate or Polybius' Fortune.[2] Eusebius himself,
the first of the great Christian historiographers, reworked this trope,
reverting to Aristotelian language to recast Christianized pagan
Fortuna as *symbebêkota*, the 'accidents' of history, while subsequent historians used different terms. Theodoret used a whole series
of Fortune words, such as *symphora*, *euklêria*, and *dysklêria*, while
Socrates and Evagrius referred to *kairos*.

We see classical models clearly at work in Socrates Scholasticus
of Constantinople, for instance, when in the introduction to his *Historia Ecclesiastica* he introduces *kairos,* echoing Thucydides 1.23.1-
3 on the proof of the importance of the Peloponnesian Wars as
expressed in earthquakes, droughts, eclipses, etc. that took place
during its course:[3]

> ... having set forth to write ecclesiastical history, we mix in with it
> also those wars which took place at critical moments (κατα
> καιρόν) ... this we do ... before all else so that it might be known
> how, when state affairs have been troubled, the affairs of the churches
> have been troubled out of sympathy also. For if anyone will observe
> closely, he will find that civil affairs of state and unpleasant affairs in
> the churches come to their acme at the same time. For he will find
> them either moved the same way or following close upon one
> another. Sometimes the affairs in the churches lead the way; then
> affairs of state follow in turn; and sometimes the reverse.

Socrates explicitly states that 'the nexus connecting troubles in
the church with troubles in the state ... is a *kairos*', events in church
and state paralleling cosmic events such as earth quakes, etc.[4] So for

---

[1] Trompf, *Early Christian Historiography*, p. 134.
[2] Chestnut, *The First Christian Histories*, p. 182.
[3] *Ibid.*, p. 184, citing Socrates Scholasticus, *Hist. Eccl.*, bk 5.
[4] Chestnut, *The First Christian Histories*, p. 184, citing Socrates, *Hist. Eccl.*,
book 5, introd.; and books 2.25-6, and 6.6.

instance, he connects the Council of the Dedication at Antioch in 341, which tried to put up the first counter-creed to the Nicene declaration, with raids by the Franks into Gaul and earthquakes in the East.[1] As Chestnut notes 'The connection between the disorders in the church and the disorders in the state was not a matter of what one today would call causal linkage; it was a sympathetic reaction of one part of the cosmos to the disturbances in some other part'.[2] Evagrius Scholasticus provided a more down to earth characterization of *kairos* as 'the opportune moment', personified, and to be grasped by the forelock:[3]

> For the Opportune Moment ('o καιρός) is swift of flight: when it is close upon one, it may be secured: but should it once have escaped the grasp, it soars aloft and laughs at its pursuers, not deigning to place itself again within their reach. And hence no doubt it is, that statuaries and painters represent the head as closely shaven behind: thus skillfully symbolizing, that when it comes up from behind one, it may perhaps be held fast by the flowing forelock, but fairly escapes when it has once got the start, from the absence of any thing which the pursuer might grasp.

One would be remiss to overstate the humanism of the universal historians and present the conception of *kairos* as kind of objectivity on their part. Evagrius' observation nicely captures the personalism which imbued their work. Their relentless pursuit of 'retributive justice', (Garry Trompf's rather euphemistic term), is expressed in the shrill voice of partisanship and doctrinal controversy; Hobbes's chief complaint against them, as Rymer, finding precedents in Hilary and Constantine's harsh words, notes in his clever preface. Not one of the Church Histories, from Eusebius on, fails to stake out an adversarial position, and defend it to the teeth: Eusebius as the glorifier of Constantine, and Rufinus as his continuator; *Athanasius as the vilifyer of Arius and Eusebius, the latter mildly Arian-leaning;

---

[1] Chestnut, *The First Christian Histories*, p. 186 n. 89, citing Socrates, *Hist. Eccl.*, 2.10.

[2] Chestnut, *The First Christian Histories*, p. 198.

[3] Evagrius, *Hist. Eccl.*, 3.26, c.f. 6.12, cited by Chestnut, *The First Christian Histories*, p. 183, who notes, n. 81: 'One such statue was the famous one by Lysippus at Sicyon, see Callistratus, *Descriptions*, 6. 428-9 K, statue of Kairos; and *Greek Anthology*, Book 16 (The Planudean Anthology), 275, statue of Kairos.'

Philostorgius as the vilifyer of Athanasius and defender of Arius; Socrates of Constantinople, a triumphalist in the tradition of Eusebius; Sozomen more sceptical; Theodoret more balanced, but celebrating the Great *Theodosius as Eusebius had celebrated Constantine, and so on.

The Church did not enjoy a pacific universality, as the historians freely admitted, nor was its continuity that of a benign orthodoxy. It was threatened by tyrants from without and heretics from within, all of them judged by portents and the punishments the wrath of God rained down upon them, from pest and plague to miracles, showers of stones and sudden death.[1] Of this humanist scholars were all too well aware, translating the contexts for retributive historiography into their own time. So, in 1668 Henri de Valois, an eminent French scholar and Gallican enthusiast, in the epistle dedicatory to Louis XIV of his edition of the *Ecclesiastical History of Socrates and Sozomen*, gives us an indication of the aspirations that drove such labour, equating the classical *schole*, or leisure, with peace, in a manner of which Hobbes's remarks in the *Historia Ecclesiastica* lines 115-20 are reminiscent:[2]

> But the Gallican Church, by a source of hope that is in no way doubtful, already promises itself peace. This Church, which for several years already, has been battered and confused by the most serious discords, is now confident, thanks to the intervention of your Majesty, lover of peace, that she will be brought back to her former concord and tranquility. At last, as a result of this peace our scholarly works are stimulated and are filled with unbelievable joy [. . . .] Because the fruits of our scholarship are disciples of peace and companions of rest and ease.

Hobbes, preoccupied by the threats and counter threats of heresy in his own day, recaptures the idiom of the early Church Histories,

---

[1] Hobbes, *Hist. Eccl.*, line 1338, for instance, uses the idiom 'drenched by a shower of stones', to be found in Pliny, *Nat. hist.* 2.38.

[2] Henri de Valois (1603-1676) *Socratis Scholastici et Hermiae Sozomeni Histori ecclesiestica* (Paris, 1668), fol. A4, cited by Jean-Louis Quantin, 'The Fathers in Seventeenth Century Roman Catholic Theology', in *The Reception of the Church Fathers in the West, from the Carolingians to the Maurists*, Irena Backus, ed. (2 vols. Leiden, E.J. Brill, 1997), vol. 2, pp. 953-76, at p. 974.

one of biting invective and perpetual wrangling even if, in their eyes, it is the story of the progressive growth of a majestic para-statal institution. He shares the position of Socrates of Constantinople, who argued, for instance that the greatest error of the Arian Eunomius was not his doctrine concerning Christ's relation to God the Father, but his claim to perfectly know and understand what God was in his *ousia*, or essential nature.[1]

From the time of Constantine, who in 313 declared Christianity *religio licita*, a religion recognized by the Roman authorities,[2] the histories of Church and Empire are incestuously entwined. Eusebius glorified Constantine in comparison with his co-ruler the tyrant Licinius, and defended his rule in terms of the promise that piety and propitiation of the appropriate God offer as security against plague and pestilence.[3] Rome as the last Empire of the prophecies of the Book of Daniel, was a preparation for God's 'final triumph' and, in his *Life of Constantine,* Eusebius foreshadows an afterlife of beatitude for Christian Martyrs who promote it,[4] and the work of the devil in those who frustrate it, chief among them being heretics.[5] Eusebius is the first to chronicle the rise of heresy from Simon Magus to Arius. He is not afraid to criticize Christian pride, sloth, hypocrisy and factionalism as provocations to persecution;[6] and if he is more restrained than his successors in cataloguing doctrinal wrangling, he lived to see less of it than they did. His failure to show that the Nicene Creed was declared explicitly against Arius, and to mention the exile of the vehemently anti-Arian Athanasius, ordered by Constantine to vacate his Bishopric of Alexandria after the Council

---

[1] Chestnut, *The First Christian Histories*, p. 176, citing Socrates, *Hist. Eccl.*, 4.7.

[2] Trompf, *Early Christian Historiography*, p. 118, to whom I am indebted for the following account.

[3] Trompf, *Early Christian Historiography*, p. 123, citing Eusebius, *Hist. Eccl.*, bk 9, 7.8, 7.11 and 7.14.

[4] Trompf, *Early Christian Historiography*, p. 129, citing Eusebius, *Vit. Const.*, 2.26.

[5] Trompf, *Early Christian Historiography*, p. 133, notes that Momigliano's claim that Eusebius's history is 'a history of the struggle against the devil', should be restricted to this context. See A. Momigliano, *The Conflict Between Paganism and Christianity in the Fourth Century* (Oxford, Clarendon Press, 1963), p. 90.

[6] Trompf, *Early Christian Historiography*, p. 132, citing Eusebius, *Hist. Eccl.*, bk 8, 1.7-8, cf.6; and bk 8, 2.4-5.

of Tyre in 335, over which Eusebius had presided, are indictments
later historians laid against Eusebius as being too soft on Arians.[1]
But the lines were not yet so tightly drawn and the great Constantine
himself had been tended on his deathbed in May of 337 by his Arian
chaplain, Eusebius of Nicomedia.[2]

The Latin translation of Eusebius completed by the presbyter
Rufinus in Roman Aquileia in 402, brought the narrative down to
Theodosius the Great, with two additional books. Rufinus added to
Eusebius' account of ten or more persecutions at least another two,
putting greater emphasis on the episcopal continuity between
Alexandria and Rome, and the eastward expansion of the Church,
and devoting considerable space to monasticism, an undeveloped
theme in Eusebius.[3] Rufinus lacked access, it seems, to the fourth
and final installment of Eusebius' history, the *Vita Constantini*, and
his history is marked by certain shifts in emphasis: he shows Constantine's reign as one of grace, despite Arianism, while excoriating
the perfidy of his successor, the Arian-sponsoring *Constantius II,
but sees *Constans I's reinstatement of Athanasius as foreshadowing
a period of peace and renewal within the Church before the period of
turmoil under Valens. For him the reign of *Gratian was indeed one
of grace (as Hobbes was to echo),[4] before the crisis under Valentinian, when the empress-dowager Justina tried to impose Arianism on
the West. His account of the efforts of Theodosius to oust the usurper
and restore the faith evokes the victories of Constantine in a previous
generation.[5] When by 415 Augustine is said to have had Eusebius'
Historia Ecclesiastica in his possession, we can safely assume that it
was in Rufinus' translation.[6]

*Philostorgius (c.368-c.439), whose work was preserved by
the bibliophile Photius, was the first of the famous line of post-
Eusebian ecclesiastical historians from the Greek East, which
included *Socrates Scholasticus (c.380-c.450), Salaminius Hermias
*Sozomen (c.400-c.450) and *Theodoret of Cyrrhus (c.393-c.458).

---

[1] Trompf, *Early Christian Historiography*, pp. 140-1.
[2] *Ibid.*, p. 141.
[3] *Ibid.*, pp. 165-6.
[4] *Hist. Eccl.*, lines 947-8.
[5] Trompf, *Early Christian Historiography*, pp. 169-70.
[6] *Ibid.*, p. 174.

But while the latter three were orthodox, Philostorgius was an Arian. Meanwhile, Athanasius, Eusebius' nemesis, had completed his *Historia contra Arianorum* sometime in the 360s, excoriating the Arian heresy as 'some great monster' rending the Christian body, and the Arian bishop Gregory, installed at Alexandria after the Council of Antioch, 337-8, as 'an outrageous robber of mendicants',[1] language familiar to us from Hobbes.[2] Athanasius is not above exploiting the ignominious end to Arius, who died from copious bowel hemorrhaging in Constantinople; and Hobbes's evocation of Arianism as a pustule that spawned a swarm of flies,[3] is also not uncharacteristic of Athanasian rhetoric, although his unsympathetic characterization of Athanasius, forced into exile, owes more to Eusebius.[4] It is to this sort of crusading anti-Arianism that Philostorgius was to respond, extolling the providential role of the Arian confessor, Eusebius of Nicomedia, at Constantine's deathbed, treating the *homoousian* clause defended by Athanasius as a pollution, finding miracles and divine portents aplenty in support of the Arian cause and in defiance of the Theodosian order, and possibly an analogue for Arius's grisly death in the death of Theodosius from dropsy.

The tendentiousness of the ecclesiastical histories of Athanasius and Philostorgius fed off retributive argument and promoted it.[5] All three orthodox Eastern post-Eusebian historians, Socrates Scholasticus, Sozomen and Theodoret, responded in turn in a chorus of reproaches against those, including Philostorgius, who impugned the Great Constantine or the Great Theodosius. While Socrates Scholasticus is the more judicious and objective in his use of source material, examining imperial letters to instance Arius's treachery before his (fittingly) ignominious death, Sozomen is the first to paraphrase *in extenso* Athanasius' letter to Serapion, to show that the citizens of Constantinople in fact took the manner of Arius' death to be an expression of divine wrath.[6] Socrates Scholasticus finds signs of

---

[1] *Ibid.*, pp. 187-8.
[2] See *Hist. Eccl.*, lines 297-302 for a typical Hobbesian catalogue of terms of abuse.
[3] Trompf, *Early Christian Historiography*, pp. 187-8.
[4] See Hobbes's *Hist. Eccl.*, lines 889-94ff.
[5] Trompf, *Early Christian Historiography*, pp. 198 ff.
[6] *Ibid.*, p. 219.

divine displeasure in the earthquake and Frankish invasion that
follow the exclusion of the *homoousion* clause from the Antiochene
Creed; Constantius' attempt to convene the synod at Nicomedia is
frustrated by an earthquake and, shocked by the apostasy of his
nephew *Julian, he dies of apoplexy.[1]

Sozomen, like Rufinus, is impressed by miracles and more cred-
ulous than Socrates, but like Rufinus is also more quietly confident
in the institutional 'progress' of the Church through the cycle of
peaks and troughs. 'Thus before Julian's rule the rewards of the
faithful are more emphasized by Sozomen than the punishments of
evil, concomitant with his picture of a slow decline from the zenith
of "the Constantinian era" to the death of Constantius.'[2] Sozomen
tells how Julian the Apostate was punished for defecating on a Christian altar by immediate corruption of his rectum and genitals, a story
Theodoret retells more elaborately. And Sozomen is the first to
provide, in the case of Julian, a Christian defence of tyrannicide; a
fact that cannot have escaped Hobbes:[3]

> Greeks and all people until this day have praised tyrannicides for
> exposing themselves to death in the cause of liberty, spiritedly stand-
> ing by their country, their family, and their friends. Still less is he
> deserving of blame, who, for the sake of God and of religion per-
> formed so bold a deed.

Theodoret is the more polemical of the three, crusading against
the impiety of Arianism as work of the Devil (*'o Daimon, 'o diabo-
los*), while portraying Constantine as 'profoundly wise'.[4] The treatment of events from the untimely death of the orthodox *Jovian and
leading up to the reign of Theodosius I, and particularly the treatment of Christian persecutions by the Arianizing Valens, is a test
case for the differences between the three. In general they tend to

---

[1] Trompf, *Early Christian Historiography*, pp. 218-19, citing Socrates, *Hist.
Eccl.*, 2.10, 2.39, 2.47.
[2] Trompf, *Early Christian Historiography*, p. 220, citing Sozomen, *Hist. Eccl.*,
Bks 1-4, at 1.1.
[3] Sozomen, *Hist. Eccl.*, 2.1-2, cited by Trompf, *Early Christian Historiography*, p. 227.
[4] Theodoret, *Hist. Eccl.*, 1.2, 4.1, 7.1, 10, 15-18, etc., cited by Trompf, *Early
Christian Historiography*, p. 220.

show Church-State relations as ones of mutual infection, rather than direct causality,[1] this infection evidenced by divine portents. So for instance, both Socrates and Sozomen have no difficulty in explaining Valentinian's death in a fit of rage as caused by the inroads of the barbarians, while for Theodoret, the reason for Valens' death while fighting the barbarians was not open to question:[2]

> How the Lord God is long-suffering towards those who rage against him, and chastises those who abuse his patience is taught precisely by the plain deeds and bad end in Valens' case. For the loving Lord uses mercy and justice like weights and scales. Whenever he sees anyone by the magnitude of his errors overthrowing the proper measure of humaneness, He prevents him from passing on to further extremes by just retribution.

Socrates closes his history with an account of the peace of the Theodosian order in the same spirit of triumphalism exhibited by Eusebius, reviewing the reign of Constantine.[3] Trompf sees this as a vindication of Byzantine caesaropapism and 'principles of reciprocity with the divine . . . found in pre-Constantinian ideology . . . but with reference to God rather than the gods', noting that 'it is with the Theodosian "establishment" that one might expect the strongest running together of divine and imperial justice, in a kind of Byzantine act of ideological synthesis'.[4] Socrates does not suggest, however, that the problem of heresy had been finally laid to rest, while Sozomen, who takes his history further, through the barbarian invasions, contrasts the pacific rule of Theodosius II in the East with disorder in the West, culminating in the sack of Rome by *Alaric, as divine retribution for the Eternal City's luxury and excess.

Theodoret goes further in insisting that the resolution of matters of state is necessarily partial to piety and, where this principle does not appear to be vindicated, he is discretely silent, as in the case of

---

[1] Chestnut's 'cosmic sympathy', see *The First Christian Histories*, p. 206.
[2] Theodoret, *Hist. Eccl.*, 5.1, quoted by Trompf, *Early Christian Historiography*, p. 231.
[3] c.f. Eusebius *Hist. Eccl.*, 1.1, cited Trompf, *Early Christian Historiography*, p. 234.
[4] Trompf, *Early Christian Historiography*, pp. 234, 238.

contemporary theological debates and particularly the Monophysite-Nestorian controversy and the 'Robber Council' of 449-50, in which he had been so heavily implicated. He chose to ignore the wailings of the exiled Nestorius – whom he had so recently defended – against *Cyril of Alexandria as 'the father of many heresies'.[1] Eschewing cosmic punishments for the wicked – he even refrains from mentioning the sack of Rome – he had his own explanation for impiety in sacred history, from which however, the lover of peace could take cold comfort:[2]

> there is no need to be astonished that the Ruler of all puts up with their savagery and impiety, for indeed, before the reign of Constantine the Great so many of the Roman Emperors raged with fury against the friends of the truth . . . .These wars and the unconquerability of the Church were predicted by the Lord, and this teaches us about [political] affairs that war brings more blessing than peace. For peace makes us delicate, easy and cowardly, while war encourages us to disdain this present order of things as flowing away. About these things, however, I have often written in other writings.

There is an uncanny likeness between the histories of Eusebius, his translator and continuator, Rufinus, the anti-Arian Athanasius and Arian Philostorgius, and later the Byzantine trio, Socrates, Sozomen and Theodoret, as narratives of the vindications of an avenging God, and the heresiography of the Puritan sects of the 1640s. Perhaps it is this observation that drives Hobbes's *Church History*, or counter-history. Like the Church Fathers themselves, he believes that the sickness of the sects has the power to affect the health of the realm. The Fathers, like the later heresiarchs, appeal to the Old Testament God, who speaks through portents and miracles, whose judgments are announced by flood and earthquake, a God of war and not of peace. But this, in Hobbes's view, is surely the old dispensation of sectarianism and violence that the new dispensation of Christ was born to remove. It is not improbable that he saw a parallel between the obsession with heresy of the authors of the ancient

---

[1] Trompf, *Early Christian Historiography*, p. 239, citing Theodoret's *Reprehen. duodec. capit. seu anathem. Cyril.*

[2] Theodoret, *Hist. Eccl.*, 39.24-6, quoted by Trompf, *Early Christian Historiography*, pp. 240-1.

ecclesiastical histories and the fanaticism of contemporary heretic hunters. So for instance, Ephraim Pagett in his *Heresiography – Or a Description of the Heretickes and Sectaries Sprang Up in These Latter Times* . . ., published in 1654, gives a list of between forty and fifty heresies, including lengthy discussions of 'Brownists,[1] Semi-separatists,[2] Independents,[3] Familists,[4] Adamites,[5] Antinomians,[6] Arminians,[7] Socinians,[8] Antitrinitarians,[9] Millenaries,[10] Hetheringtonians,[11] Antisabbatarians,[12] Trafkites,[13] Jesuits,[14] Pelagians,[15] Soulesleepers,[16] Antiscripturians,[17] Expecters or Seekers,[18] and Papists';[19] continuing with a comparison between Papists and yet more heretics, Catharists, etc.[20] Pagett notes that he includes Papists with 'late Heretickes', because 'there is a great difference between ancient Papists and the moderne since their Trent Conventicle.'[21] It is significant, perhaps, that he concludes his work with a postscript in defence of tythes which his 'Sectary' parishioners refuse to pay!

Pagett's work was based in turn on Daniel Featley's *The Dippers dipt or the Anabaptists d'nckt and plunged over head and ears* (1645) – a title that Hobbes perhaps hints at with his own short catalogue of sects and factions in the poem, beginning with 'Independents, Quakers, Presbyterians, Fifth Monarchy Men, Episcopalians',

---

[1] Pagett, *Heresiography*, p. 54 ff.
[2] *Ibid.*, p. 81.
[3] *Ibid.*, p. 82 ff.
[4] *Ibid.*, p. 91 ff.
[5] *Ibid.*, p. 102.
[6] *Ibid.*, p. 103 ff.
[7] *Ibid.*, p. 116 ff.
[8] *Ibid.*, p. 129 ff.
[9] *Ibid.*, p. 131.
[10] *Ibid.*, p. 132.
[11] *Ibid.*, p. 133.
[12] *Ibid.*, p. 134.
[13] *Ibid.*, p. 135 ff.
[14] *Ibid.*, p. 137 ff.
[15] *Ibid.*, p. 142.
[16] *Ibid.*, p. 143.
[17] *Ibid.*, p. 144.
[18] *Ibid.*, p. 145.
[19] *Ibid.*, p. 146 ff.
[20] *Ibid.*, p. 156 ff.
[21] *Ibid.*, p. 146.

and finishing with Anabaptists, to whom he refers as 'twice dipped'.[1] Judged in their own time as products of a paranoid imagination, Thomas Edwards' *Gangraena, Catalogue and discovery of many of the errors, heresies, blasphemies and pernicious practices of the sectaries of this time,* 1646, is just as obsessive; while Alexander Ross's, *Pansebeia: or A View of All the Religions of the World,* took a more academic approach to heresy, in contrast to John Davies' *Apocalypsis: Or Revelation of Certain Notorious Advancers of Heresie,* bound together with it, but came up with just as impossibly long a list of heretics.

The patristic works on heresy were not necessarily more restrained. The *Panarion* of Epiphanius, Bishop of Salamis, in volume 2 of Denis Petau's edition of *Epiphanii opera* (held in the Hardwick Hall Library at shelf mark F.3.1.), for instance, lists some 80 sects, a term Epiphanius uses flexibly to cover both formally organized groups like the Manichaeans, schools of philosophy, tendencies of thought, or more general religious of philosophical classifications, like Epicurean and Jew.[2] Alexander Ross in *Leviathan Drawn out with a Hook,* of 1652, with likely reference to the *Panarion* of Eusebius, accused Hobbes of reviving the heresies of 'Anthropomorphists, Sabellians, Nestorians, Saduceans, Arabeans, Tacians or Eucratists, Manichies, Mahumetans and others'.[3] Hobbes himself, in the person of interlocutor B in the 1668 Appendix to the Latin *Leviathan,* §88, cites Epiphanius to make an important point:

> Thus Epiphanius, in his *On the Trinity,* at the beginning of the seventh book: 'The word of God was sufficient for all believers when He said, "Go now and teach all nations, baptizing them in the name of the Father, of the Son and of the Holy Spirit, etc." But we are forced by the errors of the heretics and blasphemers to do that which is not permitted and speak of that which is ineffable and to fall into that error which is the contrary of theirs'.

---

[1] *Dibaphi* (Chambers Murray) (from Gr. *dibaphos*), literally twice dipped. See *Hist. Eccl.,* line 1560.

[2] See the Forward to *The Panarion of St. Epiphanius, Bishop of Salamis, Selected Passages,* edited by Philip R. Amidon, S.J. (Oxford 1990).

[3] See the epistle 'to the reader' prefacing Ross's *Leviathan Drawn out with a Hook . . .* (1652), cited by Collins, *Allegiance,* p. 269.

Interlocutor A comments, 'Epiphanius wrongly excuses himself, for, without threats or outright force, no one can be compelled by another's error to do that which is not allowed'.[1]

There are other clues that Ephiphanius may have been an important source for Hobbes, in particular his use of the term *pharmakon*, indicating a cure for heresy, or poison,[2] and his discussion of 'Hellenism' (hellenismos) as Graecismus. The late François Tricaud, in his excellent editorial notes to his French language edition of *Leviathan*, suggests that Hobbes's discussion of 'Grecism', Hellenism and Judaism in that work may have been taken from Epiphanius' response to Acacius and Paul, where he addresses the Pharisees, Sadducees and Essenes, in the manner of Hippolytus before him.[3] It seems highly likely that Hobbes would lump together heresiarchs ancient and modern in his *Ecclesiastical History*, which is both a history of gentilism and a history of (un)civil religion.

---

[1] See 'The 1668 Appendix to *Leviathan*', ed. Wright, pp. 365, 398 n. 110 and 399, n. 124 pp. 323-413.

[2] See *Hist. Eccl.*, line 1091.

[3] See François Tricaud, in his editorial notes to *Léviathan Traité de la matière, de la forme et du pouvoir de la république ecclésiastique et civile* (Paris, 1971), p. 750, n. 7; see also Wright, 'The 1668 Appendix to *Leviathan*', p. 399, n. 124.

CHAPTER 5

HOBBES,
PATRISTICS AND PLATONISM

5.1 HOBBES AND PATRISTICS

It is claimed that 'the last third of the seventeenth century experienced a historiographical efflorescence; it was a golden age for the study of Christian antiquity'.[1] Hobbes's *Historia Ecclesiastica* falls squarely in this period and, if anything, he is in the vanguard of English Christian antiquarians, a field which France tended to dominate. Canons of Renaissance humanist scholarship were applied just as systematically to ecclesiastical as to secular history. The desire to recover Christian teachings in their authentic purity was as strong in the field of patristics as the desire to recover pagan classical texts. Some of the Christian antiquarians were seriously pagan in their religious instincts, and Hobbes, along with his friend Selden, numbers among them. As we might expect, however, much of the pioneering antiquarian scholarship was the work of Jesuits.

Patristics were marshaled to resolve a problem set by the Council of Trent which, at its fourth session in 1546, had 'equated the Scriptures and the unwritten traditions passed down from Christ and the Apostles, and which had forbidden interpretation of the Scriptures *contra unanimen consensum Patrum*'.[2] By placing the Fathers as

---

[1] Jean-Louis Quantin, 'The Fathers in Seventeenth Century Roman Catholic Theology', in *The Reception of the Church Fathers in the West, from the Carolingians to the Maurists,* Irena Backus, ed. (Leiden, E.J. Brill, 1997), 2 vols, vol. 2, pp. 953-76, at p. 976.
[2] *Ibid.*, p. 953.

gate-keepers of the apostolic tradition, the Council had presented a challenge to all those for whom the Scriptures were the keystone of Christology; and an opportunity for scholars to meet it. The problem lay not least in the vagueness of the notion 'unanimous consensus of the Fathers', for which the Council provided no criteria, not even a list of the Fathers who might be considered to have met them. While the term 'Father' was loosely distinguished from that of 'Doctor' – a distinction Hobbes preserves in his poem – major debate centred on whether or not the authority of the Fathers could be extended up to and including the scholastics, especially Aquinas, and contemporary theologians, such as Bellarmine. It was a subject on which Catholic and Protestant patrologists were predictably to divide. Not surprisingly perhaps, the Jansenists also tended to restrict the term Father to the early Church, for suspicion of the scholastics was also widespread in France and the Spanish Netherlands. So, while in 1690 the leader of the Vaticanists at the Theology faculty in Louvain could declare that the Scholastics were 'the Fathers of that time, just as the ancient Fathers were the scholastics of their age', his Jansenist colleague, Opstraet, declared just as firmly that the line must be drawn at St. Bernard for the Latin Fathers and John of Damascus for the Greek.[1]

The divide between the Greek and Latin Fathers was itself of more than linguistic or regional significance. Because the Latin Fathers had long been accessible in a Latin speaking Church, early modern translations tended to focus on their homiletic works for the enlightenment of the less educated. But the Greek Fathers presented a repository of knowledge on the theology of the early Church and its Councils that had been largely untapped. For more than a century the Jesuits, who for reason of their on-going competition with the Pope, and because of the conaturality of their mission and spirituality with the Greek Fathers, had favoured them over the Latin Fathers. Extraordinary pioneering scholarship, focused especially on the witnesses to the Nicene Council and the anti-heresiarchs, was undertaken by a succession of great Jesuit scholars (to choose just five of the most productive from a list of 153): the polymath Andreas Schott

---

[1] *Ibid.*, p. 955.

from Antwerp (1552-1629), the Swabian patrologist Jacob Gretzer (1562-1625), Fronto Ducaeus of France (1558-1624), and his compatriots, Jacques Sirmond (1559-1651) and Denys Petau (1583-1652).[1] These were all Hobbes's contemporaries and several taught in Paris. It is highly likely that it was during his Paris sojourn with the Stuart court that Hobbes became acquainted with the new patristic scholarship. A sample of the works of leading Jesuit scholars of his day, many of which are included in Hobbes's book list for the Hardwick Hall Library (q.v.), gives some indication of possible sources for Hobbes's *Historia ecclesiastica* in the great patristic tradition of works by that name.

Andreas Schott,[2] who taught rhetoric at Louvain and Greek in Salamanca before joining the Jesuits, and whose interests included the Latin historians and poets, the Greek novel, epics, numismatics and Venetian printing, produced 71 printed works and 13 manuscripts on patristics, including an edition of Orosius's *Historiae adversus paganos*, the works of Basil of Cesarea, the life and works of Gregory of Nazianzus and many annotated works published in volume one of the *Magna Biblioteca Patrum* edited in Cologne in 1618. Jacob Gretzer another polymath and great controversialist, among his 234 published works and 45 manuscripts, edited works by Gregory of Nyssa, Hippolytus' *Chronicon*, *Anastasius of Sinai's *Hodegos*, an anti-monophysite guide, annotated the History of John Cantacuzenus, and published Manuel Calecas's treatise on 'The Errors of the Greeks'. He took an interest in heresies old and new, defending the testimony of various authorities against the Waldensians, and Jerome against the pseudo-Scaligerians.

Fronto Ducaeus,[3] who taught rhetoric and theology in Bordeaux and Paris, entering the fray against Philippe du Plessis-Mornay, edited the complete works of Gregory of Nyssa, including the

---

[1] For the account that follows I am particularly indebted to Dominique Bertrand, 'The Society of Jesus and the Church Fathers in the Sixteenth and Seventeenth Century', in Irena Backus, ed., *The Reception of the Church Fathers in the West*, vol. 2, pp. 775-838. Bertrand gives biographical notes for 153 Jesuits in Europe from Spain to the Ukraine, for the period 1500 to 1638.

[2] Item 39 in Bertrand's list, 'The Society of Jesus and the Church Fathers in the Sixteenth and Seventeenth Century', p. 903.

[3] *Ibid*., item 54, pp. 907-8.

account of his life by George of Trebizond, a new edition of the works of Basil of Cesarea, a Latin edition of the works of Athanasius for use in schools, and the 18 books of the *Ecclesiastical History* by Nicephorus Callistus. He annotated Irenaeus's work *Against Heresy*, produced translations of 77 homilies by Chrysostom on such topics as *Against the Jews, On the Incomprehensibility of God*, and on the saints, and among his manuscripts were found the works of Theodoret, plans for an edition of the Septuagint, work on some Greek Councils, two letters by Pope Gregory II on images, and works by Cyril of Alexandria.

Jacques Sirmond,[1] who taught humanities and rhetoric in Paris and was at one time the confessor to Louis XIII, published the complete works of Theodoret of Cyrrhus, the *Quaestio triplex* from Alaric's codex, and 14 opuscules by Eusebius of Cesarea. Involved in many collaborative works on patristics, as well as works relating to French chronicles and histories of the Gallic councils, he responded to Jansenist pressure in his notes on Augustine's twenty sermons, engaged in a polemic with Petau on the Synod of Sirmium, and corresponded with Justus Lipsius.

The renowned Jesuit Denis Petau (Petavius), who taught rhetoric and dogmatic philosophy in Paris for 22 years up to his death in 1652, is a likely source for Hobbes.[2] A major theologian and author of the six volume *Theologica dogmata*, Petau included among his translations of patristic works the *History* of Nicephorus of Constantinople, nineteen discourses by Themistius, Cyril of Alexandria's *Against the Books of Impious Julian*, and fragments of Julian the Apostate's *Against the Galileans*.[3] Petau also translated the complete works of Epiphanius, and Hobbes apparently uses Petau's edition of Epiphanius in the 1668 Appendix to the Latin *Leviathan*, §88, as

---

[1] *Ibid.*, item 56, pp. 909-10.

[2] See·Gianni Paganini, 'Hobbes, Valla and the Trinity', p. 14 n. 38, who comments on Petau's *Opus de theologicis dogmatibus* (1644-1650, 4 vols) as an encyclopaedia of patristic theology and much used early modern source on the Trinity, citing Dionysii Petavii, *Opus de theologicis dogmatibus auctius in hac nova editione*, t. II, Antwerpiae apud G. Gallet, 1700, at 'De Trinitate' lib. IV, pp. 182 fol. This work was listed in the Hardwick Hall Library at shelf mark X.3.1, see Appendix A.

[3] Item 93 in Bertrand's list, 'The Society of Jesus and the Church Fathers in the Sixteenth and Seventeenth Century', pp. 917-18.

noted. The Jansenist controversy led Petau to further studies in Pelagianism, Semi-pelagianism, and the works of Augustine in light of
the Tridentine decrees. He was read and admired by Grotius,
Gassendi and Mersenne and appears in the Hardwick Hall book list
prepared by Hobbes at shelf mark X.3.1. Richard Tuck suggests
Hobbes's indebtedness to Petau's *Theologicorum Deorum* (Paris,
1644 –), *Prolegomena* ch. 3, as a source in *Leviathan*, Book 4, *xlii*,
§130, as noted; and Gianni Paganini has undertaken a very scholarly
examination of Petau's influence on Hobbes in the expanded English
version of his essay on 'Hobbes, Valla and the Trinity'.[1]

Hobbes's Paris sojourn probably left an indelible imprint on his
ecclesiology every bit as much as on his scientific and philosophical
projects. Antoine Arnauld, the great Jansenist, could proudly proclaim, 'The French Church is now the most knowledgeable of all the
Catholic Churches', surpassing Rome itself where, in the words of
the Maurist, Dom Germain, Mabillon's companion, the *virtuosi*
lacked 'the taste for understanding religion and Church doctrine to
the full, in the way that we French do, feasting on it and making it
into our prime study'.[2] Patristics followed the drift of more general
seventeenth century historiographical developments. The authority
of the Fathers rested on their credentials as witnesses, based in turn
on 'the theory of historical certainty developed in the wake of Cartesianism, by Arnauld and Nicole in particular'.[3] The historical authority of the Fathers, based on their secular qualities as reliable
reporters, was carefully distinguished from their specifically theological authority. So, for instance, the notion of the Fathers as reliable witnesses was the subject of a thesis presented at Louvain in
1685 by member of the famous Dutch diplomatic family, Gommaire
Huygens, a theologian with Jansenist leanings,[4] who was a relative
of Hobbes's correspondent, Christiaan Huygens (1629-1695).

---

[1] Richard Tuck, 'The Civil Religion of Thomas Hobbes', pp. 133-4; and Gianni
Paganini, 'Hobbes, Valla and the Trinity', p. 198 ff.
[2] Quantin, 'The Fathers in Seventeenth Century Roman Catholic Theology',
p. 978.
[3] *Ibid.*, p. 965.
[4] *Ibid.*, 'p. 964, citing the *Dictionnaire de théologie catholique*, t. VI 1/1
col. 350-55 for Gommaire Huyens, 1631-1702.

172

5.2 THE PHILO-SEMITIC HOBBES

Examination of Hobbes's writings suggests, as I have elsewhere argued, that his so-called 'toleration' was not that at all, but was rather a reflex of his Erastianism.[1] Certainly Hobbes was not a tolerationist, but waged war against all sects that pretended to institutional power on the dualist model of separate spheres divided between spiritual and civil powers. The spirit kingdom is a 'Kingdome of Darkness', Hobbes relentlessly maintained, characterizing it after Homer and Virgil as a world of spectres and shades. Like Milton he believed that 'New Presbyter is but old Priest writ large';[2] which simply reversed James I's claim that that 'Jesuits are nothing but Puritan-Papists'.[3] Hobbes's Erastianism is melded to his Epicureanism, permitting tolerance of only those forms of civil religion that can deliver to the sovereign a quiescent people, happy to worship publicly according to the state cult, and privately left to believe what conscience dictates.

The fact that Hobbes and Scargill eventually escaped prosecution themselves is nevertheless testament to the relative openness with which religion could be debated in Stuart England, the relative fluidity of doctrinal positions, and the rather surprising range of views on the table at any given moment. This was also a period of great efflorescence in critical theology, due in no small part to the development of Patristics (discussed in chapter 5.1), particularly in France. Primitive Christianity, emulated by the Latitudinarians, was also believed to be characterized by doctrinal pluralism.[4] So

---

[1] Springborg, 'Hobbes on Religion', in *The Cambridge Companion to Hobbes*, ed. Tom Sorrell (Cambridge, Cambridge University Press, 1995) pp. 346-80; and Springborg, 'Hobbes's Theory of Civil Religion'; c.f., Alan Ryan, 'Hobbes, toleration and the inner life', in *The Nature of Political Theory*, ed. by David Miller and Larry Seidentop (Oxford, Clarendon Press, 1983); and Ryan, 'A more tolerant Hobbes', in Susan Mendus, ed., *Justifying Toleration* (Cambridge, Cambridge University Press, 1988).

[2] John Milton, *On the New Forces of Conscience under the Long Parliament* (1647), quoted by Charles McIlwain in his Introduction to *The Political Works of James I* (Cambridge, Mass., Harvard University Press, 1918), pp. xvii – xviii.

[3] Quoted by McIlwain, *op. cit*, p. xxvii.

[4] Rymer makes much of Christianity as the simple religion of fishermen in his Preface, lines 27-30, as already noted. See also *Hist. Eccl.*, lines 13-25.

the Jesuit, Denis Petau (Petavius), one of the greatest Patristic scholars and a probable source for Hobbes, as already noted, could argue 'that the early Christians had not believed in a stable body of doctrine which had become corrupted after Nicaea (the usual Anglican view), but had indulged instead in a wide range of deviant theologies'.[1]

This fluidity of belief also prompted Deists to review the pagan civil religions and, following the first English translation of the Koran in 1649, Islam was also endorsed in these terms. Hobbes himself praised 'Mahomet' among the 'founders and legislators of commonwealths among the Gentiles, whose ends were only to keep the people in obedience and peace'.[2] The leaders of civil religions from Numa Pompilius to 'the founder of the kingdom of Peru', claimed oracles for their semi-divine status, and so, 'Mahomet, to set up his new religion, pretended to have conferences with the Holy Ghost in the form of a dove'.[3] Hobbes's inference does little honour to either Mahometans or Christians, but his insistence that Islam is a civil religion follows a consistent line of argument among Erastians. The separatist John Goodwin convicted the Cromwellian church of 'Mahometanism' for erecting a 'State Religion';[4] while Francis Osborne (1593-1659), author of he famous *Advice to a Son* (1656), that went through many editions, and with a reputation for atheism and a 'sceptick humour' like Hobbes – rated by Aubrey as one of his many 'great acquaintance[s]' – dared to import 'Hobbesian ecclesiological and religious doctrines into his 1656 *Politicall Reflections upon the Government of the Turks*'.[5] Praising Cromwell, the 'Protector, carrying all afore him', in 1657, for creating Ejectors to control the parishes and 'eject the Obnoxious',[6] and apparently including

---

[1] See Richard Tuck, 'The Civil Religion of Thomas Hobbes', p. 134.

[2] *Lev.*, xii, §20, 57-8/69-70.

[3] *Ibid.*

[4] See Collins, *Allegiance*, pp. 170-71, citing John Goodwin, *Thirty Queries . . . Whether the civil Magistrate stands bound by way of Duty to Interose his Power or Authority in Matters of Religion* (1653), pp. 4-7.

[5] See Collins, *Allegiance*, pp. 175-6.

[6] Osborne to Draper 165?, and 11 Mar. 1657, in *Miscellaneous Works of that Eminent Statesman, Francis Osborne* (2 vols, 1722); see Collins, *Allegiance*, p. 176.

Hobbes along with his praiseworthy friends Selden and Bacon,[1] Osborne referred to princes as 'State-Leviathans' and the papacy as an 'Ecclesiastical Leviathan', draining the European nations of their martial power by manipulating 'Future feare' and 'ransacking the more tender Consciences of Dying men'.[2] By contrast he argued, under Islamic rule, 'Though the Eccesiastical and Civill Powers be both radically in the Grand Segnior; yet the pontificall Mufty hath Studied the Art to make the people beleve these two Streames, doe flow, one from a lesse, and the other from a more Sanctified fountaine'; Islam was a 'huge operation upon Obedience to the civill Magistrate', he declared.[3] Osborne was one a circle of sceptics who praised 'the Erastian philo-Semitic logic of Leviathan', among them Edward Bagshaw, who belonged to Owen's circle of Independents and is probably among the 'many favourites' Stubbe reported Hobbes having at Oxford after 1656; and who in fact corresponded with the philosopher briefly in 1658.[4]

This was a period of great interest in Orientalia and the occult. Edward Pococke (1604-91), of Corpus Christi College, Oxford, held the first Chair of Arabic at Oxford, founded by Archbishop Laud in 1636, to which was added the Chair of Hebrew in 1648. A bible scholar, whose knowledge of Arabic, Hebrew, Syriac, Samaritan, and Ethiopic enabled him to usher in a new phase of English critical biblical studies, Pococke came to the attention of Georg Vossius, and counted John Selden and John Owen among his influential friends. Selden (1584-1654), Pococke's senior, was himself a considerable Orientalist, and the two men had remarkably parallel interests. Pococke's *Porta Mosis*, comprising extracts from the Arabic commentary of Maimonides on the *Mishna* of 1655, was preceded by

---

[1] See Osborne's epistle 'to the reader', in *A Miscellany of Sundry Essays, Paradoxes and Problematicall Discourses* (1659); see Collins, *Allegiance*, p. 176, who notes that the 'B, D, and H etc' praised in the epistle 'to the reader' prefacing Osborne's *Advice to a Son*, are probably Bacon, Descartes and Hobbes.

[2] Osborne, *Miscellany*, p. 253 and *Reflection upon the Turks*, pp. 87, 9-11, 87, 91-4; see Collins, *Allegiance*, pp. 176-7.

[3] Osborne, *Reflection upon the Turks*, pp. 44, 53; see Collins, *Allegiance*, p. 177.

[4] See Bagshaw, *Saintship no Ground of Sovereignty . . .* (Oxford, 1660); see Collins, *Allegiance*, p. 238.

Selden's *De successionibus in bona defuncti secundu in leges Ebraeorum* and *Dc successione in pontificatum Ebraeorurn*, published in 1631, his *Dissertatio de anno civili et calendario reipublicae Judaicae* of 1644, and his treatise on marriage and divorce among the Jews, *Uxor Hebraica* of 1646. Pococke's *Annals of Eutychius* in Arabic and Latin of 1656 was preceded by Selden's *Eutychii Aegyptii, Patriarchae Orthodoxorum Alexandrini, Ecclesiae suae Origines. Ex ejusdem Arabico nunc primum typis editit, ac versione & commentario auxit*, held in the Hardwick Hall library.[1] The latter seems to have been Hobbes's source in the poem for information on the Council of Nicaea. Relying upon an Arabic manuscript, the Oxford Codex of Joseph of Egypt ('fl. Hegirae 790, Christi 1400'), it contains a list of the names of 307 of the 381 Bishops said to have attended the Council of Nicaea,[2] and a paper trail of the sources Joseph of Egypt might have used to establish the list.[3] The language and details of Selden's account of Constantine's handling of the council,[4] based on this source, are mirrored in Hobbes's text. Moreover, Selden's translation made a point of playing up the role of early Christian presbyters and playing down the role of bishops.[5]

Selden's *De Synedriis*, seems to have come to Hobbes's attention, perhaps at the time of writing *Leviathan*, given that the first of its three volumes was published already in 1650. For the two men came to similar conclusions on the critical matter of excommunication. *De Synedriis* was addressed to the question debated by the Westminster Assembly, whether the Jewish Sanhedrin should be a model for Christian polities and, if so, whether it set an Erastian or dualist model of church government.[6] *De Synedriis* argued emphatically in

---

[1] Selden's *Eutychii Aegyptii, Patriarchae Orthodoxorum Alexandrini, Ecclesiae suae Origines. Ex ejusdem Arabico nunc primum typis editidit, ac versione & commentario auxit*, published in his *Opera Omnia* (London, 1626, 6 vols), vol. 3, pp. 410-527, was listed in Hobbes's booklist, *q.v.*, in a 1642 folio edition.

[2] Selden's *Eutychii* (1626), vol. 3, pp. 474-98.

[3] §§13ff. (pp. 468-74) of Selden's text concern the 'Concilii Nicaeni Canonibus Arabicis'.

[4] Selden's *Eutychii*, §16, pp. 467-8.

[5] See Collins, *Allegiance,* p. 99.

[6] See Collins, *Allegiance,* p. 164.

favour of the former and against the latter, the first volume, largely
devoted to the question of excommunication, concluding that
beyond informal disciplinary measures by local congregations,
only a sovereign power had the authority to exclude Jews from
religious observance; Hobbes's position in *Leviathan*.

Selden's career also had certain parallels to Hobbes's. Although
Hobbes did not succeed in his early bid to enter the House of
Commons as a member for Derbyshire, Selden began his career as
a parliamentarian and had a large share in drawing up and carrying
the Petition of Right; and in 1629 he was one of the members
mainly responsible for the passage of the Bill against the illegal
levy of tonnage and poundage. He was briefly a supporter of the
King, to whom he dedicated *Mare Clausum* in 1635; and later a
member of the Long Parliament, representing the University of
Oxford. The same man who had in the Long Parliament opposed
the resolution against episcopacy which led to the exclusion of the
bishops from the House of Lords, and joined in the protestation of
the Commons for the maintenance of the Protestant religion
according to the doctrines of the Church of England, in 1643 participated in discussions of the Presbyterian-oriented Assembly of
Divines. And finally in 1646 Selden subscribed to the Solemn
League and Covenant. If there seems not to be much consistency in
Selden's affiliations, this is perhaps an indication of how tumultuous times were and how much trimming it took to survive. Like
Justus Lipsius (1547-1606), the Belgian philosopher and another
of Hobbes's sources, who changed from Catholicism to Calvinism
and from Calvinism to Lutheranism in order to take various University posts, and actually dared to write a book *On Constancy*,
inconstancy was his motto, the occupational hazard of the Erastian,
as we know from the case of Hobbes.

Lipsius comes to our attention in another context, and that is
Hobbes's relation to Hermeticism. A syncretistic cult centred on the
Egyptian Hermes and now believed to owe some ancestry to late
Pharaonic cults that tie it to Gnosticism, Hermeticism swept the
Renaissance world.[1] Hobbes himself has an ambiguous relation to

---

[1] For such an account see G. Fowden, *The Egyptian Hermes: A Historical
Approach to the Late Pagan Mind* (Princeton, N.J., Princeton University Press,

hermeticism. Very few hermetic works appear in the Hardwick Hall book list, in fact, and yet there are a large number of internal references to hermetic *topoi*, which we can only conclude Hobbes sourced elsewhere, perhaps in Digby's collection.[1] Horst Bredekamp, following the seminal work of Karl Schuhmann,[2] has argued that Hobbes's 'Mortal God' is heavily indebted to the Hermetic text *Asclepius*, an early source for the thesis that men have the power to create gods in their own image, of which Leviathan might be a proto-type. Francesco Patrizi, in his encyclopedic work of 1593, *Nova de Universis Philosophia*, had incorporated the complete *Corpus Hermeticum*. There we find the following passages from *Asclepius* according to Patrizi's recension:[3]

> Learn, Asclepius, of the mighty power of men. As the Lord and Father or, that most holy of names, God the creator of heavenly gods, so also is man the creator of gods, who are happy to reside in temples close to men, and not to be illuminated but to illuminate. And he not only moves the gods, but he also shapes them.

1993). The classical scholar Isaac Casaubon in *De Rebus sacris et ecclesiaticis exercitiones XVI*, of 1614, had argued on philological evidence, from the nature of the Greek, that most of the 'philosophical' *Corpus Hermeticum* can be dated post AD 300. But this view has been revised.

[1] See Chatsworth MS E2, discussed above at pp. 81-2, for discussion of Hobbes's occult wisdom; see also Patricia Springborg, 'Hobbes, Heresy and the *Historia Ecclesiastica*', and 'Writing to Redundancy: Hobbes and Cluverius'.

[2] For a treatment of the importance of Hermeticism for Leviathan, see Karl Schuhmann's pioneering essay, 'Rapidità el pensiero e ascensione al cielo: alcuni motivi ermetici in Hobbes', *Rivista di Storia della Filosofia*, vol. 40 (1985), pp. 203-27; and Horst Bredekamp's *Thomas Hobbes der Leviathan*, chapter 3. For Gianni Paganini's response to Schuhmann and Bredekamp, see, 'Alle Origini del "Mortal God": Hobbes, Lipsius e il *Corpus Hermeticum*', *Rivista di Storia della Filosofia*, vol. 61 (2006), pp. 509-32.

[3] See also Bredekamp's essay, 'Thomas Hobbes's Visual Strategies', in the *Cambridge Companion to Hobbes's Leviathan*, p. 34, citing Patrizi 1593, p. 68; for a modern edition, see Hermès Trismégiste, *Corpus Hermeticum*, ed. A. D. Nock, trans. A. J. Festugière, 4 vols (Paris, Les Belles Lettres, 1980), vol. II, *Asclepius*, VIII, 23, lines 4-8, p. 325:

> Et quoniam de cognatione et consortio hominum deorumque nobis indicitur sermo, potestatem hominis, o Asclepi, vimque cognosce. Dominus & pater, uel quod est summum, Deus, vt effector est Deorum coelestium, ita homo effector est Deorum, qui in templis sunt, humana proximitate coniuncti, et non solum illuminantur, verum etiam illuminant. Nec solum ad Deum proficit, verum etiam confirmat Deos.

It is clear that Asclepius is referring to the statue cults of ancient Egypt, where effigies were taken not merely as 'reminders' of the gods but as their living incarnation, with the power to reward and punish, to inflict or ward off evil at will; for Asclepius notes:[1]

> I mean statues that have life breathed into them, full of spirit and *pneuma*, that accomplish great and mighty deeds, statues that can read the future and predict it through priests, dreams and many other things, which weaken and heal men, create sadness and joy for every individual according to his merits.

In the *Historia Ecclesiastica* Hobbes devotes surprising space to statue cults, what statues portend as 'warnings' or 'remembrances'; what it means to 'worship' a statue; and an account of the (misguided) iconoclast movement.[2] Given his predilection for simplicity of doctrine and minimalism in speech, it comes as some surprise perhaps that Hobbes argues a positive case for statue cults, harking back to precedents in Ancient Greece and Rome. But this is, in fact, no more surprising, and perhaps related to, his startling use of metaphor and image, in particular his choice of Leviathan as the emblem of the state. Bredekamp argues that Hobbes's opening claims for Leviathan suggest that he hopes to evoke in his readers an image as powerful and terrifying as the God of Job, but under a different dispensation: that of the interim between the first and the second comings, during which God has abandoned men and they must rule themselves with institutions of their own artifice. Leviathan, the 'mortal god' of the Hermetic texts, is men's greatest creation, ruling over this intermediate zone and sharing its dual characteristics: 'By resembling the gods, man can never free himself from the memory of his own nature and origin; thus man, as created by the Father and Lord of immortal

---

[1] Patrizi 1593, p. 69 (see Hermès Trismégiste 1980, vol. II, *Asclepius*, VIII, 24, p. 326):

> Statuas animatas, sensu & Spiritu plenas, tanta & talia facientes, statuas, futurorum praescias, easque forte vates omnes somniis, multisque aliis rebus praedicentes, imbecillitatesque hominibus facientes, easque curantes, tristitiamque pro meritis.

[2] *Hist. Eccl.*, lines 1311 to 1410. See also the long treatment of statues, idols and idolatry in *Lev.*, xlv, §10-33.

Gods who resemble him, also designs even his Gods according to his own image'.[1]

Gianni Paganini, in a pioneering piece of research, has argued that the situation is more complicated however. Hobbes was undoubtedly also aware of the tradition of anti-Hermetic critique that ran from Augustine to *Bradwardine, registering the scandal to Christian theology caused by these idolatrous claims.[2] So Marsilio Ficino, translator and commentator on the *Asclepius*, despite ambivalence towards this work, is able to situate it critically. Tracing in *De voluptate* the steps of *theologia prisca* from Hermes to Zoroaster and to the 'divine Plato', Ficino underlines the capacity of man for apotheosis, given his middle position between god and the animals. But already in *De vita coelitus comparanda*, Ficino had given a critical reading of the passages from the *Asclepius* in question, stressing first that *Asclepius* is attributing to these statues demonic and not divine power,[3] and secondly trying to explain statue cults pragmatically, in terms of the difficulty Egyptian priests faced in describing divine providence, and their resort to an illicit magical explanation of the statues as numinous.[4] Moreover, according to Ficino the demons these statues represented were rather low-ranking compared with the gods themselves, aerial, not celestial, perhaps the 'thin aerial spirits' Hobbes had in mind when he discussed demons and spirits in *Leviathan*, chapter 12.[5]

---

[1] Patrizi 1593, p. 69r. (Hermès Trismégiste, 1980, *Asclepius*, VIII, 24, p. 326):
ita humanitas semper memor naturae et originis suae in illa divinitatis imitatione perseverat, ut, sicuti Pater ac Dominus, ut sui similes essent, Deos fecit aeternos, ita humanitas Deos suos, ex sui vultus similitudine figuraret.

[2] Paganini, 'Alle Origini del "Mortal God"', p. 513.

[3] Paganini, 'Alle Origini del "Mortal God"', pp. 514-15, referring to Ficino's *De vita coelitus comparanda* III, 26 (*Opera ficiniani*, Basilea, 1561, vol. 1, p. 571).

[4] Paganini, 'Alle Origini del "Mortal God"', p. 513. I thank Dr. Ivo de Gennaro, of Bocconi University and the Free University of Bolzano, for helping me with the translation from the Italian.

[5] Hobbes in his discussion of apparitions and the delusions of dreams treats these creatures of the imagination or 'fancy', which people call 'ghosts, as the Latins called them *imagines* and *umbrae*, and thought them spirits, that is thin aerial bodies'. *Lev.*, xii, §7, 54/65. The corresponding passage in the *LL* (*OL*, Curley edn, p. 65 n. 3) adds: 'But that the same thing might be both a *spirit* and *incorporeal* cannot be understood. For a spirit is determined by place and figure, i.e., by limits and some size of its own. Therefore, it is a body, however rarefied and imperceptible.'

In another passage of *De vita coelitus comparanda* more attuned to Plotinus, Paganini notes,[1]

> Ficino also proposed a more correct reading of Asclepius, insisting that the Egyptian priests did not introduce to the statue cults spirits separated from matter, that is to say demons properly speaking, but rather *mundane numina*, mundane or mortal gods, which are equivalent in a neo-Platonic optic to celestial images, in turn reflections of the idea of the ideas, and as such are intermediate in this middle ground between the intellect and the body.

Although Hobbes could not accept such a Platonist reading, he could exploit it in his own way. Ficino's 'intermediate state' of man, half god, half beast was an analogue for man since the Fall, as it was for man in the state of nature, Janus-faced as both 'homo homini lupus' and 'homo homini deus'. Ficino had in fact entitled a letter to Bracciolini 'Lupus est homo homini, non homo' (Man is a wolf to other men, not a man to other men'),[2] while Estes di Lefèvre in his commentary on the *Asclepius*, reflecting on the twin human capacities for good and evil, had argued that the mind of

---

[1] Paganini, 'Alle Origini del "Mortal God"', pp. 513-14, citing Ficino's *De vita coelitus comparanda* III, 26 (*Opera ficiniani*, Basilea 1561, vol. I, p. 571). Paganini notes other more neutral references to the Hermetic treatment of statue cults, in Ficino's *De vita coelitus*, cap. 13 (*Opera* t. I, p. 548), and in his *Theologia platonica*, XIII, 3, ed. Marcel, t. II, p. 233), referring for comment to J. B. Allen's, *Synoptic Art: Marsilio Ficino on the History of Platonic Interpretation* (Florence, Olschki, 1998), pp. 44-45. Paganini's impressive apparatus including among his sources Claudio Moreschini, *Storia dell' ermetismo cristiano* (Brescia, Morcelliana, 2000), pp. 150-51, which reproduces (with the commentary of Arthur Darby Nock and Festugière in note 197) two passages from Porphyry's *De imaginibus*, fr. 2-3, in which he rejects the view that God is present in these statues, a view, as Moreschini comments, that would be a magical doctrine 'extremely embarrassing for Christians'. On the theme of the Creation in the Hermetic tradition, see Walter Scott, *Hermetica*, 1st edn 1924-36, 4 vols; reprint (London, Dawsons, 1969), vol. IV, p. 180 ff.; Jean-Pierre Mahé, *Hermès en haute-Egypte*, 2 vols (Québec, Presses de l'Université Laval, 1978-82), vol. II, pp. 98-102, p. 223 ff., 315, 385; B. Copenhaver, ed., *Hermetica. The Greek Corpus Hermeticum and the Latin Asclepius in a new English translation with notes and introduction*, (Cambridge, Cambridge University Press 1992), pp. 238 ff., 254 ff.

[2] Ficino, *Epistolarum liber III*, in *Opera* cit., vol. I, p. 741, cited by Paganini, 'Alle Origini del "Mortal God"', p. 522, n.44. The letter is already noted by Karl Schuhmann, 'Francis Bacon und Hobbes' Widmungsbrief zu *De cive*', *Zeitschrift für philosophische Forschung*, vol, 38 (1984), p. 179.

man in the terrestrial zone is dominated not by the mind of god, but by its 'sensible shadow' ('obumbratio'),[1] which gives evil entry, transforming man who is by nature divine into the worst of beasts.[2] For Hobbes, as for Ficino and Lefèvre d'Etaples, scripture must be interpreted to mean that God had ruled men in person until the Fall, but that the fact of original sin had caused him to retreat, casting men into an intermediate state, permitting, and indeed dictating, the creation of mortal gods with the power of salvation as intermediaries. Just such a mortal god was Leviathan, an artificial substitute for the creator God, but one who could reign in the nether zone until God came to re-establish his kingdom on earth at the Second Coming. Centuries later, as Paganini remarks, Carl Schmitt, who wrote his own *Leviathan*, was able to realize the terrible potential of Hobbes's 'mortal god' for the divinization of the state.[3]

Paganini also shows that Hobbes had a source closer to hand for the hermetic 'mortal god', Leviathan, than the *Hermes Trismegistus*, Ficino or Lefèvre d'Etaples, and that was Justus Lipsius, who made explicit reference to a 'mortal god'. Hobbes specifically mentions Lipsius for the Stoic definition of the concept of 'fate', on which he comments: 'I think fit to say this much, that their error consisteth not in the opinion of fate, but in feigning a false God', i.e. in making a god out of Fate.[4] Lipsius delineated the twin zones of mortal and immortal gods more conventionally: 'man on earth is a mortal god; god in heaven is an immortal man'. Although learned in Platonist and Neoplatonist sources, he was, like Hobbes, more prudent in his interpretation of Hermeticism, which he melds to Judeo-Christian

---

[1] Paganini, 'Alle Origini del "Mortal God"', p. 523. In 1505 Lefèvre d'Etaples had published Ficino's *Pimander* and *Asclepius* in Paris with his own commentary. This observation concludes his commentary on chapter 3 of the Asclepius, in particular the final part where he distinguished the 'essential' or divine part of man from the corporeal or 'mundane'. For man is a dual animal, he says, 'Solum enim animal homo duplex est', citing Ficino, *Opera*, vol. 2, p. 1860. The exact reference (as Paganini points out, p. 523, n. 45, of which Lefèvre's is a rough translation) is to *Asclepius* 7 (*Corpus Hermeticum* vol. II p. 304 ff.).

[2] Paganini, 'Alle Origini del "Mortal God"', p. 523.

[3] Paganini, 'Alle Origini del "Mortal God"', p. 517, n. 21, citing Carl Schmitt, *Der Leviathan in der Staatslehre des Thomas Hobbes. Sinn und Fehlschlag eines politischen Symbols* (Köln-Lövenich, Günter Maschke, 1982) pp. 44, 243.

[4] Hobbes, Liberty, Necessity and Chance, (*EW* V, p. 245) cited by Paganini, 'Alle Origini del "Mortal God"', p. 524.

orthodoxy. So, for instance, the construction of the 'mortal god' as an artificial person is tempered by biblical context to yield Adam as the first 'mortal god', exercising the political prerogative of sovereignty in the primordial stage of history.[1]

A convergence of thought on two Platonist *topoi* demonstrates Hobbes's possible indebtedness to Lipsius, both indicative of what he takes from these sources and where he departs from them. The first, already noted by Schuhmann, derives the divinization of man from the ubiquitous movement of thought. The Platonist concept 'praestantia Animi' stresses as a proof of man's divinity not only the velocity and omnipresence of thought, but a capacity of the soul for transcendence that even God does not enjoy.[2] For, while God is restricted to Heaven, man can move with great speed between the spheres, cross oceans and flit in thought from one India to another, without having to move outside himself, by means of copious imagery retained in the imagination.[3] As we shall see (chapter 6.1), it is just this capacity of the mind to conduct pure thought experiments on which the important 'annihilation of the world' depends, so critical for Hobbes's solution to the problem of scepticism; while the calculation of self-interest necessary to motivate people to contract is a thought experiment of a different kind. Schuhmann has examined the possible classical sources for Hobbes's notion of the ubiquitousness and velocity of thought, including Sallust, Seneca's *De beneficiis*, Claudian, Cicero's *De finibus,* to which Paganini adds a source in Lipsius's *Physiologia* for which Hobbes's passage, except for the mention of India, is an almost exact copy; a passage echoing the *Corpus Hermeticum* in turn.[4]

The second Platonist *topos* comprises Lipsius's reflections on the command 'know thyself' ('Nosce te ipsum'), taken from Plato's *Philebus* according to Porphyry, a command repeated in the short

---

[1] Paganini, 'Alle Origini del "Mortal God"', p. 528.

[2] Karl Schuhmann, 'Rapidità del pensiero e ascensione al cielo: alcuni motivi ermetici in Hobbes', cited by Paganini, 'Alle Origini del "Mortal God"', p. 526.

[3] Th. Hobbes, *De corpore*, II, vii, 1, ed. K. Schuhmann (Paris, Vrin, 1999), pp. 75-76, corresponding to *OL* I, p. 82, cited by Paganini, 'Alle Origini del "Mortal God"', p. 510.

[4] Lipsius, *Physiologia;* corresponding to the *Corpus Hermeticum*, XI 19 (vol. I, p. 154 l. 21 – p. 155 l. 7), cited by Paganini, 'Alle Origini del "Mortal God"', p. 526.

introduction to Hobbes's *Leviathan*, precisely in the context of his 'mortal god'. 'Nosce te ipsum', now understood not as divine knowledge, is in fact the fiat that gives rise to artificial man and the construction of the 'mortal god', which is the state.[1] For 'know thyself' applied to the sovereign, rather than to the individual, elevates self-knowledge from the personal understanding of one's passions and motivations to a higher level of knowledge, whereby the sovereign, as 'mortal god' in reading himself reads the nature of man. Self-knowledge as such was a consequence of the Fall, whereupon God departed from the earth and it was left to man to fabricate a substitute. That 'mortal god', the sovereign or Leviathan, thus assumes the two consequences of original sin after God withdrew, divinity and mortality.[2]

What under the direct rule of God would have been forbidden, now becomes praiseworthy, the divinization of man. Since the problem of evil can only post-date the Fall, and is a problem that does not concern God, who knows only good, it follows that it belongs to the prerogative of the sovereign not only to know human nature, but also to set the criteria for 'mine and thine, just and unjust, useful and useless, good and evil, honest and dishonest', as the basis for civil law, as Hobbes insisted in *De cive*.[3] Although, as Paganini points out, there is a sense in which Hobbes captures the poesis of hermeticism and its extraordinary notion of the divinity of man as 'mortal god' in the period of waiting between the first and second comings, in a way that Lipsius did not,[4] this sense of poesis did not and could not extend to acceptance of the mysticism of the Neoplatonists and their extravagant language, as we shall see.

---

[1] Hobbes, *Lev.*, Introd, §3, 2/4, cited by Paganini, 'Alle Origini del "Mortal God"', p. 526.

[2] Paganini, 'Alle Origini del "Mortal God"', p. 528.

[3] *De cive*, The Latin Version, ed. by Howard Warrender, Part II 'Imperium', chapter VII, ix, p. 139, cited by Paganini, 'Alle Origini del "Mortal God"', p. 529. For Hobbes on 'just and unjust, useful and useless, good and evil', see Patricia Springborg, '*Behemoth* and Hobbes's "Science of *Just* and *Unjust*"', pp. 267-89; and for 'the science of just and unjust from an Epicurean perspective, see Springborg, 'Hobbes and Epicurean Religion'.

[4] Paganini, 'Alle Origini del "Mortal God"', p. 531.

5.3 HOBBES AND PLATONISM

If the *Historia Ecclesiastica* examines the institutional edifice of the Christian church as a countervailing power to the Prince, and the papacy as a surrogate for bishops claiming *jure divino* powers, it equally addresses the doctrinal structures by which the Church maintains and propagates itself. In the eyes of one who saw primitive Christianity as a civil religion corrupted by Greek metaphysics, much of this falls under the rubric of Platonism and Aristotelianism. While substantial work has now been done on Hobbes's relation to Aristotle,[1] the impact of Platonism on Hobbes's theory has, in my view been systematically underestimated.[2] Platonism had become very influential, but pernicious, in Hobbes's view; first, as the quintessence of a Greek metaphysics that sought the unity of classes of particulars in terms of essences, and was therefore guilty of transforming generalizations into universals; secondly, as providing the metaphysical underpinnings of the divisive (and his view, false) doctrines of 'hypostases' and 'transubstantiation' in the Roman Church;

---

[1] On Hobbes and the late Aristotelians, see the fine essays by Karl Schuhmann and Cees Leijenhorst, in particular K. Schuhmann, 'Thomas Hobbes und Francesco Patrizi', *Archiv für Geschichte der Philosophie,* vol. 68 (1986), pp. 253-79; 'Hobbes and Telesio', *Hobbes Studies,* vol. 1 (1988), pp. 109-33; 'Zur Entstehung des neuzeitlichen Zeitbegriffs: Telesio, Patrizi, Gassendi', *Philosophia Naturalis,* vol. 25 (1988), pp. 37-64; 'Hobbes and Renaissance Philosophy', in *Hobbes Oggi,* ed. Arrigo Pacchi (Milan, Franco Angeli, 1990), pp. 331-49; 'Hobbes and Aristotle's Politics', in *Thomas Hobbes. Le Ragioni del Moderno tra Teologia e Politica,* ed. G. Borrelli (Naples, 1990), pp. 97-127; and 'Le Concept de l'Espace chez Telesio', in *Bernadino Telesio e la Cultura Napoletana,* ed. R. Sirri and M. Torrini (Naples, Guida, 1992), pp. 141-67. See also the following works by Cees Leijenhorst: 'Hobbes and Fracastoro', *Hobbes Studies* vol. 9 (1996), pp. 98-128; 'Hobbes's Theory of Causality and its Aristotelian Background', *The Monist,* vol. 79 (1996), pp. 426-47; 'Jesuit Conceptions of *Spatium Imaginarium* and Hobbes's Doctrine of Space', *Early Science and Medicine,* vol. 1 (1996), pp. 355-80; 'Motion, Monks and Golden Mountains: Campanella and Hobbes on Perception and Cognition', *Bruniana e Campanelliana,* vol. 3 (1997), pp. 93-121; and *The Mechanisation of Aristotelianism.*

[2] Platonism in general and Cambridge Platonism in particular have seen a recent revival in scholarly interest. See James Hankins, *Plato and the Italian Renaissance,* 2 vols (Leiden, E. J. Brill, 1990); Sarah Hutton, ed., *Henry More (1614-1687). Tercentenary Studies* (Dordrecht, Kluwer, 1990); and G.A.J. Rogers, J.-M. Vienne, and Y.-C. Zarka (eds), *The Cambridge Platonists in Philosophical Context. Politics, Metaphysics and Religion* (Dordrecht, Kluwer Academic Publishers, 1997).

and thirdly, as propagated by the new Chairs of Greek at Oxford and Cambridge, representing yet another force capable of destabilizing the realm.

If the degree to which Hobbes's political project was targeted at the universities has been underestimated, to the same degree has his response to Platonism been understudied, and these two factors, of great importance, are interrelated. Even a brief overview of the institutional bases of Platonism can shed some light on how, just as in the case of Scargill and the Latitude men, a constellation of philosophical views was associated with specific communities of scholars, clustered together in particular Oxbridge Colleges. The creation of Chairs of Greek at Oxford and Cambridge signaled a new departure and new centres of intellectual activity. If the Latitudinarians were particularly associated with Corpus Christi College, Cambridge, the Cambridge Platonists were especially associated with Emmanuel and Christ's Colleges. The most influential of the Cambridge Platonists, Henry More (1614-1687) and Ralph Cudworth (1617-1689), were both fellows of Christ's College, while Benjamin Whichcote (1609-1683), Peter Sterry (1613-1672), John Smith (1618-1652), Nathaniel Culverwell (1619-1651), and John Worthington (1618-1671), were all one-time fellows of Emmanuel College, Cambridge.

To take Hobbes's general reaction to Platonism first, it is important to understand the larger institutional context for the reception of Platonism, which like Aristotelianism, went in waves. During the long period of the ascendancy of the Eastern Church Platonism was dominant, and Aristotelianism, the weapon of the Latin Church, only later ascendant. I cite the overview of Philip Hadot, which emphasizes the institutional basis of these schools:[1]

> At the beginning of the Hellenistic period an extraordinary proliferation of schools emerged in the wake of the Sophist movement and the Socratic experience. But beginning with the third century BC a kind of sorting out occurred. In Athens the only schools to survive were those whose founders had thought to establish them as well-organized institutions: the school of Plato, the school of Aristotle and Theophrastus, the school of Epicurus, and that of Zeno and Chrysippus. In addition to these four schools there were two movements that

---

[1] Hadot, Pierre, *Philosophy as a Way of Life: Spiritual Exercises from Socrates to Foucault* (Oxford, Blackwell, 1995), pp. 56-7.

are primarily spiritual traditions: Scepticism and Cynicism. After the institutional foundations of the schools in Athens collapsed at the end of the Hellenistic period, private schools and even officially subsidized teaching posts continued to be established throughout the empire, and here the spiritual traditions of their founders were their reference points. Thus, for six centuries, from the third century BC until the third century AD, we witness a surprising stability among the six traditions we have just mentioned. However, beginning with the third century AD, Platonism, in the culmination of a movement underway since the first century, yet again at the price of subtle shifts in meaning and numerous reinterpretations, came to absorb both Stoicism and Aristotelianism in an original synthesis, while all the other traditions were to become marginal. This unifying phenomenon is of major historical importance. Thanks to the writers of lesser antiquity but also to the Arab translations and Byzantine tradition, this Neoplatonist synthesis was to dominate all the thought of the Middle Ages and Renaissance and was to provide, in some fashion, the common denominator among Jewish, Christian, and Moslem theologies and mysticisms.

Closer to Hobbes's time Platonism took on a new life as the force from the East to which, through the agency of the Byzantine emissaries to the Florence-Ferrara Council of 1438-9 – and the manuscripts they brought with them, which formed the initial deposit of the Vatican Library – the Renaissance in many respects owed its inception.[1] It is sometimes forgotten that the ascendancy of the Latin Church under the rising power of the papacy had also meant the eclipse of Greek. Some time between the closure of the Athenian Academy by the emperor *Justinian in AD 529 and the *quattrocento*, facility in Greek had died out in the Western Empire. So, for instance, while the ecclesiastical histories of Sozomen, Athanasius, Socrates of Constantinople, Eusebius of Caesarea and Gregory of Nyssa, were written in Greek – hence the scramble in the Renaissance to translate them – many of the patristic sources were already in Latin. Most of these sources are to be found in contemporary editions in the Hardwick Hall book list in Hobbes's hand.

---

[1] On the Byzantine emissaries and their reception, see the many articles by Deno J. Geanakopolis, as well as his book: *Constantinople and the West: Essays on the Late Byzantine (Palaeologan) and Italian Renaissances and the Byzantine and Roman Church* (Madison Wisc., University of Wisconsin Press, 1989).

When the Greek language died in Latin Christendom, Platonism had more or less died with it.[1] As a magnificent demonstration of historical contingency, the Florence-Ferrara Council – a council convened to reconcile Eastern and Western Christianity in the face of the Muslim threat – reintroduced Platonism as an unintended consequence. Platonism blew like a new wind through the Western empire, due in no small part to the magnetic personality of Gemistus Pletho and his proto-nationalist, politicized Plato which caught the imagination of Marsilio Ficino and his patron, Cosimo de Medici, both of whom are reputed to have attended Council sessions. Cosimo de Medici ordered Ficino to learn Greek forthwith and embark on the translation of Platonist works, beginning with the *Hermes Trismegistus*. The translations by Marsilio Ficino of all thirty-six Platonic dialogues of the Thrasyllan canon in 1484, at the behest of his patron, ushered in the new humanism, antiquarian, metaphysical, nationalistic and Platonist.

Plato was the handbook of the Renaissance upstart prince[2] and, of all the Platonist works, the most well known was probably Castiglione's *Il cortegiano (The Courtier)*. We can only speculate about Hobbes's reaction to this aspect of Plato's reception. Perhaps as a courtier's client he could see himself in the mould, plying his trade to the Cavendishes, and through them first to the King and then to the Protector.[3] But the 'Divine Plato' was also the purveyor of a disturbing new metaphysics. Ficino had also translated the *Enneads* of Plotinus (1492) and the Hermetic *Asclepius* and *Pimander* (1471) and, in fact, Hobbes's relation to those works is not unambiguous. For he was both a humanist himself and a scathing critic of the Renaissance and its consequences. Although he shares many of the antiquarian interests of the classical humanist, and can rightly be classed with his English Antiquarian friends, Aubrey and Selden,[4] his very refusal to

---

[1] See James Hankins, *Plato and the Italian Renaissance*, 2 vols (Leiden, E. J. Brill, 1990).

[2] On Plato and the Renaissance upstart prince, see Alison Brown, 'Platonism in Fifteenth-Century Florence and its Contribution to Early Modern Political Thought', *Journal of Modern History,* vol. 58 (1986), pp. 383-413.

[3] *Hist. Eccl.*, lines 234-72; the name for the Chief of the Court dispensing justice, 'Praesidis', can in fact be read as 'Protector'.

[4] For Hobbes and the Antiquarians, see Patricia Springborg, 'Hobbes, Heresy and the *Historia Ecclesiastica*'.

grant the academic or critical distance we associate with the humanist – and which we find so pronounced in Selden's glosses on the
texts of his friends[1] – gives us pause for caution. Platonism was the
sheerest instance of the power of ideas to create new institutions and
erode old ones, and despite his cooptation of certain Platonist and
hermetic tropes already discussed, this in general was how Hobbes
treated it.

Plato was a man for all seasons. The French Protestant, Jean de
Serres (Joannes Serranus) (c. 1540-1598), had dedicated his transla-
tion of Plato made in collaboration with the famous humanist Henry
Estienne, to Elizabeth I. But in the sixteenth century only one
English translation of Plato was printed, the pseudo-Platonic
Axiochus (1592), translated by Edmund Spenser, and later included
in a collection attributed to the Huguenot leader so admired by Sir
Philip Sidney, Philippe du Plessis Mornay, entitled, *Six Excellent
Treatises of Life and Death* (London, 1607).[2] No Latin or English
translation of Plato appeared in England until the *Platonis de rebus
divinis, dialogi selecti*, printed in Cambridge in 1673, followed two
year's later by the London imprint of *Plato his Apology of Socrates
and Phaedo or Dialogue concerning the Immortality of Man's Soul,
and Manner of Socrates his death*. It is to the tradition of the 'Divine
Plato' that Hobbes's attack is particularly directed. The association
between Platonism and Catholicism went back to the first introduction of Italian Platonism to England. Humphrey, Duke of Gloucester,
who had made a foundation deposit of some 300 MSS to what was to
become the Bodleian Library in Oxford, had contacts with the trans-
lators of the *Republic*, Leonardo Bruni and Pier Candido Decembrio
(1392-1477), while Sir Thomas More's friend, John Colet (1467-

---

[1] See Selden's elaborate 'Illustrations', prefacing Drayton's *Poly-Olbion*,
reprinted in *The Works of Michael Drayton*, vol. 4, p. v. For treatment of English
mythological history by Hobbes's contemporaries, including Selden's glosses on
Drayton's *Polyolbion*, see Springborg, '*Leviathan*, Mythic History and National
Historiography', in David Harris Sacks and Donald Kelley, eds., *The Historical
Imagination in Early Modern Britain* (Cambridge, Cambridge University Press/
Woodrow Wilson Press, 1997), pp. 267-297.
[2] See Sarah Hutton, 'Plato and the Tudor Academies', in Francis Ames-Lewis,
ed., *Sir Thomas Gresham and Gresham College: Studies in the Intellectual History
of London in the Sixteenth and Seventeenth Centuries* (London, Ashgate, 1999),
pp. 106-24, especially p. 107, n. 3., p. 108, to whom I am indebted for this account.

1519) had corresponded with Marsilio Ficino. When in 1549 libraries were purged in a campaign to eliminate Catholic books, all but one of the Duke Humphrey's Plato manuscripts were destroyed.[1] The founding of the Greek chairs at Oxford and Cambridge was a turning point and we may read Hobbes's attack on the universities in the Latin *Leviathan*, in particular, in *Behemoth* and in the *Historia Ecclesiastica*, as at least in part an attack on the Platonists. As the Dutch scholar Cees Leijenhorst notes, 'Hobbes's critique of scholastic metaphysics and theology is also an institutional critique of the universities which teach these doctrines to future clergy . . . inspired by abstruse metaphysics, preach[ing] sedition and revolt instead of obedience to the legitimate sovereign'.[2] Certainly Hobbes's remarks in *Leviathan*, a 'Review and Conclusion', about his hope to see universities free from 'the venom of heathen politicians, and from the incantation of deceiving Spirits' could be read as an attack on the Platonists.[3]

It was in the new humanist foundations which pioneered the study of Greek, Corpus Christi College, Oxford, and St. John's College, Cambridge, that the impact of Plato was strongest. Cardinal Wolsey's abortive Cardinal College, whose remnants were incorporated in Christ Church, had set itself the project of translating all the Greek manuscripts of Cardinal Bessarion, an important Byzantine transmitter of Plato.[4] Corpus Christi College, founded in Oxford in 1517 by Bishop Richard Fox, who immediately established a public lectureship in Greek, won praise for its humanist curriculum from Erasmus, who had longstanding English connections, and briefly held the Chair in Greek at Cambridge. Plato was not prescribed

---

[1] Sear Jayne, *John Colet and Marsilio Ficino* (London, 1963), p. 90.

[2] C.H. Leijenhorst, *Hobbes and the Aristotelians*, pp. 33-4.

[3] See *Lev.*, ch. 46 and the 'Review and Conclusion' §16, 396/496, where Hobbes declares:

> For seeing the Universities are the fountains of civil and moral doctrine, from whence the preachers, and the gentry, drawing such water as they find, use to sprinkle the same (both from the pulpit, and in their conversation) upon the people, there ought certainly to be great care taken to have it pure, both from the venom of heathen politicians and from the incantation of deceiving spirits. And by that means the most men, knowing their duties, will be the less subject to serve the ambition of a few discontented persons, in their purposes against the State . . . .

[4] Sear Jayne, *John Colet and Marsilio Ficino*, pp. 85-6.

reading on the Greek syllabus, but readings from the 'divine Plato', could be given on feast days and the library included three editions of Plato's works, including the celebrated Aldine edition of 1513, as well as three commentaries on Plato by Proclus and Plotinus's *Enneads*.[1]

Both of Bishop Fisher's foundations at Cambridge, St. John's College, and Christ's College, were modeled on Corpus Christi at Oxford. St. John's, which established a lectureship in Greek, also boasted the first Regius Professor of Greek, John Cheke, who taught on Plato in tutorials, and later Roger Ascham, tutor to Elizabeth I. Among its other distinguished alumni were John Dee, the Queen's astrologer, and Everard Digby (b. c. 1550). The latter, father of Hobbes's friend Kenelm Digby who underwrote the cost of printing *De cive*, was a Plato scholar who relied heavily on Reuchlin's *De arte cabbalistica* (1517), and his magnum opus, the *Theoria analytica, viam ad monarchiam scientiarum demonstrans,* (1579), is referred to by C. B. Schmitt as 'the first serious, published philosophical work in Britain after the coming of the Reformation'.[2]

It is true to say that there had been a dearth of philosophers in England for at least two centuries after the death of the great late medieval scholastics, *Peter Lombard, *Ockham and *Duns Scotus, all of whom get negative mention from Hobbes in the *Ecclesiastical History*.[3] When in the sixteenth century Aristotelianism, often of a Platonizing variety, experienced a revival, a number of the most prominent thinkers were forced to resign their fellowships on the grounds of suspected Catholicism. Sir Everard Digby was one. John Case of St. John's college, Oxford, was another, his *Speculum moralium questionum in universam ethnice Aristotelis* (1585), the first book printed at Oxford University Press, where he published seven more text-books of Aristotelianism dealing with logic, ethics, politics and economics before he died in 1600. John Sanderson, fellow of Trinity college, Cambridge (B.A. 1558), appointed reader in logic was yet another; he later became a student at Douai in 1570, was

---

[1] Hutton, 'Plato and the Tudor Academies', p. 111.
[2] C. B. Schmitt, *John Case and Aristotelianism in Renaissance England* (Kingston and Montreal, McGill-Queen's University Press, 1983), pp. 47-8.
[3] *Hist. Eccl.*, lines 1643-62, and 1879-82.

ordained a priest in the Catholic church and was appointed divinity professor in the English college at Rheims. It was a reasonable expectation at this time, therefore, that Platonists were also Catholics.[1] Everard Digby was openly Catholic, and a list of his sources gives us an indication of his particular brand of Platonist metaphysics. They include Plotinus, Porphyry, Iamblichus, Proclus, Pseudo-Dionysius, Hermes Trismegistus, Apuleius and Alcinous, Ficino, Pico della Mirandolla, and the Christian Cabbalists, Reuchlin and Agrippa.[2] Sir Everard Digby's son, as we have already noted, had been the owner of the large collection of hermetic texts listed in Chatsworth MS E2, which he turned over to the Bodleian.

We have some flavour of the elevated tone of Italian Neoplatonism in Ficino's preface to his translation of the *Phaedrus*: 'Our Plato was pregnant with the madness of the poetic Muse, whom he followed

---

[1] See *The Cambridge History of English and American Literature* in 18 Volumes (1907-21), vol 4, Prose and Poetry, §6. Philosophy in English Universities; Revival of Aristotelianism in the 16th century. http://www.bartleby.com/214/1406.html.

[2] For the vast secondary literature on hermeticism see those works referred to by Paganini in 'Alle Origini del "Mortal God"', p. 12, note 45. Paganini includes among older works, David P. Walker, *Spiritual and Demonic Magic from Ficino to Campanella* (London, Warburg Institute, 1958); Frances A. Yates, *Giordano Bruno and the Hermetic Tradition*, (London, Kegan Paul, London 1964) and Yates's *The Occult Philosophy in the Elizabethan Age* (London, Routledge and Kegan Paul, 1970). Recent volumes include: R. S. Westman and J.E. McGuire, *Hermeticism and the Scientific Revolution*. Papers read at a Clark Library Seminar, Los Angeles 1977; J. S. Gill, *English Hermeticism. A critical study of contrasting responses to Hermeticism in Renaissance and Seventeenth Century Literature* (Ph.D. Thesis, Loughborough University of Technology, 1982); *Occult and Scientific Mentalities in the Renaissance*, ed. by B. Vickers (Cambridge, Cambridge University Press 1984); Claudio Moreschini, *Dall' Asclepius al Crater Hermetis: studi sull'ermetismo latino tardo-antico e rinascimentale* (Pisa, Giardini, 1985); *Hermeticism and the Renaissance: intellectual history and the occult in early modern Europe*, edited by Ingrid Merkel and Allen G. Debus, (Washington, Folger Books, 1988); Paola Zambelli, *L'ambigua natura della magia: filosofi, streghe, riti nel Rinascimento* (Venezia, Marsilio 1996); Maria Muccillo, *Platonismo, ermetismo e "prisca Theologia". Ricerche di storiografia filosofica rinascimentale* (Firenze, Olschki 1996); *Gnosis and Hermeticism from Antiquity to Modern Times*, ed. by Roelof van den Broek and Wouter J. Hanegraaf (Albany, New York, State University of New York Press, 1998); Anne-Charlott Trepp and Hartmut Lehmann, *Antike Weisheit und kulturelle Praxis. Hermetismus in der Frühen Neuzeit* (Göttingen, Vandenhoeck & Ruprecht, 2001). Martin Mulsow, *Monadenlehre, Hermetik und Deismus. Georg Schades geheime Aufklärungsgesellschaft* (Hamburg, Meiner 1998).

from a tender age or rather from his Apollonian generation. In his radiance, Plato gave birth to his first child, and it was itself almost entirely poetical and radiant.'[1] Joel Wilcox notes Ficino as the source for the Neoplatonism of Chapman's translations of *Homer*, to which Hobbes responds with his extraordinarily flat footed, and much misunderstood translations of his own. William Cowper, for instance, claimed that 'Hobbes's Homer possessed "greater clumsiness" than even Chapman, made him "laugh immoderately", and made up for its miserable poetic quality by being ridiculous'.[2] But what Cowper, along with Dryden and Alexander Pope, all of whom commented negatively on Hobbes's Homer, missed, was that his translation was deliberately deflationary, an attack on the 'Homerus Sophos' tradition in line with his attack on the 'divine Plato'.[3]

Wilcox notes of Ficino's *Ion* and Phaedrus commentary that 'this general theory of divine inspiration as found in the *Theologia Platonica* and elsewhere links the madness of heavenly rapture to the natural appetite for the true vision of God, a vision which for the Neoplatonist constitutes both the object of poetry and philosophy.'[4] So, for instance, Chapman lifted a quotation by Ficino from Ovid's *Fasti* for the dedicatory letter to Prince Henry which prefaces his *Iliad*: 'There is a god in us, we are inflamed at his rousing./ That impulse holds the kernals of the sacred mind.'[5]

This is precisely the type of dangerous Enthusiasm and puffed up language that Hobbes set about to deflate. Nowhere is it better demonstrated than in Ficino's notion of *hypostases*, possibly Hobbes's target in the *Historia Ecclesiastica* where he mocks the concept which, as the Neoplatonists used it, had the sense of essence

[1] Joel F. Wilcox, 'Ficino's Commentary on Plato's *Ion* and Chapman's Inspired Poet in the *Odyssey*', *Philological Quarterly*, vol. 64 (1985), pp. 195-209; at p. 195.

[2] See the *Letters and Prose Writings of William Cowper*, ed. James King and Charles Ryskamp, 5 vols. (Oxford, Clarendon Press, 1979-86), vol. 4, p. 369, cited by Jerry Ball in 'The Despised Version: Hobbes's Translations of Homer', *Restoration*, vol. 20, 1 (1996), p. 16, n. 7.

[3] Paul Davis makes this argument in his excellent essay, 'Thomas Hobbes's Translations of Homer: Epic and Anticlericalism in Late Seventeenth-Century England', *The Seventeenth Century*, vol. 12 (1997), pp. 231-55.

[4] Wilcox, 'Ficino's Commentary', p. 195.

[5] Marsilio Ficino, *Opera Omnia* (Basle, 1561; reprinted Turin, 1959), vol. 1, p. 287.

or principle. So Ralph Cudworth, in his *Intellectual System*, 1.1.22, had noted: 'That Plato and his followers held *treis archikas huposta-seis*, Three Hypostases in the Deity, that were the first Principles of all things, is a thing very well known to all'.[1] Ficino's account of how it is that all things proceed from the mind of God involved a descrip-tion of 'the fall of the soul into body', beginning in his commentary on the *Ion,* with its origin in God and proceeding through Mind, Reason, Opinion, Nature, to Body.[2] He identified the 'ineffable One of the pagan Neoplatonists with the second hypostasis of Mind as well, making what he calls "Angelic Mind" stand for the world of Forms'. By means of 'divine fury, a man is raised to unity until he becomes, in Ficino's starling phrase, "one God"'.[3] Wilcox goes on to expound Ficino's theory of the *hypostases*:[4]

> For Ficino divine inspiration accomplishes a specific task: it reverses the process of the fall of souls into bodies, returning it to a higher original self-unification and then to a vision of the One, the source of all unity, in accordance with his sense of the fundamental identity of knowing and being. Because the intelligible world of the Platonists is not 'peopled' with concepts but with things more real than the images of ordinary experience or concepts derived from that experience, the fall of the soul into body is a fall through all of the hypostases which make up the fulness of creation. The return to god necessarily implies a re-acquaintance with all of the entities of the intelligible world. Since the hypostasis of Body is the lowest of all created things, the fall of souls into bodies – souls which have in them innately all of the knowledge of God's mind from which they spring – makes man the unique comprehender of the whole creation, ' a little world made cunningly', as Donne writes.

The term *hypostasis* had a long history in the theological debates over Arianism, in particular in the battle that culminated in the

---

[1] *OED*, 1971 edn.

[2] Wilcox, 'Ficino's Commentary', pp. 206-8, citing Marsilio Ficino's *Ion* (*Opera Omnia*, vol. II, pp. 1281-2).

[3] Wilcox, 'Ficino's Commentary', citing Marsilio Ficino's *Opera Omnia*, vol. II, pp. 1281, and Oscar Kristeller, *The Philosophy of Marsilio Ficino*, trans. Virginia Conant (1943, reprinted Gloucester, Mass., Peter Smith, 1964), p. 68.

[4] Wilcox, 'Ficino's Commentary', p. 197, citing Ficino, *Opera Omnia*, vol. II, pp. 1282-3 and Giovanni Pico della Mirandola, 'On the Dignity of Man', in *On the Dignity of Man and other Works*, trans. Charles Glen Wallace, *et al.* (Indiannapolis, Bobbs Merrill, 1965), pp. 434-5.

Nicaean Council. The term, denoting person, personality, or personal existence, was used to make the distinction between *person* as
distinct from *nature*, as in the one *hypostasis* of Christ, distinguished
from his two *natures* (human and divine); at the same time distinguished from *substance*, as in the three *hypostases* or 'persons' of
the Godhead, which are said to be the same in 'substance'.[1] Hobbes's
use of the term *hypostasis*, in the *Historia Ecclesiastica* enables him
to couple Neoplatonism with Arianism, turning the slur of heresy
against the Neoplatonists of his day, especially Henry More, whose
works had been published from 1640 on, Cudworth, perhaps, and
their antecedents already discussed. Platonism was yet another
demonstration of the power of ideas to create and erode institutions.
And the conflation of Arianism and Platonism was also central to the
analogue Hobbes was drawing between the commotion caused by
heresy in Alexandria and the religious roots of the English civil war.
It was an identification that he was probably not the first to make.
Contemporary English senses of the term *hypostasis*, for instance,
reflected those in late Greek, as well as the usage by early modern
Neoplatonists and those who mocked them. So John Crowne's
depiction of the Neoplatonist in the Restoration drama *Sir Courtly
Nice*, is nicely Hobbesian: 'A Scholar . . . emptied by old suck-eggs
of all that nature gave me, and crumbl'd full of essences, hypostases,
and other stuff o' their baking'.[2]

While Hobbes clearly plays on central neo-Platonist themes, typically co-opting those elements that fit his theory, he excoriated the
Platonist divinization of man embraced by the Cambridge Platonists
in terms similar to his excoriation of the 'idolatry' of the Stoics. This
apparent paradox can once again be explained by his Erastianism
and the institutional threat the universities posed. Everard Digby had
first made the case that was later to engage Cambridge Platonists,
Benjamin Whichcote, Ralph Cudworth, Henry More and John
Smith, and which later became associated in particular with Nicolas
Malebranche (1638-1715), philosopher and theologian, priest of the
Oratory of St. Philip Neri in Paris, that 'we see all things in God', or

---

[1] *OED*, 1971 edn.
[2] See John Crowne *c.* 1640-*c.* 1703, English playwright, *Sir Courtly Nice, or It
cannot be* (1685), in *Dramatic Works*, 1874, vol. 3 p. 276.

that all things including the human mind and its contents, are an efflux of ideas in the mind of God. Reason permits man the ascent up the ladder of dialectic to divine wisdom, from which he descends to certain knowledge of the world, according to this view. While this might be a small step from the divinization of man, capable of great thought experiments, which Hobbes endorses, it presented a democratization of the idea that would have destabilized Hobbes's 'mortal god', Leviathan, or the state.

It is Platonism in the 'divine Plato' tradition to which Hobbes most strenuously objects, typical of the luminaries of Corpus Christi, the college of Richard Hooker, John Jewel, Henry Jackson, and John Rainolds, Greek Reader (1572-8) and President of the College (1599). Rainolds, at least five of whose works are included in Hobbes's list of the Hardwick Hall Library holdings (*q.v.*, below), was a typical humanist who believed in the mutually reinforcing wisdom of the scriptures and the pagan classical tradition, a view to which Hobbes and the Latitudinarians were hostile. In his famous lecture on the subject delivered in 1573 and published in Latin in 1613 (and in English in 1637, in Henry Jackson's translation), Rainold's claimed: 'The scriptures and profane writings are like Hippocrates' twins laughing together, weeping together, sicke together, and sound together'.[1] But Rainolds was a cautious Platonist, observing that 'Ficino "became superstitious" from reading Plato, and the "wild and graceless" Cornelius Agrippa and Nicholas Machiavelli have "polluted all Italy" with their Philosophy'.[2]

Some idea of the internationalism of Neoplatonism may be gained from the fact that Henry Jackson (1579-1640) named as his mentor the great humanist Juan Luis Vives, recruited by Cardinal Wolsey and subsequently lecturer in humanity at Corpus Christi. Vives, born in Valencia in 1492, was an influential Renaissance pedagogue, and one with a strong following in England. His works include a criticism of the studies and methods at the University of

---

[1] Hutton, 'Plato and the Tudor Academies', p. 120, citing *An Excellent Oration of the Late Famously Learned John Rainolds, DD . . . . very useful for all such as affect the Studies of Logick and Philosophie and admire profane learning*, ed. John Leycester (Oxford, 1637), p. 125.

[2] Rainolds, *An Excellent Oration*, p. 122, cited by Hutton, 'Plato and the Tudor Academies', p. 121.

Paris, in *Liber in Pseudodialecticos*; *De Ratione Studii Puerilis*, written upon the request of Catherine of Aragon to serve as a plan of study for Mary Tudor; *De Institutione Feminae Christianae*, a work commissioned by Queen Catherine which would become the leading theoretical manual on women's education of the sixteenth century; and *Satellitium*, a book of maxims for Mary Tudor.[1] Vives' monumental pedagogical work, *De Tradendis Disciplinis*, consisted of twenty books, seven books on the corruption of the Arts (included under the title of *De Causis Corruptarum Artium*); five on the transmission of the Arts (*De Tradendis Disciplinis*); the remaining eight books consisting of treatises on the Arts. Once again Vives is a thinker to whom Hobbes has an ambiguous relation, and I have elsewhere speculated that Vives may well have been Hobbes's source on the question of the relation of *verbum* and *res*, important for his nominalism.[2] As so often with Hobbes, he avails himself of the arguments of friends and enemies at will.

Vives, an eclectic Platonist who, like the others mentioned here, was well versed in Aristotle, recommended reading George of Trebizond, Giorgio Valla, Philip Melanchthon, Boethius, Martianus Capella, Apuleius, Poliziano and Greek interpreters of Aristotle in preference to the medieval commentators.[3] Jackson had himself studied with the Aristotelian logician, Richard Crakanthorpe, producing twelve books of theology and an early Platonist work, *The Eternal Truth of Scriptures* (1613). In his posthumous work, *The Primeval Estate of the First Man* (1654), Jackson, in addition to accepting the notion of a *theologia prisca*, betrayed his Aristotelian training by insisting on the logically fallacious position of most of those responsible for the 'combustion' of the Christian world, divided by sects and schisms. He in particular seeks to target predestinarian arguments by arguing a proto-Arminian and classically Cambridge

---

[1] Excerpted in Foster Watson, *Vives and the Renascence Education of Women* (London, Edward Arnold, 1912).

[2] See especially Vives, *De prima philosophia*, in his *Opera*, 2 vols, (Basle, 1555), vol. 1, pp. 532-3, trans. Richard Waswo, *Language and Meaning in the Renaissance* (Princeton, Princeton University Press, 1987), pp. 128-9. See Springborg, 'Hobbes and Epicurean Religion', p. 169.

[3] Hutton, 'Plato and the Tudor Academies', p. 118, citing Vives' pedagogical work, *De Tradendis Disciplinis* (Antwerp, 1531), IV.1.

Platonist philosophy of grace, leveling 'the charge of fallacious reasoning at the prince of the predestinarians, Theodore Bèze (Beza) himself'.[1] Jackson, not surprisingly, drew the ire of Puritan scholastics like Laurence Chaderton, William Perkins, Anthony Tuckney and William Twisse, by his recourse to Plato, 'that purveyor of "Aegyptian darkness"', Twisse commenting: 'I muse not a little to see Platonicall and Plotinicall Philosophy so much advanced by an Oxonian: as if Aristotles learning left logicians perplext in a point of sophistry and only Plotinicall Philosophy could expedite them'.[2]

It is odd that Platonism, as a philosophical movement of his time, has not been explored as a context for Hobbes's philosophy, given that he was in fact a contemporary of the leading Cambridge Platonists Ralph Cudworth (1617-1688) Henry More (1614-87), John Smith (1618-1652), Nathaniel Culverwell (1619-1651), and Richard Cumberland (1631-1718).[3] That he would have been acquainted with their works we can safely assume, given that they were systematically dedicated to refuting Hobbesian views, targeted in particular his materialism and his 'mortalism', the belief that the soul could not subsist without the body. Cambridge Platonists taught a spiritual metaphysics which turned to Cartesianism as a response to the 'materialism' of Hobbes, Boyle, Cavendish, and those who posited corporeal substance but denied immaterial substance. They argued that the concept of body proposed by the mechanists, particularly Hobbes, invited a non-mechanical explanation of its movement, which they ascribed to spiritual substance. For, if bodies consist of inert extended substance differentiated only by the size, shape and position of their constituent particles, they are incapable of self-motion. Accordingly, a motor of some kind must be posited and that, More claimed, was spirit, which drives so-to-speak the body in motion. More's theology, like that of Cudworth, was in many

---

[1] Hutton, 'Plato and the Tudor Academies', pp. 115-117.

[2] Hutton, 'Plato and the Tudor Academies', p. 117; at p. 115, citing W. Twisse, *Discovery of Doctor Jackson's Vanity* ([Amsterdam], 1631), p. 179. See also Sarah Hutton, 'Thomas Jackson, Oxford Platonist, and William Twisse, Aristotelian', *Journal of the History of Ideas*, vol. 39 (1978), pp. 635-52.

[3] Cumberland, Bishop of Peterborough from 1691, in his *De legibus naturae* (*On Natural Laws*) (1672), both propounded the doctrine of utilitarianism and explicitly opposed Hobbes's 'egoistic ethics'.

respects defensive, a reaction to materialism which saw Platonism and Cartesianism as the best redoubt against atheism. As he put it at the close of *An Antidote against Atheisme*, published a year after *Leviathan*, 'That Saying is not less true in Politicks, *No Bishop, no King,* than this in Metaphysics, *No spirit, no God*'.

More, in some ways Hobbes's most formidable adversary, in his *Enchiridion ethicum* (1667), had argued for the essential goodness of human nature, translated into virtuous action under the direction of the 'boniform faculty', through which the principles of morality are imprinted on the soul. Elaborating a philosophy of spirit diametrically opposed to Hobbesian materialism, he undertook to explain all the phenomena of mind and of the physical world as the activity of spiritual substance controlling inert matter. He thought of both spirit and body as spatially extended, but defined spiritual substance as the obverse of material extension: where body is inert and solid, but divisible, spirit is active and penetrable, but indivisible. It was in his correspondence with Descartes that he first expounded his view that all substance, whether material or immaterial, is extended. He proposed space, within which material extension is contained, as an example of non-material extension, anticipating Newton by arguing that space is infinite. More also argued that God, who is an infinite spirit, is an extended being (*res extensa*). There are, therefore, conceptual parallels between the idea of God and the idea of space, a view that he elaborates in *Enchiridion metaphysicum* (1671), maintaining the parallel even with respect to the properties of space which, analogous to the attributes of God, comprise infinity, immateriality, immobility etc. More specifically challenged Hobbes, whom he considered an atheist, and whose dismissal of the idea of incorporeal substance he considered nonsensical. Although More's philosophical project was mainly devoted to demonstrating the existence and providential nature of God by proving the existence of incorporeal substance, or spirit, he was also interested in contemporary science. For More, as for Cudworth, seventeenth century physics (the so-called mechanical philosophy), offered the most satisfactory explanation of phenomena in the physical world and for that reason he seized on Descartes' physics, recommending that Cartesianism be taught in the universities.

There were points of contact between the Platonists and Hobbes, but their philosophies of mind were diametrically opposed. Ralph

Cudworth and Henry More conceptualized the soul as a spiritual, self-active, incorporeal substance; and consciousness as a redoubling of the soul. So Cudworth proposed as a 'psychological hypothesis':[1]

> there must be in the soul one common focus or centre . . . in which all is recollected and knit together, something that is conscious of all congruities, both higher and lower, of all the cogitations, powers, and faculties of the soul . . . . Now this is the whole soul redoubled on to itself, which both comprehends itself and, holding itself as it were in its own hands, turns itself this way and that way . . . this is the . . . (autoekastos), that which is properly called 'I myself in every man'.

John Smith, by contrast, held the movement of ideas to be analogical to the movement of sensations, transforming the latter from spiritual to physical entities, at the same time making claims for human access to revealed truth that Hobbes would have considered outrageous:[2]

> the souls of men are as capable of conversing with it, though it does not naturally arise out of the fecundity of their own Understanding, as they are with any Sensible and External Objects. And as our Sensations carry the motions of Material things to our Understandings which were before unacquainted with them, so there is some Analogical way whereby the knowledge of Divine Truth may also be revealed to us.

He subscribed to the notion of spirit as an ecstatic union of the soul and divine substance, claiming that 'indeed without such an internal sensating Faculty as this is we should never know when our souls are in conjunction with the Deity or be able to relish the ineffable sweetness of True Happiness.'[3] The search for spiritual entities, vehicles of the soul, took the Cambridge Platonists in the direction of Neoplatonist pneumatology. The newly re-introduced doctrine of innate ideas and Cambridge Platonist Plotinian *nous* coalesced in a view of

---

[1] See John Muirhead, *The Platonic Tradition in Anglo-Saxon Philosophy* (New York, Macmillan), 1931, 64-5, quoting from the Cudworth MSS at the British Museum, vol. 4, p. 106.

[2] John Smith, 'Of Prophecy', *Select Discourses* (London, 1660; New York, Scholars Facsimiles and Reprints, 1979), p. 170.

[3] John Smith, 'A Discourse concerning the True Way of attaining to Divine Knowledge', *Select Discourses*, p. 2.

the world in which ideas in the mind of God that lay at the foundation of the world were held to be both present in germ in the soul and out there to be 'seen' in the world. As a consequence Cambridge Platonists described the processes of perception in a number of characteristic metaphors in which the individual is a spectator on the cosmic stage; by appealing to Platonist images of light and shadows to explain the principles of intelligibility and their surrogates; and by reference to music, harmony, numbers and specifically geometry as the fabric out of which the foundations of the world were built. Smith exhorted his followers, 'the Soul itself hath its sense, as well as the Body', declaring that 'to know the Divine Goodness, calls not for *Speculation* but Sensation, *taste and see* how good the Lord is'.[1] Cambridge Platonists' preoccupations with optic metaphors led them to seek a medium of translation between the soul and God, most simply expressed in the notion of the mind as mirror of God, from which they inferred the 'deification of man', nowhere more clearly stated than by Smith:[2]

> As the eye cannot behold the Sun . . . unless it be Sunlike, and hath the form and resemblance of the Sun drawn in it; so neither can the Soul of man behold God . . . . unless it be Godlike, hath God formed in it, and made partaker of the Divine Nature.

These were provocative views, directly hostile to the materialist metaphysics proposed by *Galileo, Gassendi, Bacon and Hobbes. This consideration, taken together with the timing of the works, most of which were published in the 1650s and 60s, suggests a direct response on Hobbes's part, in his long disquisitions on incorporeal substance, inspiration and Divine ideas in *Leviathan* and the *Historia Ecclesiastica*. Not inconsequentially, as we shall see, he melded Cartesianism to Platonism in his general attack on idealism.

---

[1] John Smith, 'A Discourse concerning the True Way', p. 3.
[2] John Smith, 'A Discourse concerning the True Way', pp. 2-3:
As the eye cannot behold the Sun . . . unless it be Sunlike, and hath the form and resemblance of the Sun drawn in it; so neither can the Soul of man behold God . . . . unless it be Godlike, hath God formed in it, and made partaker of the Divine Nature.

CHAPTER 6

THE *HISTORIA ECCLESIASTICA* AND HOBBES'S PHILOSOPHICAL PROJECT

6.1 SCEPTICISM AND HOBBES'S PHILOSOPHY

Hobbes the Deist and Hobbes the atheist have until recently over-shadowed serious consideration of Hobbes's 'First Philosophy', in which dreams and phantasms once again have a serious role to play. That the *Historia Ecclesiastica*, at least at one level, is to be read as an epitome of Hobbes's *philosophia prima*, we know from the appearance of recurrent *topoi* that dominate his works from the *Elements*, to his *Objections to Descartes* and *De corpore*. But before turning to these matters, let us note that if, in the final form in which we have it, the *Historia Ecclesiastica* was one more attempt on Hobbes's part to ensure that his philosophical legacy was understood, his *Vita carmine expressa*, in a much more condensed form, was another. There, with a rare acknowledgment of his sources, Hobbes set out his own contribution to philosophy in a paradigmatic way.[1]

Dating the fundamental formulation of his philosophy to the period 1634-37, while touring Italy and France, Hobbes declares that, 'whether sailing, riding, or driving' ('Seu rate, seu curru sive

---

[1] Hobbes *Vita carmine expressa* (London, 1679), p. 4, reprinted in *OL* I, pp. 89-90. See the excellent essay by Gianni Paganini, 'Hobbes and the Continental Tradition of Scepticism', in José R. Maia Neto and Richard H. Popkin, eds, *Scepticism in Renaissance and Post-Renaissance Thought* (London, Journal of the History of Philosophy and Humanity Books, 2004, pp. 65-105), at pp. 76-7, which I paraphrase here.

ferebar equo'), he had been constantly preoccupied with the question of 'the nature of things' ('perpetuo naturam cogito rerum'), being forced to conclude that 'only one thing in the whole universe is true, though falsified in many ways' ('Et mihi visa quidem est toto res unica mundo/Vera licet multis falsificata modis'). And that one thing is matter in motion, the 'only true basis of those things that falsely we say are something' ('Unica vera quidam, sed quae sit basis earum/ Rerum quas falso dicimus esse aliquid'). Preoccupied with the sceptical dichotomy between appearances and reality, his self-declared achievement was to establish that 'phantasmata' or the fruit of our brains ('nostri soboles cerebri'), do not correspond to anything outside the mind ('nihil extra'), but are only an effect of the movement of its inner parts. About these twin discoveries, that the fantasies of the imagination are due to the inner working or the mind; and that they have an ontological basis in matter in motion, Hobbes declares he wrote nothing ('Scribo nihil'), communicating them only in private conversations with Mersenne and his circle. Indeed, Hobbes claims, somewhat disingenuously, that he owes his discoveries to no author, no text and no adversary, apart from Nature who was always his teacher ('magistra/Quae docuit, praesens nam mihi semper erat'); and that it was precisely these twin discoveries 'that commended him to this circle of philosophers, among whom he was to be henceforth numbered' ('Is probat et multis commendat; tempore ab illo/ Inter philosophos et numerabar ego').

The significance of Hobbes's *philosophia prima* tends to be underestimated in Anglophone Hobbes scholarship, based mainly on his English works and heavily tilted towards *Leviathan* and the political philosophy. So, Quentin Skinner in response to Yves Charles Zarka in *The Amsterdam Debate*, argued:[1]

> I see no evidence that Hobbes was even faintly interested in Pyrrhonism, let alone relativism. He is not I think responding to an epistemological crisis at all . . . . Nor was he at all interested in the technical claims put forward by self avowed sceptics, whether

[1] See *The Amsterdam Debate*, (in French), Yves Charles Zarka and Quentin Skinner, 'Deux interprétations de Hobbes', *Le Débat*, vol. 96 (1997), pp. 92-107; (in English) Quentin Skinner and Yves Charles Zarka, *Hobbes: the Amsterdam Debate*, ed. Hans Blom (Hildesheim, George Olms Verlag, 2001), pp. 21-2; noted in Paganini, 'Hobbes and the Continental Tradition of Scepticism', p. 100 n. 32.

pyrrhonian or academic. What I try to show is that that points us in the wrong direction. What Hobbes is really preoccupied with is the neo-classical art of rhetoric and its view about what it is to conduct an argument.

But as I shall try to show here, Hobbes's preoccupation with the neo-classical art of rhetoric was not at odds with his epistemology, but rather a corollary of it.

The European Republic of Letters, which still tends to read Hobbes in Latin, has given the *philosophia prima* much more attention.[1] In a series of important articles Gianni Paganini has traced the aetiology of Hobbes's scepticism and his innovative solution posed in response to that 'itinerary of doubt par excellence: Descartes' *First Meditation*'.[2] Hobbes, in his *Objectiones*, was dismissive of Descartes' originality on the question of 'What can be called into doubt', folding him into company of 'Plato and other ancient philosophers [who] discussed this uncertainty in the objects of the senses'. But he nevertheless recognized the importance of Descartes' reflections and continued to address the problem in the terms in which Descartes posed it, in particular the impossibility of

---

[1] For an impressive outpouring of work on Hobbes's first philosophy from European scholars, I single out only a few items. See the many essays by Gianni Paganini listed below; see also the work of Charles Zarka, *La Décision métaphysique de Hobbes, Conditions de la politique* (Paris, Vrin, 2nd edn 1999), p. 33; Zarka, 'First Philosophy and the Foundations of Knowledge', in *The Cambridge Companion to Hobbes*, ed Tom Sorell (Cambridge, Cambridge University Press, 1996), pp. 62-85; Zarka, 'Le Vocabulaire de l'apparaitre: champ sémantique de la notion de *phantasma*', in *Hobbes et son vocabulaire: Etudes de lexicographie philosophique*, Yves Charles Zarka and Jean Bernhardt, eds (Paris, Vrin, 1992) pp. 13-29; and Zarka and Jean Bernhardt, eds, *Thomas Hobbes Philosophie première, théorie de la science et politique* (Paris: P.U.F., 1990). See particularly Hobbes's *De corpore,* introduction, édition critique latine, annotation par Karl Schuhmann, *Thomas Hobbes œuvres complètes* (Paris, Vrin, 2000); and Schuhmann's 'Phantasms and Idols: True Philosophy and Wrong Religion in Hobbes', *Rivista di Storia della Filosofia*, vol. 59, 1 (2004), 15-31. See also the works of Cees Leijenhorst, mentioned above.

[2] See Paganini, 'Hobbes and the Continental Tradition of Scepticism', p. 66; Paganini, 'Montaigne, Sanches et la Connaissance par Phénomènes: Les Usages Modernes d'un Paradigme Ancien', in *Montaigne, Scepticisme, Métaphysique, Théologie*, ed. Vincent Carraud and Jean-Luc Marion (Paris, P.U.F., 2004), pp. 107-35; and Paganini, 'Hobbes Among Ancient and Modern Sceptics: Phenomena and Bodies', in Paganini, ed., *The Return of Scepticism: From Hobbes and Descartes to Bayle* (Dordrecht, Klüwer, 2003), pp. 3-35.

finding a criterion ('nullum esse *kriterion*') to distinguish between reality and appearance, as illustrated in the case of dreams.[1] So what at first appears in *Leviathan* and the *Historia Ecclesiastica* to be a characteristic resort to the Epicurean *topos* of fear,[2] and its classical expression in the work of Horace and others, is also a serious disquisition on this epistemological problem that lies at the heart of the sceptics' dilemma. It was a problem to which Hobbes had a solution so original that it alone sufficed to admit him into the company of Mersenne and his circle, as in his *Vita* he boldly claims.

Nor was Hobbes simply reacting to Descartes. As Paganini notes, the problem of distinguishing the sensations experienced in dreams from those experienced in waking, raised also by the Epicureans as we have seen, was one of the most classical formulations of scepticism from Cicero's *Academica*, through the writings of Sextus Empiricus, to Montaigne's *Apologie de Raimond Sebond*. Hobbes had addressed it as early as the *Elements of Law*, where it holds a privileged place. There he already stated, there is 'no criterion or mark by which he [a man] can discern whether it were a dream or not . . . nor is it impossible for a man to be so far deceived, as when his dream is past, to think it real'.[3] Again in his critique of Thomas White's *De Mundo* Hobbes had expressed himself on the sceptics' problem of discriminating between appearance and reality, once again formulated in terms of the impossibility of discriminating between experience sleeping and waking in terms of sensations ('dormientium phantasmata').[4] In *Leviathan*, the short opening chapter 'Of Sense' is immediately followed by chapter 2, 'Of Imagination', in which dreams have pride of place. There he argued that

---

[1] See Thomas Hobbes, *Meditationes: Objectiones tertiae cum responsionibus authoris*, in René Descartes, *Meditationes de prima philosophia*, *Œuvres*, ed. C. Adam and P. Tannery (Paris, Vrin, 1897-1913), vol. 7, p. 171. English translation in *The Philosophical Writings of Descartes*, trans. J. Cottingham, R. Stoothoff and D. Murdoch (Cambridge, Cambridge University Press, 1984), vol. 2, p. 121, cited in Paganini, 'Hobbes and the Continental Tradition of Scepticism', p. 66 and notes.

[2] See Hobbes on dreams, *Lev.*, ii, §§5-7, 6-8/9-11.

[3] Hobbes, *Elements*, I, iii, 10, p. 12. See Paganini, 'Hobbes and the Continental Tradition of Scepticism', p. 88.

[4] Hobbes, 'De motu, loco et tempore', in *Critique du 'De Mundo' de Thomas White*, critical edition of an unpublished text, ed. Jean Jacquot and Harold Whitmore Jones (Paris, Vrin, 1973), p. 327. See Paganini, 'Hobbes and the Continental Tradition of Scepticism', p. 89.

'a Dreame must needs be more cleare, in this silence of sense, than are our waking thoughts', concluding: 'And hence it cometh to pass, that it is a hard matter, and by many thought impossible, to distinguish exactly between sense and dreaming'. The problem of illusion is not inconsequential for religion and, although avoiding the path taken by Descartes of attributing reality to illusion, Hobbes nevertheless argues that it is precisely 'From this ignorance of how to distinguish dreams and other strong fancies from vision and sense did arise the greatest part of the religion of the gentiles in time past, that worshipped satyrs, fawns, nymphs', etc.[1]

In formulating the problem of fantasms and illusion famous sceptics preceded him, notably Michel de Montaigne, whose solution in the *Apologie* is a striking anticipation of Hobbes's. The English translation by John Florio, *The Essayes of Michael Lord of Montaigne* (1603), reads:[2]

> Our phantasie doth not apply itself to strange things, but is rather conceived by the interposition of senses; and senses cannot comprehend a strange subject [substance]; nay, not so much as their owne passions: and so, nor the phantasie, nor the apparence is the subject's [substance's], but rather the passion's only, and the sufferance of the sense: which passion and subjects [substances] are diverse things: Therefore, who judgeth by apparences, judgeth by a thing different from the subject [substance].

Moreover Montaigne goes on to introduce the problem of the criterion ('instrument judicatoire'), the kernel of scepticism for Hobbes, in a passage that in Florio's translation reads:[3]

> To judge of the apparences that we receive of subjects [substances], we had need have a judicatorie instrument: to verifie this instrument

---

[1] *Lev.*, ii, §§5-8, 6-8/9-11, cited by Paganini, 'Hobbes and the Continental Tradition of Scepticism', p. 88.

[2] See Michel de Montaigne, *Les Essais*, ed. Pierre Villey (Paris, P.U.F., 1999), II, xii, 'Apologie de Raimond Sebond', 2:601; and the translation by John Florio, *The Essayes of Michael Lord of Montaigne* (1603), ed. Henry Morley (London, Routledge, 1886), p. 309a, cited by Paganini, 'Hobbes and the Continental Tradition of Scepticism', p. 88 and notes.

[3] Montaigne, *Les Essais*. I have bracketed 'subject', for as Paganini notes, p. 97 n. 30, 'Montaigne speaks of "sujet" ("subject") while thinking of substance ("subjectum") that for us would rather be the object, the thing and not the knower'.

we should have demonstratio; and to approve demonstration, an instrument: thus are we ever turning round.

What marks the radical difference between Hobbes and Descartes, apparent as early as Hobbes's *Objectiones tertiae* to Descartes' *Meditations*, and published with it, is Hobbes's refusal to grant an *a priori* correspondence between things in themselves and our representations of them. He early abandoned the notion that our representations were in any way 'copies' of the objects perceived, a presupposition maintained by Descartes even in the case of 'false illusions' induced by dreams ('veluti quasdam pictas imagines').[1] In the case of 'primary qualities' (extension, shape, size, number, place and time), that is, the 'most simple and universal' objects of cognition ('magis simplicia et universalia'), Descartes maintained, our representations were 'true' copies of reality, 'from which we form all the images of things, whether true or false, that occur in our thought'.[2] This presupposition held not only for simple cognitions but also for complex ideas – or even theories, such as mathematics, where the notions of arithmetic and geometry, Descartes also believed to be true 'images' of reality. It even held for illusions, so 'the visions that come in sleep are like paintings, which must have been fashioned in the likeness of things that are real',[3] Descartes maintained, attributing 'delusions of dreams (ludificationes somniorum)' to some malicious demon, 'devised to ensnare my judgment'.[4]

---

[1] Descartes, *Meditationes de prima philosophia*, Meditation 1, *Œuvres de Descartes*, ed. by C. Adam and P. Tannery (Paris, Cerf, 1896-1913), vol. 7, p. 19.

[2] Descartes, *Meditationes*, Meditation 1, *Œuvres*, vol. 7, p. 20: 'ex quibus tanquam coloribus veris omnes istae, seu verae, seu falsae, quae in cogitatione nostra sunt, rerum imagines effinguntur'. Paganini, 'Hobbes and the Continental Tradition of Scepticism', p. 93 n. 3, notes on 'tanquam rerum imagines', the contributions by Raul Landim Filho, 'Idée et représentation', and Edwin Curley, 'Hobbes contre Descartes', in Jean-Marie Beyssade and Jean-Luc Marion, eds *Descartes: Objecter et répondre* (Paris, P.U.F., 1994), pp. 187-203, and 149-62, respectively.

[3] 'tamen profecto fatendum est visa per quietem esse veluti quasdam pictas imagines, quae non nisi ad similitudinem rerum verarum fingi potuerunt . . .'. Descartes, *Meditationes de prima philosophia*, Meditation 1, *Œuvres*, vol. 7, p. 19.

[4] Descartes, *Meditationes*, Meditation 1, *Œuvres*, vol. 7, p. 22; English translation in *The Philosophical Writings of Descartes*, tr. by John Cottingham, Robert Stoothoff, and Dugald Murdoch (Cambridge, Cambridge University Press, 1985), vol. 2, p. 15; cited in Paganini, 'Hobbes and the Continental Tradition of Scepticism', p. 67 and notes.

Defining the *res cogitans* as immaterial substance; distinguishing between 'idea' and sensible 'image'; and resorting to the 'idea of God' to derive 'the certainty of the existence of material things' ('de materialium existentia'),[1] Descartes had introduced a route of argumentation that Hobbes systematically rejected. Because he insisted that even delusions have real referents, he was forced to introduce this *deus ex machina* in the form of a 'deceptive God' or an 'evil genius' to explain error or misconceptions. In the *Historia Ecclesiastica*, where Hobbes mockingly discusses spectres, attributing to them manipulation of the masses against their king by an 'evil genius', quite possibly he has Descartes in mind.[2]

Hobbes's is not, however, a relentless scepticism:[3]

> In *Objectiones* Hobbes does not even mention the hypothesis of the evil genius and cuts off at the roots the resort to theological conceptions. In this way, he was able to keep within the perimeter described by traditional arguments of classical scepticism and to reject those arguments that appeared as artificial and forced hypotheses even to other critics of Descartes of a 'sceptical' temper (such as Gassendi). Furthermore, even at the initial phase of doubt, Hobbes detached himself from Descartes at a very significant point. Where in the *Meditationes* Descartes describes a relationship of similarity ('imago', 'similitudo') between representations and things, if only to cast doubt on it, Hobbes takes a very different route, which leads him to consider 'conceptiones' as effects and not as images. The route he takes is that of the description of psychological entities in the more general framework of a mechanistic psychology, with all it involves in terms of the ontology of mental representations. These appear to Hobbes as 'phantasmata' regardless of whether they occur during waking or in dreams ('phantasmata, quae vigilantes & sententientes habemus'). In both cases these phantasms are 'accidents' that are not inherent to external objects, nor do they provide absolutely evidential arguments to support a real existence 'without us' ('non esse accidentia objectis externis inhaerentia, neque argumento esse talia objecta externa omnio existere'). Hobbes therefore concludes that if we follow our senses without any other reasoning 'we shall be justified in doubting whether anything exists' ('Ideoque si sensus nostros sine aliâ ratiocinatione sequamur, merito

---

[1] See Paganini, 'Hobbes and the Continental Tradition of Scepticism', p. 66.
[2] See *Hist. Eccl.*, lines 91-100.
[3] Paganini, 'Hobbes and the Continental Tradition of Scepticism', pp. 67-8.

dubitabimus an aliquid existat, necne'). Apparently, the result is the same as that of Descartes, that is total *epoche* with respect to knowledge of the external world ('accurate deinceps assensionem esse cohibendam, si quid certi velim invenire'), and in this sense Hobbes is right to claim also for himself the 'truth' of this *Meditation*. In reality, this is a result at the same time more sceptical and less sceptical than Descartes'.

What was both most radical and most innovative about Hobbes's formulation was the paradox of the 'deception of sense' underpinned by a materialist ontology, on the one hand, and its resolution by means of ratiocination, on the other. Hobbes's physics establishes the fundamental principle of atomism, that matter at rest remains at rest unless acted upon; and its corollary, that matter in motion remains in motion unless impeded.[1] It is from this axiom that Hobbes moves to sense and a sensationalist psychology in which the mind is activated by the friction exerted on the senses by matter from the external world: 'And as pressing, rubbing, or striking the eye, makes us fancy a light; and pressing the ear, produceth a din, so do the bodies also we see, or hear, produce the same by their strong, though unobserved action'.[2] Optics supplies a technical account of how perception allows the transfer of images, produced by the abrasions of the external world, from the retina to the brain: 'pressure, by the mediation of nerves and other strings and membranes of the body, continued inwards to the brain, and heart, causeth there a resistance, or counter-pressure, or endeavour of the heart to deliver itself'.[3]

But we have no grounds to assume a correspondence between our cognitions and their objects. Quite the contrary. By the 'deception of sense', Hobbes characterized the delusion whereby external stimuli, reaching the brain through 'animal spirits', and traveling in an arc from the sense organs to the nerves and then to the brain, 'rebound' to give the sensation or 'phantasma', an internal reaction, the

---

[1] *Lev.*, ii, §1, 4/7:

> That when a thing lies still, unless somewhat else stir it, it will lie still for ever, is a truth that no man doubts of. But that when a thing is in motion, it will eternally be in motion, unless somewhat else stay it, though the reason be the same, (namely, that nothing can change itself), is not so easily assented to.

[2] *Lev.*, i, §4, 4/7.
[3] *Lev.*, i, §4, 4/6.

character of exteriority.[1] So 'image and colour is but an apparition unto us of that motion, agitation or alteration, which the object worketh in the brain, or spirits, or some internal substance in the head'.[2] Framed in his materialist ontology, sensation thus becomes an illustration of matter in motion and its consequences.[3] But the 'deception of sense' presents a paradox that only reason can resolve.

Such a daring solution to the problem of freedom and necessity, which can admit the one without denying the other, was not reached by Hobbes immediately, Paganini noting that in the *Elements* he still implied that 'the deceit of the senses will be remedied by the senses themselves ("this is the greatest deception of sense, which also is by sense to be corrected") or that "ratiocination" simply starts from "principles that are found indubitable by experience"', the old Baconian formula that Hobbes was later to reject.[4] Paganini is specific about what differentiates Hobbes's phenomenalism from its predecessors:[5]

> Compared with other less radical versions (such as Galileo's distinction between primary and secondary qualities, or Descartes' . . . distinction between 'natura corporea in communi' and sensible appearances), Hobbes's reduction in the *Elements* is much more extensive, since it also involves the quantitative structure of sensory representations: not only color, sound, smell and heat, but also shape, position, and visual data attesting to geometrical properties, all sensory data in general are involved in the reduction to phenomena ('apparitions'), that are 'nothing without': 'accidents or qualities' that 'are not there' but only in the subject.

---

[1] Paganini, 'Hobbes and the Continental Tradition of Scepticism', p. 71, 79 and notes.

[2] Hobbes, *Elements* I, ii, 7, p. 5, the repetition of an almost identical sentence at *Elements* I, ii, 5, p. 4, as Paganini, 'Hobbes and the Continental Tradition of Scepticism', observes (p. 96, n. 24).

[3] Paganini, 'Hobbes and the Continental Tradition of Scepticism', pp. 71, citing *Elements* I, II, 9, p. 7, and 79.

[4] Paganini, 'Hobbes and the Continental Tradition of Scepticism', p. 71, stresses the radicalism of Hobbes's phenomenalism, remarked upon already by Richard Tuck in his essay, 'Hobbes and Descartes', in G. A. J. Rogers and Alan Ryan, eds., *Perspectives on Thomas Hobbes* (Oxford, Clarendon Press, 1988), pp. 28-9, as one of the fundamental steps in 'the invention of modern philosophy', and Descartes, Gassendi, and Hobbes's 'great novelty'.

[5] Paganini, 'Hobbes and the Continental Tradition of Scepticism', p. 71.

Paganini notes that in the *Elements*, where Hobbes rarely uses the term 'phantasm', which he employs in his mature theory, but rather the terms 'image' and 'representation', the copy theory of truth seems to linger. But in the course of chapter two of that work, he already develops the phenomenalist argument that 'sensible qualities are "seemings and apparitions only", they do not exist "without us really", although "our senses makes us think" that they are there'.[1] It is in *De corpore*, however, that he makes the connection between his materialist ontology and his sceptical epistemology for the first time. There, matter-in-motion in the physiology of the human brain is posited as the *cause* of *phantasmata* which, so far from being exact copies of the objects perceived, are representations indistinguishable from the phantasms of dreams, were it not for the active power of reason called in to verify them.[2] For, in *De corpore*, which opens with the famous thought experiment of 'the feigned annihilation of the world' ('ficta universi sublatio'), body ('corpus', Hobbes's synonym for 'substantia') 'is presented as an entity "subsistens per se", "existens", that is – by definition – existing "extra nos"', as Paganini notes:[3]

> In the same way, because it is understood not through the senses but through reason ('non sensibus sed ratione tantum'), substance is denominated 'Suppositum et Subjectum'; engaging the double meaning of 'suppositum': underlying, that lies beneath the accidents, but also conjectured, hypothesized by means of a rational inference.

What is most remarkable about the phantasms that survive the thought experiment of the annihilation of the world, is that 'they present themselves as the residue of previous experiences ... deriv[ing] therefore from an a posteriori origin that relates to the

---

[1] See Hobbes, *Elements*, I, ii, 4, p. 3: 'That the subject wherein colour and image are inherent, is not the object or thing seen'. 'That that is nothing without us really which we call an image or colour', cited by Paganini, 'Hobbes and the Continental Tradition of Scepticism', p. 95, n. 19.

[2] Paganini, 'Hobbes and the Continental Tradition of Scepticism', p. 71, citing Hobbes's *Elements*, I, ii, 4, p. 4.

[3] Paganini, 'Hobbes and the Continental Tradition of Scepticism', p. 84, citing Hobbes's *De Corpore: Elementorum Philosophiae Sectio Prima,* critical edition, notes, appendices, and index by Karl Schuhmann (Paris, Vrin, 2000), 8.1.82-3.

empirical foundations of Hobbes's entire philosophy . . .
describ[ing] the spectral reality of a world in which the whole of past
experience is reduced to memory or at best enlivened by the fatuous
light of imagination'.[1] It was a small step from here to resolving the
sceptical paradox:[2]

> if phenomena or 'accidents' are no longer considered in themselves
> as a reality external to the subject, but rather as 'effects' ('effects
> produced in the percipient subject by objects that act on the sense
> organs'), the application of a principle (not empirical, but rational)
> like that of cause permits one to indicate motion as the universal
> cause of changes, motion called upon to explain that complex
> process examined in chapter 25 of *De corpore* in connection with
> 'Phantasmatis generatio'. The principle of causality thus constitutes
> the 'dogmatic' bastion of Hobbes's entire philosophy: doubt is
> never thrown on it, indeed it represents the assumption on which is
> based the link between the 'internal' sphere of sensible perception
> and . . . 'external' reality. Bodies in movement are literally the only
> concrete 'res' that really exist, as Hobbes expounded in [his] *Vita*
> and as he had explained in *De corpore*, claiming that bodies are
> 'things' and, moreover, 'things' not 'generated', whereas 'the acci-
> dents under which they variously appear' (and among the accidents,
> phenomena, appearances, sensible qualities are in the forefront) are
> 'generated', they are not 'things'.

In other words, Hobbes has found a criterion, but perhaps not one
that the classical sceptic would recognize. His solution had been
foreshadowed by Pierre Gassendi, who arrived at dual criteria in a
formulation that also anticipates Hobbes on the 'sign' and the 'signified'.[3] On the one hand we have the senses, which can deceive, and
on the other ratiocination, which can solve the puzzle of sense, for
'we understand through ratiocination the hidden thing: that is, the
mind, the intellect or reason'.[4] Both Hobbes and Gassendi saw

---

[1] Paganini, 'Hobbes and the Continental Tradition of Scepticism', p. 85.

[2] Paganini, 'Hobbes and the Continental Tradition of Scepticism', p. 86, citing
Hobbes, *De corpore*, 25.1.267, and *De corpore* 8.20.92.

[3] For Hobbes on signs, see *Lev.*, iii, §8, 11/14, and *Lev.*, iv, §3, 14/16-17, cited
by Paganini, 'Hobbes and the Continental Tradition of Scepticism', p. 88.

[4] ('altertum quo ipsam rem latentem ratiocinando intelligamus: Mens nempe,
Intellectus, seu Ratio'). See Gassendi, *Syntagma Philosophicum*, Pars Prima, quae
est Logica, lib. II, 'De Logicae Fine', cap IV, 'Veritatis critera qui ponant', in *Opera
Omnia in sex tomos divisa*, vol. 1, Lugduni, Sumptibus Laurentii Anisson et Ioan

ratiocination as the ability to make a rational calculation, deductive reason, to be distinguished from Aristotelian induction which hypothesizes *a priori* our ability to arrive at truth on the basis of experience. Although rejecting dogmatic philosophy of the standard Platonist and Aristotelian variety, Hobbes looks for certitude elsewhere, by marrying his mechanistic psychology to a materialist ontology, and this is his stroke of genius.

In Hobbes's mechanistic psychology it is axiomatic that sensations, a term he uses interchangeably with cognitions, are *caused* by the friction on the sense organs of external stimuli, thus providing a dogmatic basis for his sceptical epistemology. It is a psychology that is both deterministic and indeterminate with respect to truth. Because they are simply a physical reaction to a physical stimulus, registering properties internal to the organism, sensations can bring with them no warranty of the durability of the external world. The 'deception of sense', whereby the responses of the receptor are read as evidence for the existence of the object perceived, would be a *cul de sac*, the experiences of dreams being as vivid and compelling as those of waking, were it not for the power of ratiocination.[1] And here Hobbes introduces the standard delusions to which the sceptic appeals in discussing the paradox of appearances versus reality: the impression that the sun moves around the earth, the reflections of objects in water, double vision, the acoustical phenomena of echoes, etc., his purpose being to show that 'by our several organs we have several conceptions of several qualities in the objects'. And although this appear to be 'a great paradox', he observes, it is important to keep the 'image' or representation – for instance the 'image of

---

Bapt. Devenet, 1658 (anastatic reprint, introduced by Tullio Gregory, Stuttgart-Bad Cannstatt, Frommann, 1964), p. 80b, cited by Paganini, 'Hobbes and the Continental Tradition of Scepticism', p. 82, and notes. That Gassendi explicitly placed himself in the sceptical tradition, is clear from the following statement (*Ibid.*):

Alioquin Sceptici vulgo admittant *ta phainomena apparentia*, seu *id quod res apparent*; ideo utramque veritatem circa id quod apparet, relinquunt ... apparentiam exsistere non dubitant (imo et existere rem quampiam sub apparentia non ambigunt, sed solum qualis ea sit minimè sciri argumentantur) et verè enunciari, iudicarique talem apparentiam exhiberi non controvertunt.

[1] Descartes, *Meditationes*, Meditation 1, *Œuvres*, vol. 7, p. 22 (English translation in *The Philosophical Writings of Descartes*, vol. 2, p. 15), cited in Paganini, 'Hobbes and the Continental Tradition of Scepticism', p. 67 and notes.

vision'. – and 'the very qualities themselves' (i.e., the objective qualities), distinct. So, he argues, 'the subject wherein colour and image are inherent is not the object or thing seen . . . their inherence is not [in] the object, but [in] the sentient'.[1] And here reason enters as the key to Hobbes's resolution of the paradox of scepticism:

> Having established the equivalence between having an idea and imagining ('ideam aliquam habere' means 'imaginari'), in the *Objectiones*, he clearly states that we have no 'idea' of substance, and this holds not only for God and the soul ('unimaginable' substances by definition) but also for what Hobbes considers as substance par excellence and in the true sense, the body understood as 'materia subjecta accidentibus & mutationibus'. Substance can be inferred only through reasoning ('sola ratiocinatione evincitur'). This statement, attributed without further clarification 'also to the old Aristotelians', casts a radical doubt on one of the cornerstones of Descartes' metaphysical realism (the theory of the 'realitas objectiva' of ideas) and more generally suggests a scenario in which, while not denying the existence of a real background made of substances and bodies, nevertheless Hobbes stresses the impossibility of representing it directly by limiting the realm of immediate perception [of] 'phantasms' to 'accidents'. This distinction between the world of essences and substances, inaccessible to direct knowledge, and the realm of 'accidents', the world of sensible phenomena, was one of the chief inheritances left by Sextus's scepticism to the neo-Pyrrhonian schools of the seventeenth century.

As Paganini remarks, here Hobbes is both more and less sceptical than his adversary, Descartes.[2] He is more sceptical in finding in sense data no evidential objectivity, and less sceptical in claiming to show the very phenomenon of sensation as simply a ramification of the rule of the physical world: matter in motion. Doubtless his ontology and epistemology owe much to Galileo, whom Hobbes had met in Florence in 1635, and whom he saluted in the dedication of *De Corpore* as the founder of modern physics ('Galilaeus primus aperuit nobis Physicae universae portam primam, natural motûs').[3]

---

[1] See Paganini, 'Hobbes and the Continental Tradition of Scepticism', p. 70, citing *Elements*, I, ii, 3-4, pp. 3-4.

[2] Paganini, 'Hobbes and the Continental Tradition of Scepticism', pp. 68-9, citing Hobbes's *Objectiones* in Descartes, *Œuvres*, vol. 7, pp. 178 and 185, notes.

[3] See Paganini, 'Hobbes and the Continental Tradition of Scepticism', p. 77.

Galileo subscribed also to the subjectivity of sensible qualities, contributing to the development of scientific instruments like the telescope, which made the new science of optics possible. Hobbes had a personal collection of telescopes and was involved in purchases of 'glasses' for his patrons. Perhaps not surprisingly, Newcastle, one of those patrons, appears also to have subscribed to the subjectivity of sensible qualities, as implied in Hobbes's reference in a letter of August 1636 – which seems to make an internal reference to Galileo – concerning: 'your Lords opinions . . . namely, that the variety of thinges is but variety of locall motion in ye spirits or inuisible bodies. And That such motion is heate'.[1]

The paradox of appearance and reality remains,[2] but Hobbes gives it a phenomenalist resolution. Because there is still no 'objective' criterion to resolve the paradox, a zone of perpetual doubt remains, to be resolved only by the thought experiments of each new generation of individuals capable of the mental calculation that the 'rerum annihilatio' requires. Or it can be resolved politically by the introduction of a sovereign, who has the power to command a solution. There is a clear analogue between the thought experiment by which the individual resolves the '"Great Paradox" of sensible knowledge',[3] and the thought experiment by means of which individuals exit the state of nature for civil society: each an exercise in rational calculation to create order out of disorder. If the erection of a sovereign is necessary to guarantee civil order, and even linguistic and normative regimes, we should not be too surprised to find that even the resolution of radical doubt can be legislated.

---

[1] See Malcolm, 'Robert Payne and the "Short Tract"', pp. 87.8, citing the Hobbes *Correspondence*, p. 33, who notes that 'the emphasis on heat suggests a particular link with the arguments of G. Galilei, *Il Saggiatore* (Rome, 1623), pp. 196-202, at pp. 201-2'.

[2] Descartes, *Meditationes*, Meditation 1, *Œuvres*, vol. 7, p. 22 (English translation in *The Philosophical Writings of Descartes*, vol. 2, p. 15), cited in Paganini, 'Hobbes and the Continental Tradition of Scepticism', p. 67 and notes.

[3] See Paganini, 'Hobbes and the Continental Tradition of Scepticism', section 2, p. 69. Paganini alludes in passing to the resort to power to resolve the problem, irresolvable in philosophical terms, of the criterion, but does not develop it. He does develop in impressive depth, however, the precedents for Hobbes's solution to the sceptical paradox in Montaigne and Gassendi, see sections 3-5 of 'Hobbes and the Continental Tradition of Scepticism', pp. 72-84.

This is not as opportunistic as it first appears, and for that reason we must treat judiciously Hobbes's response to his acolyte, Daniel Scargill's case. The resort to power, where clubs are trumps, is a brutally non-philosophical resolution to a philosophical problem. But in fact Hobbes's position is more subtle than it appears, for matter-in-motion and his materialist psychology set limits to what even a sovereign can command. Such a *de facto* solution to the problem of radical doubt cannot reach the internal court, *in foro interno*, for the internal court is governed by the necessary and involuntary responses to stimuli, belonging to processes of cognition that even the subject, him or her/self, has not the power to control, much less an external, albeit coercive, agent.

Keeping in mind the *in foro interno*, *in foro externo* distinction, in conjunction with Hobbes's resort to sovereign power to solve the problem of truth, we can now give this an ontological underpinning. Sensations or phantasms are such that their occurrence, whether in dreams or in waking, is fully determined by material cause-event sequences in which matter-in-motion, conveyed through the nerves and strings of the bodily cognitive apparatus, produces them involuntarily. No external authority has any more power over our sensations or phantasms than we do. Because these phantasms have an irreducibly subjective aspect – they are a function of the excitation of the subject in response to external stimuli – they are unreliable as a faithful representation of the object, if this were even possible. But, in the absence of a criterion, authority can supply it, and this too can be deduced.

Just as surely as the subject can deduce that in the absence of an immediate correspondence between a thing and our cognition of it, reason must make up the deficit, so, individuals in the struggle for life and death that constitutes the state of nature can calculate from their own situation to that of others and arrive at a solution of maximum benefit for minimum risk as a strategy for survival. This calculation involves the erection of a sovereign as guarantor of the individual, but unstable, pacts that individuals make between themselves. In this way the dualism of Hobbes's system, that admits a public creed and private doubt, is endemic, underpinned by a carefully elaborated materialist ontology and mechanistic psychology, spelled out in a nominalist epistemology. It is perhaps surprising that Hobbes allowed Daniel Scargill to make such a mockery of what was an epistemologically serious, if sceptical, philosophical position. For it is a corollary of Hobbes's systematic doctrine of 'the deception of sense', illustrated by appeal to dreams and other experiences of illusion, to enhance the power of reason and will. And sovereign power is the ultimate expression of will. It is short step to the Nietzchean 'will to power' and Carl Schmitt's divided world, governed by the malevolent dichotomy of 'Freund und Feind'.[1] Schmitt, architect of the juridical system of the Third Reich met his own foe in Franz Neumann, whose critical analysis of Nazism borrowed another Hobbes title: *Behemoth: The Structure and Function of National Socialism* (1942).

6.2 *THE HISTORIA ECCLESIASTICA* AND SPECIES THEORY

Caution is once again in order however, for there is a perennial tendency to vulgarize Hobbes's philosophy and render radical, aspects that are more traditional than we tend to think. This is particularly true of the religious doctrine and Hobbes's application of Renaissance techniques of philological exegesis and textual criticism to the Bible. But it is also true of his epistemology, and of this Daniel Scargill and Sir William Davenant count among the earliest and most famous vulgarizers. Hobbes's daring resolution to the paradox of the 'deception of the senses' also had important implications for poetics and the mirror theories of truth that dominated aesthetics in his day, as demonstrated in the important but little examined debate between Hobbes and Davenant that prefaces the publication of *Gondibert*. Davenant, although not immediately grasping the specifics of Hobbes's epistemology, once led through it by the hand by the master, is able to turn it to use in the propagation of the state cult.

An impressive body of recent scholarship has reaffirmed Renaissance sources for Hobbes's thought. The Renaissance, it is worth

---

[1] See Schmitt's *The Leviathan in the State Theory of Thomas Hobbes*. On Hobbes and Schmitt, see Horst Bredekamp, 'From Walter Benjamin to Carl Schmitt, via Thomas Hobbes', in: *Critical Inquiry*, vol. 25, 1999, pp. 247-266; and the forthcoming volume of essays edited by Johan Tralau as a special issue of the *Critical Review of International Social and Political Philosophy*.

remembering, was not anti-tradition but a reaffirmation of tradition that sought to cut away its superfluous accretions by means of humanist scholarship. Hobbes stands squarely in this tradition, as the *Historia Ecclesiastica* demonstrates. His approach to heresy, for instance, treats a term that he believed had departed too far from its original meaning of a sect, or, more narrowly, the taking of an opinion.[1] He discusses the merits of Latin as a *lingua franca* that has common currency and is transparent,[2] while seeing the 'Greekification of Christianity' as a route to power for the clergy who control the mysteries,[3] approaching the problem of the papacy in terms of the Pope's power to change the meaning of words.[4] These are all classically humanist positions.

Certain recurrent *topoi* chart for us Hobbes's progress in taking his characteristic route to resolving the paradox of scepticism, and they are rehearsed in the *Historia Ecclesiastica*. So, for instance, Primus's programmatic statement in the *Historia Ecclesiastica*, lines 31-4, cues us to the statement in Hobbes's *Vita* that Nature was always his teacher: 'magistra Quae docuit, praesens nam mihi

---

[1] *EW* IV, pp. 387-408; *Hist. Eccl.*, lines 19-28.

[2] *Hist. Eccl.*, lines 385-94, 1541-4. Hobbes may be signaling knowledge of Edmund Spenser's famous debate over language with Gabriel Harvey, when Spenser, in service to the Queen's favourite, Leicester, had posed to Harvey the famous rhetorical question, 'Why in God's name, may not we, as else the Greeks, have a kingdom of our own language?'. See Seth Werner, 'Spenser's Study of English Syllables and Its Completion by Thomas Campion', *Spenser Studies*, vol. 3 (1982), p. 3. Richard Helgerson prefaces *Forms of Nationhood: The Elizabethan Writing of England* (Chicago, University of Chicago Press, 1992), with this quotation, noting the following references to the Spenser-Harvey debate: Lyly's heroic poem, *Euphues* (1578), part 1 of which is Hellenizing, part 2 Anglicizing, aimed at Ascham, Spenser and Harvey; and William Webbe's, *Discourse of English Poetry* (1586). See John Lyly, *Euphues: the Anatomy of Wit; Euphues & his England* (1578-80) ed. Morris William Croll & Harry Clemons (New York, Russell & Russell, 1964). See also Gabriel Harvey, *A New letter of Notable Contents with a Strange Sonet Entituled Gorgon or the wonderfull yeare* (London, John Wolfe, 1593), a reply to Thomas Nashe's *Christ's Teares over Jerusalem*. Helgerson notes, pp. 30, 3, that Richard Stanyhurst quotes the Spenser-Harvey correspondence and Ascham's project in his (1582) hexameter translation of *Aeneid*, Books 1-4.

[3] *Hist. Eccl.*, lines 613-28, 699-702, 751-4, 1081-4.

[4] *Hist. Eccl.*, lines 871-82, 1015-30, 1071-6, 1224-90, at 1449-80, 1498-1506, 1530-41, 1581-8, 1689-1710, 1750-1910, at, 1970-2140, 2177-2224.

semper erat'. Speaking of the 'world-upside-down of civil war', Primus remarks about its causes:

> Nor am I surprised, Nature does not often make men
>   exceptionally good or bad,
> Exceptionally stupid or wise: teachers complete her work [So also
>   with religion:]

We can now read this statement in a new light as establishing the neutrality of sense experience with respect to morality, or indeed to truth, and the role of the teacher or authority in resolving the sceptical paradox, with all the attendant dangers that this *de facto* resolution can bring. In fact we have the perfect example of a *de facto* resolution in the strange Egyptian story of the 'Collar of Truth'.[1] This story of Egyptian court procedure, told also in *Behemoth*,[2] describes how, after the orderly presentation of the plaintiff's case, the calling of witnesses and the deliberation of counsel, the chief-justice, or 'Protector', of the court decides the matter by the placement of the bejeweled collar belonging to his official regalia on the documents of the winning side, beyond which there is no further contest. Winning means 'true', losing means 'false'.

In *Behemoth*, the tale is told negatively as a demonstration 'of what power was acquired in civil matters by the conjuncture of philosophy and divinity', and as a warning against priest-craft. But in the *Historia ecclesiastica*, by contrast, the tale is told positively and at much greater length, as a demonstration of the power to decide truth and falsity by political means. Having described the chief-justice's collar 'adorned with jewels which they say sparkled with an incredible light', the narrator Primus notes: 'As a consequence, as an "indicator of truth" (it was called) "truth", the name given everywhere to a winning cause'.[3] 'Indeed, when the chief-justice applied the collar to the documents, he could see as he read them whether they were true or false'.[4] Primus expresses amazement 'that there

---

[1] *Hist. Eccl.*, lines 227-72. See Diodorus Siculus, 1.75.5 (Loeb edn, London, Heinemann), p. 261.

[2] *Beh., EW* IV, p. 92.

[3] *Hist. Eccl.*, lines 235-8.

[4] *Hist. Eccl.*, lines 239-40.

could be silent justice, with no storm of advocacy, unmoved by any outside force'.[1] Secundus is less interested in this than in the fact that 'it is difficult to know whether they read the documents before the collar was placed alongside', asking 'why couldn't they have spared themselves all that work, when it didn't matter which side was right?'[2] Primus then asks, significantly, whether Secundus' reaction should be taken to mean that he thinks that when the Egyptians thought they had chosen judges 'of well-tried honesty and great distinction', they had in fact chosen 'cruel men'. And Secundus answers:[3]

> *Sec.* I'm not talking about cruel men, but unjust men, everyone acts as he pleases.
> But because it was not of much consequence whether these men were just or unjust, they were as they wanted to be.

Although on the face of it an anecdote about a curious legal system, the collar of truth is in fact a parable about civil religion. It is a powerful and disturbing analogue for the power of Constantine and his successors, the princes of early modern European nation states, in deciding between orthodoxy and heterodoxy. More than that, it is a figure for Hobbes's entire theory of truth. One can draw from it only Machiavellian conclusions. Christians committed to the Old Testament covenant as the precursor to Christianity can take little heart from Secundus' concluding question: 'But tell me, did this custom come to Egypt from the Hebrews, or was it the other way round? For the custom was common to both of them.'[4]

---

[1] *Hist. Eccl.*, lines 261-2.
[2] Diodorus Siculus does not suggest that the collar called truth has the power to reveal the truth of the writings, the placing of the collar being merely a ceremonial gesture that concludes a proper legal investigation. But, speculating on why the Egyptians adopted this procedure of 'silent justice', Diodorus sensibly concludes, 1.76.1 (Loeb edn, pp. 261-2), that it was because of the power of forensic orators to distort the truth (a view with which Hobbes would undoubtedly concur):
> they believed that if the advocates were allowed to speak they would greatly becloud the justice of a case; for they knew that the clever devices of orators, the cunning witchery of their delivery, and the tears of the accused would influence many to overlook the severity of the laws and the strictness of truth.

[3] *Hist. Eccl.*, lines 269-72.
[4] *Hist. Eccl.*, lines 273-4.

Hobbes is mindful that resolution of the paradox of scepticism by resort to authority also opens the door to systematic error. In the *Historia Ecclesiastica* we have a detailed disquisition on the medieval doctrine of 'sensible species', still taught by the universities in Hobbes's day, which he presents as an example of the errors perpetuated by teachers:[1]

> These ideas arose from the vacuous philosophy of those times which the Fathers cultivated.
> For the ancient philosophers had in those days spoken of an ingenious organization of the mind.
> Because the body is the house of the mind, it does what the mind commands; it is not the person, nor the body, nor the mind itself that executes the work.
> But everything is carried out by the proper organization of its servants, and each readily performs its own function.
> It is not the person that smells and tastes, touches, sees and hears; but the particular sense.
> It smells and tastes, it feels by touch, it sees, it hears; not the person as such, but the particular sense does that.
> Indeed an object sends its image into the eyes; and the faculty of sight sees it, the person does not.
> And no sound enters the ears, without the faculty of hearing it; there is nothing that the person himself hears.

---

[1] *Hist. Eccl.*, lines 1643-660. In *Lev.*, i, §5, 4/7, Hobbes specifically distances himself from species theory:

> But the philosophy-schools, through all the universities of Christendom, grounded upon certain texts of *Aristotle*, teach another doctrine, and say, for the cause of *vision*, that the thing seen sendeth forth on every side a *visible species* (in English, a *visible show, apparition*, or *aspect*, or *a being seen*), the receiving whereof into the eye, is *seeing*. And for the cause of *hearing*, that the thing heard, sendeth forth an *audible species*, that is, an *audible aspect*, or *audible being seen*; which entering at the ear, maketh *hearing*. Nay for the cause of *understanding* also, they say the thing understood sendeth forth *intelligible species*, that is, an *intelligible being seen*; which coming into the understanding, makes us understand.

Hobbes makes it clear (*Lev.*, i, §5, 4/7) that he takes this to be an illustration of the dangerous power of teaching institutions to resolve epistemological problems dogmatically; it being one of the instances of 'insignificant speech' in the universities that he would hope to see reformed. In *LL* he discusses 'species theory' at even greater length, using the technical language of the scholastics of species 'sent into [*intromitti*]', or 'emitted [*emitti*] to the object', and cognition 'produced by extramitting [*extramittendo*] or by intramitting [*intramittendo*] species'; see *LL*, xlvi, §21, 322/475 (Curley edn).

> Once the images have been received, the intellect considers them,
> Reason evaluates them, and memory retains them.
> In this way also the faculty of judgement judges and the faculty of
> will wills, so it is truly said that man is a microcosm.

Later in the poem Hobbes uses this medieval model of the mind to parody the work of the Church, whose self-proclaimed function is that of the 'Mystical Body' of Christ, a doctrine mobilized in the Henrician reforms that established English Protestantism.[1] The Church saw itself as an institution organized on the model of the human body, and so, for instance, Hobbes depicts the intelligencing of the Pope as a body sending out its faculties, 'servants' or missionaries, on the (false) model of an object sending out 'sensible species'. The great whale that the pope as a 'fisher of men' encounters, forcing its way into the net, is of course Leviathan; and the parable of the fishing expedition is also a parable about the contest between pope and emperor:[2]

> You cannot believe that the Popes spent their lives in leisure, and do
> not think that they had nothing further to do.
> The desires of men are always increased by desires fulfilled.
> Increasing affluence protects wealth already acquired.
> The shrewd fisherman does not neglect his customary skill, however
> great the prey entangled in his nets.
> He always pursues his own advantage. Whether he is mending his
> nets if at some point a great whale has forced its way through,
> Or perhaps thinking about hooks and new bait for fish, or seeking to
> attach some tricky device,
> Or offer them colours of bait that they like, or poisons to pollute
> clear waters.
> And having sent out his servants, he examines every shoreline to
> find which certain fish flee and which ones they love.
> Then his next concern is what he can sell, to whom and for how
> much; and what fish to keep for his own table.

So critical is the issue of species theory for Hobbes that it may indeed prove to be the philosopher's stone in resolving the thorny

---

[1] See the celebrated study by Ernst Kantorowicz, *The King's Two Bodies: A Study in Medieval Political Theology* (Princeton, Princeton University Press, 1957).
[2] *Hist. Eccl.*, lines 1241-56. Leviathan as the big fish is a thought Hobbes had already suggested at lines, 1229-30.

question of the authorship of the *Short Tract* of 1636. Karl Schuhmann, Cees Leijenhorst and Gianni Paganini defend Hobbes's
authorship of this work, held in the Cavendish collection, on philosophical grounds;[1] but Noel Malcolm, offers counter arguments,
supported by paleographic analysis, to establish the authorship of
Robert Payne, William Cavendish, Duke of Newcastle's chaplain.[2]
One argument for the *Short Tract* not being a work by Hobbes would
seem to be the author's explicit subscription to the notion of 'sensible species', which Hobbes was so scornfully to dismiss in both
Leviathan and the *Historia Ecclesiastica*.[3] So, while subscribing to
matter in motion as the fundamental principle of physics, the author
of the *Short Tract* qualifies it in a non-Hobbesian way. 'Euery Agent,
that worketh on a distant Patient, toucheth it, eyther by the Medium,
or by somewhat issueing from it self. Which thing so issueing lett be
calld Species', the *Short Tract* declares, going on to develop the standard theory of 'sensible species' as things emitted from the object
that then travel to the eye, or other relevant sense receptor.[4]

But there had been a time when Hobbes had subscribed to species
theory in fact, as he admits in the 1668 Appendix to the Latin
Leviathan.[5] Then he changed his mind, revising Medieval *species*

---

[1] J. Bernhardt, *Thomas Hobbes. Court Traité des Premiers Principes. Le Short
Tract on First Principles de 1630-1631* (Paris, P.U.F., 1988), section 2, Conclusion
8, p. 34. See also Karl Schuhmann, 'Le Short Tract, première œuvre philosophique
du Hobbes', *Hobbes Studies*, vol. 8 (1995), pp. 3-36; and Gianni Paganini, 'Hobbes,
Gassendi e la psicologia del meccanicismo', pp. 351-445.

[2] See Noel Malcolm, 'Robert Payne, the Hobbes Manuscripts and the "Short
Tract"', in *Aspects of Hobbes*, pp. 80-146. Frank Horstmann, *Nachträge zu Betra-
chtungen über Hobbes' Optik* (Ph.D. Dissertation Utrecht, 2004), pp. 327-452, has
undertaken a refutation of Malcolm's ascription of the Short Tract to Payne, and on
his own grounds. I have not seen the dissertation, but I thank Cees Leijenhorst for
informing me of it.

[3] *Lev.*, i, §5 4/7; *Lev.*, ii, §9, 7/11; and *Hist. Eccl.*, lines 1643-60.

[4] The *Short Tract*, BL, MS Harl. 6796, fols 297r and 299r, cited by Malcolm,
p. 110.

[5] See the 1668 Appendix to *LL*, §93 trans. Wright, p. 366, where Hobbes
admits, probably referring to his early Oxford education in the scholastics:

> I do recall however that at one time I thought that body was only that which
> met my touch or sight. And so I thought that body was also the image (*species*)
> of a body that appears in a mirror or in a dream or even, to my wonder, in the
> dark. But then I considered that those species disappeared, so that their exis-
> tence did not depend on themselves but on some animated entity, and they no
> longer seemed real to me but only appearances (*phantasmata*) and the effect

theory in favour of Lucretian *simulachra*, which when received by the eyes produce vision, and when received by the mind, produce dreams. Like the Epicureans he argued that the gods too emit 'simulachra', differentiated from those of mundane bodies according to their peculiar atomic structure. This revision, we should note, was almost certainly after his contact with Gassendi, the main conduit for his knowledge of Epicurean physics, and with whose work he first became acquainted as early as 1634-6, through conversations with Marin Mersenne.[1] Clearly the author of the *Short Tract* demonstrates no knowledge of the Epicurean theory of simulachra; and this would support Hobbes's authorship, if he became acquainted with Gassendi's work only around 1644, as we know he did, because it was in Paris, where the two worked alongside, that this acquaintance developed. Malcolm notes that the *Short Tract* contains a possible borrowing from Mersenne's *Harmonicorum Libri*, Mersenne's rough translation, completed in October 1635 of his own *Harmonie universelle*.[2] But this would fit with the dates for Hobbes's acquaintance with the work of Mersenne, so that what were initially arguments against Hobbes's authorship can be turned around to support it.

---

of things working on the organs of sense. And so I knew that they were incorporeal.

See also the *LL*, *OL* vol. III, p. 537, discussed by Karl Schuhmann in his, 'Le Short Tract. For Lucretius on 'simulachra' see *De rerum natura* 2.167-83, 5.156-234. *LL*, *OL* III, 537.

[1] Frithiof Brandt, in *Thomas Hobbes' Mechanical Conception of Nature* (Copenhagen, 1927), denies Leo Strauss's argument that Hobbes had met Gassendi by 1628, and that he influenced the *Short Tract*, on the grounds that there is no evidence for this claim. In any event, Gassendi had just begun his great biographical work on Epicurus at this point. See Lisa Sarasohn, 'Motion and Morality', p. 365 n.10, who conjectures that Hobbes met Mersenne in 1634, and that he may have discussed Gassendi's work now in progress, which would be significant if the *Short Tract* is dated to 1636 rather than 1630, following Brandt, and if it is in fact by Hobbes.

[2] Noel Malcolm, 'Robert Payne, the Hobbes Manuscripts and the "Short Tract"', p. 131. On the mutual influence of Hobbes and Gassendi, see Gianni Paganini's excellent essays: 'Hobbes, Gassendi and the Tradition of Political Epicureanism'; 'Hobbes, Gassendi e la psicologia del meccanicismo'; and 'Hobbes, Gassendi et le *De Cive*', in *Materia Actuosa: Antiquité, Âge Classique, Lumières; Mélanges en 'honneur d'Olivier Bloch*, ed. Miguel Benitez, Antony McKenna, Gianni Paganini, Jean Salem (Paris, Champion, 2000), pp. 183-206.

One of the most interesting and least understood *topoi* that features prominently both in *Leviathan* and the *Historia Ecclesiastica* is
Hobbes's interpretation of the parable of the talents (Mathew 25:14-
30, Luke 19:11-27), which he used both to characterize the active
power of cognition vis à vis the theory of 'sensible species' in which
the recipient is passive, and to fix the boundaries between faith and
reason.[1] Hobbes has plenty to say on these boundaries in the *Historia Ecclesiastica*, particularly on the impossibility of an idea of God,
the impossibility of reducing the extraordinary, the supernatural, to
the ordinary, the Christian mysteries to everyday experience, and so
on, vis à vis Descartes. As Paganini stresses, Hobbes does not read
the parable as referring to 'divine "gifts" in general . . . [but] rather
more specifically to tools of cognition', as demonstrated by the programmatic statement opening book 3 of *Leviathan*:[2]

> we are not to renounce our senses and experience, nor (that which is
> the undoubted word of God) our natural reason. For they are the
> talents which he hath put into our hands to negotiate till the coming
> again of our blessed Saviour; and therefore not to be folded up in the
> napkin of an implicit faith, but employed in the purchase of justice,
> peace, and true religion.

If 'sense and experience' are the talents with which we negotiate
religion, they suffer the usual limitation that the 'deception of sense'
can only be remedied by reason or authority; while authority suffers
the limitation that it can command only public obedience, not private
belief: 'For sense, memory, understanding, reason and opinion are
not in our power to change, but [are] always and necessarily such as
the things we see, hear, and consider suggest unto us; and therefore
are not effects of our will, but our will of them'.[3] Paganini makes the
brilliant observation that it follows from Hobbes's 'determinism'
that even mistaken beliefs may be beyond our control, and therefore

---

[1] I am greatly indebted to Gianni Paganini's account of Hobbes's treatment of
the parable of the talents in *Leviathan*, which opens his essay, 'Hobbes, Valla and
the Trinity', p. 183ff.

[2] *Lev.*, xxxii, §2, 195/ 245, cited by Paganini, 'Hobbes, Valla and the Trinity',
p. 183.

[3] *Lev.*, xxxii, §4, 195/246, cited by Paganini, 'Hobbes, Valla and the Trinity',
p. 185.

pointless to reward or punish, a view, as I have already suggested, that Hobbes hints at himself at the outset of *Leviathan* when he insists that 'there is no conception in a man's mind which hath not at first, totally or by parts, been begotten upon the organs of sense':[1]

> And here it should be noted that psychological determinism or causalism becomes a secure bastion protecting the private sphere, that of 'freedom' of conscience, provided that it is understood within its own limits and that 'seditious' consequences are not deduced from it. In the terms in which *Leviathan* defines it, this liberty stands on the distinction between verbal or exterior discourse (subject indeed to the sovereign, as are all other voluntary movements, in this case of that particular muscle the tongue) on the one hand, and mental discourse (which is removed from the sphere of command, but included within that wider chain of cause and effect operating upstream from the will) on the other hand.

The curious way in which Hobbes introduces the problem of heresy in the *Historia Ecclesiastica*, as if people with heretical views are unfortunate but non-culpable, supports this view of the ungovernabilty of the internal court. Moreover, his treatment of the parable of the tares in the poem is different from his treatment in *Leviathan*, to make a different point.[2] And that is that the wheat and the tares are only to be sorted on the Last Day: 'Through this parable, Christ forbids the removal of heretics before God's judgement on the Last Day', Hobbes declares.[3] In the meantime, the state must tolerate the fact that they grow up together and abstain from punishing heretics, or those guilty of mistaken beliefs for which they cannot be held responsible. The mysteries of religion are neither susceptible to 'philosophical truth by logic, . . . nor fall under any rule of natural science'. For this reason, Hobbes concluded, they are best swallowed whole 'like some wholesome pills for the sick', which then have the power to cure, 'but chewed, are for

---

[1] *Lev.*, I, §2, 3/6. Paganini, 'Hobbes, Valla and the Trinity', p. 185.
[2] Paganini, 'Hobbes, Valla and the Trinity', p. 185.
[3] *Hist. Eccl.*, lines 1139-40, concluding the discussion of the parable from lines 1129-1140. Note that the 1722 paraphrast directly connects this parable to Henry IV and the St. Bartholemew's Day massacre, as a violation of its principles.

the most part cast up again without effect'.[1] Words of which lines
1091-4 in the *Historia Ecclesiastica*, dealing with the Eucharist, are
an irreverent paraphrase:

> Don't just taste the remedy to sin with the roof of your mouth. If you
> want to be cured, open wide and swallow it like a brave
> fellow.
> For the man who chews the sacred mysteries with a logical tooth, is
> seized by dizziness, nausea and vomiting.

In the *Historia Ecclesiastica* Hobbes treats themes already set out in
Leviathan, but with juxtapositions that render orthodox doctrines
incongruous. So, for instance, when accounting for the rise of astrology as the first and most primitive form of religion, he conflates the
parable of the talents with the parable of the wheat and the tares:[2]
'And yet as tares grow in fields of wheat,[3] so ambition rejoices to be
counted among good talents'.[4] In this economical and ironical formulation, Hobbes is able both to affirm the tools of cognition as
talents with circumscribed limits, and lump together all forms of
religion, including Christianity, alongside much-castigated astrology, as overstepping those limits. And why do they overstep the
limits? First, as the product of ambition on the part of those who like
to control others through the power of religion;[5] and second, as

---

[1] *Lev.*, xxxii, §3, 196/246, cited by Paganini, 'Hobbes, Valla and the Trinity',
p. 189. In *Lev.*, 'A Review and Conclusion', §15, 395/496, Hobbes states a general
position on the citation of authorities, that 'such opinions as are taken only upon
credit of antiquity, are not intrinsically the judgment of those that cite them, but
words that pass (like gaping) from mouth to mouth'; and that 'it is an argument of
indigestion, when Greek and Latin sentences, unchewed, come up again, as they use
to do, unchanged'.

[2] *Hist. Eccl.*, lines 137-8.

[3] Matthew 13:25

[4] Matthew 25:13-30.

[5] See Lucretius, *De Re. Nat.* 1.108-11 (ed. Smith, pp. 12-13 and notes), points
out that if men understood that the soul dies with the body, 'somehow they would
have strength to defy the superstitions and threatening of the priests (*vatum*); but as
it is, there is no way of resistance and no power, because everlasting punishment is
to be feared after death'. See also *Lev.*, ii, §8, 8/11: 'If this superstitious fear of
spirits were taken away, and with it prognostics from dreams, false prophecies, and
many other things depending thereon, by which crafty ambitious persons abuse the
simple people, men would be much more fitted than they are for civil obedience'.

meeting the craving for certitude by giving unwarranted hope to those so controlled.

So we can give a different reading to the lines where he exhorts the Christian, if he wants to be 'cured', to swallow down 'the remedy to sin' by opening wide: 'For the man who chews the sacred mysteries with a logical tooth, is seized by dizziness, nausea and vomiting'.[1] In this case Hobbes manages to package together in one pill, so to speak, the Eucharist as *pharmakon* – the medicine of immortality, according to Athanasias, that communicants are instructed should not be allowed to stick to the roof of the mouth, but swallowed right down – with Lucretius' injunctions on how to induce children to take bitter medicine by sweetening the pill,[2] and his own reflections in *Leviathan* on how to deal with the mysteries: to swallow them down for fear of them regurgitating because the do not bear logical examination.

6.3 HOBBES AND THEOLOGICAL LYING

Hobbes maintains that the sceptical dilemma can only be resolved by reason and is open to manipulation by teachers, giving rise to systematic error. What then are we to make of the rendering he gives of the Nicene Creed in the poem – which reads like a catalogue of errors, most of which any sensible man, and certainly he, would reject?[3] Let us take only the first 14 verses, where Hobbes reviews six of the most tendentious doctrines, which the Nicene Council decreed compulsory 'making all those men [who refuse to accept them] heretics'.[4]

> *Pr.* First they made a heretic of anyone who dared to say that there was no God or that there were more gods than one.
> By this decree they drove out idolatry and Mani's principle of duality.

---

[1] *Hist. Eccl.*, lines 1091-4.
[2] Lucretius, *De Rerum Natura*, 1.930-41) Matthew 25:13-30.
[3] *Hist. Eccl.*, lines 647-70.
[4] *Hist. Eccl.*, lines 647-50.

So Hobbes dealt with the problem of Manicheism, which exercised so much of Augustine's energy. Second:

> They made a heretic out of anyone who would say the world was eternal; and anyone who denies it was the work of the eternal;[1]

The first of these twin propositions characterized Epicurean thought, that 'nothing is produced from nothing'. Deemed heretical by the Nicene Creed, it is in fact one of the basic axioms of atomism to which Hobbes subscribes, and which Diogenes Laertius first ascribed to Democritus:[2]

> There is nothing more true than the twin propositions that 'nothing is produced from nothing' and 'nothing is reduced to nothing', but that the absolute quantum or sum total of matter remains unchanged, without increase or diminution.

Francis Bacon, Hobbes's mentor, also explicitly endorsed Democritus's view that matter is eternal and that space is infinite.[3] The Renaissance philosopher Telesio, Bacon reports, 'frames such a system as may apparently be eternal, without supposing a chaos, or any changes of the great configuration of things', whereas Bacon himself believed that although matter was eternal, the infinity of worlds between which it was distributed suffered change and destruction. His position was not significantly different from that of Arius, at whom the second of the twin propositions, which makes a heretic out of anyone who denies that the world is the creation of God, is directed. For Arius, the finitude, mutability and corruption of

---

[1] *Hist. Eccl.*, lines 651-2.

[2] See Diogenes Laertius, 2.60, and Lucretius, 1.2.146-264.

[3] See Bacon, *Novum Organum* (The Author's Preface, I, xi-xiv and I, lxxxii) and *History is Dense and Rare* (*Works*, IV.382, IV.412). See Charles T. Harrison, Bacon, Hobbes, Boyle, and the Ancient Atomists', in *Harvard Studies and Notes in Philology and Literature*, vol. 15 (1933), pp. 195, 197. See also the 1668 Appendix to the *LL* §§7-8, in George Wright's translation, pp. 350, and 390, n.20. Gianni Paganini, in his letter to Springborg, 7/5/2002, points out that as early as his *Critique of Thomas White's 'De Mundo'* and *De Corpore* (chapter 26, §1), Hobbes subscribed to the eternity of matter.

the created world put it out of reach of the Eternal Father, as rather the work of an extraordinary intermediary.[1]

To turn now to the third tendentious doctrine, that makes a heretic of:[2]

> Anyone who denies that Jesus was God, begotten and one with the Father; and anyone who denies that the Father was unbegotten;

Once again we have twin propositions, the first of which concerns the Arian heresy and whether Christ is God coequal with the Father. This is the subject of a long reflection in the 1668 Appendix to the Latin *Leviathan*, where interlocutor B, in answer to interlocutor A's question, 'What is the difference between "begotten" (*genitus*) and "made" (*factus*)?' states:[3]

> B In saying 'made' (*factus*), we understand something made by God out of nothing, that is, a creature. For, although living creatures may be said to be both created (*creata*) and begotten (*genita*), when we say they are created (*creata*), this is understood in relation to God the Creator, who created the first male and female in every species out of the earth which He had created. But when we say a living creature is begotten (*genitus*) in the natural way, this should be understood in relation to the first things that were created, as matter. But when Christ is said to be begotten, this means begotten (*genitus*) of God the Father Himself, of the matter of the Virgin.

Here, Alexandre Matheron notes, 'Hobbes systematically applies to the *physical* generation of Jesus-Christ *as man* the formulas of the Nicene Council which concern in fact the eternal generation of the Word'. He concludes: 'this man-God engendered by God is only God in a very relative sense' and 'it is difficult, in spite of the distinction between "made" and "begotten", not to consider him as a creature pure and simple', so that 'there is certainly in Hobbes's Christology, something that resembles Arianism'.[4]

---

[1] See Athanasius, *Oratio contra Arianos*, *PG* XXVI, cols 85-6, discussed in Hefele, *Histoire des conciles*, pp. 359-69.

[2] *Hist. Eccl.*, lines 653-4.

[3] See the 1668 Appendix to the *LL* (trans. Wright), §12, p. 351.

[4] Alexandre Matheron, 'Hobbes, la Trinité et les caprices de la représentation', in *Thomas Hobbes: Philosophie première, théorie de la science et politique*, ed. Yves Charles Zarka and Jean Bernhardt (Paris, 1990), p. 383-4 (my translation).

The fourth proposition makes a heretic of:[1]

> anyone who would say that another was born from God the Father
> besides Jesus; or that Jesus was born at some definite time;

This is because, once again the Nicene Creed anathematizes those who
say 'there was a time when He was not'. Fifth, it makes a heretic of:[2]

> anyone who will say that he is a spirit without a material body; or
> that he did not have a rational mind;

Hobbes was not guilty by these terms, claiming that 'out of this, that
God is a *spirit corporeal* and *infinitely pure*, there can no dishon-
ourable consequence be drawn', and elsewhere describing God as 'a
most pure, simple, invisible spirit corporeal'.[3] In the *Historical Narration* he gives a more specific list of the heresies he has in mind
here, including the Valentinians, 'the Heresy of Apelles and others,
who made Christ a mere phantasm'.[4]

Sixth, the Nicene Creed makes a heretic of:

> anyone who denies he [God] exists in the way that light is born from
> kindled light, and both at the same time;

Hobbes, in the *Historical Narration concerning Heresy*, in a fine
display of erudition, notes of the phrase 'light from light', that 'this
was put in [to the Nicene Creed] for explication, and put in to that
purpose by Tertullian',[5] whereas Athanasius goes so far as to express
the relation of the Father and Son as 'like unto the splendour of the
sun and inseparable'.[6] In the 1668 Appendix to the Latin *Leviathan*,
Hobbes raised important objections to light symbolism for Christ

---

[1] *Hist. Eccl.*, lines 655-6.

[2] *Hist. Eccl.*, lines 657-8.

[3] See Hobbes, *Answer to Bramhall*, (*EW* IV, p. 384), cited by Gianni Paganini,
'Hobbes, Valle e i problemi filosofici della teologia umanistica', p. 44n., who notes
that Lorenzo Valla, in the *Dialectica*, I, vii, p. 636 ff. devotes a rather polemical
chapter to the aberration of Porphyry ('Substantiae distributio contra Porphyrium et
alios') namely his explicit recognition of a 'substantia incorporea'.

[4] *Hist. Eccl.*, lines 659-60.

[5] *Hist. Narr.*, *EW* IV, p. 393.

[6] Athanasius, *De decretis Nicaenae synodi*, *PG* XXV, col. 449. ff., at 453 and
notes. See Hefele, *Histoire des conciles*, 1.1.2, pp. 434-6.

that rehearse his phenomenalist theory of *phantasms* and a catalogue of standard delusions, as if to place this among them. He compares the illusion created by a kaleidoscope, which multiplies images, with the delusion of the *hypostasis*, which multiplies the persons of the Trinity.[1] So Interlocutor A asks:[2]

> What is 'Light of Light'? For it seems to me that light is an appari- tion (*phantasma*), not something that exists. For example, interpose a glass between your eye and a candle. If the surface of the glass is composed of many planes arranged in a certain way, many candles will appear to you. Still we know that there is only one true candle there and thus that all the others are empty apparitions (*phantas- mata*), idols (*idola*), that is, as St. Paul says, nothing. And it is not that any one of those candles is truer than the rest as regards their appearances; the true candle, the one placed there in the beginning, is simply none of the candles that appear. It remains itself, the cause of all those other images (*imagines*). For this reason, Aristotle dis- tinguished it from the apparition (*phantasma*) by means of the word *hypostasis*, as though the thing itself 'stood under' the image, lurking. The Latins turned this Greek word into substance. Thus both Greeks and Latins distinguish the true thing standing on its own, from the appearance (*phantasma*), which seems to stand on its own but does not and is not an entity. Is this not the true distinction between the thing itself and its appearance (*apparentia*)?

---

[1] Hobbes's 'Answer' to Davenant's Preface to *Gondibert*, ed., David F. Gladish (Oxford, Clarendon Press, 1971), p. 73 closes with an elaborate conceit based on the kaleidoscope or 'perspective glass', where he gives Davenant credit for having suc- cessfully created in his poem a display in which, as in a kaleidoscope, are mirrored the virtues of its author, distributed among its characters; a glass in which, Hobbes ironically notes, the author sees only the spectre of himself:

> I beleeve (Sir) you have seen a curious kinde of perspective, where, he that lookes through a short hollow pipe, upon a picture conteyning diverse figures, sees none of those that are there paynted, but some one person made up of their partes, conveighed to the eye by the artificiall cutting of a glasse. I find in my imagination an effect not unlike it from your Poeme. The vertues you distribute there amongst so many noble Persons, represent (in the reading) the image but of one mans vertue to my fancy, which is your owne.

For Hobbes's indebtedness to the work of Jean-François Niçeron, *La Perspective Curieuse* (1638) on the physics of the kaleidoscope, see Horst Bredekamp, *Thomas Hobbes der Leviathan: Das Urbild des modernen Staates*, pp. 87-90, and Noel Malcolm, 'The Titlepage of *Leviathan*, Seen in a Curious Perspective', *The Seven- teenth Century*, vol. 13, 2 (1998), pp. 124-55, reprinted in his *Aspects of Hobbes*, at pp. 211-17.

[2] 1668 Appendix to the *LL*, (ed. Wright), §13, p. 351.

Optics is a serious science for Hobbes and the suggestion that 'light of light' as an epithet for Christ might refer, on the analogue of the images produced by the kaleidoscope, to 'empty apparitions (*phantasmata*), idols (*idola*), that is, as St. Paul says, nothing', is pretty strong language.[1] B, while agreeing to A's suggestion that 'it was wrong for [the Fathers] to have sought to explain the mystery at all', because 'they all agreed in this, that the nature of God, like that of the Trinity and of the angels, as Athanasius added, was incomprehensible', answers that '"Light of Light" is therefore placed in the Creed only as an aid to faith'. George Wright translator of the 1668 Appendix, notes:[2]

> Hobbes's insistence that this expression is metaphoric is prompted by his aversion to the metaphysics of light. Among Christians, Tertullian and Clement of Alexandria prepared the way for Augustine's elaborate and profound combination of Platonic and Plotinian elements in describing Christ as divine light. Pseudo-Dionysius' *Hierarchia caelestia* became a kind of handbook of later Christian light symbolism, and the theory of divine illumination proved immensely influential, evidenced in its use by Avicenna, Isaac Israeli, Robert Grosseteste, Roger Bacon, Alexander of Hales, Bonaventure, Marsilio Ficino, Giordano Bruno, Pico della Mirandola and Jacob Böhme. Hobbes's own studies in optics must have made it clear to him that such speculation could not be supported scientifically, so that its use as a productive site for theology was problematic. Galileo had argued in a similar way regarding the celestial motions he had discovered.

---

[1] The mirror of the imagination is a metaphor to which Hobbes subscribes: 'memory is the World (though not really, yet so as in a looking glass)', he observed ('Answer', to Davenant's Preface to *Gondibert*, p. 81). Mirror theory, governed by the analogue of the retina in optics, had been raised to a neurological science in Hobbes's lifetime by Thomas Willis, author of two important works: *Cerebri anatome: cui accessit nervorumque descriptio et usus* (1664), illustrated by Sir Christopher Wren, and *De anima brutorum quae hominis vitalis ac sensitiva est* (1672). Willis, a medical doctor, foundation member of the Royal Society, and fellow of the Royal College of Physicians from 1666, argued that the corpus callosus of the brain acted like a retina, or perhaps a kaleidoscope, assembling images directed to it by the optic nerve. I would like to thank Prof. Renato G. Mazzolini (Ordinario di Storia della scienza), Dipartimento di Scienze Umane e Sociali, Università degli Studi di Trento, for this advice.

[2] Wright notes to the 1668 Appendix, p. 391 n. 33.

Edwin Curley, in his now celebrated piece that revisits the issue of Hobbes's scepticism, detects a certain mocking deliberateness in Hobbes's exposure of these paradoxes.[1] The 1668 Appendix to the Latin *Leviathan* is an excellent example, I would suggest. It begins innocuously enough, Interlocutor A setting the agenda by stipulating a simple criterion for the truth of religious dogmas in terms of whether or not they congrue with Holy Scripture:[2]

> [1]A. I should like you to explain the Nicene Creed to me. I ask not so that I may grasp the matters in question with my intellect, but that I may understand these words of the faith in a way that is in agreement with the Holy Scriptures

It quickly emerges, however, that essential articles of faith do not pass this simple test. So Interlocutor A asks whether such terms as 'incorporeal substance,' 'immaterial substance,' or 'separated essences' are to be found in the Holy Scriptures, and B replies:

> [95]B. They are not. But, the first of the Thirty-nine Articles of the faith, published by the Church of England in the year 1562, expressly states, 'God is without body and without parts'. And, this must not be denied. Also, the penalty for those who do deny it is established as excommunication.

> [96]A. And, it will not be denied. Nonetheless, in the twentieth article, it is stated that nothing ought to be enjoined as a belief by the church that could not be derived from the Holy Scriptures. How I wish this first article had been derived in that way! For, I still do not know in what sense something can be called greatest or great that is not body.

At §90 Hobbes puts into the mouth of Interlocutor A the observation: 'almost all those theologians who published explanations of the Nicene Creed use definitions taken from the logic and metaphysics of Aristotle, when they ought to have proven the holy Trinity from Sacred Scripture alone'.[3] And he goes on to express incredulity

---

[1] Curley, 'Calvin and Hobbes', pp. 267-8, citing *OL*, vol. III, ch. 46, §10.
[2] I cite the 1668 Appendix to the *LL* in Wright's translation, *Interpretation*, vol. 18, 3 (1991), pp. 324-413.
[3] §90, 1668 Appendix to the *LL* (*OL*, vol. III, p. 536).

that 'the Nicene Fathers, so many of whom were philosophers, did not bring into the creed those terms of art which they used in their explanations.'[1] But of course of course, as Interlocutor B at §8 establishes, the Nicene Creed is not entirely devoid of Greekification. In a passage paralleling that in the *Historia Ecclesiastica* at lines 653-4 already cited, Interlocutor B points out that, on the one hand, we have the 'unbegotten' God the Father:[2]

> God, who was made neither by anyone nor by Himself, cannot be changed or suffer alteration, neither from Himself nor from any other. Indeed He is changeless and utterly without parts, devoid of that Aristotelian mixing. All these attributes, simple, immutable, and eternal, as they are deduced from the words of the creed, so are they also predicated of God in the Holy Scriptures in those very words.

On the other hand we have God 'the begotten not-in-time', 'one Lord, Jesus Christ, the only-begotten Son of God': 'The natural son of God, or Him begotten of God, from the beginning, that is, from everlasting'.[3] A and B try to resolve the paradox between them by construing the eternity of the 'only begotten Son of God' in terms of John 1:1, the evangelist famous for his Greek concept of *logos* or the eternity of the Word (*verbum*).[4] Interlocutor A ventures an interpretation of *verbum* as 'the eternal decree of God for the establishment of the world and the redemption of man', but interlocutor B cautions: 'I do not know what the Fathers felt in this matter, but I doubt they thought that, lest they approach too near the doctrine of the Stoics, whose word *hemarmene* among the Greeks and *fatum* among the Latins means the same as eternal decree.'

Once again we are left with serious doubts about the coherence of the Nicene Creed; and Hobbes's claim in the Latin *Leviathan* that it escaped contamination by Greek philosophy is clearly falsified.[5] This is what David Berman refers to as 'theological lying', cases in which the author states an official position and then sets about to

---

[1] 1668 Appendix to the *LL*, §90 (*OL*, vol. III, p. 536).
[2] §8, 1668 Appendix to the *LL*, (ed. Wright), p. 351.
[3] 1668 Appendix to the *LL*, §9, p. 351.
[4] 1668 Appendix to the *LL*, §§18-26, pp. 352-3.
[5] *OL*, vol. III, p. 536, cited by Curley, 'Calvin and Hobbes', p. 268.

subvert it. Hobbes's itemization of the Nicene Creed in the *Histori-cal Narration*, the 1668 Appendix to the Latin *Leviathan*, and in the *Historia Ecclesiastica*, reads like a catalogue of disbelief. He sys-tematically addressed the Nicene Creed, that most central and minimal set of doctrines for the conforming Anglican, item by item, as if to demonstrate that he could not accept most of them. It is not hard to see how Scargill could take 'swallowing down the pill' to simply mean obeying authority and reserving private judgment. If, according to Hobbes, reason and sense could not validate religious mysteries, they could not strictly speaking invalidate them either. This was taking the gap between the dispensation of Reason and the dispensation of Faith to intolerable extremes, even for the Latitude men, minimalist as to content of the Christian mysteries, but placing emphasis on authority and tradition. For Hobbes, however, the epis-temic impossibility of excluding *arcana* and the magical aspects of delusion is a corollary of the sceptics' dilemma. For, if there is an unbridgeable gap between appearance and reality, there is no sure criterion to discriminate between illusion and delusion either – given that reason cannot be invoked as a criterion in the realm of faith – another problem for religious orthodoxy. Hobbes demonstrates an interest in various aspects of magic, as well as witch-craft, fairies, and the spirit-world,[1] and we know from the list of manuscripts to be found in the Chatsworth archive that he had possible access to an incomparable collection of sources on the occult in the safekeeping of his friend and promoter, Sir Kenelm Digby.[2]

It is a small step from Hobbes's resort to a *de facto* solution to 'the Great Paradox of sensible knowledge', to admitting other possible solutions to the problem of appearances and reality, faith and reason, all reached by paths of ratiocination on the analogue of the resolution of the deception of sense by the thought experiment of 'rerum anni-hilatio' or 'the feigned annihilation of the world'. The marveling primitives of Lucretius, observing the night sky and contemplating other worlds, are a paradigm case, and so is the astrologer, on whom

---

[1] Discussed in Springborg, 'Hobbes, Heresy and the *Historia Ecclesiastica*'.
[2] See the Chatsworth MS E2 analysed by Arrigo Pacchi in, 'Una "biblioteca ideale" di Thomas Hobbes: il MS E2 dell'archivio di Chatsworth', pp. 5-42, dis-cussed above at pp. 81-2.

their marvelings confer power. Both make their appearance in the *Historia Ecclesiastica*.[1] We cannot exclude that Hobbes was a relativist and that he saw in the oriental religions, in which he took a particular interest,[2] solutions to the paradox of existence that followed their own reasoned route. And while he pours scorn on priestcraft of all types, Egyptian, Hebrew, Greek, Roman and Christian, and particularly the Pope as supreme Pontiff or great Magus,[3] he does so just because he understands the legitimately important role authority plays in legislating a resolution to the existential paradox. Nonorthodox solutions had an even greater fascination for Hobbes than orthodox, just because they demonstrate the possibility of other worlds. But they also had to be condemned as dangerous, because they involved a conflict of authority, hence the venom with which he attacks all forms of heterodoxy (except of course his own).

---

[1] *Hist. Eccl.*, lines 121-30.
[2] See the many texts on magic and the occult in Chatsworth MS E2 from the Digby collection, already mentioned.
[3] *Hist. Eccl.*, lines 1223-6, 1449-60, 2185-96.

CHAPTER 7

HOBBES AND THE POETS[1]

7.1 HOBBES, THE IMAGE AND AESTHETICS

The thesis that Hobbes was indeed, as he was received, an atheist and an Erastian,[2] and that he set out purposefully to undermine the religious belief of the elite, while recommending the propagation of civil religion among the people as an instrument of political pacification, receives support in surprising contexts. Consistent with the basic tenets of Epicureanism, and its aristocratic disdain of the people but endorsement of civil religion as a sop to them, these principles were made operational in a Machiavellian project promulgated by Hobbes's acolyte, the Poet Laureate William Davenant, in which Hobbes may well have seen himself participating. Acknowledging in his preface to *Gondibert* of 1651 his great debt to Hobbes's

[1] This chapter draws on the findings of my project, 'Hobbes and the Poets', funded by the Australian Research Council Large Grant Scheme, grant no: A79602887, awarded for the calendar years of 1996 to 1998; and by a Folger Institute grant-in-aid in 1993, for which I express grateful thanks, both to the University of Sydney and to the Folger Shakespeare Library. See Springborg, '*Leviathan*, Mythic History and National Historiography'; Springborg, 'Hobbes and Historiography: Why the future, he says, does not Exist', in *Hobbes and History*, ed. G.A.J. Rogers and Tom Sorell, London, Routledge, 2000, pp. 44-72; Springborg 'Classical Translation and Political Surrogacy: English Renaissance Classical Translations and Imitations as Politically Coded Texts', *Finnish Yearbook of Political Thought,* vol. 5, 2001, pp. 11-33; and Springborg, 'Classical Modelling and the Circulation of Concepts in Early Modern Britain', *Contributions*, vol 1, no 2 2005, pp. 223-44. I express grateful thanks to the publishers for permitting me to draw on this material.
[2] See Collins, *Allegiance,* p. 252.

238 INTRODUCTION

theories of psychological conditioning,[1] Davenant, in his *Proposition for Advancement of Moralitie, By a new way of Entertainment of the People'*, addressed to Prince Charles and published three years later, proposed a programme to promote the state cult by separate strategies: pacification of the people by shows and spectacles enlisting the full panoply of visual forms of persuasion, emblem books, royal processions, coinage, and extraordinary theatrical displays; and co-optation of the elite through the arts and sciences.[2]

Davenant's *Proposition* closely parallels another advice book from Hobbes's circle, also addressed to Prince Charles, Newcastle's, *Letter of Instructions to Prince Charles for his Studies, Conduct and Behaviour*. William Cavendish (1593-1676), Earl, Marquis, and Duke of Newcastle, was a patron of the arts as well as being a military man, who saw himself in the Renaissance mould, mounting a number of didactic projects, musical, iconographic, theatrical and equestrian.[3]

---

[1] William Davenant, *A Discourse upon Gondibert. An Heroick Poem . . . With an Answer to it by Mr. Hobbs*. (Paris, Chez Matthiev Gvillemot, 1650 [Hobbes's Answer dated January 10, 1650]). See Cornell Dowlin, *Sir William Davenant's Gondibert, its Preface, and Hobbes's Answer: A Study in Neoclassicism* (Philadelphia, n.p., 1934); see also Robert D. Hume's authoritative account of Davenant's role in *The Development of English Drama in the Late Seventeenth Century* (Oxford, Oxford University Press, 1976), and the biography by Mary Edmond, *Rare Sir William Davenant* (Manchester, University of Manchester Press, 1987).

[2] Sir William Davenant, *A Proposition for Advancement of Moralitie, By a new way of Entertainment of the People*, London, 1653/4 [British Library 527 d. 17; Bodleian Library 8o L82 Med (2)], pp. 1-5. Published as the Appendix to James R. Jacob and Timothy Raylor, 'Opera and Obedience', *The Seventeenth Century*, vol. 6, no. 2 (1991), pp. 205-50, at pp. 241-9.

[3] Newcastle's plays included, *The Varietie, A comedy lately presented by his Majesties Servants at the BlackFriers* (London, printed for Humphrey Moseley, 1649), and *The Country Captaine, A comoedye lately presented by his Majesties Servants at the Blackfreyers* (London, printed for Humphrey Moseley, 1649, bound with *The Varietie*). For his musical endeavours see Lynn Hulse, 'Apollo's Whirligig: William Cavendish, Duke of Newcastle and his Music Collection', in the special issue of *The Seventeenth Century* (vol. 9, no. 2, 1994), on *The Cavendish Circle*, edited by Timothy Raylor, pp. 213-46. Hobbes-style theories of psychological conditioning were also mobilized in micro-contexts such as the Earl of Newcastle's manual on how to train horses. See William Cavendish, 1st Duke of Newcastle's *Méthode Nouvelle et Invention Extraordinaire de Dresser les Chevaux* (Antwerp, printed by Jacques Van Meurs, 1657), dedicated to Charles II, and undoubtedly indebted to the famous manual on horsemanship, Antoine de Pluvinel's *L'Instruction du Roy* (1625). See also Newcastle's posthumous, *A General System of Horsemanship in all its Branches* (London, Printed for J. Brindley, 1743, 2 vols).

His advice book expounding the three pillars of Machiavellian policy, good arms, good laws, and civil religion, displays both Machiavellian pragmatism and Hobbesian nominalism, counseling his prince to read history, 'and the best chosen histories, that so you might compare the dead with the living; for the same humour is now as was then; there is no alteration but in names, and though you meet not with a Caesar for Emperor in the whole world, yet he may have the same passions'.[1] Newcastle proceeds to a discussion of pacification of the multitude which emphasizes social distance, court etiquette, and ways to instill it.[2]

> To lose your dignity and set by your state, I do not advise you to that, but the contrary: for what preserves you Kings more than ceremony. The cloth of estates, the distance people are with you, great officers, heralds, drums, trumpeters, rich coaches, rich furniture for horses, guards, marshals men making room, disorders to be laboured by their staff of office, and cry 'now the King comes'; I know these maskers the people sufficiently; aye, even the wisest though he knew it and not accustomed to it, shall shake off his wisdom and shake for fear of it, for this is the mist is cast before us and maskers the Commonwealth.

Like Newcastle, Davenant was explicit both that sensationalist psychology was his rationale and crowd control his game. The language, like that of Lucian's Gallic Hercules and Hobbes's *Leviathan*, is of eyes and ears and means to reach them by persuasion.[3] Thinking undoubtedly of his own poem *Gondibert*, Davenant claims that poetry, worked 'into the channell of Morality', could be a 'great commander of mindes, and like Hercules in the Embleme

---

[1] See Newcastle's, *Letter of Instructions to Prince Charles for his Studies, Conduct and Behaviour.* Reprinted [from a copy preserved with the Royal Letters in the Harleian MS., 6988, Art. 62] as Appendix II to the *Life of William Cavendish, Duke of Newcastle*, by Margaret, Dutchess of Newcastle, ed C. H. Firth (London, 1907), at p. 186. See also William Cavendish, 1st Duke of Newcastle, *Ideology and Politics on the Eve of Restoration: Newcastle's advice to Charles II,* transcribed and introduced by T.P. Slaughter (Philadelphia, University of Pennsylvania Press, 1984).

[2] Newcastle's, *Letter of Instructions to Prince Charles*, p. 186.

[3] For Hobbes and the Gallic Hercules, see Springborg, 'Hobbes's Biblical Beasts', §4, pp. 363-9.

draw all by the Eares'. Spectacle is thus a program of pacification in general:[1]

> since there hath not been found a perfect meanes to retaine the people in quiet (they being naturally passionate and turbulent, and yet reducible) and that Perswasion must be join'd to Force, it can be compass'd no other way then by surprisall of their Eyes and Ears.

Hobbes through Cavendish patronage enjoyed membership of shifting and overlapping circles of humanists and new scientists, some gathered around the Stuart court, others around aristocratic patrons such as the Great Tew circle, centred on Lord Faulkland and the baronial Cavendishes' own scientific circles. From 1622, when he joined the Virginia Company,[2] Hobbes also enjoyed the fellowship of politically active poets, playwrights and projectors who were

---

[1] Davenant's, *Proposition*, ed. Jacob and Raylor, pp. 221 and 238. Davenant's reference to the Gallic Hercules recalls *Lev.*, xxi, §5, 108/138, where Hobbes notes that in creating the 'artificial man, which we call a commonwealth', men 'by mutual covenants' necessarily create those 'artificial chains, called civil laws . . . fastened at one end to the lips of that man, or assembly, to whom they have given the sovereign power, and at the other to their own ears'. See Springborg, 'Hobbes's Biblical Beasts', for further explorations of this image. The image of the Gallic Hercules, as described in Lucian's text of that name, was ubiquitous, featuring in the triumphal entry of Henry II into Paris in 1549, with the Gallic Hercules, clad only in an animal skin, as the effigy of the king, mounted on a pediment and accompanied by four statues representing the estates, chained by their ears to the lips of the king. The explanatory cartouche reads: 'we are pulled and we follow freely'. See Lawrence M. Bryant, 'Politics, Ceremonies and Embodiments of Majesty in Henry II's France', in Heinz Duchhardt, Richard Jackson and David Sturdy (eds), *European Monarchy, its Evolution and Practice from Roman Antiquity to Modern Times* (Stuttgart, Franz Steiner Verlag, 1992), pp. 127-54.

[2] On Hobbes and the Virginia Company, see Noel Malcolm, 'Hobbes, Sandys, and the Virginia Company', *The Historical Journal*, vol. 24 (1981), pp. 297-321; reprinted in Malcolm, *Aspects of Hobbes*, pp. 53-79. Malcolm, notes that the Virginia Company was generally anti-Catholic Spain, Britain's main commercial rival, and hoped that James I would take a tougher role against the Hapsburgs in support of his crusading Protestant relatives in Palatinate, Princess Elizabeth and Prince Frederick. In this connection, Malcolm speculates, that Cavendish may have circulated to the Virginia Company letters from Micanzio (in Hobbes's translation) increasingly critical of James I's policy. Malcolm, *Aspects of Hobbes*, p. 71, citing Vittorio Gabrieli, 'Bacone, la riforma e Roma nella versione Hobbesiana d'un carteggio di Fulgenzio Micanzio', *The English Miscellany*, vol. 8 (1957), pp. 195-250, at p. 248.

fellow members,[1] notably: the playwright brothers Killigrew, Thomas (1612-83), Master of the Revels after 1673, and his brother Henry Killigrew (1613-1700), Master of the Savoy after the Restoration; Nicholas Ferrar (1592-1637), relative of Sir Walter Ralegh and one of the Virginia Company's most active members; Sir Edward Sackville, 4th Earl of Dorset KG (d. 1652), friend of Edward Herbert, Lord Cherbury, (1582/3-1648), who wrote an Epitaph to Sackville's still-born son;[2] Sir Edwin Sandys (1561-1629) a founder of the Virginia Company, leading parliamentarian and opponent of James I; his brother, George Sandys (1578-1644), Virginia Company Secretary and poet; and John Donne (1572-1631), chaplain to James I and metaphysical poet.

The humanist projects mounted by these circles, whose members were officially or unofficially enlisted in the national identity formation of Great Britain, were not just national but translocal, representing the English response to the Renaissance, that great efflorescence of humanist scholarship connecting them to fellow-humanists on the Continent. Great Britain, the product of the union of the Crowns of England and Scotland of 1603, was celebrated by Michael Drayton (1563-1631), author of *Poly-olbion* (literally, *Great Britain*) of 1613,[3] which set out to map the land mythologically and chorographically. Drayton had been preceded in this great mapping project by William Camden (1551-1623), author of *Britannia*, the first topographical and historical survey of all of Great Britain. Begun in 1577 with the encouragement of the great map-maker, Abraham Ortelius,

---

[1] 'Projectors' is used in the early modern sense of one that plans a project, specifically, a promoter. See Kathleen Lesko's forthcoming edition of John Wilson, the Restoration playwright, *The Projectors*. Note also the observation by L. C. Knight on Philip Massinger's drama, that 'the Projector scenes in *The Emperor of the East* [1632], and Timoleon's speeches to the senate in *The Bondman*, I, iii [show] Massinger also had keener *political* interests than most of his fellows'. L. C. Knight, *Drama and Society in the Age of Jonson* (London, Chatto and Windus, 1937), pp. 270-300.

[2] *Epitaph on sir Edward Saquevile's Child, who dyed in his Birth*, by Edward, Lord Herbert of Chirbury, *Occasional Verses of Edward, Lord Herbert* (1665), Boledleian Library, Bliss A.98. (Wing H1508).

[3] Michael Drayton, *Poly-Olbion, or A chorographicall Description of the Tracts, Riuers, Mountaines, Forests, and other Parts of this renowned Isle of Great Britaine . . . .* London, Mathew Lownes et al., 1613, reprinted in *The Works of Michael Drayton*, William Hebel, ed., (Oxford, Basil Blackwell, 1933), vol. 4.

it officially chronicled and mapped the land, county by county and shire by shire. Hobbes's country house poem, *De Mirabilibus Pecci*,[1] written in 1636 he tells us, was also inspired by the chorographical work of Camden in *Britannia*; while the publication of *Poly-olbion* coincided with that of *The Theatre of the Empire of Great Britaine*, by John Speed, England's most famous map-maker, who published his atlas in 1612.[2]

Poly-Olbion was typical of the Renaissance humanist, executed with all the trappings that heroic poets of antiquity and their archaizing counterparts of modernity could bestow, including learned glosses by John Selden, Hobbes's close friend, and a set of mythologizing maps. This was a perfect case of cosmopolitan localism, in which the resources of antiquity and modernity were jointly plundered to fabricate a particular identity out of a global class.[3] In some of the more deliberate efforts to accomplish collective identity formation through persuasion, eloquence and the power of the image, we see the reach for empire as the nation writ large. So Davenant, who early in the 1650s was to be found counseling Prince Charles, the future Charles II, on his management of the state cult, in his plays later in the 1650's celebrated national heroes and colonizers like Sir Francis Drake in support of 'Cromwell's "imperial western design"'.[4]

Davenant like Edmund Waller, mentioned in Rymer's preface as an important influence on Hobbes, belonged to the Louvre faction

---

[1] *De Mirabilibus Pecci*, written Hobbes tells us in 1636 and dedicated to his patron, William Cavendish Earl of Devonshire, like the *Elements*, for which he was laying the groundwork at the time, also dedicated to his patrons, was initially circulated only within the Newcastle and Cavendish circles. It appeared in print for the first time in 1678, and then without Hobbes's permission, published in Latin and English under the title, *De Mirabilibus Pecci: Being the Wonders of the Peak in Darbyshire, and translated due to public demand, it is claimed, by an unnamed 'Person of Quality'* – a translation licensed to Roger L'Estrange, the Restoration censor on September 3, 1677. My speculation is that it was translated by Charles Cotton Jr. See below.

[2] 'Speedes Mappes of England, fol.' is listed at T.3.2 in the general section of MS EIA, the Hardwick Hall booklist, while 'Speedes Chronicle, fol.' is listed at T.3.1.

[3] See Patricia Springborg, 'Classical Modelling and the Circulation of Concepts in Early Modern Britain', pp. 223-44, especially pp. 228, 235.

[4] Jacob and Raylor, 'Opera and Obedience', p. 213.

centred on Charles I's consort, Henrietta Maria, during the Stuart exile. But like the Cavalier poets, Sir John Suckling (1609-1642), Thomas Carew (1594-1640),[1] Charles Cotton Sr. (d. 1658) – and even Newcastle and Hobbes – he also numbered among the 'sons of Ben' (Jonson), an interlocking circle of literateurs with whom Hobbes was loosely connected.[2] Charles Cotton Sr was a friend of Jonson (1572-1637), John Donne (1572-1631), John Selden (1584-1654), Sir Henry Wotton (1568-1639), Izaak Walton (1593-1683) – who wrote biographies of Donne, Wotton and George Herbert, and co-authored *The Compleat Angler* with Charles Cotton Jr. – John Fletcher (1579-1625), Henry Glapthorpe, Robert Herrick (1591-1674), Richard Lovelace (1618-1657), William Davenant, and Edward Hyde, Lord Clarendon (1609-1674). Charles Cotton Jr. (1630-1687), anonymous translator of Hobbes's *De cive*,[3] and famous as the translator of Michel Montaigne, came to know Davenant, Lovelace and Walton, through his father.[4] Aston Cockayne

---

[1] Thomas Carew, *The Poems of Thomas Carew with his Masque Coelum Britannicum*, ed. Rhodes Dunlap (Oxford, Clarendon Press, 1949); see introduction pp. xiii-lix on Carew's life and work.

[2] Hobbes allegedly consulted Ben Jonson on the epistle dedicatory to his translation of Thucydides of 1629. Note the important comment on Ben Jonson by William Petty, Hobbes's acquaintance: William Petty to Samuel Hartlib, 1649, Hartlib Papers, 50H28/1/28a 'Ephemerides 1649': 'What Verul[am's] Natural History is in Phil[osopy] the same Parallel for Ethics or Moral Histories is most exactly couched in Ben Jonson's works, to the Readers admiration expressing the Characters of all humours and behauiours whatsoeuer'. For the cross-referencing between Jonson and Newcastle, see the excellent essay by Anne Barton, 'Harking Back to Elizabeth: Ben Jonson and Caroline Nostalgia', *ELH*, vol. 48 (1981), pp. 706-31. Earl Miner, *The Cavalier Mode from Jonson to Cotton* (Princeton N.J., Princeton University Press, 1971), p. 5, notes the interlinking Cavalier clubs and coteries, from Jonson's Tribe, the Mermaid Club, to Inns of Court and Faulkland's Great Tew. See also David Rigg's biography, *Ben Jonson: A Life* (Cambridge Mass., Harvard University Press, 1989).

[3] See Noel Malcolm, 'Charles Cotton, Translator of Hobbes's *De cive*'.

[4] See MS.CAT. [Calendar of] The Cavendish-Talbot Manuscripts, Folger Library (Z6621.F61.C3), p. xviii. This archive of letters and miscellaneous documents of the Cavendish-Talbot families, 1548-1607, mostly comprises those letters to Elizabeth, Countess of Shrewsbury, 1520-1608, addressed either as Lady Cavendish, Lady St. Loe, or as Countess of Shrewsbury, and are written from Welbeck, Chatsworth, the court, Buxton, etc., concerning the running of her estates, the building of Chatsworth and the education of her children, Charles, William and Mary. They are an important and unexplored source for Hobbes's patronage circle.

(1608-1683/4), Cotton Sr.'s cousin and dedicatee of Cotton Jr.'s poem, *The Wonders of the Peake*, written with acknowledgement to Hobbes's *De mirabilibus pecci*,[1] knew Donne, Drayton, for whom he wrote an elegy, George Sandys (1578-1644), the translator of Ovid's *Metamorphoses*, Thomas May (1595-1650), the translator of Lucan, Philip Massinger (1583-1640), William Habington (1605-1654), Thomas Randolph (1605-35), and Suckling; while Cotton Jr.'s mother, Lady Olive Stanhope, was the subject of an elegy written by Michael Drayton.[2] Despite recent focus on Hobbes's Renaissance humanism, the painstaking work necessary to construct the prosopography of members of these literary circles, and Hobbes's personal and quasi-institutional connections to them, has yet to be undertaken.[3]

Drayton, perhaps less powerful in these coteries than his rivals, in his letter 'To the Generall Reader', prefacing *Poly-Olbion*, made an extraordinary case for the merits of print culture as opposed to scribal publication, that put him at odds with Hobbes[4] and Donne, for

---

[1] Buxton, in his brief commentary on Cotton's poem, notes that it was first published in 1681, following the publication of Hobbes's *De Mirabilibus Pecci* in 1678, 'with an English translation on facing pages "by a Person of Quality" whom there is no reason to identify with Cotton'. But is there any good reason not to consider Cotton as a candidate for Hobbes' translation, especially as he is now established to have been the translator of *De Cive*? (See Malcolm, 'Charles Cotton, Translator of Hobbes's *De Cive*'.) Cotton's furious poem addressed to the 'turncoat' poet Waller, in this collection, p. 113: *To the Poet E. W.*, MS 1689, is also of interest. Edmund Waller is identified in the MS as author of *A Panegyrick to my Lord Protector*, a poem which was published in 1655, but written in 1653. This, in combination with his outspoken Francophobia, suggests that Cotton's disposition towards Hobbes and his connections to the Louvre faction may have been ambiguous.

[2] The Cavendish-Talbot Manuscripts, Folger Library (Z6621.F61.C3), p. xix.

[3] Another important and unexplored archive is the MS.CAT., Calendar of the Bagot Papers, Folger Library, Z6621.F61.B4; a collection of 1076 letters and documents of the Bagot family of Blithfield, Staffordshire, purchased from Sotheby's July 4-5, 1955. Letters, 1557-1671, mostly written in the life of Richard Bagot (d. 1597), sheriff of Staffordshire, deputy lieutenant, commissioner for recusants, commissioner of array and J. P; and his son Walter (1557-1623), indicate works the county family performed for the Crown. Lord Burghley; George Talbot, Earl of Shrewsbury; his son, Gilbert, Earl of Shrewsbury; Robert Devereux, Earl of Essex; and Sir John Fortescue, number among the correspondents.

[4] See Hobbes's airy dismissal of printing in *Leviathan*: 'The invention of printing, though ingenious, compared with the invention of letters is no great matter.' *Lev.*, iv, §1, 12/15.

instance, courtier's clients who jealously protected their monopoly of knowledge and feared that print culture would take it out of their hands. Drayton noted:[1]

> In publishing this Essay of my Poeme, there is this great disadvantage against me; that it commeth out at this time when Verses are wholly deduc't to Chambers, and nothing esteem'd in this lunatique Age, but what is kept in Cabinets, and must only passe by Transcription . . . ; such I meane, as had rather read the fantasies of forraigne inventions, then to see the Rarities and Historie of their owne Country delivered by a true native Muse.

This reads as a plea for localism against the machinations of the Transmontani,[2] as well as a protest against the *arcana imperii* tradition of state secrets and royal mystique; an impression strengthened by the frequent mention of Machiavelli and Bodin in Selden's commentary on the poem. And yet *Poly-Olbion*, with its mythological trappings and arcane glosses is itself an essay in surrogacy.

---

[1] Michael Drayton, letter 'To the Generall Reader', prefacing *Poly-olbion* (1610).

[2] Charles Cotton Jr., in his *Wonders of the Peake*, making reference to Davenant, and possibly Hobbes as Francophiles, brands them as 'Transmontani' (from the term used by the Romans for Gaul as the land 'across the mountains') in their affiliations:

> For all that pass the Portico this way
> Are Transmontani, as the Courtiers say . . . .
> To bub old Ale, which nonsense does create,
> Write leud Epistles, and sometimes translate
> And keep a clutter with th' old Blades of France,
> As D'Avenant did with those of Lombardy,
> Which any will receive and none will buy
> And that has set H.B. and me awry.

See the modern edition of his poem in *Poems of Charles Cotton* with an introduction by John Buxton (London, Routledge, 1958), pp. 52-94; commentary, pp. 265-8, at p. 97. Charles Cotton Jr. was the recipient of a copy of *Gondibert* inscribed by the author, which read: 'Will: Davenant. Tower: Decemb.19, 1651'. See Noel Malcolm, 'Charles Cotton, Translator of De Cive', *Aspects of Hobbes*, p. 243, citing J. G. McManaway, 'The "lost" Canto of Gondibert', *Modern Language Quarterly*, vol. 1 (1940), pp. 63-78, at p. 65 n. The juxtaposition of Davenant's *Gondibert*, set in Lombardy, and his problem with his publisher, Henry Brome [H.B.], because of verses (by Davenant) that 'any will receive but none will buy' may also be evidence that the 'lost' Canto of *Gondibert*, dedicated to Charles Cotton Sr., and for which Cotton Jr. wrote commendary verses, was in fact written by Cotton Jr., my own speculation.

Celebrations of the land, of the Union, of localism, of the
common law of England and of the *Ecclesia Anglicana*, jostled with
projects in natural philosophy, optics, mathematics and the new
science, to rewrite the *ars humanis* for a tolerant, urbane, court-
centred, non-sectarian, cosmopolitan culture that would, its advocates hoped, bring to fruition the promise of Elizabethan days,
while putting behind them the structural fragility of the Elizabethan
polity. These were projects in which Hobbes, it seems, was a participant. The earliest letters in his *Correspondence* find him conspiring in the transmission of state gossip – if not in fact state secrets –
on the progress of the King's cause in the Low Countries.[1] As
Bacon's emanuensis and Cavendish's translator he was privy to
information on foreign policy that he did not hesitate to dispense as
patronage when required. We find him on two occasions, either
writing to, or showing information from privileged sources to a
third party.[2] He privately circulated Latin poems for the edification
of his peers; he translated histories for those who kept 'curiosities
in cabinets'; and he commented upon poetics and aesthetics in the
service of the state.

In Hobbes's preface to *The Iliads and Odysses of Homer* of 1673,
we find a counterpart to Drayton's appeal against secrecy and surrogacy, but argued the other way, as a defence of closet history, and
epic poetry fit for a gentleman's cabinet. Discussing the 'virtues
required in an heroic poem, and indeed in all writings published',
Hobbes remarks:[3]

> A sixth virtue consists in the perfection and curiosity of descrip-
> tions, which the ancient writers of eloquence call icones, that is
> images. And in an image is always a part, or rather a ground of the
> poetical comparison .... For a poet is a painter, and should paint
> actions to the understanding with the most decent words, as painters

---

[1] Mason to Hobbes, Dec. 10, 1622, first recorded in F Tönnies, 'Contributions
à l'histoire de la pensée de Hobbes', *Archives de philosophie*, vol. 12, cahier 2,
(1936), p. 81; reprinted in Hobbes *Correspondence*, pp. 1-4.
[2] *Ibid.*, and Aglionby to Hobbes 1629, Hobbes *Correspondence*, p. 778, which
reports about the treasonous treatise by Dudley II found in Robert Cotton's library;
and in the same letter reports the pending match between Countess of Oxford, his
patron and Thomas Bruce, brother of Chrisian, Countess of Devonshire.
[3] Hobbes, *EW* X, iii.

> do persons and bodies with the choicest colours, to the eye; which if
> not done nicely, will not be worthy to be placed in a cabinet.

Defending the ancient *pictura poesis* tradition as a criterion for the worthiness of poetry and histories to be kept in cabinets, is curiously old fashioned, placing them in the same category as the curiosities of the antiquarians, Hobbes's friends Herbert of Cherbury, John Selden, and John Aubrey. But in some senses Hobbes was old fashioned, a representative of the antique mentality as measured by his subscription to the principle 'history is the teacher of life' – 'Historia Magistra Vitae' – of which the *Historia Ecclesiastica* may be seen as yet another expression.[1]

Surrogacy was the sea in which the Renaissance courtier swam; and the imagery of locking cabinets was ubiquitous. Sir Thomas Browne, another of Hobbes's associates, who wrote a work entitled *Natures Cabinet Unlock'd* (1657), was also author of the famous *Pseudodoxia Epidemica*, which attracted satirical commentary, under the title, *Arcana Microcosmi: Or, The hid Secrets of Man's Body discovered* (1652), by Alexander Ross, who was to excoriate Hobbes in *Leviathan Drawn out with a Hook*, of 1652. The courtier's world was the field of *arcana* par excellence; and if human artifice must be concealed behind closed doors, and nature's secrets tightly locked in drawers, *arcana imperii* could also include maps. So, 'in Philip II's Spain, Pedro de Esquival's great cartographic survey of the Iberian peninsula was kept in manuscript, locked in the Escorial as 'a secret of state'.[2]

Hobbes was himself no stranger to surrogacy. The earliest extant letter we have in the Hobbes *Correspondence*, dated December 10, 1622 and written to Hobbes by Robert Mason, a Fellow of St. John's College, Cambridge, discourses on the uses of secrecy in politics, employing coded language typical of subterfuge, for instance, rivers which might represent the sites of printing presses, or the *patriae* of

---

[1] See Reinhart Koselleck, for whom this principle is the marker of a pre-modern mentality, in 'Historia Magistra Vitae: The Dissolution of the Topos into the Perspective of a Modernized Historical Process', in *Futures Past: On the Semantics of Historical Time*, tr. Keith Tribe (Cambridge, Mass., MIT Press, 1985), pp. 21-38.

[2] Richard Helgerson, *Forms of Nationhood: The Elizabethan Writing of England* (Chicago, University of Chicago Press, 1992), p. 146.

248

famous authors like Machiavelli and Sarpi, as we have previously seen. Referring to previous correspondence with Hobbes, Mason writes:[1]

> there are many things, as your letter discreetly intimates, whereof it becomes us to be ignorant, so I would be loath to be thought so great a stranger to ye commonwealth I liue in as not to know what ye greater sort of men do, that wish a prosperous successe to ye designes both of their Prince & Countrey, which I hope henceforth to haue from you, so no matter though it be at ye sixt, seventh, or 50th hand. The proceedings in Commonwealths as they come into ye knowledg of ye subiect are not unfitly compared to ye currents of rivers, for as all rivers run into ye Sea, & yet some are carryed with a more slow & swift torrent as their chanels are more or lessed indented, & some there are we read of, that haue secret passages vnder ye earth into the sea, So all affairs of State at length fall into ye discours of ye multitude, yet some sooner according to the rectitude of their relations, others later, as their truth is empesht by ye turnings and twinings it finds in the braines of some partiall & affected Relations. Other affairs again of deeper consequence are (as they ought to be) more closely & secretly managed & not so much as whispered of, nay they are kept even from ye subtlest Politicians, till of a sudden they let themselve out both into rumor & admiration. Arcana imperij nihil moror. periculum intelligere.[I do not object to the existence of state secrets; one must understand the danger.]

Secrecy is evoked in Hobbes's early warning to his patron in the Preface to his translation of Thucydides of 1629, to beware of the multitude and its fickleness and to use this private history as a weapon against public intransigence:[2]

> Though this translation have already past the censure of some, whose judgments I very much esteem: yet because there is something, I know not what, in the censure of a multitude, more terrible than any single judgment, how severe or exact soever, I have thought it discretion in all men, that have to do with so many, and to me, in my want of perfection, necessary, to bespeak my candour.

---

[1] Mason to Hobbes, Dec 10, 1622, Hobbes *Correspondence*, pp. 3-4. The translation of the Latin epigram is Malcolm's.
[2] Hobbes, *EW*, VIII, p. vii.

'There is no news at court but of maskes', Hobbes reported to the Marquis of Newcastle, in January, 1633/4, introducing in one line a *topos* that has largely been ignored in Hobbes scholarship.[1] Anne of Denmark had introduced the court masque to Britain and Jonson's masques have been described as a compendium of 'Platonic meanings, mythological references and humanistic doctrines', for which he drew on Caesare Ripa's *Iconologia*, or *Descrittione di Diverse Imagini*, published in Rome, 1603.[2] *The Masque of Blackness*, 1605, the first and unsuccessful collaboration between Inigo Jones and Ben Jonson, and the epithalamium masque in the form of a Roman marriage ceremony, *Hymenaei*, of January 1606, celebrating the luckless marriage of the young Earl of Essex and Lady Frances Howard, involved striking visual effects requiring elaborate stage machinery. Jones claimed in 1614 to have been present at the enthronement of Camillo Borghese, Pope Paul V, at Castle St. Angelo in 1605, where he would have observed such spectacle; and an inscription dated 1607 from the Catholic scholar Edmund Bolton is addressed to Jones as one 'through whom there is hope that sculpture, modeling, architecture, painting, acting and all that is praiseworthy in the elegant arts of the ancients may one day find their way across the Alps into our England'.[3]

Poetics, aesthetics and image making were the stock-in-trade of the Renaissance humanist. The *pictura poesis* theory of representation famous from Horace's *Ars Poetica* was much in vogue and employed by Elizabethan and Jacobean theorists of poetics, presupposing a mirror theory of truth. Historiographers and rhetoricians from Lucian, Quintilian and Cicero to Ralegh, Spenser and Sidney, had invoked it. Lucian, in *How to Write History*, had argued that the

---

[1] Hobbes to the Marquis of Newcastle, 26 January, 1633/4, calendared in *H.M.C. Thirteenth Report*, Appendix, Part 1: *The Manuscripts of His Grace the Duke of Portland, preserved at Welbeck Abbey*, vol. 2, 1893, p. 124.

[2] James Lees-Milne, *The Age of Inigo Jones* (London, B.T. Batsford, 1953), pp. 25-7. These mechanical wonders possibly inspired Davenant in his descriptions of elaborate mechanical spectacle in the Preface to *Gondibert*, dedicated to Hobbes, and in his *Proposition for Advancement of Moralitie*.

[3] Lees-Milne, *The Age of Inigo Jones*, pp. 27-8, who notes, p. 52, that Inigo Jones, like Ben Jonson and Lord Arundal, whose father, grandfather and great-grandfather had been condemned to death for Catholicism, forfeiting titles and estates, apostatized.

historian must adopt the stance of the impartial spectator, the images
he supplied 'in no way displaced, dimmed or distorted',[1] a metaphor
adopted by Gerhard Vossius in 1623 to define history as the mirror
of humanity ('speculum vitae humanae').[2] History as a mirror was a
medieval gloss on Cicero's trope *historia magistra vitae*, said to
characterize ancient historiography. Not only did it give rise to a specific political genre, mirrors for princes (*speculum regum*), but it was
an opportunity for more wide-ranging explorations of the relation of
history to truth, the role of judgement in history, history and memory,
raised by Cicero in his famous claim: 'History indeed is the witness
of time, the light of truth, the life of the memory, the messenger of
antiquity; with what voice other than that of the orator should it be
recommended for immortality ?'.[3]

In reflections on the writing of history, whether mythic or
national, *pictura poesis* representation found a powerful role in
explaining how the images conjured up by historians translated into
behavioural stimuli for readers and how historical *exempla*, therefore, could produce a moral effect; none more powerful than in
Hobbes's own explanations of the image. From his early preface to

---

[1] See Lucian, *Works*, ed. A. M. Harmon (London, Heinemann, Loeb Classical
Library, 1959), vol. 6, ch. 39. On the 'speculum vitae humanae', see Reinhart Koselleck's 'Perspective and Temporality: A Contribution to the Historiographical Exposure of the Historical World', in *Futures Past: On the Semantics of Historical Time*,
tr. Keith Tribe (Cambridge, Mass., MIT Press, 1985), pp. 130-55.

[2] *Gerhard Vossius, a familiar figure of the London literary scene, was probably an unacknowledged source for Hobbes's *Hist. Eccl.*, as noted.

[3] 'Historia vero testis temporum, lux veritatis, vita memoriae, magistra vitae,
nuntia vetustatis, qua voce alia nisi oratoris immortalitati commendatur?' Cicero,
De oratore, 2.9.36. See Reinhart Koselleck, 'Historia Magistra Vitae', p. 23 ff. The
mirror of the imagination is a metaphor to which Hobbes subscribes: 'memory is
the World (though not really, yet so as in a looking glass)', he observed ('Answer',
to Davenant's Preface to *Gondibert*, p. 81). Mirror theory, governed by the analogue
of the retina in optics, had been raised to a neurological science in Hobbes's lifetime
by Thomas Willis, author of two important works: *Cerebri anatome: cui accessit
nervorumque descriptio et usus* (1664), illustrated by Sir Christopher Wren, and *De
anima brutorum quae hominis vitalis ac sensitiva est* (1672). Willis, a medical
doctor, foundation member of the Royal Society, and fellow of the Royal College of
Physicians from 1666, argued that the corpus callosus of the brain acted like a
retina, or perhaps a kaleidoscope, assembling images directed to it by the optic
nerve. I would like to thank Prof. Renato G. Mazzolini (Ordinario di Storia della
scienza), Dipartimento di Scienze Umane e Sociali, Università degli Studi di Trento,
for this advice.

his Thucydides to his late preface to his Homer, we have a consistent
account; he chose his historians according to the venerable principle
historia magistra vitae: 'as having in them profitable instruction for
noblemen, and such as may come to have the managing of great and
weighty actions'.[1] Thucydides was the greatest of all because,
without intruding himself into the narrative as a moralist, he could,
through images, simulate in his reader the passions that drove the
historical actor, and thus keep history alive in the eternal present of
sensation.[2] In his preface to *The Iliads and Odysses of Homer*,
Hobbes gave one of his most succinct accounts of the power of the
image of which Thucydides and Virgil were such masters:[3]

> And in an image is always a part, or rather a ground of the poetical
> comparison. So, for example, when Virgil would set before our eyes
> the fall of Troy, he describes perhaps the whole labour of many men
> together in the felling of some great tree, and with how much ado it
> fell. This is the image. To which if you but add these word, 'So fell
> Troy' you have the comparison entire; the grace whereof lieth in the
> lightsomeness, and is but the description of all, even the minutest,
> parts of the thing described; that not only they that stand far off, but
> also they that stand near, and look upon it with the oldest spectacles
> of a critic, may approve it.

Hobbes's refusal to accept a copy theory of truth (see chapter 6.1),
may seem an obstacle to his embracing such an episteme. But he

---

[1] Hobbes, *Eight Bookes of the Peloponnesian Warre Written by Thvcydides the
Sonne of Olorvs Interpreted with Faith and Diligence Immediately out of the
Greeke* (London, 1629), *EW* VIII, v.

[2] *EW* VIII, vii:

> It hath been noted by divers, that Homer in poesy, Aristotle in philosophy,
> Demosthenes in eloquence, and others of the ancients in other knowledge, do
> still maintain their primacy: none of them exceeded, some not approached, by
> any in these later ages .... But Thucydides is one, who, though he never
> digress to read a lecture, moral or political, upon his own text, nor enter into
> men's hearts further than the acts themselves evidently guide him: is yet
> accounted the most politic historiographer that ever writ.

[3] Hobbes's preface to his Homer (*EW* X, iii): *The Iliades and Odysses of Homer.
Translated out of the Greek into English. With a large Preface concerning the
Vertues of an Heroick Poem; written by the Translator: Also the Life of Homer.* The
Third Edition. London, for Will Crook, at the green Dragon without Temple-Bar,
next Devereux-Court, 1686 [Folger H2552 Homerus]. See the frontispiece, showing
Cameo's of Homer (top), Hobbes (bottom) and standing martial, sword-bearing
figures. Legend gives the date (1677) and publication details of the first edition.

was able to accommodate historiography to phenomenalism nevertheless, once again taking his cue from a classical source, but in this case the rhetorician Quintilian:[1]

> There are certain experiences which the Greeks call fantasia, and the Romans visions, whereby things absent are presented to our imagination with such extreme vividness that they seem actually to be before our eyes. It is the man who is really sensitive to such impressions who will have the greatest power over the emotions . . . . From such impressions arises that *energeia* which Cicero calls illumination and actuality, which makes us seem not so much to narrate as to exhibit the actual scene, while our emotions will be no less actively stirred than if we were present at the actual occurrence.

Quintilian equivocates on whether phantasmata are real or illusory, stressing that his theory of illumination applies regardless. Illumination can create the illusion of truth, and it can create it for the past as well as for the present. Illumination makes use of illustration, as Hobbes's acquaintance in the Virginia Company, George Sandys, its newly appointed treasurer, in his elaborate *Ovid's Metamorphosis Englished, Mythologized and Represented in Figures* of 1623, demonstrated. Reputed to be the first work of English poetry written in the Americas, Sandys completed two books of his translation of Ovid's *Metamorphoses* en route to Maryland to take up his post, 'amongst the rorering of the seas, the rustling of the Shroude, and the clamour of the sailors'.[2] Once in Virginia he translated eight more, taking the completed manuscript with him on his return to England, where it was published in 1626 and republished in 1632 in a magnificent folio edition. Mindful perhaps of the limits to literacy in the New World, and reflecting on the earliest forms of writing as pic-

---

[1] Quintilian, *Institutio Oratoria*, trans. H. E. Butler (Cambridge, Mass., Harvard University Press, 1953), vol 2, pp. 433-7, noted by David Johnston in, *The Rhetoric of Leviathan* (Princeton, Princeton University Press, 1986), p. 19. On Hobbes on phantasms, see, Yves Charles Zarka, 'Le Vocabulaire de l'apparaitre: champ sémantique de la notion de *phantasma*', in *Hobbes et son vocabulaire*, pp. 13-29.

[2] See Richard B. Davis, *George Sandys, Poet Adventurer: A Study in Anglo-American Culture in the Seventeenth Century* (New York, Columbia University Press, 1955), p. 140.

tographs, Sandy prefaces his work with a frontispiece that is itself an iconographic marvel, accompanied by the following statement:[1]

> I have attempted (with what Successe I submit to the Reader) to collect out of Sundrie Authors the Philosophicall sense of these fables of Ouid, if I may call them his, when most of them are more antient then any extant Author, or perhaps then Letters themselves; before which, as they expressed their Conceptions in Hieroglyphics, so did they their Philosophie and Diuinite under the Fables and Parables: a way not un-trod by the sacred Pen-men; as by the prudent Law-giuers, in their reducing of the old World to ciuilitie, leauing behind a deeper impression, then can be made by the liuelesse precepts of Philosophie.

Hobbes's philosophical focus on the image and its epistemology, laid out as early as *The Elements of Law* of 1640,[2] and expounded in his exchange with Davenant prefacing *Gondibert*,[3] produced an aesthetic optic with startling results.[4] The shocking image of Leviathan, the hybrid 'mortal God', recalling the Hermetic Asclepius and Machiavellian hybrids, the fox/lion and the *centaur, both man and beast,

---

[1] I cite the second edition of Sandys' *Ovid's Metamorphosis Englished, Mythologized and Presented in Figures* (Oxford, 1632). See Sandys' epistle to the reader, p. x.

[2] Hobbes, *Elements*, I, ii, §10, p. 26.

[3] Sir William Davenant, *A discourse upon Gondibert*. In 1651 the complete *Gondibert* was published in three books, followed in 1653 by Sir John Denham's *An Essay in Explanation of Mr. Hobbes . . .*; and in 1655 by Davanant's *Gondibert Vindicated*. Denham's essay appeared in *Certain Verses written by Severall of the Authours Friends; to be Reprinted with the Second Edition of Gondibert* (London, 1653). The relation these works bear to one another has been insufficiently investigated. Sir John Denham (1615-1659), author of the famous country house poem, *Cooper's Hill* (1642), who served Queen Henrietta Maria as an envoy in Paris, once listed himself, along with Davenant's rival stage-producer Thomas Killigrew and Killigrew's brother-in-law William Crofts, as 'dire foes' of Davenant's *Gondibert*, as A. H. Nethercot, *Sir William D'Avenant, Poet Laureate and Playwright-Manager* (Chicago, University of Chicago Press, 1938), p. 244, notes.

[4] Horst Bredekamp discusses not only the Hermetic encoding of *Leviathan*, but demonstrates the way in which the frontispiece relates to the tradition of Archimboldesque images – named for Guiseppe Archimboldo, inventor of those ambiguous composite images beloved of the Baroque, such as a fruit basket that looks like a human face. See Bredekamp, *Thomas Hobbes der Leviathan*, pp. 39-59. On the shock value of hybrids see Johan Tralau, 'Leviathan, the Beast of Myth: Medusa, Dionysos, and the Riddle of Hobbes's Sovereign Monster', in the *Cambridge Companion to Hobbes's Leviathan*, pp. 61-81.

signaled a new departure. The biblical beasts of Hobbes's *Leviathan* and *Behemoth* were calculated to cause a stir, and Hobbes's collaboration with the engraver of the frontispiece to *Leviathan* suggests a carefully crafted shock. Without doubt designed to appeal to an elite schooled in Hermetic and pagan iconographic codes, it appealed also to the lay public accustomed to 'reading' Emblem books.[1]

The notion of politically coded texts is an important one.[2] While Leo Strauss's general thesis about the hidden meaning of texts may be over-extended, one can nevertheless see that the conditions of censorship and Draconian punishment for political and ecclesiastical non-conformity in early modern Europe encouraged surrogacy.[3] The *Historia Ecclesiastica* may be seen as a further chapter in Hobbes's programme of political surrogacy – music and masques for the masses and heroic poetry for the elite – that continued through his last works, the translations of Homer, as we have seen.

7.2 LITERARY SOURCES AND STYLISTICS

The question remains whether Hobbes's *Ecclesiastical History* really is a serious history at all, or whether it is indeed a show of

---

[1] The most famous of the emblem books was the *Emblematum liber* by the famous Milanese glossator, Andrea Alciato (1492-1550), written between 1523 and 1531. When in 1523 Alciato first refers to his 'little book of epigrams', it seems that he is describing in large part a series of translations and imitations he was making of short poems from late Hellenistic sources, of which many of his emblems are direct translations. Some of the earliest versions of Alciato's emblems in English are found in two works, by Thomas Palmer and Geffrey Whitney. Palmer's *Two Hundred Poosees* is a manuscript emblem book (1566) that rewrites many of the Alciato emblems; while Whitney's *A Choice of Emblemes*, published in Leiden in 1586 by Christopher Plantin, instead of translation, often resorts to paraphrase. See http://www.mun.ca/alciato/comm.html#publ. On the frontispiece illustration to *De cive* as the imitation of an image illustrating Horace from a Dutch Emblem book, see Maurice Goldsmith, 'Hobbes's Ambiguous Politics'.

[2] See Patricia Springborg, 'Classical Translation and Political Surrogacy'.

[3] See the important and only lately published work on Hobbes's ecclesiology by Leo Strauss, 'Die religionskritik des Hobbes', *Gesammelte Schriften*, Bd. III, hrsg. v. Heinrich und Wiebke Meier (Weimar/Stuttgart, J. B. Metzler Verlag, 2001), pp. 262-369, translated into French by Corine Pelluchon as, *La critique de la religion chez Hobbes. Une contribution à la compréhension des Lumières (1933-1934)* (Paris, P.U.F., 2005).

Renaissance rhetoric or even a baroque burlesque, as the English
paraphrase would suggest. For to treat the poem as belonging to
Hobbes's philosophical project does not rule out rhetorical purposes,
for which Quentin Skinner has given such an excellent account. It
has not been previously commented upon that Hobbes's poem
appears to undergo a name change between 1671 and 1688, and this
may give us a clue. Given as *Historia Ecclesiastica Romana* in
Wheldon's account book, Crooke's catalogue, and the title pages of
the Harley and Grund MSS (i.e., as late as 1685), the work is
renamed *Historia Ecclesiastica Carmine Elegiaco Concinnata*[1], *A
Church History in the form of an Elegiac Poem*, on the title page of
the 1688 printed edition. The reference to the Roman Church in the
earlier title is consistent with Aubrey's claim that the poem concerns
the *History of the Encroachment of the clergie (both Roman and
Reformed) on the Civil Power*, but clearly does not fulfill the brief of
the title of the paraphrase, to tell the *True Ecclesiastical History from
Moses to the Time of Luther*. The name change to *Historia Ecclesiastica Concinnata* could be significant on a number of counts. The
term *concinnata*[2] was indicative of a certain heroic style, and may
have been added by Thomas Rymer, author of the Preface to the
1688 printed edition, which bears the new title. It is just possible that
the change could also have been made by Hobbes, to suggest that
once the original purposes of the poem had been served, and the heat
of the heresy debate had passed, he hoped to preserve it for posterity
as a state of the genre humanist literary piece that was also an
epitome of his philosophy.

From its dramatic opening the poem alerts us to its literary pretensions and display of classical sources. It begins in pastoral mode,
the interlocutors, Primus and Secundus, singing of war and peace in
the tradition of the famous singing shepherds of Theocritus' idylls,
and the rhetors answering one another of Horace's *Odes* and Virgil's,

---

[1] The subtitle of the *Hist. Eccl.*, added possibly by Rymer, is not to be found in
the MSS.

[2] According to Lewis and Short's *Latin Dictionary*: 'In the 'Asianic' style of
pathetic prose, simplicity of syntactical structure is compensated by elaborate
rhetorical artifices of "concinnitas". Virgil shows both the narrative simplicity and
this type of rhetorical stylization, which Cicero notes Gorgias was the first rhetorician to use.'

Eclogues.[1] Secundus reflects upon the transformative powers of war
to corrupt discourse, a moral 'world upside-down' reminiscent of
Thucydides,[2] the Greek historian favoured by the Renaissance whom
both Hobbes and Lorenzo Valla had translated. The use of the dialogue form is typical of humanist 'invectives', of the type that Valla
had made famous and, despite the pastoral beginning, the poem
quickly turns to disputation. So Poggio Bracciolini, in his *Historia
convivialis* of 1450, had presented his critique of Lorenzo Valla in
the form of pseudo-classical invectives, after the style of the spurious *invectivae* of Sallust and Cicero, a form already sanctioned by
Petrarch. It was the idiom in which Valla in turn replied, answering
Poggio's criticisms in 'a philological cross-examination of the plaintiff Poggio', a style derived in part from Quintilian and 'in keeping
with his [Valla's] forensic bent'.[3] There is much to suggest Valla as a
model for Hobbes as we shall see.

Primus quickly introduces religion or superstition as the cause of
war, in particular the English Civil War, and although Hobbes's
Behemoth, written around the same time, gives just such an account,
in the *Historia Ecclesiastica* it is delivered in an entirely different
mode. Nor are the Epicureans Hobbes's only classical source for a
history of religion as superstition. When, for instance, at lines 93-4
of the poem, Hobbes details the horrors of the sleeper, waylaid by
spectres 'striking terror with their eyes, their claws and their threats'
he seems to evoke Horace's Fury of *Epodes* 5.92-4, who assails the
fearful sleeper with slashing nails. Similarly 'the magician, the
astrologer, the diviner and the soothsayer',[4] are stock characters from
Greek and Roman comedy, to whom the anti-clerical Renaissance
turned for its characterization of priests. Hobbes's catalogue of
snake-oil salesmen, 'Astrologer, pimp, Chaldean, Philosopher and
lying Jew', is particularly reminiscent of Juvenal *Satire* 3.58-83,

---

[1] See especially Virgil *Ecl.*1.36.
[2] Compare *Hist. Eccl.*, lines 9-12, with See Hobbes's *Thucydides* bk 3, §82
(ed. David Grene), pp. 204-5.
[3] See Marsh, 'Grammar, Method, and Polemic in Lorenzo Valla's "Elegantiae"', *Rinascimento, Rivista dell' Instituto Nazionale di Studi sul Rinascimento*,
vol. 19 (1979), pp. 91-116, at p. 108, citing Book II of the *Antidota* from Valla's
Opera omnia, ed. E. Garin, vol. I, p. 274.
[4] *Hist. Eccl.*, lines 105-6.

who asks just how Greek these charlatans in fact are, and whether all
this oriental hocus-pocus can truly be laid at the Greeklings' door:[1]

> Now let me turn to that race which goes down so well/ with our mil-
> lionaires, but remains *my* special pet aversion,/ and not mince my
> words. I cannot, citizens, stomach/ a Greek-struck Rome. Yet what
> fraction of these sweepings/ derives, in fact, from Greece? For years
> now Syrian/ Orontes has poured its sewerage into our native Tiber –
> / its lingo and manners, its flutes, its outlandish harps/ with their
> transverse strings, its native tambourines,/ and the whores who hang
> out round the race-course . . . . All of them lighting out for the
> Cities' classiest districts/ and burrowing into great houses, with a
> long-term plan/ for taking them over. Quick wit, unlimited nerve, a
> gift/ of the gab that outsmarts a professional public speaker –/ these
> are their characteristics. What do you take/ that fellow's profession
> to be? He has brought a whole bundle/ of personalities with him –
> schoolmaster, rhetorician,/ surveyor, artist, masseur, diviner,
> tightrope walker, / magician or quack, your versatile hungry Greek-
> ling/ is all by turns.

In locating the genre of, and literary sources for, Hobbes's poem
there is no better place to begin than with Thomas Rymer, who wrote
the Preface to the posthumous 1688 printed edition.[2] Rymer subscribes to the method of 'loaded citation' so well described by Lisa
Jardine as characteristic of Renaissance writers.[3] It is the method of

---

[1] Juvenal, *The Sixteen Satires*, Peter Green trans. (Harmondsworth, Penguin, 1974), *Satire* 3, lines 58-83, p. 89.

[2] For the humanist tradition to which Hobbes belongs, by far the most important modern source is Quentin Skinner's *Reason and Rhetoric in the Philosophy of Hobbes* (Cambridge, Cambridge University Press, 1996), and his many essays, collected in *Visions of Politics*, especially vol. 3, *Hobbes and Civil Science*.

[3] See Lisa Jardine, 'Lorenzo Valla and the Intellectual Origins of Humanistic Dialectic', *Journal of the History of Philosophy*, vol. 15 (1977), pp. 143-64, at p. 156, speaking of Lorenzo Valla as one who:

> habitually employs a strategy of loaded citation, popular with Renaissance writers; the passage cited or quoted in the text acquires most of its force only when referred back to its source (and the full reference is invariably, if occasionally inaccurately, given in the text). Clusters of citations imply a particular sectarian point of view. In every case in which I shall be concerned to show Valla's philosophical bias from the published (historically influential) text, by excavating such loaded quotations and clusters of citations, the first, suppressed version makes the point more explicitly; identifying quotations and sources is not here a matter of parading erudition, but part of the excavation necessary when sensitive issues have been driven underground.

Hobbes himself. 'The passage cited or quoted in the text acquires
most of its force only when referred back to its source', while 'clus-
ters of citations imply a particular sectarian point of view'. This is
the stock-in-trade of surrogate discourse of the type in which Hobbes
engages, as I elsewhere discuss.[1] By unacknowledged citation
Hobbes cues us to a wide range of classical and scholastic sources,
while Rymer notes Hobbes's specific indebtedness to Marin
Mersenne, Pierre Gassendi and Edmund Waller. So, for instance,
Hobbes makes unacknowledged in-text references to the following
sample of classical works, authors listed in order of frequency:

Horace: *Epode*, 5.92-4 (line 93), *Epode* 12.5 (line 1820), *Epode*
2 (line 2231), *Satires* 1.10.18 (line 570), *Sat.* 2.3.247, 275 (line
1286) *Sat.* 1.3.40 (line 1820) *Sat.* 2.3.82-3 (line 1840), *Sat.* 2.3.25
(line 1932), *Sat.* 2.6.87, 93-7 (line 2206); *Sat.* 1.6.52-3 (line 2232);
Ars poetica 361 (line 1488), *Ars poet.* 78 (line 1588), *Ars poet.* 31,
(line 1948); *Ode* 1.31.7 (line 1837), *Ode* 1.12.58-60 (line 2140);
Ode 1.11.1-8 (line 2154), *Ode* 1.22 (line 2236); *Epistles*, 1.2.23-6
(line 1892), *Epist.* 1.6 (line 1917), *Epist.* 1.2.32-3 (line 1941), *Epist.*
1.1.41-2 (line 1948).

Virgil: *Eclogues* 1.36. (line 2), *Ecl.* 3.104. (line 148), *Ecl.* 3.93.
(line 396 and 1234); *Ecl.* 3.1. (line 966), *Ecl.* 1.66 (line 1273);
Aeneid. 9.59 (line 464); *Aen.* 9.59-66 (line 489), *Aen.* 7.19-20 (line
1267), *Aen.* 2.211 (line 1759), *Aen.* 4.73 (line 2140), Virgil's *Georgics* 2.458-9, (line 534), *Georg.* 3.9. (line 2027).

Homer: *Odyssey* 11.49 (line 87), 17.485-7 (line 177); 8.266 ff.
(lines 350 and 1264), bk 9 (lines 1200 and 1895), 17.317 (line 1237),
10.210 ff (line 1267). 9.415ff. (line 1289), 10.210 ff. (line 1892);
10.187ff. (line 1894).

Rymer fills in some of the classical sources, citing Horace,
Satires 1.4.4, and 1.1.23-7, *Sat.* 1.4.39-44, *Odes* 2.17.6 and *Epistles*,
1.19.19; Vergil's *Aeneid.* 1.739, Lucretius 1.926; *Odyssey*, 11.29,
and Juvenal, *Satire* 1. He mentions as models for Hobbes's poetics
Horace's *Ars Poetica*, 97, Ovid's, *Fasti*, Homer and Virgil. It is
Rymer who identifies Diodorus Siculus bk 4 and Aelienus as the
provenance of Hobbes's account of the strange 'Egyptian custom of
deciding disputes by means of the "Collar" and the Gem as the

---

[1] See Springborg, 'Classical Translation and Political Surrogacy', pp. 11-33.

"touchstone of truth"'. This custom practiced in Meröe in Upper Egypt, which was sometimes confused geographically with Ethiopia in the seventeenth century, is described in the *Historia Ecclesiastica* and in *Behemoth*,[1] for which Rymer notes contemporary sources, including 'the very famous Selden,[2] and Marsham',[3] but fails to mention John Spencer's *Dissertatio de Urim et Thummimm*, as already noted. Rymer is particularly useful in identifying some of Hobbes's ecclesiastical sources, Greek sources probably consulted in Latin translations, like those anthologized by John Christopher-son, Bishop of Chicester (d. 1558), in the *Historiae ecclesiasticae scriptores Graeci*, ed. (Cologne, 1570).

Declaring the author of the *Historia Ecclesiastica* to be no juvenile (punning perhaps on Juvenal the satirist as a one of Hobbes's sources), Rymer introduces Hobbes as the old man ('*senex*'), mentioned in the titles of works by Cicero, Ovid and Petrarch,[4] who decides to set his most mature reflections in verse. Rymer dares to set Hobbes the poet in the tradition of 'the oracles of Phoebus, Pythagoras, "the first teacher of wisdom"', Ovid's *Fasti*, and Horace on the *Ars poetica*, sources to which Hobbes makes internal

---

[1] *Hist. Eccl.*, lines 227-76, and *Beh.*, *EW* VI, p. 92 ff.

[2] John Selden was a fellow member of Magdalen Hall with Hobbes, and the two later became close friends (see Aubrey, I, p. 369). Letter 18, Hobbes *Correspondence*, p. 32, records Hobbes as reading Selden's *Mare Clausum* in 1636, soon after it was published, a fact noted in Skinner, 'Thomas Hobbes and the Renaissance *studia humanitatis*', pp. 74, 206n. Hobbes's source for the numbers of those who attended the Nicene Council is almost certainly Selden's *Eutychii Aegyptii*, already noted; and Selden's works were held in the Hardwick Hall Library.

[3] "Sir John Marsham, (1602-1685), author of the *Diatriba chronologica*, 1649, and the *Chronicus Canon Ægyptiacus, Ebraicus, Graecus, et disquisitiones*, 1672, accused Eusebius of doctoring the Hebrew chronologies to disguise the importance of ancient Egyptian wisdom, a position with which Hobbes can be assumed to be sympathetic, given his oft-repeated argument (*Historia Ecclesiatica* lines 155-6, 159-60, 167-8, 217-18, 273-6, 335-6), that Egyptian wisdom came first. Marsham mentions Spenser's *Dissertatio de Urim et Thummum*, as previously noted, but probably too late to be a source for Hobbes.

[4] See Cicero's *De Senectute* and Ovid's *Senex*. In the *Senili* 4:5, Petrarch significantly asks: 'Who is there in dealing with such doubtful matters, daring to affirm with assurance that the intention of those authors was absolutely this rather than that, in works which they composed a thousand years ago?'; see Thomas M. Greene, trans., 'Petrarch and the Humanist Hermeneutic', in Giose Rimanelli and Kenneth John Atchity, eds, *Italian Literature, Roots and Branches: Essays in Honor of Thomas Goddard Bergin* (New Haven, Yale University Press, 1976), pp. 201-24.

reference. But there is a proviso, Rymer points out: Hobbes's style is that of 'everyday language', 'a plain and native simplicity', compared with the 'heroic wind' of the 'polished style', someone who 'cared little for ornamentation and poetic colouring'. These comments are particularly pointed, referring to debates over stylistics to which he cues us terminologically, and which require review. For, to rely for Hobbes's sources exclusively on Rymer's explicit attributions would be to ignore the Renaissance line of transmission of classical scholarship, about which both he and Hobbes, respecting the canons of the day, were largely silent.

Renaissance authors may go unmentioned but Hobbes, like Rymer, employs various methods of indirect acknowledgement to introduce celebrated Renaissance debates to the inner circle of cognoscenti, for whom the *Historia Ecclesiastica* was presumably written. Hobbes belongs firmly to the tradition post-dating the great classical 'discoveries' in the *quattrocento* of the works of Quntilian and Lucretius, and is apparently aware of the Renaissance scholars who recirculated these texts, Poggio Bracciolini,[1] Guarino Veronese,[2] Leonardo Bruni, both of the latter teachers of the renowned Lorenzo Valla.[3] Hobbes appears to rehearse arguments in the debates reported by Angelo Decembrio from the court of Leonello d'Este in the 1440s, which were to be replayed at the important Ferrara-Florence Church Council of 1438-9, for instance. These debates concerned language, the importance of the vernacular and the role of a *lingua franca* in the establishment of empire, all of which find mention in the poem, as they do in debates to which we know Hobbes contributed.[4]

---

[1] The works of Quintilian were rediscovered in their entirety by Poggio Bracciolini in 1416. See R. Sabbadini, *le scoperte dei codice latini e greci ne' secoli xiv e xv*, 2 vols (Florence, 1905, repr. 1967), II, pp. 247-248; Winterbottom, M. 'Fifteenth-Century Manuscripts of Quintilian', *Classical Quarterly* 17 (1967), pp. 339-69.

[2] For the full text of Quintilian with Greek annotations of Aulus Gellius, rediscovered by Guarino in 1431, see Sabbadini, *Codice* I, 97.

[3] See Sarah Gravelle, 'Lorenzo Valla's Comparison of Latin and Greek and the Humanist Background', *Bibilothèque d'Humanisme et Renaissance*, vol. 44, 2 (1982), pp. 279-80.

[4] *Hist. Eccl.*, lines 384-90. See Hobbes's exchange with William Davenant, prefacing *Gondibert*, as well as Davenant's *A Proposition for Advancement of Moralitie*, discussed in chapter 7.1.

The printed edition of Hobbes's *Historia Ecclesiastica* bears the subtitle *Carmine Elegiaco concinnata*, 'A Poem in Elegiac Mode', not to be found in the MSS and perhaps Rymer's addition, as already noted. The term *concinnata*[1] places Hobbes's work squarely in the Renaissance tradition of Elegance, centred around Lorenzo Valla, who, in the prefaces to his *Elegantiae,* provided a programme of linguistic reform based on philological and forensic precision, for which his most important sources were Quintilian, the works of the later Roman jurists and the newly recovered *Attic Nights* of Aulus Gellius. Valla's wide-ranging reforms included not only philology and grammar, but a comparative study of Greek and Roman linguistic styles and philologically based Biblical exegesis. It is no exaggeration to claim that Hobbes's own efforts at Biblical exegesis in books 3 and 4 of *Leviathan,* as well as in the *Historia Ecclesiastica*, trace a direct line of descent from Valla through Erasmus, who read and annotated Valla's *Elegantiae* at the age of eighteen, and who discovered and published Valla's *Adnotationes in Novum Testamentum* in 1505. An early indication of the impact of Valla's linguistic theory on the young Erasmus is to be found in his letter on the decline of studies of 1489, further developed in his *Antibarbari,* a work which directly targets the 'barbarous' philosophical terminology of the English theologians, *Ockham and Duns Scotus, who come in for invective along similar lines in Hobbes's poem.[2] Erasmus's *Anti*

---

[1] *concinnitas* (rhet.), a rhythmical style. In the 'Asianic' style of pathetic prose, simplicity of syntactical structure is compensated by elaborate rhetorical artifices of 'concinnitas'. Virgil shows both the narrative simplicity and this type of rhetorical stylization, which Cicero notes Gorgias was the first rhetorician to use. One of the features of this style is its division (*incisim*) into members (*membratim*), and the use of antithesis to juxtapose them. While Latin takes the theory of *concinnitas* from the Greeks, the device itself was native to Italian soil. 'The logically constructed period with inner harmony and balance of its constituent parts (*concinnitas*) received its ultimate refinement when the arrangement of the words was made to conform to a rhythmical pattern'. See L. R. Palmer, *The Latin Language* (London, Faber & Faber, 1968) pp. 132-3, 116.

[2] For a direct echo of the terminology of Valla and Erasmus in Hobbes, see *Hist. Eccl.*, lines 1867-8, 1879-84, and *Lev.,* xlvi, §40, 379/467:

> the writings of School-divines are nothing else, for the most part, but insignificant trains of strange and barbarous words, or words otherwise used than in the common use of the Latine tongue, such as would pose Cicero, and Varro, and all the grammarians of ancient Rome. Which, if any man would see proved, let him (as I have said once before) see whether he can translate any School-divine into any of the Modern tongues, as French, English, or any

Barbari, although written earlier, was published only in 1520. Petrarch had been the first of a long line of Italian humanists, including Valla, Leonardo Bruni[1] and fourteenth century theological writer, Coluccio Salutati,[2] to single out the British logicians for their 'barbarous' Latin, meaningless abstractions and hair-splitting distinctions.[3] As a consequence, Ockham, *Bradwardine and Suiseth[4] were 'the main butt of humanist ribaldry and vituperation down to the seventeenth century'.[5] Humanist attacks on scholasticism, and particularly the logicians, were succeeded by a later generation of critics, including Gassendi and Chillingworth, Hobbes's contemporaries and associates.

Some of the humanists, notably Erasmus and Vives, had strong English connections, while Lorenzo Valla, the model of the humanism they venerated, introduced to England an important line of European anti-clerical and anti-papal polemic that stretched from Marsilius of Padua to Erastus. Hobbes could not have been unacquainted with Valla and the tradition of thinking that he represents. His *De*

---

other copious language. For that which cannot in most of these be made intelligible is not intelligible in the Latin. Which insignificancy of language, though I cannot note it for false philosophy, yet it hath a quality, not only to hide the truth, but also to make men think they have it, and desist from further search.

Compare with Gassendi (*Exerc.* 1.1.9, 110b.):

Voces commenti sunt barbaras, phrasesque loquendi ineoptas, quibus intra Scholarum cancellos ita intumescunt, ut rideant caeteros mortales, quod non assequantur illarum mysteria. Miseri! qui non percipiunt garritum hujusmodi mullius esse extra Scholas usus . . . . Ecce enim significatus vocabulorum ita detorserunt, ut verba etiam vulgaria, dum ab istis usurpantur, dixeris tibi videri chymaerarum bombinantium: non vulgi, quem penes loquendi arbitrium ac norma est.

[1] Bruni, an eminent Italian humanist, was born of poor parents at Arezzo, the birthplace of Petrarch, in 1369, dying at Florence in 1444.

[2] *De lab. Herc.*, 1.1.4.

[3] The English had a poor reputation as Latinists up to the 17th century, see Binns, J. W. *Intellectual Culture in Elizabethan and Jacobean England: the Latin Writings of the Age* (Leeds, Francis Cairns Ltd, University of Leeds, 1990). But Renaissance humanist accusations focused particularly on the logicians and their importation of Greek terminology, Hobbes's charge against them also.

[4] Richard Swineshead (Suiseth, Calculator) *fl. c.* 1350.

[5] Lisa Jardine, 'Humanist Logic', in Charles B. Schmitt, Eckhard Kessler and Quentin Skinner, eds., *The Cambridge History of Renaissance Philosophy* (Cambridge, Cambridge University Press, 1988), pp. 173-198, at p. 177.

falso credita et emendita constantini donatione had become an 'authentic bestseller of humanist Europe', having been translated into English by William Marshall and published in 1534 on the initiative of Thomas Cromwell, principal secretary to Henry VIII, and Hobbes was clearly familiar with it.[1] The parallel between the shape of Hobbes's corpus and that of Valla, is striking. Valla and Hobbes both produced translations of Thucydides, Hobbes likely using Valla's translation from Greek to Latin as a crib for his own translation from Latin to English. Hobbes's 'Letter to the Reader' prefatory to his translation of Thucydides (1628), reproves Valla, both for his Latin and for the textual apparatus: 'the Latin of Laurentius Valla . . . was not without some errors; and he [used] a Greek copy not so correct as now is extant'. To claim to outdo Valla in methods of textual criticism is a typical piece of Hobbesian audacity, designed quite probably to throw the reader off the scent.[2] The parallels do not stop there. Both published works on the problem of the will, while Valla's famous exegetical work, the *Commentary on the New Testament*, edited by Erasmus, is clearly imitated by Hobbes, who takes some of his philological examples from Valla in the long chapters of *Leviathan* devoted to Biblical exegesis.[3] Valla's last work, the *Encomium* of St. Thomas Aquinas, which also marked Valla's last public appearance, was characteristic of his provocative, polemical style, in turn. Invited to deliver the *Encomium* to an audience of Dominicans in the Church of Santa Maria sopra Minerva at Rome to celebrate the saint's anniversary, he delivered instead an anti-encomium, a critique of St. Thomas's style

---

[1] Gianni Paganini, 'Thomas Hobbes e Lorenzo Valla. Critica umanistica e filosofia moderna', *Rinscimento, Rivista dell' Instituto Nazionale di Studi sul Rinascimento*, 2nd series, vol. 39, 1999, pp. 515-68, at p. 520 n. 9, argues that Hobbes was acquainted with Valla's famous exposure of the (supposed) Donation of Constantine, as a forgery, the 1620 citing the *Horae Subsecivae* (pp. 327-9). But Valla is not listed in the Hardwick Hall book list, whereas a local source is: Richard Crackenthorpe's *Defence of Constantine: with a treatise of the Popes temporall monarchie, wherein, besides divers passages touching other Counsels, both General and Provinciall, the second Roman Synod, under Sylvester, is declared to be a meere Fiction and Forgery* (London, 1621), held at shelf mark K.1.12 (*q.v.*).

[2] *EW* VIII, p. viii.

[3] See Valla's, *Adnotationes in Novum Testamentum*, in *Opera omnia*, ed. E. Garin (Torino 1962).

and his penchant for logic that advocated a return to the theology of
the Fathers of the church; a path along which Erasmus, Luther and
Hobbes were to follow him.[1]

These parallels point to a similarity of intention between these
thinkers that has yet to be fully explored, but which our commentary on the poem makes an effort to address. As already noted, the
term *concinnitas*, which appears in the title of the 1688 printed
edition of the *Historia Ecclesiastica*, is probably not incidental. It
may cue us, to an important debate about precise language conducted between Valla and his critics, Poggio Bracciolini, Paolo
Cortesi, and the Neopolitans Panormita and Fazio, as to whether
the appropriate terminology for discourse put precision above
classical canons of style, and the degree to which popular usage
should be admitted. So for instance, Poggio, although in his *De
avaritia* (1428) implicitly challenging the medieval tradition of
etymological glossing, and particularly Isidore, was 'scandalized
by Valla's animadversions on the most ancient and hallowed representatives of Latin erudition', Varro, Gellius, Donatus and
Priscian.[2] This was the line taken by Paolo Cortesis, who, in *De
doctis hominibus* of 1489, praised Valla's philology, but attacked
his grammatical theory:[3]

> Valla sought to formulate the import of words, and he taught an
> approach, albeit incorrect, to the structure of discourse. But in fact
> there is a different basis for composition, which Valla either omitted

---

[1] Valla, *Encomium S. Thomae Aquinatis,* p. 394. Valla's most important works
comprise, in chronological order, *De voluptate/De vero bono* (1431) *Epistola de
insigniis et armis* (1437), *De libero arbitrio* (1439), *Dialecticae disputationes*
(1439), *De falso credita et ementita Constantini donatione declaratio* (1440), *De
professione religiosorum (1442), Apologia adversus calumniatores* (1444), *De ele-
gantiis linguae Latinae* (1444), *Gesta Ferdinandi regis Aragonum* (1445/46), *In
Latinam Novi Testamenti interpretationem adnotationes* (ca. 1448), *Oratio in principio sui studii* (1455), and his *Encomium* (1455).

[2] See David Marsh, 'Grammar, Method, and Polemic in Lorenzo Valla's "Elegantiae"', pp. 96-97, citing Poggio's letter to Niccolo about the *De avaritia*, in
Poggio. Bracciolini, *Opera omnia*, ed. R. Fubini (Torino 1964), 3, p. 35, where
Poggio claims to have even 'cited (pseudo)-Isodorean Decretals in order to cite a
favourite authority of the clergy' (Marsh, 'Lorenzo Valla's "Elegantiae"', p. 97n.).

[3] P. Cortesi, *De hominibus doctis dialogus,* ed. M. T. Graziosi (Rome 1973),
p. 40, cited by Marsh, 'Lorenzo Valla's "Elegantiae"', p. 103n.

or did not know. For ornate, sweet, and uncorrupted Latin style requires a certain periodic composition which creates an audible harmony (*concinnitas ad sonum*).

Shifting the meaning of the term 'elegance', away from Valla's etymological and forensic focus to purely stylistic considerations, the Venetian Francesco Negri, in his syntactical and stylistic manual *Regulae elagantiarum* published in Paris in 1498, joined Cortesi in defining elegance as 'delightful harmony of words which fills the ear with sweet sounds (elegantia est venusta verborum concinnitas, dulcem auribus sonum afferens)'.[1]

Did Rymer – if it was he who revised the title to include the term concinnitas – believe that Hobbes was on the side of Valla's critics, and an advocate of elegance rather than linguistic precision? Poggio Bracciolini, in his *Historia convivialis* of 1450, had opened the question which Valla was later to discuss at length, whether Latin was the popular language of the ancient Romans, venturing interpretations of Quintilian that provoked from Valla a vigorous response. It is a matter to which Hobbes alludes in his discussion of Latin as a *lingua franca* in *Historia Ecclesiastica* lines 385-90. Valla, taking the opportunity to answer Poggio's earlier criticisms of his *Elegantiae*, quoted as the flagship of his attack the famous passage from *Institutio oratoria*, 1.6.3, where Quintilian states that 'usage is the surest guide in speaking, and language should be used just as a coin with a public stamp'. Quintilian's *topoi*, language as a means to popular commerce (publica forma), and usage (usus, consuetude) as a linguistic criterion, feature prominently in Valla's reply to Poggio, the *Antidota in Pogium* of 1452. But they had already informed his grand project, the *Repastinatio dialectice et philosophie*, completed 1439, which in the various printed editions became known as the *Dialecticae disputationes*.

---

[1] *Regulae elegantiarum Francisci Negri*, in A. Dati, ed. *Elegantiarum linguae latinae praecepta* (Lugduni 1589), p. 402, cited by Marsh, p. 103n. As Marsh, 'Lorenzo Valla's "Elegantiae"', notes (p. 103): 'The Ciceronians of the late Quattrocento thus re-interpreted the word *elegantia* in terms of their own stylistc ideal of full periods and aural harmonies, and the semantic import of Valla's notion has been obscured ever since'.

These are issues on which once again Hobbes, contemptuous of 'insignificant speech' and classical pedantry, would seem to come down on Valla's side. Valla's use of 'the playful approbria of the traditional invective to introduce each new argument'[1] cues us to the format of Hobbes's *Historia Ecclesiastica*. In book IV of the *Elegantiae* Valla had addressed the very issues with which Hobbes was later to deal, the application of philology to the study of a Scripture-based Christian theology and linguistic reform based on Paul and the Church Fathers. Moreover, the *Elegantiae*, composed during Valla's period of service at the court of Alphonse of Aragon (1435-46), had engaged him in disputes with the Neapolitans Panormita and Fazio that left their mark on a later generation of Neapolitan humanists. So, for instance, in the dialogues of Giovanni Pontano, and particularly his 'Lucianic depiction of the grammarians' in *Charon*, the polemics between Valla and the Neapolitan humanists resound.[2] Pontano's second dialogue, the *Antonius*, named for his mentor Panormita, takes as its model the young Valla's now lost *Comparatio*, a polemic over the relative merits of Cicero and Quintilian on the subject of oratory. Pontano in this dialogue depicting a debate in the Neapolitan Academy, not surprisingly, takes the side of his mentor against Valla, less to attack Quintilian than to defend Cicero. But in the second discussion of the Academy, Pontano, following the example of Valla, defends Virgil against unfavourable comparisons with Pindar and Homer made by the ancient grammarians Gellius and Macrobius.[3] The dialogue concludes with lyrics and a mock-epic poem, the *iter Napolitanum*, a journey poem related by a member of the Academy, Iurazio Suppazio, who narrates travels in Italy by friends, purportedly in search of a wise man, but which is largely a comical survey of local Italian customs, and ends by describing

---

[1] Marsh, 'Lorenzo Valla's "Elegantiae"', p. 108.

[2] Marsh, 'Lorenzo Valla's "Elegantiae"', pp. 108-10, citing Giovanni Pontano, *Dialoghi*, ed. C. Previtera (Florence 1943), p. 35. Marsh notes the common ground between Valla and Pontano in their 'mocking contempt for Isidorean etymologies'.

[3] Marsh, 'Lorenzo Valla's "Elegantiae"', pp. 110, citing Giovanni Pontano, *Dialoghi*, pp. 66, 67-74. This was also an issue taken up by Davenant, who similarly defended the merits of Virgil against unfavourable comparison with Homer in his Preface to *Gondibert,* with which Hobbes in his 'Answer' to the Preface, appears to concur.

'violent encounters with grammarians who thrash Suppazio for alleged errors in his Latin':[1]

> Even when Suppazio complains that he has been lacerated by fierce grammarians as if by a bear or a lion, he derives the image from Valla's account of polemics with the earlier generation of Neapolitan humanists, and when the dialogue ends with the declaiming of a mock-epic poem in which present members of Pontano's circle do battle in Virgilian guise, the hexameter polemics merely elaborate Valla's previous quotations from the *Aeneid* in attacking his adversary Poggio.

The genre and style of the *iter Napolitanum* put us distinctly in mind of another Virgilian mock-heroic journey poem, Hobbes's *De Mirabilibus Pecci*, while the themes it addresses are rehearsed in Hobbes's own work on poetics, the curious and little examined exchange with Davenant that prefaces the latter's heroic poem, *Gondibert*.

In fact we have considerably more material on Hobbes and poetry than Rymer would suggest, including the description in his *Vita* of the Cavendish library, that mentions not only indigenous historians as well as Greek and Latin, including Thucydides; but the poets, Homer and Virgil, Horace, Sophocles, Plautus, Euripides, and Aristophanes among its contents.[2] More importantly, we have an extensive disquisition on poetics by Hobbes in his 'Answer' to the Preface dedicatory of the Poet Laureate, Davenant's *Gondibert*,[3] addressed to him, as I have elsewhere discussed.[4]

---

[1] Marsh, 'Lorenzo Valla's "Elegantiae"', pp. 110, citing Giovanni Pontano, *Dialoghi*, pp. 86-94. As Marsh notes, p. 113n. Valla, in his *Antidota* cites Virgilian descriptions of combat as appropriate to his polemic with Poggio. See Valla, *Opera omnia*, I, p. 336.

[2] Hobbes's *Vita*, lines 77-84, *OL* I, p. xvii; and in Curley's translation, pp. liv to lxiv, see at p. lv-lvi, lines 75-84.

[3] See Davenant's *Gondibert*, including Hobbes 'Answer'. For the context for this extraordinary exchange, see the preface to the modern edition, Gladish's, *Sir William Davenant's Gondibert*, pp. xiv, xv, etc.

[4] See my essay, '*Leviathan*, Mythic History and National Historiography'.

A SURVEY OF THE MSS AND PRINTED TEXTS

This edition of the *Historia ecclesiastica* is based on the 1688 first printed edition, STC H2237, reproduced with few changes in Molesworth *OL* vol. 5, pp. 341-408; and listed in Hugh MacDonald and Mary Hargreaves, *Thomas Hobbes: A Bibliography*, as item 101 (p. 75). Copies of the 1688 edition are held in the British Library (B.L.);[1] two copies are held in the Bodleian (Bodl.),[2] one of them Aubrey's autographed copy;[3] two are held in the Cambridge University Library (U.L.C.);[4] one in John Meynard Keynes's Library at King's College, Cambridge (Keynes);[5] and one in the Folger Shakespeare Library.[6] All these copies appear to come from the same printing. They have notable characteristics, in common: the punctuation is often smudged, and always in the same places. For instance, the question marks, commas, semicolons and colons are usually in a

---

[1] BL 702.b.29. This copy has been rebound, but is otherwise in good condition and identical to the Bodleian and Folger copies. It has no annotations.

[2] The Bodleian copies, Bodl. 8o S 174 (2) Th. and Bodl. Ashmole 1637, the latter with John Aubrey's autograph, have marbled covers and velum spines, are in good condition, and in every other respect identical to the BL 702.b.29 and the Folger copy. They have no annotations.

[3] Inscribed as Jo: Aubrey R.S.S. No annotations.

[4] CUL P.6.30 and Syn. 8.68.27 (1). These copies lack the marbled covers of the Bodleian and Folger copies but are in good condition and otherwise identical. They have no annotations.

[5] To this copy I was unable to gain access.

[6] Identical to the Bodleian copies, but with new end papers. No annotations. This may well have been Charles Cotton's copy, bought by the Folger from the Chatsworth estate in the 1930s together with other Hobbes material, including a copy of Hobbes's country house poem, *De Mirabilibus Pecci*, bearing the inscription *ex dono authoris*, that was almost certainly Cotton's. Again no annotations.

heavy type, but the periods closing verses are often placed so close to the final word as to be almost indistinguishable: so at lines 30, 60, 80, 90, 96, 97, 100, 182, 188, 210, 212, 230, 232, 234, 238, 240, etc. At other places bleed-through, smudges, or the imprint of the type block can look like punctuation: as at lines 19, 147, 149, 523, 285. All copies have a heavy comma after 'primùm', at line 147. At 570 '(Si modo Philosophus, Simius esse potest)', the brackets appear to be entered by hand; while at line 1187 '(putas)' they are very light, and at lines 1746 'erat.)' and 1983 'hominis.)', the periods inside the closing parenthesis are almost impossible to see. At line 590 the capital E of Ethnicus is has a large smudge in the Folger, Ashmolean and Aubrey editions. The copy text, as finally established from all these copies, is referred to here as '1688'.

MacDonald and Hargreaves preface their entry for the *Historia Ecclesiastica* with a quotation from John Laird, *Hobbes* (London, Bouverie House, 1934, no page number given), about the dating of the work: 'Probably begun about 1659, but written, for the most part, some years later. The preface is by T. Rymer of Gray's Inn. The verses were a sort of sequel to the *Leviathan*, the history being compiled from Cluverius's *Historia Universalis*'.[1]

Three manuscript versions of the text are extant:

1. BL Harl. 1844, referred to in the copy text as **A**, but here usually referred to as 'Harley' for easier identification. The manuscript, in two hands, lacks end-papers and is missing its title page, the title and interlocutors being entered at the top of the first page of the poem in the second hand. The last four lines are in the corrector's hand, as if the last page had also been lost. The catchword *Et* on the previous page is in the first hand, suggesting that the last page once probably existed also in the first hand. The MS is heavily corrected, with marginal restorations of material lost in the gutter when it was too tightly bound, as well as interlinear corrections. These are indicated in our copy text by giving the uncorrected variant as **uA**.

---

[1] On the question of Hobbes and Cluverius, and which Cluverius, see Springborg, 'Writing to Redundancy: Hobbes and Cluverius' and chapter 4.2 above. MacDonald and Hargreaves appear to rely on Molesworth, who in this matter, as in others, is unreliable.

2. Grund MS. Bibliotheca Thotiana VII, 'ThottsSml. 4o Nr 213. Hobbes, Historia ecclesiastica Romana'. Referred to in the copy text as **B**, but here usually referred to as 'Grund', for easier identification, this MS, held in the Royal Copenhagen Library, is in an excellent state of preservation, is copied in a clear neat hand and has few corrections.

3. Vienna MS, Stiftung Fürst Liechtenstein, Vienna MS N-7-6, referred to in the copy text as **C**, but here usually referred to as 'Vienna'; also in a clear neat hand, a copy of the 1688 printed edition.

We express enormous gratitude to Dr. Noel Malcolm, of All Soul's College College, Oxford, who put his expert knowledge of the Hobbes manuscripts, Hobbes's hand and that of his amanuensis, James Wheldon, at our disposal by undertaking an analysis of the manuscripts and their relation to the 1688 printed edition. His conclusions are presented here more or less verbatim under points 1 to 4:

1. Harley and Grund were both copied from the same MS source; however, Grund copied more observantly and intelligently, while the copyist of Harley was less careful and seems not to have followed the meaning of the Latin.

2. The common source for Grund and Harley was once owned by Lord Vaughan, as Grund makes clear; it was almost certainly not the fair-copy MS produced by James Wheldon, but more likely a rather hastily made copy from it.

3. 1688 was based on a different source, a superior version of the text, presumably closer to the original fair-copy MS prepared for Hobbes (i.e., lacking the errors introduced by Vaughan's copyist), and seems to have incorporated subsequent improvements made by Hobbes or Rymer.

4. Harley was at some stage bound, but the pages were over-cropped, the binding was too tightly sewn, and material was lost in the gutter. Subsequently a corrector undertook to restore the lost material as marginalia, and to correct the entire manuscript to the standard of the 1688 printed edition.

5. The Vienna MS (**C**) post-dates the 1688 printed edition, reproducing its title page, and is a more or less exact replica of it, with minor modifications in punctuation (e.g. lines 1234, etc., e.g., 1373 where **C** sometimes substitutes a colon for a period, spelling

and capitalization). While it was not obligatory to include the variants of the Vienna MS, as post-dating 1688, we have chosen to do so to complete the MSS record and allow readers to judge for themselves about its likely provenance.

For these reasons, which are further elaborated below, and following the advice of Professors Donald Russell and Noel Malcolm, we have taken the 1688 printed edition as our copy text, as that most representative of the author's intention, recording material variants from the Harley (**A, uA**), Grund (**B**) and Vienna MSS (**C**).

(1) There is a mass of evidence that Harley and Grund were copied from the same source. Again and again they have the same errors: 'sterile' for 'utile', 'eris' for 'eis', 'dolosus' for 'stultus', etc. The fact that the two MSS differ in minor matters of punctuation, accentuation and capitalization is not significant: it looks as if Grund was both more likely to copy what he saw and more consistent in his understanding of the principles of versification (principles which the copyist of Harley may not have understood at all). In the long and relatively straight forward narrative sections given over to one speaker, usually Primus, e.g., lines 210-230, 1120-1225, 1240-90, etc., the relative absence of variants (and misreadings) is noteworthy. In these passages the punctuation of **A** and **B** closely coincides and **A** is less often corrected to 1688, whereas **C** follows 1688.

The fact that not every substantive error in Harley is replicated in Grund is not a reason to dismiss the hypothesis of a common source: Harley was more likely to misread what he saw. Thus in line 2017 Grund correctly read what was in front of him as 'decrerant', but Harley mis-read it as 'deerant' (or possibly 'decrant' – it is somewhat obscured by the correction). In line 80 what they both saw was a badly written 'terribiles' which looked like 'tertibiles': Harley misread it as 'testibiles', while Grund wrote 'ter', started the upstroke of a 't', but then thought about it, realised what the word was meant to be, and changed that letter into an 'r'. Harley also seems to have been more casual and sloppy in his reproducing of the cues for 'Pr.' and 'Sec.' And he was more likely to omit a word through inattention, or even to omit whole lines as, for example, in the case of lines 1928-31. Here it seems that the eye of the Vaughan MS copyist had jumped up a line, repeating 'Machina Regis' as from the line-ending above (instead of 'ferrea Martem'), raising the possibility

that the Vaughan MS from which Harley and Grund were copied was
itself a copy of a copy. Harley's eye jumped to the second occurrence, in turn, this time omitting the two lines in between, while
Grund copied correctly what he had in front of him. (The possibility
that Harley was not copying the Vaughan MS, but rather a copy of it,
which was itself exact in almost every detail, with the exception of
one or two cases of such misreadings and errors, must be seriously
considered. But whether or not we posit an extra intermediary MS of
this sort, the relationship between Harley and Grund remains essentially the same for our purposes.)

(2) We know from Grund's title page that the MS he copied was
owned by Vaughan, and said to be signed by Hobbes. Given the evidence of Wheldon's letter, one might imagine that this MS was the
fair-copy MS produced by Wheldon.[1] Indeed, as already noted,
Wheldon's personal account book contains an entry for writing out
this work in the autumn of 1671: 'Giuen me by M[r] Hobbes for
writing a booke, Historia Ecclesiastica Romana £1'.[2] But the nature
of the misreadings preserved in Harley and Grund suggests that the
MS from which they were copying is unlikely to have been a fair
copy in Wheldon's hand. His fair hand was a neat, rounded italic of
exceptional clarity, and had they copied directly from it, the numerous errors that arise from misreadings could not have arisen at all.
(Thus 'sterile' for 'utile', 'eris' for 'eis', 'finitione' for 'sine fine',
etc., etc.) A particularly revealing misreading occurs at line 253,
where Grund and Harley have 'luce deferendum' instead of 'laude
ferendum'. Looking at Grund, one can see exactly how this ocurred:
in the original MS the word 'laude' must have been broken at the end
of the line, thus:

    Lau
    de ferendum

    In some hands, 'lau' can look very like 'luce' (this is true of
Grund's hand, as it happens, in the reverse: his 'luce' can be quite

---

[1] Aubrey, *Brief Lives*, I, p. 382: 'For those Latine verses you mention about
Ecclesiasticall Power, I remember them, for I writ them out, but know not what
became of them, unlesse he presented them to judge Vaughan, or burned them, as
you seem to intimate'.
[2] Chatsworth, MS Hardwick 19, entries for Sept. and Oct. 1671.

easily read as 'lau'). However, in Wheldon's hand 'uce' and 'au' have clearly different forms. Given this and all the other evidence of misreadings, we are forced to conclude that the MS from Vaughan's library was not the Wheldon MS, but a much less legible copy made from it. (Or even, conceivably, a copy of a copy: one might suppose that the first copy made from Wheldon was not very legible, and the second – the one seen by Harley and Grund – preserved certain misreadings of the first in a fixed form.)

This raises the question why Wheldon, in his letter to Aubrey of 16 January 1679/80, should apparently suppose that it was his own MS that ended up in Vaughan's hands. The answer might be quite simple: when he writes 'unlesse he presented them to judge Vaughan, or burned them, as you seem to intimate', *both* the possibilities he mentions are covered by 'as you seem to intimate'. In other words, the suggestion had come from Aubrey, who had no doubt heard on the grape-vine that Vaughan possessed a MS copy of this work and assumed it was Wheldon's, while Wheldon himself simply does not know what happened to his fair copy but grants that either of the possibilities Aubrey suggests is plausible. Aubrey and Wheldon in their exchange seem not to canvass the possibility of more than one copy, but it is our assumption that Harley and Grund were made from a copy inferior to Wheldon's fair copy, and that it remained in Vaughan's library until at least 1685, when Grund copied it.

It is our further assumption that the copy listed in the possession of Crooke in his 'Supplement' of June 1675 was in fact Wheldon's fair copy, providing the copy text for the 1688 printed edition. This assumption is also consistent with Aubrey's letter to Wheldon of 16 January 1679/80, for clearly Wheldon's fair copy was not a presentation text in the usual sense, with a substantial Dedicatory Preface to the Judge, or Wheldon would have been certain that Vaughan was the intended recipient, rather than merely speculating that he was. The 1688 printed edition also lacks a dedicatory preface. Anxiety on Hobbes's part, and his desire to minimize incriminating evidence until the storm about heresy blew over, may have conspired to prevent a formal presentation copy. He may even have given Vaughan his verses in an earlier copy, for safekeeping. What we can establish with some degree of certainty on the basis of Malcolm's analysis (once again, more or less verbatim) is the following:

(3) There is a mass of evidence to suggest that 1688 was based on a different MS from Harley and Grund. That MS was obviously superior insofar as it preserved many correct readings in places where the Vaughan MS had misread things. In some of these cases, of course, an intelligent editor, given the garbled version present in Harley and Grund, could have deduced what the correct version should have been (although certainly not in all – e.g. 'laude ferendum'); but in other cases, such as 'ferrea Martem' instead of the repeated 'Machina Regis', it seems much more reasonable to suppose that the compositor of the 1688 edition had a different and superior version of the text to work from.[1]

We can assume that the person who prepared 1688 was a moderately good classicist – better than Grund, far beyond Harley, and possibly better than Hobbes – and a person capable of independently applying rules of punctuation and grammar and changing the text accordingly. This would account for some of the variation between 1688 and Harley and Grund. Rymer, who in his Preface sets about to establish his credentials as a classicist, is the most likely candidate. Hobbes is sloppy in his syntax and his use of tenses. Note the casual and inaccurate syntax of lines 1533-8. Although it is true to say of Neolatin in general that punctuation is no sure guide to syntax, the punctuation in the poem is very uncertain (punctuation to lines 425-6, is particularly misleading). It is also noteworthy that both Grund and 1688 (and therefore corrected Harley) are more heavily punctuated than uncorrected Harley, which suggests intervention by the editor of 1688.

(4) Malcolm in his memorandum further discusses the changes made to Harley: all the corrections, and all the restorations of material obscured in the gutters seem to be derived from 1688, as already noted. To say that the corrector of Harley was working from 1688 does not mean, however, that he made every necessary correction, or that he made no mistakes when copying this material. But there

---

[1] E.g. line 385: 1688 has atque, A and B have et, atque scans, et does not. The further analysis of these 4 points regarding the copy text and MSS, reports verbatim the communication Malcolm to Springborg, 27/1/2005. But the matters of line-numbering and the distribution of the speakers are the speculations of Springborg, in the latter case on the basis of discussions with Professor Donald Russell.

are no variants that *could not have* been derived from 1688, or that *must have* been derived from Grund instead. Many of the changes are tiny, involving punctuation and even capitalization; it is highly unlikely that these could have been derived from any source other than 1688. The compositors (and/or the printing-house's regular scholar/hack/editor) would have made small changes in such matters as they set the work; only rarely, in this period, was a MS followed in every detail of punctuation, capitalization, etc., and those rare cases would typically involve a demanding author – whereas the author was dead in this case.

The motivation of the Harley corrector remains to be explained. Why would anyone make such changes to a MS once the printed edition was available? The most likely explanation is that whoever owned this MS copy of the text discovered that it was defective (and was irritated by the constraints of the binding), and took the opportunity to correct it. We do not know when this happened: perhaps the 1688 edition was no longer available in bookshops. Booksellers' lists for *Leviathan* show a steep rise in prices where supply could not meet demand.[1] But even if the printed text of *Historia Ecclesiastica* were still available, the owner of the MS may have wanted to save a few shillings by doing this simple conversion-job himself. This is not only a perfectly normal scenario; it is the only scenario that plausibly accounts for these corrections. The corrections are certainly not in Hobbes's hand, nor that of Wheldon; and they are, in the great majority of cases, clearly not changes made by an author improving a draft, rather, they are corrections to a corrupted text. One would not expect such exact correspondence in small matters of capitalization etc. between a MS and a printed edition in normal cases of the former being used as the basis for the latter; nor, furthermore, was this MS itself used as printer's copy – it is not marked up by the printer.

In sum then, the 1688 printed edition is our copy-text; the apparatus records material variants (**mv**) from Harley and Grund; and

---

[1] See Noel Malcolm's table itemizing the relative costs of the 'Head', 'Bear' and 'Ornaments' editions of *Leviathan*, in 'The Printing of the "Bear": New Light on the Second Edition of Hobbes's Leviathan', *Aspects of Hobbes*, p. 343. The 'Head' easily won the contest, reaching 30 shillings in 1668, up from 8*s.* 6*d.* in 1651.

only in rare cases have we promoted readings from Harley or Grund to the text (indicated by **sc** for 'silent correction').[1] The marginalia are a case in point, and deserve mention. The editor of 1688 seems to have preferred to place the marginalia he found in his MS in a glossary (reproduced by Molesworth), but in our edition these are incorporated in brackets, although we have also appended the 1688 glossary.

Mention must be made of line-numbering. The 1688 edition erroneously numbers line 58 as 60, which throws off the numbering by two, and later misnumbers lines 1229-30, which throws the count off by four. The error is repeated in **C** but corrected in Molesworth (which otherwise follows 1688), while **A** and **B** have no line numbering, which is problematic for the scenario I earlier advanced that they are copies of the MS on which Hobbes was working as recorded by Aubrey, which 'numbered every 10th line'. Lines 1229-30 of the 1688 printed text, which include the references to *Leviathan* and *Behemoth*, present another puzzle. They are interpolated in **A**, by being noted in a large and uncertain hand at the foot of the page. Included in the text of **C** and 1688, but missing in **uA** and **B**, these two lines are strong evidence for a common source for **uA** and **B** which predated the 1688 printed edition to which **A** was subsequently corrected. Perhaps the interpolation was made by Rymer, or even by the printer, to advertise these works. The *Historia Ecclesiastica* was printed anonymously in 1688, might these two lines be also intended to indicate that Crooke was the printer?

A further feature of the text remains to be discussed, and that is the distribution of the speakers raised by Professor Donald Russell, who notes that this is most uncertain and that, even in 1688, the distribution seems to be erroneous. Lines 607-8, for instance, read as if they should be distributed to Secundus. Line 1035 reads as if Primus should begin here, but no text gives it. Lines 1043 to 1050 are also problematic: lines 1043-4 quote what the Monophysites say, lines 1045-6 give the Catholic reply, and lines 1047-8 a response to the reply. The passage reads as if lines 1043-4 and 1047-8 should be distributed to Secundus, and lines 1045-6 and lines 1049ff. to Primus.

---

[1] Line 1609 is a noteworthy example, where **uA** and **B** have laeserit (grammatically necessary to parallel nolit) but 1688 (copied in **A** and **C**) have laeserat.

At lines 1485 to 1490 the distribution is again uncertain: Primus should perhaps take lines 1485-6 and 1491 ff., Secundus lines 1489-90. Again at line 1505: Does Secundus interject the question 'Why' here, and again at line 1597, to be answered by Primus? At lines 1791-1800 the distribution of the speakers is again unsure, and again at lines 1969 to 1975. It seems more likely that Secundus should not resume at line 1969, but that Primus breaks off the long sequence of '*if*'-clauses enumerating the qualities of a good teacher, by asking, 'But who is so skilled . . . .?' Then at lines 1971-3 Secundus says it is all a trivial act, and Primus denies this by saying (lines 1973-4) 'I shall think this man deserving of any amount of honour: the public good demands that he should be respected.' Finally, does Primus return at line 2205? And does Secundus return at line 2225?

These uncertainties, determined in terms of the sense of the passages, are accompanied by great variation in the distribution of the speakers between MSS **A** and **B** and the 1688 printed edition, and may throw some light on the relation between them. Once again the variants in uncorrected Harley (**uA**) and Grund (**B**) are most similar, while corrected Harley closely tracks 1688 and the Vienna MS (**C**) is virtually identical with it. So for instance *Pr* is missing from uA and B, but present in 1688 and **C**, at lines 17, 41, 167, 395, 705, 757, 779, 1095 and 1387 (where *Pr* is however missing from **C** in both cases), and from lines 1427, 1671, and 2067. Similarly, *Sec* is missing from uA and B at lines 1 and 49 (added in both as marginal insertion), at lines 189 and 628 (where *Sec.* is in both cases entered at the beginning of the line below), and from lines 1447 and 1711, but present in 1688 and **C** in all these cases.

Such striking parallels once again suggest that Harley and Grund are working from a different MS source from 1688, and cannot reasonably be accounted for in terms of scribal error. The same cannot be said, however, for variations between Harley and Grund in the distribution of speakers, and here, once again, Harley departs more often from 1688 than Grund, suggesting, where Grund and 1688 are the same, a coincidence between the Vaughan MS and the MS from which the 1688 typesetter was working, and in the case of differences between uncorrected Harley and Grund, scribal errors on the part of the Harley copyist who was, presumably working from the same MS as Grund. Cases were *Pr.* and *Sec.* are missing from uncorrected Harley (**uA**) but present in Grund (**B**), are to be found at lines

69, 75, 79, 109, 111, 147, 153, 258, 262, 425, 950, 1553, 1565, 1723, 1872, and 1927. The accuracy of the copyist of the Vienna MS, **C** is vastly superior to that of Harley, as registered by the fact that there are only two instances in which the distribution of the speakers is different from 1688, and that is at lines 1489 and 1951.

I have taken the distribution of speakers as an illustration of the pattern outlined by Noel Malcolm in his analysis of the Harley and Grund MSS and their relation to the 1688 printed edition. Prompted by the extraordinary rate of discrepancies in what should have been a relatively simple matter (deciphering the names of the interlocutors presents the copyist with one of his easier tasks!), I offer the following hypothesis. Wheldon's fair copy was made at a time when Hobbes, whose palsied hand made it difficult for him to write, was probably dictating his texts. As the Chatsworth baker, Wheldon had no Latin, and would almost certainly have had the Latin checked, but possibly he was less careful about the distribution of the speakers. The fact that even in the case of the printed edition the distribution of the speakers is highly questionable then, is still consistent with our assumption that it was made from Wheldon's fair copy. The editor, Rymer, may have intervened to improve the text, but in the case of the distribution of the speakers did not revise it very well. On the basis of Donald Russell's rather negative assessment of Hobbes's talents as a Latin poet, as evidenced by the *Historia Ecclesiastica* (the Latin of Hobbes's country house poem, *De Mirabilibus Pecci*, is in Professor Russell's estimation superior, perhaps because it was closer to his schooling in the subject), it seems likely, in any event, that the published edition would have required intervention by a careful editor, who did not, however, manage successfully to address the problem of the distribution of the speakers.

(BY PATRICIA SPRINGBORG)

ECCLESIASTICAL SOURCES
IN THE HARDWICK HALL LIBRARY

Rymer in his preface identifies a number of sources for the *Historia Ecclesiastica*, editions for which can be located with some certainty in the Hardwick Hall Library which Hobbes played an important role in assembling and recording. Noel Malcolm has confirmed that the Chatsworth Library book list, Chatsworth MS E1A, is in Hobbes's own hand, and was drawn up in the 1620s to record the contents of the Hardwick Hall Library, but also includes additions made by Hobbes in the 1630s after he returned to the Cavendish household.[1] Many of the items are Continental imprints, and only to be found in French and German bibliographic sources. A smaller number are to be found in the French and German STCs (references to the STC catalogue are to the English STC unless otherwise noted). The book list MS E1A is divided between general authors and a separately listed 'Theological Library'. I address the latter, giving the list in an abbreviated form to focus on works relevant to the *Historia Ecclesiastica* and its concerns.

What follows is the list, then, alphabetized in Hobbes's own way, indicating those editions which I have been able positively to identify. In each case I give the entry as Hobbes lists it, as given and without italics: author, title, identified as folio or quarto, and shelf mark, where noted (items cross-referenced on the list have no shelf mark under secondary entries). Identification is then indicated

---

[1] Letter Malcolm to Springborg, 1/10/2000. See also J. Hamilton, 'Hobbes's Study in the Hardwick Hall Library', *Journal of the History of Philosophy,* vol 16 (1978), pp. 445-53.

by = and the full bibliographic entry and source that allowed me to locate it (in the form that it is cited, to allow easier checking), and followed by a question mark in cases I am not sure about. I should note that in some cases I was assisted by a penciled STC number on the Chatsworth List.

LIBRI THEOLOGICI

Augustini Opera. 5 vol. fol. G.3.3. etc. = *Augustini Opera*, á Bâle, chez Jean d'Amerbach, 1ˢᵗ edn, 1489-95, 12 parts in 5 folio vols (Brunet, vol. 1.)

Augustini Epitome. fol. N.5.3. = *Augustini Epitome de Johannes Piscatorius*, Augsburg, 1537?

St Augustine of the Cittie of God. Engl. fol. K.2.3. = *Of the Citie of God with the learned comments of Jo. Ludovicius Vives.* Englished by J. H[ealey]. London, 1610, fol. (STC 916); 2ⁿᵈ edn. 1620, fol. (STC 917).

St. Augustines Enchiridion. Engl. 12o. L.2.39. = *Saint Augustine his enchiridion to Laurence, or, The chiefe and principall heads of all Christian religion by Augustine, Saint, Bishop of Hippo.* London: Printed by Humfrey Lownes, for Thomas Clarke, 1607 (STC 2nd ed. 921.5).

Ambrosii opera. 3 Vol. fol. G.3.13 etc. = 1ˢᵗ edn of the works of Ambrose, á Bâle, chez Jean d'Amerbach, 1492, 3 vols in fol.; or possibly Ambrose's *Works*, 6 tomes in 3 vols. fol. ed. Dom Basa, text with corrections, Rome, 1579-87? (see Brunet, vol. 1.)

Athanasii opera. Gr. Lat. fol. 2 vol. G.3.11, etc. = Athanasius, *Operum*, tomus II, Gr. and Lat., Heidelberg, 1600, fol. (German STC C77.h.3 (I)).

Arnobius. vide Tertulliana = (cross reference missing) *Arnobii disputationes adversus gentes*. Romae 1542 in fol. (Brunet, vol. 6, p. 977); or *Terulliani opera*, Paris, 1675 fol. (Brunet vol. 6, p. 963).

Alcoran fol. N.5.18 = Ryer ([André] Sieur du) *L'Alcoran de Mahomet. Translaté d'Arabe en Francois* . . . Paris, chez Antoine de Sommaville, 1649?

Antiquitates Ecclesia Brittanica. fol. W.2.9. = James Ussher, *Britannicarum ecclesiarum antiquitates*, Dublin 1639, fol.?

Aquinus Summa. Fol. K.3.8. = Aquinas Prima secunde. (& Secunda secunde.) [Summa theologica.] 2 vol. (in I). Venetiis, per B. Locatellum, 1495-1506?

Biblia Junii et Tremolii. fol. G.2.1. = *Biblia lat. a Tremelio et Fr. Junio*, Hanoviae, 1624 fol. (Brunet, vol 6, p. 35).

Biblia Septuaginta Interp. fol. G.3.1. = the full Biblia Septuaginta are all multi-volume, but possibly, given Hobbes's interest in the Book of Job, Patrick Young, (Patricius Junius, Bibliothecarius regius). *Catena Graecorum Patrum in beatum Job collectore Niceta, Heracleae Metropolita, ex duobus MSS. Bibliothecae Bodleianae codicibus, graece nunc primum in lucem edita, et latina versa. Accessit ad calcem textus Jobi [char], iuxta veram et germanam Septuaginta Seniorum interpretationem, ex venerando Bibliothecae Regiae MS. codice, et totius orbis antiquissimo ac praestantissimo.* 1637?

Basilii opera. fol. H.3.15 = several possibile editions: *Basilii Magni Caesariensis episcopi Eruditissima opera, quorum catalogum in sequenti pagella deprehendes. Monodia Gregorii Nazianzeni. Interpretes: Iohannes Argyropilus. Georgius Trapezuntius. Raphael Volaterranus. Ruffinus presbyter. – Coloniae: ex officina Eucharii, anno 1531*; fol.; or *Omnia D. Basilici Magni Archiepiscopi Caesareae Cappadociae, quae ad nos extant, opera, iuxta argumentorum congruentiam in tomos distincta quatuor, ab Iano Cornario . . . interpretata, iterumque recognita & castigata, ac duobus libris contra Eunomij apologeticum aucta: . . .* Hieronymus Froben, 1552, or the Jesuit edition: S. *Patris nostril Basilii magni, . . . Opera quae latine extant omnia. Nunc demum praeter caeteras editiones solerti industria, nec minus accurata collatione ad fidem Graecorum aliquot exemplarium synceriori lectioni restituta, multisque libris aucta. Accedunt notae rr.pp. Frontonis Ducaei & Andreae Schotti, Societ. Iesu theologor. Cum indicibus copiosis – sumptibus Antonii Hierat,* 1617?

Bedae Venerab. oper. 3. vol. fol. J.3.11. etc. = *Opera Bedae Venerabilis presbyteri Anglosaxonis.* Basel, 1563. 3 vols.

Biblia Hebrae. 2. vol. 4°. G.1.2 = *Biblia Hebrae Chaldae, Graeca & Latina,* ed. Robert Estienne, Paris, 1540?

Biblia Lat. 4°. G.1.17. = many possible one volume editions.

Bellarmini Controuersia. 3 vol. fol. L.3.13.etc. = Antwerp 1611 edn, 3 vol. fol. (Brunet vol. 1).

Beza Testamentum. Gr. Lat. 4°. G.1.16. = *Jesu Christi Domini Nostri Novum Testamentum, sive Novum Foedus, cujus Græco contextui respondent interpretationes duæ: una, vetus; altera, Theodori Bezæ* . . . . Cantabrigiae: Ex officina Rogeri Danielis, 1642. fol. (the first Greek-Latin edition of Beza's New Testament to be printed in England) (Wing, rev., 2728A.)?

Beza Tractatus Theologici fo. J.2.1. = No work of that title, probably Beza's *Loci aliquot communes et theologici* (Frankfort [1538]; Eng. transl., under the title *Comon places of scripture ordrely and after a copendious forme of teachyng set forth*, by R. Taverner, London, 1538)?

Bernardi opera. fo. G.3.2. = St. Bernard *Opera omnia* . . . Lugduni, I. Giunti, 1538.

Bedae. *Historia Ecclesiastica* Angliae. 12o. W.1.22. = Beda *Venerabilis, Historiae ecclesiasticae gentis Anglorum*, libri V in tribus praecipuè MSS. Latines. 1644, Canterbury, fol. 2 parts in 1 vol. (STC B1662)?

Bellarminus de Scriptoribus Eccls. 4°. L.3.20. = *De scriptoribus ecclesiasticis liber unus*, Roberto card. Bellarmino e Societ. Iesu auctore, Coloniae Agrippinae, sumptibus Bernardi Gualtheri, 1613.

Bellarminus de Translatione Imperii. 8°. O.3.19. = Bellarminus, R. *De translatione Imperii Romani a graecis ad francos, libri tres*. Köln, Gymnich, 1599.

Concordantia Bibliorum. fol. M.5.12. = *Concordantiae Graecolatinae Testamenti Novi* . . . [ed. R. H. Stephanus & others.] Oliva P. Stephani, 1600.

Chrysostomi opera 10 vol. Lat. fol. H.3.1.etc. = *Joannis Chrysostomi* . . . . *Opera nunc primum Graece et Latine edita* (per Frontum Ducaeum). 10 vols Paris, 1603-1617, Claudius Morellus, fol.

Clementis Alexand. op. fol. G.3.9. = *Clementis Alexandris Opera*, ed. P. Victorius, Florence, 1550, or *Clementis Alexandris Opera Graece et Latina*, ed. D. Heinsius, Lugduni Batavorum, J. Patius, 1616?

Cypriani op. fol. H.3.13. = *Cypriani Opera*, apud Seb. Gryphium Lugduni, 1544; or Erasmus' *Cypriani Opera*, Basel, 1558 (John Fell's famous *Cypriani Opera*, Oxford, 1682 is too late)?

Historia Concilii Tridentini. Lat. fol. W.2.10. = possibly a Latin version of Paolo Sarpi's *Historia del Concilio Tridentino*, fol.

appresso G. Billio, 1619 (Brunet, 21760, 1619); tr. N. Bent as, *The History of the Council of Trent*, J. Bill, 1620 fol (Brunet, 21761, 1620); an earlier version of *Historia Concilii Tridentini Pio IV. pontifice romano, inde a sessione XVII. ad finem usque celebrati*, 1672; Or, one of the many editions of *Sacrosancti Concilli Tridentini, canones & decreta*, e.g. [with Index librorum prohibitorum] 2 pt., Venetiis, 1615 8o. (German STC 1489.cc.47).

Crackenthorpe. Defence of Constantine. 4o. K.1.12. = Richard Crackenthorpe, *The Defense of Constantine: with a treatise of the Popes temporall monarchie, Wherein, besides divers passages, touching other Counsels, both General and Proviciall, the second Roman Synod, under Sylvester, is declared to be a meere Fiction and Forgery*. London, 1621. 4°,

Chemnitii Examen Concilii Trident. fol. H.2.14 = Martinus Chemnitius *Examen Concilii Tridentini*, Frankfurt am Main, 1578; tr. Martinus Chemnitius (Lutheran divine), *On the Council of Trent*, English out of Latin (STC 5116). (see following items by Chemnitius).

Concilia, 5. vol. fol. K.3.10.etc., = an edition of *Concilia Generalia, et Provincialia . . . . Item Epistolae Decretales, et Romanor. Pontif. vitae . . .* Cologne, 1618, Gr. & Lat. 2o 4 tom. [tom. 1,2,4 are in 2 pt., tom 3 in 3 pt.]. (German STC C1174)?

Cyrilli Alexandr. oper. Lat. fol. G.3.8. = Cyril of Alexandria: *Opera omnia . . . per G. Hervetum . . . e graeco conuersis . . .* Parisiis, apud M. Sonnium, 1575.

Chemnitii Harmon. Euang: 3. vol. 4o. H.1.7. etc. = *Harmonia Quatuor Evangelistarum*, by Martin Chemnitz, completed posthumously by Lyser and Gerhard, 1628.

Cavalarii Effigies Paparum. 8o W.1.14. See *Pontificium romanorum effigies*a J. B. de Cavallerino, Romae, 1580, 8o [portraits of 130 popes from St. Peter to Gregory XIII] (Brunet, 21607, see later entry under *Pontificium*).

Chemnitii Theologia Jesuitica. 8o M.4.14. = No work of this title by Martin Chemnitz is recorded, but it is possibly Chemnitz's masterpiece, the *De Duabus Naturis in Christo* of 1578, addressing the hypostatical union.

Chemnitii Loci Communes. 8o. 3 vol. M.4.15. etc. = Martinus Chemnitius *Loci Theologici*, modelled on Philip Melanchthon's *Loci Communes*, first published after his death by Polycarp Leyser in

1591. Subsequent editions Frankfurt and Wittenberg, 1653 (German STC).

Damasceni op. fol. F.3.6. = *Joannis Damasceni opera*, ed Jacques de Billy, Paris, 1577.

Dorothei Histor. Eccl. vide Eusebius. = *Eusebii. Pamph. Historia Ecclesiastica cum Sozomeno et Socrate, Theod. Lect., Evag., et Dorothei Tyri vitis Prophetarum et Apostolorum ex ejusdem Musculi interpretatione et Theodoreti H. E. ex versione Joach. Camerarii.* Basle, 1549. Fol. (Dorothei is mentioned in Selden's *Eutyches*, but not included in Christopherson's anthology, q.v.)

Dordrectanae Synodûs Canones. 4o. H.1.18. = Latin edition of the Canons of the Synod of Dordt November 13, 1618 – May 9, 1619, possibly the *Acta Synodi Dordracenae*, Lugd. Bat. 1620?

Erasmus Paraphrase on ye Gospell. fo. Engl. K.2.11 = *Paraphrase of Erasmus upon the Newe Testamente*, London, 1548, fol., (translation of Erasmus, *Paraphrases in Novum Testamentum*, 1517), or 1551-2 edn, London, E. Whitchurch, (STC 2866)?

Epiphanii Op. 2. Vol. fol. F.3.1. etc. = *Epiphanius: Opera omnia, Gr. et Lat., Dionysius Petavius ex veteribus libris recensuit, Latine vertit et animadversionibus illustravit.* Paris, 1622, 2 vols. fol.

Eusebii et aliorum Histor. Eccla. fol. Lat. = *Eusebii. Pamph. Historia Ecclesiastica cum Sozomeno et Socrate, Theod. Lect., Evag., et Dorothei Tyri vitis Prophetarum et Apostolorum ex ejusdem Musculi interpretatione et Theodoreti H. E. ex versione Joach. Camerarii,* Basle, 1544, 1549, fol. 2nd edn. Basle, 1557, fol.

Evagrius Histor. Eccl. vide Eusebius = see above.

Eutychius Histor. Cum notis J. Selden. fol. W.2.12. = *Eutychius patriarch alexdr. Ecclesiae sune origines, ex ejusdem Arabico numc premium typis edidet ac versione ac commentario auxit J. Selden.* London, 4o, 1642 (Brunet 21545).

Episcoporum ang. Catalogus. vide Godwin. 4o. = *De praesulibus Angliae commentarius (De archepiscopius Ebroracensibus)* 4o in 8s. by Francis Godwin, Bp. 1616 (STC 11941).

Flacius Clavis Scriptura. fol. M.5.13 = Flacius, Matthias Illyricis, 1520-75, *Clavis scripturae sacrae*, 1567 (STC 10532).

Friar Minors. A Chronicle of that order. 4o. W.1.8. = Friar Angelo Clareno (c. 1260-1337), famous *Chronicon seu Historia septem tribulationum Ordinis Minorum*; possibly also Friar Thomas of Eccleston, *De Adventu Fratrum Minorum in Angliam*, 1258-1259

(Chronicle of the arrival of the Friars Minor in England); Friar Jordan of Giano, *Chronicle* (particularly of the Franciscan mission in Germany), 1262; or Friar Salimbene de Adam from Parma, *Chronicle*, 1282-1287?

Gregory Nyssene op. fol. H.3.41. = Gregory, St. of Nyssa: *Opera . . . additae I. Ducaei . . . notae . . .* Coloniae Agrippinae, sumptibus A. Hierat, 1617?

Gregory Nazianzenus op. fol. H.3.39. = Gregorius (Nazianzenus), *Divi Gregorii Theologi, Episcopi Nazianzeni Opera*, Basel, 1550 fol. (Brunet); or Gregory, St, of Nazianzus: *Opera omnia . . . Latina facta sunt J. Billii . . . labore.* Parisiis, apud J. Benenatum, 1569?

Gregorii Papae op. 2 Vol. fol. H.3.11. etc. = Gregory I, St., Pope: *Opera.* 2 vol. Basileae, Froben, 1564.

Hieronymi op. 3, vol. fol. J.3.8. etc. = Erasmus, Desiderius (1469-1536) edn of Eusebius' Works of St. Jerome: *Divi Eusebii Hieronymi Stridonensis, opera omnia accessit his in epistolarum tomos nova Scholiorum,* per Erasmum Roterodamun instauratio . . . Paris, 1534?

Hieronymi Natalis Annot. in Ev. cum Eiconibus. fol. L.5.12. = Hieronymi Natalis (Jerome Nadal, S. J.) *Adnotationes et Meditationes in Evangelia quae in sacrosancto Missae sacrificio toto anno leguntur; cum Evangeliorum concordantia historiae integritati sufficienti.* Antwerp, 1595 (illustrations to the Spritual Exercises of Ignatius Loyola).

Hospiniani Historia Jesuitica. fol. W.2.11. = Rudolf Hospinian (pseudonym for Rudolf Wirth, 1547 – 1626), *Historia Jesuitica,* 1619.

Hilarii op. fol. J.3.4. = Hilary, Saint, Bishop of Poitiers, *Opera,* Paris, 1631?

Innocentii Papae. oper. fol. F.3.7. = *Innocentii III. Romani Pontificis Opera omnia,* 1552?

Justini Martyris op. fol. K.3.21. = Langius, Johannes Silesius, *Diui Justini Philosophi et Martyris Christi Operum,* Basel, 1565?

Joverii Sanctiones Ecclesiasticae. fol. K.3.15. = John Laski, 1456-1531) Primate of Poland, *Sanctiones ecclesiasticae tam expontificum decretis quam ex constitutionibus synodorum provinciae excerptae, in primis autem statuta in diversis provincialibus synodis a se sancita,* Krakow, 1525 (includes most of the canons and decrees of the early synods)?

Josephus. Grae. Lat. fol. W.3.18. = *Flavii Josephi opera quae extant* . . . Geneva, Petrus de la Rouiere, 1611 (the first bilingual, Greek, Latin, edition of Josephus)?

Index expurgatorius. 4o. W.1.4. = *Index librorum prohibitorum*, first published 1564 by authority of Pius IV.

Jesuitarum Historia. Vide Orlandinum = Orlandini, N. *Historiae societatis Jesu* . . . . 1ˢᵗ part, Ignatius, Rome, 1615 or Antwerp 1620?

Impostures in Casting our of Divels. 4o. K.1.25. = Samuel Harsnett, *A Declaration of egregious popish impostures, to with-draw the harts of her Majesties subjects from their alleagance and from the truth of Christian religion professed in England, under the pretence of casting out of devils.* London, printed by James Roberts, 1603.

De studiis Jesuitarum abstrusioribus. 8o. W.1.25. = [Johannes Cambillion], *De studiis jesuitarum abstrusoribus.* Anon 12o [Eliots Court Press] 1609 (STC 4469.5).

Keckermanni Systema Theologica. 8o. M.4.1. = Keckermann, Bartholomaeus, *Systema theologiae tribus libris adornatum, in appendice a Operum omnium tomus secundus*, Geneva, 1614.

Lutheri opera 7. vol. fol. H.2.3. etc. = *Opera Latina varii argumenti ad reformationis Hist. pertinentia*, Latin, 7 vols. 1545-1558, with many subsequent reprintings.

Lactantius fol. K.3.3. = *Lactantii Firmiani de diuinis institutionibus libri septem. Eiusdem de ira dei ad Donatu. De opificio dei & formatione hominis [&c.]. Ite Tertuliani Apolegeticus aduersus getes.* Publisher Ven. cura O. Scoti, per B. Locatellum 1494, fol.

Pet. Lombardus. 4o. G.1.5. = Petrus Lombardus, *Sacratissima sententiarum totius theologie quadripartita uolumina* . . . .Venetiis, per Gregorium de Gregoriis, 1514.

Lennard. History of ye Waldenses. 4o. W.1.9. = Jean Paul Perrin, *The bloudy rage of that great Ante-christ of Rome . . . against the true church of Christ . . . In the historie of the Waldenses and Albigenses . . .* tr. S. Lennard. f. N. Newberry, 1624 (STC 19768.5).

P. Martyr. in Lib. Judicu. fol. H.2.11. = Vermigli, Peter Martyr, Reformer (1499-1562), *Commentary on the Book of Judges*?

P. Martyr. in Lib. Regum. fol. H.2.12. = Vermigli, Peter Martyr, Reformer (1499-1562), *Commentary on 1 Kings*?

P. Martyris Loci Communes. fol. H.2.10. P. Martyris *Loci Communes*, 5ᵗʰ edn, fol., Basil, 1608?

Monumenta patrum. 2. Vol. fol. K.3.15. = Jean-Baptise Cotelier (Cotelierius), *Ecclesiae Graecae Monumenta*. Paris. apud Franc. Muguet 1677, 2 vols (vol. 3, 1686)?

Mornaei Mysterium Iniquitatis. fol. J.2.12. = Philippe de Mornay, French Huguenot leader (1549-1623), *Le mystère d'iniquité* (Saumur, 1611, fol.) (Brunet vol 6).

Morney. Mystery of Iniquity. Eng. fol. K.2.15. = Mornay, Philippe De, *The mysterie of iniquitie: that is to say the histoire of the papacie*. Englished by S. Lennard, 1612 fol. (STC 18147).

Mornaeus de Ecclesiâ. 8o. L.4.9. = Philippe de Mornay, *A Treatise of the Church* (trans), various French, English translations (STC 18156a.5 – 18161.5).

Mercurius vide Trismegistus = Selections from Francesco Patrizi's translation of the *Corpus Hermeticum*, published as *Hermes Trismegistus Opuscula*, London, 1611 (reprinted 1628).

Missale Romanum. 4o. G.1.15. Many editions of the Roman missal were printed after its promulgation by Pius V in 1570 in execution of the decree of the Council of Trent.

Mirror of Popish Subtiltyes. vide Abbot. = Robert Abbot, Bishop of Salisbury, *A Mirror of Popish Subtilties*, London, 1594. (STC 52 1594).

Moulin agt. Coeffettau. 4o.K.1.10. = *Pierre du Moulin the Elder against R. Bellarmine, N. Coëffeteau and other doctors*. Oxford, 1613 (STC 7306).

Moulin. Confutation of Purgatory. 8o. M.3.15. = Pierre de Moulin the Elder. *The Waters of Siloe. To quench the Fire of Purgatory*. 1636 (STC 7343).

Moulins Letter to ye Papistes. 8o. M.3.14. = Pierre de Moulin the Elder. *A letter unto them of the Romish Church*. tr. 1621 (STC 7331).

Moulins de Monarchiâ Pap. Temp. 8o. L.4.25. = de Moulin, *De Monarchia temporali pontificis Romani* [Eliots Court Press] 1614. (STC 7335).

Magdeburgensium Historia Eccl. 7 vol. W.2.1. etc. = Matthias Flacius, Ludovici Regis, 1524, 9 vols, tr. M. A. Cassiodorus: 2 Magdeburg edns. 1549 C. Rôdinger, 4o (German STC BL4827.c.22 and BL4828 a. 25).

Origenis op. fol. K.3.14. = *Origenes Adamantii Operum pars secunda complectens ea maxime quae ipse in Novum Testamen-*

tum est commentatus, ex quibus antehac a nobis aediti apparent
jam commentarii in Evangelium Joannis, tum dialogi aliquot
adversus Marcionatas, praeter quos denuo libri adversus Celsum,
diversi denique tractatus e regia Bibliotheca deprompti. – Parisiis,
1572. G. Ghaudière, in fol.?
Orlandini Historia Jesuitarum. 4o. W.1.3 [q.v]. = Nicolo Orlandini,
Historia Societatis Jesu, Rome 1614, 2nd edn (with Francesco
Sacchini), Antwerp, apud Filios Martini Nutij, 1620 (Brunet,
vol. 4, 231)?
Patrum Monumenta. 2 vol. fol. K.3.6. etc. = an earlier edition of J. B.
Coteleri, Ecclesiae gr. Monumenta, Paris, 1677-81, 8o.? (Brunet,
vol. 6, 820).
P. Latina de Vitis Pontificum. Fol. W.2.14. = *Le vite de pontifici ed*
imperatori Romani, da Fr. Petrarca. Florentinae. 1478 in fol.?
(Brunet 21604)
Perkinsi Problema. 4o. H.I.13 = Guilielmi Perkinsi, *Problema de*
Romana fidei ementito catholicismo. Cambridge, 1604 (STC
19734).
Parsons. Answer to ye 5th part of Cookes reports. 4o. J.1.28. = Robert
Parsons, an Answere to the fifth part of Reportes lately set forth by
syr E Cooke. [St Omer] 1606. 4o. (STC 19352).
Perrorii op. 2 Vol. fol. L.5.8 etc. = G. Perrot defender of Jesuits S
Omers. See also *De Studiis Jesuitarum* (STC 4469.5).
Philo Judaeus. fol. M.5.8. = Philo Judaeus, *De Vita Contemplatavia,*
ed. Sichardus, 1527 (Latin trans of the Hebrew)?
Controversies inter Pap. Et Venetos. 2 vol. 4o. W.1.5. etc. = Paolo
Sarpi's *Historia del Concilio Tridentino,* published under the
pseudonym Pietro Soave Pollano, London, 1619?
Petavius 2 Vol: Fol. X.3.1. = Dionysius Petavius, *De theologicis dog-*
matibus, Paris, 1644-50?
Pontificum Roman: effigies. W.1.14 = *Pontificum romanorum effi-*
gies. Romae 1580 [portraits of 230 popes from St. Peter to
Gregory XIII]. (Brunet 21607).
Reignolds for Marriage after divorce. 4o. = John Rainolds *A Defense*
of the judgment of the Reformed churches [touching adultery and
remarriage] wherein both R. Bellarmin and an English pamphlet
are confuted [Dort, G. Waters] 1609 (STC 20607).
Reignoldi Lectiones in Lib. Apocry. 2 vol. 4o. G.1.3.etc. = John Rainolds, *The Prophecy of Obadiah opened and applied in Sundry*

Sermons, 2 parts, Oxford, 1613, 1620, 4o (STC 20619); or John Rainolds, *The prophesie of Haggai, interpreted and applyed in sundry sermons*. – London: by W.W. for W. Lee, 1649?

Reignolds and Hart. 4o. K.1.8. = John Rainolds and John Hart, *The summe of the conference betvveene Iohn Rainoldes and Iohn Hart, touching the head and the faith of the church*. London, W. Hall for T. Adames, 1609

Reignoldi Theses 8o. L.4.12. = John Rainolds, *Sex theses de sacra scriptura, et ecclesia*. Oxford, Printed by Joseph Barnes, 1613. (STC 20624).

Reignoldus de Idololatria Roma. 8o. L.4.13. = John Rainolds, *De romanae ecclesiae idolatria in cultu sanctorum, religuarum . . . libri duo*. 4o in 8s. Oxford, 1596 (STC 20606).

Sanderus de Monarchiâ Ecclâ. fol. L.5.11. = Nicholas Sanders, *Fidelis servi, unà cum errorum examine in septimo libro de visibili ecclesiae monarchia a N. Sandero conscripta*. 1573. 8o (STC 21691).

Sutclivius de Missâ. 4o. G.2.19 = Sutlivii, Mathiae, *De missa papistica . . . adversus R. Bellarminum, libri quinque*, 2 pts, 1603. 4o in 8s (STC 23456).

Sutclivius de Ecclesiâ. 4o. G.1.20. = Sutlivii, Mathiae, *De Catholica orthodoxa, et vera Christi ecclesia*, libri duo, 4o, 1592 (STC 23455).

Sempell of Tithes. 4o. K.1.26. = Sir James Sempell, *Sacrilege sacredly handled. That is, according to the Scripture only. An appendix answering some questions of J. Scaligers Diatribe, & J. Seldens History of Tythes*. 1619, 4o (STC 22186).

Seldens History of Tithes. 4o. K.1.24. – John Selden, *The History of Tithes*. London 1618. 4o (STC 22172).

Sleydens Commentaries. Eng. fol. W.2.16 = [Sleidanus, Johannes] Philippson, Johannes, *A famouse cronicle of oure time, called Sleidanes Commentaries concerning the raigne of the emperour Charles the fift*. Tr. J. Davis, 1560. fol. (STC 19848).

Sands his Sermons. 4o. L.3.12. = Sermons of Edwin Sandys, Bishop of Worcester (1559), London (1571) and Archbishop of York (1577)?

Vsher de Ecclesiâ. 4o. H.1.12 = *Jac. Usserii britannicarum ecclesiarum antiquitates*. Londoni 1687. fol. (Brunet), or James Ussher, *The Reduction of the Episcopacy unto the Form of Synod-*

ical Government, Received in the Ancient Church: Proposed in the Year 1641, as an Expedient for the Prevention of Those Troubles, which afterwards did arise about the matter of Church-Government, vol. 12 of The Whole Works of the Most. Rev. James Ussher, D. D., Lord Archbishop of Armagh, and Primate of All Ireland (Dublin, Hodges and Smith; London, Whittaker and Co., 1847)?

Vogelii Thesaurus Theologicus. 8. L.4.24. = *Thesaurus Theologicus ex sola sacra scriptura depromtus, in quo unico tomo omnes loci theologici testimoniis verbi dei explicantur et confirmantur (. . .) autore M. Matthaeo Vogelio . . .,* Tübingen, 1592

J. [John] Whites way to ye Church. 4o. K.1.33. = .John White D.D., *The Way to the True Church.* London, Richard Field for William Barret, 1608. 4o. (STC 25394, 1608).

J. [John] Whites defence of ye way. 4o. K.1.34. = (STC 25390, 1614). = .John White D.D., *The Way to the True Church.* London, Richard Field for William Barret, 1615. 4o. (The fourth impression, to which is annexed the Author's Protestation made upon his deathbed, touching his opinion in the present controuersies. MS. Notes)?

Fr. [Francis] Whites. The Orthodox way Justifyed. 4o. K.1.35. = Francis White, Bishop of Ely, *Orthodox Faith and the Way to the Church,* 1617 (STC 25380).

History of the Waldenses. 4o. vide Lennard [W.1.9.] = Jean Paul Perrin, *The bloudy rage of that great Ante-christ of Rome . . . against the true church of Christ . . . In the historie of the Waldenses and Albigenses . . .* tr. S. Lennard. F. N. Newberry, 1624 (STC 19768.5).

Whitaker against Reynolds. 8o. M.3.33. = William Whitaker (1548-1595) *(A) disputation on Holy Scripture, against the Papist, especially Bellarmine & Stapleton*?

Zozomeni Histor. Eccla. vide Euseb. = *Eusebii. Pamph. Historia Ecclesiastica cum Sozomeno et Socrate, Theod. Lect., Evag., et Dorothei Tyri*; or Zozomenus Hermias, *Historiae ecclesiasticae libri IX,* Latin, in Christopherson, John, *Historiae ecclesiasticae scriptores Graeci.* 1570, (German STC C.80.i.3) *q.v.*?

APPENDIX C
(BY NOEL MALCOLM)

GEORG GRUND, A BIOGRAPHICAL NOTE

Georg Grund spent most of his career in the service of the Danish crown; but he was not born a Danish subject, and the evidence of his one surviving diplomatic report shows that his maternal language was German. (This is also suggested by his name: Danes spelt it 'Grundt', but he himself used the German spelling, 'Grund'.)[1] He was born in Stade, a small town (formerly a Hanseatic port) on the Elbe, roughly 20 miles west of Hamburg, probably in the period 1659-63.[2] He was most probably a son or nephew of the lawyer Joachim Grund. Originally from Lübeck, Joachim had been a student at the universities of Helmstedt (in 1648-50) and Franeker (in 1657).[3]

---

[1] Just Juel, his Danish successor as envoy to Peter the Great, spelt it 'Grundt': J. Juel, *En rejse til Rusland under Tsar Peter: dagbogsoptegnelser af viceadmiral Just Juel, dansk gesandt i Russland, 1709-1711*, ed. G. L. Grove (Copenhagen, 1893), p. 141. For Grund's own spelling see the titlepage of his MS transcript of Hobbes's *Historia ecclesiastica*, and I. I. Shcherbachev, ed., *Zapiski Iusta Iulia, datskago poslannika pri Petr Velikom (1709-1711)* (Moscow, 1899), p. 7 (n.). A German might also have spelt it 'Grundt', but a Dane would have been less likely to spell it without the 't'. Although all other records give only 'Georg' as his first name, T. O. Achelis names him 'Elias Kay Georg' in the matriculation records of his two sons: *Matrikel der schleswigschen Studenten, 1517-1864*, 3 vols. (Copenhagen, 1966-7), i, pp. 277, 290.

[2] Grund's place of birth is supplied by the entry for his matriculation at the University of Helmstedt, where he is described as 'Grund, Georgius, Stadensis': W. Hillebrand, ed., *Die Matrikel der Universität Helmstedt, 1636-1685*, Veröffentlichungen der historischen Kommission für Niedersachsen und Bremen, ix, Abt. 1, Bd ii (Hildesheim, 1981), p. 221. The approximate date of birth given here is inferred from the date of this matriculation: see my comments on this, below.

[3] See J. Moller, *Cimbria literata, sive scriptorum ducatus utriusque Slesvicensis et Holsatici . . . historia*, 3 vols. (Copenhagen, 1744), i, p. 221; Hillebrand, ed., *Die Matrikel*, p. 58 ('Lubecensis'); and T. J. Meier, ed., *Album promotorum Academiae Franekerensis (1591-1811)* (Franeker, 1972), p. 35. Georg Grund's second son

Joachim Grund became a 'Syndikus'of Stade in 1659, and was a member of a delegation sent by the town to Stockholm in 1662; he left Stade in 1671, to take up an appointment at the 'Obertribunal' in Wismar (a small town to the east of Lübeck).[1] His relations with the authorities in Stade thereafter were not good: he spent the next 21 years litigating against them for the payment of expenses he had incurred while in their service.[2]

Stade was in the territory of the Duchies of Bremen and Verden, which had been under Swedish rule since 1648; between 1674 and 1687 the 'Chancellor' of Stade was Esaias von Pufendorf (brother of the philosopher and jurist Samuel), who was in the service of the Swedish crown.[3] But Denmark also had a strong influence on Stade: the opposite bank of the Elbe, to the north, was Danish territory, and from 1676 to 1680 Stade was occupied by pro-Danish forces – members of an alliance against Sweden that included Denmark, Brandenburg, and Braunschweig-Lüneburg. Wismar had also come under Swedish rule in the Thirty Years' War, being placed under the jurisdiction of the Swedish Governor-General of Pomerania. It too was captured by Brandenburg and Denmark at the end of 1675, and kept under Danish control for the next five years. Both Stade and Wismar were returned to Swedish rule in 1680.[4]

On 27 April of that year, Georg Grund matriculated at the University of Helmstedt, in the territories of the Duke of Braunschweig-

---

was christened 'Joachim': see below, n. 21. Georg himself did not study at Franeker, but a 'Gerhardus Hermannus Grundt, Stadensis, iur. cand.', possibly a younger brother, matriculated there in 1692: see S. J. Fockema Andreae and T. J. Meijer, eds., *Album studiosorum Academiae Franekerensis (1585-1811, 1816-1844)* (Franeker, 1968), p. 257.

[1] Details of the 1662 mission to Stockholm are in B.-C. Fiedler, *Die Verwaltung der Herzogtümer Bremen und Verden in der Schwedenzeit, 1652-1712: Organisation und Wesen der Verwaltung* (Stade, 1987), p. 213: I am very grateful to Dr Jan Lokers, of the Niedersächsische Staatsarchiv, Stade, for this reference. For the other details of Joachim Grund's appointments I am indebted to Dr Jürgen Bohmbach, of the Stadtarchiv, Stade. The 'Obertribunal' in Wismar was the highest court in Sweden's German territories, having replaced the Imperial 'Kammergericht' (see F. Techen, *Geschichte der Seestadt Wismar* (Wismar, 1929), p. 206).

[2] Information from Dr Jürgen Bohmbach.

[3] See H. Wohltmann, *Die Geschichte der Stadt Stade an der Niederelbe* (Stade, 1956), pp. 156, 169-70.

[4] Techen, *Geschichte der Seestadt Wismar*, pp. 205, 224-7; Wohltmann, *Geschichte der Stadt Stade*, p. 178.

Lüneburg; whether this choice of university reflected merely a family tradition, or whether it signified any particular sympathy for Denmark and the Danish alliance, can only be guessed at.[1] Helmstedt was, in any case, one of the leading universities in the northern German lands, the stronghold of a liberal and humanistic Lutheran culture. Grund studied law there, and in 1681 he performed (and published) a legal disputation, *De poenis*, under the Professor of Jurisprudence, Johann Eisenhart.[2] For a student to have done this in only the second year of his university studies would have been highly unusual; it seems very likely, then, that this was not the first university Grund attended, though the place of his earlier studies remains unknown. (Hence the conjectural dating of his birth given above, based on the assumption that he was aged between 17 and 21 at the time of his matriculation at Helmstedt.)

The next trace of Grund's activities is the inscription on the titlepage of his manuscript copy of Hobbes's *Historia ecclesiastica*, which shows that he was in London in 1685. Unfortunately, nothing more is known of this visit. Perhaps Grund was performing the sort of post-university *peregrinatio academica* that brought many young men from northern Europe to see the sights, visit the libraries and meet the learned men of London, Oxford and Cambridge.[3] Alternatively, he may have been acting already as a tutor-cum-travelling-companion to a young nobleman. He certainly fits the profile of such a travelling tutor, as described by the leading modern expert on the study-tours of Danes during this period: 'Sometimes the tutor was a

---

[1] Hillebrand, *Die Matrikel*, p. 221. When Stade had fallen to the besieging anti-Swedish forces in 1676, the University of Helmstedt had held a formal celebration of the event: see J. Cellerarius, *Panegyricus ... post felicem expugnationem stadensis civitatis* (Helmstedt, 1676).

[2] *De poenis* (Helmstedt, 1681): there is a copy in the Yale University Law Library, foreign law pamphlet collection, vol. 98, no. 3. On Eisenhart (1643-1707) see C. G. Jöcher, *Allgemeines Gelehrten-Lexicon*, 4 vols. (Leipzig, 1750-1), ii, cols. 300-301.

[3] For examples of young Scandinavians making such visits to England during this period, and details of the sorts of people and places they visited, see E. Seaton, *Literary Relations of England and Scandinavia in the Seventeenth Century* (Oxford, 1935), pp. 164-81, and the two major works by Vello Helk: *Dansk-norske studiere-jser fra reformationen til enevaelden, 1536-1660* (Odense, 1987), and *Dansk-norske studierejser, 1661-1813*, 2 vols. (Odense, 1991) (at i, pp. 124-8, on the places visited).

German student, who had originally been appointed as a tutor in the
home, to facilitate the study of the language. Quite a few of these
tutors later made their careers in Denmark . . .'[1] Of the known
Danish visitors to England in or around 1685, only one, the nobleman Vincents Lerche (1666-1742) was likely to have had an
entourage large enough to include a travelling tutor; but there is no
documentary evidence to connect him with Grund.[2] Clear evidence
of Grund's employment emerges only seven years after the visit to
England. In 1692-3 he accompanied Christian Gyldenløve (an ille-
gitimate son of the Danish King Christian V) on his foreign travels,
and between 1696 and 1698 he similarly accompanied Prince Carl of
Denmark.[3]

Prince Carl's tour included six months spent at Montpellier (a
university town, famous for its medical faculty) during 1697; at the
end of that year the Prince moved to Italy, and most of 1698 was
spent at the University of Bologna.[4] We may guess that Grund spent
some of his time at both universities attending lectures or otherwise
pursuing his own intellectual interests. Two pieces of evidence
suggest that those interests included medicine: one is the fact that he
was later appointed to the Commission for Public Health in Copenhagen (see below), and the other is a letter from Queen Charlotte
Amalie to Carl von Ahlefeldt (the nobleman who was the chief attendant of Prince Carl on his travels) in Montpellier in 1697, in which

[1] Helk, *Dansk-norske studierejser, 1536-1660*, p. 27.

[2] Lerche travelled in Germany, France (where he spent the winter of 1684-5),
Italy, England and Holland; he was accompanied by a 'hovmester' or chamberlain,
Vilhelm Helt (see Helk, *Dansk-norske studierejser, 1661-1813*, ii, pp. 139, 178).
Other Danes in England in or around 1685 include the theologian Hans Bartholin;
the future bishop Jens Bircherod and his brother Hans Husvig Bircherod; the future
civil servant Christian Hansen Leegaard; the theologian Christopher Nicolaisen
Lund; and the theologian Hans Steenbuch (*ibid.*, ii, pp. 66, 75-6, 176, 183, 253).

[3] See Helk, *Dansk-norske studierejser, 1661-1813*, ii, p. 91; R. Aereboe, *Autobiografi (1685-1744)*, ed. G. L. Grove (Copenhagen, 1889), p. 102; G. L. Grove,
ed., *Des Kgl. Dänischen Envoyé Georg Grund's Bericht über Russland in den
Jahren 1705-1710*, Zapiski imperatorskoi akademii nauk (Mémoires de l'Académie
Impériale des Sciences de St-Pétersbourg), ser. 8, vol. iv, no. 7 (St Petersburg,
1900), p. v. The entry on Christian Gyldenløve in the *Dansk biografisk leksikon*, 3rd
edn., 16 vols. (Copenhagen, 1979-84), v, pp. 402-03, states that he spent most of the
period 1691-4 in France, some of it in a Danish regiment in the service of Louis XIV.

[4] See F. Ahlefeldt Laurvig, *Prins Carls rejse* (Copenhagen, 1925), at pp. 64-5.

she expressed gratitude for 'the prescription which I received from Grund'.[1]

In 1704 Grund was appointed a member of the newly established 'College of Commerce' in Copenhagen; in the following year he was sent as Danish envoy to the court of Peter the Great. He was recalled at the end of 1708, but various delays occurred, and he left Russia only in 1710.[2] The one piece of writing by Grund that has come down to us, apart from his university disputation, is the long report on conditions in Russia which he compiled at the end of his embassy. Here, in the section on religion, we find an approach to ecclesiastical matters which suggests that Grund had indeed absorbed the lessons of Hobbes's *Historia ecclesiastica*. He began by pointing out approvingly that religion in Russia was organized 'in such a form, that the Tsar is *summus pontifex* [Pope] in his country, and therefore controls all the ways in which the temporal power of the Church must be used to support the state, for the sake of good order.'[3] He noted that one aspect of this 'special policy' was to tolerate very low levels of education among the monks and priests: the Russians had observed that too much reading only encouraged pointless disputes among the clergy, which could lead to the formation of new sects, thus causing more harm than good.[4] To illustrate the advantages of Peter the Great's caesaropapism he told the cautionary story of the great dispute between Patriarch Nikon and Tsar

---

[1] Laurvig, *Prins Carls rejse*, p. 88 (letter dated 11 September 1697): 'Den Recept, som jeg har faaet af *Ground*'.

[2] Grove, ed., *Des Envoyé Grund's Bericht*, p. v. For a modern edition of this report, with Russian translation, see G. Grund, *Doklad o Rossii v 1705-1710 godakh*, ed. Y. I. Bespiatykh (Moscow and St Petersburg, 1992); however, Bespiatykh does not add any biographical details concerning Grund's earlier or later life.

[3] Grove, ed., *Des Envoyé Grund's Bericht*, p. 31: 'solcher Gestalt, das der Czaar Summus Pontifex in seinem Lande, und daher die Handhabung alles deszen hat, worin die Weltliche Macht der Geistlichen in einem Reiche zu hülffe kommen mus, damit es ordentlich darin zugehe'. This report is in German; Grund's successor as envoy to Russia, the Danish vice-admiral Just Juel, wrote his reports in Danish (p. iv).

[4] Grove, ed., *Des Envoyé Grund's Bericht*, p. 31: 'Wobey die Ruszen dan diese besondere politiqve haben umb in dem bisherigen Stand unverändert zu verbleiben, dasz sie die Bekandte Ignorantz der Münche und Pfaffen sehr dulden, damit durch vieles Scrupuliren und gegensprechen, so aus der Lesung vielerley Schrifften und Bücher, öffters herrühret, nicht neue Secten unter Ihnen aufkommen, und also Ihrer Meinung nach mehr Unheil als Nutzen daraus entspringen möge ...'.

Alexei Mikhailovich (Peter's father) in the 1650s, in which Nikon had tried to raise the authority of the Church above that of the state. According to Grund, the Patriarch 'became so full of ambition, because of his learning, that he wanted to have himself declared the Pope of Russia'; the Tsar was on the point of agreeing to this, when he was reminded by his sister Sophia 'that after such a declaration was made in the Latin Church, the Roman Emperors were soon obliged to leave Rome and hand it over to the Pope'. Tsar Alexei had therefore changed his mind; nevertheless, 'the ambition of this priest caused much harm and damage to Russia.'[1] Grund's discussion of the state of religion in Russia ended with some admiring comments on Peter the Great's ecumenist tendencies. He noted that the Tsar had 'abolished many *adiaphora* [indifferent matters in religion], and brought his Church into conformity, so far as possible, with others . . . It is quite clear that the Tsar would like to bring it about that Russians, Catholics and Protestants should be less opposed to one another than they have been hitherto.'[2]

After his return to Copenhagen Grund was appointed chairman of the Commission for Public Health; he won admiration for his hard work during the plague of 1711, when a third of the population of Copenhagen died. He later became a provincial governor at Bredstedt (in Schleswig-Holstein, north of Husum) and a member of the upper court in Gottorp (also in Schleswig-Holstein, east of Husum and west of Schleswig). A sign of the enhanced social status he had acquired is given in the record of the matriculation (at Jena Univer-

---

[1] Grove, ed., *Des Envoyé Grund's Bericht*, p. 32: 'der wegen seiner Gelartheit so voller ambition gewesen, das Er sich zum Pabst von Ruszland hat wollen declariren lassen, auch den Czaarn dazu schon so weit induciret gehabt, das es zur öffentlichen declaration damit würde gekommen seyn, wan nicht des Czaaren damahligen Schwester, so auch Sophia . . . dem Czaren diesen Einwurf gemachet hatte: das nach solcher declaration in der Lateinischen Kirchen, die Römischen Kayser Rom bald hatten qvitieren und denen Päbsten überlaszen müszen. Welches zwar den Czaarn so sehr frappiret, dasz Er von solchem project auf einmahl gantz wieder abgegangen, Aber doch hatte die Ambition dieses Pfaffen in Ruszland viel Unheil und Schaden Verursachet . . .'
[2] Grove, ed., Des Envoyé Grund's Bericht, p. 33: 'viele adiophora [*sic*] abgeschaffet und seine Kirche so viel möglich gewesen mit anderen conformiret . . . Dieses aber erhellet wohl daraus, das der Czaar es gerne dahin bringen wolte, dasz die Ruszen, den Catholischen und Protestanten nicht mehr so feind sein solten, als sie bishero gewesen.'

sity, in 1728) of his elder son, Georg, who called himself 'Georgius de Grund, Eques Holsatus'. Another son, born at Bredstedt in 1715, matriculated at Jena in 1734, described as 'nobilis'. Their father, Georg Grund, died on 18 September 1729.[1]

POSTSCRIPT

How and when Grund's manuscript of Hobbes's *Historia ecclesiastica* passed into the possession of Otto Thott is not known, but the simplest explanation – that it was sold by Grund's executors, and purchased then by Thott – is perfectly possible in chronological terms. Thott (1703-85) spent the years between 1723 and 1727 travelling, studying at Halle and Jena, and visiting France, Holland and England (where he spent some time at Oxford). By the time of his return to Copenhagen in 1727 he was already a keen collector of books and manuscripts. However, his collection was destroyed in the Copenhagen fire of 1728, and he had to start building it up again.[2] If Grund's library was sold off in the following year, we may indeed assume that Thott would then have been in a buying mood.

---

[1] For the details of Grund's career, and date of death, see *ibid.*, p. v; Aereboe, *Autobiografi*, pp. 102-03. For the sons' matriculation records see Achelis, *Matrikel*, i, pp. 277 (Georgius), 290 (Joachimus Benedictus). Although the attendance of both sons at Jena might suggest that the father had also studied there, his name is absent from the records of that university: see G. Mentz, R. Jauernig and O. Köhler, eds., *Die Matrikel der Universität Jena*, 3 vols. (Jena, Leipzig, 1944-90), ii (for 1652-1723).

[2] All these details are from the entry on Otto Thott in the *Dansk biografisk leksikon*, xiv, pp. 558-60. That entry notes that by the time of his death his astonishingly large collection contained roughly 200,000 titles; his manuscripts were bequeathed to the Royal Library, while his printed works were sold at auction (many of them being purchased by the Royal Library). See also K. Bogh, *Det kongelige Bibliothek gennem 300 år* (Copenhagen, 1980), pp. 7-8.

HOBBES:

Historia Ecclesiastica

Translation by
PATRICIA SPRINGBORG, PATRICIA STABLEIN AND PAUL WILSON

HISTORIA
ECCLESIASTICA
CARMINE ELEGIACO
CONCINNATA

AUTHORE
THOMA HOBBIO Malmesburiensi.

Opus Posthumum.

_____Fraudesque dolique
Insidiaeque &t vis, amor scleratus habendi.
Ovid. Met.

AUGTUSTAE Trinobantum:
Anno Salutis, MDCLXXXVIII.[a]

---

[a] A, BL Harl. 1844, title page reads:
Historia Ecclesiastica
Romana.
Autore
Pereximio Viro
THOMA. HOBBESIO
Malmesburiensi.
B, Royal Copenhagen Library Thotts Sml., 4o Nr. 213 title page reads:
HISTORIA
ECCLESIASTICA ROMANA.
consignata
à
THOMA HOBBESIO.
Ex Bibliotheca
My Lord Vaugan.
exscripsit
Londini
Georgius Grund
Ad 1685
C replicates the title page of the 1688 printed edn, including the epigram from Ovid,
but gives the date as 1678. (C also includes the 1688 Preface missing from A and B.)

A CHURCH HISTORY

IN THE FORM
OF AN ELEGIAC POEM[1]

BY THE AUTHOR
THOMAS HOBBES of Malmesbury

A Posthumous Work

_____there emerged deceits and tricks
and betrayals and violence and wicked lust of ownership
Ovid. Met.

London
In the Year of Salvation, MDCLXXXVIII

---

[1] A, BL Harl. 1844, title page reads:
History of the Roman Church,
By the Author
That Esteemed Man
THOMAS HOBBES
of Malmesbury
B, Royal Copenhagen Library Thotts Sml., 4o Nr. 213 title page reads:
HISTORY OF THE ROMAN CHURCH
signed by Thomas Hobbes.
From My Lord Vaughan's Library
copied
in London
George Grund
AD 1685
C, the Vienna MS, replicates the title page of the 1688 printed edn, including the epigram from *Ovid, but gives the date as 1678. (C also includes the 1688 Preface, missing from A and B.)

HISTORIA ECCLESIASTICA.
DIALOGUS.
SECUNDUS, PRIMUS, *Interlocutores.*[a]

Sec.[b] Quid fers,[c] *Prime,*[d] novi?[e] Visendae quae fuit urbis[f]
    Causa tibi,[g] modò[h] qui ruris amator eras?[i]
Pr.[j] Rus mihi carcer erat;[k] quo quamvis non male clauso,[l]
    Intravit bello praetereunte Metus.
Verum tu quid agis, qui magnâ[m] tutus in urbe
    Invito,[n] Musis,[o] Marte,[p] *Secunde,*[q] vacas?
Sec.[r] Non facio magni Musas,[s] doctasve sorores,[t]
    Sunt illae nostri tristis origo mali.
Nonne vides rerum totus mutetur ut ordo?
    Utque pium dicunt,[u] quod fuit ante scelus?   **10**[v]
Perfidiam,[w] caedes, perjuria,[x] furta,[y] rapinas,[z]
    Nonne vides civis dicier acta boni?[aa]
Quam Christus dixit sinceram Relligionem[ab]
    Monstrant perspicuè[ac] tradita jussa[ad] Dei:[ae]
Addas à[af] Christi sperandam morte salutem,[ag]
    Munera servatae Relligionis habes.
Pr.[ah] Nunc impossibilem quandam formatur in artem,[ai]
    Non Pietas[aj] vitam,[ak] Theologia[al] dabit.

---

[a] A has this title inserted above the text on page numbered 2 (2r):
Historia Ecclesiastica. Dialogus.
Secundus. Primus. Interlocutores.
[b] mv uA *Sec.* missing • [c] A B fers • [d] A B Prime C Prime, • [e] A B novi, • [f] A Urbis • [g] uA tibi B Tibi • [h] uA B C modo • [i] uA B eras: • [j] mv uA *Pr.* missing • [k] A B erat, • [l] A B clauso • [m] uA B magna • [n] uA B Invito • [o] uA B Musis • [p] uA B Marte • [q] mv uA B secunde C Secunde, • [r] mv uA *Sec.* missing • [s] uA Musas B musas • [t] uA sorores B sorores. • [u] A dicunt; • [v] Line numbers in 1688 and C number every tenth line but A and B have no line numbers. • [w] uA B Perfidiam • [x] uA B perjuria • [y] uA B furta • [z] uA B rapinas • [aa] mv uA boni B boni; • [ab] A relligionem B religionem C relligionem. (throughout A and B forms of religio, in C relligio, are used uncapitalized) • [ac] A C perspicue • [ad] mv A B justa (read jussa) • [ae] A B Dei. C Dei • [af] A a • [ag] uA B salutem C salutem; • [ah] mv uA *Pr.* missing • [ai] A B artem • [aj] A B C pietas • [ak] uA B C vitam • [al] uA Theologia (uA B have the form theologia throughout)

ECCLESIASTICAL HISTORY
A DIALOGUE
SECUNDUS, PRIMUS,[2] Interlocutors

Sec. What news do you bring Primus? Why are you visiting the city, you
who were up to now a lover of the countryside?[3]

Pr. The country was a jail for me. However well enclosed, fear still
entered it as the war passed by.

But what are you doing, Secundus, safe in the big city in spite of the war,
are you devoting your time to the Muses?

Sec. I don't care much for the Muses, or the learned sisters,[4] they are the
dismal source of our troubles.

Don't you see that the whole order of things is being altered? That what
was once a crime, they now call upright?   **10**

Don't you see that treachery, slaughter, perjury, theft and pillage are called
the acts of a good citizen?[5]

The commands[6] of God which have been handed down clearly show what
pure religion Christ preached.

If you add the salvation to be expected from the death of Christ, you have
the rewards of preserved religion.

Pr. Now that religion is shaped into some impossible system, theology,
not piety is to give us life.

---

[2] The use of the dialogue form is typical of humanist 'invectives'. See Springborg Introduction, chapter 7.2.

[3] Hobbes's interlocutors imitate the famous singing shepherds of Theocritus,
the rhetors answering one another of Horace's *Odes* and Virgil's, *Eclogues*, especially *Ecl.*1.36. The dramatic setting has the English Civil War still in progress and
they sing of 'arms and the man', as in the opening lines of Virgil's *Aeneid*.

[4] See Cooper, *Thesaurus*: *Musae*: for humanities. Horace: *amicus Musis*: 'a studient: one geuen to learnyng'.

[5] See Hobbes's translation of *Thucydides* bk 3, §82 (ed. David Grene), pp. 204-
5 on the power of war to corrupt discourse: 'The received value of names imposed
for signification of things was changed into arbitrary. For inconsiderate boldness
was counted true-hearted manliness; provident deliberation, a handsome fear;
modesty, the cloak of cowardice; to be wise in everything, to be lazy in everything',
etc.

[6] mv A B *justa Dei*: the observances due to God.

Deque Dei dicunt naturâ[a] dogmata vana[b]
   Pastores,[c] populo[d] non capienda rudi.   **20**
Excutitur natura Dei secreta.[e] Sciendum[f] est
   Quid, Quando,[g] Quare,[h] Quomodo[i] vult et agit.[j]
Praeter Opus,[k] Leges[l] sanctas,[m] Nomenque[n] timendum,[o]
   Scire valent homines[p] de Deitate nihil:[q]
Sed nostri voluere viri praescire videri,[r]
   Quid Deus extremum judicat ante diem.
Unus,[s] ab aeterno pendere,[t] ait,[u] omnia verbo,[v]
   Alter,[w] ab arbitrio multa venire suo:[x]
In partes veniunt omnes quibus utile[y] bellum est:[z]
   Sic Doctis[aa] debes inde sequuta[ab] mala.   **30**
Nec miror,[ac] Natura[ad] homines raro[ae] facit ipsa
   Egregiéve[af] bonos, egregiéve[ag] malos,[ah]
Egregiè[ai] stultos, aut egregiè[aj] sapientes;[ak]
   Perficit[al] inceptum quodque Magister[am] opus.[an]
Ostendit Natura[ao]Deum;[ap] summeque colendum,[aq]
   Sed cultus veri non docet illa modum.
Sec. Quae nescit Natura,[ar] potestne docere Magister?[as]
Pr. Quid ni,[at]Doctorem[au] si docet ipse Deus?[av]
Sec. Quem vero[aw] docuit Deus, et quo teste sciemus[ax]
   Credibili,[ay] quenquam sic docuisse Deum?[az]   **40**
Pr.[ba] Primus erat Moses,[bb] cui testes Signa[bc] fuere
   Edita in Aegypto,[bd] retrogradoque[be] mari;[bf]

---

[a] uA B C natura • [b] B vana. • [c] uA B C Pastores • [d] A Populo • [e] uA secreta •
[f] A sciendum • [g] A B C quando, • [h] A B C quare, • [i] A B C quomodo • [j] uA B
agit • [k] uA B opus C opus, • [l] uA C leges B léges • [m] C sanctas • [n] uA B C
nomenque • [o] uA timendum B timéndum • [p] A homines, • [q] uA B nihil • [r] uA
B C videri • [s] uA B Unus • [t] uA B pendere • [u] uA B ait • [v] C verbo. • [w] uA B
C Alter • [x] A B suo • [y] mv uA B sterile (read utile) • [z] A B est • [aa] B C doctis
• [ab] A B secuta • [ac] uA B miror A miror. • [ad] B C natura • [ae] A B rarò • [af] uA B
C Egregieve A Egregiévè • [ag] uA C egregieve • [ah] uA B malos • [ai] uA B C
Egregie • [aj] uA C egregie B égregie • [ak] A B sapientes • [al] mv A B Perfidiae
(read perficit) • [am] B C magister • [an] A opus • [ao] A B C natura • [ap] uA B Deum
• [aq] A colendum • [ar] A B natura C natura, (natura generally uncapitalized throughout) • [as] B C magister? • [at] uA B ni mv C ni? • [au] uA B doctorem • [av] mv uA B
Deus! • [aw] B C verò • [ax] mv B sciemus. • [ay] uA B C Credibili • [az] mv uA B
Deum. • [ba] mv uA *Pr.* missing • [bb] uA Moses B Mosés, • [bc] A B C signa •
[bd] uA B Aegypto • [be] A Retrogradoque • [bf] A B mari.

And pastors teach empty dogmas about the nature of God that are not
    intended to be understood by uneducated people.   **20**

The hidden nature of God is examined. They try to know what, when,
    why, and how He wills and acts.

Beyond his work, his sacred laws and his name to be feared, men cannot
    know anything about the Deity,

But our fellows wanted to appear to know beforehand what God decides
    prior to the Last Day.[7]

One man says everything depends on His eternal word,
    while another says that many things occur through one's own free will.

Everyone for whom war is useful joins one party or the other,[8]

So you owe to the learned the evils that have followed from it.   **30**

Nor am I surprised, Nature does not often make men
    exceptionally good or bad,

Exceptionally stupid or wise: teachers complete her work.[9]

    [So also with religion:]

Nature[10] shows us that God exists and is to be greatly worshipped, but she
    does not teach us the due manner of true cult.[11]

Sec. Can the master teach things which Nature does not know?[12]

Pr. Why not, if God Himself teaches the teacher?

Sec. But whom did God teach, and by what credible witness are we to
    know that God taught anyone in this way?   **40**

Pr. Moses was the first, whose witnesses were the miracles performed in
    Egypt, and in the sea that turned back.[13]

---

[7] Romans, 8:29; 11:2.

[8] Mv uA B *sterile* (to read: 'Everyone for whom war is sterile'). A follows
1688, substituting *utile* for uA B *sterile*, crossed out in A.

[9] mv A B *Perfidiae* (A B read: a work of deception teachers have completed).

[10] *Natura* (despite the circumflex indicating ablative) must be in the nominative.

[11] Hobbes *Lev.*, xxxi, §9, 189/238 ff. discusses worship, in Latin *cultus*, distinguishing between the honour due to God according to the laws of natural reason, and forms of worship commanded at will by the state (*Lev.*, xxxi, §38, 192/242).

[12] Scansion requires 'nature' to be in the ablative.

[13] Exodus 14:21.

Proximus huic Aron frater;[a] summusque[b] sacerdos
    Doctus voce Dei est,[c] ordine quique suo.[d]
Tum Testamenti veteris[e] his adde Prophetas,[f]
    Et Jesum Christum,[g] qui fuit ipse Deus;[h]
Postremò[i] Paracletus,[j] id est,[k] Ecclesia[l] Christi
    Credenda est veri verba docere Dei.[m]
Sec.[n] Adde et Phanaticos[o] hujus nova lumina secli;[p]
    Et Romae,[q] si vis,[r] adjice Pontificem,[s]   50
Sed scio,[t] non docuit pugnantia dicere secum
    Verba Deus. Lex sunt, et nisi clara nihil,[u]
Perspicuè[v] descripta tenet[w] quaecunque requirit,[x]
    In libris sacris,[y] lex Vetus[z] atque Nova.[aa]
Quorsum igitur doctae lites? Sententia[ab] dispar[ac]
    Doctorum parti demit utrique fidem.
Me sequere ad Regnum[ad] Coelorum[ae] clamitat Alter,[af]
    Imo me potius,[ag] clariùs[ah] Alter[ai] ait.[aj]
Vela ratis sanctae jactantur in aere[ak] scisso:[al]
    Ejicitur Pietas[am] simplicitasque foras.   60
Rex noster nobis et[an] Moses est, et Aäron;[ao]
    Nescio,[ap] Doctores qualia regna volunt.
Omnes alloquitur Dominus per Biblia sacra;[aq]
    Verbaque,[ar] clam nobis, nulla susurrat eis.[as]
Dic mihi,[at]*Prime,*[au] precor,[av] secli[aw] studiose vetusti,[ax]
    Et severe satis Censor[ay] in Historia,[az]

---

[a] uA B frater • [b] C sumusque (error) • [c] uA B est • [d] A suo • [e] A C Veteris •
[f] A B Prophetas • [g] B Christum • [h] A B Deus C DEUS. • [i] A C Postremo •
[j] A Paracletus B Paracletus: C paracletus, • [k] uA id est missing, rectified in A •
[l] B C ecclesia • [m] A B Dei • [n] mv uA *Sec.* missing • [o] A Fanaticos C Fanaticos,
• [p] uAB secli A secli. • [q] uA B Romae • [r] uA B vis • [s] B Pontificem. • [t] A B
scio • [u] A B C nihil • [v] C Perspicue • [w] A B tenet, • [x] A B requirit • [y] uA B
sacris • [z] mv uA B C vetus • [aa] mv uA B nova. • [ab] A B sententia • [ac] A B
dispar, • [ad] A B C regnum • [ae] A B C coelorum • [af] mv uA Alter missing; A
Alter, B alter C alter, • [ag] uA B potius • [ah] A B C clarius • [ai] uA B C alter •
[aj] The 1688 edition erroneously numbers this line 60, which throws off the numbering by two. The error is repeated in C but corrected in Molesworth which otherwise
follows 1688. • [ak] A C aëre • [al] mv uA B scite • [am] A C pietas • [an] mv uA B et
missing • [ao] mv uA B est Moses et Aaron (word order) • [ap] uA B Nescio • [aq] A
B sacra: • [ar] uA B Verbaque • [as] mv uA B eris. • [at] uA B mihi • [au] uA B Prime
C Prime, • [av] uA B precor • [aw] uA seculi (error) • [ax] uA B vetusti • [ay] uA B C
censor • [az] uA B historia C historia.

Next came Aaron, his brother; and the High Priest was taught by the
voice of God, each in his own turn.[14]

Then add to these the Prophets of the Old Testament,
and Jesus Christ who was Himself God.

Finally the Paraclete, that is the Church of Christ, must be believed to
teach the words of the true God.

Sec. Add also the Fanatics, the new lights of this age, and, if you wish,
throw in the Pontiff of Rome.   **50**

But I know that God did not teach to preach contradictory words. They
are the Law, and unless they are clear, they are nothing.

The Old Law and the New contain everything it requires, clearly set down
in Holy Scripture.

To what purpose then are these learned disputes? The differing opinion of
the Doctors takes away the credibility of each party.

One keeps shouting, 'Follow me to the Kingdom of Heaven',
'Oh No', the other says louder, 'follow me instead'.

The sails of the holy boat[15] are tossed about in the rent air, and piety and
simplicity are thrown overboard.   **60**[16]

Our king is for us both a Moses and an Aaron;
I do not know what sort of kingdoms the Doctors want.

The Lord speaks to everyone through the Holy Bible and he whispers to
them no words secretly from us.

Tell me Primus, I pray, since you have an interest in ancient times and are
a tough enough critic in historical matters,

---

[14] Numbers 1:1 ff.

[15] The baque of St. Peter, i.e., the Church.

[16] Line 58 is numbered in the 1688 edn as 60. This uncorrected fault throws the
count off by two until a similar error at line 1586 throws it off by four for the rest of
the poem. Molesworth corrects these errors.

Quis fuit ille hominum qui se (nisi[a] Rex fuit idem)[b]
  Esse Deo-doctum[c] dicere primus erat ?[d]
Pr.[e] Scis ut Aristoteles[f] trutinata[g] cacumina rerum
  In duo divisit,[h] Stultitiam[i] atque Dolum.[j]   **70**
Est Dolus in rebus, sunt certi denique stulti,[k]
  Utris conveniunt Regia sceptra magis ?
Et melius defendet uter Stultusne[l] Dolosum,[m]
  Anne Dolosus[n] eum[o] qui caret ingenio ?[p]
Sec.[q] Arma Deo-doctis[r] ipsorum Lege[s] negantur ;[t]
  Vita truces gladios tam pretiosa fugit.
Ergo quibus telis, quibus artibus, et quibus armis[u]
  Nos hi defendent, bellaque nostra gerent ?[v]
Pr.[w] Quos tu forte[x] times hostes,[y] non dico nec arma ;[z]
  Sunt hostes alii,[aa] terribilesque[ab] magis.   **80**
Est Mundo[ac] nostro Mundus[ad] conterminus alter,[ae]
  Nostri dissimilis,[af] perpetuusque comes :[ag]
Qui Phoebum nunquam vidit[ah] nunquamque videbit,[ai]
  Quantuncunque[aj] gradum grandiat ille suum ;[ak]
Quemque habitat[al] populus numerosus,[am] qui neque mortem
  Nec morbum norunt ;[an] Spirituale[ao] genus ;[ap]

---

[a] mv uA nisi (parenthesis missing) • [b] mv uA B idem (parentheses missing) C idem.) • [c] mv uA B Deo doctum C DEO-doctum • [d] mv uA B erat. • [e] mv uA *Pr.*missing • [f] sc mv 1688 Aristotelis • [g] mv A B trutinando (read trutinata) • [h] uA B C divisit • [i] uA B C stultitiam • [j] uA B C dolum. • [k] A B stulti; • [l] uA B C stultusne • [m] uA B C dolosum, • [n] mv uA B stultus (error) C dolosus • [o] A C eum, • [p] mv C ingenio • [q] mv uA *Sec* missing • [r] uA B Deodoctis • [s] A B C lege • [t] uA B negantur • [u] A armis. B armis, • [v] mv uA B C gerent. • [w] mv uA *Pr.*missing • [x] A fortè B forté • [y] uA hostes B hostés • [z] uA B arma, • [aa] uA B alii • [ab] mv A B testibilesque (read terribilesque) • [ac] uA B C mundo • [ad] uA B C mundus • [ae] B alter • [af] uA B dissimilis • [ag] A B comes. • [ah] A C vidit, • [ai] ~ A videbit • [aj] A B Quantum cunque C Quantumcunque • [ak] A suum. • [al] mv uA B habitant • [am] mv B uA spectra populus numerosus (spectra crossed out in A) • [an] uA B norunt • [ao] uA B C spirituale • [ap] uA B genus

Which man (if he was not also a king), was the first to claim that he was
    taught by God?

Pr.   You know how Aristotle, having examined extremes, divided them
    into two types, folly and treachery.[17]   **70**

Treachery can be found in many places, and fools moreover are a
    constant, but which of the two is better suited to royal power?

Shall the fool defend the deceitful man better? Or shall the deceitful man[18]
    defend better the man who lacks intellectual ability?

Sec.   Arms are denied to God-taught men by their own law: so valuable a
    life shuns the cruel sword.

So by what missiles, by what skills, and by what weapons shall these men
    defend us and wage our wars?

Pr.   Those you are possibly afraid of, I do not call enemies or weapons.
    There are other formidable enemies.[19]   **80**

There exists another world coterminous with our world,[20] unlike our
    world, yet its constant companion.

A world which has never seen the sun, and never will see it,
    however much Phoebus might enlarge his course.

A numerous population[21] inhabits that world knowing neither death nor
    sickness; they are a spirit race:[22]

---

[17] Possibly *Aristotle, *Eth. Eud.* 1221a12 on categories.

[18] mv A substitutes *dolosus*, deceitful, for uA *stultus*, stupid.

[19] mv 1688 terribilesque A, B testibilesque; A, B would read: 'There are other
attested enemies'.

[20] On the parallel world of the gods in Epicurean theory see Cyril Bailey, *The
Greek Atomists and Epicurus*, p. 362 ff. and Joseph Moreau, 'Epicure et la Physique
des Dieux', *Revue des Études Anciennes*, vol. 70 (1968), pp. 286-94.

[21] mv uA B habitant spectra populus numerosus: Spectres inhabit that world, a
numerous population etc.

[22] Invernizzi notes of the list of names that follows, drawing on the 1688 Glossary (pp. 604-5 of this edition): 'The first four names invented by Hobbes allude to
the psychic origin of the belief in demons: the names Umbri, Somnites, signify
respectively sons of the Shades and sons of Dreams; the Ameninees, Atheneentes,
derive from the Greek words Amenenos (without force without consistency) and
Asthenes (weak)'. Note that Cooper's 1565 *Thesaurus* lists none of these terms.

Umbri, Somnites, Amenenees,[a] Astheneentes[b]
  Et Cacodaemonii,[c] Daemoniique[d] alii;
Quotquot et hinc homines nostri moriuntur ad illos,[e]
  Nec Regum Leges[f] id prohibere valent.   **90**
Hi nobis hostes, hi nos terroribus implent,[g]
  Defessos[h] animos[i] nec relevare sinunt.[j]
Invadunt homines noctu,[k] somnoque ligatos[l]
  Terribiles oculis, unguibus,[m] atque minis.
Attamen ad lucem,[n] percussi pectoris agmen
  Spectrorum,[o] ventis ocyùs,[p] omne,[q] fugit.[r]
Sed quoniam metuebat ab his,[s] quod erat metuendum,[t]
  Et sperabat ab his omnia,[u] turba levis,[v]

---

[a] mv uA B Armenenus • [b] mv uA B Asthenienses, • [c] mv uA B Lacodemoniis •
[d] uA B Demoniique C daemoniique • [e] mv uA ad illos missing; B ad illos • [f] uA
B C leges • [g] A implent • [h] mv C Defensos (error) • [i] A animos, • [j] A sinunt •
[k] uA B C noctu • [l] B legatos, • [m] A Unguibus B C unguibus • [n] uA B lucem •
[o] uA B Spectrorum • [p] uA B ocyus • [q] A B omne • [r] A B fugit • [s] B his • [t] A
B metuendum • [u] uA B omnia • [v] uA B levis

The Shades, the Dream fiends, the Amenenees,[23]

the Asthenentes,[24]the bad Demons[25] and the other Demons;

And all our men from here who go to them in death,

the laws of kings are incapable of preventing it.   **90**

These are our enemies, these fill us with horrors,

and they do not allow exhausted souls relief,[26]

Striking terror with their eyes, their claws[27] and their threats, they fall

upon men at night when they are bound in sleep.

Nevertheless, at first light, the whole procession of spectres, with stricken

breast, take flight, swifter than the winds,

But since the fickle crowd feared from them what it needed to fear, and

expected all things from them,

---

[23] mv uA B: Armenenus A corrected to 1688 Amenenees. The Amenenees are *Homer's νεκύων ἀμενηνά κάρηνα 'the powerless heads of the dead', from *Odyssey* 11.49.

[24] mv uA: B: Asthenienses, A corrected to 1688, Astheneentes, αςθενεντες from *astheneis* (Gr. adj.) weak, feeble; sick; poor, insignificant. See the 1688 Glossary (pp. 604-5), 'invalidi, languescentes'.

[25] mv uA B: Lacodemoniis – i.e. Spartans. A corrected to 1688: Cacodaemonii. See Thomas, *Dictionarium Linguae Latinae*, 'Cacodaemon, onis: f.g. Val. Max. An evill spirit or devill.'

[26] Lucretius in *De Rerum Natura*, 1.102-3, notes how priests capitalize on the vulnerability of humans to superstition, by inventing nightmares and fears of eternal torments and urges us (1.130-5, pp. 10-15, tr. W. H. D. Rouse, commentary by M. F. Smith, London, Heinemann, 1975, Loeb edn) to:

> examine with keen-scented reasoning, of what spirit is made and the nature of the mind, and what thing it is that meeting us when awake terrifies our minds whilst we are labouring under disease, or buried in sleep, so that we seem to see and to hear in very presence those who have encountered death, whose bones rest in earth's embrace.

Hobbes *Lev.*, ii, §8, 8/10-11, declared:

> From this ignorance of how to distinguish dreams, and other strong fancies, from vision and sense did arise the greatest part of the religion of the gentiles in time past, that worshipped satyrs, fawns, nymphs, and the like;.... And for fairies and walking ghosts, the opinion of them has I think been on purpose, either taught or not confuted to keep in credit the use of exorcism, of crosses, of holy water, and other such inventions of ghostly men.

[27] Horace *Epodes*, 5.92-4 (Penguin edn, p. 54):

> I shall/ waylay you by night as a Fury; my shade
> shall slash at your faces with crooked nails,
> as Manes are empowered to do;

*Socrates of Constantinople believed that the *Emperor Julian had been slain by 'snaky-haired female spirits called the Erinyes' (Socrates, *Hist. Eccl.*, iii.21); see Chestnut, *The First Christian Historians*, p. 180, who recounts that Socrates took seriously other classical pagan demons, recording (*Hist. Eccl.*, iv.19) that 'an *Alastôr* spelled out the letters ΘΕΟΔ in the famous episode of the magic tripod that foretold the name of Valens' successor'.

Ars non magna fuit,[a] jam fraenis ore receptis,[b]
    Ducere perdomitos[c] quâ[d] voluere viâ.[e]   **100**
Sufficiebat enim,[f] conjunctis foedere agyrtis   **Montinbanchi**[g]
    Cum sibi sit populi concilianda fides,[h]
Alter[i] ut alterius virtutem magnificaret,[j]
    In speciemque Artis[k] verba locare nova :[l]
Hinc Magus, Astrologus, Divinus,[m] Sortilegusque,[n]
    Creditur indoctis,[o] esse Propheta Dei ;[p]
Talibus et cupiunt Regni committere jura,[q]
    Aut Praeceptores[r] Regis habere sui.
Sec.[s] Scire velim fontem sceleratae qui fuit artis,
    Primaque[t] quae tantae fraudis origo fuit.[u]   **110**

---

[a] B fuit • [b] A B receptis • [c] A B perdomitos, • [d] uA B C qua • [e] B via. • [f] uA B enim • [g] sc mv B (and Molesworth) marginal gloss : Montinbanchi • [h] mv A B fides. • [i] A Alter, • [j] A B magnificaret • [k] A B C artis • [l] uA nova. B nova. • [m] uA divinus A B C Divinus • [n] uA B sortilegusque A C Sortilegusque • [o] uA B indoctis • [p] uA B Dei • [q] ~ A jura B jura. • [r] A Praeceptores, • [s] mv A *Sec.* missing • [t] A Primaque, • [u] mv A B fuit

It took no great skill, once their mouths took the bit – to lead those
    subdued by what road they wished.   **100**
For it was sufficient for mountebanks conspiring together,[28] when they
    had to secure the people's trust,
To magnify one another's virtues and assign new words to produce an
    appearance of art.
For this reason the magician, the astrologer, the diviner and soothsayer,
    are all believed by the uneducated to be the prophets of God.[29]
And to such men the people want to entrust the laws of the realm, or else
    to have them as mentors of their own king.
Sec. I would like to know the source of their pernicious skill and the first
    beginnings of such great fraudulence.[30]   **110**

---

[28] See the 1688 Glossary (pp. 604-5), and Molesworth's note 1, p. 352 to line 101:
[agyrtai, simpliciter, qui populum congregant: item, circulatores circum-
foranei, qui congregata multitudine pharmaca aliqua ostentant, eaque praed-
icantes divendunt. Vide GLOSSARIUM.]
agyrtai, simply, those who gather men together: likewise, those who circulate
around the forum or market place, who having gathered them together, show
to the multitude drugs or cosmetics, which the preachers sell in lots.
B: inserts Montinbanchis in the margin beside agyrtis, indicating that in 1685 already
the connection to a Mountebank was made; see the 1688 Glossary (pp. 604-5).
Hobbes's 'conjunctis foedere agyritis' may be a mocking echo of Lucretius `com-
munia foedere pacis' violated by regicides (*De rerum natura*, 5.1155), a passage
commented upon in *Pierre Gassendi's *Syntagama* p.790b. See Paganini, 'Hobbes,
Gassendi, and the Tradition of Political Epicureanism', *Hobbes Studies*, vol 14
(2001), p. 7.
[29] See Juvenal *Satire* 3.58-83 (Juvenal, *The Sixteen Satires*, Peter Green tr.
(Harmondsworth, Penguin, 1974), p. 89):
    Now let me turn to that race which goes down so well/ with our millionaires,
    but remains *my* special pet aversion,/ and not mince my words. I cannot, citi-
    zens, stomach/ a Greek-struck Rome. Yet what fraction of these sweepings/
    derives, in fact, from Greece? For years now Syrian/ Orontes has poured its
    sewerage into our native Tiber – / its lingo and manners, its flutes, its out-
    landish harps/ with their transverse strings, its native tambourines,/ and the
    whores who hang out round the race-course. . . . All of them lighting out for
    the Cities' classiest districts/ and burrowing into great houses, with a long-
    term plan/ for taking them over. Quick wit, unlimited nerve, a gift/ of the gab
    that outsmarts a professional public speaker –/ these are their characteristics.
    What do you take/ that fellow's profession to be? He has brought a whole
    bundle/ of personalities with him – schoolmaster, rhetorician,/ surveyor, artist,
    masseur, diviner, tightrope walker, / magician or quack, your versatile hungry
    Greekling/ is all by turns.
[30] See Ovid's characterization in *Metamorphoses* I.130-1 of the Iron Age, a
period of brutal war, of 'deceits and tricks and betrayals and violence and wicked
lust of ownership', the epigram chosen for the 1688 title page.

Pr.[a] Orbe fuit toto quondam sapientia vultu
    Uno,[b] jus Patriae[c] scire et amare suae;[d]
Quam docuit Natura,[e] peritior Arte[f] Magistra,[g]
    Commoda quae jussit quaerere quemque sua.
Ergo suae causa conspiravere[h] salutis
    Exigui multi magnus ut esset homo;[i]   **Origo Civitatum**[j]
Cunctorumque opibus[k] communem ut pelleret hostem,[l]
    Servaret pacem, justitiamque domi.
Regibus hinc vires,[m] populo sunt otia nata;[n]
    Artibus ingenuis otium origo fuit.   120
Tunc astra,[o] et coelum mirantibus,[p] orta libido est
    Quaerere quid faciunt, quo properantque loci;[q]
Qua[r] nobis facit arte diem Sol,[s] Lunaque[t] mensem,
    Annum complures aedificantque Dies.[u]
Nec leges tantum Stellarum[v] quaerere;[w] frontes[x]
    Inspiciunt;[y] utrum[z] prospera,[aa] necne ferant.
Dama Viatorem sic spectat praetereuntem,
    Fortuitus quoniam nescit,[ab] an hostis eat.[ac]
Hinc primo[ad] nobis Ars utilis Astronomorum,
    Ingenii puri filia nata fuit;[ae]   130
Haec cum[af] Deliquium[ag] certa praediceret hora[ah]
    Phoebi[ai] vel[aj] Phoebes, res faceretque fidem:[ak]

---

[a] mv uA *Pr.* missing • [b] uA B Uno • [c] A B C patriae • [d] uA B suae, • [e] uA B natura C natura, • [f] uA B C arte • [g] uA B C magistra, • [h] A B conspiravére • [i] uA B homo • [j] sc mv A B marginal heading inserted at line 116 • [k] A B opibus, • [l] uA B hostem • [m] uA B vires • [n] uA B nata, • [o] uA B C astra • [p] uA B mirantibus • [q] mv uA B loco • [r] A Quâ • [s] mv uA B sole, (error) • [t] uA B C lunaque • [u] A B C dies. • [v] A B C stellarum • [w] uA B C quaerere, • [x] uA fontes (error) • [y] uA B Inspiciunt, • [z] mv uA B utrum missing; marginal addition in A but with no indication where it should be inserted in the text • [aa] uA B prospera • [ab] A B nescit • [ac] mv uA B erat. • [ad] B primò • [ae] A B fuit. • [af] A cùm • [ag] A B C deliquium • [ah] A B hora, • [ai] A Phoebi, • [aj] mv C et • [ak] A B fidem.

Pr. At one time wisdom had a single manifestation throughout the whole
world,[31] to know and love the law of one's country;
Nature, a more experienced teacher than art, taught this and ordered
everyone to seek his own advantage.
Therefore, for the sake of their own safety, many small men united so
· there could be one great man;[32]   **origin of the state**[33]
And so that he could rout the common enemy with all of their resources,
conserve peace and maintain justice at home.
From this source originated power for kings and leisure for the people; and
leisure was the wellspring of the liberal arts.[34]   **120**
Then, from marveling at the stars and sky, the desire arose to ask what
they are doing, and to what place they are hurrying;[35]
By what skill the sun makes the day for us, and the moon the month, and
many days build up a year –
And not only to inquire into the laws of the stars: they also examine their
aspects to see if they bring good fortune or not.
In the same way a deer watches a passing traveler because she does not
know whether he is passing by chance or whether he is an enemy.
From this, the practical art of the astronomers, the daughter of pure
intellectual activity, was first born to us.[36]   **130**
When this art predicted an eclipse of the sun or the moon at a definite
time, and the event gave credence to the prophecy –

---

[31] 'Orbe fuit toto quondam sapientia vultu Uno' echoes Ovid, *Metamorphoses*
1.6: 'unus erat toto naturae vultus in orbe' ('the whole revolving face of the globe
was one in nature').

[32] *Leviathan* as the product of social contract.

[33] A, B marginal note, *Origo Civitatum.*

[34] See Ovid, *Met.* 1.100: 'mollia per agebant otia'; and *Lev.*, xlvi, $6, 368/455:
'*Leisure* is the mother of *philosophy*; and *Commonwealth*, the mother of *peace* and
leisure.'

[35] mv uA B: in or from what place they are hurrying.

[36] C.f. *Epicurus Rational Sentences* (Κγριαι Δοχαι), XI (Bailey, *Epicurus, the
Extant Remains*, p. 97):
> If we were not troubled by our suspicions of the phenomena of the sky and
> about death, fearing that it concerns us, and also by our failure to grasp the
> limits of pains and desires, we should have no need of natural science.

and *Κγριαι Δοχαι*, XII (*loc. cit.*):
> A man cannot dispel his fear about the most important matters if he does not
> know what is the nature of the universe, but suspects the truth of some mythi-
> cal story. So that without natural science it is not possible to attain our plea-
> sures unalloyed.

See also *Lev.*, chapter 12 on the origins of religion in native curiosity and fear.

Si quo,[a] quodque,[b] loco coeli se ostenderet astrum,
  Et quando, et nomen dicere promptus erat,[c]
Quantus erat stupor bipedum, quanti faciebant[d]
  Astronomum![e] Socius[f] creditur esse Dei.
Attamen ut tritici,[g] crescunt zizania,[h] in arvis,[i]
  Ambitio ingeniis gaudet adesse bonis.[j]   **Origo Astrologiae**[k]
Nam cum se tanto senserunt esse in honore,[l]
  Et sua dicta,[m] velut dicta valere Dei,[n]   140
Uti stultitiâ[o] populi voluere,[p] timeri[q]
  Quaerunt,[r] humanum despiciuntque genus.
Credi scire futura volunt quaecunque;[s] quia astris
  Sunt inscripta,[t] aiunt, nec legit astra alius.[u]
Nec modo praedicunt adversa et prospera Regum,[v]
  Sed modicis etiam fata parata viris.[w]
Sec.[x] Dic quibus in terris primùm,[y] quo sole,[z] lutoque
  Egregio[aa] ingenia haec nata fuisse putas?[ab]

---

[a] uA B quo • [b] A B quodque • [c] A B erat. • [d] B faciebant, • [e] mv uA B
Astronomum; • [f] uA B socius • [g] uA B tritici • [h] A B zizania • [i] A B arvis •
[j] A B bonis • [k] sc mv A B marginal heading • [l] ~ A honore • [m] uA B dicta •
[n] B Dei • [o] A B C stultitia • [p] mv A B voluere. • [q] A B Timeri • [r] uA B
Quaerunt • [s] uA B quaecunque, • [t] uA B inscripta • [u] uA B alius • [v] uA
Regum C regum, • [w] B viris • [x] mv uA *Sec.* missing after first being inserted in
the line above and deleted • [y] uA B primum C primum, • [z] uA B sole • [aa] A
Egregiò B Egrégio • [ab] mv B putas

If he [the astronomer] was ready to say at what point in the sky each star
would appear and when, and to give it a name,

How great was the amazement of those bipeds, how highly they used to
regard the astronomer! He was believed to be an ally of God.

And yet as tares grow in fields of wheat,[37] so ambition rejoices to be
counted among good talents,[38]   **origin of Astrology**[39]

For when the astronomers realized that they were held in such great esteem
and that their words were valued as if they were the words of God, **140**

They wanted to exploit the stupidity of the people. They try to be feared
and they despise the human race.

They want it believed that they know all the future; because these things,
they say, are written in the stars, and others cannot read the stars.

Not only do they predict the misfortunes and successes of kings, but also
the fate prepared for men of lesser rank.

Sec. Tell me, in what lands, under what sun, and from what marvelous
clay, do you think these abilities first sprang forth?[40]

---

[37] Matthew 13:25.

[38] Hobbes conflates the Biblical parable of the wheat and the tares, Matthew
13:24-27, with the parable of the talents, Matthew 25:13-30. For Hobbes's curious
treatment of the parable of the talents, see Paganini, 'Hobbes, Valla and the Trinity',
British Journal for the History of Philosophy, vol. 40 (2003), pp. 183-4, who
stresses that this was not an interpretation given to the parable by the Protestant
reformers. Paganini, 'Thomas Hobbes e Lorenzo Valla. Critica umansitica e
filosofia moderna', *Rinscimento, Rivista dell' Instituto Nazionale di Studi sul
Rinascimento*, 2nd series, vol. 39 (1999), pp. 515-68, at p. 543, notes a moderation in
tone in the *Historia Ecclesiastica* and a plea for toleration with regard to heretics, by
appeal to Christ's recommendation that the wheat and the tares should not be separated until the last day.

[39] A, B: marginal title inserted, *Origo Astrologiae*, the Origin of Astrology.

[40] An echo of Virgil *Eclogues* 3.104 – perhaps an example of what Rymer in his
Preface refers to as 'parodia'. See also Diodorus Siculus, *Bibliotheikeis Historikeis*
(Library of History), 3 vols, trans. C.H. Oldfather (London, Heinemann, 1946-52),
1.7, pp. 24-7:

> while all that was mud-like and thick and contained an admixture of moisture
> sank because of its weight into one place; and as this continually turned upon
> itself and became compressed out of the wet it formed the sea, and out of what
> was firmer, the land, which was like the potter's clay and entirely soft. But as
> the sun's fire shone upon the land, it first of all became firm, and then, since
> its surface was in a ferment because of the warmth, portions of the wet swelled
> up in masses in many places, and in these pustules covered with delicate mem-
> branes made their appearance. And while the wet was being impregnated with
> life by reason of the warmth in the manner described, by night the living
> things forthwith received their nourishment . . . .

Pr. Ne dubites,[a] illic[b] ubi summa potentia[c] solis[d]
   Semper erat, tellus et bene cocta fuit;[e]   **150**
Multus ubi serpens[f] et corpore nascitur ingens,[g]
   Ingenio vincens[h] quicquid habebat ager.[i]
Sec.[j] Aethiopas dicis, quos,[k] sunt qui dicere primos
   Non dubitant hominum,[l] quos generavit humus.[m]
Ast ego cum multis deductas esse putavi
   Artes Aegypto quasque Mathematicas:[n]
Cernere[o] ubi stellas longus concedit Horizon;[p]
   Adnictant quoties, quo coeuntque[q] loco.
Nonne Aegyptia erat pretio sapientia quondam[r]
   Ingenti? Et[s] Graecis non erat inde sua?[t]   **160**

                                                   Origo Artium[u]

Quo nisi in Aegyptum[v] Plato, Thales, Pythagorasque,[w]
   Atque alii plures,[x] eximiique viri,
Et vacuus,[y] nec habens longas[z] quo falleret horas,
   Ad mercandum artes ibat et ingenium?

---

[a] uA B dubites • [b] uA B illic, • [c] B poténtia • [d] B solis, • [e] uA B fuit. • [f] A B serpens, • [g] A ingens • [h] A B vincens, • [i] mv uA B ager • [j] A *Sec*. Reinserted after uA insertion in the line above was deleted • [k] uA B quos • [l] uA B hominum • [m] mv A B C humus • [n] A B Mathematicas. • [o] mv uA B Cerne (read cernere) • [p] uA B horizon • [q] mv A B coëunte C coëuntque • [r] mv uA quondam missing • [s] uA B et • [t] mv A B sua. • [u] sc mv A B marginal heading • [v] A Aegyptum, • [w] A B C Pythagorasque • [x] A B plures • [y] uA B C vacuus • [z] A longas,

Pr. So that you are in no doubt, it was in that place where the power of
the sun was always at its greatest, and where the earth was
thoroughly scorched,[41]   **150**
Where is born many a serpent, huge in body and superior in cunning to
anything the land contained.

Sec. You're speaking of the Ethiopians, whom some do not hesitate to
claim were the first men to whom the earth gave birth.[42]
And yet I, along with many others, thought that all the mathematical arts
came from Egypt:
Where the long horizon allows one to see the stars, how often they
twinkle, and when they come together.[43]
Wasn't the wisdom of Egypt once highly valued?[44]   **origin of the arts**
And did not the Greeks get their wisdom from there?   **160**
Where else but to Egypt did Plato, Thales and Pythagoras and many other
distinguished men go[45]
To purchase arts and intellect – yes, and idle men who had nothing to help
them pass the long hours?[46]

---

[41] Ovid, *Metamorphoses* 2.1-328, Phaeton drove Apollo's fiery chariot too
close to the earth, cooking it and turning men black.

[42] Allusion to the etymology of *homo* from *humus* (e.g. Quint. 1.6.34). For
*Ethiopians as the first men see Diodorus 3.2.

[43] Diodorus, 1.9.6. According to Hobbes's theory the twinkling of the stars 'is
generated by the continuous dilating and contraction of the luminous body, pushing
aside pockets of air or water, which simultaneously push their contiguous parts. . . .
Hobbes defines the pulse which is generated by the light source as a *conatus* or
endeavour'. See Leijenhorst, *Hobbes and the Aristotelians*, p. 75, citing *Elements of
Law*, 1.2.8 (*EW* IV, p. 6): 'And further, that that motion whereby the fire worketh, is
dilatation, and contraction of itself alternately, commonly called scintillation or
glowing, is manifest also by experience'. Hobbes's interest in astrology, central to
Epicurean theory, is evidenced by his early poem, *De motibus solis, aetheris et telluris* (Toronto MS 3064, printed in *Anti-White*, pp. 441-7), by his early work on
comets, and by his purchase of telescopes, which he later sold to William Cavendish.

[44] A, B: marginal heading, *Origo Artium*. Whether the provenance of early scientific wisdom was Egyptian or Greek was debated by Diodorus Siculus, whether
Egyptian or Hebrew, was a 17c. topos addressed by *Sir John Marsham, (1602-
1685), author of the *Diatriba chronologica*, 1649, and the *Chronicus Canon Ægyptiacus, Ebraicus, Graecus, et disquisitiones*, 1672. Marsham is noted in Rymer's
Preface as a probably source for Hobbes. For the general context of this debate, to
which Newton was to contribute so importantly, see John Gascoigne, '"The Wisdom
of the Egyptians" and the Secularisation of History in the Age of Newton'.

[45] Diodorus, 1.96.2-3, 1.98.1; Strabo 17.1.29.

[46] See *Lucian, *Philosophers for Sale*, and *Lev.*, xlvi, §7, 369/455, where
Hobbes claims precisely of the Greeks, that 'they that had no employment, neither
at home nor abroad, had little else to employ themselves in but either (as St. *Luke*

Haec etiam Mosi placuit sapientia,[a] cum vix
    Nomen fama satis noverat Aethiopum.[b]
Pr.[c] Aegyptus Graecos, Graeci docuere Latinos,[d]
    Artes;[e] atque etiam (non nego) sacra sua.
Sed tamen Aethiopes, priùs[f] Aegyptum:[g] Fuit illa
    Limus,[h] quando ingens fama erat Aethiopum.[i]   **170**
Aethiopes coluere Deos, Urbes habuere,
    Rexerunt,[j] et erant artibus egregii,
Aegypto nondum prognatâ:[k] nam pietatis
    Mercedem hanc illis apposuere Dii.
Nam quantis,[l] quotiesque,[m] Deos epulis meruere,[n]
    Essent ut placidi, submadidique sibi:[o]
Neptunum imprimis,[p] si vis cognoscere,[q] testis[r]
    Natus in Aegypto certus Homerus erit.[s]
Gratus ob haec,[t] limum[u] delatum flumine Nilo
    Neptunus ripis addidit Aethiopum;   **180**
Firmavit Phoebus;[v] missoque à[w] montibus altis
    Ignoto nobis Jupiter imbre rigat.

---

[a] uA B sapientia • [b] uA Aetyopum A Aethyopum (uA consistently uses the form Aetyopus corrected to Aethyopus, which will not be further noted) C Aethiopum: • [c] mv uA B *Pr.* missing • [d] uA B latinos, • [e] uA B Artes • [f] A B C prius • [g] A B Aegyptum. • [h] mv uA B Limes • [i] mv A Aethyopum B C Aethiopum • [j] uA B Rexerunt • [k] A B C prognata: • [l] B quantis • [m] uA B quotiesque • [n] A meruêre B C meruere • [o] A B sibi, • [p] uA B imprimis • [q] uA B C cognoscere • [r] A B testis, • [s] A erit B erit, • [t] uA B haec • [u] A B Limum • [v] uA B Phoebus, • [w] A B a

This wisdom also pleased Moses, at a time when fame scarcely knew the
    name of the Ethiopians.[47]

Pr. Egypt taught the Greeks their skills and (I don't deny it) their own
    religious beliefs,[48] the Greeks did the same for the Latins.

Nevertheless, the Ethiopians taught Egypt first: Egypt was mud when the
    fame of the Ethiopians was immense.[49]   **170**

The Ethiopians worshipped gods, had cities, were rulers, and were
    outstanding in the arts,

When Egypt had not yet been born, for the gods presented them with this
    reward for their piety.

If you want to know with what feasts and how often they served the gods
    (especially Neptune),

In order to make them peaceful and slightly drunk,[50] Homer, who was
    born in Egypt, will be a reliable witness.[51]

Grateful on account of these things, Neptune added to the Ethiopian
    shores mud brought down by the river Nile,   **180**

Phoebus made it firm, and, having sent rain unknown to us from the high
    mountains, Jupiter gave it water.[52]

---

says, Acts, 17.21) *in telling and hearing news*, or in discoursing of *philosophy* publicly to the youth of the city.'

[47] For the contrary view that Ethiopians, not Egyptians, first discovered astrology, see Lucian, *De astrologia* 3-4. For Hobbes's section on the Ethiopians in
general, see Diodorus 3.2-3.

[48] Herodotus, 2.58.

[49] Diodorus 3.3.2 (Loeb edn, vol. 2, p. 93):
For, generally speaking, what is now Egypt, they maintain, was not land but sea
when in the beginning the universe was being formed; afterwards, however, as the
Nile during the times of its inundation carried down the mud from Ethiopia, land
was gradually built up from the deposit.

[50] See Homer, *Il.* 1.423, 23.205; *Od.* 1.222-6, 5.202. Hobbes collapses two
reports of Diodorus, the first of which 1.12.7-13.2 (Loeb edn, vol. 1, pp. 37ff.,
reports that Zeus, Hephaestus, Demeter and Oceanus are said to 'visit all the inhabited world, revealing themselves to men in the form of sacred animals', as vouched
for by Homer, *Odyssey* 17.485-7: 'the poet, who visited Egypt and became
acquainted with such accounts as these from the lips of the priests, in some place in
his writings sets forth as actual fact what has been said'. See also *Iliad*, 1.423-4,
cited by Diodorus, 3.3, (Loeb edn, vol. 2, p. 91):
    For Zeus had yesterday to Ocean's bounds
    Set forth to feast with Ethiop's faultless men,
    And he was followed there by all the gods.

[51] Homer as an Egyptian is one of the alternatives given in various late Lives,
e.g. *Vita V* 10, *VI* 23, *VII* 1-2 (T. W. Allen, *Homeri Opera*, Oxford, 1912).

[52] Diodorus, 1.7.

Nam surgens Nilus, dum campos contegit undis
     Nunc etiam Aegyptum dum rigat aedificat.[a]
Quam simulatque pati potuit,[b] coepere colonis
     Exercere suis Aethiopes Domini.[c]
Atque suas populo leges,[d] ritusque dedere,
     Et sibi subjectos sic tenuere diu.
Sec.[e] Quis fuit Aethiopum status? Tum[f] summa potestas
     Cujus erat? Regis solius an populi?   **190**
Pr. Nomine Regis erat, sed regnavere Sophistae,[g]
     Quos deceptores diximus Astrologos.
Hos quia sermones cum Dîs[h] conferre putabat
     Plebs stupida,[i] ignorans[j] atque futura tremens,[k]
Regum Electores voluerunt[l] esse suorum;[m]
     A solis,[n] ipsi,[o] Dîs[p] voluere regi.
Et sic Sacrifici Regem,[q] fictique Prophetae
     Per multos annos dantque reguntque suum.[r]
Quid faceret Rex quoque die, quid qualibet hora,
     Quando dormiret, quosque cibos caperet;[s]   **200**
Quodque[t] magis mirum est,[u] quando discedere vita
     Debebat Rex, nec quaerere quîv meruit,[w]
Audax dictabat Nebulonum[x] Ecclesia stultis:[y]
     Parebant[z] Reges,[aa] Lex valuitque diu.
Donec Alexandri paulò[ab] post tempora magni,[ac]
     Rex fuit Aethiopum nobilis Ergamenes;

---

[a] A B aedificat C aedificat: • [b] mv uA potuit missing; marginal addition but with no indication where it is to be inserted; B potuit • [c] C domini • [d] uA B leges • [e] mv A B *Sec.* entered at the beginning of the line below • [f] A tum • [g] A B C Sophistae • [h] A B Diis C Dis • [i] C stupida • [j] A ignorans, • [k] A tremens • [l] mv uA B noluerunt (error) • [m] uA B suorum • [n] A B solis • [o] A B ipsi • [p] uA B Diis C Dis • [q] uA B Regem • [r] A B suum • [s] A B caperet. • [t] mv uA B Quidque (error) • [u] B est • [v] uA B C qui • [w] A meruit. • [x] A B nebulonum • [y] uA B stultis • [z] mv uA B Parabat (error) • [aa] C reges; • [ab] C paullo • [ac] A B magni

In fact the rising Nile, as it covers the plains with its waves, while it
provides water, at the same time it also builds up Egypt.[53]
And, as soon as it could bear it, the Ethiopian rulers began to cultivate it,
using their own farmers,
And they gave their own laws and rituals to the people and, in this way,
held them subject for a long time.
Sec.[54] What was the political regime of the Ethiopians? Whose was the
supreme power? The king's alone, or the people's? 190
Pr. It was nominally that of the king, but the Sophists, those deceivers
we've called Astrologers, ruled.
Because the stupid people, knowing nothing and fearing the future,
thought that these men conversed with the gods,
They wanted them to be the electors of their own kings; they themselves
wanted to be ruled by the gods alone.
So, for many years, priests and false prophets chose their own king and
they directed
What the king would do each day and at any hour, when he would sleep,
and what food he could take. 200
And what is even more amazing, that audacious congregation[55] of
nobodies dictated to fools,
When the king ought to die, and he was not entitled to ask why.[56] Kings
obeyed and this law was in force for a long time,
Until, shortly after the time of Alexander the Great, the noble Ergamenes
was king of the Ethiopians;[57]

---

[53] Diodorus, 1.10.

[54] mv A, B: line 189, *quis fuit Aethiopum status? tum summ potestas*, is spoken
by Primus; Secundus begins, *Cujus erat? Regis solius an populi.* Primus returns
with *Nomine Regis erat, sed regnavere Sophistae*, etc. Molesworth follows the 1688
edition in assigning lines 189 and 190 to Secundus, Primus staying with *Nomine
Regis erat.*

[55] *Ecclesia*, church, which Hobbes defines in the Greek sense as a popular
assembly. See *Lev.*, xxxix, §2, 248/315:

> [A] Church (when not taken for a House) signifieth the same that *ecclesia* sig-
> nified in the Grecian commonwealths, that is to say, a congregation or an
> assembly of citizens, called forth to hear the magistrate speak unto them, and
> which in the commonwealth of Rome was called *concio*, as he that spake was
> called *ecclesiastes*, and *concionator*.

[56] Diodorus, 3.6.1-2.

[57] *Ergamenes, king of the Ethiopians in the reign of Ptolemy II Philadelphus
(BC 285-46), had been educated in Greece. C.f. Diodorus, 3.6.3.

Qui regum[a] vitam pendere à[b] gentis iniquae
　　　Arbitrio, indignum censuit esse viro.
Hic igitur misso delevit milite stirpem
　　　Omnem, latrones[c] anticipatque[d] sacros.　　　　　　　　　210
Sic ratione dolum detexit, et ense abolevit[e]
　　　Ergamenes sapiens, nobilis Ergamenes.[f]
Ex illo Aethiopum fit tempore pectus apertum,
　　　Humanaeque capax gens rationis erat.
Et simulatque Dei coepit doctrina doceri,
　　　Christi cum primis hi subiere jugum.
Ad Graecos[g] artes venere bonaeque,[h] malaeque,[i]
　　　Ante ex Aegypto[j] quam fuit Ergamenes.
Una Sacerdotis gens semper habebat honorem[k]
　　　Aegypto, Sophiae sanguis origo fuit.　　　　　　　　　220
Natos quisque sua pater instituebat in arte;[l]
　　　Ingenii fuit his una Magistra domus.
Sed numerosa domus, namque illis tradita alendis
　　　Ex tribus Aegypti partibus una fuit:[m]
Doctaque stillabant praeceptis ora profundis,
　　　Quae sitiens hausit Graecus,[n] et Assyrius.
Mos erat unus eis ad sydera laude ferendus,[o]
　　　Nempe,[p] in judiciis quem tenuere modum.
Nullus erat strepitus, nec vox audita clientis,
　　　Patronis nullus,[q] causidicisque locus.　　　　　　　　230
Nam triginta viri jus cognitionis habebant[r]
　　　De re quae nondum,[s] cuja[t] liquebat,[u] erat.[v]
Conspicuis totidem[w] delecti ex urbibus omnes;[x]
　　　Unus et adjectus,[y] Praesidis esse loco.

---

[a] A B Regum • [b] uA B a • [c] A B Latrones • [d] A Anticipatque • [e] A B abolevit,
• [f] C Ergamenes • [g] mv uA graecas B Graecas • [h] B C bonaeque • [i] A B
malaeque • [j] B Aegypto, • [k] A B honorem, • [l] uA B arte, • [m] A B fuit. • [n] A
B Graecus • [o] uA ferendas, (error) • [p] A B Nempe • [q] C nullus • [r] A B
habebant, • [s] uA B nondum • [t] mv uA B cujus • [u] uA B liquebat • [v] A B erat,
• [w] A B totidem, • [x] A B omnes, • [y] uA B adjectus C adiectus

He thought it unworthy of a real man that the life of kings should depend
    on the will of an unjust race.

Consequently, having sent in the army, he destroyed the whole tribe, and
    outwitted those holy robbers.   **210**

In this way wise Ergamenes, noble Ergamenes, exposed their evil intent
    by reason and destroyed it by the sword.[58]

From that time he opened the hearts of the Ethiopians so that they became
    a race capable of human reason.

And as soon as the doctrine of God began to be taught, these people were
    among the first to submit to the yoke of Christ.

Arts both good and bad came to the Greeks from Egypt before
    Ergamenes' time.

One priestly clan always held high office in Egypt. The source of wisdom
    was blood.   **220**

Each father instructed his sons in his own skill. One house was the
    teacher of intellectual ability to these people.

But the house was populous, for a third of Egypt had been handed over
    for the maintenance of these people.

Their learned lips dripped with profound maxims,[59] which the thirsty
    Greek and Assyrian drank in.

One practice of theirs which should certainly be extolled to the stars was
    the manner in which they conducted judicial enquiries.

There was no din, nor was the voice of the client heard, there was no
    place for patrons and none for advocates.   **230**

For thirty men had the right of judgement with respect to property whose
    ownership was not yet clear.

That number of men was chosen from important cities, and one was
    added to hold the position of chief-justice.[60]

---

[58] Diodorus, 3.5.4.

[59] An echo of Lucretius, 5.1131-5 (1975 Loeb edn, tr. W. H. D Rouse, pp. 466-7) on ambitious men responsible for the slaying of kings: 'their wisdom comes from the lips of others, and they pursue things on hearsay rather than from their own feelings. And this folly does not succeed at the present, and will not succeed in the future, any more than it has succeeded in the past.'

[60] The name for the Chief of the Court dispensing justice, 'Praesidis', can in fact be read as 'Protector'. See: *praeses praesidis* (m. f.), guardian, defender, protector; president, head, chief. (Cooper) 'he that hath authoritie in a province nexte under a king: lieutenaunt: a provost: a vice-roy: he that hath the tuition and protection of a thing or countrey: a defendour (Cicero: *libertatis praeses & custos Tribunis plebis*: "the tribune was as a protectour and defendour of common libertie"'.

Distinctum gemmis Praeses collare ferebat,[a]
    Quod vix credibili luce micasse ferunt.
Ergo (Index[b] Veri)[c] Veri[d] quoque nomen habebat,
    Victrici causae nomen ubique datum.
Illud enim praeses cum scriptis applicuisset,
    Vera an falsa (legens) sint ea scripta videt.[e]   **240**
Ergo suam quicunque petit rem quam tenet alter,[f]
    Et patriâ[g] lege[h] ut restituatur Agit,[i]
Is Quid[j] sit factum, quo Pacto,[k] et Quando,[l] simulque
    Quid Testes[m] dicant, quid Ratione[n] ratum[o] est,
Et documenta sui juris ferre omnia scripto,
    Et non ambiguo,[p] debuit hisce viris.
Hique legunt secum,[q] quo vult petitore eunte;[r]
    Nullus non scripti pensitat omnem apicem.[s]
Copia Scripturae fit;[t] respondere jubetur[u]
    Qui tenet et causam verificare suam.   **250**

---

[a] mv A B gerebat, • [b] A B (index • [c] uA B C veri) • [d] uA B C veri • [e] A B videt, • [f] A alter • [g] A B C patria • [h] A B lege, • [i] A B C agit, • [j] A B C quid • [k] uA B C pacto • [l] A B quando C quando, • [m] A B C testes • [n] A B C ratione • [o] mv uA B verum • [p] uA B C ambiguo • [q] uA B secum • [r] sc mv 1688 A and C beante (which is meaningless); uA B eunte • [s] uA B apicem, • [t] uA B fit, • [u] A B jubetur,

The chief-justice wore a collar adorned with jewels which they say
    sparkled with an incredible light.[61]
As a consequence (as an 'indicator of truth') it was called 'truth', the
    name given everywhere to a winning cause.[62]
Indeed, when the chief-justice applied the collar to any documents, he
    could see as he read them whether they were true or false.[63]   **240**
So, whoever brought an action to recover something which another held,
    and proceeded according to ancestral law to have it restored to him,
Was required to tell these men what had happened, how and when, and at the
    same time what the witnesses say and what was determined by reason,
And was required to bring all the evidence for his case written in
    unambiguous language before them.[64]
And these men read it for themselves, the plaintiff proceeding as he will,[65]
    and no one failed to consider every letter of the writing.
An abundance of written evidence was tendered. The defendant was
    ordered to respond and prove his own case.   **250**

---

[61] Diodorus, 1.75.5 (Loeb edn. p. 261):
    The [chief justice] regularly wore suspended from his neck by a golden chain
    a small image made of precious stones, which they called Truth; the hearings
    of the pleas commenced whenever the chief justice put on the image of Truth.
Note also that *Lorenzo Valla makes much of the strap or band that 'strap that
usually surrounds our imperial neck' ('quod imperiale circumdare assolet collum'),
mentioned in *Gratian's Decretum §2, along with the 'purple mantle and scarlet
tunic, and all the imperial raiment' marking the pope's change of status after Constantine's gift. See *The Treatise of Lorenzo Valla on the Donation of Constantine,
Text and Translation into English*, ed. Christopher B. Coleman (New York, Russell
and Russell, 1922, reprinted Toronto, University of Toronto, 1993), pp. 14-15.

[62] Hobbes gives a twist to the story told by Diodorus: because the stone was
called 'truth', the outcome to which it was applied as a touchstone was necessarily
'true'. If the *praeses* is a figure for the Protector, Hobbes could be making a point
about Cromwell's Erastianism (see Introduction), according to which what the
Prince deems is true is in fact true, on the principle 'cuius regio eius religio').

[63] Diodorus, 1.75.3-4 and Aelian, *Varia Historia* 14.34. The strange fable of
Egyptian justice is also related by Hobbes in *Behemoth*, EW IV, 92.

[64] Diodorus, 1.75.6 (Loeb edn, p. 261):
    the custom was that the accuser should present in writing the particulars of his
    complaint, namely, the charge, how the thing happened, and the amount of
    injury or damage done, whereupon the defendant would take the document
    submitted by his opponents in the suit and reply in writing to each charge, to
    the effect either that he did not commit the deed, or, if he did, that he was not
    guilty of wrongdoing, or, if he was guilty of wrongdoing, that he should
    receive a lighter penalty.

[65] sc mv 1688, A C *beante*; uA B *eunte*; beante is meaningless but eunte could
be read as a gloss on *meante*: 'the plaintiff proceeding as he will'.

Tum scripto rursus petitor respondet,[a] et ille
    Qui tenet huic iterum. Denique ter fit idem.[b]
Se. Nil video hic magni, nec magna laude ferendum;[c]
    In qua parte orbis non reperitur idem?
Pr.[d] Sed neque miror ego.[e] Fertur[f] sententia. Nemo
    Obloquitur. Praeses judicat,[g] at tacitus.[h]
Namque ut consessum est,[i] scriptum effert Praeses utrumque[j]
    Collocat in mensam, separat atque manu.
Detractum collare sacrum scripto admovet uni:[k]
    Et certus litis terminus ille fuit.   260
Justitiam tacitam sine tempestate forensi[l]
    Miror;[m] quam nunquam vis aliena movet.[n]
Se.[o] Hoc rectè,[p] sed utrum legissent[q] scripta priusquam
    Collare appositum est, noscere difficile est.
Parcere enim tanto cur non potuere labori,
    Cum nil[r] referret[s] pars utra justa fuit?
Pr. Tune ita inhumanos potuisti credere lectos
    Spectatae fidei,[t] praecipuosque viros?
Se. Non ego inhumanos homines dico, sed iniquos.[u]
    Ut quid cuique libet[v] sic quoque quisque facit.   270

---

[a] uA B respondet • [b] A idem • [c] mv A B luce deferendum; (transcription error, see Malcolm's note in Appendix C) • [d] mv uA *Pr.* missing • [e] uA B ego • [f] uA fertitur • [g] A B judicat • [h] uA B tacitus • [i] uA B est • [j] B utrumque, • [k] A B uni, • [l] A forensi, B forénsi, • [m] A B Miror • [n] A movet • [o] A *Sec* moved to line 263 from uA line 262 • [p] uA B rectè • [q] mv uA B legisset (error) • [r] uA B nihil • [s] A B referret, • [t] C fidei • [u] A B iniquos • [v] A B libet,

Then the plaintiff answered back in writing, and the defendant again in turn. Finally the same procedure was repeated.[66]

Sec. I see nothing special here, or that deserves great praise. In what part of the world is the same procedure not encountered?

Pr. I am not surprised either. The verdict is handed down. No one protests it. The chief-justice passes judgement, but does so in silence.

For, when they have taken their seats, the chief-justice brings forward the documentation for both sides, places it on the table, and separates it with his hand.

Having taken off the sacred collar, he places it on the documents of one party; and that is the definite end to the dispute.   **260**

I admire this silent justice, with no storm of advocacy, unmoved by any outside force.

Sec. That is all well and good. But it is difficult to know whether they read the documents before the collar was placed alongside.

In fact, why couldn't they have spared themselves all that work, when it didn't matter which side was right?[67]

Pr. Could you have believed that chosen men of recognized honesty and great distinction could be so cruel?

Sec. I'm not talking about cruel men, but unjust men; everyone acts as he pleases.[68]   **270**

---

[66] Diodorus, 1.75.7 (Loeb edn. p. 261):
After both parties had twice presented their statements in writing to the judges, it was the duty of the thirty at once to declare their opinions among themselves and of the chief justice to place the image of Truth upon one or the other of the two pleas which had been presented.

[67] Neither Aelian nor Diodorus suggests that the collar called truth has the power to reveal the truth of the writings, the placing of the collar being a ceremonial gesture that concludes a proper legal investigation. However, Diodorus does speculate on why the Egyptians adopted such a procedure, expressing sentiments with which Hobbes would probably concur. Diodorus, 1.76.1 (Loeb edn. pp. 261-2):
This was the manner, as their account goes, in which the Egyptians conducted all court proceedings, since they believed that if the advocates were allowed to speak they would greatly becloud the justice of a case; for they knew that the clever devices of orators, the cunning witchery of their delivery, and the tears of the accused would influence many to overlook the severity of the laws and the strictness of truth.

[68] For Hobbes, like Epicurus, the thesis that justice was conventional, arising from pacts between men, does not mean that it is relative, to behave as one pleases. Epicurus, elaborated his position in important Sentences, *Ratae Sententiae* XXXI to XL, trans. Bailey in *Epicurus, the Extant Remains*, p. 103. See also Springborg, '*Behemoth* and Hobbes's "Science of *Just* and *Unjust*"', *Filozofski vestnik*, special issue on Hobbes's *Behemoth*, ed. Tomaz Mastnak, vol. 24, no. 2, 2003, pp. 267-89

Sed quia non multùm[a] refert[b] aequine,[c] an iniqui
     Hi fuerint, fuerint, ut sibi[d] cunque placet.[e]
Sed dic,[f] Aegyptum mos hic,[g] venitne ab Hebraeis,[h]
     An contra?[i] quoniam par fuit his,[j] et eis.
Pr. Nescio.[k] At alterutrum si fortè[l] necesse putarem,
     Aegypti (dixîm)[m] mos fuit ille prius.
Et maribus pueris praeputia scindere circum,[n]
     Autor Niliacus,[o] non Abrahamus erat.
Se. Verumne est ergo[p] quod rerum sola novarum
     (Ut vulgo dicunt) Africa mater erat?   **280**
Pr. Deinde Sacerdotum[q] numerus,[r] cum crescere coepit[s]
     Doctorumque fuit turba molesta sibi,[t]
Ibat in Assyriam pars magna vocata.[u] Sciendi[v]
     Sortem venturam tanta libido fuit.
His multas urbes terrasque dedere colendas[w]
     Assyrii.[x] Cura[y] his Relligionis[z] erat,[aa]
Nomine Chaldaeis:[ab] Nomen[ac] venerabile quondam,
     Ut Magus,[ad] ut Sapiens,[ae] utque Mathematicus.

---

[a] A B C multum • [b] C refert, • [c] uA B C aequine • [d] mv uA B tibi • [e] C placet: • [f] uA B dic • [g] uA B hic • [h] A Hebraeis C Hebraeis. • [i] mv uA B contra, • [j] uA B his • [k] uA B Nescio, • [l] A C forte • [m] uA B dixerim • [n] A B circum • [o] uA B Niliacus • [p] A ergo, • [q] A C sacerdotum • [r] A B C numerus • [s] C coepit, • [t] A B sibi mv C tibi, • [u] mv uA vocata • [v] uA sciendi • [w] A B colendas, • [x] mv uA B C Assyrii, • [y] uA C cura B Cura • [z] A B relligionis • [aa] A B erat. • [ab] uA B Chaldaeis. • [ac] uA B nomen • [ad] uA B Magus • [ae] uA B sapiens

But because it is not of much consequence whether these men were just or unjust, let them be as they wanted to be.

But tell me, did this custom come to Egypt from the Hebrews, or was it the other way round?[69] For the custom was common to both of them.

Pr.   I don't know. But if perchance it were necessary that I should think one over the other, that custom (I would say) was Egypt's first.

The originator of circumcision was also from the Nile and not Abraham.[70]

Se.   Is it true, therefore, as they say everywhere, that Africa alone was the mother of innovation?[71]   **280**

Pr.   Then when the number of priests began to grow and the mass of learned men became a source of trouble for themselves,

Having been called to do so, a large proportion went to Assyria, so great was the desire to know their fate to come.

The Assyrians gave them many cities and land for cultivation.

Responsibility for religious matters fell to these men.

They were known as Chaldeans.[72] It was once as respected a name as magician,[73] Wiseman and mathematician.

---

[69] John Spencer, Master of Corpus College, Cambridge, at the time of Scargill's forced Recantation, had also discussed the provenance of 'the collar of truth' in his *Dissertatio de urim and thumum* (1669), later developing the controversial thesis that the Hebrew priesthood had encouraged idolatry and superstition on the Egyptian model, in *De legibus Hebraeorum* (London, 1685). *Urim* and *thummum* was a form of priestly divination (Exodus 28:30) discussed also by Hobbes in *Leviathan*, ch. 42 (*EW*, vol. 3, p. 557), and in *Behemoth* (*EW*, vol. 6, p. 279). Spencer was likely to be known to Hobbes, if only through Scargill. See Jon Parkin, 'Hobbism in the Later 1660s: Daniel Scargill and Samuel Parker', *The Historical Journal*, vol. 42, 1 (1999), pp. 92-3, and Springborg Introduction, chapter 3.2.

[70] On Abraham as the originator of circumcision see Gen. 17:10, Paul Rom. 4:9-12.

[71] Source of the proverb, Pliny *Nat. Hist.* 8.42.

[72] The Chaldeans, natives of the fertile Crescent, whose language was the biblical Syriac or Aramaic, became synonymous with soothsaying, astronomy, magic and cheating in every form. See Butler's *Hudibras*, 1664, 'he stole your cloak and pick'd your pocket, Chows'd and Caldees'd you like a blockhead' (*OED*, 1971 edn, 1.252).

[73] For instance, one of the participants at the *Council of Nicaea, James of Nisibis, was known as the Thaumaturg, a magician or conjurer, because of his reputation for raising men from the dead. See *Histoire des conciles, d'après les documents originaux*, trans. and augmented by Henri Leclercq, 11 vols. (Paris, 1907-49), vol. 1.1.2, p. 413. The OED (1971 edn) gives 18th century sources for the term as applied by the Catholic Church to its miracle working saints – note in particular, M. Davies, *Athen. Brit.*, 1.125: 'Petavius . . . attainted . . . Origen's wonder-working scholar Gregory the Thaumaturg'. Hobbes may have used Petavius' translation of Ephiphanius of 1622, as Wright notes, 'The 1668 Appendix to *Leviathan*', p. 399, n. 124.

Sed quando gentem^a Romanus vicerat illam,
    Niliacum populum subdideratque levem,^b   **290**
Venerat et Romam Chaldaeus;^c tunc inhonestum^d
    Chaldaei nomen,^e Philosophique fuit.
Nam Regum mortes,^f audax,^g bellique futuros
    Eventus,^h promptus dicere solus erat.ⁱ
Perfidiae coeptis audacibus atque pericli
    Plenis,^j spem solitus vendere solus erat,^k
Matronis suasor,^l vates,^m adjutor et idem
    Chaldaeus semper turpis amoris erat.
Astrologus, Leno,ⁿ Chaldaeus,^o Philosophusque,^p
    Judaeus,^q mendax^r atque Mathematicus,   **300**
Sortilegus,^s Vanus,^t Deceptor,^u Veneficusque,^v
    Nomina certa scias unius esse viri;^w

---

^a A Gentem • ^b mv A B sevem (read levem) • ^c uA B Chaldaeus, • ^d A inhon-
estum, • ^e A C nomen B nomen. • ^f uA B mortes • ^g uA B audax • ^h uA B
Eventus • ⁱ mv A B C erat • ^j uA B Plenis • ^k C erat • ^l uA B suasor • ^m uA
B Vates • ⁿ uA B Leno • ^o uA B C Chaldaeus • ^p uA B C Philosophusque •
^q uA B C Judaeus • ^r A C mendax, • ^s uA B Sortilegus • ^t uA B vanus • ^u uA
B deceptor • ^v A Veneficusque B veneficusque • ^w A Viri. B viri. C viri,

But when the Romans had conquered that race and had subdued the
fickle[74] Egyptian people, **290**

And the Chaldeans had come to Rome, from then on the name of
Chaldean and philosopher was not respected.

For that bold man alone was ready to pronounce on the deaths of kings
and the future outcomes of war.

When deeds of treachery, daring and full of danger were undertaken, he
was usually the only one selling hope.

Seducer of married women and prophet,[75] the same Chaldean was always
the promoter of base love.[76]

Astrologer, pimp, Chaldean, Philosopher and lying Jew; as well as
Mathematician, **300**

Soothsayer, good-for-nothing, cheat and poisoner, you might know these
are the set names for one type of man.[77]

---

[74] mv A B *sevem*, to read: savage Egyptian people.

[75] Hobbes's uses the term *vates*, referring contemptuously to priests after the
manner of Lucretius *De rerum natura* 1.102-3 (ed. Smith, pp. 10-11), who uses the
term to warn Memmius, the aristocratic backslider to whom the poem is addressed:
'You will yourself some day or other seek to fall away from us [i.e., the Epicureans],
overborne by the terrible utterances of priests (*vatum*)'. On Hobbes's Epicureanism
see, Arrigho Pacchi, 'Hobbes e l'epicureismo', *Rivista Critica di Storia dell
Filosophia*, vol. 33 (March 1975), pp. 54-71; and Patricia Springborg, 'Hobbes's
Theory of Civil Religion', Proceedings of the Conference on *Pluralismo e religione
civile*, Università del Piemonte Orientale, Vercelli, Italy, May 24-25, 2001, ed.
Gianni Paganini and Edoardo Tortarolo, Milano: Bruno Mondadori, 2003, pp. 61-
98; and Springborg, 'Hobbes and Epicurean Religion', in *Der Garten und die
Moderne: Epikureische Moral und Politik vom Humanismus bis zur Aufklarung*,
ed, Gianni Paganini and Edoardo Tortarolo (Stuttgart-Bad Cannstatt: Rommann-
holzboog Verlag (2004), pp. 161-214.

[76] This stereotype of the Chaldean was also applied to *Arius, slandered for
lewdness, avarice and relations with loose women. See *Theodoret, *Hist. Eccl.* bk
1. ch. 4, *PG* LXXXII, col. 909, cited Hefele, *Histoire des conciles*, 1.1.2, pp. 356-7.

[77] See Seneca's evaluation of astrology in *Epist. Mor.* 88.15, and one of the earliest critiques in a fragment of Ennius quoted in Macrobius, *Sat.* I.62. Cicero, *On
Divination* 1.58.132, quoting Ennius, asserted: I do not recognize fortune-tellers, or
those who prophesy for money, or necromancers, or mediums, whom your friend
Appius [Claudius, colleague of Cicero in the augural college] makes it a practice to
consult.
    In fine, I say, I do not care a fig
    For Marsian augurs, village mountebanks
    Astrologers who haunt the circus grounds,
    Or Isis-seers, or dream interpreters:
– for they are not diviners either by knowledge or skill, –
    But superstitious bards, soothsaying quacks,
    Averse to work, or mad, or ruled by want,
    Directing others how to go, and yet

Quem Româ[a] Reges potuerunt pellere saepe,[b]
  Pulsum non potuit Roma tenere foras.
Sec. Claudius,[c] ut nosti,[d] Ptolemaeus qui fuit author[e]
  Magni operis, minimè[f] vanus habetur homo;[g]
Astronomus priscoque et nostro tempore clarus,
  Ille Genethliacae[h] conditor artis erat.
Is,[i] quod ab astrorum dependent omnia nutu,[j]
  Fortunam et sobolem syderis esse docet.[k]   **310**
An stellas torpere putas[l] sine viribus;[m] aut vim
  Non efferre satis posse putabo suam,[n]
Quae tamen ad nos usque ferunt lucem atque calorem,
  Et mutant faciem temperiemque soli?

---

[a] uA B C Roma • [b] ~ A B saepè • [c] uA B Claudius • [d] uA B nosti • [e] A B Author • [f] A B minime • [g] ~A homo • [h] B genethliacae • [i] uA B Is • [j] uA nutu • [k] A B docet, • [l] A putas, • [m] A B viribus • [n] A B suam.

Kings could often banish him from Rome, but having been driven out,
Rome could not keep him out.[78]

Sec. As you know, Claudius Ptolemeus,[79] who was the author of great
works, is considered the least worthless man among them;

As an astronomer famous in ancient times, and also in our own day, he
was the founder of the art of calculating horoscopes.

He teaches that because all things depend on the will of the stars, Fortune
is also an offspring of the constellations.[80]   **310**

Or do you think that the stars are inert and powerless, or am I to think that
they cannot project their light far enough,

When (in fact) they carry light and heat to us and change the face and
temperature of the earth?[81]

> What road to take they do not know themselves;
> From those to whom they promise wealth they beg
> A coin. From what they promised let them take
> Their coin as toll and pass the balance on.

[78] Astrology was associated with the East, Semites and Jews, hence the term
Chaldean. Cato in 149 BC warned against consulting Astrologers and in 139 BC the
first expulsion of Astrologers from Rome was recorded. Three expulsions of the
Jews from Rome are recorded, in 139 BC, AD 19 and during Claudius' principate.
See H.J. Leon, *The Jews of Ancient Rome* (Philadelphia, The Jewish Publication
Society of America, 1960).

[79] *Claudius Ptolemeus (fl. AD 127-48), astronomer, mathematician and geographer, was famous for refining the earth-centred theory of the universe advanced
by Aristotle, and Hobbes may have singled him out among the astronomers out of
deference to *Galileo Galilei (1564-1642), who opposed Ptolemy's system. Hobbes
visited Galileo in Florence in the Spring of 1636.

[80] Note that this is Lucan's universe of Fortune. See *Pharsalia* 6.607-10, tr. Jane
Wilson Joyce (Ithaca, NY, Cornell University Press, 1994), p. 160:
> Though sidereal rays have decreed/ a particular death, yet it is granted to my
> skill/ to impose delays; again, though every star has forcast/ old age for a man,
> we with our herbs snap his life in half.

[81] Lorenzo Valla, in the chapter *De corpore* of the various redactions of his
Dialecticae, discusses star theory and theories about the sun's heat and light with
reference to a range of classical sources, including Ovid's *Metamorphoses* 2.727-9,
Seneca's *Naturae Questiones* 2.57, Aristotle and Pseudo-Aristotelian *De Mundo*.
See Valla, 'De corpore', *Repastinatio*, bk 1, §15, p. 422, lines 10-13, and *Retractio
totius dialectice*, bk 1, §11, in *Laurentii Valle Repastinatio dialectice et philosophie*,
ed. G. Zippel, 2 vols (Padua, Antenore, 1983), vol. 1, p. 98, lines 5-25. Valla rejects
the Aristotelian position that motion produces heat in favour of the theory that friction creates heat. Valla therefore concludes (*Repastinatio*, p. 100, lines 5-18, tr.
Trinkaus, 'Lorenzo Valla's Anti-Aristotelian Natural Philosophy', *I Tati Studies*,
vol. 5 (1993), pp. 279-325, at p. 289):
> Therefore the sun would be sufficient for providing heat both to us and the
> world aided by the cause I mentioned above: that fire is generated from a col-
> lision and heat from compression, especially of the moisture which having
> been attached to the earth heats up and is exhaled.

Nilne frequens coeli facit observatio,[a] nonne[b]
  Id quod saepe fuit,[c] nos docet id quod erit?
Pr. Non.[d] Scit[e] enim quid erit nisi qui sciat omnia[f] nemo;[g]
  Omni contribuunt omnia namque rei.
Nescit Ephemeridum confector postera quid sit
  Allatura dies;[h] decipit ille sciens.   320
Et cùm[i] praedicit mala publica,[j] cogitat illa
  Quo pacto faciat;[k] dignus et est laqueo.
Sec. Verum cur habuit Chaldaeos Graecia nullos,
  Graecia Romanis nota Magistra[l] viris?[m]
Pr. Ob multas causas. Non fallit Aruspicem Aruspex;[n]
  Callida Graecorum natio tota fuit;[o]
Nec deceptores fictos habuere Prophetas,
  Sed proprios sibimet;[p] nempe genus[q] Logicum;[r]
Ars erat hisce malam,[s] victricem[t] reddere,[u] causam[v]
  Dicendo,[w] quarto propria et illa modo.   330
Adde quod et pauper dominis subjecta Latinis[x]
  Natio tota fuit;[y] non erat unde darent.

---

[a] uA B observatio • [b] B nonne, • [c] uA B fuit • [d] uA B Non, C Non • [e] C scit • [f] uA C omnia, • [g] A B nemo, • [h] uA dies A B C dies, • [i] A B C cum • [j] uA B publica • [k] uA B faciat • [l] B C magistra • [m] A Viris? • [n] A Aruspex B Aruspex, C aruspex; • [o] A B fuit. • [p] uA B sibimet, • [q] A Genus • [r] uA B logicum. A Logicum. • [s] uA B malam • [t] A Victricem • [u] uA B reddere • [v] A B causam, • [w] uA B Dicendo • [x] mv uA B Lavinis C latinis • [y] uA B fuit,

Is frequent observation of the skies worth nothing, doesn't what often
    happened in the past teach us what is going to happen?

Pr. Not at all. In fact no one knows what will happen unless he knows
    everything, for all things affect every single thing.

The man who prepares almanacs[82] does not know what the next day will
    bring; if he says he knows he's lying.   **320**

And when he predicts public harm, he is contemplating the means by
    which he can bring it about; and he deserves the noose.

Sec. But why did Greece, that well known teacher of Roman manhood,
    have no Chaldeans?

Pr. For many reasons. One soothsayer[83] doesn't trick another. The whole
    Greek race was shrewd.

And they did not have false prophets to deceive but their very own,
    namely the logicians.

Their art was to make the bad cause victorious by speech, and that art
    belongs properly to the fourth figure.[84]   **330**.

On top of that their whole race was poverty-stricken, subject to Latin
    overlords;[85] there were no resources with which to give anything.[86]

Trinkaus notes, pp. 288-9, n. 15, that 'Valla's statement asserting that Aristotle
incorrectly claims that motion produces heat but that in fact friction causes it may
be compared with Galileo Galilei's statement in his *Il Saggiatore* 44' (*Opere di
Galileo Galilei*, ed. Brunetti, vol. 1, pp. 763-4).

  [82] **Ephemerides*, diaries, a term particularly designating the royal journal of
Alexander the Great kept by Eumenes of Cardia providing information about
Alexander's daily life. (*OCD*, 1970 edn, 386-7). Note that the 1722 paraphrast
(p. 22) refers to Eumenes, as 'the grand Projector of th' *Ephemeris*'. Among
Hobbes's contemporaries Edmund Spenser wrote *The Shepherd's Calendar* (1579),
and Milton and Hartlib *Ephemerides*. See Stephen Clucas, 'Samuel Hartlib's
Ephemerides, 1635-1659'.

  [83] **Haruspex*, a soothsayer, who foretold future events from the inspection of
the entrails of victims, a diviner among the Etruscans, who introduced the practice
to the Romans. (Lewis & Short).

  [84] The fourth figure of the syllogism, the so-called **figura galenica*, of dubious
validity, also referred to by Hobbes in *De Corpore*, *LW* 4.11. For the Galenical
figure in logic, see Reid 1774, *Aristotle's Logics* bk 3, §2: 'It (the fourth figure of
the syllogism) was added by the famous Galen, and is often called the Galenical'
(*OED*), and Joseph, *Introduction to Logic*, pp. 325-30.

  [85] uA B *Lavinis*. Lavinia, the daughter of Latinus and wife of Aeneas (Livy 1.1
ff.; Varro 1.11.5. §144; Virgil *Aeneid* 6.764; Ovid *Met.* 14.449, 570), gave her
name to a city of Latium founded in her honour (Lewis & Short).

  [86] Literally, they had not the wherewithal.

Namque Impostori[a] non est locus ille salubris[b]
    Qui lucri sterilis, fertilis ingenii est.[c]
Aegyptus Graecis ultro non attulit artes[d]
    Ingenuas;[e] Graeci sed petiere Viri.[f]
Pythagoras,[g] Thales, Plato,[h] plures;[i] nec petiere
    Aegypti fraudes,[j] nec sacra Niliaca,[k]
Nec demonstrandi praecepta,[l] nec Officiorum;[m]
    Sed mensurandi quicquid in orbe fuit.   **340**
Se.[n] Quis Graecos reliquas artes docuit?[o] Quis[p] Elenchos?
    Quis morum normam,[q] justitiaeque dedit?[r]
Pr: Socratis inventum Dialectica[s] dicitur esse,
    Una quidem,[t] dici quae solet Ironia.

---

[a] A B C impostori • [b] C salubris. • [c] C est • [d] uA B artes, • [e] uA Ingenuas B Ingénuas • [f] B C viri. • [g] B Pythagoras • [h] B Plato • [i] uA B plures C plures, • [j] B fraudes • [k] A B Niliaca. • [l] B C praecepta • [m] uA B officiorum, C officio-rum; • [n] mv uA *Sec.* missing • [o] uA B docuit • [p] uA B quis • [q] A B normam • [r] mv uA B dedit. • [s] uA B dialectica • [t] uA B quidem

In fact, a place barren of wealth and rich in genius, is not a healthy place
    for imposters.

Egypt did not bring her liberal arts to the Greeks of her own accord;
    rather the Greeks sought them out.

Pythagoras, Thales, Plato[87] and others; nor did they seek the delusions of
    Egypt, or the Nilotic mysteries.[88]

They weren't seeking the rules of demonstration, or ethical principles, but
    rules for measuring whatever was in the world.[89]   **340**

Se. Who taught the Greeks the remaining arts? Who taught them the art
    of refutation? Who gave them the rules of morality and justice?

Pr. It is said that one kind of dialectics, was the invention of Socrates;
    the one usually called Irony,[90]

---

[87] Juxtaposition of *Pythagoras, *Thales and *Plato as sceptical thinkers is
probably not incidental, and here again Hobbes was preceded by Valla. Lisa Jardine
notes that Valla endorses Lactantius's claim (*Divinae institutiones* 3.2, Migne
6.352-3) regarding Pythagoras, 'who first coined this name [philosophos] since he
was a little wiser than those before him who thought themselves wise, and understood that no human knowledge could attain to wisdom'. (See Jardine, 'Lorenzo
Valla and the Intellectual Origins of Humanistic Dialectic', *Journal of the History of
Philosophy*, vol. 15 (1977), p. 156, citing S. I. Camporeale, *Lorenzo Valla: filosofia
e religione nell 'umanisimo italiano* p. 405). Valla then goes on to contrast this view
with the Aristotelians, adding: 'How much superior was Socrates, that second
father of philosophy, after whom all philosophers wished to be called Socratics:
"this much alone I know", he said, "that I know nothing"' (Camporeale, p. 406).
Here Valla echoes Lactantius (3.6, Migne 6.361) who made of Socrates' claim 'I
know only that I know nothing', 'an example of the liar paradox: "If Socrates
knows only that he knows nothing, and he knows that, then he knows nothing"'
(cited Jardine, p. 163).

[88] The Pharaonic religion to which, long-standing legend has it, Pythagoras,
Thales and Plato were initiated by Egyptian priests.

[89] The Ancient Egyptians developed geometry as a rapid method for recalculat-
ing property boundaries after the annual inundation of the Nile.

[90] *Socrates' *eironeia* is his (deceptive) assertion that he knows nothing, but see
Aristotle's discussion of Socratic irony, where the term 'irony' is consistently associated with contemptuous or arrogant treatment of others. *Nicomachean Ethics* bk
II, ch. 7, 1108a20-2, 'opposes arrogance (*alazoneia*) and irony (*eirôneia*) as two
forms of *prospoiêsis*, one tending to more (*epi to meizon*), the other to less (*epi to
elatton*)'. So 'Socratic irony' to him signifies a kind of wilful disdain of convention,
and is no better than *alazoneia*. Plato also uses the term negatively, e.g., Thrasy-
machus in *Republic* 337a or Callicles in *Gorgias* 489e, where *eironeia* means
evasion as a deliberate tactic to get the better of one's opponents by pretending to
have no answer to the questions one poses. See Michel Narcy, 'What is Socratic
Irony?', citing I. Vahlen (*Philologus*, 21 [1864], p. 153-4).

Nam tantum rogat,[a] et vult se nil[b] scire videri,
    Perpetua atque atrox hostis alazonibus,[c]   **Jactatoribus**[d]
Quae ducebat eos sensim,[e] quaerendo,[f] sequendo,
    Non perceptibiles molliter in laqueos,[g]
Mulciber ut Martem quondam fertur tenuisse,[h]
    Turpiter implicitum ridiculumque Deum.   **350**
Inde fuit magnis exosus civibus,[i] atque
    Ingenio vitam perdidit ipse suo.
Primus et ille fuit patrias concludere in Artem
    Leges,[j] mensurans jus ratione sua.
Et quia rem populi malè[k] curans,[l] sed sua rectè,[m]
    A populo Sapiens[n] audit ubique loci.[o]
Rectores stultos ridens nimis ambitiose,
    Nec juvit,[p] civis nec bonus ipse fuit.
O utinam,[q] matulâ,[r] mortem prius oppetiisset,[s]
    Ictus ab insana conjuge turpe caput,   **360**
Quam de Justititiâ[t] coepisset sermocinari,[u]
    Et vitae dominis scribere jura suae.
Namque ab eo multi didicerunt,[v] publica primò[w]
    Censuris,[x] cives,[y] subdere jura suis,[z]
Scribereque ad vulgus praecepta Politica[aa] stulti
    Certatim,[ab] ut stultos gloria vana jubet,

---

[a] uA rogat • [b] uA B nihil • [c] A Alazonibus B alazonibus • [d] sc mv A B cross-reference x Alazonibus to marginal notation x Jactatoribus • [e] uA B sensim • [f] uA B quaerendo • [g] A B laqueos. C laqueos • [h] A B tenuisse • [i] A Civibus, • [j] uA B Leges • [k] A B male • [l] uA B curans • [m] uA rectè C recte, • [n] uA B sapiens • [o] C loci, • [p] uA B juvit • [q] uA B utinam • [r] uA B matula C matula, • [s] A B oppetiisset • [t] A justititiâ B justititia C iustitia • [u] uA B sermocinari • [v] uA B didicerunt • [w] A C primo • [x] uA B Censuris • [y] A B cives • [z] A B suis. • [aa] A B C politica • [ab] uA B C Certatim

For it merely asks questions, and wants to seem to know nothing, a
    perennial and unyielding enemy to braggarts,[91]
An enemy, who gradually, by probing and pursuing, used to lead them
    softly into imperceptible snares.
In the same way [Vulcan] the Softener[92] is reported to have once held
    Mars[93] captive, a shamefully entangled and ridiculous god.[94]   **350**
For this reason Socrates was hated by the powerful citizens, and lost his
    life on account of his own cleverness.
He was also the first to embrace ancestral law in an art, measuring right
    by his own reasoning.
And because he attended to public affairs badly, but his own well, he was
    spoken of as a Wise Man by people everywhere.
Laughing too ostentatiously at stupid rulers, he did not please them, nor
    was he himself a good citizen.
If only he had met his death earlier, struck on his ugly head with a pot[95] by
    his mad wife,[96]   **360**
Before he began to discourse[97] about justice and write laws for those who
    were the masters of his life.
In fact many citizens first learned from him to submit public laws to their
    own criticism.
And from him fools learned to vie in writing political precepts for the
    mob, as empty glory commands the foolish,

---

[91] sc mv A B cross-reference x *Alazonibus* to marginal notation x *Jactatoribus* (*iactor* from Gr. *aladzon -onos*), braggards, swaggerers, imposters; vagabonds. See above for Aristotle's discussion of *alazoneia* and *eirôneia*.

[92] *Mulciber, literally, Vulcan, the Softener, Vulcan in a specific mode or figuratively, fire. Again an allusion to an ancient etymology connecting *Mulciber* with *mollere*. See Maltby, *A Lexicon of Ancient Latin Etymologies*, p. 394.

[93] *Mars, god of war, the father of Romulus; figurative, war, conflict.

[94] See Homer, *Odyssey* 8.266 ff. *Mars and *Venus are having an assignation and Vulcan, who comes upon them, captures them in an intricate net hand wrought from his underworld workshops, and exposes them to the gods.

[95] *Matula*, pot (cooking or chamber).

[96] For Socrates' wife Xanthippe, see Diogenes Laertius 2.36. She was a favourite with irreverent Cynics. This sort of low humour characterized the 'rowdy boys', 'sons of Ben' (Jonson) and the Tityre Tus (see Raylor, *Cavaliers, Clubs and Literary Culture*).

[97] 'sermocinari' = διαλέγεσθει, to debate or discourse, c.f. Quintilian 9.2.31, a term used also by Valla who proposed replacing the empty abstractions of metaphysics with an empirical science of discourse ('scientia sermocinantes'). See Valla's *Dialectica* in his *Opera omnia*, ed. E. Garin vol I, p. 732, cited by Gravelle, 'Lorenzo Valla's Comparison of Latin and Greek and the Humanist Background', *Bibliothèque d'Humanisme et Renaissance*, vol. 44, 2 (1982), p. 283.

Et,[a] Libertatis[b] specioso nomine,[c] Leges[d]
    Negligere, et Reges esse putare lupos.
Quos inter Stagyrita[e] fuit,[f] licet ipse Tyranni
    Doctor erat magni,[g] magnus[h] Aristoteles.   370
Quem Cicero,[i] et Seneca,[j] Tacitusque[k] et mille secuti,
    Reges nos nostros[l] dedocuere pati.
His Democraticis lectis Authoribus,[m] et qui
    Nil Libertatem[n] significare putant[o]
Praeterquam vice quemque sua regnare,[p] nefanda[q]
    In Regem cives arma tulere suum:[r]
Quo bello periere virûm[s] prope millia centum,
    Et victus tandem Rex jugulatus erat.
Quod fieri facinus plebs nunquam passa fuisset,[t]
    Maxima ni Cleri[u] pars animasset eos;[v]   380
Grex Aristotelis fuit hic;[w] Metaphysicus atque
    Physicus,[x] et Logicus,[y] Rhetoricusque[z] simul;[aa]
Et quorum mandris[ab] nunc est Academia nomen,[ac]
    Noster erat Pastor summus Aristoteles.[ad]

---

[a] uA B C Et • [b] uA B C libertatis • [c] uA B nomine • [d] uA C leges • [e] A B C stagyrita • [f] uA B fuit • [g] uA B magni • [h] A Magnus • [i] uA B C Cicero • [j] uA B Seneca • [k] A Tacitusque, • [l] A Nostros • [m] uA B Authoribus C autoribus, • [n] uA B C libertatem • [o] C putant, • [p] A B regnare • [q] A B nefanda, • [r] A B C suum. • [s] mv uA B viri • [t] A B fuisset • [u] B C cleri • [v] uA B eos, • [w] uA B hic • [x] uA B C Physicus • [y] uA B logicus • [z] B Rethoricusque • [aa] A B simul. • [ab] A B mandris, • [ac] A nomen. • [ad] C Aristoteles:

And under the high-sounding name of Liberty were taught to despise the
    law and to regard kings as wolves,[98]
Among whom was the Stagyrite, the great Aristotle, although he himself
    was the teacher of a great tyrant.[99]   **370**
Cicero, Seneca and Tacitus and a thousand others followed him in
    teaching us not to submit to our kings.
It was after having read these democratic authorities, the same ones who
    thought liberty means nothing other than
Each man reigning in his turn,[100] that citizens took up abominable arms
    against their own king.
During that war almost a hundred thousand men perished and the king,
    finally defeated, had his throat cut.[101]
The common people would never have allowed that crime to be committed
    if the greatest part of the clergy had not incited them: [102]   **380**
This was the herd of Aristotle, metaphysicians, natural philosophers,
    logicians and rhetoricians, all at the same time.
And our Aristotle was the supreme shepherd of those whose folds now
    bear the name of the Academy.

---

[98] Hobbes's form of words, 'libertatis specioso nomine, Leges/ Negligere, et
Reges esse putare lupos', is strongly reminiscent of Lucretius *De re. nat.*, 5.1130-
40, which treats those who 'desire to hold the world in fee and to rule kingdoms' as
the cause of regicide and civil war; causing men 'who hang on their lips', 'to regard
their kings as wolves' ('Reges esse putare lupos'). Taken in conjunction with lines
11-12 (Perfidiam, caedes, perjuria, furta, rapinas, Nonne vides civis dicier acta
boni?), Hobbes's claim also echoes a famous passage from Pierre Gassendi's formulation of Epicurus' *Ratae Sententiae* XXXIII, which in turn contains the reference to the proverb cited by Hobbes in *De Cive*: '*Hominem esse homini lupum*'. See
Paganini, 'Hobbes, Gassendi et le *De Cive*', pp. 191-2; and Tricaud, '"Homo
homini Deus", pp. 61-70.
[99] Aristotle taught Alexander the Great. Hobbes's use of the term *Tyrannus*
shows typical Renaissance slippage. Machiavelli, who avoids the term in *The
Prince*, using rather the term *il Principe* for Nabis of Sparta and Petruzzi of Sienna,
in the *Discourses* 3.6 refers to Petruzzi as *tirrano*. In Aristotle's own time, tyrant
was an honorific form of address, in fact.
[100] On the 'democratical principles of Aristotle and Cicero' as the cause of 'the
rebellion we now talk of', see *Beh.* p. 43.
[101] Charles I, King of Great Britain, was beheaded on January 1, 1649. Hobbes
gives here the same figure for English Civil War casualties that he gives in *Behemoth*. See the Introduction by Stephen Holmes to the reissued Tönnies edn, p. 95.
[102] In *Beh.*, pp. 2-3, Hobbes gives a different catalogue of those who turned the
public against the King. 'The seducers were of divers sorts', first Papists, then
*Presbyterians and third, *Independents, *Fifth-monarchy-men, *Quakers and
Adamites, all claiming independent, and in some cases democratic, authority.

Se. Non tanti puto scire fuit Graecè[a] atque[b] Latinè;[c]
    Nec nova vox pretio sanguinis empta placet,
Quo nobis minus esse licet felicibus[d] absque
    Linguis externis,[e] quàm[f] fuit Assyriis?
Cur contenta sua fuit unâ[g] Graecia Lingua[h]
    Garrula, nec petiit verba Latina[i] prior?   390
Quare qui linguam solam addidicere Latinam,[j]
    Illam nec valde,[k] praetereaque nihil,[l]
Dicuntur Docti;[m] qui scit bene pluribus uti[n]
    Dicitur Indoctus,[o] Plebs,[p] Idiota,[q] Rudis?[r]
Pr.[s] Quaeritur hoc rectè;[t] nempe hac latet anguis in herba;[u]
    Fons erat hic nostri[v] principiumque mali.
Nam Graecis,[w] Sapiens,[x] simul ac[y] virtute virorum
    Septem, praeclari nomen honoris erat,
Incoepit[z] multis,[aa] quibus otia suppetiere[ab]
    Libertasque[ac] animi[ad] Philosophia coli,[ae]   400

---

[a] B Graece C graece • [b] mv A B et (1688 atque scans, et does not: possibly the common neolatin abbreviation for atque, ac, misread) • [c] uA B latine C latine; • [d] mv A B fidelibus (read felicibus) • [e] uA B externis • [f] A B C quam • [g] A B C una • [h] A B lingua, C lingua • [i] uA B C latina • [j] uA B C latinam, • [k] B valde • [l] A B nihil. • [m] uA B docti, C docti; • [n] A uti; • [o] A B C indoctus, • [p] A B C plebs, • [q] uA B idiota C idiota, • [r] uA B C rudis? • [s] mv uA B *Pr.* missing • [t] uA B rectè, C recte; • [u] A B herba, • [v] A B nostri, • [w] uA B Graecis • [x] uA B C sapiens, • [y] A B simulac • [z] mv A Incepit • [aa] mv uA B a multis • [ab] mv uA B suppetivere • [ac] uA liberasque • [ad] B C animi, • [ae] A coli. B coli

Se. I wouldn't think knowing Greek and Latin was so important, nor is it
a good thing that a new language is acquired at the price of blood.[103]
Why is it less possible for us to be successful[104] without foreign languages
than it was for the Assyrians?
Why was garrulous Greece satisfied with her own single language, and
did not attempt to learn Latin earlier?[105]   **390**
Why are those who have learned Latin as their only language, and not
very well, and have learned nothing else
Considered learned[106], while the man who knows how to use many languages
well is said to be uneducated, common, ignorant and uncultured?
Pr. Your point is well taken. A snake certainly hides in this grass.[107] Here
was the source and beginning of our trouble.
For among the Greeks, as soon as the name 'Wise' began to be specially
honoured because of the excellence of seven men,[108]
Philosophy began to be cultivated by the many men for whom the leisure
and freedom of mind were available.[109]   **400**

---

[103] See *Lev.*, xxi, §9, 111/141, 'Of the Liberty of Subjects':
And by reading of these Greek, and Latin authors, men from their childhood
have gotten a habit (under a false show of liberty,) of favouring tumults and of
licentious controlling the actions of their sovereigns; and again of controlling
those controllers, with the effusion of so much blood; as I think I may truly
say: there was never any thing so dearly bought, as these western parts have
bought the learning of the Greek and Latin tongues.

[104] mv 1688 *felicibus* A B *fidelibus* (faithful) which does not scan.

[105] Lorenzo Valla stressed the significance of a single Latin language for Roman
hegemony. See the introduction to his manual on Latin style, the *Elegantiae* (translated by Alan Fisher in 'The Project of Humanism and Valla's Imperial Metaphor',
Journal of Medieval and Renaissance Studies, vol. 23 (1993) pp. 301-22, at p. 302):
Often when I consider the exploits of our own ancestors and those of others,
whether kings or *populi*, it seems to me that ours have surpassed all the rest in
propagating not only their authority but their language.

[106] Petrarch was the first of a long line of Italian humanists, including Valla
(*Encom.*, 394), Bruni and Salutati (*De lab. Herc.*, 1.1.4), to single out British logi-
cians for their 'barbarous' Latin. Lisa Jardine, 'Humanist Logic', in Charles
B. Schmitt, Eckhard Kessler and Quentin Skinner, eds., *The Cambridge History of
Renaissance Philosophy* (Cambridge, Cambridge University Press, 1988), pp. 173-
198, at p. 177.

[107] 'Latet anguis in herba', Virgil, *Eclogues* 3.93.

[108] Jean Bodin, possibly Hobbes's source, refers favourably to the seven sages
of Greece in bk 2, chs 4-5, of *The Six Books of the Republic*, although he calls two
of them tyrants because they took their realms by force.

[109] Lucretius' *De re. nat.* bk 5 and Seneca's Ninetieth Letter on the progress of
civilization; see *Lev.*, xlvi, §6, 368/455.

Mundum hi,[a] non libros legerunt, ingenioque
      Incoepit causas quaerere quisque suo,
Nullius addictus[b] jurare in verba Magistri,
      Solus enim his[c] primis Author[d] erat Ratio,[e]
Horum Epicurus erat, Plato, Zeno, Democritusque,[f]
      Pyrrho,[g] Aristoteles, nescio quotque alii,[h]
Digni laude viri,[i] quorum sapientia juvit[j]
      Humanum multâ[k] commoditate genus.
Hujus,[l] post illos,[m] devenit gloria laudis[n]
      Ad quotquot primos[o] hi docuere viros.[p]   **410**
Hos tamen aequales ne credas esse Magistris;[q]
      Ingenio quoniam non sapuere suo.
His successerunt alii,[r] verùm[s] inferiores;[t]
      Atque artes lento sic periere pede.
Philosophis sed honos habitus non omnibus idem est[u]
      A cunctis;[v] unum hic praetulit, ille alium.[w]
Et distinxit eos nomen quandoque Magistri,
      Et quandoque Scholae,[x] quo docuere loco.[y]
Hinc Stoa, et hinc Peripatus,[z] multarum haeresiumque
      Obvia sunt veteri[aa] nomina in historia.   **420**
Se. Haeresis, oro,[ab] quid est? Nam me convicia[ac] tantum
      Fecerunt magnum[ad] crimen ut esse putem.

---

[a] uA B C hi • [b] A B addictus, • [c] A his, • [d] uA B author C autor • [e] uA B ratio. C ratio, • [f] A B C Democritusque • [g] uA B Pyrho, • [h] A B C alii. • [i] A Viri, • [j] A B juvit, • [k] uA B C multa • [l] uA B C Hujus • [m] A B illos • [n] A B laudis, • [o] A B primos, • [p] A Viros B viros • [q] A B Magistris, C magistris • [r] uA B alii • [s] uA B C verum • [t] uA B inferiores • [u] uA est, • [v] uA Cunctis A Cunctus; B cunctis C cunctus, • [w] uA alium: • [x] B C scholae, • [y] uA loco: • [z] uA B Peripatus • [aa] A Veteri • [ab] A B oro • [ac] A B convitia (variant) • [ad] A B magnum,

These men read the world not books,[110] and each undertook to investigate
    causes by means of his own natural intelligence,
Obliged to swear by the words of no master.[111] For Reason alone was the
    authority for these distinguished men.
Among them were Epicurus, Plato, Zeno and Democritus, Pyrrho,
    Aristotle, and I don't know how many others.
These were men worthy of praise, whose wisdom helped the human race
    to great advantage.[112]
After them, the glory of this praise came down to however many
    outstanding disciples they taught,   **410**
However you should not believe these men were equals to their teachers,
    for they did not have wisdom by their own intelligence.[113]
Others succeeded them, but they were inferior; and so the arts slowly
    died.
But the same respect was not accorded to all philosophers by everybody;
    this man preferred one philosopher, that man preferred another.
Sometimes the name of their teacher distinguished them, and sometimes
    the name of the School at which they taught.
Hence the Stoa, the Peripatos and the names of many sects[114] are
    encountered in ancient history.   **420**
Se. A sect? What's that pray? For to me the mere invective makes me
    think it is a great crime.

---

[110] Reference to a celebrated passage in the essays of Galileo Galilei *The Assayer [Saggiatore], Opere,* 6.232 (see Invernizzi, note).

[111] Horace, *Epist.* 1.1.14.

[112] Molesworth's notes, p. 360, refer us to *Lev.*, xlvi, §7, 369/455, where Hobbes makes the same claims of the Greek philosophers.

[113] c.f. the 1668 Appendix to the *LL*, §109, (tr. Wright, p. 368):
    For it is true, I think, that Plato and Aristotle, Zeno and Epicurus, the sects' originators, were truly philosophers according to the capacity of the pagans; that is, they were men devoted to truth and virtue. And it is for this that their names have justly shone in the glory of their wisdom throughout nearly all the world. But I do not think that we should call their sect-followers philosophers, for, apart from the opinions they knew their masters held, such men themselves understood nothing. They lacked knowledge of the principles and lines of reasoning upon which the teaching they professed rested. Nor did they at all conduct themselves in life after the manner of philosophy, except that they let their beards grow and wore a thread bare pallium. For the rest they were greedy, haughty and irascible, complete strangers to civic affection.

[114] *haeresis* (Gr. *'airesis*) [Souter], perhaps oftener in early mss *heresis* (= *'eresis, ai*), guild (of sailors) [*Cod. Theod.* 13.6.9.]; school, sect (rarely of pagans, sometimes of Jews, but most often) of Christians who are opposed to the doctrines of the Catholic Church; heretical opinions, heresy.

Pr. Doctorum Docti[a] pugnans cum Dogmate[b] Dogma,[c]
    Haeresis à[d] Graeca gente vocata fuit.
Se.[e] Cujus erat quaeso legis violatio? natae,
    Haeresis,[f] an positae? Crimen ut esse sciam?[g]
Pr. Neutrius. Errat homo, quia nemo libenter;[h] et omnis
    Libera apud Graecos Philosophia fuit.
Hi converterunt Pietatem in Theiologiam[i]
    Primi,[j] spernentes[k] tertia verba Dei.   430
Mox illis bellum peperit sententia discors,
    Pugnari et coeptum est fustibus et baculis.[l]
Nec Graecis tantùm[m] fuit haec sapientia cordi,[n]
    Semina dissidii[o] sparsit ubique loci.[p]
Quantum orbis[q] patuit Romanus,[r] rixa erat inter
    Coecos, de,[s] Quis[t] habet lumina clara magis.
Quorum olim[u] mores,[v] lepidus,[w] depinxit ineptos[x]
    Lucius,[y] et postquam desiit esse Asinus.[z]
De quorum vitiis,[aa] ut dignum est,[ab] stultitiaque,[ac]
    Quantumvis Rhetor,[ad] dicere nemo potest,[ae]   440
Vile genus,[af] lucri cupidum, nil turpe recusans
    Auri suaveolens[ag] unde veniret odor;[ah]
Infima faex plebis, pauper gens,[ai] atque superba,[aj]
    Nullius frugi, nil nisi barba gravis.
Frontibus austeris obsceni,[ak] totaque vita[al]
    Ipsorum,[am] contra quam docuere,[an] fuit.

---

[a] A docti, B Docti, C docti • [b] A B C dogmate • [c] A B dogma C dogma, • [d] A a • [e] mv uA *Se.* missing • [f] A B C Haeresis • [g] mv uA B sciam. • [h] A C libenter, B libenter • [i] A B Theologiam • [j] A B Primi • [k] mv A sperantes (read spernentes) • [l] A B C baculis • [m] A B C tantum • [n] A B cordi • [o] A dissidii. B dissidii, • [p] mv C loci • [q] A Orbis • [r] mv uA B Romanus patuit (word order) • [s] uA B C de • [t] uA B quis • [u] B olìm • [v] uA B mores • [w] uA B lepidus • [x] A ineptos. • [y] uA B C Lucius • [z] A B C asinus. • [aa] uA B vitiis • [ab] A B est • [ac] A B stultitiaque • [ad] uA Rhetor B Rethor C rhetor • [ae] A B potest. • [af] A B genus • [ag] uA suaviolens, B suaveolens, • [ah] uA B odor. • [ai] uA B gens • [aj] C superba • [ak] uA B obscoeni • [al] A B vita, • [am] uA B Ipsorum • [an] uA B docuere

Pr. The fighting of learned men against learned men, doctrine against doctrine, was called 'sect' by the Greeks.[115]

Se. Of what law, I ask you, was a 'sect' a violation? Of a natural law or one imposed, so that I can know it to be a crime?

Pr. Neither. Because no man errs deliberately, and among the Greeks all philosophy was free.

These men were the first who transformed piety into theology, taking little account of[116] the three words of God.[117]   430

Soon discordant opinion among them gave birth to war, and it began to be fought with clubs and sticks.

And this wisdom was not only dear to the heart of the Greeks. It spread the seeds of division everywhere.

However far the Roman world extended, the quarrel was among the blind about who had the clearer eyes.

At one time witty Lucius[118] represented the absurd behaviour of these men, and also after he stopped being an ass.

No-one, however good a rhetorician, could adequately describe the faults and folly of these men.   440

Low types, greedy for gain, and refusing no vice from which the sweet smell of gold might come,

They were the lowest dregs of the masses,[119] poor folk, insolent and of no use, nothing but a weighty beard.[120]

They were repulsive men, austere in appearance, and their whole life was contrary to what they taught.

---

[115] Diogenes Laertius 1.20, defined the term sect in terms of adherence to a fixed set of doctrines, referring at 1.19 to the nine Greek philosophical Schools, cited in Hippobotus' work *On Philosophical Sects*.

[116] mv A sperantes 'hoping' (ungrammatical).

[117] *tertia verba Dei.* See the 1688 Glossary (pp. 604-5), and Molesworth's note, [*vide Glossarium*], *Glossarium: Tertia Verba Dei – Sacra Scriptura. In lib. De. Cive, cap. XV, triplex verbum Dei: 1. Rationale, 2. Sensibile, 3. Propheticum.* See [Souter], the three-fold word of God, (1) *rationale*, [revealed] by reason (2) *sensibile*, [revealed] by the senses, (3) *propheticum*, of the prophets (*q.v.* Hobbes, *De Cive*, ch. 15).

[118] Lucius refers to the work *Lucius, or the Ass*, attributed to Lucian*, and telling the same story as Apuleius' *Golden Ass*. Hobbes appears to concur with the attribution.

[119] See Lucan, *Pharsalia* 9.455-9, on religion falling into disuse, and Rome becoming the sewer of the world: 'mundi faece repletam' (7.405).

[120] c.f. the 1668 Appendix to the *LL*, §109, (tr. Wright, p. 368), cited above, on the followers of the great philosophers in no way matching the wisdom or virtue of the founders of the sects, Plato, Aristotle, *Zeno and Epicurus.

Se.[a] Nunc quoque Centauros[b] videor,[c] Lapithasque videre,[d]
    Clamosae quoties audio verba Scholae.[e]
Nec non Theiologûm[f] libris convicia[g] foeda
    Miror, et indignor, cumque rubore lego.   **450**
Nam qui Theiologis[h] dissentit,[i] protinus audit[j]
    Passim Blasphemus, Atheus,[k] Haereticus.
Improba non dicet mulier convicia[l] summa,
    Si non se laesam sentiat[m] esse prius.
Pr. Non laesum credis[n] Clerum,[o] sapientia quorum
    Spernitur,[p] et parvi ducitur ingenium?
Virtute Ingenii[q] dominari[r] est summa voluptas;[s]
    Te,[t] quibus hanc tollis,[u] posse placere putas?
Et quibus est commissa teipsum cura docendi,
    An diversa putas[v] hisce docere leve?   **460**

---

[a] mv uA B *Sec.* missing • [b] B centauros • [c] A B videor • [d] A B videre • [e] A B
C scholae • [f] A B Theologum B Theologùm C Theiologum • [g] A B convitia
(variant) • [h] uA B Theologis • [i] uA dissentit • [j] A B audit • [k] A C Athaeus,
• [l] A B convitia (variant) • [m] mv uA B sentiet • [n] mv uA B credis esse • [o] uA B
clerum • [p] A B Spernitur • [q] A B C ingenii • [r] mv uA B dominare • [s] A B
voluptas, • [t] A B Te • [u] uA B tollis • [v] A putas,

Se. Now too, whenever I hear the teachings of some noisy School, I
seem to see Centaurs[121] and Lapiths.[122]
I am astonished at the foul invective in the books of the theologians, and I
am angry and read them with shame.   **450**
For whoever dissents from theologians immediately hears from all sides,
'blasphemer', 'atheist' and 'heretic'.[123]
Even a wanton woman wouldn't utter the most forceful invective unless
she first felt that she had been harmed.

Pr. Don't you think that the clergy, whose wisdom is scorned and whose
intelligence is considered paltry, has been harmed?[124]
Given that the greatest pleasure is to dominate by the excellence of one's
intellect, do you think that you can satisfy those from whom you take
this pleasure away?
Or do you consider it a frivolous matter to teach something different from
those who have been entrusted with teaching you?   **460**

---

[121] Machiavelli used the image of the *centaur to capture human nature, part
man, part beast, in the *The Prince* (Harmondsworth, Penguin, 1961, p. 99), a variant
on the 'homo homini lupus, homo homini deus' theme. But Hobbes uses the
analogy of the centaur differently, to refer to simple as compared with compounded
imaginings, and here he follows Cicero, *De nat. deor.*, 1.38.105: 'si tantum modo ad
cogitationem valent, nec habent ullam soliditatem nec eminentiam, quid interest
utrum de hippocentauro an de deo cogitemus?' See *Lev.*, ii, §4, 6/9:

> as when from the sight of a man at one time, and of a horse at another, we con-
> ceive in our mind a Centaur. So when a man compoundeth the image of his
> own person with the image of the actions of another man, as when a man
> imagines himself a *Heracles*, or an *Alexander*, (which happeneth often to
> them that are much taken with reading of romances) it is a compound imagi-
> nation, and properly but a fiction of the mind.

[122] Nestor in the *Iliad*, 1.261-71, uses the example (*paradeigma*) of the
*Lapiths, who took his advice in their fight against the Centaurs, in his speech to
resolve the dispute between Agamemnon and Achilles. The *paradeigma*, an
example narrating past events, was one of two types of proof (the other being the
enthememe), outlined in Aristotle's *Rhetoric*, 1393a. See Kennedy, *Classical
Rhetoric*, pp. 9-15, and *Art of Persuasion*, pp. 35-40, who notes that Homer is weak
at arguing from proof. Cited in Peter Toohey, 'Epic and Rhetoric: Speech-making
and Persuasion in Homer and Apollonius', University of New England, Armidale,
Australia (http://www.cisi.unito.it/arachne/num1/toohey.html), p. 2.

[123] Hobbes refers to the charges of atheism brought against him personally in the
1660s. See Springborg Introduction, chapter 3.1.

[124] A, B: *laesum credis esse Clerum*, perfect pass. infin., as opposed to perf.
pass part., in 1688 text; possibly amended for versification. *Clerus*, as often, is a
collective (= Gr. *kleros*), the clergy.

Sunt quibus est etiam doctrinae gloria,[a] Panis;[b]
   Non laedis,[c] faciens hosce perire fame?
Si mandrita,[d] pecus subreptum viderit iri,[e]
   Non vis ut fures clamet adesse gregi?
Sec: Pastorem verò[f] rectè[g] non increpat alter[h]
   Pastor, nec furem fur bene, parque parem.
Pr. Confiteor. Verum quid agemus? Relliquiae[i] sunt[j]
   Antiquae nobis insipidaeque Scholae.[k]
Tempore namque illo, quo nostrae Praeco[l] salutis,[m]
   In Graecis sparsit semina,[n] Paulus,[o] agris,[p]   470
Maxima erat mundo falsorum Philosophorum
   Copia; nequitiae *Plemmyris,[q] illa fuit.[r]

                              *Mare plenum seu aestus maximus[s]

Quorum non paucos Ecclesia sancta vocavit[t]
   Ad mensam. Crevit sic parasita Fides,[u]
Victum communem[v] ut Christi cultoribus esse
   Sensit egens nebulo, nomine Philosophus,[w]
Rebus in adversis succurrere et omnibus omnes,[x]
   De grege[y] Christicolûm[z] se simulavit ovem.[aa]
Acceptusque fuit.[ab] Quid ni? Fuit[ac] utilis ille
   Militiae Christi; dux fuit et sapiens.   480
Namque Orator erat,[ad] doctusque abducere ab hoste,[ae]
   Si cui forte duces,[af] non placuere sui.

---

[a] uA B gloria • [b] uA B panis, • [c] uA B laedis • [d] uA B C mandrita • [e] A iri •
[f] A C vero • [g] A C recte • [h] A B alter, • [i] A reliquiae B Reliquiae • [j] mv C
sunt. • [k] A C scholae. • [l] uA B C praeco • [m] A B C salutis • [n] uA B semina •
[o] uA B Paulus • [p] A B agris mv C ayris, (error) • [q] uA B plemmyris • [r] A B fuit
• [s] sc mv A B marginal gloss on plemmyris, missing in 1688 • [t] A B vocavit, •
[u] uA fides A B Fides. C fides, • [v] B communem, • [w] ~ A Philosophus • [x] A B
omnes • [y] A Grege • [z] uA B C Christicolum • [aa] C ovem • [ab] uA B C fuit •
[ac] mv uA B Fuit missing; A fuit • [ad] uA erat • [ae] A B C hoste • [af] mv uA B
ducens,

There are some for whom the glory of teaching is their bread and butter;
  so aren't you harming them by making them die from hunger?
If a shepherd saw that his cattle were about to be stolen, wouldn't you
  want him to shout out to the flock that thieves were coming?[125]
Sec. But it is not right that one herdsman should rebuke another, it is not
  proper that one thief should rebuke another, or one man his peer.
Pr. I concede your point. But what are we going to do? Ours are the
  leavings of an ancient and worthless School.
For at the time when the Paul the Evangelist spread the seeds of our
  salvation in Greek fields,   **470**
There was throughout the world the greatest abundance of false
  philosophers; the tide of wickedness was at the full.[126]
The Holy Church called more than a few of them to her table.[127]
  The faith grew as a parasite.
As soon as some poor good-for-nothing, philosopher in name only,
  realized that the disciples of Christ had their living in common,
And that in adversity everyone helped one another,[128]
  he pretended to be a sheep from Christ's flock.
And he was accepted. And why not? He was useful in the service of
  Christ; he was a leader and a wise man.   **480**
For he was an orator, and clever enough to seduce away from the enemy
  anyone who did not like his own leaders.[129]

---

[125] Echoes of Zechariah 13:7, Matthew 26:31 and Virgil *Aen.* 9.59.

[126] mv A, B: Marginal gloss (indicated with a cross) on the term *Plemmyris* meaning: Mare plenum seu aestus maximus. See the 1688 Glossary (pp. 604-5), and Molesworth's note, to line 472, p. 362: (*pleimmuris, maris aestuans accessus.* Vide Glossarium.) The text in the Glossary, *Plemmyris – Mare plenum, seu aestus maximus,* which corresponds to A, B. *Plemmyris:* from Gr. (f.) *pleimmuris* flood, the flood-tide of the surging sea.

[127] See Clement of Alexandria (b. AD 150, fl. 175-210), *Exhortation to the Greeks,* ch. 5, 'The Witness of Philosophy', ed. Butterworth, pp. 145-63. Hefele, *Histoire des conciles,* 1.1.2, p. 337, notes that Clement, an early church father, sometimes verges on heresy himself.

[128] See *Prudentius' *Psychomachia* on the tillers of Christ, *Prudentius, Works,* ed. H. J. Thomson, 2 vols, Loeb edn, (London 1949); and *The Latin Glosses on Arator and Prudentius in Cambridge, University Library,* Ms Gg.5.35, Studies and Texts 61 (Toronto, 1983).

[129] mv uA B *ducens,* 'the one leading him'.

Idem doctus erat duri vibrator Elenchi,[a]
     Et dilemma anceps torsit utraque manu.[b]
Eminus è Cathedra telis pugnare peritus,
     Cominus[c] et furcis[d] vincere doctus erat.[e]
His igitur multis usa est Ecclesia[f] Christi ;[g]
     Nam docti multo sunt in honore bonis ;
Et curanda ferè[h] traduntur ovilia magna[i]
     His solis,[j] sanctas hi Synodosque regunt.[k]   **490**
Nam licet in Synodis Patres, Sanctique[l] piique,[m]
     Atque proba noti simplicitate viri,
Philosophos numero superarent, attamen illos
     Vincere suffragiis non potuere suis.
Attonitus verbis peregrinis Philosophorum[n]
     Vir simplex contrà[o] dicere non potuit.

---

[a] B C elenchi, • [b] A manu • [c] C Comminus • [d] mv A furiis (read furcis) • [e] A B erat, C erat: • [f] B C ecclesia • [g] ~ A Christi uA B Christi, • [h] A C fere • [i] A B magna, • [j] C solis • [k] A regunt C regunt: • [l] A B C sanctique • [m] A Piique B piique • [n] B Philosophorum, • [o] B C contra

The same fellow was a trained wielder of harsh debate, and he hurled a
   two-horned dilemma with both hands.
He was experienced at fighting at a distance with missiles from the Chair,
   and he was taught to win with a fork[130] in hand to hand fighting.[131]
So the Church of Christ employed many of these men because
   knowledgeable men are held in high regard by honest men;
And the great flock[132] is handed over in general to the care of these men
   alone and they rule the holy Councils,   **490**
For although the holy and pious Church Fathers and men noted for their
   honesty and integrity
Outnumbered the philosophers, they nevertheless could not defeat them
   on the strength of their votes.
Thunderstruck by the strange speech of the philosophers, plain-spoken
   men were not able to contradict them.[133]

---

[130] mv A reads *furiis* ('with furious rage'), but 1688 *furcis*, 'with a fork', is
more likely. The *OED* notes that Hobbes uses 'fork' (*furcis*) for dilemma in
Behemoth.

[131] C.f. Hobbes's reference to the missiles launched from the papal seat
('e cathedra') with Lorenzo Valla's comments on the militancy of the Pope
(*The [Supposed] Donation of Constantine*, ed. Coleman, pp. 178-9):

> And so, that he may recover the other parts of the Donation, money
> wickedly stolen from good people he spends more wickedly, and he supports
> armed forces, mounted and foot, with which all places are plagued, while
> Christ is dying of hunger and nakedness in so many thousands of paupers.

[132] The clergy are compared to Turnus, characterized by rapacious fury in
Virg. *Aen.* 7.462-66: 'Out of his wits, he roared for weapons and hunted for them
by his bedside and all through the house. In him there rioted the bloodthirsty lust
of the blade, the accursed lunacy of war, and, above all, anger'. In *Aen.* 9.59-66,
at the siege of the Trojan camp, Turnus is compared to a raging wolf lying in wait
outside an impenetrable sheepfold.

[133] See the report given in the *Ecclesiastical History of Socrates Scholasticus
in VII Books* (3rd edn London 1729), bk 1, ch. 8, of several logicians demonstrating their forensic skills before the council commenced session. Reprimanded by
an 'honest well-meaning cleric', who maintained that 'neither Christ nor his
Apostles taught us the art of disputing, nor vain subtleness, or fallacies, but a plain
opinion which is to be guarded by faith and good works', they thereupon desisted.
Cited by Martinich, 'On the Proper Interpretation of Hobbes's Philosophy',
Journal of the History of Philosophy, 34 (1996), pp. 273-83, who notes at p. 281
that Socrates Scholasticus is a likely source for Hobbes.

Christi vera Fides,[a] Essentia[b] quid sit ab Ente
   Abstracta,[c] ignorans,[d] obstupefacta tacet.
Non ita Philosophi Patres; sed quisque Magistri
   Dogmata conatur reddere vera sui.   **500**

---

[a] uA B fides C fides, • [b] A Essentia, • [c] uA B Abstracta • [d] A ignorans

The true faith of Christ, not knowing what Essence[134] might be extracted from Being,[135] kept stupefied silence.[136]
So the Fathers were not philosophers; but each tries to make the teachings of his own teacher true.[137] **500**

---

[134] Hobbes uses the term *essentia*, the being or essence of a thing (from the Greek *ousia*). (See Quintilian, *Institutes* 2.14.2, 3.6.23, 8.3.33). Paganini, in a masterpiece of textual archeology, 'Hobbes, Valla e i problemi filosofici della teologia umanistica: la riforma "dilettica" della Trinità', in L. Simonutti, ed. *Dal necessario al possibile. Determinismo e libertà nel pensiero anglo-olandese del XVII secolo* (Milan, FrancoAngeli, 2001), pp. 11-45, at pp. 36-42, argues that Hobbes's discussion of *essentia* follows that of Lorenzo Valla in the *Dialectica*. See *Opera omnia*, ed. E. Garin, vol I, ch. v, p. 653ff., and *Repastinatio dialectice et philosophie*, ed. Zippel, vol. 1, ch. 5, pp. 36-41, entitled 'Inter "essentiam" et "esse" nihil interesse . . .', where Valla argues that attributions of essence are typically illicit inferences drawn from the verb to be. As a consequence, Valla argued, many uses of the term *essentia*, including that of Boethius, involved confusing *essentia* and *substantia*. Valla's important revision of Aristotle's ten categories in favour of Quintilian's three, substance, essence and quality, had been re-elaborated by Pierre Gassendi in the *Syntagma*, which Hobbes was able to discuss with his colleague and friend in Paris in the 1640s, as it was being written. See Gassendi's *Syntagma philosophicum*, in his *Opera Omnia* (Lyon, 1658), vol. 1, p. 181b., cited by Paganini, p.36ff.

[135] Hobbes uses *ens*, a thing; formed, like *essentia* after the Gr. *ousia*, by Flavius (or Fabianus) (according to Quintilian, *Institutes* 8.3.33), but first used by Caesar (according to Priscian, 18.8.75), *entia* (= *ta onta*) (Quintilian 2.14.2). Thomas, *Dictionarium Linguae Latinae*, references (Quintilian), Beeing. But it is not to be found in Elyot. For Hobbes's position on essence as an abstraction from attributes, see *Hist. Narr.*, *EW* IV, pp. 393-5. In the *Answer to Bramhall*, (*EW* IV, p. 304), Hobbes comments, 'If he mean *essence* the same with *ens*, τὸ 'όν, I approve it. Otherwise, what is *essence*? There is no such word in the Old Testament'. Lorenzo Valla, who retained *essentia* as one of his three categories, could barely tolerate the term *ens*, which he defined as 'that thing which is' ('ea res quae est'), an attribution made properly only of God: '*Ens* is said ineptly of any thing other than God, and therefore the great among the Latins spurned this word not without reason'. Valla, *Opera omnia*, ed. Garin, vol 1, p. 647. See Gravelle, 'Lorenzo Valla's Comparison of Latin and Greek', p. 283 and Paganini, 'Hobbes, Valla e i problemi filosofici della teologia umanistica', p. 40n.

[136] The Fathers demonstrated by the fallacy of trying to derive essences from names that they were not philosophers but dogmatists, regurgitating the doctrines of their teachers. See Hobbes's parody in the Appendix to the *LL*, §76 (Wright trans., p. 363), referring specifically to the term 'essence':
> The essence of an entity concretely, take some white entity, is the name of the white itself, but considered only insofar as it is an entity. Generally, abstracts are names of concrete objects when they are thought of separately from the other names of the same object. A white entity for example, is white. If we now were to consider the white in a white object separately from the entity, we say whiteness, for pedagogical reasons, in place of white; or we say, being white.

[137] See the 1668 Appendix to the *LL*, §76 (tr. Wright, p. 363):
> In the primitive church, up to the time of the Council of Nicaea, most of the teachings about which the Christians then disagreed concerned the doctrine of the Holy Trinity. For although everyone held that the mystery of the Trinity

Scinditur in partes Ecclesia;[a] risit at hostis[b]
    Elanguitque jacens debilitata Fides.[c]
Esse novae princeps[d] fuit ingens gloria Sectae[e]
    Philosopho,[f] sine qua non erat unde ederet.
Sic Doctrinarum[g] nascuntur mille colores,[h]
    Dum nebulo fama nobilis esse cupit.
Nascitur hinc odium, et pugnandi magna libido;[i]
    Sed pacem servant arma negata Gregi.[j]
Mutua sed jaciunt convicia;[k] credit utrique
    Ethnicus,[l] et Christi dulce jugum refugit.   **510**
Alter et alterius dum damnat dogmata,[m] natum est
    Nomen et Haeretici,[n] Catholicique viri.[o]
Nam cum finisset[p] Synodi sententia litem,
    Vincere Catholicum, vinci erat Haereticum.[q]
Consensere tamen signati nomine Christi[r]
    Contra Gentiles[s] lignicolasque viros.[t]
Ergo miles[u] erat[v] quoties bellum fuit inter
    Ipsos Romanos Christicola egregius.[w]

---

[a] A B Ecclesia, mv C ecclesiae; (error) • [b] A B hostis, • [c] uA B fides. C fides •
[d] A Princeps • [e] A B sectae, • [f] uA B C Philosopho • [g] B C doctrinarum • [h] A
B colores • [i] A B libido • [j] A B gregi. C gregi • [k] uA convitia A B convitia; •
[l] A B Ethnicus • [m] uA B C dogmata • [n] A haeretici B haeretici. C haeretici, •
[o] mv uA B veri. • [p] mv uA B finissent (error) • [q] B Haereticum C haereticum. •
[r] A Christi, B Christi. • [s] B C gentiles • [t] B viros • [u] A Miles • [v] A B erat, •
[w] uA B egregius

The Church is torn apart by factions, but the enemy laughed and faith
    grew faint and lay crippled.

To be the leader of a new sect was a great source of glory for a
    philosopher, without which he could not eat.

So a thousand forms of doctrines sprang up, as long as the rascal wanted
    to have great fame.

From this hatred was born and a great lust for fighting; but the denial of
    arms to the flock preserved peace.

Yet they hurled mutual invectives; the pagan believed both sides and fled
    the sweet yoke of Christ.   **510**

And while one man condemned the doctrines of another, the names
    heretic and Catholic were born.

In fact, when a judgement of the Council ended the dispute, to win was
    Catholic, to lose was heretical.[138]

Nevertheless, sealed in the name of Christ, they made common cause
    against the pagans and idol-worshippers.[139]

As a consequence, whenever there was war among the Romans
    themselves, the Christians[140] made outstanding soldiers.

---

was incomprehensible, nonetheless, trusting the philosophy of his masters, each man dared to explain it after his own manner. From this there arose at first arguments, then disorders; then, to avoid scandal and establish peace in the church, synods were called, convoked without the order of those in power but through the voluntary drawing together of bishops and pastors, as they were able with the lessening of persecution.

[138] See the 1668 Appendix to the *LL*, §123 (tr. Wright, pp. 369-70):
In these councils, the participants defined what one was to believe concerning the faith in any controverted area. That which was defined was called the catholic faith; what was condemned, heresy. For, with respect to the individual bishop or pastor, the council was the catholic church, that is, the whole or universal church. So also was their opinion the catholic opinion, while a specific teaching held by an individual pastor was heresy. And it is from this, as much as I have gleaned from the historical sources, that the name 'Catholic Church' derives. And in every church, the words 'catholic' and 'heretic' are relative terms.

[139] *lignicola* [Souter] worshipper of wood (i.e. wooden statues) (*Vita Cae. Arel.* [AD 600] 1.55 [*Mon. Ger. Hist. Script. Merou.* 3 i.e. Annals of the Merovingians]. On the pagan worship of idols made of wood and stone, including the cult of Sarapis, see Clement of Alexandria, *Protreptikos pros Helleinas* (Exhortation to the Greeks), ch 4, 41-42, on 'The Worship of Statues', specifically on wooden statues. Clement notes that Ares in old times was worshipped [metonymically] as a spear.

[140] *Christicola* [Lewis & Short], worshipper of Christ; a poetic designation for Christian (Prud. *Cath [emerina* Calendar of Daily Life] 3.56, 8.80; Prud. *contra Symmachum*, 2.1002; Prud. *peri Stephanon*, 3.72.

Hi Constantinum fecerunt vincere, et ille,[a]

    His,[b] non credentum[c] sanguine lavit humum;   520

Cunctaque falsorum destruxit templa Deorum,

    Unius et sanxit publica sacra Dei;[d]

Pastoresque gregum magno dignatus honore est[e]

    Praecipuos; Christi cultor et ipse fuit.[f]

Summe temporibus Ecclesia floruit illis,[g]

    Agrorum sanctis[h] proprietasque redit.

Inque dies crevit grex Christi;[i] accessit ad illos[j]

    Omnibus è[k] terris innumerus populus,[l]

Principis exemplo,[m] vel prosperitate vocati[n]

    Temporis,[o] aut aliqua voce Ministerii.   530

Jamque nihil deerat[p] quod gentem reddere Christi

    Foelicem[q] posset[r] ni sibi deesse velit.

Sec. Defuit (haud dubium est) quod erat. Qui non bona norit

    Ipse sua,[s] aut nescit[t] quid juvet aut noceat,

Hunc nec agri nec opes foelicem[u] reddere possunt,[v]

    Nam sibi divitiis ipse molestus erit.

Pr. Est ita.[w] Divitias[x] dederit si numen avaro[y]

    Quantum optat magnas, ambitiosus erit.[z]

Si rerum curam commiserit ambitioso,[aa]

    Vult dici sapiens, atque superbus erit.[ab]   540

Esse datam dicet, sicut par est,[ac] sapienti,

    Debitaque ingratus, quae capit,[ad] esse putat.

Annis usa fuit paucis Ecclesia pace,

    Quando commisit lis nova Philosophos.[ae]

---

[a] A B ille • [b] A B His • [c] mv A B C credendum (read credentum) • [d] A B Dei. • [e] A B est, • [f] C fuit, • [g] A B illis • [h] A B sanctis, • [i] uA Christi • [j] A illos. • [k] A e • [l] A B populus. C populus • [m] uA B exemplo • [n] ~ A vocari (marginal restoration of uA vocati in the gutter, error) • [o] uA Temporis • [p] A B deerat, • [q] A C Felicem • [r] A B posset, • [s] uA sua • [t] A nescit, • [u] A B C felicem • [v] A possunt • [w] uA B ita • [x] uA B divitias • [y] A avaro, B avaro. • [z] A B erit • [aa] uA B ambitioso • [ab] A B erit, • [ac] A B est • [ad] uA B capit • [ae] B Philosophos,

They made Constantine[141] victorious, and he bathed the earth in the blood
    of those who did not believe them.[142]   **520**
And he destroyed all the temples of false gods and decreed the public
    worship of the one God.[143]
And he thought the most prominent pastors of the flocks worthy of the
    greatest honour; and he was a worshipper of Christ himself.
The Church flourished extremely well at this time and ownership of
    landed property returned to pious men.
From day to day the flock of Christ grew; countless men from every land
    joined them.
Induced by the example of the emperor, or the prosperity of the times, or
    by some call of a minister,   **530**
Now there was nothing lacking to make Christ's people happy, if it did not
    choose to fail itself.
Sec. In itself it did fail, no doubt of that. If a man doesn't know his own
    blessings,[144] or is unaware of what is good or harmful to him,
Neither property nor wealth can make him happy, and in fact he will be a
    trouble to himself because of his riches.
Pri. That's right. If divine will gives the greedy man as much great
    wealth as he might desire, he will want power.
If God entrusts responsibility for affairs to the ambitious man, he will
    want to be called wise but will be arrogant;   **540**
He will say it was granted, as is due to a wise man, and the ungrateful
    fellow thinks anything he gets is owed to him.
For a few years the Church enjoyed peace, until a new quarrel brought the
    philosophers into conflict.

---

[141] *Constantine the Great, Roman Emperor. (c. AD 280-337, emperor from
306).

[142] See Valla's address to the Pope, in *The [Supposed] Donation of Constantine*,
ed. Coleman, pp. 176-7:
> What if you despoil our temples? You *have* despoiled them. What if you
> outrage maidens and matrons? You *have* outraged them. What if you derench
> the city with the blood of its citizens? You *have* drenched it. Must we endure
> all this? Nay, rather, since you have ceased to be a father to us, shall we not
> likewise forget to be sons?

[143] 'Constantine having defeated Maxentius in the battle of the Mulvian Bridge
(312), with the Edict of Milan in 313, made Christianity the official religion of the
empire' (Invernizzi note). It was Constantine who began the practice of forced con-
versions which corrupted belief.

[144] Virgil, *Georgics* 2.458-9, 'O fortunatos nimium, sua si bona norint, agricolas!'

Inter Alexandrum certatur,[a] et inter[b] Arium,[c]
    Inter,[d] id est,[e] Ephorum,[f] Presbyterumque[g] suum,[h]
Christus an aequalis Patri fuit,[i] an minor illo,[j]
    Illi,[k] par visus, huic,[l] minor esse Deo.
Ad mensam coeptum est,[m] atque inter pocula quaeri:[n]
    (Ad mensam esse solet libera lingua mero.)[o]   **550**
Hinc abit ad Cathedras[p] sacra controversia sanctas,
    Sectumque in partes concitat inde gregem.
Mox et Alexandri celebri pugnatur in urbe,
    Et diversa furens[q] miles in arma ruit:[r]

---

[a] A B certatur • [b] mv uA B inter missing • [c] A B Arium • [d] uA B Inter • [e] uA B est • [f] uA B C Ephorum • [g] A B presbyterumque • [h] ~ A suum • [i] uA B fuit • [j] uA B illo • [k] uA B C Illi • [l] A B huic • [m] A B Coeptum est ad mensam (word order) • [n] A B quaeri • [o] A B mero) • [p] uA B C cathedras • [q] A B furens, • [r] A B ruit,

The dispute was fought out between Alexander[145] and Arius,[146] that is
between a Bishop[147] and his own Elder,[148]
Over whether Christ was equal to or lesser than the Father,[149] to the former
he seemed equal to God, to the latter lesser than God.
The matter began to be discussed at dinner and when drinking[150] (at
dinner, wine usually loosens the tongue),   **550**
From here the religious controversy went to the sacred Sees, and from
there stirred up the flock, dividing it into factions.
Soon there was fighting even in the crowded city of Alexandria, and
crazed soldiers rushed to join the opposing forces.[151]

---

[145] *Bishop Alexander of Alexandria. See *Sozomen, *Hist. Eccl.*, bk 1 ch. 15.
See Hefele, *Histoire des conciles* 1.1. bk 2, p. 352, citing *PG* LXVII, col. 906.

[146] *Arius, a 'subordinationist', for whom Christ and the Holy Ghost, proceeded
from, and therefore were subordinate to, God the Father, was condemned at the
Council of Nicaea (AD 325. Hobbes accuses him of sedition but not of heresy. For
Hobbes the reason for calling the *Nicene Council was, significantly, a power struggle between an elder (Presbyter), Arius and a bishop (ephor) Alexander. See the
1668 Appendix §124 (tr. Wright, p. 370):
> The reason for calling the Council of Nicaea was Arius, elder of Alexandria.
> When the bishop of that city, Alexander, had said that the Son of God was
> *homoousios*, that is, of the same substance with the Father, Arius contradicted
> him. And then, with a large number of elders present, in the rising heat of their
> argument, he also denied the divinity of Jesus Christ. As a result, shortly
> thereafter civil strife and bloodshed were born in Alexander's city. Then, in
> order to preserve the peace, Emperor Constantine the Great convoked the
> famous Council of Nicaea . . . .

[147] 'Ephor' ('ἔφυρος) is sometimes used in Christian texts for bishops: Lampe
s.v. 2c. See the 1688 Glossary (pp. 604-5), and Molesworth's note, p. 364: *Vide
Glossarium.*

[148] *presbyter -eris* (m.) [Souter], (= Gr. *presbuteros*) elder.

[149] 'The controversy began at Alexandria in AD 318. The reference to the banquet
which immediately follows takes its origin perhaps from the fact that Arius first
expounded his doctrine in a work, probably in verse, entitled the *Thalia* (*The Banquet*).

[150] Hobbes mocks both Plato's *Symposium* and Arius's famous work in prose
and verse, the *Thalia* (*Banquet*), of which only fragments remain in the work of
Athanasius, *Orat. contr. Arian.*, bk 1 chs 4, 6, and *De syn. Arimin.*, ch. 15, *PG*
XXVI, cols 16, 24, 705, discussed in Hefele, *Histoire des conciles*, 1.1.2, pp. 375-8.
Composed as songs to lure sailors travelers and artisans to his doctrines (Hefele,
p. 376), the work was popular among Alexandrian sailors and rabble rousers. Both
Arius and his disciple Eutyches the Archimandrite earned for their followers,
including monks and hermits, the reputation of hard-drinking revelers and 'belly-
lovers', as Gregory of Nazianus comments, *Palatine Anthology*, VIII, 175-269, c.f.
poems 165-75, cited by Gregory, *The Urban Crowd in the Religious Controversies
of the Fifth Century AD*, PhD Thesis (U. of Michigan, Ann Arbor Microfilms,
1971), pp. 221-5, at p. 224).

[151] Two of the teachers of Socrates of Constantinople, Helladius, a priest of
Zeus, and Ammonius, a priest of the Ape God, participated in the anti-Christian

Rex Constantinus multos jam,[a] militiaeque
    Florem,[b] civili clade perire videns,[c]
Ut Regem decuit prudentem, tollere causam[d]
    Dissidii studuit, et stabilire Fidem;[e]
Convocat ex omni terrarum parte suarum[f]
    Doctos Rectores, Praesbyterosque Viros.   **560**
Ordinis et primi tunc convenere Trecenti[g]
    Octodecimque[h] graves eximiique Senes.[i]
Haec Nicena fuit Synodus[j] Patrum[k] generalis.[l]
    Primaque Romani totius orbis[m] erat.

---

[a] uA jam • [b] uA Florem • [c] uA B videns A videns. • [d] A B causam, • [e] uA B
fidem C fidem; • [f] A B suarum, • [g] uA B trecenti, A Trecenti, C trecenti • [h] mv
uA B Octodecim • [i] uA B senes. C senes, • [j] A C synodus • [k] C patrum • [l] A
Generalis, C generalis, • [m] A Orbis

The Emperor Constantine, seeing many men, and the flower of his army,
   now being killed in civil conflict,
Applied himself, as a prudent monarch should, to removing the cause of
   the conflict and restoring stability to the faith;
He called together from all parts of his empire learned bishops[152] and
   elders.[153]   **560**
At that time three hundred and eighteen men of the highest rank,
   including influential and distinguished old men, assembled.[154]
This was the Nicaean Council and it was the first general Council of the
   Church Fathers in the Roman world.[155]

---

riots in Alexandria of 389 AD. Socrates Scholasticus (*Hist. Eccl.*, v. 16) records
Helladius's boast to have killed nine Christians with his own hands during the riot
(See Chestnut, *The First Christian Historians*, p. 179).

   [152] *rector -oris* (m.) [Souter] (eccl.) bishop, (Hilary, Damas., Ambrosiast. [AD
366-84]); ruler (God) (August., Cassiod.). (Cooper), a ruler or governour: he or she
that governeth.

   [153] See Hefele, *Histoire des conciles*, 1.1.2 n. 1, pp. 405-6, on the point in patristic sources that Constantine alone called the Council without Papal involvement.

   [154] Hefele notes that Hobbes's contemporary and friend, *John Selden, gives a
list of the attendants at the Nicene Council translated from later Arabic commentary,
in his *Eutychii Aegyptii, patriarchae orthodoxorum Alexandrini. . . . ecclesiae suae
origines* (London, 1642), p. 71. (See Hefele, *Histoire des conciles*, 1.1.2. pp. 409,
449, and notes.)

   [155] The Nicene Council of AD 325. In parallel passages, both in *Behemoth* and
the 1668 Appendix to the *LL*, Hobbes stresses that the doctrinal pronouncements of
Nicaea reflected the relatively lax censorship regime under Constantine, where
Bishops (Rectores) and Elders (Presbyteros) were able to convene councils and
synods, 'convoked without the order of those in power', to express their dissenting
views. See *Beh. EW* VI, p. 176:

   B. The first general Council, held at Nicæa, declared all to be heresy which
   was contrary to the Nicene Creed, upon occasion of the heresy of Arius, which
   was the denying the divinity of Christ. . . .
   A. I see by this, that both the calling of the Council, and the confirmation of
   their doctrine and church-government, had no obligatory force but from the
   authority of the Emperor.

See also the 1668 Appendix §124 (tr. Wright, p. 370, my emphases):

   [124]B. In the primitive church, up to the time of the Council of Nicaea, most
   of the teachings about which the Christians then disagreed concerned the doctrine of the Holy Trinity. For, although everyone held that this mystery was
   incomprehensible, nonetheless, trusting the philosophy of his masters, each
   man dared to explain it after his own manner.
   From this, there arose at first arguments, then disorders; thereafter, to avoid
   scandal and establish peace in the church, synods were organized, *convoked
   without the order of those in power but through the voluntary drawing
   together of bishops and pastors*, as they were able with the lessening of persecution.

Cum consedissent,[a] in Bouleuterion[b] intrat
                              (locus ubi Patres consedebant.)[c]
   Princeps,[d] in medio stansque salutat eos.
Consurgunt Patres, sed eos jubet ille sedere;[e]
   Nec voluit Princeps ipse sedere prior.
Ingenium nunc disce virorum Philosophorum[f]
   (Si modo Philosophus,[g] Simius[h] esse potest)   **570**
Disce quid ad mores confert legisse Platonem,[i]
   Aut Aristotelem,[j] aut Biblia sacra Dei,[k]
Si legis ut doceas, et non ut vivere discas;[l]
   Virtutem nihil est scire,[m] nisi facias.[n]
Urbem Nicenam venere à[o] finibus orbis,[p]
   Ut fieret cunctis unica certa Fides,[q]
De Christo, cultuque Dei per saecula[r] Patris
   Aeterni,[s] libris conveniensque sacris.
Sed quid fecerunt? Pastoris crimina Pastor
   Accusat,[t] Patrem dedecoratque Pater.[u]   **580**
Defert ad Regem sua quisque inscripta libellis[v]
   Jurgia. Doctrinae cura nec ulla fuit.
Hac iter esse[w] putas ad pacem? Ecclesia numquid[x]
   Moribus his sponsa est immaculata Dei?[y]

---

[a] A B consedissent • [b] B bouleuterion • [c] sc mv A B marginal gloss on Bouleuterion missing in C and 1688. • [d] uA B Princeps • [e] uA B sedere • [f] A B
Philosophorum, • [g] B philosophus • [h] uA B C simius • [i] A B Platonem • [j] B
Aristotelem • [k] A B Dei • [l] A B discas, • [m] uA B scire • [n] uA B facias • [o] A
a • [p] A Orbis B orbis • [q] uA B fides. C fides, • [r] A B C secula • [s] uA B Aeterni
• [t] uA C Accusat • [u] A B Pater C pater. • [v] A B libellis, • [w] mv uA B interesse
• [x] A B numquid, • [y] mv A Dei;

Once they were in session, the Emperor entered the council chamber[156]
and, standing in their midst, greeted them.[157]

The Fathers stood up, but he ordered them to be seated, for the Emperor
did not want to be seated before they were.[158]

Learn now the talent of philosophical men (as long as an ape can be a
philosopher),[159]   570

Learn what reading Plato or Aristotle contributes to morals, or even the
holy Bible of God

If one reads it in order to teach and not to learn how to live: To know
virtue means nothing unless you practice it.

They came to the city of Nicaea from the ends of the earth, so that a
united and true Faith might be established for all.[160]

A faith concerning Christ, and the worship of God the Father eternal
throughout the ages, and conforming to the holy books.   **580**

But what did they do? One Pastor made accusations against another, and
one Church father dishonoured another,

Each one brought to the Emperor his own written opinion[161] on the dispute
in the form of pamphlets, there was no concern for doctrine.

---

[156] A, B, marginal gloss on *Bouleuterion*: 'Locus ubi Patres consedebant'
('place where the Fathers deliberated'). See the 1688 Glossary (pp. 604-5), and
Molesworth note p. 364: Vide Glossarium.

[157] *Eusebius of Caesarea's *Vit. Const.*, PG XX, col. 1061. Hefele, *Histoire des
conciles*, pp. 408-9, n. 2, reviews conflicting testimony about the site.

[158] Eusebius, *Vit. Const.*, PG XX 1064, cited in Hefele, *Histoire des conciles*,
1.1.2 p. 423.

[159] For *simius*, ape, as a term of abuse for imitators, see Horace, *Satires*, 1.10.18.
'neque simius iste' ('don't be an ape'). Petrarch, in a letter to Boccaccio, uses the
example of his copyist and aspiring poet, Giovanni Malpaghini to expound on the
principles of true imitation: 'Thus we may use another man's conceptions and the
color of his style, but not his words. . . . The first procedure makes poets, the second
makes apes'. Petrarch, *Le familiare*, 23.19, cited by Greene, 'Petrarch and the Humanist Hermeneutic', in Giose Rimanelli and Kenneth John Atchity, eds, *Italian Literature, Roots and Branches: Essays in Honor of Thomas Goddard Bergin* (New Haven,
Yale University Press, 1976), p. 209. Possibly also a play on the name of Simmias, the
Theban philosopher who engages Socrates in the Phaedo 84b-86d and 91c-95a concerning an 'absolute essence of all things', an essence of beauty and of goodness of
which man has an innate recognition; these 'essences', or 'ideas' being his 'inborn
possession'. Diogenes Laertius 2.15.124 reports 23 extant works by Simmias.

[160] The Council was situated at Nicaea and Constantine put state vehicles and
beasts of burden at the disposal of his bishops, precisely to ensure as many as possible attended. See Eusebius, *Vit. Const.*, PG XX, cols 1060, 1064, cited in Hefele,
Histoire des conciles 1.1.2, p. 407.

[161] Eusebius *Vit. Const.*, PG XX, cols 1064-8, Sozomen, *Hist. Eccl.*, 1.17.3-4,
ed. Bidez, p. 195.

Quid Constantinus fecit? Capit ille Libellos,[a]
    Atque legit, lectos[b] condidit inque sinum.[c]
Sanctorum invidiam miratur,[d] et ambitionem,
    Sordes,[e] mollitiem,[f] et facta pudenda virûm,[g]
Deinde gravis culpae, sed leniter,[h] admonet illos,[i]
    Et docet ut ridens Ethnicus illa videt.   590
Certè[j] ego si vestro vidissem ex ordine quemquam
    Talia peccantem[k] qualia fertis, ait,
Non modo rem turpem tacuissem,[l] veste[m] sed ista
    Texissem. Christi sic puto poscit honor.
Vos precor ergo[n] Patres[o] nunc uni incumbite paci;[p]
    Cumque unus simus Grex,[q] sit et una Fides.[r]
Consulite Ergo Gregi.[s] Fidei componite formam;[t]
    Atque illam faciam[u] ne sit inanis ego.[v]
Dixit. Et illato coram omnibus igne libellos
    Comburi Patrum jussit edace nigros.   600
Sec. Heu, quantum experti praestat sapientia Regis
    Doctorum libris,[w] ingenioque Scholae.[x]
Quid fecere Patres postquam essent igne libelli[y]
    Combusti, nec erat jam locus invidiae?

---

[a] A B C libellos • [b] A B Lectos • [c] A B sinum • [d] A B C miratur • [e] uA Sordes
• [f] uA B mollitiem • [g] uA virûm B virûm. • [h] A B leniter • [i] ~ A illis (error) •
[j] A B C Certe • [k] A peccantem, • [l] A B C tacuissem • [m] A veste, • [n] A Ergo •
[o] A B Patres, C patres • [p] uA B paci, • [q] uA C grex, • [r] uA C fides. • [s] uA
gregi. B grégi. C gregi: • [t] A formam B formam, • [u] A B faciam, • [v] uA B ego
• [w] uA B libris • [x] A B Scholae C scholae. • [y] B libelli,

Do you think this way was the path to peace? Surely the Church could
    never be the immaculate spouse of God with this sort of behaviour;
What did Constantine do? He took the pamphlets, read them and having
    read them, stored them in his pocket,
He was amazed at the jealousy and ambition of these holy men, their
    meanness, weakness and reprehensible deeds.
He then admonished them gently for their serious faults and warned them
    that the pagans were watching these events and laughing.[162]   **590**
'If I saw someone of your rank committing the sort of sins you allege', he
    said,
'I would certainly not only have kept silent about the foul deed, but I would
    also have concealed it in these clothes. The honour of Christ I believe
    demands this.
I therefore beg you, Fathers, devote your effort to a united peace; and
    since we are one flock, let there be one faith.
Consider the flock, therefore. Establish a form for the faith and I shall
    ensure that it does not remain without effect.'
He finished speaking. And he ordered that once a consuming fire had been
    brought, the blackened pamphlets of the Fathers be burned in the
    presence of all of them.[163]   **600**
Sec. Goodness, the wisdom of the experienced King is so superior to the
    books of the learned and the ingenuity of its School!
What did the Fathers do after their pamphlets were burnt in the fire and
    there was no place left for ill-will?

---

[162] Sozomen records that pagan philosophers attended the Council and participated in the discussions. See his *Hist. Eccl.*, 1.18, ed. Bidez, p. 199-203; see also
Hefele, *Histoire des conciles*, 1.1.2, p. 121 3. Note that while the Christianization of
the Empire was not yet complete, the ridicule of pagans was still a topos. See
Augustine, with respect to the natural sciences: 'Now it is a disgraceful and dangerous thing for an infidel to hear a Christian. . . talking nonsense on these topics;
and we should take all means to prevent such an embarrassing situation, in which
people show up vast ignorance in a Christian and laugh it to scorn.' Augustine,
Literal Meaning of Genesis (*De Genesi ad Litteram*), trans. John Hammond Taylor
(New York, Newman Press, 1982) vol. 1, pp. 42-3.
[163] See Hefele, *Histoire des conciles*, 1.1.2. pp. 409, 449; Eusebius *Vit. Const.*,
PG XX, col. 1069, cited Hefele, *Histoire des conciles*, 1.1.2, p. 427; and Sozomen,
Hist. Eccl., 1.17.5, ed. Bidez, p. 197. Hefele, 1.1.2, p. 449, notes: 'Hobbes's narrative of the Council's deliberations does not depart much from what has been handed
down by tradition. That Constantine had spurred the Fathers to find a common
accord and that he had burned before the Council the *libelli*, are facts also recorded
by Rufinus, *Hist. Eccl.*, *PL*, vol. 21, cols. 468ff. See also the works of Sozomen and
Socrates, which derive in large measure from Rufinus.'

Pr. Nescio. Non extant[a] Synodi decreta. Quod extat[b]
    Indignum multis creditur esse fide.
Quorsum Philosophi spectat Comoedia[c] victi?[d]
    Cur hostis ficto vulnere succubuit?
Dogmata sed constat Synodum damnasse[e] Ariana,[f]
    Nam visum est,[g] Jesum,[h] Patribus,[i] esse Deum.   **610**
Doctrinas etiam ante Arium damnasse fere omnes,
    Adversas Fidei[j] quam[k] Sacra[l] Scripta[m] docent.
Sed dum verba Dei tentant exponere frustra[n]
    Verbis Graecorum, Philosophoque modo,[o]
Non intellectae periere Patrum rationes,
    Haeresis et crevit[p] tanto Ariana magis.
Jussus Ab-aeterno genitum,[q] si dixeris,[r] ecquid
    (Multoties repetens) concipis inde rei?

---

[a] B exstant • [b] A exstat • [c] uA B Comoudia C comoedia • [d] A Victi? • [e] A damnâsse • [f] A B Ariana • [g] uA B est • [h] uA B Jesum • [i] A B Patribus • [j] A fidei, B C fidei • [k] mv A B quas • [l] A B C sacra • [m] A C scripta • [n] B frustra, • [o] ~ A modo • [p] A B crevit, • [q] uA B genitum • [r] uA B dixeris

Pr. I don't know. The decrees of the Council are not extant.[164] The
evidence which survives is considered by many to be unreliable.[165]
What is the purpose of the comedy of the defeated philosopher? Why did
the enemy succumb to a feigned blow?[166]
But it is agreed that the Council condemned the Arian doctrines, for it
seemed to the Fathers that Jesus is God.[167]   **610**
And that it also condemned almost all the doctrines before Arius (all)
which Holy Scripture shows to be contrary to the faith.
But while they tried in vain to expound the word of God using the
language and philosophical method of the Greeks,[168]
The Fathers' arguments, not being understood, were to no avail and the
Arian heresy increased all the more.[169]
If you would say, having been told to do so, 'begotten from eternity' (repeating
it many times over), would you understand anything by that?[170]

---

[164] Selden's *Eutyches* (*Eutychii Aegyptii, Patriarchae Orthodoxorum Alexandrini, Ecclesiae suae Origines*, 1626, p. 468) records that although the reported disputes of the Council filled forty books, the decrees and canons it issued numbered only three books.

[165] Hefele, *Histoire des conciles*, 1.1.2, p. 409 n.4, discusses the destruction of documentation for the Nicene Council by the Arians, and the way in which the form of the Nicene decrees themselves had later to be reconstituted from scraps of evidence.

[166] See Sozomen, *Hist. Eccl.*, 1.18.2-4, who uses this form of words to describe the mock defeat in debate by a philosopher of a simple old man. Note that lines 607-8 read as if they should be distributed to Secundus.

[167] The doctrine that Jesus, second person of the Holy Trinity is consubstantial (*homoousian*) with the Father, which Arius denied.

[168] Constantine's opening address was in Latin but, as a participant in the philosophical debates, he spoke the Greek of the pagan philosophers. See Hefele, *Histoire des conciles*, pp. 427-9. But here Hobbes refers specifically to Greek theological terminology, **hypostasis, *homoousion, ens*, etc. which he discusses later at length.

[169] With the accession in AD 353 of *Constantius II, who took the epithet Augustus, the Arians came back into favour. An Arian himself, a great warrior and opponent of Athanasius, he initiated persecutions against Nicenists. But Constantine, in the final years of his reign, had also supported the Arians. See Sozomen on the renewal of the Arian heresy, *Hist. Eccl.* (bk 3 ch. 1); on Arianism as favoured by Constantius (bk 4 ch. 2); and on Constantius' persecutions (bk 4 chs 20-1).

[170] Hobbes mocks the language of the Council in the spirit of orthodox critics, like Gregory of Nyssa, who in *De deitate filii et spiritu sancti*, PG XLVI, col. 557 (tr. Gregory, *The Urban Crowd*, p. 1), quipped:

> If you demand your change, someone philosophizes to you on the Begotten and the Unbegotten. If you ask the price of bread you are told, 'The Father is greater and the Son inferior'. If you ask, 'Is the bath ready?', someone answers, 'The Son was created from nothing'.

The Council's debate on the relation between the Unbegotten (*agennitos*) Father and the Begotten (*gennitos*) Son, critical to Arianism, is raised in Athanasius, *De Synodis*, PG XXVI. cols 706, 708, cited in Hefele, *Histoire des conciles*, 1.1.2, p. 368 n. 1.

Sec. Quî[a] possum? superat captum generatio Christi[b]

    Nostrum, quâ[c] Deus est, utque puto,[d] Angelicum.[e]   **620**

Sed possum jussus non contradicere. Possum

    Credere, si dederit qui jubet ipse fidem.

Pr. Dicit Aristoteles Ens est Essentia;[f] dicunt

    Doctores nostri[g] quod Deus est Deitas.[h]

Inque Deo[i] Sapiens[j] Sapientia,[k] velle volens est,[l]

    Quodque Deo tribui debeat[m] id Deus est.

Quem potes ex verbis sic junctis sculpere sensum?[n]

    Sec.[o] Audio verba, meras sed video tenebras.

Tune Fidem[p] Christi stabilitam dixeris esse[q]

    Principis imperiis,[r] ingeniisve[s] Patrum,   **630**

Per nova,[t] prolatam,[u] nil significantia verba,

    Et quae divinis sunt aliena libris?

Istane perpetuam procurant credita vitam,

    Perpetuamve[v] dabunt ista negata crucem?

Antiquos Dominus nos jussit adire Prophetas,

    Cum sit salvatrix inde petenda Fides?[w]

In Veteri[x] sacro legiturne Essentia[y] libro?

    Non.[z] Neque[aa] repperies talia verba Novo.[ab]

Nam neque Christus eo, Christi nec Apostolus usquam[ac]

    More loqui jussit, sicve[ad] loquutus[ae] erat.   **640**

Progenies Noachi sic est fortassse loquuta,[af]

    Tunc cum cessarent[ag] aedificare Babel.

---

[a] uA B C Qui • [b] A B Christi, • [c] uA B C qua • [d] uA B puto • [e] C Angelicum • [f] A B Essentia, • [g] A B C nostri, • [h] A B Deitas, • [i] B Déo • [j] A C sapiens • [k] C sapientia, • [l] A B est. • [m] A B debeat, • [n] uA B sensum, • [o] A B *Sec.* misplaced in line below • [p] A B C fidem • [q] A B esse, • [r] uA B imperiis • [s] mv A B ingeniisque • [t] A B nova • [u] uA B prolatam • [v] mv uA B Pertuamve (error) • [w] uA B fides? mv C fides. • [x] B vetri (error) C veteri • [y] B *essentia* C essentia • [z] uA B Non, • [aa] A B Nec • [ab] uA B C novo. • [ac] A B usquam, • [ad] A sive • [ae] A B locutus • [af] A B locuta, • [ag] mv A B cessassent

Sec. How could I? The begetting of Christ, in virtue of which he is God,
exceeds our grasp, and also that of angels, I think. 620

If I am so ordered, I *can* refrain from contradicting it. I *can* believe if the
one who commands me gives me a creed.[171]

Pr. Aristotle says that Being is Essence; our Doctors tell us that God is
Divinity,

And that knowing in God is Wisdom, and willing in God is will. And
what ought to be attributed to God is God.[172]

How can you carve out meaning from words joined together like this?

Sec.[173] I hear words, but I see mere darkness.

Would you say that the faith of Christ was determined by the edicts of the
emperor or the ingenuity of the Fathers, 630

When it was advanced through new words signifying nothing, and foreign
to the holy Scriptures?

Does believing such things guarantee eternal life, or will denying them
bring eternal torment?

Did the Lord command us to consult the ancient prophets, when the faith
that gives salvation is to be sought from here?[174]

Is the word 'essence' found in the book of the Old Testament? No. Nor
will you find such words in the New Testament.

For nowhere did Christ, or an Apostle of Christ, speak or tell us to speak
in that fashion.[175] 640

Perhaps the descendants of Noah spoke that way, once they stopped
building the tower of Babel.[176]

---

[171] See Hobbes's *Answer to Bramhall*, (*EW* vol. IV, p. 339): 'to obey is one thing,
to believe is another. Laws only require obedience; belief requires teachers and arguments drawn either from reason, or from some thing already believed', a position epit-
omized by Daniel Scargill, a self-professed Hobbist, who declared to his accusers that
he could not be accused of atheism because his most central belief was to profess
whatever the state commanded of him. See Springborg Introduction, chapter 3.2.

[172] Echoes of Job 12:13, 'With Him are wisdom and might'; and Daniel 2:20,
'wisdom and power belong to Him'; and Luke 20:25, 'Render unto Caesar the
things that are Caesar's and unto God the things that are God's'.

[173] A B *Sec.* misplaced in line below.

[174] i.e., from the Nicene Creed. In the Molesworth edition, p. 366, there is no
question mark.

[175] The importation of Greek philosophical terms which are not to be found in
the Bible was also an issue for the Church Fathers. See Hefele, *Histoire des conciles*, 1.1.2, p. 434 ff.

[176] Nimrod, the offspring of Noah, was credited with building the Tower of
Babel, See Genesis 10:8-12, 11.

Sed missa haec facio, desidero namque quid actum est[a]
    Scire, quod Haeresium spectat ad Historiam.[b]
Dic nunc[c] quas isto signarunt nomine Patres[d]
    Doctrinas, et quae poena statuta quibus.
Pr. Haereticum primò[e] faciunt,[f] qui,[g] dicere nullos,[h]
    Aut uno plures,[i] auserit,[j] esse Deos.
Hoc expellebant Decreto[k] Idololatriam,[l]
    Manetis,[m] rerum Principiumque duplum.   **650**
Haereticum faciunt[n] qui Mundum dixerit esse[o]
    Aeternum;[p] aeterni quique opus esse negat;[q]
Qui Jesum negat esse Deum, Genitumque,[r] et eundem[s]
    Cum Patre;[t] et ingenitum qui negat esse Patrem;[u]
Quique alium natum esse Deo Patre praeter Iesum[v]
    Dixerit; aut ipsum tempore natum aliquo;
Quique ipsum dicet,[w] solido sine corpore,[x] spectrum,
    Vel rationalem non habuissse animam;

---

[a] A B est, • [b] B C historiam. • [c] A nunc, • [d] A B Patres, • [e] A C primo • [f] C faciunt • [g] uA B C qui • [h] uA B C nullos • [i] A B C plures • [j] A B C auserit • [k] A B C decreto • [l] uA B Idololatriam • [m] uA B Manetis • [n] A B faciunt, • [o] A B esse, • [p] uA B Aeternum, • [q] uA B negat • [r] A B Genitumque C genitumque • [s] B eundem, • [t] A B Patre, • [u] A patrem • [v] A Jesum B Jesum, • [w] mv uA B dicit • [x] uA B corpore

But I'll pass over these matters.[177] I really want to know what happened
    because it is relevant to the history of heresies.
Now tell me which doctrines the Fathers designated with that name, and
    what punishment was established for which.
Pr. First they made a heretic of anyone who dared to say that there was
    no God or that there were more gods than one.
By this decree they drove out idolatry and Mani's principle
    of duality.[178]   **650**
They made a heretic out of anyone who would say the world was
    eternal;[179] and anyone who denies it was the work of the eternal;[180]
Anyone who denies that Jesus was God, begotten and one with the
    Father;[181] and anyone who denies that the Father was unbegotten;[182]
And anyone who would say that another was born from God the Father
    besides Jesus; or that Jesus was born at some definite time;[183]
And anyone who will say that he is a spirit without a material body;[184] or
    that he did not have a rational mind;[185]

---

[177] let pass, to pass over in silence (Cicero: *ut haec missa faciam*) (usually with
a *quod* clause, typical of Cicero's letters).

[178] *Mani (c. AD 215-76), the Persian religious leader and founder of the heretical sect of Manichaeism, began in around 245 to preach his doctrine of the double
worlds of good and evil at the court of the Persian king Sapro (Shahpur) I. He travelled widely but was eventually crucified by his Zoroastrian enemies. (*Chambers
Biographical Dictionary*).

[179] That 'nothing is produced from nothing', is one of the basic axioms of atomism
to which Hobbes subscribed. See 1668 Appendix to the *LL* §§7-8, tr. Wright, pp. 350,
and 390, n.20. As early as his *Critique of Thomas White's 'De Mundo'* and *De Corpore*
(chapter 26, §1), Hobbes had debated the eternity of the world, as Gianni Paganini
emphasizes (personal communication from Paganini to Springborg, 7/5/2002).

[180] The view of Arius, see Athanasius, *Oratio contra Arianos*, PG XXVI, cols
85-6, discussed in Hefele, *Histoire des conciles*, pp. 359-69.

[181] See the 1668 Appendix to the *LL*, tr. Wright, §12, p. 351, and interlocutor
B's, answer to interlocutor A's question, 'What is the difference between "begotten"
(*genitus*) and "made" (*factus*)?'.

[182] Athanasius ridiculed Arius's position on the unbegotten nature of God the
Father, as making him in fact lesser to the begotten Son. See Athanasius, *De
synodis*, PG XXVI, col. 708, and the discussion in Hefele, *Histoire des conciles*,
pp. 368-9 and notes.

[183] The Nicene Creed anathematizes those who say 'there was a time when He
was not'.

[184] See Hobbes, *Answer to Bramhall*, (*EW* IV, p. 384), discussed in Springborg
Introduction, chapter 6.3.

[185] Hobbes, in the *Hist. Narr.* (*EW*, IV, p. 393), gives a more extensive list of the
heresies he has in mind here: the Valentinians, 'the Heresy of Apelles and others,
who made Christ a mere phantasm'.

Aut illo negat esse modo[a] Genitum[b] quali generatur
    Lumen ab accenso Lumine,[c] et ambo simul;   **660**
Quique Deum carnem[d] quo sumpsit tempore nostram[e]
    Descendisse negat Virginis[f] in gremium;
Quique negat Genitum[g] genitori ὁμοοῦσιον esse
    Ingenito;[h] aut natum Virgine[i] Matre[j] negat;[k]

---

[a] mv A B illo modo negat esse (but even 1688 is not correct and the line would only scan if genitum or illo were omitted) • [b] A C genitum, B genitum • [c] A B lumine; • [d] A B carnem, • [e] B C nostram, • [f] uA B C virginis • [g] A B C genitum • [h] uA B Ingenito, • [i] B C virgine • [j] B C matre • [k] A negat

Or anyone who denies he exists in the way that light is born from kindled
light,[186] and both at the same time;[187] **660**
And anyone who denies that God, when he assumed our flesh, descended
into the womb of the Virgin;
And anyone who denies the begotten to be of 'the same Substance'[188] as the
unbegotten Father; or who denies he was born of a Virgin Mother;[189]

---

[186] See *Hist. Narr.* (*EW*, IV, p. 393) on the phrase 'light from light', discussed in
Springborg Introduction, chapter 6.3. See Wright's comment on the 1668 Appendix
to the *LL*, p. 352 and notes.

[187] i.e., both Father and Son at the same time.

[188] Hobbes uses the Greek 'ομοούσιον, of one substance, adopted by the
Council of Nicaea against the Arians. The term had been debated at the three Councils of Antioch, 264-9, which engaged the anti-Trinitarian Paul of Samosata (see
Hefele, *Histoire des conciles*, 1.1.2., pp. 195-206). It was central to the Arian debate
on whether the relation between members of the Trinity is that of ομοούσιον, of one
substance, or 'ομοιοῦσιον, of like substance. But because the Gnostics and Paul of
Samosata had used it, the Origenists, who had no sympathy with the Arians, preferred to use 'ομοῦσιον, like substance, to have more room to differentiate the
Godhead. See the Oxford *Dictionary of the Christian Church*, ed. F.C. Cross (rev.
edn, Oxford 1974). See also Athanasius in *De decr. Nic. syn.*, *PG* XXV, col. 449ff.,
De syn., *PG* XXV, col. 767 and the *Epist. ad Afros*, *PG* XXVI, col. 1038. See also
*Hilary, *De Trinitate*, *PL* X, cols 25-472. Athanasius in *De decr. Nic. syn.* notes a
general lack of enthusiasm for this term, which is not found in the Bible, although
some foundation for its use may be found in John.10.30, *Ego et Pater unum sumus*,
and John 16.15, *Omnia quaecumque habet Pater, mea sunt*. But St. Augustine in
Contra Sermonem Arianorum reports that Arians called orthodox people 'Homou-
sianos'. (See discussion in Hefele, *Histoire des conciles*, 1.1.2., p. 434, citing Tertullian, *Adversus Praxean*, *PL* II, col. 157. See also Stead, '"Homoousios" dans la
Pensée de Saint Athanase'.) The Jesuit Denis Petau (Petavius, 1583-1652), also
uses the expression in *Dialogo I Maximi, qui sub Athanasii titulo editus est*. See
Dionysii Petavii, *Opus De Theologicis dogmatibus* (Amsterdam, apud G. Galet,
1700), lib. IV, cap. V, §iv to t. II, p. 205b, where he adds a reference to Marius Vic-
torinus' *in tractatu de Homoüsio recipiendo* (Petau cap. V, §xiv, p. 209a). Both the
1688 printed editions and the MSS use a 17c. symbol for the ού in'ομοούσιον.
Gianni Paganini (personal communication from Paganini to Springborg, 7/5/2002)
notes that Petau favours the Latin transcription 'homoüsiou' (with diaeresis on the
first u) adopted, for instance, by Hilary when he refers to the proceedings of the
Paris Council, published in the year 362 (see Petau §xv, p. 209). Petau observed that
the Toledo Council also made use of the Latin form of the word 'homousios' (Petau
§xvi, p. 210a) as did Jerome who, in *Chronico*, spoke of 'homousio' (Petau, IV, VI,
§212a). *Rymer in the 1688 Preface notes Hilary and Jerome as Hobbes's sources,
and Petau was also an important source for him.

[189] Hobbes formulates a central paradox of the Nicene Creed, which claims at
once that God the Son is of the same substance as the unbegotten Father, and yet
commands us to believe he was born of the Virgin Mary and takes human shape.
Hobbes seems to be saying that the distinction between like substance, and unity

Et qui pro nobis passum nostraque salute
      Esse negat; vel qui mortem obiisse negat;[a]
Et qui post mortem non surrexisse fatetur;[b]
      Vel negat ad dextram[c] nunc residere Patris;[d]
Aut negat inde iterum venturum, ut judicet omnes[e]
      Viventesque homines,[f] quique obiere diem.   **670**
Hos facit Haereticos[g] Synodus Nicena.[h] Sed[i] Acta
      Nicenae Synodi[j] non valuere diu.
Nam Constantini successor 'ὁμοῦσιον' illud
      (Areii[k] fautor) noluit esse ratum.
Sic nec habebat adhuc constantem Ecclesia[l] pacem,
      Nec certam Patres quam voluere Fidem.[m]

---

[a] A negat • [b] A B fatetur • [c] A dextram, B Dextram • [d] A Patris B Patris, C patris. • [e] A B omnes, • [f] C homines • [g] A haereticos • [h] A B Nicena, • [i] A B sed • [j] A C synodi • [k] A B Areij • [l] C ecclesia • [m] A fidem. B Fidém. C fidem

And anyone who denies he suffered for us and for our salvation; and
anyone who denies that he died;

And anyone who does not acknowledge that after death he rose again; or
anyone who denies he now resides at the right hand of the Father;

Or denies that from there he will come again to judge all men, both the
living and the dead. **670**

The Nicene Council makes all these men heretics, but the acts of the
Nicene Council did not remain in force for long.

For Constantine's successor[190] (a supporter of Arius) did not want the
homoousion clause[191] to be ratified.[192]

So the Church still did not have the stable peace or the sure faith that the
Fathers wanted.

---

of substance, is to no avail in resolving this paradox. This raises the question
whether in fact Hobbes subscribes to the Nicene doctrine as the official doctrine
of the Anglican Church at all (see Springborg Introduction, chapter 6.3). In
Lev., xvi, §12 82/103 Hobbes had developed a theory of the Trinity that sidesteps
the homoousios/homoiousios debate by construing the relationship of the persons
of the Godhead in the form of roles, or incumbents of an office; a conception
strikingly similar to that of Lorenzo Valla, but which Hobbes felt obliged
to retract in the 1668 Appendix to the *LL*. §11-14 (*OL* III, p. 362, Curley edn,
p. 543), without however truly abandoning it.

[190] Hobbes refers to Constantius II (318-361), son of Constantine the Great,
who ruled in his own right in 353 after the death of his brothers *Constans I (320-
350) and *Constantine II (316-40).

[191] 'ὁμοῦσιον = 'ὁμοούσιος, of the same substance, c.f. 'ὁμοιούσιος, of
similar substance. See §127 of the 1668 Appendix to the *LL*, ed. Wright, p. 370:
'The reason for calling the Council of Nicaea was Arius, elder of Alexandria.
When the bishop of that city, Alexander, had said that the Son of God was
homoousios, that is of the same substance, with the Father, Arius contradicted
him.' Wright comments (p. 405), 'Both the 1668 text and Molesworth's edition
bear the word *"homousios"*, not the correct form *"homoousios"'*. Wright hazards
the guess: 'This may stem from a peculiarity of Dutch orthography or of Blaeu's
Greek type, for it is surely wrong to think that Hobbes would hope to pass over in
silence the distinction between *homoousios* ("of the same substance") and
homoiousios ("of like substance")'. But Wright is mistaken. When Hobbes uses
'ὁμοῦσιον for 'ὁμοούσιος he is following a Latin model (Souter s.v. *homousion*,
homousianus), see note 188 and Paganini to Springborg 7/5/2002.

[192] Note that several of the cosignatories to the Nicene decrees in fact deliberately substituted the barely distinguishable Greek characters *homoiousios* for
homoousios, proving themselves to be heretics. See Hefele, *Histoire des conciles*,
1.1.2., pp. 446-8 and notes, citing the Arian *Philostorgius, *Hist. Eccl.*, extant only
in the extensive *Epitome* by *Photius. See the *Epitome of the Historia Ecclesiastica
of Philostorgius*, pp. 433-4.

Sec. Non rectè[a] Patres mysteria dicere verbis[b]
    Tentarunt, animis non capienda suis.
Namque hominem esse Deum,[c] factis cognoscere solis;
    Testibus et solis cernere facta,[d] licet;[e]   680
Facta ferebantur Christi miracula multa;
    A solo fieri[f] quae potuere Deo.
Illa quibus mediis fiunt comprendere[g] mente[h]
    Nemo,[i] praeter eum[j] qui facit illa,[k] potest.
Omne genus morbi verbi virtute fugavit,
    Illum jussa levis sustulit unda gravem.
Illius ad vocem posuerunt flabra protervi
    Venti, compressis et siluere animis.
Defunctis vitam;[l] privatis lumine visum
    Restituit,[m] claudis[n] (voce) gradumque dedit.[o]   690
In vinum[p] mutavit aquam. Bis multiplicatum[q]
    Ad populum panem numine fertque suo.
Quorum Factorum[r] testes habuere probatos[s]
    Niceni Patres, queis habuere fidem,[t]
Matthaeum,[u] Marcum, Lucam, Petrum,[v] atque Johannem,
    Discipulosque alios. His habuere Fidem.[w]
Quî[x] potuere Patres[y] igitur de re manifesta,[z]
    Et tam confessa, credere non eadem?
Pr. Scis Graecos numero reliquos superasse,[aa] et in illis
    Sectam Aristotelis praevaluisse aliis.[ab]   700

---

[a] A B C recte • [b] A verbis, B verbis; • [c] uA Deum B Déum • [d] uA B facta •
[e] A B licet. • [f] A fieri, • [g] mv uA B C comprehendere • [h] A mente, • [i] uA B
Nemo • [j] A eum, • [k] uA B illa • [l] C vitam • [m] A Restituit • [n] A Claudis •
[o] A dedit • [p] A Vinum • [q] A B multiplicatum, • [r] uA B C factorum • [s] A B
probatos, • [t] A B fidem; • [u] B Matthaeum • [v] A B C Petrum • [w] uA B C
fidem. • [x] A B C Qui • [y] A C patres • [z] A B manifesta • [aa] B C superasse •
[ab] C aliis

Sec. It was not right that the Fathers tried to put into words mysteries
     which their own minds could not comprehend.[193]
For only from his deeds can one know a man to be God; and only from
     witnesses can one determine what those deeds were.[194]   680
Many miracles were reported as deeds of Christ, which could only have
     been done by God alone.
No-one, except the one who made them, can mentally comprehend by
     what means those miracles were performed.
He put to flight every kind of sickness by the power of his word; upon his
     command the light waves supported his weight.[195]
At his voice gusts of violent wind abated, and holding their breath fell
     silent.[196]
He restored life to the dead;[197] sight to those deprived of vision and (by
     his voice) gave to the lame the power to walk;[198]   690
He changed water into wine.[199] And he brought to the masses bread
     multiplied many times over by his own divine power.[200]
The Nicene Fathers had reliable witnesses of these acts, witnesses in
     whom they had trust;
Matthew, Mark, Luke, Peter and John,
     and the other Disciples. They had faith in these men.
How, then, were the Fathers not able to believe the same things about
     such clear and incontrovertible matters?
Pr. You know that the Greeks outnumbered the rest; and that among
     them Aristotle's School prevailed over the others.[201]   700

---

[193] Hobbes shares the position of Socrates of Constantinople, who argued, for
instance (*H.E.*, iv.7), that the greatest error of the Arian Eunomius was not his doctrine concerning Christ's relation to God the Father, but his claim to perfectly know
and understand what God was in his *ousia*, or essential nature. (See Chestnut, *The
First Christian Historians*, p. 176).
[194] Hobbes seems to make a special case for the validity of Christian belief,
based on witnesses, prophets, miracles and Scripture, only to then undermine it.
(See *Hist. Eccl.*, lines 39-47 above).
[195] Matt. 14.
[196] Acts 17:11.
[197] Matt. 9:5; Mark. 2.
[198] John 5:1-16.
[199] The Wedding Feast at Cana, John 4:3-26.
[200] Mark 6:42. Matt. 14:13.
[201] Hobbes's mention of the various factions making up the Council, Greeks,
Aristotelians, Jews, follows debate on the composition of the Council, between
Athanasius, *Epist. ad Afros*, PG XXVI, col. 1031, and Eusebius of Caesarea, *Vit.
Constant, PG* XX, (see Hefele, *Histoire des conciles*, 1.1.2. pp. 409, 449, and notes).

Judaeus Signis;[a] Graecus cedebat[b] Elenchis,[c]
    Ut qui quaerebat non 'ὅτι sed διότι,[d]
Sec. Sed quo fine,[e] Dei[f] dum propria facta fatentur,[g]
    Quaerebant fieri[h] quo potuere modo?
Pr.[i] Scilicet in synodo docti,[j] indoctique fuerunt;[k]
    Doctos[l] quos fecit lectio Aristotelis.
Indocti verò,[m] qui nil[n] aliud didicissent[o]
    Quam pro se Christum mortem obiisse crucis,
Et quorum nullos servabant scrinia libros,[p]
    Excepto tantum Codice utroque sacro.   710
Hi quia non audent[q] adversum dicere Doctos;[r]
    Dicere nec contra Biblia sacra volunt,[s]
Contenti sanctam Triadem firmasse,[t] simulque
    Non uno plures in Triade esse Deos;[u]

---

[a] A B C signis; • [b] mv uA B credebat • [c] uA Elenchis C elenchis, • [d] uA διότι C διότι. • [e] uA B fine • [f] uA B Dei, • [g] A fatentur B fatentur. • [h] A B C fieri, • [i] mv A B *Pr.* missing • [j] uA B docti • [k] A B fuerunt, • [l] A Doctos • [m] B verò C vero, • [n] uA B nihil • [o] A B didicissent, • [p] A B libros C libros. • [q] A audent, • [r] mv uA B Doctis, C doctos; • [s] C volunt • [t] A firmâsse, • [u] uA Deos C deos;

The Jew yielded to[202] miracles; the Greek to refutation, as one who sought
    not 'the that' but 'the wherefore'.[203]

Sec. But why, since they acknowledged the deeds of God were entirely his
    own, did they seek to know the means by which they could have been
    done ?[204]

Pr.[205] Of course there were educated and uneducated men in the Council;
    reading Aristotle made them educated.[206]

The uneducated, in fact, were those who had learned nothing other than
    that Christ died for them on the Cross,[207]

And whose bookcases held no books except the Old and New
    Testaments.   710

Because they didn't dare to contradict the educated men, and did not wish
    to speak against the holy Bible,

These men were content to affirm the holy Trinity, and at the same time
    that there was not more than one God in the Trinity.[208]

---

[202] mv 1688 *cedebat* uA B *credebat* (to read: the Jew believed in, etc.).

[203] Terms given in Greek: non ὅτι sed διότι. 'The traditional distinction, which
also Hobbes uses in *De Corpore* 6.1.2.' (Invernizzi note). On the terms ὅτι and
διότι Lorenzo Valla, speaking of the traps forced on theologians by the Greek language, noted in the third recension of his *Dialectica* 164.6-10 (tr. Monfasani, 'Was
Lorenzo Valla an Ordinary Language Philosopher?' p. 311):

> Here an observation forces itself upon us concerning the Greek language,
> which is otherwise very rich, yet in this respect in some way defective. For
> since there are three things, as the rhetoricians tell us, which enter into an
> inquiry: 'whether it is', 'what it is' and 'of what sort it is', they [the Greeks]
> employ the last of these for what is 'which is'. . . .

[204] Hobbes suggests that the Greeks violated the principle of God's ineffable
essence, that his works cannot be explained in human causal terms.

[205] mv A B *Pr.* missing.

[206] See the 1668 Appendix to the *LL*, §89 (tr. Wright, p. 365: 'For of those very
theologians who published explanations of the Nicene Creed, almost all used definitions selected from the *Logic* and *Metaphysics* of Aristotle, although they ought to
have explained the Holy Trinity from Sacred Scripture alone'.

[207] This is the chief tenet of Christianity according to Hobbes, see the closing
lines of the poem.

[208] Hobbes flags his own unorthodox theory of the three persons of the trinity as
three different orders representing God the Father, of *Lev.*, xlii, §3, 267/334:

> But a person (as I have shown before [ch. xvi]) is he that is represented, as
> often as he is represented; and therefore God, who has been represented (that
> is personated) thrice, may properly enough be said to be three persons
> (though neither the word Person, nor Trinity, be ascribed to him in the Bible).

Hobbes's position, which he withdrew under threat of heresy charges in the *LL*
(see 1668 Appendix), was remarkably similar to that of Lorenzo Valla, presented in
the *Dialecticae disputationes*, the title under which the various versions of his

Solliciti nimium de verbis esse timebant,
    Ne quis eos Doctus[a] diceret esse rudes.
Namque ignorabant peregrina vocabula quantum
    Ad res mutandas,[b] dissidiumque valent.
Sec. Damnatos autem[c] quae tandem poena sequuta[d] est ?[e]
    Cujus ad arbitrium? Principis anne Patrum ?[f]   **720**
Pr. Aspera poena satis,[g] citraque gravissima mortem.[h]
    Peccanti Clero[i] poena erat exilium.[j]
Peccanti Laico[k] via claudebatur ad omne
    Civilis vitae,[l] militiaeque decus;
Nec Patrum arbitrio (quibus accusare dabatur)[m]
    Legibus at[n] scriptis Principis Imperio.[o]
Sec. Crimen erat,[p] fateor, Synodi[q] contraria dictis,[r]
    Cum fuerint lata lege probata,[s] loqui.
Cur tamen impietas dicenda sit,[t] haud bene cerno;
    Nam non es,[u] si non impius esse velis.   **730**
Et qui credebant[v] se Biblia[w] sacra sequutos,[x]
    Esse proculdubio se voluere pios.

---

[a] uA B C doctus • [b] C mutandas • [c] A B autem, • [d] A B secuta • [e] mv A B est, • [f] mv A Patrum • [g] uA B satis • [h] A mortem B C mortem, • [i] B C clero • [j] C exilium • [k] B laico • [l] A B C vitae • [m] ~ A dabatur (closing bracket of the parenthesis missing) • [n] mv A B ac (read at) • [o] A B C imperio. • [p] uA B erat • [q] A synodi • [r] A B dictis • [s] A B probata • [t] A B sit • [u] uA B es • [v] A credebant, • [w] A biblia • [x] A secutos,

They were afraid of being too bothered by words, lest some educated man
    might call them unsophisticated.
For they did not know how much power foreign terms had for changing
    things and for dissension.[209]
Sec. But what punishment finally awaited those who were condemned?
    And according to whose decision? The Emperor's or the Church
    Fathers'?   **720**
Pr. A harsh enough punishment, the most severe this side of death. The
    penalty for an offending cleric was banishment.[210]
For an offending layman the way was barred to every honour of civic and
    military life;
And not by the decision of the Fathers (who were allowed to bring
    charges), but by the authority of the Emperor in written laws.
Sec. I acknowledge that it was an offence to contradict the findings of the
    Council, once its proposals had been approved by law.
But I can't understand why it should also be called impiety. For you're not
    impious if you do not choose to be.   **730**
And those who believed they were following the holy Bible without doubt
    wanted to be pious.[211]

Repastinatio dialectice et philosophie (completed 1439), were circulated in printed
editions. (On the various printed editions see G. Zippel, 'Note sulle redazioni della
"Dialectica" di Lorenzo Valla', *Archivio storico per le provincie parmensi* vol. 9
(1957), pp. 301-15). Valla claimed that since the term *persona* connoted the qualities and attributes of a person, or a character or role in a drama, the three persons of
the Trinity could only be interpreted as three roles played by a single Deity, a position he had to defend against the charge of heresy brought by the Inquisition – see
S. I. Camporeale, *Lorenzo Valla: umanesimo et teologica* (Florence, Istituto
Nazionale di Studi sul Rinascimento, 1972) pp. 123-76.

[209] In the 1668 Appendix to the *LL*, §17 (tr. Wright, pp. 352), interlocutor A
remarks: 'there follows then that great article, which brought so many disorders into
the ancient church, so many banishments and killings: "of one substance with the
Father, by whom all things were made"'. For the debate of the Nicene Council on
substantia, *homoousios* and the *Logos* in which Eusebius of Caesarea participated
on the losing side ('he hoped to avoid the precision of the word *homoousios* and the
strict definition of the doctrine of the Logos', Hefele, p. 436), see Hefele, 1.1.2,
pp. 432-6, 440-1, citing Athanasius *Epist. de decret. syn. Nic.*, *PG* XXV, col. 448;
Theodoret, *Hist. Eccl.* bk 1, ch. 12, *PG* LXXXII, col. 915; and Gelasius of Cyzicus,
Historia Concilii Nicaeni bk 2, ch. 34, in Mansi, ed., *Sacrorum conciliorum nova et
amplissima collectio.*

[210] Hobbes is referring to excommunication.

[211] The passage that follows concerns the early Christians and appears to be a
dialogue, lines 733 to 736, *Pr.*; lines 737-8, *Sec.*; 739-40, *Pr.*; 741-4 *Sec.*; 745ff.
Pr.

Illo,[a] damnati quam magnos,[b] tempore,[c] honores,
     Quantas divitias deseruere,[d] puta;
Quo vixere metu, quantos subiere dolores,[e]
     Ut conservarent[f] quam tenuere Fidem![g]
Anne Fidem[h] quisquam[i] tanti facit Impius?[j] Illis
     Regnare est summum,[k] divitiaeque bonum.
Errarunt. Synodi doctrinam cernere sanctae
     In scriptis caeci[l] non potuere sacris.   **740**
Ergone caecus[m] homo damnabitur Impietatis,[n]
     Quando non (jussus Lege[o] videre) videt?
Cur non et patria[p] jubeatur cedere simus,
     Si non et nasum corrigat ille suum?

---

[a] uA B C Illo • [b] A B magnos • [c] A C tempore B témpore • [d] A B deseruere •
[e] A B dolores • [f] A B conservarent, • [g] uA fidem. B Fidem. C fidem! • [h] A C
fidem • [i] mv uA B quisquam missing • [j] A B C impius? • [k] uA B summum •
[l] A B C coeci • [m] A B C coecus • [n] A impietatis B Impietatis C impietatis, •
[o] uA B C lege • [p] A Patria

Remember that at that time the condemned forfeited great honours and
   much wealth.
What fear they lived with, what pain they suffered in order to preserve the
   faith they held!
Does any impious man value Faith so highly? For impious men riches
   and power are the highest good.
They went astray. Like blind men they could not find the doctrines of the
   Council in Holy Scripture.[212]   **740**
Should the blind man therefore be condemned for impiety when he cannot
   see (what he is commanded in law to see)?[213]
Why should a snub-nosed man not be commanded to leave his country, if
   he does not straighten his own nose?[214]

---

[212] This contradicts Hobbes's otherwise stated position that the decrees of the
Nicene Council were not in fact infected by Greek philosophy, one of the grounds
for his subscription to the orthodox Anglican view that essential doctrine comprised
the thirty-nine articles and the doctrines of the first four Church Councils. In the *LL*,
published as the *Historical Narration* was being written, Hobbes notes that the
Council of Nicaea had condemned 'not only Arius, but also all heresies which had
arisen since the birth of Christ, summing up briefly the orthodox faith in the creed
called Nicene, taken from the Scripture itself, with no admixture of Greek philosophy at all'. See E. Curley, 'Calvin and Hobbes, or Hobbes as an Orthodox Christian', *Journal of the History of Philosophy*, 34 (1996), pp. 267-8, citing *OL*, vol. III,
ch. 46, §10. This is not strictly speaking true, *homoousios* makes its way into the
creed, even if, as Professor Martinich in his reply to Curley claims, only at the insistence of the Emperor Constantine, and it conotated a range of philosophical concepts, Aristotelian 'substance', 'essence' and so on, as we see above, lines 497-502
(Martinich, 'On the Proper Interpretation of Hobbes's Philosophy'; and Curley,
'Reply to Professor Martinich').

[213] This follows from Hobbes's *in foro interno, in foro externo* distinction,
which stipulates that public religious observance lies in the power of the prince,
taken together with his sensationalist psychology. Cognition is sense driven; so
people, who are free as to their private beliefs, cannot be condemned for not understanding impossible and improvable postulates about the (unknowable) divinity;
anymore than the blind man can be condemned because he cannot see.

[214] C.f. Aristotle, *Rhetoric* 1.4, 1360a:
   Thus, democracy loses its vigour, and finally passes into oligarchy, not only
   when it is not pushed far enough, but also when it is pushed a great deal too
   far; just as the aquiline and the snub nose not only turn into normal noses by
   not being aquiline or snub enough, but also by being too violently aquiline or
   snub arrive at a condition in which they no longer look like noses at all.
Hobbes probably combines the reference to Aristotle with allusions to Socrates,
renowned for a snub-nose, forced to leave Athens, and to the expulsion of the Greek
philosophers from Rome under Domitian in AD 89 and 95 (*OCD*, 1970 edn, 'Domitian', 360). Possibly also a play on the name for Ovid, Naso 'the nose'. C.f. Aristotle,
Physics 2.1-2: on definitions of the things and of their attributes. '"Odd" and "even",
"straight" and "curved", and likewise "number", "line", and "figure", do not involve

Aequum erat,[a] in tenebris verborum,[b] ignoscere si quis
     Cavit ne plures diceret esset Deos.
Inter Non-genitum,[c] Genitumque[d] in tempore nullo,[e]
     Quid sit dissidii[f] non capit omnis homo.[g]
Nec quorum lingua Verbum[h] substantia[i] dici,
     Aut animo possit qua ratione capi.   **750**

---

[a] A B C erat • [b] uA B verborum • [c] uA B C non-genitum, • [d] uA B C genitumque • [e] A B nullo • [f] A dissidij • [g] C homo, • [h] C verbum • [i] B Substantia

It would have been fair, given how obscure the wording was, to overlook it, as long as someone took care not to say there was more than one God.[215] What might be in dispute between the 'the not-begotten' and 'the begotten not-in-time', not all men understand.[216] Nor (does everyone understand) in whose language the Word[217] can be a 'substance', or how it can be understood in the mind.   **750**

---

motion; not so "flesh" and "bone" and "man"-these are defined like "snub nose", not like "curved"'. See also Aristotle, *On Sophistical Refutations*, sect. 3, part 31, which reads as a display of the sophistries he, and Hobbes, were keen to refute:

> For 'concave' has a general meaning which is the same in the case of a snub nose, and of a bandy leg, but when added to either substantive nothing prevents it from differentiating its meaning; in fact it bears one sense as applied to the nose, and another as applied to the leg: for in the former connexion it means 'snub' and in the latter 'bandyshaped'; i.e. it makes no difference whether you say 'a snub nose' or 'a concave nose'. Moreover, the expression must not be granted in the nominative case: for it is a falsehood. For snubness is not a concave nose but something (e.g. an affection) belonging to a nose: hence, there is no absurdity in supposing that the snub nose is a nose possessing the concavity that belongs to a nose.

[215] Hobbes is speaking to his own case, where he was accused of heresy for an unorthodox doctrine of the trinity. He does not wish to be accused like Socrates, who was condemned to death for leading youth astray and introducing strange gods, for which he was brought to trial before a popular jury in 399 BC (*OCD*, 1972, p. 998).

[216] Hobbes addresses this issue most fully in the 1668 Appendix to the *LL*, §§8-20 ff. (tr. Wright, pp. 351-3), 'changeless and utterly without parts, devoid of that Aristotelian mixing'. On the other we have God 'the begotten not-in-time', 'one Lord, Jesus Christ, the only-begotten Son of God' (§9, p. 351); 'The natural son of God, or Him begotten of God, from the beginning, that is, from everlasting'. Interlocutors A and B try to resolve the paradox (§§18-26, pp. 352-3) by construing the eternity of the 'only begotten Son of God' in terms of John 1:1 on the eternity of the Word (*verbum*), understood as 'the eternal decree of God for the establishment of the world and the redemption of man'. But that 'the Word' could satisfy the stipulation of 'persons', sharing the same substance, calls into question the coherence of the Nicene Creed and Hobbes's claim in the *LL* (*OL*, vol. III, p. 536) that it escaped contamination by Greek philosophy.

[217] 'Logos' being both words in general and the divine Word, Jesus Christ. C.f. the 1668 Appendix to the *LL*, §17 (tr. Wright, pp. 352), where interlocutor A remarks: 'there follows then that great article,. . . "of one substance with the Father, by whom all things were made"'. To which interlocutor A replies (§18, p. 352), 'And utterly true it is, made manifest in St. John's clear words (John 1:1): "in the beginning was the Word, and the Words was with God, and the Word was God"; and, "all things were made through it".' For the debate of the Nicene Council on *substantia*, *homoousios* and the *Logos* in which Eusebius of Caesarea participated on the losing side ('he hoped to avoid the precision of the word *homoousios* and the strict definition of the doctrine of the Logos', see Hefele, *Histoire des conciles*, 1.1.2, pp. 432-6, 440-1, citing Athanasius *Epist. de decret. syn. Nic.*, *PG* XXV, col. 448; Theodoret, *HE* bk 1, ch. 12, *PG* LXXXII, col. 915; and Gelasius of Cyzicus, *Historia Concilii Nicaeni* bk 2, ch. 34, in Mansi, ed., *Sacrorum conciliorum nova et amplissima collectio*.

Vox Hypostasis[a] sonat ut substantia Graecis;[b]
　　Qui dicit tres sunt,[c] tres ait esse Deos.

---

[a] A C hypostasis • [b] C Graecis, • [c] B sunt

The Greek word for substance is 'hypostasis';[218] one who says there are three hypostases says there are three Gods.[219]

---

[218] *Hypostasis* in italics in Molesworth (p. 369). *Hypostasis*, Greek for foundation or groundwork, although in general a synonym for substance, was a technical metaphysical and theological term in Neoplatonist and early Christian usage for a Person of the Trinity. See Hefele, *Histoire des conciles* on 1.1.2, p. 368 n. 1, citing Athanasius, *Orat.I contra Arian.*, ch 6, *PG* XXVI, col. 24. At the Council of Ferrara/Florence of 1438-9, convened to explore possible unity between the Greek and Latin Churches, the differing position of the Orthodox and Latin camps with respect to the persons of the Trinity was summed up as 'one in three' and 'three in one' (see Deno J. Geanakopolos, *Byzantine East and Latin West: Two Worlds of Christendom in Middle Ages and Renaissance* (Oxford, Oxford University Press, 1966), Chapter 3, 'The Council of Florence (1438-39) and the Problem of Union between the Byzantine and Latin Churches', pp. 99ff. See Hobbes's 1668 Appendix to the *LL*, in *OL* III, p. 534, on the Ciceronian use of the term person, 'not only in the theatre, but even in the court and in the church'. In his *Answer to Bramhall*, (*EW* vol. IV, p. 311), referring to the usage of 'persona' in Cicero, *De oratore* 2.24, Hobbes notes:

> In the same sense we use the word [person] in English vulgarly, calling him that acteth by his own authority, his own person, and him that acteth by the authority of another, the person of that other. And thus we have the exact meaning of the word *person*. The Greek tongue cannot render it: for πρόσωπον is properly a face, and metaphorically, a vizard of an actor upon the stage. How then did the Greek Fathers render the word *person*, as it is in the blessed Trinity? Not well. Instead of the word *person* they put *hypostasis*, which signifies substance; from whence it might be inferred, that the three persons in the Trinity are three divine substances, that is, three Gods. The word πρόσωπον they could not use, because face and vizard are neither of them honourable attributes of God, nor explicative of the meaning of the Greek church. Therefore the Latin (and consequently the English) church, renders *hypostasis* everywhere in Athanasius his creed by *person*.

[219] In the 1668 Appendix to the *LL*, §82, (tr. Wright, p. 364) Hobbes is more explicit: 'For if, with the Greek Fathers, we used the word hypostasis in place of person, since hypostasis and substantia mean the same thing, in place of three persons, we make three divine substances, that is, three Gods.' Jerome, in a well-known passage (Ep. 57 ad Damasum), had already expressed reservation about speaking of 'three hypostases for three persons', as Hobbes was undoubtedly aware from his source, Denys Petau. See Dionysii Petavii, *Opus De Theologicis dogmatibus* (Amsterdam, apud G. Galet, 1700), vol. 2, bk 4, p. 187b, cited in Gianni Paganini, 'Hobbes, Valla and the Trinity', p. 199. And in §88 of the 1668 Appendix to the *LL*, (tr. Wright, p. 365), Hobbes quotes at length the fruitless efforts recorded in the first book of Peter Lombard's *Sentences*, 23, ch. 14, to make sense of the three hypostases. Commenting on Augustine's *De trinitate*, bk 7, ch. 4, as Hobbes notes, Lombard had declared:

> For the Greeks understand substance differently from the Latins. The Latins say 'one essence or substance, three persons'. In our language, essence is properly understood differently from substance. And so that it might be understood at least 'as a mystery', whenever someone asked what the three things were, it was incumbent upon us that some reply be made. Thus, when asked who or what the three were, we set about the task of finding some name by which to embrace the three. But nothing occurred to us, for the supereminence of the Godhead exceeded our power of customary speech.

Regnorum medici,[a] verborum discite vires,
  Dementem populum Lex[b] sine mente facit.
Dic nunc cur Synodus[c] non sanxit et Haeresin[d] esse[e]
  Verbum,[f] Scripturas[g] esse negare,[h] Dei.
Pr.[i] Jus Indicendi[j] Synodum tunc Caesar habebat[k]
  Solus, et indixit[l] cum Synodo esset opus.
Tunc opus est autem cum turbant Dogmata[m] pacem.[n]
  De Libris[o] Sacris[p] quaestio nulla fuit.   760
Quaestio talis enim Scriptura judice nunquam[q]
  Finiri,[r] aut (alio judice) teste potest.
Quare si Patres[s] certassent,[t] Haereticique,[u]
  Dictavit libros[v] quos Homo,[w] quosque Deus,[x]
Vir bone nonne vides,[y] ut Judice Caesare,[z] Verba[aa]
  Essent nulla Dei non placitura sibi?
Si tunc[ab] Haereseos[ac] Synodus damnasset[ad] et illum,
  Scripturas,[ae] verbum,[af] qui negat esse,[ag] Dei,
Consilium Patrum periisset Philosophorum,
  Resque ignota foret spirituale forum.   770
Ergo Fidem[ah] tenebris visum est involvere densis,[ai]
  Proque Dei verbo subdere verba sua;
Ut sic dum Reges regeret Scriptura[aj] Fideles,[ak]
  Scripturam regerent,[al] ut voluere,[am] Patres.
Primus ad Imperium[an] Clero fuit hic gradus,[ao] unde
  Sacra vident placitis subdita scripta suis.

---

[a] uA B medici • [b] uA B C lex • [c] A C synodus • [d] A C haeresin • [e] A B C esse, • [f] A B Verbum • [g] A C scripturas • [h] A B negare • [i] mv uA B *Pr.* missing • [j] A B C indicendi • [k] A B habebat, • [l] A indixit, • [m] A C dogmata • [n] A pacem B pacem, • [o] A B C libris • [p] A B C sacris • [q] A nunquâm B nunquam, • [r] A B Finiri • [s] A C patres • [t] A B certassent • [u] A haereticique B Haereticique C haereticique, • [v] A libros, • [w] A B homo C homo, • [x] ~ A Deus • [y] uA Vides B vides • [z] uA B Caesare • [aa] A C verba • [ab] sc mv 1688 Nunc A B C nunc but sense requires tunc • [ac] A C haereseos • [ad] A damnâsset • [ae] uA B C Scripturas • [af] B verbum • [ag] A B esse • [ah] A C fidem • [ai] A densis • [aj] A B C scriptura • [ak] A B C fideles, • [al] uA B regerent • [am] uA Voluere B C voluere • [an] A B C imperium • [ao] uA B gradus

You healers of kingdoms,[220] learn the power of words, for law without
    sense makes the people mad.
Now tell me why the Council didn't decree that it is also heresy to deny
    the scriptures are the word of God.
Pr. At that time the Emperor alone had the right to convene a council
    and, when there was need for a council, he convened it.
It was needed then, at the time when dogmas were disturbing the peace.
    There was no question concerning the Holy Books.   **760**
For such an issue can never be determined by Scripture as judge or as a
    witness (with another as judge).[221]
For that reason, if the Fathers and heretics had come into conflict over
    which books man had dictated and which God had dictated, don't
    you see my good man,
That with the Emperor as judge, words which did not please him would
    not be considered the words of God?[222]
If at that point the Council had condemned of heresy also those who
    denied the Scriptures were the word of God,
The deliberation of the philosophical Fathers would have come to nothing,
    and their spiritual forum would have been a thing unknown.   **770**
So it was resolved to envelop faith in dense darkness and substitute their
    own word for the word of God,
So that as long as Scripture controlled faithful kings, the Fathers might
    control the Scripture as they pleased.
It was the first step toward supremacy for the clergy who, from then on,
    see the Holy Scriptures subordinated to their own opinions.

---

[220] See Thucydides 6.14 for the use of medical metaphors for the state, favoured
by Plato and Epicurus, the latter known to his followers as a sage who was both
doctor and healer. See Jean Salem, *Tel un dieu parmi les hommes: l'ethique d'Epicurus* (Paris, Vrin, 1989), Introduction, pp. 9-34. Lorenzo Valla opens *De Voluptate*
by referring to himself as healer, suggesting that 'those who refuse the presciption
of the great doctors may perhaps accept our own'. He affirms that this is the method
he intends to follow in this work, asking 'What are my remedies?', and answering,
'I shall reveal them only after I have indicated who are sick'. See Maristella de
Panizza Lorch's edition of Valla's *De Voluptate*, translated as *On Pleasure*, p. 49.

[221] In 'A Review and Conclusion', *Lev.*, §15, 395/495, Hobbes openly admits
that there is no place for witnesses in the determination of true or false doctrine:
'For first, all truth of doctrine dependeth either upon reason or upon Scripture. . . .
Secondly, the matters in question are not of fact, but of right, wherein there is no
place for witnesses'.

[222] The principle of *cuius regio eius religio.*

Sec. Dic mihi quam causam populi conversio tanti,
     Regibus invitis, tam celeremque habuit?[a]
Pr.[b] Imprimis fecit numeroso cognita teste,
     Occiso Domino reddita vita fidem.[c]   **780**
Tum quòd tot[d] Christus miracula fecerat ipse,
     Tantaque discipuli[e] tam manifesta sui.
Quodque suam lucem Christi doctrina ferebat
     Secum,[f] cogentem simplicitate sua.
Adde quòd[g] ad Christum[h] populo veniebat ab omni,[i]
     Si cui Sacrifici[j] non placuere sui.[k]
Israelitarum[l] sic regnum transtulit olim
     Fastus Elidarum junctus avaritiae.[m]
Turba frequens erat haec[n] et habebat nomina multa[o]
     Nobilium, notos divitiisque viros.   **790**
Traxit et (ut dixi)[p] multos aequatio vitae,
     Mensaque communis queis erat una Fides.[q]
Doctis,[r] Indoctis,[s] Fidis simul[t] et Simulatis,[u]
     Haec paupertatis dulce levamen erat.
Crescentem numerum[v] jam non mirabere;[w] Namque[x]
     Crevit vera Fides,[y] Hypocrisisque[z] simul.
Denique summus honor Doctis[aa] fuit[bb] in grege Christi;
     Maxima Christicolis haec fuit ambitio.
Sed quod non fuerant eadem, at contraria docti,
     Principium primum seditionis erat.   **800**
Sec. Quos doctos narras? Quoniam nec Apostolus ullus,[cc]
     Discipulusve fuit, quod scio,[dd] Philosophus.
An quibus ingenium breve erat[ee] sed barba profunda;[ff]
     Quorum asper sermo,[gg] lubrica vita fuit;[hh]

---

[a] mv uA B habuit. • [b] mv uA B *Pr.* missing • [c] A fidem • [d] mv A B tot missing • [e] A B discipuli, • [f] A Secum • [g] A B C quod • [h] A christum • [i] ~ A omni • [j] A B C sacrifici • [k] C sui: • [l] A C Israëlitarum • [m] mv uA B amicitiae. C avaritiae • [n] B haec, • [o] A multa; B multa, • [p] uA B ut dixi (no parentheses) • [q] uA B C fides. • [r] uA B Doctis • [s] A jndoctis, B C indoctis, • [t] A simul, • [u] A B C simulatis, • [v] A numerum, • [w] A mirabere. B mirabere, • [x] A Namque, B namque • [y] A B C fides • [z] A C hypocrisisque • [aa] B C doctis • [bb] B fuit: • [cc] A B ullus • [dd] uA B scio • [ee] A C erat, • [ff] A B profunda. • [gg] uA B sermo • [hh] A B fuit

Sec. Tell me what was the reason for the conversion of so many people,
when kings were against it, and why it occurred so quickly?

Pr. First, the fact that life had been restored to the slain Lord, which was
known by numerous testimony, created faith, **780**

Secondly, because Christ himself had performed so many miracles and his
disciples such great and manifest ones.

And because Christ's teaching brought its own light, which by its
simplicity convinced people as he did.

In addition, because men from all nations came to Christ[223] when their
own priests did not satisfy them.

So the pride and avarice[224] of the sons of Eli[225] once brought about the
transfer of the kingdom of the Israelites.[226]

This crowd was large in number and included many names of nobles and
men noted for their wealth. **790**

Equality of life and the common table (as I have said) attracted many,
who had a single faith.

For the educated, the uneducated, the faithful and those pretending to be
faithful alike, this was sweet solace for poverty.

Don't be amazed now at the increasing number. In fact true faith grew and
hypocrisy grew at the same time.

In the end, the highest office among the flock of Christ was for the
educated; this was the greatest ambition for Christians.

But because the learned had not learned the same things, but things at
variance with one another, this was the first source of sedition. **800**

Sec. Which learned men are you talking about? Because no apostle or
disciple that I know of was a philosopher.

Do you mean those whose intelligence was shallow as their beards were
long, whose talk was harsh as their life was slippery,

---

[223] Note the significance of the deliberate substitution of a lower case christus in
A: *christus* (= Gr. *christos*), the annointed one, the Messiah; Jesus Christ.

[224] Mv A B *amicitiae*, to read 'of friendship'; read instead 'of greed', like 1688.

[225] *Elidarum* = 'of the sons of Eli', *Elides* being a patronymic formed in the
normal Greek way (Pelides = son of Peleus = Archilles), possibly a neologism
created by Hobbes.

[226] 1 Samuel 2:12-26, 3:19-21, 'because Eli's sons, Hophni and Phinehas, were
worthless men and had become corrupt beyond hope'.

Et quos ad fraudes damnarat Inedia[a] viles,
     Re stultos, falso nomine Philosophos?
Pr. Hos ipsos.[b] Quorum multos Ecclesia[c] habebat.[d]
     Quicquid cepissent[e] retia,[f] Piscis[g] erat.[h]
Ex horum numero fiebat Episcopus, ut quis
     Insignis Logicus,[i] Rhetoricusve[j] fuit.   810
Qui veteris[k] certant[l] imbuti errore Magistri,[m]
     Verba Dei ad Sectam ducere quisque suam.
Verborum pugnam parit ignorantia discors,
     Quam nexus[n] rerum conciliare solet.
Horum quisque tamen sapiens sibi tam vehementer
     Esse videbatur,[o] tamque superbus erat,
Ut non Philosophos prae se contemneret omnes,[p]
     Ut pecudes totidem,[q] quae ratione carent.[r]
Philosophos (iisdem si non didicere Magistris)
     Spurcabant ipsos,[s] quo potuere,[t] luto.   820
Qua[u] freti virtute? Modo quoniam,[v] atque Figura
     Scibant[w] disserere, et ludere in ambiguo.
Haec illis Logica, Ratio, Sapientia,[x] Virtus,
     Ambitio,[y] Spes,[z] et gloria summa fuit.
Deque sacris verbis[aa] dum disceptatur,[bb] in Artem[cc]
     Vertitur ignotam debilitata Fides.[dd]
Ars ignota fuit,[ee] quae nunc est Theiologia.[ff]
     An circumscripsit quis sine fine[gg] Deum?[hh]

---

[a] A B C inedia • [b] uA B ipsos • [c] C ecclesia • [d] C habebat • [e] mv A coepisset B coepissent • [f] uA B retia • [g] A B C piscis • [h] B erat • [i] uA B logicus • [j] mv A B C Rhetoricusque • [k] A Veteris • [l] A Certant • [m] A B Magistri C magistri • [n] A Nexus • [o] C videbatur • [p] ~ A omnes • [q] B C totidem • [r] mv C carent • [s] uA B ipsos • [t] A B potuere • [u] A Quâ • [v] A B quoniam • [w] uA B Scibant • [x] A sapientia B C sapientia, • [y] uA B Ambitio • [z] uA B C spes • [aa] uA B C verbis, • [bb] A B disceptatur • [cc] ~ A Artem uA B Artem, C artem • [dd] A C fides. • [ee] B fuit • [ff] uA B Theologia • [gg] mv A B finitione instead of 1688 C sine fine • [hh] mv C Deum

And whom hunger condemned to cheap frauds – fools in reality, falsely
    called philosophers?[227]

Pr.   Those very men. The Church had many of them. Whatever its net
    caught was considered fish.[228]

One of their number would be made a bishop according to how
    distinguished he was as a logician or rhetorician.   **810**

Every one of them was tainted with the error of an ancient teacher, and
    struggled to arrogate the word of God to his own sect.

Conflicting ignorance generates a war of words which a binding-together
    of interests usually reconciles.[229]

However, each of these men considered himself wise with such
    vehemence, and was so arrogant

That he disparaged all non-philosophers compared with himself, as so
    many cattle lacking reason.

They sullied their fellow philosophers, if they weren't taught by the same
    masters, with what mud they could.   **820**

On the basis of what ability?[230] They knew only how to argue by Mood
    and Figure and play with ambiguity.[231]

To those men, this was the height of logic, reason, wisdom, virtue,
    ambition, hope and glory.

As the holy words are made subject of debate, faith is crippled and
    transformed into an unknown science.

The unknown science is what is now Theology. Can anyone delimit God
    who is infinite?[232]

---

[227] See Hobbes's echo of *Metamorphoses* I.130-1: '*there emerged deceits and tricks and betrayals and violence and wicked lust of ownership*' (fraudesque dolusque insidiaeque et vis et amor sceleratus habendi). Lorenzo Valla, whom Hobbes may also cite, had applied the epigram specifically to the belligerent popes, boasting: 'Let me tell why the Roman pontiffs show fraud and craft (fraus dolusque) rather than ignorance in using war instead of law as their arbiter'. See Valla's *[Supposed] Donation of Constantine*, ed. Coleman, pp. 172-3.

[228] Note the English proverb 'all is fish that comes to the net'.

[229] Hobbes echoes the language of Lucretius' *De rerum natura*, though in many respects the chain of causes and the interconnectedness of human affairs that he emphasizes here is a thoroughly Stoic notion.

[230] This reads like an intervention from Secundus.

[231] Hobbes refers to the modes of syllogistic logic.

[232] Mv A B *finitione* substitute for 1688 C *sine fine* to read: 'Can anyone delimit God with a definition?', perhaps better to capture Hobbes's intention.

Quae,[a] de Natura[b] Divina[c] dicere fas est,
  Quaeque tacere decet, Pagina[d] Sacra[e] docet.   830
Discipulus Christi discernitur agnitione,
  Et cultu, Sacri quem docuere libri ;
Et vita,[f] quae sit divinae congrua Legi.[g]
  Non à[h] Naturae[i] cognitione Sacrae.[j]
Sec. At cur Niceni tanto conamine quondam
  De Christo,[k] Physicè[l] disseruere Patres,
Cum nihil in tota Scriptura[m] clarius extet[n]
  Quàm[o] Salvatoris[p] cùm[q] caro,[r] tùm[s] Deitas ?
Pr. Cur nisi quod puduit quicquam nescire videri
  Philosophum, aut victum discere,[t] vera licet ?   840

---

[a] A B C Quae • [b] A B C natura • [c] A C divina • [d] uA C pagina • [e] A C sacra •
[f] A B vita • [g] uA B legi, C legi. • [h] A B C a • [i] A B C naturae • [j] A C sacrae.
• [k] uA B Christo • [l] A C physice • [m] A scripura (error) C scriptura • [n] A exstet,
B extet, • [o] A B C Quam • [p] A B C salvatoris • [q] uA B C cum • [r] A caro B
Caro C caro, • [s] uA B tum • [t] uA B discere

The Holy Writing[233] teaches what can be said about the divine nature and
     what one should keep silent about.[234]   830

The disciple is set apart by his acceptance of Christ and by the worship
     which the Scriptures have taught him;

And by a life which conforms to Divine Law; but not by an
     understanding of the nature of the divine.

Sec. Why then did the Nicene Fathers at one time debate scientifically
     with such effort about Christ,

When nothing in all of Scripture stands out more clearly than that our
     Saviour was not only flesh but also deity ?[235]

Pr. Why indeed? Unless it was because it shamed a philosopher to seem
     not to know something, or to be defeated and learn – even if what he
     learned was the truth?   840

---

[233] Literally, *Pagina sacra*, 'the sacred page', reminiscent of Valla's witty discussion of the term 'page' in *The [Supposed] Donation of Constantine* (ed. Coleman, p. 133), at the point where the claim is made that the document was confirmed by Constantine's own hands: "'The page, moreover, of this imperial decree, we, confirming it with our own hands, did place above the venerable body of the blessed Peter/'". Of which Valla remarks, 'Was it paper or parchment, the "page" on which this was written? Though, in fact, we call one side of a leaf, as they say, a page; for instance, a pamphlet has ten leaves, twenty pages'.

[234] Silence about Christian mysteries beyond understanding is a subject addressed in the Latin elegiac poem of 1852 lines by John of Salisbury (c. 1115-1180), the 'Entheticus' (*De dogmate philosophorum*), apparently intended as an introduction to the *Policraticus*, and covering practically the same ground in briefer form. See Michael Wilks, 'John of Salisbury and the Tyranny of Nonsense' at p. 278. John of Salisbury a diplomat at the papal court of Pope Eugene III, and private secretary to Theobald, Archbisop of Canterbury, may well have been an important source for Hobbes. His *Metalogicus* is a philosophical treatise in four books, in defence of the study of logic and philosophy against a group of obscurantists whom he nicknamed *Cornificians*. The *Policraticus*, in eight books, deals, as its sub-title (*De nugis curialium et vestigiis philosophorum*) indicates, partly with philosophy and learning in a proto-humanist manner. And he wrote a *History of the Papacy, Historia Pontificalis*, first published by Arndt (*Monumenta Germaniae Historica*, xx, 517-45, 1868), and identified as the work of John, by Giesebrecht (Bay. Akad. d. Wissensch., Munich, 1873, 124) (*Catholic Encyclopaedia*).

[235] By insisting on the divinity of Christ, Hobbes makes the point that he is not an Arian, despite his reputation based on the unorthodox trinity of his 1651 *Leviathan*. There (*Lev.*, xlii, §3 267-9/334-5), Hobbes's case for the Trinity as God the Father and two orders of representative, God the Son and the Holy Ghost, is similar to the doctrine of 'subordinationism' and Arius's three hypostases. It is also strikingly similar to the Trinitarian doctrine of Lorenzo Valla, as Paganini has carefully demonstrated in 'Hobbes, Valla e i problemi filosofici della teologia umanistica', at pp. 24-30. Hobbes meekly retracted the potentially heretical doctrine in the 1668 Appendix to the *LL*; but on these dangerous points, including the doctrine of free will, Hobbes's position was not considered by contemporaries to differ significantly from that of Arius.

Dum pugnant freti veteris ratione Magistri,[a]
    Non tenuere novam vasa vetusta fidem.[b]
Causa Potestatis[c] tamen haec discordia Patrum,
    Principium et Regni Spiritualis[d] erat.
Nam Constantinus populis dum reddere[e] pacem[f]
    Nititur,[g] atque unam constabilire Fidem,[h]
Lex (inquit) fiet quicquid statuetis;[i] et illam
    Curabo ne quis transgrediatur ego.
Hinc vulgò[j] visum est,[k] in rebus Relligionis,[l]
    Consensu Regis non opus esse sui.   **850**

---

[a] ~ A Magistri C magistri, • [b] ~ A fidem • [c] A C potestatis • [d] A B C spiritualis • [e] B reddére • [f] A B pacem, • [g] uA B C Nititur • [h] A C fidem, • [i] uA B statuetis • [j] A vulgo • [k] uA B C est • [l] A relligionis B Relligionis C relligionis,

While they were fighting, relying on the reasoning of an old master, old vessels did not contain the new faith.[236]

However, this discord among the Fathers was the origin of their power, and this was the beginning of the spiritual kingdom.[237]

For while Constantine strove to restore peace to his peoples, and establish a single faith,

He said, 'Whatever you decide will be made law and I myself will ensure that no one transgresses against it.'[238]

From this it was generally held that in religious matters there was no need for the agreement of the king.   **850**

---

[236] Hobbes's play on the proverb 'old wine in new bottles' may be with reference to the Schools of *medieval logic. The corpus logicum in the 12th and 13th centuries comprised the logical works of Aristotle and Boethius, together with the Isagoge of Porphyry, and was divided into two parts, the Logica vetus and the Logica nova, the latter becoming known during the course of the 12th century (c.f.: Grabmann, 'Aristoteles im 12. Jahrhundert', pp. 123-162). See 'A Review and Conclusion', *Lev.*, §14, 395/495, for Hobbes's declaration of his willingness to express novel religious doctrines in the interests of truth (including his unorthodox doctrine of the Trinity), which utilizes a new wine in new bottles metaphor:

> In that part which treateth of a Christian commonwealth, there are some new doctrines, which (it may be) in a state where the contrary were already fully determined were a fault for a subject (without leave) to divulge, as being an usurpation of the place of a teacher. But in this time, that men call not only for peace, but also for truth, to offer such doctrine as I think true (and that manifestly tend to peace and loyalty) to the consideration of those that are yet in deliberation is no more but to offer new wine, to be put into new cask, that both may be preserved together. And I suppose, that then, when novelty can breed no trouble, nor disorder in a state, men are not more generally so much inclined to the reverence of antiquity as to prefer ancient errors before new and well proved truth.

[237] For Hobbes's refutation of the Church's temporal power, based on the doctrine of twin kingdoms, terrestrial and spiritual, see *Lev.*, xlii, §128, 317/394:

> But spiritual commonwealth there is none in this world. For it is the same thing with the kingdom of Christ, which he himself saith is not of this world, but shall be in the next world, at the resurrection, when they that have lived justly and believed that he was the Christ shall (though they died *natural* bodies) rise *spiritual* bodies; and then it is, that our Saviour shall judge the world, and conquer his Adversaries, and make a spiritual commonwealth. In the meantime, seeing there are no men on earth whose bodies are spiritual, there can be no spiritual commonwealth amongst men that are yet in the flesh (unless we call preachers, that have commission to teach and prepare men for their reception into the kingdom of Christ at the resurrection, a commonwealth, which I have proved already to be none).

[238] For this view of Constantine see Richard Crackenthorpe's *The Defense of Constantine: with a treatise of the Popes temporall monarchie, Wherein, besides divers passages, touching other Counsels, both General and Proviciall, the second Roman Synod, under Sylvester, is declared to be a meere Fiction and Forgery* (London, 1621), listed in the Hardwick Hall catalogue in Hobbes's hand at shelf mark K.1.12.

Unus,[a] habebatur Princeps[b] quoque,[c] de grege,[d] Caesar,[e]
　　Seque suae Synodo subdere visus erat.
Utque alii,[f] poterat,[g] si dissensisset ab illa,[h]
　　Haereticus dici Legibus ipse suis.
Non illum Domini Sancta[i] depellere Coena
　　Hactenus audebant. Spes (sed inermis) erat.[j]
Hinc quoque praesumptum est conscripta Oracula[k] libris[l]
　　Sacra, Sacerdotis[m] solius ore loqui.
Quaeque,[n] ad Scripturas[o] spectarat[p] libera Sacras,
　　Ad Patres spectat nunc pavefacta Fides.[q]　　　　　　　　　　860
Lege Dei dupla facta est Ecclesia biceps,
　　Lex una est animis,[r] altera corporibus.
Atque duplex homines terrebat poena misellos,
　　Cognita poena omnes, credita poena pios.

---

[a] A B Unus • [b] A B Princeps, • [c] uA B quoque • [d] uA B grege • [e] A B Caesar
• [f] uA B alii • [g] uA poterat B potérat • [h] A B illa • [i] B C sancta • [j] A erat •
[k] A B C oracula • [l] A libris. • [m] A C sacerdotis • [n] A B C Quaeque • [o] B C
scripturas • [p] mv C spectarant (error) • [q] uA C fides. • [r] C animis

The Emperor also was regarded as one of the flock, and had seemed to
subject himself to his own Council.[239]

And just like any other person, if he disagreed with the Council, he
himself, by his own laws, could be called a heretic.

They did not yet dare to banish him from the Lord's Supper.[240] There was
still hope (but it was defenseless),[241]

Henceforth, too, it was taken for granted that the holy oracles written in
the scriptures could speak only through the mouth of the priest.

The Faith, which when it was free, used to look to holy scripture, is now
frightened and looks to the Fathers.   **860**

The Church was made two-headed by a double law of God, one law for
souls, and another for bodies.[242]

And a double punishment terrified poor men, the known punishment
terrified everyone, punishment which was a matter of belief terrified
the pious.

---

[239] Violating, in Hobbes's view, the principle *cuius regio eius religio.*

[240] Hobbes addresses the right of excommunication, denied by Erastians, in
Lev., xlii, where he produces a novel theory. See Johann P. Sommerville, *Thomas
Hobbes: Political Ideas in Historical Context* (London: Macmillan, 1992),
pp. 127-33, 196-7, at p. 131. Hobbes took excommunication to forbid men to associate with or even 'eat with a man excommunicate' (*Lev.*, xlii, §30, 278/348). Consistent with Anglican policy, he argued the Sovereign could never be excommunicated (*Lev.*, xlii, §28, 278/347-8). Note that the regicide of Charles I and conciliar
doctrines of the right of resistance also lie behind Hobbes's comments. Lorenzo
Valla, in the opening lines of *De falso credita. . . donatione*, also called into question the power of the Pope to excommunicate, as belonging to temporal power
which he denies to the church. See *The [Supposed] Donation of Constantine*,
pp. 20-1.

[241] In the *Historical Narration* (*EW* IV p. 402), Hobbes notes: '*There was no
doctrine which tended to the power ecclesiastical, or to the reverence of the
clergy, the contradiction whereof was not by one Council or another made heresy,
and punished arbitrarily by the Emperors with banishment and death.*'

[242] Hobbes follows an important line of European anti-clerical and anti-papal
polemic against the temporal power of the Church that stretched from Marsilius of
Padua to Erastus. It includes Lorenzo Valla, who began his *[Supposed] Donation
of Constantine* (ed. Coleman, pp. 20-3), by attacking the two-fold power of the
pope: 'the supreme pontiff [is] armed not only with the temporal sword as are
kings and princes, but with the spiritual also, so that even under the very shield, so
to speak, of any prince, you cannot protect yourself from him'. 'But there is no
reason'. An English edition of Valla's work by Thomas Godfray, *A treatise of the
donation or gyfte. . . by Constantyne emperour of Rome* (1534) had become a
virtual best-seller.

Sec. Magna fuit,[a] fateor, Synodorum prisca Potestas;[b]
    Atqui res,[c] Synodus,[d] rara brevisque fuit;[e]
Nec Papae potuit concedere,[f] Regia[g] jura;
    Nec quamvis poterat,[h] id voluisse puto.
Pr. Per quatuor Synodos primas,[i] centumque per annos,
    Per Regum[j] inscitiam, per populumque levem,[k]   **870**
Creverat obscurè[l] Papae furtiva Potestas,[m]
    Donec Romano Principe major erat.
Nimirum,[n] Piscator[o] erat, piscemque[p] petivit;
    Et Piscatorum[q] coetus erat Synodus.
Sed pro pisce fuit rerum suprema potestas;[r]
    Capturam facilem turbida praebet aqua.
Cuncta fuere priùs[s] tenebris turbisque replenda,[t]
    Terrarum Domini quam potuere capi.
Et partes aliquas sibi vult fortuna relinqui,[u]
    Quae summi tacita est actio certa Dei.   **880**
Sec. Verum quo pacto,[v] de paupere Philosophastro,[w]
    Obtinuit,[x] terris,[y] proximus esse Deo?
Pr. Historiae filum quod nunc subtile retexo,[z]
    Ostendet breviter,[aa] perspicuéque[bb] satis.
Finita synodo statim nova dogmata surgunt,[cc]
    Quamque priùs[dd] fuerat acrior ira redit.

---

[a] uA B C fuit • [b] A B potestas. C potestas; • [c] uA B res • [d] uA B Synodus • [e] A B fuit. • [f] uA B C concedere • [g] A C regia • [h] sc mv A B poterat, 1688 and C substitute poterant, for the metre, but unnecessarily, even classical writers sometimes lengthen vowels at this point of the line; sense requires poterat • [i] uA B primas • [j] C regum • [k] A levem • [l] A C obscure B obscuré • [m] A C potestas, • [n] A C Nimirum • [o] A C piscator • [p] A Piscemque • [q] A B C piscatorum • [r] uA B potestas, • [s] A B C prius • [t] ~ A replenda • [u] ~ A relinqui • [v] A B pacto • [w] A B Philosophastro • [x] uA B Obtinuit • [y] uA B terris • [z] A B retexo • [aa] C breviter • [bb] A C perspicueque • [cc] ~ A surgunt • [dd] A B C prius

Sec. I acknowledge that the early power of the Councils was great, but the
  Council was a rare and short-lived event;

And it could not cede royal rights to the Pope; nor do I think, even if it
  was able to, it would have wanted that.

Pr. During the first four Councils, and for a hundred years, due to the
  lack of attention by Emperors and the fickleness of the people,   **870**

The power of the Pope (power that was stolen), secretly increased, until
  he was more powerful than the Roman Emperor.[243]

Of course he was a fisherman and he looked for fish; and the Council was
  an assembly of fishermen.[244]

But instead of fish, power was his most important concern; muddy water
  provides an easy catch.

All things had to be filled with shadows and disturbances before the rulers
  of the lands could be captured.[245]

And fortune, which is the silent but sure action of the supreme God,
  wanted some role reserved to herself.[246]   **880**

Sec. How from being a poor pseudo-philosopher did he succeed in
  becoming second to God on earth?

Pr. The delicate thread of history I am now unraveling will reveal an
  answer concisely and clearly enough.

Immediately after the Council ended, new doctrines arose and anger more
  violent than before returned.

---

[243] This is Hobbes's closest reference to the *Donation of Constantine*, on which
he does not dwell, preferring to give an institutional account of the rise of papal
power; most likely because he accepted Lorenzo Valla's famous exposure of it as a
forgery, if Paganini, 'Thomas Hobbes e Lorenzo Valla', p. 520 n.9, is right.

[244] *Synodus Piscatorum*: Hobbes may be punning on the name of the Calvinist
casuist, Johann Piscator (1546-1625), friend of Samuel Hartlib (1595-1662), the
intelligencer, whom Hobbes may have known personally. See also the concluding
chapter of Isaak Walton and Charles Cotton's *The Compleat Angler* (1653) (1653),
ed. Jonquil Bevan (Everyman edn, 1993), ch. 21, a dialogue between 'Piscator and
Venator', on which the following passage seems to be an elaborate play.

[245] Note the language of Hilary, *Ad Const. August.*, *PL* X. col. 558.

[246] The concept of Fortune, *Tychê*, so important in Polybius (1.4), but rejected
by Thucydides, although he uses the word 28 times, was Christianized by Eusebius,
who uses Aristotle's term, *symbebêkota*, the 'accidents' of history. Among subsequent ecclesiastical historians, Theodoret used a range of words for Fortune, such as
symphora, *euklêria*, and *dysklêria*', while Socrates and Evagrius appealed to the
term beloved of Graeco-Roman historians, *kairos*, the decisive moment'. See
Chestnut, *The First Christian Historians*, pp. 38, 182-3. Hobbes's use of the term
raises doubts about claims that he was a determinist.

Post Constantinum,[a] rexit Constantius Orbem,[b]
    Catholicos vexans; Namque Arianus erat.[c]
Ille et Athanasium Magnum terroribus implens,[d]
    Martyrium,[e] vitâ,[f] fecit amare minus.   **890**
Exul ab Aegypto,[g] Constantis castra per Alpes,[h]
    Gallorumque adiit frigida rura senex.
Judice te,[i] meritò,[j] latas à[k] Principe Leges,[l]
    Ausus,[m] doctrinae post-posuisse[n] suae.
Proximus huic,[o] mundi[p] tenuit Julianus habenas,[q]
    Antè[r] quidem Christi[s] qui simularat ovem;[t]

After Constantine Constantius[247] ruled the world, harassing the Catholics;
   for he was an Arian.[248]
He filled the great Athanasius[249] with fear, and made him love martyrdom
   less than life.[250]   **890**
From Egypt, the old man went in exile through the Alps to visit Constans'
   camp and the chilly countryside of Gaul[251] –
Deservedly so, as you would judge, because he had ventured to give less
   weight to the laws promulgated by the emperor than to his own teaching.
After Constans, Julian held the reins of the world.[252] Before he had
   pretended to be one of Christ's flock;[253]

---

[247] Constantius II, Roman Emperor, AD 318-61, second son of Constantine the
Great, ruler of the East, in 337 instituted a rebellion and lynched Julian Constantius,
half brother of Constantine the Great, to gain greater power. For most of his reign he
battled the Persians without and usurpers within. He died in 361, while moving to
suppress the rebellion of Julian in Paris, whose father he had slain (*OCD*, 1970, 282).

[248] See Hilary, *Contra Constantium Imperatorem*, *PL* X, col. 577-606 on the persecutions of Constantius II, who was raised and lived in Antioch, the great centre of Arianism. See also Frend, 'The Church in the Reign of Constantius II (337-361)', in
L'Église et l'Empire au IVᵉ siècle, ed. Albrecht Dihle, pp. 73-111; T. D. Barnes, 'Christians and Pagans in the Reign of Constantius', in *L'Église et l'Empire au IVᵉ siècle*, ed.
Albrecht Dihle (Geneva, Fondation Hardt, 1989), pp. 301-43; and George Ostrogorsky,
History of the Byzantine State (New Brunswick, N.J., rev. edn, 1969), pp. 48-9.

[249] *Athanasius, known as the great (295-373), was a deacon of Bishop Alexander during the Council of Nicaea and then he himself was Bishop of Alexandria. For
his extremist positions he was sent into exile at Trier already during the reign of
Constantine (325-337). (Invernizzi note.)

[250] Sozomen, *Hist. Eccl.*, 3.9-11.

[251] Constans I, although a Nicenist, to placate his brother, Constantius II, the
Arian, permitted Athanasius to return to his See in 346.

[252] *Julianus Flavius Claudius, termed 'the Apostate' (331-363), emperor from
361 AD. Lorenzo Valla in *The [Supposed] Donation of Constantine* (ed. Coleman,
pp. 66 9) uses Julian as a test case to prove that Constantine had not in fact given
away his power to the Pope, citing Eutropius, *Breviarum ab urbe condita*, 10.16.1:
   Of a thousand witnesses one may suffice; Eutropius, who saw Constantine,
   who saw the three sons of Constantine who were left masters of the world by
   their father, and who wrote thus in connection with Julian, the son of Constantine's brother: "This Julian, who was subdeacon in the Roman church and
   when he became Emperor returned to the worship of the gods, seized the government, and after elaborate preparations made war against the Parthians; in
   which expedition I also took part".
Hobbes's use of the image 'reins of the world' is probably not innocent either. For
Valla makes much of the absurdity in the *Donation* §4 of Gratian's *Decretum*, that
'holding the bridle of his horse, out of reverence for the blessed Peter', Constantine
could have 'performed for [the Pope] the duty of squire' (*ibid.*, pp. 16-17, 120-3).

[253] It is true that Julian only openly professed his paganism on being acclaimed
Augustus by his troops in 360. (*OCD*, 1970, 567-8). On a minion of Julian as a 'wolf
climbing into the fold' see Photius's *Epitome of the Historia Ecclesiastica of*

Sanctorum nunc[a] hostis erat;[b] verùm[c] ille pepercit
    Fortunis,[d] sacri corporibusque gregis.
Sed fecit[e] quod pejus erat. Nam Templa Deorum
    Surdorum pridem diruta restituit;   **900**
Atque Idolorum cultum revocavit ineptum.[f]
    Sic iterum ritus convaluere mali.
Christicolas autem sanxit non esse docendos[g]
    Ingenuas artes, bella paratque animis.
Sec. Non tutam forsan[h] Pietatem viderat inter
    Grammaticos, Logicos, Rhetoricosque viros.
Scilicet[i] his,[j] patrias amor est reprehendere leges,
    Et statum rerum vertere,[k] summa Venus.
Non minùs[l] ingenii committit gloria Doctos,[m]
    Quàm[n] Reges rapti dedecus imperii.[o]   **910**
Pr. At frustra cultum permisit Rex Julianus
    Gentibus antiquum, nemo ubi sacra dabat.
Quisque suum Taurum,[p] Vitulum,[q] comedebat et Agnum;[r]
    Sacrificus rarus, victima cara[s] fuit.

---

[a] mv uA B hic instead of nunc • [b] A erat, B erat. • [c] A B C verum • [d] A B For-
tunis • [e] A fecit, • [f] A B ineptum, • [g] A B docendos, • [h] mv A B forsan. • [i] A
B C Scilicet • [j] uA B his • [k] B vertere • [l] A B C minus • [m] uA C doctos, •
[n] A B C Quam • [o] A B Imperii.C imperii, • [p] uA B C taurum, • [q] uA B C
vitulum • [r] uA B C agnum, • [s] mv C rara

Now he was an enemy of the pious; but actually he spared the persons
    and the property of the sacred flock.
Yet he did what was worse. For he rebuilt the temples of those deaf gods
    which had long before been destroyed;   **900**
And he restored the senseless worship of idols, so that evil rituals
    flourished again.
Moreover Julian decreed that Christians should not be taught the liberal
    arts, and prepared to attack their minds.[254]
Sec. Perhaps he had seen that piety was not secure among the
    grammarians, logicians and rhetoricians.[255]
Of course for these men it was a delight to thwart the laws of one's
    country, and to overthrow the state was for them the highest pleasure.
Pride in their intelligence brought the learned into conflict no less than the
    infamy of stolen power brings kings into conflict.   **910**
Pr. But the Emperor Julian gave permission for people to practice the
    ancient religions in vain, because no one gave sacrificial offerings.[256]
Each man ate up his own bulls, calves and lambs. Sacrificing priests were
    rare, beasts for sacrifice were expensive.

Philostorgius, ed. Walford, p. 479. Hilary saw Constantius as much a wolf in sheep's clothing as Hobbes saw Julian, see Hilary, *Contra Constantium Imperatorem, PL* X. cols.586-8.

[254] Amm. Marc. xxii.10.7 and xxv.4.20. See Chestnut, *The First Christian Histories*, p. 178, who notes that Ammianus Marcellinus, although a devoted hagiographer of Julian, was appalled by his exclusion of Christians from schools. Ostrogorsky, *History of the Byzantine State*, says of Julian, who exploited the divisions among the Christians (p. 50):

> In his efforts against them he remained primarily the leader of a cultured pagan aristocracy of neoplatonic philosophers and rhetoricians whose beliefs he himself shared.

Note that neoplatonists did not believe in the wide dissemination of the liberal arts, for to them knowledge was a privilege of initiates.

[255] In 362 Julian forbad Christians to teach grammar, rhetoric or philosophy logic; c.f. Bowersock, *Julian the Apostate*, pp. 83-4.

[256] For the reign of Julian, see Sozomen, *Hist. Eccl.*, (ed Bidez), bk 5 and bk 6, chs 1-2, and Photius's *Epitome of the Historia Ecclesiastica of Philostorgius*, bk 7. See Ostrogorsky, *History of the Byzantine State*, p. 50, of Julian:

> The pains which he took to revive pagan cults, even sacrificing to the gods himself in person, provoked scornful astonishment and not only in Christian circles. Like all attempts to bolster up old ways simply because they are old and to oppose innovation because it is innovation, his attempts were doomed to failure.

Frigebant arae,[a] desertaque Templa silebant:[b]
    Catholicum,[c] de Diis dicere pauca,[d] fuit.
Et dum quisque suam rem solam curat et urget,
    De dubia dixit Relligione nihil.
Et quia desuerat[e] populus Diis sacrificare,
    Fit nova Relligio, quae fuit antè[f] vetus.   **920**
At mox à[g] Persis Rex[h] caeditur hostibus (hostis,[i]
    Dicebat clerus,[j] quod fuit ille Dei.)[k]
Tunc etiam Gotthi coeperunt arma movere,
    In sibi vicinos Imperii populos.
Fortisan injustè,[l] sed non tamen absque colore
    Justitiae; satis est Regibus ipse color.
Gentibus et tandem posuerunt nomina victis,
    Non audita priùs,[m] quae voluere Duces.[n]
Vandalus hinc, Gotthusque,[o] Herulusque,[p] Hunnusque,[q] et Alanus[r]
    Ad Boream fines occupat Imperii.[s]   **930**

---

[a] A B arae • [b] A B C silebant. • [c] uA C Catholicum • [d] uA C pauca • [e] mv A
desierat • [f] A B C ante • [g] A a • [h] C rex • [i] A B C hostis • [j] A Clerus, B C
clerus • [k] A B Dei) • [l] uA B injuste, • [m] uA B prius C prius, • [n] uA C duces. •
[o] A C Gothusque, B Gothusque • [p] A B Herulusque • [q] A B C Hunnusque • [r] ~
uA B Alanus. C Alanus, • [s] A C imperii.

The altars went cold and the deserted temples fell silent. To say few
words about the gods became universal practice.[257]

While each man took care of and promoted solely his own interests, he
said nothing about this doubtful religion.

And because the people had stopped sacrificing to the gods, what was
previously the old religion became the new religion.   **920**

But soon the emperor was killed by Persian enemies[258] (according to the
clergy because he was an enemy of God).

Then the Goths[259] also began to wage a war against peoples of the Empire
who were their neighbours.[260]

Perhaps unjustly, but not however without the appearance of justice; and
for kings the appearance is enough.

And finally, when these tribes were conquered, they gave them names
which had never been heard before, but which the leaders wanted.[261]

So the Vandal[262] and the Goth,[263] the Herulian[264] and the Hun[265] and the
Alan[266] occupied the borders of the empire to the north.[267]   **930**

---

[257] On the failure of Julian to resuscitate pagan rites, see Sozomen, *Hist. Eccl.*,
bk 5, ch. 16.

[258] Of the Persians see Ostrogorsky, *History of the Byzantine State*, p. 51: 'In
Constans' day it was already clear that the Persians were the predominant influence
in the Mesopotamian region'.

[259] On the *Goths, see Sozomen, *Hist. Eccl.* bk 6, chs 37-40, at 37. The great Goth
bishop, Ulphilas, entered into communion with the Arians at Constantinople, but this
was no obstacle to their willingness to make war on the Roman Empire of the East.

[260] In fact the invasion of the Goths had started in the 3rd century AD with their
occupation of Asia. Hobbes reconstructs the events of the barbarian invasions in a
roughly approximate manner. See Invernizzi note.

[261] See Sozomen, *Hist. Eccl.*, bk 9, ch. 12.

[262] The *Vandals, a Germanic people originally based in southern Scandinavia,
around AD 200.

[263] The *Goths another Germanic people based in southern Scandinavia, who
began moving into the Roman Empire at the beginning of the Christian era.

[264] The *Heruli, a Germanic peoples.

[265] For the *Huns, see Sozomen, *Hist. Eccl.*, bk 6 ch. 37. Theodoret, *Hist. Eccl.*,
bk 4, ch. 37 and Philostorgius, the Arian, also treat the Huns (*Hist. Eccl.*, bk 2, ch. 5
and bk 11, ch 8, see Photius's *Epitome of Philostorgius*). See also Ammianus Marcellinus, bk 31, ch 2.

[266] For the *Alans, see the Roman History of Ammianus Marcellinus, bk 22, ch
8; see also Sozomen, *Hist. Eccl.*, bk 9 ch. 12, who lists the Alani among the Suevi
and the Vandals.

[267] For the *Grosse Volker Wanderung* from the 3rd century on, see Pauly
Wassova, and Walter Pohl, *Die Awaren: ein Stepppenvolk in Mitteleuorpa, 567-822*
(Munich, C.H. Beck, 1988); see also Ostrogorsky, *History of the Byzantine State*,
pp. 60-3.

Nominibus variis, una sed origine[a] Gotthi,[b]
    Nascitur ex una pustula multa lue.[c]
Et tandem Italiam crebris successibus implent,[d]
    Et miscent verbis verba Latina[e] suis,
Et Gentem[f] genti.[g] Romanam possidet urbem
    Gotthus;[h] sed doctus sacra Latina priùs.[i]
Atque[j] sui Gotthis (ut Graecis atque Latinis)
    Catholicique inerant, Haereticique viri.
Post hunc regnavit Jovianus mensibus[k] octo,[l]
    Christicolis demptas reddidit ille Scholas.[m]   **940**
Catholicus fuit ille quidem, sed legibus uti
    Aequis Catholicos,[n] Haereticosque jubet.
Quo facto moritur;[o] tanquam si sceptra tulisset,[p]
    Esset ut in tuto libera cuique Fides.[q]
Romana accipiens tunc fraena Valentinianus
    De sacra[r] mutat Relligione nihil.[s]

---

[a] A Origine • [b] uA B Gothi A Gothi; C Gothi. • [c] mv uA B lues. • [d] A implent
B implént, • [e] A B C latina • [f] B C gentem • [g] A Genti. • [h] uA B Gothus C
Gothus; • [i] A B C prius. • [j] A B (Atque • [k] A Mensibus • [l] A Octo; • [m] B C
scholas. • [n] uA B Catholicos • [o] uA B moritur, • [p] A B tulisset • [q] A C fides. •
[r] A Sacra • [s] A Nihil.

Although they had various names, the Goths had a common origin, many
pustules come from a single disease.

And finally, as a result of their frequent invasions, they filled Italy, and
they mixed Latin words with their own words,

And the Latin race with their own race. The Goths occupied the city of
Rome,[268] having first learned the Latin rites.

And the Goths (like the Greeks and Latins) had among them their own
Catholics and heretics.

After Julian, Jovian[269] ruled for eight months, and returned to the
Christians the Schools that had been taken from them.   940

He was in fact a Catholic, but he ordered Catholics and heretics to abide
by the same laws.[270]

Having done this, he died, just as if he had only borne the sceptre in order
to ensure that Faith should be free and safe for all.

Valentinian,[271] then took over the reins of Rome and did not alter religious
practice at all.[272]

---

[268] 'Hobbes alludes to the celebrated sack of Rome of 410, conducted in fact by
the Visigoths according to King Alaric. The Goths in general were Arians (c.f., lines
1005ff.)' (Invernizzi note).

[269] *Jovian, an ardent Christian, who secured a peace treaty with the Persians in
exchange for giving up its claims to Armenia as well as considerable territory in
Mesopotamia, ruled in 363-4. Socrates (*Hist Eccl.*, ii, 24-6) presents him as settling
the re-emergent orthodox-Arian controversy, which Sozomen, although devoting
several chapters to his reign (*Hist. Eccl.*, bk 6 chs 3 to 6), does not mention. See
Ostrogorsky, *History of the Byzantine State*, p. 51 and Trompf, *Early Christian Historiography*, p. 228.

[270] Jovian recalled *Athanasius from exile to put an end to the doctrinal disputes
against the Trinity, but in his brief to Jovian, *Ad Jovianum de fide* (*PG* XXVI, cols
811-24), Athansius had reintroduced the thorny issue of *homoousios* to which Jovian
refused to subscribe, admitting a semi-Arian construction of the Trinity. Theodoret,
Hist. Eccl., also records Athansius's letter to Jovian (in Mansi, ed., *Sacrorum conciliorum nova et amplissima collectio*, vol. 3, p. 366). On these issues and Jovian's
legislation and law of toleration, see Hefele, *Histoire des conciles*, 1.2.5, p. 973 n. 2,
citing Sozomen, *Hist. Eccl.*, bk 6, ch. 4; and Socrates, *Hist. Eccl.*, bk 3, ch. 5, *PG*
LXVII, col. 454. The Constitution of Jovian is extant in the Theodosian Code.

[271] *Valentinian I (321-375), Roman Emperor ruling jointly from 364 with his
brother *Valens, whom Hobbes does not name, (Invernizzi note).

[272] In fact the theological debates continued under Valentinian, who was Orthodox and had been imprisoned and exiled under Julian, and Valens who was Arian and
initiated persecutions which saw the eventual death of Athanasius in AD 373. A
plethora of theological councils was convened under Valentinian and Valens, including the councils of Lampsachus, AD 365; of Nicomedia, AD 366; at Smyrna and in
general throughout Asia Minor. See Sozomen, *Hist. Eccl.* bk 6 ch 7-40 and Hefele,
Histoire des conciles, 1.2.5, pp. 973-87, citing Athanasius, Theodoret, and Hilary.

Nec qui successit cui nomen Gratia[a] fecit.[b]
    Paci juncta fides dulcis utrique fuit.
Sec. Quem tulit effectum concessa licentia tanta?
    Pr.[c] Nec pax consequitur nec bene certa Fides.[d]   **950**
Qui non audebant Deitatem tollere Christo,[e]
    Spiritui Sancto tollere non dubitant.
Impietatis erat tantae Macedonius Author,[f]
    Qui Byzantinas ore regebat oves.
Audax Orator;[g] torrentis more sonorus,[h]
    Turbidus atque celer,[i] non tamen altus erat.
Jamque iterum in partes Ecclesia scinditur. Iras
    Aeternae vitae mutua cura facit.[j]
Sec. Unde meae vobis commissa est cura Salutis[k]
    Theiologi? Sine me consulitisne[l] mihi?[m]   **960**
Cur non et sine te liceat mihi cogere quemque
    Vestrum,[n] quod sperat,[o] quaerere more meo?

---

[a] uA C gratia • [b] B fecit • [c] mv A *Pr.* omitted • [d] A fides, B Fides, C fides. •
[e] A B Christo; • [f] B C author, • [g] uA B Orator, C orator; • [h] A B sonorus • [i] A
Celer, B celer • [j] mv uA B fuit. • [k] A B C salutis • [l] mv uA B consuluistisne •
[m] mv C mihi • [n] A B C Vestrum • [o] uA B C sperat

Nor did the Emperor who succeeded him, whose name was Gratian.[273]
The combination of faith and peace was sweet to both of them.[274]

Sec. What effect did the granting of such great freedom have?

Pr. Neither peace nor sufficiently firm faith resulted,[275]   **950**

Men who did not dare take divinity away from Christ, did not hesitate to take it away from the Holy Spirit.

The instigator of such great impiety was Macedonius[276] who ruled the Byzantine flock by the strength of his voice.

He was a bold orator, loud, turbulent and swift like a raging river, but he was nevertheless not deep.[277]

And so now the Church was again torn into factions. Concern on all sides about eternal life bred anger.

Sec. When was concern about my salvation entrusted to you, oh Theologians? Are you consulting my interest without consulting me?   **960**

Why am I not to be allowed, without your leave, to compel any of your people to look for what he hopes for in *my* way?[278]

---

[273] Gratian (359-383), succeeds his father in 375, together with his step-brother, Valentinian II, of whom little is said.

[274] Sozomen, *Hist. Eccl.*, bk 7, chs 1-2. Gratian, the son of Valentinian I, was Orthodox like his father, promulgating his own law of toleration to all but the Manicheans, Photinians, and Eunomians (see Hefele, *Histoire des conciles*, 1.2.5, pp. 984-5).

[275] Gratian's tolerance was sorely tried by the aggressive Macedonian Arians, resulting in three major councils, at Antioch in AD 378, and the councils of Milan and Saragossa in AD 380 (see Hefele, *Histoire des conciles*, 1.2.5, pp. 984-7).

[276] *Macedonius was a priest at Constantinople around 335 and was implicated in the tumultuous events of Bishop Paul, later exiled from the city. Whatever his true theological position might have been, he was considered the instigator from 360 of the debate over the Holy Spirit, whose divine status he denied. (Invernizzi note). For the heresy of Macedonius, an Arian, see Sozomen, *Hist. Eccl.*, bk 3, ch. 3, bk 4, chs 21-27, and bk 5, ch. 4.

[277] Note the Orthodox and even-handed Sozomen, a lawyer who could present both sides fairly, and perhaps commended himself to Hobbes for that reason, reports in the *Hist. Eccl.*, bk 3, ch. 3, that the Arian Macedonians themselves believed Bishop Paul of Constantinople was more skilled than Macedonius as an orator, but that Macedonius was held in high regard for his integrity compared with the licentiousness of Bishop Paul.

[278] *Lev.*, xlvi, §37, 378/466, addresses the following 'error', which is:
> To extend the power of the law, which is the rule of actions only, to the very thoughts and consciences of men, by examination and inquisition of what they hold, notwithstanding the conformity of their speech and actions. By which men are either punished for answering the truth of their thoughts, or constrained to answer an untruth for fear of punishment . . . . But to force him to accuse himself of opinions, when his actions are not by law forbidden, is against the law of nature (and especially in them, who teach that a man shall

Quod si praeceptis rem tantam credere vestris[a]
    Insanus cupiam,[b] quis mihi ductor erit?
Nam dum continuò[c] pugnatis,[d] nescio cujum
    Sum pecus; et videor neutrius esse mihi.
Hoc scio,[e] sum Christi, qui jussit regibus[f] omnes
    Auscultare suis. Rex mihi rector[g] erit,[h]
Rex mihi rector[i] erit Vocis;[j] Mens[k] libera soli
    Parebit domino,[l] quo velit ille modo.   **970**
Jam Divina[m] Libro[n] defixit Gratia Sacro[o]
    Quam servabo Fidem;[p] si tamen ille velit.
Quam (puto) Doctorum sententia nulla refiget;[q]
    Sed nec eo Patriae[r] jura tenebo minus.
Quid nobis Arius, quid Athanasius? Reperitur
    In solo sacro Codice[s] plena[t] salus.
Unde igitur Patrum[u] discordia tanta profecta est,
    Si non ambitio maxima causa fuit?
Indignum Doctis[v] non Reges esse putabant
    Philosophi; pecudum nos habuere loco.   **980**

---

[a] A B vestris, • [b] C cupiam • [c] A C continuo • [d] uA B pugnatis • [e] uA B C scio • [f] A Regibus • [g] A Rector • [h] A erit. • [i] A Rector • [j] A C vocis; B Vocis, • [k] uA C mens • [l] C domino • [m] A B C divina • [n] uA C libro • [o] uA C sacro. • [p] uA fidem, B C fidem; • [q] A B refiget, • [r] A C patriae • [s] A C codice • [t] mv A plenae • [u] A C patrum • [v] A B C doctis

But if I insanely desire to entrust such a great matter to your control, who
will be my leader?

In fact, while you continually fight, I don't know whose flock I belong
to,[279] and I see myself belonging to neither side.

But this I know, I belong to Christ, who commanded all men to obey their
own kings. My king will be the guide for me.

My king will be the master of my words.[280] My unfettered mind will obey
my lord alone, in whatever manner he wishes.   **970**

Divine Grace has already fixed firmly in the Holy Bible what faith I shall
observe, provided that my lord wishes it.[281]

No opinion of the Doctors (I believe) will cancel that faith, yet I shall not
uphold the laws of my country any less.

What is Arius to us, what is Athanasius to us? Full salvation is found in
the sacred texts alone.

But what then was the origin of such great discord among the Church
Fathers if ambition was not the most prominent cause?

The philosophers thought it was unworthy of educated men not to be
kings; they considered us cattle.[282]   **980**

---

be damned to eternal and extreme torments if he die in a false opinion concerning an article of the Christian faith). For who is there, that knowing there
is so great danger in an error, whom the natural care of himself compelleth not
to hazard his soul upon his own judgement, rather than that of any other man
that is unconcerned in his damnation?

[279] Virgil *Ecl.* 3.1.

[280] In the 1668 Appendix to the *LL* (ed. Wright, §132-3, p. 371) Hobbes stakes
out a radically Erastian position on state-sanctioned religion. In the English *Lev.*,
xlvi, §42, 379/468, Hobbes makes a startling claim which points in the same direction: 'For disobedience may lawfully be punished in them that against the laws
teach even true philosophy'. 'Is it because they tend to disorder in government, as
countenancing rebellion or sedition?', he asks: 'Then let them be silenced, and the
teachers punished, by virtue of his power to whom the care of the public quiet is
committed (which is the authority civil).'

[281] A bald restatement of Daniel Scargill's position. See Springborg Introduction, chapter 3.2. But see also *Luther, The Reformation Writings of Martin Luther,
Bertram Lee Wolf, tr. (London, 1956), 2 vols, vol. 1, p. 117:
   The social corpus of Christendom includes secular government as one of its
   component functions. This government is spiritual in status although it dis-
   charges a secular duty. It should operate freely and unhindered upon all the
   members of the Christian corpus.
Marsilius, Luther and Hobbes all agree that the state has a monopoly of government,
ecclesiastical and civil.

[282] Hobbes is attacking the Platonist position of rule by experts. See Alison
Brown, 'Platonism in Fifteenth-Century Florence and its Contribution to Early
Modern Political Thought', *Journal of Modern History* vol. 58 (1986) pp. 383-413.

Pr.[a] Post hunc Theudosiusque,[b] puerque Valentinianus
    (Theudosius Magnus) Sceptra[c] habuere simul.[d]
Vicerat hic Gotthos,[e] et eos servire coegit[f]
    Victos,[g] sed certa conditione,[h] sibi.
Hic et Iberinis victas ejecerat arvis
    Gentes Vandalicas, Haereticum populum;[i]
Imperii summa meruit virtute coronam;[j]
    Jure etiam tenuit cum sibi dante pari.
Catholicus fuit et multum praebebat honorem
    Praelatis sanctis[k] de grege[l] Catholico.[m]   **990**
Nec nisi concordi censebat milite bella
    Contra concordes,[n] prospera,[o] posse geri.

---

[a] mv uA *Pr.* missing • [b] mv A B Theudosius • [c] A C sceptra • [d] A B simul •
[e] uA B C Gothos • [f] A B coegit, • [g] uA Victos • [h] uA B conditione • [i] A
populum, B populum. • [j] A B coronam • [k] A Sanctis • [l] A Grege B gregè •
[m] mv A B Catholico • [n] uA B concordes • [b] uA B prospera

Pr. After Gratian Theodosius the Great[283] and the boy Valentinian[284] ruled at the same time.

Theodosius had conquered the Goths and forced them in defeat to be his slaves, but under fixed conditions.[285]

He had also defeated the Vandal tribes[286] and expelled this heretic people from the Spanish plains;[287]

He earned the imperial Crown through his supreme courage;

and he even held it by a right equal to that of him who bestowed it.[288]

Theodosius was a Catholic and he paid great honour to the holy prelates of the Catholic flock,[289]   **990**

He believed also that only by a united soldiery could successful wars be waged against united adversaries.[290]

---

[283] Theodosius the Great, Roman Emperor, c. 346-95, an Orthodox Christian and rigorous defender of the Nicene Creed. Sozomen devotes an entire book to Theodosius, *Hist. Eccl.*, bk 7, chs 1-29; see also the Arian view of him represented by Philostorgius, *Hist. Eccl.*, bk 9 chs 15-19, bk 10, chs 1-12, and Hefele, *Histoire des conciles*, 1.2.5., pp. 987-8.

[284] 'Valentinian II, 371-92, in reality always played a role much subordinate to Theodosius (347-395), emperor from 379' (Invernizzi note).

[285] See Ostrogorsky, *History of the Byzantine State*, pp. 52-3:
Once the Goths had been driven back behind the Balkan Mountains, the Emperor concluded an agreement (*foedus*) with them. The Ostrogoths were to settle in Pannonia, the Visigoths in the Northern districts of the diocese of Thrace. They were granted complete autonomy, exemption from taxation, and a high rate of pay for their military services; they were to be enlisted as *foederati* in the imperial service. Many even chose to serve directly under the Emperor. . . . All the same this solution only meant that a hostile Germanic invasion had been converted into a peaceful one. . . . Theodosius' policy towards the Goths had another side to it, for it entailed a considerable drain on the exchequer.

[286] The *Vandals, a Germanic people originally based in southern Scandinavia, had reached Silesia around AD 200.

[287] Valentinian I had ruled the West for himself and given the East to his younger brother, Valens. Theodosius I in contrast made his elder son Arcadius ruler of the East and assigned the West to the younger Honorius. But Hobbes seems to have confused Theodosius I and *Theodosius II. It was the latter who had the confrontation with the Vandals, who reached Spain about 411, but even he did not beat them.

[288] Note that Theodosius I was regent during Valentinian II's minority, but he ruled as full emperor *de facto*, rather than *de jure*, in other words, by his deeds he made himself worthy of equal status, without exceeding the law.

[289] Note Ostrogorsky, *History of the Byzantine State*, p. 53:
Theodosius ardently upheld the Nicene creed and supported orthodoxy with all his strength, bitterly opposing both pagans and heretical Christian sects. It was during his reign that Christianity became the state religion, thus gaining a position of monopoly, while other religions and beliefs were denied the right to exist.

[290] See Ostrogorsky, *History of the Byzantine State*, p. 53, of Theodosius's army after the conquest of the Goths and his policy of appeasement:

His Synodum[a] causis indixit. Episcopus omnis
    Constantinopolin,[b] jussus adire,[c] venit.
Spiritus hîc Sanctus decernitur esse colendus
    Ut Deus,[d] et credi de numero esse Dei.[e]
Hîc[f] quoque firmantur Synodûs[g] decreta Nicenae
    Omnia; Christicolûm[h] perficiturque Fides.[i]
Post hunc successit Honorius, Arcadiusque,[j]
    Principe Theudosio natus uterque patre.[k]   **1000**
In partes iterum Regnum discinditur. Ille
    Occiduas Aquilas,[l] hic Orientis habet.

---

[a] A C synodum • [b] uA B Constantinopolim • [c] uA B adire • [d] A B Deus • [e] B
Dei • [f] A B C Hic • [g] uA B Synodus mv C synodi • [h] A B C Christicolum •
[o] ~ A Fides C fides. • [j] A B Arcadiusque • [k] A B Patre • [l] uA C aquilas,

And he called a Council for this reason.[291] Every bishop came to
Constantinople, having been commanded to attend.[292]
At this Council[293] it was decided that the Holy Spirit should be
worshipped as God, and should be believed to be counted as God.
The Synod also confirmed all the decrees of the Nicene Council; and the
faith of Christians achieved its definitive form.
After him Honorius[294] and Arcadius,[295] both sons of the Emperor
Theodosius, then succeeded to the throne,[296]   **1000**
And again the kingdom was split into two parts. Honorius having
command of the West,[297] Arcadius of the East.[298]

The German element in the army became so predominant that the greater
number of the troops came from this source, and the most important comman-
ders were German.

[291] Theodosius called the *Council at Constantinople in 381, and subsequent councils at Bordeaux in 385, Trier in 386, Rome in 386, Telepte or Zelle in 418, Antioch in
388 or 389, Sida in 390, and two councils of Carthage between 386 and 390, councils
at Rome and Milan in 390, Capua in 391, a series of councils beginning with Hippo in
393, and Nimes in 394, dying in 395. See Hefele, *Histoire des conciles* 2.1.8, pp. 1-97.

[292] 'The first Council of Constantinople was held in 381. Hobbes does not make
mention of the Edict of Thessalonica of 380 which imposed the Catholic faith on the
Emperor's subjects' (Invernizzi note).

[293] Hobbes uses *synodus -i* (f.), first introduced at line 490, (= Gr. *sunodos*),
college of priests (*Inscr. Orell.* 1.1, 21.60, 26.27); an ecclesiastical assembly or
council (*Codex Just.* 1.3.23; Amm. 15.7.7), a synod. But the more usual Latin term
for council is *concilium*. This usuage, taken together with his repeated use of the
term Presbyter, suggests Hobbes sees a parallel with the (Presbyterian) Westminster
Assembly of Divines of July 1643, which debated whether the Jewish Sanhedrin
should be a model for Christian polities and, if so, whether it set an Erastian or
dualist model of church government (see Springborg Introduction, chapter 5.2).

[294] *Honorius, (384-423), younger son of Theodosius I. See Sozomen, *Hist.
Eccl.*, bk 9 ch. 16.

[295] For *Arcadius (371-408), see Philostorgius, *Hist. Eccl.*, bk 10 ch. 5, bk 11
chs 3-6.

[296] Honorius in the Occident, Arcadius in the Orient. The *Hist. Eccl.* of Socrates
Scholasticus and Eusebius (completed by Rufinus) take us only this far, concluding with
the promulgation of the Theodosian Code, AD 439, an ambitious synthesis of the con-
stitutions from Constantine on. See Chestnut, *The First Christian Historians*, pp. 168-
9, 196. Hereafter Hobbes's early sources comprise Sozomen, Theodoret and Evagrius.

[297] Literally, 'the former held the Eagles of the West, the latter of the East'. Each
legion of the Roman army had a chapel at its permanent station where the statues of
the gods and emperors and the standards of the unit, and particularly the eagle associated with the *genius* and *virtus* of the legion, were venerated (*OCD*, 1970, p. 1011).

[298] Ostrogorsky, *History of the Byzantine State*, pp. 53-4, notes that even though
Theodosius was from the far Western empire, he judged the East more important,
putting his elder son, Arcadius, in charge there, and reserving the West for the
younger Honorius.

Tunc Gotthis ducibus concessa à[a] Caesare pridem
    Audent Romani jura[b] negare Duces.[c]
Corripiunt enses Gotthi, Romamque petentes
    Accipiunt Urbem[d] sub ditione sua;[e]
Aequassetque[f] solo fortassis Alaricus Urbem
    Dimidii mundi[g] quae caput antè[h] fuit,[i]
Si non Romanus venientibus obvius isset
    Papa,[j] ferens Christi jura,[k] praecesque suas.   **1010**

---

[a] A a • [b] mv uA B jure • [c] A C duces. • [d] B C urbem • [e] A suâ; •
[f] A Aequâssetque • [g] A mundi, • [h] A B C ante • [i] A fuit. B fuit • [j] A Papa •
[k] A B jura

Then the Roman generals dared to deny the generals of the Goths the
rights granted them long ago by the emperor.[299]
The Goths took up their swords, advanced on Rome and had the city in
their power.[300]
Perhaps Alaric[301] would have razed to the ground the city which once was
capital of half the world[302]
Had the Roman Pope not gone to meet the advancing Goths, bearing the
authority of Christ and his own entreaties.[303]   **1010**

---

[299] See Ostrogorsky, *History of the Byzantine State*, pp. 54:
Under Theodosius' sons there was continual rivalry between the rapid succession of regions who governed for the weak Arcadius, and the powerful
German Stilicho who controlled the West for more than ten years in the name
of the young Honorius. A severe crisis threatened to undermine the policy
towards the Goths which Theodosius had initiated.

[300] Invernizzi notes: 'Hobbes's narrative suggests some perplexity because, as
is seen above [lines 935-6] the sack effectively had taken place. *Pope Innocent I
was not even at Rome in this period. Hobbes perhaps conflates the sack of 410 with
the two descents on Rome of Alaric in 408 and 409, which were concluded without
the sack of the city. Otherwise it refers to the fact that Alaric effectively spared some
churches, in particular Sts Peter and Paul Outside-the-Walls, buildings which served
as asylums to citizens in flight from the sacking. Perhaps Hobbes really confuses the
events of Alaric with those of Atilla'. The matter is more complex than this,
however, for even among the early ecclesiastical historiographers the sack of Rome,
as a 'critical event' is treated very differently. As noted in Springborg, introduction,
chapter 4.3, Socrates Scholasticus, *Hist. Eccl.* book v, uses it as an example of 'the
'critical moment', while Evagrius ignored it. See Chestnut, *The First Christian Historians,* pp. 186, 217.

[301] *Alaric, Visigoth leader, an Arian, besieged Rome three times from 408 to
410.

[302] See Sozomen, *Hist. Eccl.*, bk 9 chs 6-7, Philostorgius, *Hist. Eccl.*, bk 12 chs
2-3. See Ostrogorsky, *History of the Byzantine State*, pp. 54-5:
The Visigoths rose under Alaric and ravaged the entire Balkan peninsula to
the walls of Constantinople and the southernmost regions of Greece. Dis-
sention between the two Roman governments prevented effective opposition,
and peace was only bought at a price: the eastern government appointed
Alaric as the imperial *magister militum per Illyricum* while the Goth Gainas
received the office of *magister militum praesantalis* and entered Constantinople with his troops. This provoked an anti-German party in the Byzantine
capital which grew steadily in strength, and by the beginning of the fifth
century had succeeded in gaining control of the situation. . . . The eastern half
was soon free of Alaric who withdrew with his army to Italy, and after three
attempts at investing Rome took the city by storm in 410.

[303] Sozomen, *Hist. Eccl.*, bk 9 ch. 7, mentions the embassy sent by Pope Innocent to Alaric, which held him off for a while, but did not prevent his eventual siege
of Rome.

Sed flexus pietate viri,[a] Rex cessit,[b] et ipsum
      Protegere incolumi jussit in urbe gregem;
Sic tamen ut tantum jus danti[c] subditus esset,
      Et successuris Regibus Italiae.[d]
Hoc quoque nactus erat, dum miles crederet illi
      De Verbo Domini; deque salute sua,[e]
De Fidei[f] mercede;[g] quot essent gaudia coelis,[h]
      Et bona Catholicis[i] quanta parata viris;[j]
Quantus amor fratrum;[k] quam suavis cantio,[l] quando
      Concinit Angelicus,[m] Catholicusque Chorus.[n]   1020
Haereticis contrà[o] quas servant Tartara poenas;[p]
      Quas ignis flammas,[q] quas[r] tenebrasque[s] simul;
Ardentesque animas,[t] etiam clam corpore, quàmque[u]
      Aeterni colubri vulnera saeva dolent.
De forma et vultu tortoris, ut illius ore
      Spiret saevities, emineantque minae.
Haec inquam miles cum crederet, eligeretque
      Idem,[v] cui Romae[w] sceptra gerenda daret;
Ne[x] dubita quin eligeret quem Papa volebat,
      Dummodo Catholicum;[y] si numerusque sinat;   1030

---

[a] uA B viri • [b] uA B C cessit • [c] mv A dandi • [d] A Italiae • [e] A B sua. • [f] A C fidei • [g] A B mercede, • [h] A B coelis • [i] A B Catholicis, • [j] A B viris, • [k] A B fratrum • [l] B cantio • [m] A Angelicus • [n] A C chorus. • [o] A B C contra • [p] uA B C poenas • [q] A B flammas • [r] mv A B quasque • [s] mv A B tenebras • [t] uA B animas • [u] A B C quamque • [v] uA B Idem • [w] A B Romae, • [x] A B Nec • [y] A B Catholicum,

But bowing to the piety of this man, the king of the Goths withdrew and
ordered his army to protect the flock in the city as yet unharmed;[304]
But on condition that he should be subordinate to the person who granted
such a right, and to the kings who would succeed him in Italy.
Even so, the concession was obtained only as long as the army had trust
in the Pope concerning the Word of God and their own salvation;[305]
Concerning the rewards of faith, how many joys there were in heaven,
and how great were the comforts prepared for Catholics;
How great the love of brothers, how sweet the song, when the angelic and
Catholic chorus sing together;   1020
On the other hand, what punishments Hell has in store for heretics, what
flames of fire and at the same time what darkness;
And souls burning, even without the body, and how the cruel wounds of
the eternal serpent give them pain;
And about the form and appearance of the torturer, that he fiercely
breathes and threats emanate from his mouth.
When the army believed all this, as I said, and was able to choose the man
to whom it would give the power to rule Rome,[306]
Do not doubt that it would choose the candidate the Pope wanted, so long
he was a Catholic and if the majority approved,   1030

---

[304] See Sozomen, *Hist. Eccl.*, bk 9, ch. 9., who records that in 410 Alaric took
Rome, entering and plundering the city, but left its buildings standing. Out of respect
for the Apostle Peter, he refused to desecrate the church built over his tomb, a placatory gesture which earned his acceptance. Invernizzi notes: 'While Alaric laid siege to
Rome in AD 408 and 409 without sacking the city, the siege of Atilla in 410 did conclude by sacking the city, although certain churches outside the walls were spared'.

[305] Lines 115-26 list the things the soldiers have to believe. The construction is
careless and not easy to translate.

[306] Note that the 1722 paraphrase rewords all this as advice from the Pope to the
king about what he should believe. But the point of Hobbes ascribing it to the army
is that, were not the army already won over, kings could not fall. In fact in all the doc-
trinals struggles to AD 500 the Bishop of Rome plays a minor role compared with the
emperors and the bishops of Alexandria and Constantinople. *Pope Leo I's intervention in the struggle with the Eutychians at the *Council of Chalcedon, called by Eutyches the Archimandrite in 448, who accused the orthodox party of being the heretics
(see Hefele, *Histoire des conciles*, 2.1.10, pp. 514-16), and on the written invitation
of the devout emperor and empress, Marcian and Pulcheria, in AD 450, marks a new
departure (see Hefele, *Histoire des conciles* 2.1.10, pp. 631-46; and Gregory, *Urban
Violence*, pp. 212-68). See also Hefele, *Histoire des conciles* 2.1.11, pp. 667-9, on the
division of power between the imperial bureaucracy and the papal legates. While the
emperor presided to see that the council complied with the rules, the council recognized the superiority of the pope by deference to his legates, without whose participation and authorization nothing was legal, further recognizing his suzerainty by
requesting written endorsement by the pope for its acts.

Si quoque non alii Regni[a] tribuisset habenas[b]
    Qui prior in manibus jure tenebat eas.
Sec. Theiologi verò[c] concordes,[d] credo,[e] fuere
    Jam de Personis[f] in Deitate[g] tribus;
Vel tacuere metu legum, quas sanxerat ante,[h]
    Theudosius,[i] multas,[j] Haereticisque malas.
Pr. Verum ut Theudosius naturae Legibus[k] ille
    Magnus concessit, fitque timente minor,
Veste nova rursus prodit vetus[l] Haeresis;[m] Unà[n]
    Secum prodibat docta caterva virûm.   **1040**
Hi clamant Christos plures non esse, sed unum;[o]
    Naturasque negant unius esse duas.

---

[a] A B C regni • [b] C habenas, • [c] C vero • [d] uA B concordes • [e] uA B C credo
• [f] A B C personis • [g] C deitate • [h] A B ante C ante, • [i] A B C Theudosius •
[j] A multas • [k] A B C legibus • [l] A vetusque • [m] A B haeresis. C haeresis; •
[n] B Una C una • [o] uA B unum,

And provided also that the man who previously held the reins of the
kingdom in his hands by right had not already given them to another.

Sec. But the theologians I believe were now of one mind about the three
persons of the deity,

Or else they were silent through fear of the laws, which Theodosius had
earlier decreed, and many harmful to heretics.[307]

Pr. But actually, when the great Theodosius yielded to the laws of nature
and became less than those who feared him,[308]

An old heresy once again returned, but dressed in new clothes.[309]

A learned band of men came forward with it, at the same time.   **1040**
These men proclaimed that there were not many Christs, and they deny
that one being could have two natures.[310]

---

[307] Theodosius in 380 published the famous edict in which he threatened
heretics and exhorted all his subjects to profess the orthodox faith. Thereafter he
confiscated the property of those who refused to conform, publishing new edicts in
381. See Hefele, *Histoire des conciles*, 1.2.5, p. 988.

[308] i.e., he was tolerant. On Hobbes's relatively more lenient position on tolerance in the *Hist. Eccl.*, compared with *Leviathan*, see Paganini, 'Thomas Hobbes e
Lorenzo Valla', pp. 538-9, who points to Hobbes's use of Matthew 13:24-27, the
parable of the wheat and the tares to argue that Christ had recommended that the
wheat and the tares were not to be separated until the last day. See also Johann Sommerville, 'Hobbes, Selden, Erastianism, and the History of the Jews'; and Franck
Lessay, 'Hobbes and Sacred History', pp. 147-59.

[309] For the long struggle between *Nestorius and *Cyril of Alexandria (d. AD
444) that culminated in the deposition of Nestorius at the *Council of Ephesus of
431, see Hefele, *Histoire des conciles* 2.1.9, pp. 233-422. For the struggle with the
*Monophysites between Theodoret supporter of Nestorius and leading critic of
Cyril; Eutyches the Archimandrite, who began on the side of Cyril against the
Nestorians but ended up leader of the Monophysite heresy; and the orthodox Irenaeus, see Hefele, *Histoire des conciles*, 2.1.10, pp. 499-554, citing Cyril *Contr.
Nest.*, bk 2 ch. 6, *PG* LXXVI, col. 84ff.; Theodoret's *Epist. LXXX, Ad Eutychium*
and *Eranistes seu Polymorphus* AD 447 (*PG* LXXXIII, cols 1276 ff. and 27ff.). The
latter, which translates as *The Beggar or Multiform*, comprises three philosophical
dialogues on the theological significance of these variants of the Arian heresy, all of
which turned on the issue of Christ being made flesh, depicting the Monophysites as
beggars, and passing off their doctrines as gathered by scraps from diverse heretical
sources; see also Irenaeus, *Adversus Haereses*, bk 3 ch. 19, *PG* VII, col. 938
(Hefele, *Histoire des conciles*, 2.1.10 pp. 499-503 and 2.1.9, p. 219).

[310] Hobbes alludes to the Monophysite heresy, initiated by Eutyches the Archimandrite. See Ostrogorsky, *History of the Byzantine State*, p. 58:

> The theological school of Antioch taught that there were two separate natures
> co-existent in Christ. The chosen vessel of the Godhead was Christ, the man
> born of Mary – hence the contention that Mary was not the Mother of God
> (*theotokos*) but the Mother of Christ (*Christotokos*). In sharp opposition to this
> rationalist conception was the mystical Alexandrian teaching of God made
> man in whom the divine and human natures were united.

Dicite utram vultis, nam possum[a] credere utramvis;[b]
     Res est difficilis credere utramque simul.
Catholicus regerit[c] cur non potes impie utramque?[d]
     Anne ignota tibi est Unio[e] Hypostatica?[f]
Nota.[g] Et[h] ob hoc ipsum non possum credere utramque;[i]
     Una est, quas unit Unio[j] Hypostatica.[k]
Concilium rursus placuit generale vocari;
     Et resonat rixis urbs[l] Ephesina sacris.[m]   **1050**
Unde redit tristis ter[n] victaque pars Ariana,[o]
     Non convicta tamen;[p] sed neque muta diu.

---

[a] mv A uB possem • [b] A B utramvis • [c] A B regerit, • [d] mv ~A utramque •
[e] uA B C unio • [f] uA Hypostatica • [g] uA Nota • [h] uA et • [i] uA B utramque, •
[j] uA B C unio • [k] uA B C hypostatica. • [l] A Urbs • [m] A Sacris. • [n] mv A B tres
• [o] ~ A Ariana • [p] uA B tamen,

[311]Declare which nature you want, for I can believe one or the other, the difficult thing is to believe both natures at the same time.

The Catholic insists, 'why can't you believe both natures, you impious man? Don't you know about the Hypostatic Union?'[312]

I do know about it, and for that very reason I cannot believe both natures. The Hypostatic Union brings together both natures so that they are one.[313]

It was resolved to call a general Council again, and the city of Ephesus echoed with holy quarrels.[314]   1050

So the ill-humoured Arian faction returned, again defeated but not refuted and not silent for long.[315]

---

[311] Lines 1043-4 quote what the Monophysites say, lines 1045-6 give the Catholic reply, and lines 1047-8 a response to the reply. The passage reads as if lines 1043-4 and 1047-8 should be distributed to Secundus, and lines 1045-6 and lines 1049ff. to Primus.

[312] In the *Hist. Narr.* (*EW* IV, p. 401) Hobbes argued:

> In the general confession of faith contained in the creed called the Nicene Creed, there is no mention of *hypostasis*, nor of hypostatical union, nor of corporeal, nor of incorporeal, nor of parts; the understanding of which words being not required of the vulgar, but only of the pastors, whose disagreement else might trouble the church; nor were such points necessary to salvation but set abroach for ostentation of learning, or else to dazzle men, with design to lead them towards some ends of their own.

Noted in Gianni Paganini, 'Hobbes, Valla e i problemi filosofici della teologia umanistica', p. 43n.

[313] The expression 'hypostatic union' goes back to Cyril, Bishop of Alexandria, who had used it to attack the positions of Nestorius, Patriarch of Constantinople from 428 to 439. See the 1575 Latin edition Cyril of Alexandria's *Opera omnia*, listed in the Hardwick Hall book list at shelf mark G.3.8. Hobbes's most likely source for the hypostatic union was Martinus Chemnitz, *De duabus naturis in Christo: de hypostatica earum unione: de communicatione idiomatum, et aliis quæstionibus inde dependentibus, libellus, ex Scripturæ sententiis, & ex purioris antiquitatis testimonijs . . . studio . . . Martini Chemnicii* of 1578. The chief works of Chemnitz, a German Protestant Theologian (1522 1586) from Wittenberg, follower of Luther and Melanchthon, appear in the Hardwick Hall book list and this work may well be the *Chemnitii Theologia Jesuitica* listed at shelfmark M.4.14 (*q.v.*).

[314] This passage actually refers to two councils at Ephesus. The first being the third general council of 431 where Nestorius who was patriarch of Constantinople but an Arian believing in two separate natures coexistent in Christ, was condemned as a heretic by theologians led by Cyril, patriarch of Alexandria, called pharaoh, who was a Monophysite. The second council at Ephesus in 449 was later known as 'the Robber Council'. See Hefele, *Histoire des conciles*, 2.1.9, pp. 219-377, at 219, citing Tertullian, *Adversus Praxeam*, ch 27, *PL* II, col. 214; Origen, *Contra Celsum*, bk 3 ch 41, and *De Principiis*, bk 3 ch. 6, in *PG* XI cols 972 and 256. See also Ostrogorsky, *History of the Byzantine State*, pp. 58-9.

[315] 'Hobbes commits an error here. The Council of Ephesus (431) did not condemn the Monophysites (which then were not yet explicitly manifested as such), but on the contrary, the Nestorians. One can rather say that it was exactly the condemnation of Nestorius that set the basis for the development of Monophysitism.

Pòst[a] etenim,[b] Synodum[c] tenuit pars illa,[d] vocante
    Principe,[e] quo dubium, sed tenuere tamen;
Quae sua suffragiis stabilivit dogmata multis.[f]
    Sic lance aequata Theiologia stetit.
Et nisi Catholici Chalcedone consuluissent,
    Essent nunc illi forsitan Haeretici.[g]
Cuncta sed[h] ad normam Synodo revocantur ab illa
    Nicenae Fidei,[i] Catholicumque modum.[j]   **1060**
Haeresin, in plures formas[k] quae vertitur una,[l]
    Quam quondam Proteus, vincula nulla tenent:[m]
In Calcedonia Synodo damnata repressa est,
    Sed tamen ut verbis mox reditura novis:[n]

---

[a] A B C Post • [b] uA B etenim • [c] A C synodum • [d] A B illa; • [e] uA B Principe • [f] ~ uA multis; B multis C multis, • [g] A C haeretici. • [h] B séd • [i] A B fidei, C fidei • [j] A modum • [k] A formas, • [l] uA B una • [m] uA B tenent. • [n] A B novis.

Afterwards, in fact, that faction held a council;[316] – it is uncertain what
    emperor summoned it[317] – but they held it nevertheless;[318]
The faction established its doctrines with many votes,[319] and so Theology
    stood balanced on a level scales.
And had the Catholics not deliberated at Chalcedon[320] perhaps now they
    would be the heretics.[321]
All matters were restored by that Council to the norm of the Nicene Faith
    and to Catholic practice,   **1060**
Yet no chains could hold heresy, which, though it was all one, kept
    changing into more forms than Proteus[322] of old:
It was condemned in the Council of Chalcedon[323] and suppressed, but only
    to return later in different terms.

The first explicit condemnation of Eutyches took place later, at Constantinople in 448 in a local council.' (Invernizzi note).

[316] Hobbes refers to the *Robber Council, the second Council of Ephesus of 449 which, under the presidency of Dioscorus, Patriarch of Alexandria after Cyril's death in 444, briefly defeated the opposition and declared for monophysitism. See Hefele, *Histoire des conciles*, 2.1.10, pp. 584-606, citing the anonymous 5th century work, *Breviculus historiae Eutychianistarum*, PL LVIII, col. 929ff.

[317] The 'Robber Council' was in fact called by both Theodosius II and Valentinian III, ruling jointly, in March 449.

[318] Hefele, *Histoire des conciles*, 2.1.10, pp. 555-606, at p. 555-6, notes that doubts were expressed before the council was even called. The Pope, *Leo I, had wanted the council to be convened in Rome, because he feared the peace of the church was at risk. Although initially planning to attend, the letter of invitation was deliberately sent too late and he was represented by his legates with letters, including the famous dogmatic letter to Bishop Flavian.

[319] The Robber Council was so named by Catholics because of the way in which they were rapidly voted into the minority, and it was not recognized as an Ecumenical Council. See Invernizzi note.

[320] See Hefele, *Histoire des conciles*, 2.2.11, pp. 649-50, on the *Council of Chalcedon, AD 451.

[321] The Council of Chalcedon began in 451 and closed with the solemn condemnation of the Monophysites. Hobbes's conflation of the Monophysites and the Arians, was common. See Invernizzi note. See also Pope Leo I's famous letter of AD 449 to Flavian, the orthodox bishop of Constantinople, where he reviews the doctrinal controversies of the Nestorians and Monophysites, to reestablish orthodoxy, cited in Hefele, *Histoire des conciles*, 2.1.10, pp. 569-79.

[322] *Proteus, a minor sea god, who has the power to take all manner of shapes.

[323] See Ostrogorsky, *History of the Byzantine State*, p. 59:
    The standing patriarchal synod at Constantinople, the *synodos eudemousa*, condemned Eutyches [an Alexandrian] as a heretic, and Pope Leo I showed himself to be in agreement with the patriarchate of Constantinople by declaring in his famous *Tome* that the incarnate Christ was a single Person in whom two perfect natures could be distinguished.

Namque unam jussi personam dicere Christi,
    Scilicet ut nobis[a] esse, nec esse duas;[b]
Non plures una voluerunt dicere Christi[c]
    Esse voluntates;[d] unica quippe Patri est.
Graeca vocavit eos Ecclesia Mounothelitas;[e]
    (Haeresis[f] Imperio posthuma at illa fuit)[g]   1070
Nataque cum Synodos[h] generales Papa vocabat,
    (Neglecto dudum Principe) jure[i] suo.
Sec. Ille Voluntatem[j] Christi qui fecerit unam[k]
    Ut debet, quamvis crederet esse duas,[l]
Salvus erit.[m] Nihil haec vitae subtilia prosunt;[n]
    Zona[o] viatoris respuit hanc maciem.[p]
Non populum Veteris[q] docuit sic Foederis[r] author;
    Tale nihil dixit Sancta[s] Cathedra[t] Sinae.[u]
Sed contrà;[v] De me frustra quicunque loqueris,
    Non impunè[w] feres. Sum. Tibi sit satis hoc.   1080
Vos,[x] ô[y] Doctores Graeci,[z] cur dicitis uni
    Tres Hypostases[aa] simplici inesse Deo?

---

[a] A nobis, • [b] A duas. • [c] A Christi. C Christi, • [d] uA B voluntates, • [e] A B Mounothelitas • [f] mv A B Heresis • [g] sc mv A B 1688 fuit, (closing bracket missing) • [h] A C synodos • [i] B Jure • [j] A B voluntatem C voluntatem. • [k] A B unam, • [l] A B duas • [m] C erit: • [n] uA B prosunt, • [o] mv uA B Zana (error) • [p] A maciem, • [q] mv uA B foederis (transcription error) C veteris • [r] A B C foederis • [s] A B C sancta • [t] A B C cathedra • [u] A B Sinae • [v] A B C contra; • [w] A C impune • [x] A B Vos • [y] A o B ò • [z] uA B Graeci • [aa] A C hypostases

For when they were ordered to say that Christ was one person, as we are,
and not two persons,

Some wanted to say the will of Christ was one, not many, just as that of
the Father is a single will.

The Greek Church called those men Monothelites[324] (but that heresy
appeared after the end of the Empire),[325]   **1070**

And it arose when the Pope summoned the general councils by his own
authority (the authority of the emperor having long been disregarded).

Sec. The man who attributed to Christ one will, as he ought, will be
saved, even if he believed there were two,[326]

These subtleties are of no benefit to one's life; the wayfarer's money belt
spurns such poor stuff,[327]

The author of the Old Covenant[328] did not teach the people in this manner,
and the Holy Seat of Sinai said no such thing,

But on the contrary: 'Whoever takes my name in vain will not go
unpunished.[329] I am.[330] Let that be enough for you.'   **1080**

O Greek Doctors, why do you claim there are three persons in one single
God?[331]

---

[324] *Monothelitism arose in the 7th century as an attempt to reconcile orthodox
and Monophysite theologies by maintaining that, while Christ possessed two
natures, he had only one will. It was condemned as a heresy by the Third Council of
Constantinople in AD 680.

[325] Hobbes must mean at the end of the Western Empire, i.e., after AD 476.

[326] The initiator of this heresy was Sergius, Patriarch of Constantinople from
610 to 638. He was condemned by the Council of Constantinople of 680-1. With
regard to the Council convoked under the Pope's own authority (Martin I) c.f. lines
1631ff. (Invernizzi note).

[327] *argumentum ad crumenam:* (An argument to the purse); An appeal to one's
interest, a term in classical rhetoric.

[328] The covenant between God and Moses. See Ps. 105:26-45; Exodus 16:9-21,
31-2.

[329] The Seventh Commandment, Exodus 20, Deuteronomy 5:6-21: 'Thou shalt
not take the name of the LORD thy God in vain'.

[330] Exodus 3:14: 'And God said unto Moses "I am that I am".'

[331] Here Hobbes judges the Nicene Creed much more harshly than in the *Hist.
Narr.* (*EW* IV, p. 398), where he argued: 'And thus also it is expounded in the Creed
of Athanasius, who was present in that Council [Nicene], by these words, *not con-
founding the persons, nor dividing the substances*; that is to say, that God is not
divided into three persons, as man is divided into Peter, James and John; nor are the
three persons one and the same person.' Gianni Paganini, in 'Hobbes, Valla e i problemi filosofici della teologia umanistica', p. 44, notes that Hobbes is making a point
about the refusal of the Fathers to employ the Aristotelian language of genera and
species to insist that the relation between 'persons' of the Trinity is not that of different species of God, or different embodiments of the same substance; see *Hist.*

Quî[a] scitis ? Si non scitis,[b] ne dicite frustra :[c]
     Nuda Libri[d] Sacri[e] sint tibi verba satis.
Esse Deum Christum liber hic declarat apertè,[f]
     Atque Deo-genitum :[g] Quî[h] queat esse rogas ?
Stulte,[i] prius videas,[j] an possis[k] noscere ab actu
     Ipse tui Patris,[l] quòd[m] generandus eras.
Tu,[n] qui musca quid est,[o] aevum nescibis[p] in omne,
     Quid siet,[q] expectas,[r] improbe,[s] scire,[t] Deus ?   **1090**
Pharmaca peccatis summo ne tange palato.[u]
     Sanari si vis,[v] injice fortis hians.

---

[a] A B C Qui • [b] uA B scitis • [c] A B frustra • [d] uA B C libri • [e] uA B C sacri • [f] A B C aperte, • [g] A Deo genitum B Deo genitum. C Deo genitum ; • [h] uA B Qui C qui • [i] uA B Stulte • [j] uA B videas • [k] mv A B poscis • [l] A C patris, • [m] A B C quod • [n] uA B Tu • [o] uA B est • [p] mv A nescitis • [q] uA B siet • [r] uA B expectas • [s] uA B improbe • [t] uA B scire • [u] C palato: • [v] A B vis

How do you know? If you don't know, don't speak in vain. Let the plain words of the Holy Bible be enough for you.[332]

This book openly declares Christ is God, and begotten of God. Do you ask how that can be?[333]

Fool, first consider whether you can yourself know that you were begotten by the act of your father.[334]

You, who will not know in an eternity what a fly is, do you expect, vile man, to know what God is?   **1090**

Don't just taste the remedy[335] to sin with the roof of your mouth. If you want to be cured, open wide and swallow it like a brave fellow.[336]

Narr. (*EW* IV, p. 398): 'They went to establish the doctrine of *one individual God in Trinity*; to abolish the diversity of species in God, not the distinction of *here* and *there* in substance.'

[332] Hobbes, in his *Answer to Bramhall*, (*EW* vol. IV, p. 314) stated his constantly reiterated position, 'When the nature of a thing is incomprehensible, I can acquiesce in the Scripture: but when the signification of words is incomprehensible, I cannot acquiesce in the authority of a Schoolman'. In the 1668 Appendix to the Latin *LL*, Hobbes restated bluntly the 'ex sola scriptura' principle (*OL* III, p. 536): 'sanctam Trinitatem ex sola Scriptura Sacra ostendere'. See Gianni Paganini, 'Hobbes, Valla e i problemi filosofici della teologia umanistica', p. 42n. Once again the judgment of the Nicene Creed in *Hist. Narr.* is less harsh (*EW* IV, p. 401), Hobbes observing that, 'In the general confession of faith contained in the creed called the Nicene Creed, there is no mention of *hypostasis*, nor of hypostatical union, nor of corporeal, nor of incorporeal, nor of parts'. This line of argument seems to congrue with the position of A in the 1668 Appendix to the *LL*, §90 (*OL*, vol. III, p. 536), who finds to his astonishment (perhaps mock astonishment) that the Nicene Creed is not infected by Greekification (see Springborg Introduction, chapter 6.3). But it is contradicted in the *Hist. Eccl.*, at lines 739-40, where Hobbes claims that because of Greekification the pious 'went astray': 'Like blind men they could not find the doctrines of the Council in Holy Scripture'. But as we see, Hobbes at *Hist. Eccl.* lines 739-40 contradicts this statement.

[333] See the discussions of 'begotten' at lines 617-18, 653-4, 747-8 and notes.

[334] Hobbes notes of paternity in *Lev.*, xx, §5, 103/129: 'For in the condition of mere nature, where there are no matrimonial laws, it cannot be known who is the father unless it be declared by the mother; and therefore the right of dominion over the child dependeth on her will, and is consequently hers.'

[335] *Pharmakon*, according to the Arndt & Gingrich's Greek dictionary, was a term for poison, magic potion, charm; medicine, remedy, drug; but in the Christian era it had a special reference to the Eucharist as *pharmakon, Athanasias*, the medicine of (i.e. means of attaining) immortality. At line 1252, Hobbes employs the same term when referring to the lures and potions used by the fisherman, mimicking the language of Walton's *Complete Angler*, pp. 137-9. Note also the relation between *pharmaca* and the title of the famous work, The *Panarion* of *Epiphanius, Bishop of Salamis, a 'Medicine Chest' for heresy. See the Forward to *The Panarion of St. Epiphanius, Bishop of Salamis, Selected Passages*, edited by Philip R. Amidon, S.J. (Oxford 1990).

[336] Lucretius, *De Rerum Natura*, lines 1.930-41, after proclaiming as his task 'to loose the mind from the close knots of superstition', connecting *religio* with *religare*,

Nam Sacra qui Logico[a] mandit mysteria dente,
　　　Hunc vertigo capit,[b] nauseaque,[c] et vomitus.
Pr.[d] Philosophis illis Nicenis nota fuerunt
　　　Haec satis, et scibant[e] quid sacra verba docent.

---

[a] uA B Logico • [b] uA B capit • [c] A B C nauseaque • [d] mv uA B C *Pr.* missing
• [e] mv uA B sciebant

For the man who chews the sacred mysteries with a logical tooth, is
seized by dizziness, nausea and vomiting.[337]

Pr. These things were sufficiently understood by the Nicene
Philosophers; and they knew what the sacred words teach.

'to bind fast', as the commentator notes, goes on to argue that, because 'the subject
is so dark and the lines I write so clear, I touch all with the Muses' grace', so that:

> as with children, when physicians try to administer rank wormwood, they first
> touch the rims about the cups with the sweet yellow fluid of honey, that unthink-
> ing childhood be deluded as far as the lips, and meanwhile may drink up the
> bitter juice of wormwood, and though beguiled be not betrayed, but rather by
> such means be restored and regain health, so now do I: since this doctrine com-
> monly seems somewhat harsh to whose who have not used it, and the people
> shrink back from it, I have chosen to set forth my doctrine to you in sweet-
> speaking Pierian song, and as it were to touch it with the Muses' delicious
> honey, if by chance in such a way I might engage your mind in my verses, while
> you are learning to see in what shape is framed the whole nature of things.

Lucretius, *De Rerum Natura*, trans. W. H. D. Rouse, commentary by M. F. Smith,
(London, 1975), pp. 78-9.

[337] Francis Bacon's essays, published in full as *The Essayes or Counsels, Civill
and Morall, of Francis Lo. Verulam, Viscount of St. Alban* (London 1625, reprinted
1972, ed. Michael J. Hawkins), which Hobbes translated into Latin, include 'Of
Studies', which reads:

> Some books are to be tasted, others to be swallowed, and some few to be
> chewed and digested: that is, some books are to be read only in parts; others
> to be read, but not curiously; and some few to be read wholly, and with dili-
> gence and attention.

See *Lev.*, xxxii, §3, 195/246: 'For it is with the mysteries of our religion, as with
wholesome pills for the sick, which, swallowed whole, have the virtue to cure, but
chewed, are for the most part cast up again without effect'. Note that this passage
follows Hobbes's claim, *Lev.*, xxxii, §2, 195/245, that:

> we are not to renounce our senses, and experience, nor (that which is the
> undoubted word of God) our natural reason. For they are the talents which he
> hath put into our hands to negotiate till the coming again of our blessed
> Saviour; and therefore not to be folded up in the napkin of an implicit faith,
> but employed in the purchase of justice, peace, and true religion.

See Gianni Paganini, 'Hobbes, Valla e i problemi filosofici della teologia umanistica',
pp. 11-45, who reviews the case for these passages as expressions of scepticism on
Hobbes's part, arguing rather that Hobbes is convinced that when some doctrine contradicts reason, we should first suspect the misunderstanding of words, and only second
the incomprehensibility of the doctrine. This is the point of Vallaean philological clar-
ification, to show that humanist method as well as rational philosophy can provide an
interpretation of words that avoids a conflict with reason (personal communication
from Paganini to Springborg, 7/5/2002). In *Lev.*, 'A Review and Conclusion', §15,
395/496, Hobbes argues with respect to classical authorities (4) that 'such opinions as
are taken onely upon credit of antiquity are not intrinsically the judgment of those that
cite them, but words that pass (like gaping) from mouth to mouth'; (5) that 'it is many
times with a fraudulent design that men stick their corrupt doctrine with the cloves of
other men's wit'; (6) 'I find not that the ancients they cite took it for an ornament, to do
the like with those that wrote before them'; (7) 'it is an argument of indigestion, when
Greek and Latin sentences, unchewed, come up again, as they use to do, unchanged'.

Sed doctrina Dei non expediebat eorum
      Consiliis, mundi[a] quos agitabat amor.
Nec populum mundi tanta dulcedine cepit,[b]
      Quantâ[c] venalis gratia Pontificum.   **1100**
Namque suos Christus jubet omnes invicem[d] amare,[e]
      Et bona vicinis omnia velle suis.
Quae bona non tua sunt,[f] Formae spectator et Auri,[g]
      Ne cupias,[h] inquit, si meus esse cupis.
Omnibus ô[i] legem duram moechis et avaris,
      Quam,[j] mundanorum quis tolerare potest?
Irasci vetat, et veniam donare petenti,[k]
      (Et puto si veniam non petat)[l] ille jubet.
Christe,[m] vetas,[n] ne quis sapientem se putet esse,
      Despiciatve rudem simplicitate virum;[o]   **1110**
Aequa quidem,[p] verùm[q] tibi dura,[r] Scholastice, lex[s] est,[t]
      Qui cupis ingenio subdere cuncta tuo.
Discipulis Dominus,[u] non,[v] dixit,[w] cogite quemquam,[x]
      Invitis quoniam gratia spreta perit.
Condere nec Leges[y] jussit, nec habere tribunal
      In terris;[z] sed eos ire,[aa] docere,[bb] jubet.

---

[a] A mundi, • [b] mv A coepit, • [c] A B C Quanta • [d] mv B inviem (error) • [e] A B amare • [f] uA B sunt • [g] uA auri B Auri C auri, • [h] uA B cupias • [i] A B o C ô • [j] uA B C Quam • [k] A B petenti • [l] mv uA B petet) • [m] uA B Christe • [n] uA B vetas • [o] A virum. B virum • [p] uA B quidem • [q] uA B C verum • [r] uA B dura • [s] A Lex • [t] uA B est • [u] uA B Dominus • [v] A B non • [w] A B dixit • [x] A quenquam C quemquam • [y] uA B C leges • [z] uA B terris, • [aa] uA B ire • [bb] A B docere

But the teachings of God did not advance the policies of those driven by
    love of the world.

Nor did they capture the people of the world with as much charm as the
    venal favour of Grace from the Pontiffs.[338]   **1100**

For Christ commands all his followers to love one another and wish all
    good things for their neighbours.

What goods are not yours, connoisseur of beauty and wealth, you must
    not covet, He says, if you wish to be mine.[339]

Oh what a hard law for all adulterers and greedy men! Who among the
    worldly can bear it?

Christ forbids us to grow angry, and commands us to forgive those who
    seek forgiveness (even, I think, those who don't seek it).[340]

O Christ, you forbid anyone to think himself a wise man or to despise the
    rough man in his simplicity.   **1110**

In fact this is a just law, but it is certainly hard for you, Schoolman, keen
    to subject everything to your intellect.

The Lord did not tell his disciples, 'compel anyone',[341] because Grace,
    rejected by those who receive it against their will, has no efficacy.

He didn't command them to establish laws, or conduct a tribunal on earth;
    rather he commanded them to go out and teach.[342]

---

[338] A *coepit*, 'begin', possibly an error; c.f., B and 1688 edn, *cepit*, 'seize, take'. See also line 808, parallel variant.

[339] In the spirit of the 9th and 10th Commandments of the Decalogue, but there is no specific passage of the Evangelists to which these words refer. Perhaps a loose paraphrase of Luke 18.23 or Mark 10.17-22 (Invernizzi note).

[340] Note, the parable of the woman taken in adultery, John 8:1-11.

[341] II Corinthians 6.1 ff. Johann Sommerville, in 'Hobbes, Selden, Erastianism', p. 187 n. 110, notes that 'Christ's role (in Hobbes's system) was to give only advice, not orders', an issue that Hugo Grotius in *De jure belli ac pacis*, bk 1, ch. 2, had argued at length to the opposite conclusion.

[342] The Church's mission is persuasive and non-governmental, a time of preaching called by Christ himself the regeneration, 'which is not properly a kingdom (and thereby a warrant to deny obedience to the magistrates). . .' (*Lev.*, xli, §4, 263/329). Emphasis on the Church's mission as spiritual and non-governmental was typical of Pre-Reformation Renaissance critics. Lorenzo Valla, in the preface to his translation of Thucydides, which Hobbes, in the Preface to his own Thucydides (*EW*, vol. 8, viii), claimed to have read, had made the same case. See Lorenzo Valla, *Oraciones y Prefacios*, ed. Francesco Adorno, p. 278, cited Connell, 'Lorenzo Valla: A Symposium', p. 4. The antinomy between '*Imperium*' and '*Evangelium*' is a central *topos* of Valla's *[Supposed] Donation*, and the title of one of its sections. See Gianni Paganini, 'Thomas Hobbes e Lorenzo Valla', pp. 522n, citing Valla's *De falso credita et emendita constantini donatione*, ed Setz, pp. 217-19, §3.

Non placet hoc munus sapientibus; esse meretur
     Qui Rex summus (ait) Ludimagister[a] erit?
Si peccatorum quem poenitet, atque salutem
     Concredat Christo[b] non variante fide,   1120
Salvus erit, sacris si fas est credere libris,[c]
     Durum est Romanus Clericus[d] omnis ait.
Illene salvus erit[e] qui non intelligit utrum
     Christus homo, fuerit factus,[f] an induerit?
Qui Genitum[g] esse nequit[h] distinguere ab esse Profectum,[i]
     Aut nescit Genitus[j] quî[k] Deus esse potest?
Si datur hoc Laicis,[l] frustra est sapientia nostra,
     Atque animas nostras corpora crassa regent.
Semina,[m] Christus ait, bona quidam[n] severat arvis
     Agricola, at veniens mox inimicus homo,   1130
Nocte latens,[o] agro Zizania sevit eodem.[p]
     In segetem semen crevit utrumque simul.
Mirantes servi, dubiique quid esset agendum,
     Ut mos est, Dominum consuluere suum.
Evelline jubes istas radicitus herbas?
     Vel si non placet hoc, dicito quid facimus.[q]
Ille,[r] simul crescant dum Messis[s] venerit,[t] inquit,
     Igni fasciculos inde parate meo.
Haereticos Christus vetat hac sub imagine tolli,[u]
     Ante diem extremum,[v] judiciumque Dei.[w]   1140
Doctrinae vestrae si frater forte repugnet;
     Molliter hunc verbis instrue,[x] Paulus ait,[y]

---

[a] B C ludimagister • [b] A B Christo, • [c] A B libris C libris. • [d] A B C clericus • [e] A B erit,C erit; • [f] mv A B factus fuerit, (word order) • [g] A B C genitum • [h] B néquit • [i] A C profectum B Profectum • [j] A C genitus, B genitus • [k] uA B C qui • [l] uA B Laicis • [m] uA B Semina • [n] mv A C quidem • [o] C latens • [p] A B eodem • [q] mv C facimus? • [r] uA B Ille • [s] A B C messis • [t] uA B venerit • [u] A B tolli • [v] A B extremum • [w] C DEI • [x] uA B instrue • [y] A B ait

This mission doesn't please the wise man. Shall one who deserves to be a
  supreme king (he says) be a Schoolmaster?
If someone who repents of his sins and entrusts his salvation to Christ
  with unwavering faith, **1120**
Will be saved, if the Holy Bible can be believed, "'It is hard", says every
  Roman cleric:[343]
Will he be saved if he does not know whether Christ was made man, or
  assumed human form,
If he cannot distinguish "begotten" from "proceeded from",[344] or if he
  does not know by what means God could be begotten?[345]
If it were given to laymen, our wisdom would be worthless and our dull
  bodies would rule our minds.'
Christ said, 'A farmer once sowed good seeds in his fields, but an enemy
  soon approached, **1130**
And avoiding notice during the night, sowed tares in the same field. Both
  types of seed grew into crops at the same time.
The servants were surprised and uncertain about what should be done, so
  as was their custom, they consulted their Master.
'Do you want us to tear out these weeds by the roots? If you don't want
  this, tell us what we should do.'
The farmer said, 'Let the crop grow up together, until the harvest-time
  comes, then prepare bundles for my fire.'[346]
Through this parable, Christ forbids the removal of heretics before God's
  judgement on the Last Day.[347] **1140**
If it happens that a brother should disagree with your teachings, prepare
  him by talking gently, Paul said,

---

[343] The cleric's speech follows to line 1128.

[344] The distinction between 'begotten' and 'proceeded from' lay at the heart of
the problem of *Subordinationism, i.e., whether the relationship between the three
persons of the Trinity was one of equality, or whether the Son and the Holy Ghost
proceeded from, and were lesser to, the God the Father.

[345] Refer to the discussion at lines 617-18, 653-4, 747-8 and notes.

[346] Paraphrase of Matthew 13:24ff. Note that Hobbes in *Lev.*, xliv, §3, 334/412,
use the parable to different effect, speaking of 'the enemy in the night', sowing
'the tares of spiritual errors. . . by mixing with the Scripture divers relics of the
religion and much of the vain and erroneous philosophy of the Greeks (especially of
Aristotle)'.

[347] Note that the 1722 paraphrase directly connects this parable to Henry IV and
the St. Bartholemew's Day massacre.

Si Deus illius velit illucescere menti,
     Ne non inveniat gratia sera locum.
Non magni fecere Patres textum hunc,[a] neque multo
     Pluris eis rectae[b] Lex rationis erat.
Maxima quando meo mea res sit agenda periclo,
     Mene vetas uti,[c] tu,[d] ratione mea?
Daemonis inferni si te duce labor in ignem[e]
     (Quod ne contingat, nescio quid prohibet)[f]   **1150**
Praecipit,[g] ut redimas,[h] Lex aequi,[i] corpore corpus,[j]
     Proque[k] salute mea perdere velle tuam.
Haec dictat ratio si coget.[l] Det mihi[m] qui vult
     Consilium;[n] sed qui coget iniquus erit.
Sec. Haereticis leges tibi non placet esse molestas,[o]
     Doctrinae nulli crimen inesse putas?
Quas caedes,[p] nescis,[q] nuper doctrina nefanda
     Egressa Oxonio,[r] Cambrigiâque[s] dedit?

---

[a] uA B hunc • [b] mv A recte (read rectae) • [c] uA B uti • [d] A B tu • [e] C ignem, • [f] C prohibet.) • [g] B Praecipit • [h] uA B redimas • [i] uA B aequi • [j] A B corpus • [k] mv uA B pro • [l] mv uA B cogitet. • [m] A mihi, • [n] uA B Consilium, • [o] uA B molestas • [p] A B caedes • [q] uA B nescis • [r] uA B Oxonio • [s] A B C Cambrigiaque

So that if God wants to enlighten his mind, grace may find an occasion
　　even at a late hour.[348]

The Church Fathers did not take great account of this text, nor was the
　　law of right reasoning of much more value to them.

Do you forbid me from employing my own reasoning, when what is most
　　important to me has to be pursued at my own peril?[349]

If under your leadership I fall into the fire of the infernal demon (and I do
　　not know what prevents it from happening)　　　　　　　**1150**

The law of equity enjoins that you redeem one body with another and that
　　for the sake of my salvation you be willing to lose your own.[350]

Reason tells us these things, if reason compels us. Give me counsel who
　　may, but whoever coerces me will be my enemy.

Sec. It does not please you that there should be laws irksome for heretics,
　　but do you think there is no doctrine that is criminal?

Don't you know what bloodshed the abominable teaching which came out
　　of Oxford and Cambridge recently brought about?[351]

---

[348] II Timothy 2.24 ff. St. Paul was singled out by Lorenzo Valla for his eloquence: 'He spoke accurately and with words both appropriate and beautiful and
exactly as suited the majesty of content; he excelled Demosthenes himself.' Valla,
Adnotationes in Novum Testamentum, in *Opera omnia*, ed. E. Garin (Torino 1962),
vol I, p. 880, cited by Sarah Gravelle, 'Lorenzo Valla's Comparison of Latin and
Greek', p. 282. There is a likely line of transmission from Valla, through Erasmus,
who edited Valla's *Adnotationes*, to Hobbes, whose style of Biblical exegesis in
Lev., bks 3 and 4 is in the Vallean-Erasmean tradition.

[349] Note the use of the legal principle, 'whose case whose peril', (Cooper) '[Cicero:
cuja res est: ut optima conditione sit is, cuja res est, cuium periculum: 'to whome
the matter appertaineth . . . ; Cicero: *cuja interest*: 'whome the matter toucheth')]'.

[350] Hobbes, who is a mortalist, mocks the doctrine of hell, by holding Christian
equity to the principle of *lex talionis*: 'an eye for an eye'.

[351] Hobbes refers to the Civil War and the role that the universities played, Oxford
being more high church and royalist, Cambridge more republican. Leijenhorst,
Hobbes and the Aristotelians (pp. 33-4), notes that 'Hobbes's critique of scholastic
metaphysics and theology is also an institutional critique of the universities which
teach these doctrines to future clergy . . . inspired by abstruse metaphysics,
preach[ing] sedition and revolt instead of obedience to the legitimate sovereign'. See
Lev., ch. 46 and the 'Review and Conclusion' §16, 396/496, where Hobbes declares:
　　For seeing the Universities are the fountains of civil and moral doctrine, from
　　whence the preachers, and the gentry, drawing such water as they find, use to
　　sprinkle the same (both from the pulpit, and in their conversation) upon the
　　people, there ought certainly to be great care taken to have it pure, both from
　　the venom of heathen politicians and from the incantation of deceiving spirits.
　　And by that means the most men, knowing their duties, will be the less subject
　　to serve the ambition of a few discontented persons, in their purposes against
　　the State . . . .

Occidit Carolum doctrina Academica Regem,[a]
    Multosque insignes nobilitate viros.   **1160**
Necnon Henrici, doctrina Pontificali,[b]
    Gallorum Reges occubuere duo.[c]
[d]Curam qui pacis suscepit cunque tuendae,[e]
    Doctorum duris legibus ora premat.
Pr.[f] Quid potuit doctrina mali ex hoc tempore vidi,[g]
    Et vidi Leges[h] quàm[i] valuere parùm.[j]
Infecto sed sera venit medicina popello
    Multo ;[k] qui,[l] quae sunt Principis,[m] arma tenet.
Regi cui praesens non est exercitus, illi
    (Seu vult,[n] seu non vult[o]) ensifer est[p] populus,[q]   **1170**
Ut nil sit[r] quod agant leges. Nihil est resecandum ;[s]
    Optima demulcens est medicina manus.
Exigat ad Leges[t] pacem,[u] convicia[v] tollat
    Rex ;[w] dubitare potes quin Schola inermis erit ?
Caetera sit calamus[x] liber, sit libera lingua,[y]
    Si mores saltem non docet illa malos.
Non loquitur Pietas[z] perplexa. Sed insidiarum
    Signum non fallax est tenebrosa phrasis.
Nam Christus lux est ;[aa] ad eum venientibus ipse
    Praelucens claro lumine monstrat iter.   **1180**
Numquid divinae,[ab] sunt pars,[ac] aenigmata,[ad] legis,[ae]
    Ingeniovè[af] salus est tribuenda meo ?

---

[a] A Regem C regem • [b] A B Pontificali • [c] A Duo. • [d] mv B *Pr*: • [e] uA B tuendae • [f] mv B *Pr*: missing (placed 2 lines above) • [g] A vidi B vidi. • [h] A B C leges • [i] A B C quam • [j] uA B C parum. • [k] uA B Multo, • [l] A B qui • [m] uA C principis B Principis • [n] C B vult • [o] A vult,) • [p] mv uA B esse • [q] A populus • [r] A sit, • [s] A B resecandum • [t] uA leges, A Leges, • [u] uA pacem • [v] A convitia (variant) • [w] uA B Rex, • [x] A Calamus • [y] A lingua B lingua. • [z] A C pietas • [aa] A B est, • [ab] uA B divinae • [ac] uA B pars • [ad] uA B aenigmata • [ae] A B legis • [af] A B C Ingeniove

Academic teaching killed King Charles and many distinguished men from
    the nobility.[352]   1160
And indeed, two kings of France by the name of Henry[353] lie dead because
    of Pontifical teaching.
Whoever took upon himself the charge of defending peace, should shut
    the mouths of the Doctors with harsh laws.
Pr. I have learned from these times what havoc teaching can wreak, and
    how little the laws were worth,
But the cure comes too late when the mass of the people, who hold the
    arms that belong to the king, have already been infected.
If the king does not have a standing army,[354] the people carries arms,
    whether he likes it or not.   1170
With the result that the laws have no effect. No surgery is needed, the best
    medicine is a soothing hand.
The King should enforce peace according to the laws and do away with
    controversy. Can you doubt that the Schools would then be
    disarmed?
In other matters let the pen be free, and let there be free speech, so long as
    it does not teach bad morals.[355]
Piety does not speak in a confused manner. But dark diction is an
    unfailing sign of snares.
For Christ is the light. He shows those approaching him the way by
    shining before them with a bright light.   1180
Surely riddles are not a part of divine law, or salvation attributable to my
    intellect?[356]

---

[352] Hobbes refers to the execution of Charles I on 30 January 1649.

[353] Henry III of France (1551-89) was assassinated by the Dominican Clement,
and Henry IV (1553-1610), was assassinated by Ravaillac (Invernizzi note).

[354] *praesens exercitus*: standing army, a great source of contention in the
17th century.

[355] As Gianni Paganini notes, 'Thomas Hobbes e Lorenzo Valla', p. 540,
Hobbes's remarks on freedom of expression are an example of the greater religious
tolerance of the *Hist Eccl.* compared with *Lev.*, where '*The Greatest Liberty of Subjects, dependeth on the Silence of the Law*' (bk 2, ch. 21, marginal subheading); a
principle with which, however, the *Hist. Eccl.*, is here consistent.

[356] In the 1668 Appendix to the *LL.*, §88, (tr. Wright, p. 365) Hobbes notes that
Cardinal Bellarmine remarks 'in the first book of his *On Christ*: "Our doctors do not
debate after the manner of philosophers in order to demonstrate the Trinity, but so
that they might solve the riddles of the philosophers".'

OEdipodas solos salvandos credimus esse ?
     Aut Christi tenerae Sphinge[a] regentur oves ?
At Sphinges[b] nequeunt,[c] aenigmata Conciliorum
     Primorum quatuor,[d] solvere mille decem.
Cur agit ergo (putas) Nicena Ecclesia Sphingem,
     Si non ut tollat Regibus imperium ?
Sustulit imperium,[e] passus non debita jura,[f]
     Constantinorum primus,[g] habere Patres.   **1190**
Inde suos populus[h] coepit contemnere Reges,
     Portantes unâ[i] Pontificale jugum.[j]
Atque utri vellet,[k] Domino servire,[l] duorum,[m]
     Suetus,[n] vix patria lege regendus erat.
Nam quoties patrias leges sibi frangere visum est,[o]
     Fracturae,[p] leges opposuere Dei.
Et quoties servire Deo minus expediebat,[q]
     Excussit populus liber utrumque jugum.

---

[a] A B Spinge (variant) • [b] A B Spinges • [c] uA B nequeunt • [d] uA B quatuor •
[e] uA B imperium • [f] A C jura • [g] uA B primus • [h] mv C populos (error) • [i] uA
B C una • [j] A jugum, C iugum • [k] A B vellet • [l] uA B servire • [m] A B duorum
• [n] uA C Suetus • [o] A B C est • [p] uA B Fracturae • [q] uA B expediebat

Do we believe that only Oedipuses[357] should be saved? Will the tender
    flock of Christ be ruled by a Sphinx?[358]

But even ten Sphinxes cannot solve the thousand riddles of the first four
    councils.

Why then (do you think) the Nicene Church played the Sphinx, if not to
    take sovereign power away from kings?[359]

It was the first of the Constantines who did take away the sovereign power
    by allowing the Fathers rights to which they were not entitled.   **1190**

From that point the people begin to disparage their own kings for
    collectively bearing the Pontifical yoke,[360]

And accustomed to serve whichever of the two masters they wished, the
    people were governed with difficulty by their ancestral law.

In fact whenever it seemed in their interests to break the laws of their
    country, they pleaded the law of God in justification for the breach.

And whenever it was less expedient to serve God, the unrestrained people
    shook off both yokes.

---

[357] *Oedipus, proverbially a solver of enigmas. Oedipus was famous for solving the riddle of the *Sphinx (Lewis & Short). The derivation of Oedipus is from the Greek, *oidipodas*, meaning swollen foot, from *oidao*, to cause to swell, and *podas*, foot. In the legend Oedipus' feet were injured by being pinned together when he was exposed as a baby (Sophocles, *Oedipus Tyrannus* 1032-4). However, the juxtaposition of Oedipus and the Pope possibly recalls Lorenzo Valla's account of the false etyomolgy of Peter, from Petrus, meaning rock, by 'pontiffs [who] are not informed on these points, when they do not know about their own name!... And "petra is stupidly explained by them through a Latin derivation, as from "pede trita" (trodden by foot)!' See *The [Supposed] Donation of Constantine*, ed. Coleman, pp. 154-5.

[358] In the 1668 Appendix to the *LL*, §100, (tr. Wright, p. 367), referring to the distinction between 'proceeds from the Holy spirit' and 'born of the Holy Spirit', and in answer to the question (§99) 'To what purpose has the Roman Church distinguished between these words?', interlocuter B answers, 'I do not know. But you know that at one time the sphinx spread terror among the people by means of a riddle.' Hobbes in Letter 68, August 1654, refers to Francis Bacon, who in *De sapientia veterum*, ch. 28, treats the parable of the Sphinx as a question of the nature of science, and the science of man as containing many riddles. See Hobbes's *Correspondence*, Malcolm ed. (Oxford, 1994), vol. 1, pp. 195, 198n, citing Bacon, *Works*, vi, pp. 677-80.

[359] C.f. lines 771-4, where Hobbes notes that the Nicene Council shrouded the word of God in riddles to maintain its power.

[360] C.f. lines 849-60.

Exitiosa fuit nimia ista licentia paci;[a]
    Sed populo Lotus,[b] militibusque fuit.[c]   **1200**
Prona igitur facilisque fuit victoria Gotthis,[d]
    Qui Romam Mystae supposuere suo.
Jamque potestatis Papa esset culmen adeptus,
    Si non Gotthorum Rex metuendus erat.
Namque à[e] Romanis Aquilis Oriente remotis,
    Non ulla apparens causa timoris erat.
Illas miles aves fecit[f] quacunque[g] volare,
    Vellet;[h] sunt et aves quas jubet ille bonae.
Non caret auspicio quodcunque inceperit ille[i]
    Cui non invitae subjiciuntur aves.   **1210**
Jamque probans vires Papa excommunicat ipsum
    Induperatorem,[j] nomine Anastasium.

---

[a] uA B paci • [b] A B Lotus • [c] A fuit • [d] A B Gothis • [e] A a • [f] C fecit, • [g] C quacunque, • [h] A Vellet, • [i] C ille, • [j] uA B Induperatorem

This excessive freedom was ruinous to peace, but it was the Lotus[361] for
    the people and the army.   **1200**
Victory was therefore swift and easy for the Goths, who put Rome under
    their own priest (mystagogue).
The Pope would then have reached the height of power, if the king of the
    Goths had not been a source of fear.[362]
For, from the Roman Eagles which were far away in the East, he had no
    apparent cause for fear.
The soldiery[363] made those birds fly whichever way it wanted, and the
    birds it commanded were kindly:[364]
Whatever is attempted by a man to whom the birds are willingly subject
    does not lack happy auguries.   **1210**
And then the Pope,[365] in a show of strength, excommunicated the Emperor
    himself, Anastasius.[366]

---

[361] Possible reference to the *Odyssey*, the beginning of book 9, prefacing the
Cyclops episode. Odyssey and his comrades ravaging cities in Asia Minor had come
across the Lotus eaters (*Lotophagi*). Odysseus has to retrieve his shipmates for fear
they would forget their homeland, the implication here being that, sated with
victory, they forget their patriotic duty.

[362] *Theodoric the Great (454-526), founder of the kingdom of the Ostrogoths,
encouraged to invade Italy by the Emperor of the East (Invernizzi note). See Ostrogorsky, *History of the Byzantine State*, pp. 68-9, on the power vacuum left by the withdrawal of the Roman Emperor into the East where the seat of Empire was now Byzantium, whence the garrisons were also removed. The *Germanic tribes ruling now in
the West, nevertheless acknowledged the overlordship of Rome, now ruling in the
East under *Justinian, who saw it as his sacred mission to reclaim the lands in the
West.

[363] Hobbes uses *miles* for soldiers of Christ in the Erasmian sense. See
Erasmus's *Enchiridion militis christiani* (*Handbook of the Christian Soldier*), 1504.

[364] Hobbes is referring to the auguries, and may well be playing with Lorenzo
Valla's etymology of the imperial title: 'Augustus, as consecrated, from "avium
gustus" (the taste, or appetite, of the birds), a customary step in consulting omens'.
Valla comments, 'Better might the supreme pontiff be called Augustus from
"augere" (to augment), except for the fact that when he augments his temporal he
diminishes his spiritual power'. See *The [Supposed] Donation of Constantine*, ed.
Coleman, pp. 160-1.

[365] *Anastasius I, Emperor (491-518), had been excommunicated by Gelasius I,
Pope from 492-6, for his support of Acacius, formerly Patriarch of Constantinople,
who had followed a policy of compromise with Monophysitism, and had himself
been excommunicated by Pope Felix III in 484. Hefele, *Histoire des conciles*,
2.2.12, pp. 939-46; Ostrogorsky, *History of the Byzantine State*, pp. 64-8.

[366] Lines 1211-12 are more or less repeated at lines 1503-4, after a long digression on the Renaissance papacy, perhaps an indication of the poem having been
picked up and put down.

Sec. Cur? *Pr.* Chalcedoniae Synodi decreta teneri
  Non fecit, quantum Catholicum decuit.
Post hunc Justinus, post illum Justinianus
  Regnavit, Papis et placuere suis.
Quorum hic imprimis Romani Codice juris
  Insignis,[a] longo tempore jura dedit.
Foelix[b] eximiis belloque et pace ministris,[c]
  Quorum virtutes[d] credidit esse suas.   **1220**
Huic Gotthos Latiis Belisarius expulit arvis,
  (Quanquam uxore minor) maximus ille ducum.[e]
Pontificum pulsis Effulsit[f] gloria[g] Gotthis;
  Sub coelo rerum maxima,[h] Papa fuit.
Cedunt arma mitrae, concessit Episcopus omnis,[i]
  Etsi quisque sibi jus cupiebat idem.

---

[a] uA B Insignis • [b] A B C Felix • [c] uA B ministris • [d] A Virtutes • [e] A Ducum
B Ducum. • [f] A B C effulsit • [g] B Gloria • [h] A B C maxima • [i] ~A omnis

Se. Why ? *Pr.* Anastasius had not enforced the decrees of the Council of Chalcedon as much as it behooved a Catholic.

After him Justin[367] ruled, and after him Justinian, and they both pleased their Popes.

Of the two, Justinian,[368] especially distinguished for his codex of Roman Law,[369] ruled for a long time.

Having excellent ministers in war and in peace, he believed that their excellence was in fact his own.   **1220**

On his behalf, Belisarius,[370] the greatest of the generals (although inferior to his wife),[371] drove the Goths from the Latin plains.[372]

Once the Goths were routed the glory of the Pontiffs shone. The Pope was the greatest thing under heaven.

Arms yielded to the mitre;[373] every bishop conceded to the Pope, although each coveted for himself the same right.[374]

---

[367] *Justin I, the Elder, 450-527, emperor from 518. See Hefele, *Histoire des conciles*, 2.2.13, pp. 1046-53.

[368] Justinian (AD 483-565), Byzantine Emperor. Clearly control of the church and the universities would have rated him high in Hobbes's eyes, but Justinian is generally believed to have committed too much of his resources to theological disputes. See the Byzantine Procopius (c. AD 500-65), *Secret Histories*, on Justinian; and Hefele, *Histoire des conciles* 2.2.13, p. 1120ff.

[369] Justinian strove to resolve the confusion governing the old law (*jus vetus*), all the statutes, senate decrees and judicial opinions ratified under the Republic and early Empire, whose bulk and uncertainty had defeated the earlier codifiers, Theodosius II and Valentinian. At the same time he attempted to reconcile the old law to the new law (*jus novum*), comprising the ordinances issued by the Emperors during the middle and later Empire in the Empire, in his famous codification of AD 529, which abrogated all laws not so reconciled (*Encyclopaedia Britannica*, 11ᵗʰ edn, 1910-11, vol 15, pp. 596-602). Hobbes refers to the old law (*jus vetus*), and the new law (*jus novum*), at line 53.

[370] *Belisarius (AD c. 505-565), one of Justinian's most famous generals, subjugated not only the Ostrogoths in Italy (540) but also the Vandals in Africa. Invernizzi notes that Hobbes's suggestion about his wife is historical fact.

[371] For Belisarius, to whom Procopius was *adsessor*, or legal adviser, and his wife, Theodora, see Procopius, *The Secret History*. Theodora was actually a Monophysite; see Hefele, *Histoire des conciles*, 2.2.13, pp. 1142-45.

[372] In 534 Justinian sent Belisarius to Africa to destroy the kingdom of the Aryan Vandals who were oppressing the Catholics there. The success of his campaign and the return of North Africa to the power of the pope was honoured at the Council of Carthage, 536. See Hefele, *Histoire des conciles* 2.2.13, pp. 1136-39.

[373] Note that Hobbes's description is consistent with the iconography of the frontispiece of *Leviathan*, which shows the mitre, the excommunication court and the trident, representative of forked dilemmas, ranged on the ecclesiastical side against the secular emblems of power in the form of the sword, the scepter, the canon and the club.

[374] Note that Hobbes correctly describes church/state relations under Justinian, while taking up his persistent theme of power-seeking bishops.

Cessit, sed tardè,[a] Constantinopolitanus,[b]
Aequali quanquam dignus honore fuit.
[c]Leviathan naribus, Behemothque[d] receperat hamum;
Et Rex et Populus servus uterque fuit.   **1230**

---

[a] uA tarde B tardè C tarde, • [b] mv A Constantinopolitatius (error) B Constantinopolitanus • [c] mv lines 1229-30 are interpolated in A at the foot of the page,
included in the text of C and 1688, but missing in uA and B. • [d] A C Behemotque

Even the Patriarch of Constantinople yielded, if tardily, although he was
   equally deserving of honour.
[375]Leviathan,[376] like Behemoth, [377] had again taken the hook in the nose;[378]
both the king and the people were slaves.[379]   **1230**

---

[375] Lines 1229-30 are interpolated in A and 1688, but missing in uA and B. They
signal a long digression on Papal expansionism in Hobbes's day, lines 1230 to 1500.
   [376] *Leviathan* (Cooper) 'a dragon of the sea. It is taken in holy Scripture for the
divell'. The precise significance of the biblical title for Hobbes's master work, has
been much debated, most notably by Carl Schmitt, *Der Leviathan in der Staatslehre
des Thomas Hobbes. Sinn und Fehlschlag eines politischen Symbols* (Stuttgart, Klett-
Cotta, 1995), p. 32 ff. See Patricia Springborg, 'Hobbes's Biblical Beasts', *Political
Theory* vol. 23 no 2 (1995) pp. 353-75, where I speculate (pp. 359-60) that Hobbes
may (among many possibilities) have had a precise source in John Calvin's *Commentary vpon the Prophecie of Isaiah* (London, 1609), dedicated to Henry, Prince of
England, son of James I and Princess Elizabeth, his wife, where Calvin breaks with the
rule of Reformation biblical criticism to give an allegorical interpretation of Leviathan
as a figure both for the Devil and the King of Egypt. Commenting on Isaiah 27:1 ('In
that day the Lord will visit Leuiathan that pearcing Serpent, and Leuiathan that
crooked Serpent, with his sore and great and mightie sword: and will kill the Dragon
that is in the sea'), Calvin remarks: 'For mine owne part I make no question but by
way of Allegorie he speakes here of Satan and his whole kingdome, describing it
under the figure of some monstrous beast'. His interpretation of Leviathan as a figure
for tyrants is quite explicit (*Commentary vpon the Prophecie of Isaiah*, p. 260b):
> The prophet speakes heere of Gods judgement in generall, and so compre-
> hends the whole kingdom of Satan. For hauing spoken before of the
> vengeance of God against tyrants and vnbeleeuers which had shed innocent
> blood, he now passeth on further, and publisheth the edict it selfe. The word
> *Leuiathan* is diuerslie expounded, but generallie it signifies a serpent, or the
> whales and fishes of the sea, which are as monsters in regards of their excel-
> liue greatnes. Now howsoeuer this description agrees to the king of Egypt, yet
> vnder the one he meant to comprehend all the enemies of the Church.

   [377] *Behemoth* (Cooper), the dyvell, and signifieth a beaste'. See Luther in his
Magnificat, discussing the demonization of 'the proud', those 'forlorn people' of
the Book of Job: 'Sometimes it calls them adders who stop their ears lest they hear
[Ps. 58:4]; sometimes stubborn unicorns [Ps 22:21]; sometimes roaring lions [Ps.
7:2]; sometimes great immovable rocks [Jer. 5:3]; and sometimes dragons [Ps.
74:13]; and much else besides'. *Leviathan* and *Behemoth* are demonizations too:
> Equally well are they depicted in Job 40 and 41, where the same kind of
> people are called Behemoth [Job 40:10ff, 41.10ff]. Behema means a single
> animal, but behemoth means a number of such animals, in other words, a race
> which has an animal mind, and does not allow the spirit of God in it.

Luther, *Magnificat*, in *The Reformation Writings of Martin Luther*, vol. 2, p. 231. See
Patricia Springborg, 'Hobbes's Biblical Beasts', p. 360.
   [378] See Job 41:1-2 (King James Version): 'Canst thou draw out Leviathan with
a hook? or his tongue with a cord *which* thou lettest down? Canst thou put a hook
in his nose? or bore his jaw through with a thorn?' See also Psalms 74:14; 104:26
and Isaiah 27:1.
   [379] A has these two lines added at the foot of the page in the second scribal hand,
with an indication that they are to be inserted following line 1228. B does not

Sec. Amplius Ergo nihil Papae restabat agendum
    Quàm[a] genus humanum luce beare sua;[b]
Et post terrarum,[c] coelorum quaerere regnum,[d]
    Ut serpens,[e] sapiens;[f] simplicitate puer.
Pr. Τῶν δ' 'ἕτερον μέν 'ἑ δῶκε πατήρ,[g] 'ἕτερον δ' 'ανενέυσε,[h]
    Nempe datum prius est, posterius minimè.[i]
Omnia Pontifices superarunt cnodula[j] quotquot[k]
    Producit tellus calliditate sua.
Sed Regnum duplex,[l] Carnale,[m] et Spirituale,[n]
    Non nimiae signum simplicitatis erat.   **1240**

---

[a] A B C Quam • [b] uA sua B sua. • [c] uA B terrarum • [d] A regnum B Regnum • [e] C serpens • [f] uA B C sapiens • [g] uA πατήρ • [h] A 'ανένευσε • [i] A B minime C minime. • [h] C cnodola • [k] A B quotquot, • [l] uA B duplex • [m] uA B C carnale • [n] uA B C spirituale

Sec. So nothing further remained for the Pope to do but bless humankind
with his own light,[380]

And, after the kingdom on earth, seek the kingdom of heaven,[381] as wily as
a snake, but with the simplicity of a child.[382]

Pr. 'The father granted him one prayer and denied him the other'.[383]
Without doubt the first was granted, the latter not at all.[384]

The popes by their own cunning overcame all the monsters[385] that the
earth produces.

But the double realm, bodily and spiritual, was not a mark of excessive
simplicity.[386]   **1240**

---

include these lines, although the 1688 edition does. This suggests that Grund made
his copy in 1685 without sighting a corrected scribal copy, whereas Harleian Ms A
was corrected to the 1688 printed edition which included these lines, perhaps later
interpolations.

[380] Thus usurping the light of Christ, see lines 1179-80.

[381] The Pope as Lucifer.

[382] Virgil, *Ecl.* 3.93. The 'Divine Hilary', in a passage cited by Rymer's Preface as
a source for Hobbes, had declared in *Against Constantius Augustus*, with direct reference to the doctrinal wrangling of the post-Nicene Church: 'Either we condemn
matters foreign in ourselves, or we condemn our own matters in condemning the
foreign, and biting one another we are finally mutually consumed'. The translations of
the Fathers from the Greek into Latin published by the Bishop of Chichester John
Christopherson (d. 1558), *Historiae ecclesiasticae scriptores Graeci* (1570), a likely
source for Hobbes, included the 3 bks of Eusebius's *De vita Constantini Magni*, as well
as Socrates of Constantinople's discussion of the Blessed Hilary's *De Trinitate* in his
Hist. Eccl, bk. 3, ch. 8. Lorenzo Valla, perhaps with reference to Hilary, in *The [Sup-
posed] Donation of Constantine* (ed. Coleman, pp. 24-5), boldly enquired of the Pope:
'what should I call him, a good shepherd, or a deaf viper which would not choose to
heed the voice of the charmer, but to strike his limbs with its poisonous bite?'.

[383] Homer, *Iliad*, 16.252, Achilles' prayer to Zeus that the Trojan attack on the
Achaian ships be repulsed by Patroclus and that Patroclus be preserved, which Hobbes
gives in the Greek, 'Τών δ' 'έτερον μέν 'έ δῶϰε πατήρ, 'έτερον δ' 'ανένευσε.'.

[384] Achilles prayer was answered with respect to the turning back of the Trojans,
but Hector slew Patroclus.

[385] *Cnodula*, [Autenrieth] Gr. *knodalon* (n.) wild animal, dangerous animal,
monster (*Odyssey*, 17.317). In the 1688 Glossary (pp. 604-5) *Animalia magnitudine,
aut qualitate noxia*, simply translates the Greek. (See cognate *knodon knodontos*,
teeth; two projecting teeth on the blade of a hunting spear; or of a double-edged
sword.) These lines echo that section of the Book of Job that introduces Leviathan
and Behemoth, to which Hobbes refers in *Lev.*, xxxviii, §27, 166/210:

> the two last verses of the one and fortieth of *Job*, where God, having set forth the
> great power of *Leviathan*, calleth him King of the Proud. 'There is nothing',
> saith he, 'on earth to be compared with him. He is made so as not to be afraid.
> He seeth every high thing below him, and is King of all the children of pride'.

[386] Reference to the dual kingdoms, spiritual and temporal, on the basis of which
the papacy claimed dual power. See above lines 869-72 and 1517-20 and *Lev.*, xli,
§§3-6, 262-5/328-331.

Nec Papas credas egisse per otia vitas,[a]
    Nec quod agendum ultra nil habuere putes.[b]
Vota hominum semper votis augentur adeptis;[c]
    Accedens partas copia servat opes.
Piscator solitam non spernit callidus artem,[d]
    Quantavis praeda retibus implicita.
Res agit ille suas semper.[e] Vel[f] retia sarcit,
    Si quo[g] perrupit[h] magna balena loco.[i]

---

[a] uA B vitas • [b] A B putes, C putes • [c] uA B adeptis • [d] uA B artem • [e] mv C semper • [f] C vel • [g] mv A qui • [h] A Perrupit • [i] A B loco

You cannot believe that the Popes spent their lives in leisure, and do not
think that they had nothing further to do.

The desires of men are always increased by desires fulfilled.[387] Increasing
affluence protects wealth already acquired.

The shrewd fisherman does not neglect his customary skill,[388] however
great the prey entangled in his nets.[389]

He always pursues his own advantage.[390] Whether he is mending his nets
if at some point a great whale[391] has forced its way through,[392]

---

[387] Hobbes postulates as 'a general inclination of all mankind, a perpetual and
restless desire of power after power, that ceaseth only in death', *Lev.*, xi, §2, 47/58,
which closely parallel's Machiavelli's definition of the lust for power in the *Prince*.

[388] Compare the Pope as a cunning Fisherman (Piscator), with Walton's ideal
Angler in *The Complete Angler*, (1653), ed. Jonquil Bevan (London, Everyman edn,
1993), p. 39, a work widely regarded as allegorical:

> And let me tell you, that in the Scripture, Angling is always taken in the best
> sense; . . . he that views the ancient Ecclesiastical Canons, shall find hunting
> to be forbidden to Churchmen . . . and shall find Angling allowed to clergy-
> men as being a harmless recreation, a recreation that invites them to contem-
> plation and quietness.

Walton's disquisition on simplicity in *The Compleat Angler*, ch 1, 'The First Day:
A Conference Betwixt an Angler, a Falconer and a Hunter, each commending his
Recreation' (Everyman edn, p. 13) leads into a discussion of which of these sports
is the more worthy use of leisure.

[389] Walton refers to the arts of the Angler (pp. 89-90, 94), speaking of the ingenious Angler who knows how to tie a fly compared with the dullard. It turns out that
Walton's Angler is not quite as high-minded as he would have us think, if in fact he
uses 'night-hooks' (p. 99) and some of the other lures he details.

[390] Hobbes seems to be following Walton's train of thought, commenting on the
venality of the Pope in direct contrast to the simplicity enjoined by Christ on his disciples. See Walton, *op. cit.*, pp. 34-44, where the Piscator comments on the moral
faithfulness of creatures of land and sea to promises, talking of turtle doves pledg-
ing their eternal troth and the faithfulness of fishes (pp. 34-5). This belongs to the
defense of fishing, where Walton, quoting David: 'They that occupy themselves in
deep waters, see the wonderful works of God', comments 'indeed such wonders,
and pleasures too, as the land affords not'. Walton goes on directly to refer to the
Apostles as simple fishermen who use their time to teach the doctrines of Christ:
'and, in their sufferings, to preach freedom from the incumbrances of the law, and a
new way to everlasting life: this was the employment of these happy fishermen'.

[391] Walton, p. 105 talks about the art of catching 'over-grown fish', speaking
about huge fish in several places. They come out at night (pp. 107-8) and 'will rise
at a dead mouse, or a piece of cloth, or anything that seems to swim across the water,
or be in motion'. Walton (p. 105) discusses the huge fish as being perhaps a trout, or
even a salmon that has not returned to the sea and whose colour has changed, but
others think he is not.

[392] A *qui Perrupit . . . loco*: 'if somehow in a place'; c.f. B and 1688 edn, *quo
perrupit . . . loco*, 'if in some place . . .'.

Aut hamos fortasse novas[a] meditatur,[b] et escas[c]
     Piscibus,[d] aut aliquod nectere fraudis opus.   **1250**
Aut illis placitos escarum adhibere colores,[e]
     Noxia vel nitidis Pharmaca[f] quaerit aquis.
Omniaque emissis scrutatur litora servis,
     Quae fugit,[g] et quae,[h] quis litora piscis amat.
Tum quos,[i] et quibus, et quanti vendat nova cura est;
     Et mensae[j] pisces[k] quos retinere suae.

---

[a] mv uA B novos • [b] A B meditatur • [c] A B escas, • [d] uA Piscibus • [e] A B colores • [f] A pharmaca • [g] A B fugit • [h] A B quae • [i] uA C quos • [j] A menses (error) • [k] A pisces,

Or perhaps thinking about hooks and new bait for fish, or seeking to
    attach some tricky device,[393]   **1250**
Or offer them colours[394] of bait that they like, or poisons [395] to pollute clear
    waters.[396]
And having sent out his servants,[397] he examines every shoreline to find
    which certain fish flee and which ones they love.
Then his next concern is what he can sell, to whom and for how much;
    and what fish to keep for his own table.[398]

---

[393] Note that the punctuation is misleading in A B and 1688: *quaerit* (line 1252) governs both *nectere* (line 1250) and *adhibere* (line 1251).

[394] Note that the 1722 paraphrase itemizes the brilliant lures and flies in language that closely imitates the passage in Walton on flies to tie attractive a trout (pp. 96-7). Note also *colores rhetorici* as a more rhetorical form of bait and lure, to which Hobbes refers in his 'Answer' to Davenant's Preface to *Gondibert*, lines 250-65, *EW* IV, pp. 51-2.

[395] See Martial's *Epigrams* 4.30.1-5: *Piscator, fuge; ne nocens*, quoted in Walton's *The Compleat Angler*, chapter 5 (p. 108):
    Angler! would'st thou be guiltless? then forbear:
    For these are sacred fishes that swim here,
    Who know their sovereign, and will lick his hand,
    Than which none's greater in the world's command;
    Nay more they've names, and when they called are,
    Do to their several owner's call repair.
Hobbes's use of the term *pharmaca* for potions to catch fish, recalls line 1091, where the term is used mockingly to refer to the Eucharist. See also Molesworth's note 1, p. 352 to line 101, where the term is used to refer to the 'drugs or cosmetics, which the preachers sell in lots'. Walton, p. 137-9 discusses the making of pastes to catch a carp; on p. 185 he talks about strong-smelling oils 'to be excellent to tempt fish to bite'. Sir Henry Wotton is a chemical man to whom Walton presented a bottle from Sir George Hastings of such *pharmaca*. Walton then proceeds to refer to the Rosicrucians and the Philosopher's Stone, in terms of finding oils that attract fish.

[396] Walton, pp. 187-9, discusses slime and objects and creatures found in water that can be used to bait fish.

[397] In other words, with the bates and lures, perhaps including live bait attached to the hook. This is an allegory for the Pope, for whom even bishops, as we recall from line 1227, are servants. Walton claims, p. 170, 'There is also another fish called a POPE, and by some a RUFFE'.

[398] This is an allegory of the Pope as Prince. It is also a Last Judgment parable, about which fish to keep and which to throw back. Walton has a lot to say about what fish to keep and what to give away (p. 167). Athenaeus, in the 15-volume work entitled *Deipnosphistai*, that was written sometime after AD 228, in which a group of learned men converse at a banquet, and that is the model for this sort of Table Talk, gives recipes on how to treat and cook different kinds of fish.

Quos sale conspergat, compluri quos sale duret;
    Et quis marcescens abjiciendus erit.
Adde quod et multis cura est,[a] et maxima,[b] natis
    Perduraturas aedificare casas.   **1260**
Circumstant similes curae Papam;[c] similisque
    Ars est;[d] et semper res agit ille suas.
Principibusque parat nova vincula relligionis
    Tenuia,[e] quae faciet fortia stultities.[f]
Doctrinisque novis sarcit, si postulat usus,
    Aut levius reddit relligionis onus.[g]
Aut aliquod monstrum doctrinae,[h] è[i] pyxide Circes,[j]
    Ornat,[k] ita ut Pytheus crederet esse suum.
Absurdumve aliquod sustentat dogma bifurcis,
    Unde stupens capitur, qui fuit ante catus.[l]   **1270**

---

[a] uA est • [b] uA maxima • [c] A B Papam, • [d] A B est, • [e] uA B Tenuia • [f] C stultities: • [g] A opus, crossed out and replaced with onus. mv C opus. • [h] uA Doctrinae • [i] A B e • [j] A B Circes • [k] uA B Ornat • [l] A catus,

Which fish he should sprinkle with salt;[399] and which he should preserve
    with a large quantity of salt;[400] and which fish is rotten and should be
    thrown away.[401]
To these many concerns, add this, the greatest, to build enduring houses
    for his children.[402]   **1260**
Similar concerns surround the Pope, and his skill is similar; he too always
    pursues his own advantage.
And for princes he prepares new chains of religion, delicate, but which
    their stupidity will make strong.[403]
If necessity demands, he mends his nets with new teachings or lightens
    the burden of religious belief,
Or embellishes some monstrosity of a doctrine from Circe's box,[404] in such
    a way that Pythian Apollo[405] might believe it was his own.
Otherwise he holds up some absurd dogma with two prongs,[406] by which a
    once clever man, stupefied, is ensnared,   **1270**

---

[399] Walton, p. 139, identifies the carp as the fish one sprinkles with salt, having
used paste and oil and a scarlet lure to catch it.

[400] Walton follows the discussion about the Pope fish (pp. 170-71) with a discussion of the 'BLEAK, or fresh-water Sprat' which is caught with a Paternoster
line (6 small hooks tied along a line), and salted to make anchovies.

[401] Walton, pp. 54-5, on the Chavender or Chub fish as the fish that has to be
thrown away if not eaten immediately.

[402] A reference to Papal nepotism in the Renaissance.

[403] An echo of *Odyssey* 8.266ff. and Homer's description of the nets designed by
Vulcan to trap Venus and Mars: 'Not even a god could see them, so fine and subtle
were they'.

[404] For *Circe (Gr. *Kirkei*), see Homer, *Odyssey* 10.210 ff. and Virgil's *Aeneid*,
7.19-20. The *pyxis* is a container suitable for poison: Juvenal 13:25, Cic. *Pro Cael.*
65. Cf. line 1397 for Circe's pyxis.

[405] Hobbes means the Pope's doctrines are as obscure as the Delphic oracles.

[406] A dilemma, as illustrated by twin forks in the frontispiece for *Leviathan*; and
a possible hint at the 'forked tongue', a term especially reserved for the prolixity of
the Greeks. So, Angelo Decembrio, reporting learned conversations at the court of
Leonello d'Este in the 1440s, which seem to have rehearsed some of the arguments
of the Ferrara-Florence Council of 1438-9, puts into the mouth of the illustrious
Guarino Veronese, Valla's teacher, an address to the courtier Giovanni Gualengo:
    You speak truly, Gualengo, and elegantly recognize the three forked tongue of
    the Greeks. There are among the Greeks many words which express a joined
    threefold sense, not in the way the barbarians use forms for singular and diverse
    signs of things, which they intend to express the meaning of diverse things.
    And this manner of writing, or rather painting in signs, continued until defini-
    tion in the Roman fashion; so that in earlier days, you find no reflection existed
    on the grammatical art, still less on the oratorical or poetic.
See Decembro, *De Politia Litteraria*, VII, 81, f. 146, cited in Sarah Gravelle, 'Lorenzo
Valla's Comparison of Latin and Greek and the Humanist Background', pp. 279-80.

Debet et ad gentes[a] longinquas mittere scitum
    Quales sunt;[b] illis qualis et esca placet.
Indo,[c] namque Scythae, divisoque orbe Britanno,[d]
    Est anima, et salvam rem cupit esse suam.
Et Novus Orbis[e] habet, tellusque[f] Incognita,[g] multas
    Nec nigras animas, corpora nigra licet.
Argentique habet illa,[h] et flavi frusta metalli;[i]
    Haec sibi ne pereant Papa cavere solet.
Quos premet,[j] et quibus indulgebit,[k] id est,[l] sale sparget[m]
    Reges et proceres,[n] abjicietve,[o] putat,   **1280**

---

[a] A Gentes • [b] A B sunt, • [c] uA B Indo • [d] uA B Britanno • [e] uA B C novus orbis A novus Orbis • [f] mv B tullusque (error) • [g] uA B incognita C incognita; • [h] uA B illa C illa; • [i] uA B metalli, • [j] C premet • [k] uA B indulgebit • [l] A B est • [m] A B sparget. • [n] B Proceres, • [o] C abjicietve

And he is bound to send to remote peoples, to enquire who they may be,
  and the sort of bait that pleases them.
For the Indian,[407] the Scythian,[408] and the Briton in his separate world,[409] all
  have a soul, and the pope wants their salvation to be his business.[410]
The New World, also the unknown land, has many souls and they are not
  black, though their bodies may be black.[411]
It has nuggets of silver and yellow gold which the Pope always makes
  sure are not lost to him.[412]
He considers which kings and leaders he will pressure, to which he will
  grant indulgence by sprinkling them with salt, and which ones he will
  throw away,   **1280**

It is worth noting that Lorenzo Valla, following Cicero's treatment in the *Prior Academics* (2.29.95), discusses the *dilemma* together with the self-referential paradox, using
three central examples from the developed account of anecdotes involving
antestrephon or *dilemma* to be found in Aulus Gellius's newly discovered *Noctes Attica*
(5.11.1-14). See Lisa Jardine, 'Lorenzo Valla and the Intellectual Origins of Humanistic
Dialectic', p. 160, citing Valla, *Opera omnia*, ed. E. Garin (Torino 1962), vol. I, p. 744.

[407] *Indus* can also be translated, Indian, Hindu, Ethiopian, Arab, according to
Cooper's *Thesaurus*.

[408] The Scythians* were movable and a metaphor for the East. Note Hobbes's
echoes of *Pharsalia*, 8.210-395 (Joyce edn, p. 239), where Magnus [Pompey] has to
find a new world in the East in which to function, as does the Pope. See especially
Pharsalia, 8.215-17:
> Be not ashamed, while seeking support for Magnus [Pompey], to probe/ the
> Mede's remote homesteads, the Scythian hinterlands,/ to cross into a whole
> new world and carry my message.

[409] An echo of Virgil, *Ecl*. 1.66. Hobbes may be referring to Papal Bull *Inter
Coetera* dated May 4, 1493, ratified as the Treaty of Tordecilla in 1494, whereby the
Pope divided the New World between the Spanish and Portuguese empires.

[410] It follows from *The [Supposed] Donation of Constantine* (ed. Coleman,
pp. 28-9) that the Pope would fall heir to all the Western provinces of the Roman
Empire, as Lorenzo Valla, pointed out. Can any sane man imagine, Valla asks, Constantine 'giving with Rome Italy, not a province but the mistress of provinces;
giving the three Gauls; giving the two Spains; the Germans; the Britons; the whole
West; depriving himself of one of the two eyes of his empire?'

[411] On the 'scientific' treatment of race in terms of colour during this period, see
Renato Mazzolini, 'Anatomische Untersuchungen über die Haut der Schwarzen
(1700-1800)', in *Die Natur des Menschen: Probleme des Physischen anthropologie
und Rassenkunde (1750-1850)*, Gunter Mann and Franz Dumont, eds (Sömmerring
Forschungen, 6) Stuttgart, Gustav Fisher Verlag, 1990, pp. 169-87.

[412] Reference to the gold and silver of the New World. See also Ovid's depiction
of the Iron Age, *Metamorphoses*, 1.137-40, pp. 12-13:
> Not only did men demand of the bounteous fields the crops and sustenance
> they owed, but they delved as well into the very bowels of the earth; and the
> wealth which the creator had hidden away and buried deep amidst the very
> Stygian Shades, was brought to light, wealth that pricks men on to crime.

Et quos post mortem (sed longo tempore)[a] Divis
    Debet sacratos[b] adnumerare suis.
Ut sale durati,[c] durent[d] hi pluribus annis,
    Non magno pretio[e] quos sibi pauper emat.[f]
Denique,[g] quod primum est[h] claras non negligit ille
    Natis, cognatis, aedificare casas.
Plures Pontificum sunt curae;[i] quas numerare
    Difficile est, mentem ni juvet ordo meam.[j]
Ostia sed fusci stabo Polyphemus ad antri,[k]
    Utque foràs[l] tendit[m] quemque notabo dolum.[n]   **1290**
Sec. Haec[o] nimium[p] vereor[q] ne sit narratio longa;
    Fraus potuit doctos nulla[r] latere Senes.[s]
O quantum fraudis,[t] sexcentos posse per annos,[u]
    Milleque ab ingeniis surgere,[v] credis,[w] opus?[x]
Tempus adest coenae,[y] serum est percurrere[z] cuncta;[aa]
    Crastina, si vis tu, finiet illa dies.
Pr. Non serum est, meus ecce bonus[ab] Chronometra[ac] quid inquit;[ad]
    Praecisè sextam[ae] dimidiamque[af] notat.
Septima sermoni finem faciet nota nostro,[ag]
    Otia ne non det[ah] crastina forte dies.   **1300**
Praeter Judaeos,[ai] Gentes[aj] Idola colebant,
    Omnes, et domibus plura habuere suis.
Aurea divitibus stabant, et eburna Sacellis,[ak]
    Aut ex argento,[al] aut aere Corinthiaco,[am]
Aut stabat summi Parius lapis arte Magistri
    Factus.[an] Materiam nam superabat opus.[ao]

---

[a] C tempore (closing parenthesis missing) • [b] A Sacratos • [c] A B durati • [d] sc mv A B C 1688 durant but sense requires durent • [e] A B C pretio, • [f] ~A emat • [g] A B Denique • [h] A B C est, • [i] A B curae, • [j] ~A meam • [k] uA B antri • [l] uA B C foras • [m] A B tendit, • [n] ~A dolum • [o] sc mv1688 Hac • [p] mv uA B nimirum • [q] mv uA Veneror, (error) B veneror (error) • [r] mv A nullos • [s] A B senes, • [t] uA B fraudis • [u] A B annos • [v] uA B surgere • [w] uA B credis • [x] mv C opus. • [y] A C Coenae, • [z] A percurere • [aa] A B cuncta • [ab] mv A bonus missing • [ac] uA B C chronometra • [ad] A inquit • [ae] A sextam, • [af] B dimidiamque horam, horam scratched out, C dimidiumque • [ag] A B nostro C nostro; • [ah] A det, • [ai] uA B Judaeos • [aj] uA B gentes • [ak] uA sacellis • [al] A argento • [am] A B Corinthiaco. C Corinthiaco; • [an] A Factus, • [ao] mv A opus

Which after death (but a long time after), he should beatify and add to the
number of his saints.

So that, preserved with salt, they last for a great many years, so that the
poor man can buy them for himself at a moderate price.[413]

Finally, and this is most important, the Pope does not overlook building
splendid houses for his children and relatives.

The concerns of the Popes are many, and they are too difficult to
enumerate unless my mind is assisted with a list.

But I will stand as Polyphemus[414] at the mouth of the dark cave, and I will
take note of each trick as it goes forth.   **1290**

Sec. I am afraid that such a report would be much too long; no trick can
have escaped the notice of those learned old men.

O how many acts of fraud do you think could arise over one thousand six
hundred years from these geniuses?

It's almost dinner time. It's getting late to run through everything. We'll
do it tomorrow, if you like.

Pr. It's not late. Look at what my good watch[415] says, it shows half past
six exactly.

We'll end our chat at seven,[416] in case tomorrow offers no leisure.   **1300**

Except for the Jews, all races used to worship idols, and they had many in
their own houses.

Gold and ivory idols stood in opulent shrines of silver or Corinthian
bronze.

Or there stood idols of Parian marble,[417] fashioned by the skill of the
greatest master. Indeed the workmanship surpassed the materials.[418]

---

[413] At least at one level this concerns the sale of indulgences.

[414] See *Odyssey* 9.415ff. Polyphemus counted each sheep as it went out of the
cave. *Polyphemus:* (Cooper) 'a gygant that had one eye in his foreheade, which was
put out by Ulysses'.

[415] A reads simply *Chronometer*; c.f. B and 1688 edn, which read *bonus
Chronometer*, 'good Chronometer', *bonus* possibly added for the metrics.

[416] The seventh hour figures importantly in John.8:20.

[417] Paros, the second largest of the Cyclades, and a center of Aegean trade, was
famous for its white marble (*OCD*, 1970, p. 784). Cooper: 'a touche stone'.

[418] Parody of Ovid, *Met.* 2.5.

Ingenium nullum,[a] potuit facundia nulla
    Eripere haec avidis tam pretiosa viris.[b]
Quid faciet Praeco[c] (quoniam miracula cessant.)[d]
    Quî[e] potuit verbo conciliare fidem?   1310
Nam si non illis simulachra[f] indulta fuissent,
    Judaeum Graecus vix coluisset homo.[g]
Ergo coli sapiens permisit Doctor;[h] at illa
    Sub certa tantum conditione coli.[i]
Nempe ut mutarent divorum nomina.[j] Nolunt
    Vel Solis[k] dici, vel simulachra Jovis,[l]
Vel Phoebi, Martis, Lunae, Veneris,[m] vel Amoris,
    Mercurii, Bacchi, Palladis,[n] aut Cereris.

---

[a] C nullum • [b] mv A B viris • [c] uA C praeco • [d] B cessant) • [e] uA B C Qui •
[f] A C simulacra • [g] A homo • [h] uA B Doctor, c doctor; • [i] C coli • [j] A
nomina, • [k] uA b C solis • [l] A B Jovis • [m] A C veneris, • [n] A B C Palladis

No ingenuity, no eloquence, could wrest such costly idols from covetous
    men.
What could the preacher do (seeing that miracles have ceased)? How
    could he promote the faith with words? **1310**
In fact if they had not been permitted to have statues, the Greeks would
    hardly have worshipped a Jew,[419]
So the wise Doctor allowed statues to be worshipped, but they could be
    worshipped only under certain conditions.
In particular, that they would change the names of the gods. They didn't
    want them to be called statues of the Sun or of Jupiter,
Or of Phoebus Apollo, Mars, the Moon, Venus, or Cupid, Mercury,
    Bacchus, Pallas Athena or Ceres;

---

[419] Hobbes's highly unorthodox claim may refer to Paul, I Corinthians 8.4, where Paul remarked: 'We know that idols do not really exist in the world and that there is no god but the One. And even if there were things called gods, either in the sky or on earth – where there certainly seem to be 'gods' and 'lords' in plenty – still for us there is one God, the Father, from whom all things come and for whom we exist.' The slight ambiguity in Paul's text as to the existence of the pagan gods, is attributed by Paul Tillich to the fact that the Christian attitude to the pagan gods reflected the mentality of the Old Testament, where, among the early Hebrew prophets, pagan gods were recognized as powers competing with Jahweh, but inferior in terms of their capability to determine the future, hear prayers and dispense justice. See Tillich, *Christianity and the Encounter of the World Religions*, p. 31 ff., cited by Wright, pp. 389-90, n. 13. Paul, I Corinthians 8.4 was discussed by Hobbes in the opening sections of the 1668 Appendix to the *LL*, §§4-6 (trans. Wright, p. 350), where interlocutor A compares the existence of the Christian God with that of the pagan gods:

> [B] He is something real, not merely an appearance (phantasma), like that which is called a specter, or like the spirits, (daemones) worshipped by the pagans, those which the Apostle Paul calls nothing.
>
> [5] A. Yes, I remember that the apostle calls the graven images (idola) nothing but not that he says the same thing of the spirits (daemonia) of the heathen.
>
> [6] B. Do you think it is those images graven in gold and ivory and wood that he calls nothing? It is rather those spirits (daemonia) that are worshipped under the images. Besides, an idol properly so called is not the material thing itself, but the apparition (phantasma), that is, the idea or conception of the thing. It was in order to reflect their ideas of what their gods were like that the Greeks fashioned the images; they rarely adopted the ideas or conceptions of their gods from the images themselves. God too is distinguished from names by that word, being (ens). For the thing man is one thing; the name man, another.

Not only does Hobbes's text cast into doubt his belief in God, but the fact that he interprets the function of the verb 'to be' merely that of identifying objects for the purpose of naming them, but consistently maintains there is no necessary connection between names and things, gives ontological space for this doubt. Hobbes's later discussion of Christian statue cults once again puts Christianity on a par with idol worship; see lines 1375-1400.

Sed Christi,[a] Petri, Pauli, Sanctaeque Mariae,[b]
    Aut alio quovis[c] nomine Apostolico.   1320
Sic Fidei[d] verae comes ire Idololatria
    Permissa est;[e] vera[f] plus placuitque Fide.[g]
Quam nullus Princeps est ausus tempore[h] longo
    Laedere, nec sibi grex senserat esse male.
Sed veluti properae curae subnascitur ulcus[i]
    Acre, quod ad tempus non breve saepe latet,
Et tandem erumpit;[j] sic morbum Rex Leo primus
    Sensit,[k] nec potuit jam superare malum.
Sed tamen hinc natum est bellum calamare Sophistis,[l]
    Temporis illius qui docuere Fidem.[m]   1330
Hoc bello victi cessarunt Iconomachi,[n]
    Non concedentes,[o] sed siluere diu.
Hac arte effectum est,[p] ne quando cerneret artem
    Stulta,[q] stupens,[r] et hians plebs in Imaginibus.[s]
Numina nec tantùm[t] Gentes[u] fictilia amabant,[v]
    Sed Festos[w] etiam concelebrare dies;[x]
Tollere quos quicunque esset conatus ineptus,[y]
    Fecisset madidum saxeus Imber[z] eum.

---

[a] A B Christi • [b] A B Mariae • [c] mv A quamvis (error) • [d] uA B C fidei • [e] uA est A est, • [f] A verâ • [g] uA C fide. • [h] B témpore • [i] mv uA ullus • [j] uA erumpit B erumpit, • [k] uA Sensit • [l] uA Sophistis • [m] uA B C fidem. • [n] uA B Iconomachi • [o] B C concedentes • [p] B est • [q] uA Stulta • [r] A B C stupens • [s] ~ A Imaginibus • [t] A B C tantum • [u] B C gentes • [v] A B amabant • [w] uA B C festos • [x] A B dies. • [y] A B ineptus • [z] A B C imber

But rather statues of Christ, Peter, Paul, Holy Mary, or in any other
    apostle's name.[420]   **1320**

So idolatry was allowed to travel as the companion of true Faith, and in
    truth it was more satisfying than true faith.

No prince dared attack idolatry for a long time, and the flock didn't
    consider this a bad thing.

But just as an ulcer becomes inflamed underneath a hasty healing,
    because it often lies hidden for a long time

And finally breaks out; so the Emperor Leo[421] was the first to recognize
    the disease but then could not overcome its ill effects.

But a war of the pen was nevertheless started over this by Sophists of the
    time who taught the Faith.   **1330**

The icon-fighters were defeated in this war and stopped their activities;
    they were not giving up, but kept quiet for a long time.

This trick was effective in ensuring that the masses, foolish, stupefied and
    gaping at images, did not detect it.[422]

Nor did the nations only love their clay gods, but they also loved to
    celebrate their feast days.

If any foolish man had tried to take them away he would have been
    drenched by a shower of stones.[423]

---

[420] This follows the account given in *Lev.*, xlv, §29, 363/448 ff., and *OL*, iv, p. 383 (Curley edn, p. 449) of the Christian practice, learned by the early Christians from the Gentiles, of fabricating material idols, simulacra. Hobbes speculates that early converts, because of 'the immoderate esteem, and prices set upon the workmanship of them', preferred 'to retain them still in their houses', simply rebaptizing them, renaming 'an image of the *Virgin Mary* and her *Son* our Saviour, which before perhaps was called the image of Venus, and Cupid' (*Lev.*, xlv, §33, 365/451). See Karl Schuhmann, 'Phantasms and Idols: True Philosophy and Wrong Religion in Hobbes', *Rivista di Storia della Filosofia*, 59, 1 (2004), 15-31, at p. 25.

[421] Invernizzi cites Leo III, the Isaurian, 675-741, emperor from 717, who started the iconoclast movement in 726, but it is more likely *Leo I (457-74), who followed Marcian, and was the first emperor to receive his crown from the Patriarch of Constantinople.

[422] Ostrogorsky, *History of the Byzantine State*, pp. 160-1, notes that after Justinian the veneration of icons became a cult in the Byzantine church, but that it was not without its critics and 'that it was contact with the Muslim world which first fanned the smoldering distrust of icons into open flame'. The iconoclasts were known as 'Saracen-minded'.

[423] i.e. soaked in his own blood. For a shower of stones see Pliny, *Nat. hist.* 2.38.

Hinc Chronicus festus (tunc Saturnalia) nunc est
    Catholicus festus, nomine Carnevale.   1340
Nonne etiam mensis Maii[a] primum meministi,[b]
    Te puero, juvenes concelebrare diem ?
Ut Phallum arboreum (membrum navile) ferebant
    E sylvis,[c] medio quem statuere foro ;
Utque illum circa juvenes duxere Choreas
    Aptus vir bellis, apta puella viris ?
Hunc festum Gentes[d] olim Priapeia[e] vocabant,[f]
    Optatum pueris Virginibusque[g] diem.[h]
Nondum defecit vetus Ambarvalia[i] festus
    (Festus,[j] at innocuous,[k] permanet ille dies.)[l]   1350
Et quem rurales finita messe coloni[m]
    Cum Baccho Cereris concelebrare solent,

---

[a] A Maij B May (error) C Maji (error) • [b] A meministi • [c] uA B sylvis • [d] A B C gentes • [e] uA B Priapea • [f] ~ A vocabant • [g] A B C virginibusque • [h] C diem • [i] sc mv A B 1688 Ambervalia C Ambarvalia • [j] uA B Festus • [k] A B innocuus • [l] A B C dies) • [m] A Coloni

For this reason, the feast of Chronos[424] (known then as the Saturnalia),[425] is
now the Catholic festival, known as Carnivale.[426]   **1340**

And don't you also remember that when you were a boy the young people
celebrated the first of May ?

Don't you remember how they carried the wooden phallus (a pole-like
member)[427] from the forest, and stood it in the middle of the
marketplace,

And how the young people led a dance around it, the men are ready for
war, the girls are ready for men ?[428]

In times past people called it the festival of Priapus[429] and boys and girls
looked forward to the day.

The old holiday, the Ambarvalia,[430] has not yet fallen into disuse (this
festive and harmless day still lives on).   **1350**

And the feast of Ceres and Bacchus, which farmers in the country used to
celebrate when the harvest was finished,

---

[424] Hobbes spells *Cronos as Chronos: an ancient derivation of the god's name
to suggest that it really meant Time: see Cicero, *De natura deorum*, ed. A. S. Pease
(Cambridge, Mass., Harvard University Press, 1955), vol. 2, p. 64, where the editor
has a long note.

[425] The *Saturnalia* of December 17, was historically associated with a mock
king and the overturning of authority by the temporary releasing of slaves. The feast
among the ancients was associated with Chronos (see Macrobius, *Sat.* 1.7.36-7), but
by the 4th century AD most of its elements had been transferred to Christmas and
New Year's Day. (*OCD*, 1970, pp. 955-6).

[426] Hobbes is mistaken, the feast of Chronos, or *Chronia*, became the Christian
Carnivale, but the *Saturnalia* became the Christian Christmas.

[427] No parentheses in Molesworth. Phallic imagery associated with fertility festivals and the god *Priapus.

[428] A version of the Maypole.

[429] Priapus, a phallic fertility god.

[430] *Ambarvalia (misspelled *Ambervalia* in the *Hist. Eccl.* A B and 1688, but
not in *Lev.*) was a rural festival involving a procession around the fields to pray for
a good crop, derived from the Roman *Terminalla* and *Ambarvalia,* festivals in
honour of the god Terminus, and the goddess Ceres. It survives in some parishes and
'perambulation' is mentioned with approval in Izaak Walton's *Life of Hooker*
(1665). Note lines 1338 ff. recapitulate *Lev.*, xlv, §38, 367/453:

> The Church of Rome imitates them [the Heathens] also in their *holy days*.
> They had their *bacchanalia*; and we have our *wakes*, answering to them. They,
> their *saturnalia*; and we our *carnevals*, and Shrove-Tuesdays liberty of Ser-
> vants. They their procession of *Priapus*; we our fetching in, erection and
> dancing about *May-poles* (and dancing is one kind of worship). They had their
> procession called *Ambarvalia*; and we our procession about the fields in the
> *Rogation week*.

Temporibus priscis sunt Bacchanalia dicta,[a]
     Cum Vini colerent ebrietate Deum.[b]
Multa tulere patres legi contraria[c] Christi,
     Dum populum properant conciliare sibi.
Nec sic venisset fortasse Proselyta[d] multus,
     Si non à[e] causis[f] pluribus actus erat.[g]
Vita Sacerdotum cunctis odiosa erat,[h] illis
     Ingenii aut morum gratia nulla fuit.   1360
Nam tristi gravitate superbus Hypocrita[i] quem non
     Offendit,[j] quamquam caetera doctus homo?[k]
Qui spretis aliis sapiens vult solus haberi[l]
     Et dici, quamvis nil sciat ille boni;[m]
Justa sibi[n] solvi qui postulat omnia, summo
     Adque[o] datum punctum,[p] jure Geometrico;[q]
Ipse tamen solvit sua,[r] libertate Poetae;[s]
     Hunc socium vitae dixeris esse bonum?
Compulit ad Christum,[t] vita improba Sacrificorum
     Multos foelices[u] ingenuosque viros.   1370
Quippe parùm[v] possunt insulsos ferre,[w] pudico
     Ingenio nati, non inopesque[x] viri.
Sed multò[y] plures traxit communio victus,[z]
     Quanquam illos inopes,[aa] contiguosque fami.[ab]
Sec. Siste gradum.[ac] Quoniam[ad] nec adhuc,[ae] in imagine Christi,[af]
     Aut Sancti,[ag] quicquam[ah] cerno ego inesse mali.[ai]
Non ego,[aj] si flector, si verba effundo precantum,
     Sique[ak] meos oculos detinet effigies;[al]
Non illi flector, non alloquor, aut colo. Solum
     Oro Deum, nomen cogito mente Dei.   1380

[a] C dicta • [b] mv A Deum B Déum • [c] A Contraria • [d] uA proselyta • [e] A B a • [f] A Causis • [g] B erat • [h] uA B erat • [i] A C hypocrita • [j] uA B Offendit • [k] uA homo • [l] mv A haberi? • [m] uA boni • [n] sc mv 1688 tibi (error) • [o] mv A B Atque • [p] uA B punctum • [q] uA geometrico, B Geometrico, • [r] uA B sua • [s] uA B Poetae • [t] uA B Christum • [u] A C felices B foelicés • [v] A B C parum • [w] uA B ferre • [x] B innopesque • [y] A B C multo • [z] A B victus • [aa] uA B innopes C inopes • [ab] C fami: • [ac] mv A B gradum • [ad] A B quoniam • [ae] A B C adhuc • [af] A B C Christi • [ag] A B Sancti C sancti, • [ah] A B quicquam, • [ai] mv uA B modi (error) • [aj] uA B ego • [ak] mv uA B Sicque • [al] A effigies.

Was in ancient times called the Bacchanalia, and then they worshipped
the god of wine with drunkenness.[431]
The Fathers put up with many things contrary to the law of Christ while
they hastened to win the people over to their side.
And probably not many converts would have come forth, if they had not
been driven by a number of reasons.
The lifestyle of the priests was detestable to everyone, their minds and
morals were nothing good. 1360
In fact was there anyone the arrogant hypocrite didn't offend with his
sullen dignity, even if he was learned in other respects? –
The man who, scorning others, wants to be considered and spoken of as
the only wise man, even though he knows nothing of goodness,
Insisting that everything should be paid to him with mathematical
exactness, precisely on time,[432]
Yet with poetic license exempting himself – could you say this man is a
good companion for life?
The corrupt lifestyle of the priests attracted many successful and
intelligent men to Christ, 1370
Because fools could barely be tolerated by men born with a modest
disposition yet not without means.
But the community of the means of life attracted many more, albeit the
poor and those near starvation.[433]
Sec. Stop right there, because up to now I have not seen anything
inherently evil in statues of Christ and the Saints.
No, if I kneel and pour forth the words of those praying, and the statue
holds my eyes,
I am not kneeling to that statue, addressing or worshipping it. I am
praying to God alone, I am reflecting upon the name of God in my
mind. 1380

---

[431] *Bachanalia* was the Latin term for the Greek *orgia*, a festival which had a
specific club identity.

[432] A, B, *sibi*; c.f. 1688 edn, *tibi*, an error.

[433] Hobbes refers in particular to the mendicant order. Note the abrupt break in
the text at line 1375, where *Sec.* answers not to the question of recruitment to the
Church on the basis of a common table, but rather to an unspoken question about
statue cults, resuming again the topic of iconoclasm from lines 1311-38. The long
disquisition on images and statue cults possibly relates to the speaking statues of the
Egyptian priests in the *Corpus Hermeticum* (see Springborg Introduction,
chapter 5.2), given that in the poem Egyptian priests are often surrogates for priestcraft in general (see lines 170-340). But at lines 1407-8 the discussion of images
belongs to the *topos* of the papacy and fisherman's lures, begun at line 1241.

Tune[a] Deos Romae credis simulachra videri?
    Quid faciunt ergo tot simulachra? Monent.
Quod fuit olim Serpens Aeneus[b] Israelitis,[c]
    Atque Sacerdoti[d] quod Cherubinus erat,
(Ante illos,[e] Dominoque Authore,[f] precatio facta est)[g]
    Hoc Sancto, Sancti praestat imago,[h] viro.
Pr.[i] Difficile esse putas homini,[j] praesertim Idiotae,
    Credere in effigie posse latere Deum?
Naturam humanam nimium nescire videris.[k]
    Credere (crede mihi) quidlibet[l] ille[m] potest.   1390
Nam simul ac hominem possedit cura futuri,[n]
    Temporis, ipse suum consuluitque metum,[o]
Credere pronus erit spem qualemcunque ferenti,
    Atque[p] sequi multos[q] quâ[r] videt ire[s] via.
Credebant Gentes habitare in imagine numen,[t]
    An minùs[u] illorum est vivida nostra fides?
Quòd[v] simulachra monent,[w] color est è[x] pyxide Circes
    Sumptus,[y] et Idolo[z] cuilibet aptus erit.

---

[a] A Tu ne • [b] A C aeneus • [c] uA Israëlitis B Israelitis C Israëlitis, • [d] A Sacerdoti, • [e] uA B C illos • [f] uA B Authore C authore, • [g] mv C est, (closing bracket missing) • [h] A B C imago • [i] mv uA B C *Pr.* missing • [j] A B homini • [k] A B videris, • [l] mv uA B C quilibet • [m] mv uA B illa • [n] A B futuri, • [o] A metum; • [p] A Atqui (error) • [q] A B multos, • [r] A B qua • [s] sc mv A B C ire (infin. of eo, to go) 1688 ira (error). See Molesworth's note, p. 386, '[Sic. Quaere ire?]' suggesting a correction of ira to ire. • [t] C Numen, • [u] A B C minus • [v] A B C Quod • [w] uA B monent • [x] A e • [y] uA B Sumptus C Sumtus (error) • [z] A C idolo

Do you believe statues are considered gods in Rome? What is the point of
    so many statues? They are reminders.[434]
What the bronze serpent once was for the Israelites, and what the
    Cherubim was for the priest[435]
(prayer was offered before them and was offered on God's authority), this
    is what the image of a saint offers to a saintly man.
Pr. Do you think it is difficult for someone, especially an uneducated
    man, to believe God can lie hidden in a statue?
You don't seem to know too much about human nature, the uneducated
    man (believe me) can believe anything.   **1390**
For as soon as concern about the future takes hold of a man, and he
    reflects upon his own fear,
He will then be disposed to believe anyone bringing hope of any kind,
    and to follow the many on whatever path he sees them take.[436]
The Gentiles believed divinity inhabited statues, and is our faith less
    lively than theirs?[437]
The counsel[438] the statues give is a colour taken out of Circe's box[439] and
    will be fitting for any idol.

---

[434] Alternatively 'warning'. See *Elements of the Law, EW*, vol. 4, p. 67 and *Lev.*,
xlv, §23, 361/446, where Hobbes cleverly turns his view on worship and idolatry to
use against the doctrine of transubstantiation:

> To worship God in some peculiar place, or turning a man's face towards an
> image or determinate place, is not to worship or honour the place or image, but
> to acknowledge it holy – that is to say, to acknowledge the image or the place
> to be set apart from common use.... And therefore is not idolatry, no more
> than it was idolatry to worship God before the brazen serpent.... But to
> worship God as inanimating or inhabiting such image or place – that is to say
> an infinite substance in a finite place – is idolatry.

[435] Exodus 25.17-22 and Numbers 21.8-9.

[436] A, B, *ire*, infin. of *eo*, to go; c.f. 1688 edn, *ira*, anger, clearly an error. See
Molesworth's note, p. 386.

[437] Lucretius, *De rer. nat.* 6.75 was willing to allow that it is right for men to
approach the shrines of the gods with placid hearts, and 'to receive with tranquil peace
of spirit the images (*simulacra*) which are carried to men's minds from their holy
bodies', as if condoning popular or state-sanctioned religion. Hobbes uses the term *simulachrum* at lines 1311, 1316, 1381, 1405 and 1653 in a principally Lucretian sense.

[438] Alternatively 'warning', referring back to line 1382.

[439] Hobbes, in his 'Answer' to Davenant's *Preface*, lines 252-64 (Molesworth edn,
EW IV, pp. 51-2), developing the theme that 'Poets are Paynters', observes of the poet:

> That which he hath of his owne, is nothing but experience and knowledge of
> Nature, and especially humane nature; and it is the true and naturall Colour.
> But that which is taken out of Bookes (the ordinary boxes of Counterfeit Com-
> plexion) shewes well or ill, as it hath more or less resemblance with the natu-
> rall, and are not to be used (without examination) unadvisedly....That which
> giveth a Poeme the true and naturall Colour consisteth in two things, which

Nil facit exemplum Serpentis,[a] nec Cherubini,[b]
    Quos fieri et statui jusserat ipse Deus.   **1400**
Respice mandatum Domini. Tibi sculptile,[c] dixit,[d]
    Non facies. Populus fecerat illa[e] Deo.
Cessantis quondam pluviae signum fuit Iris;[f]
    Sanati morsus Aeneus[g] ille Draco.[h]
Sec. Nec colui Simulachra,[i] nec esse colenda putabam;[j]
    Attamen assensu laetus abibo tuo.
Persequere inceptum,[k] quibus insuper artibus usi
    Sunt Piscatores[l] ordine quasque refer.[m]
Pr. Est aliud genus Idoli subtilius omni
    Materia, quali vita carere nequit.   **1410**
Aëre[n] simplicius, subtilius aethere puro;[o]
    Mobile;[p] sed nullo quod queat esse loco.

---

[a] A B serpentis • [b] A cherubini B Cherubini • [c] uA sculptile B sulptile (error) mv C sculptibile, • [d] uA B dixit • [e] B illas (error) • [f] B Iris, C iris • [g] C aeneus • [h] A C draco. • [i] A C simulachra, • [j] A B putabam • [k] C inceptum; • [l] A C piscatores, B piscatores • [m] sc A B C refer. 1688 refer, • [n] A Aeëre B C Aere • [o] uA B puro • [p] uA B Mobile,

The examples of the serpent or the Cherubim are of no avail; God himself
    had ordained that they should be created and established.   **1400**
Consider God's commandment. He said, 'Thou shalt not make thyself any
    graven image'.[440] Yet the people had made graven images to God.
The rainbow was once the sign that the rains were over,[441] and the bronze
    serpent that the bite was healed.[442]
Sec. I have not worshipped images, and never thought they should be
    worshipped, but I shall go away happy if I have your approval.
Go on with your planned account and relate also all the arts the Fishermen
    have used.
Pr. There is another kind of image; finer than any substance, which life
    cannot do without.[443]   **1410**
Lighter than Air, finer than pure Ether; mobile, yet unable to occupy any
    place.[444]

---

are; *To know well*, that is, to have images of nature in the memory, distinct and
cleare; and *To know much*.

[440] Exodus 20, 23.
[441] The rainbow personified as the goddess Iris.
[442] Numbers 21:6-9, at 9: 'Moses accordingly made a bronze serpent and mounted
it on a pole, and whenever anyone who had been bitten by a serpent looked at the
bronze serpent, he recovered.' For Hobbes's discussion of images and idols, with specific reference to the Bronze serpent and Cherubim, see *Lev.*, xlv, §23, 361/446.

[443] Hobbes's discussion of this 'kind of image; finer than any substance' (*genus
Idoli subtilius omni Materia*), may be with direct reference to Duns Scotus, known
as *Doctor Subtilis*, and mentioned at line 1868.

[444] At lines 1409, 1413, 1415, and 1674 Hobbes uses the term *idolum* to refer to
images or ideas as the indispensable vehicle of the imagination. Ref. also *Lev.*, xlv,
§14, 358/444:

And these are the images which are originally and most properly called *ideas*,
and *idols*, and derived from the language of the Graecians, with whom the
word Εἴδω signifieth to *see*. They are also called PHANTASMS, which is, in
the same language, *Apparitions*. And from these images it is that one of the
faculties of man's nature is called the imagination. And hence it is manifest
that there neither is, nor can be, any image made of a thing invisible.

On idols and phantasms as a semantic field, see especially Zarka, 'Le Vocabulaire de
l'apparaitre' and Schuhmann, 'Phantasms and Idols'. Schuhmann notes, p. 19, that
'phantasm' is the term Hobbes uses for cognition in general and that in its general
meaning 'the term "idol" is just another word for "phantasm"', as Aristotle used it
(p. 23), while in its restricted sense it refers to 'a statue or picture of some heathen god,
such as "the idol Moloch" (*EW* III, p. 447) or "the idol Rimmon" (*EW* III, p. 493)'.
Schuhmann references (p. 23) the frequency of Hobbes's quotation of Paul, 1 Cor. 8:4,
that 'an idol is nothing' (at *EW* III, pp. 150, 382, 645; *OL* III, pp. 457, 481, 512, 515,
537, 563; *EW* IV, p. 308; *EW* V, p. 211; *EW* VII, p. 79). The account in the *Hist. Eccl.*,
that follows sets out succinctly Hobbes's theory of images, idols, phantasms and ideas
as unexamined sense data, refined into knowledge by ratiocination. *Idolum* in Bacon's
Novum Organum, describes the four kinds of false learning as 'Idols of the Tribe (tacit

Talibus Idolis[a] non est macilentior umbra;[b]
    Namque patente oculo[c] cernitur umbra nigra.[d]
Illa Idola[e] oculis nunquam cernuntur apertis,
    Sed tantum clausis attonitisve metu.
Sicut subtilis[f] magis est sapientia per se[g]
    Quam quisquam sapiens,[h] re bonitasque bona;[i]
Sic etiam subtilior est Idololatria
    Quam dico, quàm[j] quae materialis erat.   **1420**
Sec. Haec[k] aenigmaticè[l] quamvis narrasse videris,[m]
    Attamen ut capiam[n] non opus OEdipode est.
Namque mera indoctae coluerunt Somnia[o] Gentes[p]
    Picta Sacerdotes quo voluere modo.
Nocturnum populum nemo non viderat. Unde
    Advenere tamen nescius omnis erat.[q]

---

[a] A C idolis • [b] uA B umbra, • [c] A B oculo, • [d] ~A nigra • [e] A C idola • [f] A Subtilis • [g] A B C per se, • [h] uA B sapiens • [i] uA B bona, • [j] A B quam • [k] mv uA B Sed • [l] mv A aenigmatice? A aenigmatice • [m] A B videris. • [n] A B capiam, • [o] A B C somnia • [p] A B Gentes, C gentes • [q] A erat

No shadow is thinner than such spectres. For, indeed, a dark shadow is
discernable to the open eye.[445]

But these spectres are never perceived by the open eyes, but only when
closed or struck with fear.[446]

Just as wisdom is in itself more impalpable than any wise man and
goodness more impalpable than any good thing,

So also this idolatry of which I speak is more impalpable than the material
kind.[447]   1420

Sec. However enigmatically you have expressed these things, I don't need
to be an Oedipus to understand them.[448]

In fact uneducated races worshipped mere dreams, embellished[449] in
whatever way the priests wanted.

Everyone had seen the people of the night. But where they come from, no
one knew.[450]

---

agreement to preserve comfortable illusion), Idols of the Cave (errors of unconscious
habit), Idols of the Marketplace (imprecise vocabulary), Idols of the Theatre (traditional systems of thought)'. See John Tobin's comment in his edition of *George
Herbert, The Complete Poems*, (Harmondsworth, Penguin 1991), p. 449, n. 12.

[445] Cicero, *De nat. deor.* 1.18, 49. Lucretius, *De re. nat.*, 5.1167-9. See Moreau,
'Epicure et la Physique des Dieux', p. 287n.

[446] See 'Of Religion', *Lev.*, xxii, §7, 53/64-5:

> And for the matter or substance of the invisible agents so fancied, they could
> not by natural cogitation fall upon any other conceit but that it was the same
> with that of the soul of man, and that the soul of man was of the same sub-
> stance with that which appeareth in a dream to one that sleepeth, or in a
> looking-glass to one that is awake; which men, not knowing that such appari-
> tions are nothing else but creatures of the fancy, think to be real and external
> substances (and therefore call them ghosts, as the Latins called them *imagines*
> and *umbrae*, and thought them spirits, that is thin aerial bodies).

For a discussion of the relation between idols, demons and matter, see also Zarka,
'Le Vocabulaire de l'apparaitre'.

[447] i.e. than the material kind of idolatry. This admission of the power of impal-
pability, perhaps with reference to Francis Bacon's 'idola fori, theatri', etc. in
Novum Organum, takes us by surprise.

[448] Oedipus won kingship by solving the riddle of the sphinx. Note George
Herbert's address to Bacon on the occasion of the publication of *Novum Organum*, in
Herbert, *The Complete English Poems*, p. 319, where the Pontiff is referred to as, 'rerum
unicus magister, at non Artium', 'fugator idolem', 'subtilitatis Tenebra', i.e., as 'fleeing
idols', a 'pontifex of truth rather than pontifex of lies', and 'a penetrator of subleties'.

[449] We expect *ficta*, 'made up, invented', but Hobbes uses *picta* (Lewis &
Short), painted, coloured, of various colours; (of style), ornamented, ornate; merely
painted, i.e., deceptive, but perhaps not invented.

[450] Once again the 'shades' and 'spectres' of Roman popular religion in Virgil,
etc., which Hobbes discredits along Epicurean lines, but more harshly in the *Hist.
Eccl.*, (see lines 85-100 and notes), than in *Lev.*, ii, §8, 8/10; here as the work of
'corrupt philosophers' playing on people's fear of the unknown.

Pr.[a] Hinc metus ignoti,[b] doctrinaque Daemoniorum,
    Subdita corruptis Philosophisque Fides.[c]
Respexitque Fides[d] ex[e] illo tempore Patrum
    Dogmata, non Sacri[f] quae docuere Libri.   **1430**
Sic populus trepidus pendebat ab ore Magistri;
    Coeperunt Regum jussa valere parùm.[g]
Cara nimis pauci versabant Biblia. Nondum
    Artis erat libros multiplicare Typis.[h]
Inque Patrum manibus mansere Oracula[i] Sancta,[j]
    Quorum praeceptis tunc didicere loqui.
Deinde quod in Templis[k] curabant commemorari
    Doctorum quaedam nomina amica sibi,
Expediebat eis. Spes ostentata[l] triumphi,[m]
    Militiae est semper maxima causa bonae.   **1440**
Sec.[n] Sed quid,[o] an in Templis,[p] et dum celebrantur honores
    Divini, fas est concelebrare hominem[q]
Quem pius ignoras sit an impius,[r] ignibus atris
    Subtùs,[s] an in coeli luce beatus agat?
Regibus infesto signabis nomine Fastos?[t]
    Becchetti[u] stabit Fatum in Ephemeride?

---

[a] mv uA B *Pr.* missing • [b] uA B ignoti • [c] uA C fides. • [d] A C fides • [e] C ea (error) • [f] A C sacri • [g] uA B C parum. • [h] A Typis • [i] uA oracula • [j] A B C sancta, • [k] A B C templis • [l] A Ostentata • [m] uA B triumphi • [n] mv uA B *Sec.* missing • [o] uA B quid • [p] A B C templis, • [q] A B hominem. C hominem, • [r] uA B impius • [s] uA B C Subtus • [t] uA fastos? • [u] B Béecchetti

Pr. Hence fear of the unknown, and the doctrine of Demons, and faith
    subjected to corrupt philosophers.
And from that time faith turned its attention to the dogmas of the Fathers
    and not to what the Bible taught.   **1430**
So the anxious people hung on the word of a teacher; the commands of
    Kings began to have little force.
Too few turned to the expensive Bible. Multiplying books by printing was
    not yet a trade.[451]
And the sacred oracles remained in the hands of the Fathers, by whose
    precepts they were taught to speak.[452]
Then it was expedient for them that they took care to have the names of
    learned men well disposed to them
Commemorated in their churches. Holding out hopes of victory is always
    the greatest reason for a good campaign.   **1440**
Sec. But what does it matter whether it is right to celebrate a man in
    churches, and while the holy sacraments are being solemnized,
When you don't know whether he is pious or impious, whether he is
    dwelling in the black fires below, or blessed in the light of heaven?
Will you mark the calendar[453] with a name inimical to Kings? Will the
    death of Becket[454] stand in the calendar?

---

[451] Hobbes notes the importance of printing to the Reformation. But in *Lev.*, iv, §1, 12/15, in a different context perhaps, he had declared that 'The invention of *printing*, though ingenious, compared with the invention of *letters* is no great matter'.

[452] The Council of Trent in 1546 insisted that the Scriptures must be interpreted in the light of the consensus of the Church Fathers, explicitly forbidding interpretations '*contra unanimen consensum Patrum*'. See Quantin, 'The Fathers in Seventeenth Century Roman Catholic Theology', in *The Reception of the Church Fathers in the West, from the Carolingians to the Maurists*, Irena Backus, ed. (Leiden, E.J. Brill, 1997), 2 vols, vol. 2, pp. 953-76, at, p. 953.

[453] *Ephemerides*, diaries, a term particularly designating the royal journal of Alexander the Great kept by Eumenes of Cardia providing information about Alexander's daily life. (*OCD*, 1970 edn, 386-7). Note that the 1722 paraphrast (p. 22) refers to Eumenes, as 'the grand Projector of th' *Ephemeris*'. Among Hobbes's contemporaries Isaac Casaubon, John Milton and Samuel Hartlib wrote *Ephemerides*, which often reported on Hobbes. See Clucas, 'Samuel Hartlib's Ephemerides, 1635-1659', and Noel Malcolm, 'The Printing and Editing of Hobbes's *De Corpore*: A Review of Karl Schuhmann's Edition', *Rivista di storia della filosofia*, vol. 59 (2004), pp. 329-57, at p. 344 n. 50.

[454] *Thomas Becket, 1118-1170, Archbishop of Canterbury, Chancellor of Henry II, whose martyrdom, ordered by the king, is celebrated on December 29. The case of Becket was one of three salient cases of Papal intervention in the affairs of England, as listed in the epic and poetic chronicle of Thomas May, Hobbes's contemporary, *The Reigne of King Henry the Second, Written in Seaven Bookes, by his Majesties Command* (1633).

Pr. Quod stetit id[a] stabit, vim legis dum tenet Usus.[b]
     Et populos recta pro ratione regit.[c]
Papa sed ad magnam spem cor[d] dilatat, et orbis
     Totius imperium cogitat esse suum.   1450
Et juris titulos extorquet Codice sacro;[e]
     Supponi sibi vult[f] omnia Jure[g] Dei.
Nominibusque capit Regum Regalia[h] jura.[i]
     (Saepe Fidem[j] gignit nomen inane rei.)[k]
Pontificem dici vult se, quo nomine quondam
     Augustus Romae coeperat Imperium.[l]
Quodque fuit Moses Judaeis, et quod Aaron[m]
     In toto Christi postulat esse grege.
Utque vocant trepidae summi Jovis[n] arma Tonantis[o]
     Gentes,[p] Censuras sic vocat ille suas.   1460

---

[a] mv A B hoc replaces id • [b] A B C usus. • [c] A B regit • [d] mv A cor missing • [e] A B sacro • [f] mv uA B vult sibi (word order) • [g] mv uA B jura • [h] A C regalia • [i] A B jura, • [j] A C fidem • [k] A B rei) • [l] A B C imperium. • [m] A B C Aaron, • [n] B C jovis • [o] uA C tonantis B tonantis, • [p] uA Gentes

Pr. What has stood will stand,[455] so long as usage has the force of law,
And governs the people instead of right reason. But the Pope's heart
 swelled with great hope,[456] and he thought that dominion over the
 whole world was his.   1450
He extracted from the sacred texts legal pretexts,[457] for he wanted
 everything to be subject to him by the law of God.[458]
And he took royal rights in the names of kings (an empty name often
 generates belief in a thing).
He wanted to be called Pontiff, the title by which Augustus had earlier
 seized sovereign power over Rome.
And what Moses and Aaron were to the Jews, he claimed to be for the
 whole flock of Christ.
And the Pope gave to his own censures the name that frightened nations
 give to the arms of Jupiter the Thunderer on high.[459]   1460

---

[455] *stare decisus.*

[456] According to Hobbes's psychology, based on inertial motion, sense experience causes an alteration of the brain, which we refer to as passion, registered in turn in the heart, as seat of the emotions, which dilates with pleasure and constricts with pain. See *De corpore* (*EW* IV, chs 1-10). For Hobbes's theory of inertial motion see Leijenhorst, *Hobbes and the Aristotelians*, and Sarasohn, 'Motion and Morality'.

[457] Hobbes is referring to the cooptation of Roman law by the canon lawyers.

[458] Hobbes concludes his account of the institutional rise of papal power by showing that with capitulation after capitulation by Christian emperors, the Pope was able to present his sovereignty as if by divine right. See Gianni Paganini, 'Thomas Hobbes e Lorenzo Valla', p. 543.

[459] i.e. *fulminatio*, used of acts of excommunication. Hobbes, referring to the Pope invoking his powers of interdict and excommunication, uses *censura*, from *censeo*, (Chambers Murray) the office of censor, censorship, used literally by Cicero, Ovid and Livy. Coleman, in the preface to his edition of Valla's *[Supposed] Donation of Constantine*, p. 8, notes that *censura* is one of the usages peculiar to the chancellery of Stephen II (III) Bishop of Rome 752-7, and of Paul I (757-67) that mark the 8ᵗʰ and 9ᵗʰ century Italian documents believed to be the provenance of the forgery, but probably unknown to Valla (See the exhaustive linguistic analysis of Paul Scheffer-Boichorst, 'Neue Forschungen über die Konstantinische Schenkung', cited by Coleman, p. 6n.). The earliest known manuscript of *The [Supposed] Donation of Constantine*, is the *Codex Parisiensis* Lat. 2778, belonging to the 8ᵗʰ century Collectio Sancti Dionysii of the monastery of St. Denis in France; while the collected Pseudo-Isodorean Decretals, the form in which the *Donation* became known to the wider world, also came from France. These manuscripts were not available to Valla, who used Gratian's *Decretum*, though possibly to Hobbes, who earlier reproved Valla for failing to use the best available manuscripts for his translation of Thucydides, complaining that Valla's translation was 'not without some errors' and taken from 'a Greek copy not so correct as now is extant'. See Quentin Skinner, *Reason and Rhetoric in the Philosophy of Hobbes*, pp. 238-9.

Nec Majestatis contentus nomine, nomen
     Sanctius assumit,[a] conveniensque Deo.
Sec. Quin siet impietas nec parva haec, nolo negare.[b]
     Censuras rectè[c] fulmina forte vocat.
Nam sicut Fulmen,[d] si quando se insinuarit[e]
     In commissuras parjetis igne suo,[f]
Disjungit lapides, si non et disjicit,[g] et sic
     Quod fuerat firmum debile reddit opus;[h]
Sic quoque dissociat cives Censura[i] timenda
     Illis qui stultè[j] Phasmata vana timent.[k]   1470
Pr. Ad genus omne boni mundani carbasa praebent;
     Ad visas,[l] velis omnibus,[m] itur opes.
Ut capiant populos, cogant et ovescere Reges,
     Quoque modo possint parta tenere student;[a]

---

[a] A B assumit • [b] A B negare • [c] B C recte • [d] A B C fulmen, • [e] mv A insin-
uâvit (uA insinuarit) B insinuavit • [f] mv A B suo. • [g] A disjicit • [h] mv A B
opus. • [i] B censura C censura, • [j] A B stulte • [k] B timent; • [l] uA B visas •
[m] uA B omnibus

Not content with the name of Majesty, he assumed a more sacred name,
and one appropriate to God.

Sec. I don't want to deny that this constitutes impiety and no small
impiety, but perhaps he rightly calls his censures thunderbolts.[460]

For just as a thunderbolt, if ever it penetrates the joints of a wall with its
fire,

Dislodges stones, if not breaking them up as well, and in this way renders
a construction which had been strong weak,[461]

So too a censure commanding fear in those who foolishly fear ghosts
divides the citizenry.[462]   **1470**

Pr. The Popes set their sails towards every kind of worldly good;
proceeding with all sails aloft at the sight of wealth.[463]

They applied themselves diligently to take peoples captive, to force kings
to become sheep, and to keep their acquisitions in any way they could,

---

[460] C.f. *Lev.*, xlii, §31 279/349:
> The name of *Fulmen excommunicationis*, (that is *the thunderbolt of excommunication*) proceeded from an imagination of the Bishop of Rome, which first used it, that he was king of kings – as the heathen made Jupiter king of the gods, and assigned him, in their Poems and Pictures, a thunderbolt wherewith to subdue and punish the Giants that should dare to deny his power.

Lorenzo Valla in his *[Supposed] Donation of Constantine*, ed. Coleman, pp. 176-7, used the same language for the Pope's punitive powers, implying like Hobbes that papal coercion betrayed the Church's mission, which is non-governmental:
> But do you attend to your priestly functions; and don't stand in the north, and thundering there hurl your lightning and thunderbolts against this people and others.

[461] Hobbes's form of words (lines 1465-8: 'Nam sicut fulmen, si quando se insinuâvit/ In commissuras parjetis igne suo./ Disjungit lapides, si non et disjicit, et sic/ Quod fuerat firmum debile reddit opus'), echoes Lucretius, *De rer. nat.*, 6.83-9: 'unde volans ignis pervenerit aut in utram se/ verterit hinc partim, quo pacto per loca saepta/ insinuarit, et hinc dominatus ut extulerit sc.' 'You may not. . . tremble to see from which direction the flying fire has come,. . . how it has penetrated through walled places, and how after taking complete possession it has won its way out.' See Lucretius, *De rer. nat.*, ed. Smith, pp. 498-9.

[462] The passage on lightning in Lucretius (see note 461 above) concerns Etruscan augural practices (C.f. Cicero *De div.*, and Pliny *HN* 2.143) and begins with Lucretius' admonition (6. 83-4): 'the law and aspect of the sky have to be understood; storms and bright lightnings have to be sung'. See Lucretius, ed. Smith, *De rer. nat.*, pp. 498-9.

[463] Ovid *Metamorphoses* 1.130-40: Ovid's Iron Age, 'this age of baser vein' sees 'Men now spread their sails to the winds' in search of lands to conquer for their mineral wealth. 'And the ground, which had hitherto been a common possession like the sunlight and the air, the careful surveyor now marked out with the long-drawn boundary-line'. Hobbes applies it to fortune-hunting Popes in the New World. Note that he sets the great expansion of the Papacy late, to coincide with the Christianization of the New World.

Queis opus est multo stratagemate perficiendis,
    Nequitia docta, Philosophaque Fide.[b]
Suevit ut in Templis,[c] audisti, Ecclesia Patrum
    Prima,[d] satellitium[e] commemorare suum.[f]
Nunc autem Papis dominantibus,[g] adnumeratur[h]
    Divis,[i] quisquis eis profuit arte sua.   1480
Reddita sic rursus populo est Idololatria,[j]
    Nemoque non Divum[k] coepit habere sibi.
Sec. Romani moris fuit haec imitatio prisci[l]
    Ut qui Caesaribus par tribuere decus.
Sed non tam temerè[m] tantos concedit honores
    Papa,[n] sed ut vitas Signa[o] probare videt;[p]
Nec subitò,[q] sed cum vita decesserit annis
    Permultis quenquam sanctificare solet.
Pr.[r] Nec mirum. Praesens mendacia respuit aetas,
    Ad quae posteritas sera coacta tacet.   1490
Jam fuit aeternae nimium via commoda vitae.
    Durum erat[s] in tota Relligione nihil.
Externus labor omnis erat, nec erat gravis. Intus
    Nescitum est cujus Relligionis[t] erant.
Qui servit Clero, qui Clero praedia donat,[u]
    Clero magnificas[v] aedificatque domos,
Is Pius est. Divumque[w] olim referetur in Album;[x]
    Aeterna est illis vita in Ephemeride.
Papa licet rigidus divini exactor honoris
    Non erat, et facilem praestitit esse Fidem,[y]   1500
Non ita neglexit placidè[z] sua jura et honorem;[aa]
    Sed summus,[ab] si quis deroget,[ac] ultor erat.

---

[a] A B student, • [b] uA fide. C fide • [c] uA C templis, • [d] C Prima • [e] A Satellitium • [f] C suum • [g] uA dominantibus • [h] A B adnumerantur, • [i] uA Divis •
[j] A B Idololatria • [k] uA B C divum • [l] C prisci, • [m] A B C temere • [n] uA Papa
• [o] uA B C signa • [p] uA videt • [q] A B C subito, • [r] mv C *Pr.* missing • [s] A
Erat • [t] A C relligionis • [u] A B donat • [v] mv A B manifestas C magnificus
(error) • [w] mv A Divum • [x] uA B Album • [y] A B C fidem, • [z] A B C placide •
[aa] A B honorem • [ab] uA B summus • [ac] uA B deroget A deroget;

Their enterprise required many stratagems, learned wickedness, and
    philosophical Faith, to be successful.

You have heard how the early Church of the Fathers used to
    commemorate its own supporters in its churches.

But now when the Popes were ruling, whoever profited them by his skill,
    was counted among the saints.   **1480**

So idolatry was brought back to the people, and there was no one who did
    not take a saint for himself.

Sec. This was an imitation of the ancient custom of the Romans, who
    bestowed similar honours on the Caesars.[464]

[465]But the Pope did not concede such great honours so rashly, but only if
    he saw signs to commend their lives.

Nor was he in the habit of canonizing an individual immediately, but only
    very many years after he had died.

Pr. That's not surprising. The present age rejects lies on which later
    posterity is forced to be silent.   **1490**

By that time the way to eternal life was too easy. There was nothing
    demanding in the whole religion.

All effort was external and it presented no burden. It was not known what
    people's innermost religious beliefs were.

Whoever served the clergy, whoever gave the clergy property and built
    them ostentatious dwellings,

That one was considered pious. One day he would be placed in the record
    of the saints; there was eternal life for such men in the calendar.

Although the pope was not a rigid taskmaster concerning the honour of God,
    and although he guaranteed that faith should be a light burden,   **1500**

He did not so quietly neglect his own office and rights but, If anyone
    detracted from these, he was the supreme avenger.[466]

---

[464] After the Augustine period *Divus* was used as an epithet for the deceased
Roman emperors by historians and on coins and inscriptions (Suet. *Domitian*, 23)
[Souter]. Note that in lines 1480 to 1502 the worldly Renaissance Church qualifies
as a civil religion: it had simple religious beliefs that did not divide the citizenry,
making a distinction between the external and internal courts, i.e., between what
people were required publically to profess and what they could privately believe.
Thereafter, lines 1502 ff., Hobbes switches abruptly back to the 5th and 6th centuries
and the dialogue broken off at line 1228 with the insertion of *Leviathan* and *Behemoth*.

[465] The distribution of the speakers is uncertain: Primus should perhaps take
lines 1485-6 and 1491 ff., Secundus lines 1489-90.

[466] An epithet for Mars.

Gentis Anastasius Romanae[a] erat Induperator,[b]
    Ille tamen sacro fulmine tactus erat.
Cur? Quia passus erat violari Chalcedonensis
    Articulos Synodi,[c] saepius admonitus.[d]
Sed confirmata est Synodus sub Justiniano,[e]
    Haereticae Fidei[f] terribilisque fuit.
Namque is Theiologus doctus cupiebat haberi,[g]
    Atque suo Princeps Codice plenus erat.   **1510**
Ille tulit leges primus, quibus Haeresis[h] (etsi
    Congrua Scripturis)[i] morte luenda foret.

---

[a] mv uA Romae • [b] B Induperator. • [c] uA B Synodi • [d] A admonitus • [e] A B
Justiniano • [f] uA B C fidei • [g] ~A haberi • [h] A B haeresis • [i] A B C scripturis)

Anastasius[467] was emperor to the Roman people, and yet he was struck by
a holy thunderbolt.[468]

[469]Why ? Because although repeatedly warned, he had allowed the articles
of the Council of Chalcedon[470] to be violated,

But the Council was reinstated under Justinian,[471] and he was terrible to
heretical faith.

For he wanted to be considered a learned theologian[472] and the
completeness of his rule was shown by his own Codex. **1510**

He was the first to make laws under which heresy (even if it was in
accordance with the scriptures) was to be punished by death.[473]

---

[467] *Anastasius I, Emperor (491-518); These lines recapitulate lines 1212ff.

[468] A play on 'Fulmen excommunicationis, (that is the thunderbolt of excommunication)' (*Lev.*, xlii, §31 279/349), see lines 1460-64 and notes. Anastasius was
attacked by Pope Hormisdas for his Monophysite tendencies and refusal to uphold
the Council of Chalcedon, provoking a revolt against him by Vitalian, a commander
of Lower Moesia. This led to protracted skirmishing and negotiations with the
papacy, broken off by an insolent letter to Hormisdas dated 11 July, 517, from Anastasius who continued to persecute the advocates of union with Rome and was excommunicated. On 9 July 518 Anastasus died suddenly in the midst of a thunder storm.

[469] Does Secundus interject the question 'Why' here and again at line 1597, to
be answered by Primus?

[470] For the *Council of Chalcedon, see lines 1057-60 and note.

[471] See lines 1217 ff. Justinian forced all his subjects to be baptized by law under
pain of confiscation of property, and put relentless pressure on Arians inside and
outside the empire making war on the Vandals and the Ostrogoths (Invernizzi note).
See Ostrogorsky, *History of the Byzantine State*, pp. 77-8:

> Justinian was the last Roman Emperor to occupy the Byzantine throne. He was
> at the same time a Christian ruler filled with the consciousness of the Divine
> source of his imperial authority. His strivings towards the achievement of a uni-
> versal Empire were based on Christian, as well as on Roman, conceptions. For
> him the *imperium romanum* was to be identified with the Christian *oekoumene*,
> and the triumph of Christianity was as sacred a mission as the restoration of
> Roman supremacy. No ruler since Theodosius the Great had made such an
> effort to convert the Empire and to root out paganism. Though numerically the
> pagans were not strong at this time, they still had considerable influence in
> learning and culture. Justinian therefore deprived them of the right to teach, and
> in 529 he closed the Academy in Athens, the centre of pagan neoplatonism.
> The scholars who were driven out found a refuge at the court of the Persian
> King of Kings, bringing with them the fruits of Greek learning.

[472] See Ostrogorsky, *History of the Byzantine State*, p. 77:

> Even in matters of belief and ritual the final decision rested with him [Justin-
> ian], and he summoned church councils, wrote theological treatises and com-
> posed church hymns. In the history of the relations between Church and State,
> the age of Justinian is the high-watermark of imperial influence in religious
> matters. . . .

[473] Hobbes is anticipating the laws on burning heretics, *De Haeretico Comburendo*, treated in lines 2171-2 (see also the 1688 Glossary, pp. 608-9).

Ille sibi,[a] et Papis multos jugulavit honestos
    (Quales nos hodie dicimur) haereticos.
Ille metu solvit, detraxit fraenaque Papis,[b]
    Expulsis Gotthis[c] Regibus Italia.[d]
Ille Potestatem[e] Papalem Spiritualem[f]
    Inflavit, pestis quae fuit imperii.
Alter damnabat sanctos,[g] spoliabat et alter;[h]
    Regnum Papa petens;[i] Rex,[j] ut avarus,[k] opes.   **1520**
Jamque animo Papae dolor unicus haesit, habere
    Constantinopoli Praesulem honore parem.
Attamen obtinuit paulò[l] post,[m] Principe Phoca,[n]
    Primatum ad nostros quem tenet usque dies.[o]
Nam Rex Tiberius successit[p] Justiniano,
    Cui vitam dempsit Sceptraque[q] Mauritius;
Mauritio Phocas;[r] Phocaeque Heraclius armis.[s]
    Proditor is fuit, hic Mounothelita[t] fuit.[u]
Phocas Catholicus Primatum[v] Spiritualem[w]
    Papae concessit; participi[x] sceleris.   **1530**

---

[a] uA B sibi • [b] A B Papis • [c] A B C Gothis • [d] mv A B Italia • [e] A C potestatem • [f] B C spiritualem • [g] A Sanctos, • [h] A B alter • [i] uA B petens, • [j] uA B Rex • [k] uA B avarus • [l] A paulo C paullo • [m] uA post • [n] A B Phoca • [o] ~A dies • [p] A Successit • [q] A B C sceptraque • [r] A B Phocas, • [s] A B armis • [t] sc A Mounothelita B C 1688 mounothelita • [u] mv A fuit • [v] B C primatum • [w] A C spiritualem • [x] mv uA B parcipiti (error)

For his own sake and on behalf of the Popes, he cut the throats of many
honest heretics (such as we are said to be today).[474]
He released the Popes from fear and loosened the curb on them by
expelling the Gothic kings from Italy,[475]
He inflated papal spiritual power, which was the ruin of imperial
power.
The one damned the virtuous and the other robbed them, the pope seeking
dominion, the greedy emperor seeking wealth.   1520
By now only one grievance remained in the mind of the Pope, that the
Bishop of Constantinople was considered his equal in honour.[476]
However, not long afterwards he gained from Emperor Phocas the
primacy he has held continuously to our time.
The Emperor Tiberius succeeded Justinian,[477] Maurice killed him and took
his kingdom;[478]
Phocas did the same to Maurice and Heraclius to Phocas by force of
arms; Maurice was a traitor, Heraclius a Monothelite,[479]
The Catholic Phocas conceded spiritual primacy to the Pope, his partner
in crime.[480]   1530

---

[474] Hobbes's reference to allegations of heresy against himself. See Introduction.

[475] Hobbes reprises the expulsion of the Goths from Italy, of lines 1221-8ff.

[476] For about a century the Patriarch of Constantinople had been using the title
'oecoumenical Patriarch'. Pope Gregory I, at the end of the 6th century, strongly
protested this usage. After considerable strain, Emperor Phocas addressed an
edict to Pope Boniface III, recognizing the Apostolic Church of St. Peter as sovereign over all Christian churches. See Ostrogorsky, *History of the Byzantine
State*, pp. 83-4.

[477] Hobbes is mistaken, Justinian's nephew, Justin II (565-78) succeeded him,
and not Tiberius II, who reigned from 578-92.

[478] Tiberius was followed by *Maurice (582-602) and Phocas (602-10).

[479] Phocas (602-10) had effectively favoured Monothelitism, but the decree of
648 in favour of the *Monothelites is from *Constans II. See also Ostrogorsky,
pp. 85-112. *Heraclius (610-41), was the first medieval Byzantine emperor to
pursue Monothelite policies. But he ultimately failed to conciliate the heavily
Monophysite Eastern states, which were lost anyhow, due to the Arab conquest of
Syria and Palestine by 638 and of Egypt soon after. The battle against the Persians
throughout the reigns of Phocas, Maurice, and Heraclius was not assisted by the
fact that the Monophysite provinces, the Syrians, Armenians, Egyptians and
Ethiopian Copts, were all anti-Chalcedon and preferred to go with the Persians
than the Roman Pope.

[480] See 1668 Appendix to the *LL*, §130 (tr. Wright), Hobbes sees Phocas' regime
as a turning point:
    [130]B. [A]fter that, the Roman Church by its decrees arrogated to itself the
    inability to err as to the articles of the faith. And then, Emperor Phocas granted

Plus ultra nihil est. Res est altissima terris
     Papa,[a] sibi visus vix minor esse Deo.
Solaque cura manet quo pacto debeat uti
     Fortunae fluxu, muneribusque frui;
Quantos indueret[b] radios splendoris, et esset
     Stella quibus foelix, stella maligna quibus;
Regna quibus deceat dare,[c] vendere,[d] tollere,[e] quique
     Exaltandus erat, quique premendus erat.
Promere sed lumen Libri,[f] atque abscondere Sacri,[g]
     Ipsius arbitrio,[h] maxima cura fuit.   **1540**

---

[a] A C Papa • [b] sc A B C 1688 induerat – pluperfect instead of subjunctive; read indueret • [c] A B dare • [d] uA B vendere • [e] uA B tollere • [f] A B libri C libri, • [g] A B sacri C sacri, • [h] uA B arbitrio

There was no one above him. The Pope, considering himself as hardly
less than God, was the highest thing on earth.

His only remaining concern was how he should use the flow of fortune,
and enjoy its gifts;

What great rays of splendour[481] to assume,[482] and to whom he should be a
star of good omen or bad;

To whom he ought to give or sell kingdoms (or take them away), who was
to be exalted and who to be put down.

But the Pope's greatest concern was to bring forth, or to hide, the light of
the Holy Bible, by his own decision.[483]   **1540**

---

supremacy over all bishops to the pope. And, as the power of the empire in
Italy began to wane and with the Christian princes seized by fear of the Saracens, the pope, already mightily increased in riches and power, called general
councils upon his own authority, without regard for the authority of the emperors and kinglings of Italy. He even dared to excommunicate some kings and
emperors as heretics.

See also Ostrogorsky, *History of the Byzantine State*, on Phocas, p. 84:

His markedly conciliatory policy towards Rome culminated in an edict
addressed to Pope Boniface III in which he recognized the Apostolic Church
of St. Peter as the head of all the churches. A column erected in the Roman
forum with an inscription praising the Byzantine tyrant showed the remarkable favour which Phocas enjoyed in Rome.

[481] Likening a monarch to the sun was a renowned Renaissance trope, made
notorious by Tommaso Campanella and the Sun King Louis XIV, whom he influenced. As a form of flattery it became dangerously hyperbolic in court masques of
the early 17th century, which marshaled the new techniques of Italian stage production and lighting to startling effect. For instance, Ben Jonson's welcome to James I
and Christian of Denmark to Theobalds in 1606 included an encomium to both
kings as suns (Jonson, *Works*, ed. Herford and Simpson, vol. 10, p. 401), while
James I is flattered in similar terms in Jonson's *Entertainment of the King and
Queen* at Theobalds in 1607 (Jonson, *Works*, vol. 7, p. 158), and as he 'that in his
owne true circle, still doth runne;/ And holds his course as certain as the sun', in
Jonson's *Oberon* (Jonson, *Works*, vol. 7, p. 353). In the Jonson-Jones court production, *Luminalia*, the radiant Queen even displaced Apollo, 'who hath resigned the
pow'r of making day' (see Roy Strong and Stephen Orgel, *Inigo Jones, The Theatre
of the Stuart Court*, eds (Berkeley Ca., University of California Press, 1973), 2 vols,
vol. 2, p. 708). Hobbes had contact with Jonson, whom he consulted over the dedicatory preface to his translation of Thucydides; and the complete collection of Inigo
Jones's drawings is housed at Chatsworth.

[482] A B 1688 induerat – pluperfect instead of subjunctive; read indueret. Note
the casual and inaccurate syntax of lines 1533-8.

[483] In this way the arbitrariness of the Pope parallels that of the Egyptian High
Priest and dispenser of Justice, discussed in the parable of the jewel of truth, lines
227-74, who simply decides by fiat what is right and what is wrong.

Namque per hoc tempus cessavit lingua Latina[a]
     Romae, quae longo tempore Babel erat;
Inque unam linguas multas conflaverat aetas;[b]
     Italica haec vulgo nomine dicta fuit.

---

[a] A B C latina • [b] A B aetas,

For during this period the Latin language disappeared at Rome,[484] which for a long time was a Babel;[485]
Time had conflated many languages into one and this language was generally called Italian.[486]

---

[484] Possibly an acknowledgement by Hobbes of the arguments of those, including Lorenzo Valla and Eusebius of Caesarea, who credited the Catholic Church with revival of the Latin tongue. Eusebius *Hist. Eccl.*, 2.2.4, mentioning the legendary praise of Christianity by the emperor Tiberius, claimed that 'heavenly providence had put this in his mind in order that the word [*logos*] of the gospel might have an unimpeded beginning, and traverse the earth in all directions', cited by Carlo Ginsburg, *History, Rhetoric, and Proof* (Hanover, N.H., Brandeis University Press, 1999), p. 66. In Valla, for whom Eusebius was an important source, *logos* translates as *lingua latina*. Valla developed these arguments in *Oratio in principio studii*, his inaugural lecture at the University of Rome, October 18, 1455, where, comparing the Latin tongue to a currency that encouraged the exchange and circulation of ideas, he noted that the sheer size of the Roman Empire invited emulation and competition. The Roman Church, by preserving the Latin tongue as a sacred and administrative language, had allowed the arts and sciences to flourish once again in Europe under the patronage of the popes. See Lorenzo Valla, *Orazione per l'inaugurazione dell'anno accadmico 1455-1456*, p. 198, cited by Ginsburg, p. 70n.:

> Et enim post collapsum imperium qui in grammatica, dialectica, rhetorica nisi nugas scripsit? quis orator hoc dignus nomine extitit? quis historicus, poeta, iurisconsultus, philosophus, theologus ulli veterum comparandus? Parum dico: nonne apud plerasque nationes tam in iudiciis quam extra iudicia scribitur illitterate, id est non latine? nonne singule pene civitates suum ius civile vernacula lingua condidertunt? Quod cum fit, quid aliud quam ius civile romanum exterminatur et pro nihilo habetur? Ita dum lingua latina abiicitur, omnes propemodum cum illa liberales abiiciuntur artes, ut licet videre ex Asia atque Africa, ex quibus quia lingua latina cum imperio eiecta est, ideo omnes bone artes pariter eiecte sunt et pristina barbaries rediit in possessionem. Quo cur in Europa non contingit? Nempe, ut reddam quod tertium est quod initio promisi, quia id fieri sedes apostolica prohibuit. Cuius rei sine dubio caput et causa extitit religio christiana.

Ginsburg, observing (p. 66) that this is one of the first known references to Europe in a cultural, rather than a geographical, sense, notes (p. 70) that Pope Pius II, who spoke several times of Europe, for instance in his letter to Mehemet II, 'was clearly aware of Valla's text'. The parallels between Valla's text and Hobbes's *Hist. Eccl.*, are striking.

[485] Babel occurs in the Vulgate only in Gen. 11:9, for Babylon, the term used elsewhere in the Vulgate. (*Catholic Encyclopedia*).

[486] Hobbes correlates national power with the development of a single tongue. Angelo Decembrio, whose *De Politia Litteraria*, reporting learned conversations at the court of Leonello d'Este in the 1440s, was not published until 1462, had also correlated the development of language and consciousness, postulating 'an inchoate stage of language among the early Romans when few words served for many things'. See Decembrio, *De Politia Litteraria*, VII, 81, f. 146, cited by Sarah Gravelle, 'Lorenzo Valla's Comparison of Latin and Greek and the Humanist Background', p. 280.

Sic qui doctrina caecus[a] fuit antè[b] popellus,[c]
    Cogitur officiis surdus adesse sacris.
Clerus cognoscet solus Scriptura[d] Precesque[e]
    Quid dicunt. Populus dicere discat[f] Amen.[g]
Uni cunctorum[h] commissa est cura salutis,
    Romani loquitur Praesulis ore Deus.   **1550**
Quod si concedas,[i] quid prosunt[j] Biblia[k] sancta?
    Salvus eris, si quae jusserit ille facis.
Sec.[l] Non erat ambitio, sed erat sapientia, vulgò[m]
    Scripturas sacras quod vetuere legi.[n]
Nonne Dei populum vetuit conscendere montem[o]
    Flammantem Moses inde videre Deum?
Nuper ut in partes fracta est Ecclesia nostra
    Vidisti;[p] Sectae[q] quotque fuere hominum?[r]
Independentes,[s] Tremuli, Presbyteriani,[t]
    Quintimonarchistae,[u] Praesulici, Dibaphi.[v]   **1560**

---

[a] A B coecus • [b] uA C ante • [c] A B popellus • [d] A Scriptura, C scriptura • [e] A C precesque • [f] A discat, • [g] uA C amen. • [h] A Cunctorum • [i] A B concedas • [j] mv A B possunt • [k] A biblia • [l] mv uA *Sec.* missing • [m] A C vulgo • [n] A B legi, • [o] A B montem, • [p] uA B Vidisti, • [q] A sectae • [r] mv C hominum • [s] uA B Independentes • [t] uA B Presbyteriani • [u] A QuintiMonarchistae, • [v] A C Dibaphi

So the mob who were previously blind to doctrine were now forced to
    attend the sacred liturgies deaf.
Only the clergy will know what the Scriptures and the prayers say. The
    people may learn to say, 'Amen'.
To one man was entrusted responsibility for the salvation of everyone.
    God spoke through the mouth of the Roman Prelate.   **1550**
If you concede that, what good is the Holy Bible? You will be saved if
    you do what that man orders.
Sec. It was not ambition but wisdom by which they forbad the Holy
    Scriptures to be read by ordinary people,
For didn't Moses forbid the Chosen People to ascend the burning
    mountain, and see God from there?[487]
Have you seen how our Church recently has been split into factions, and
    how many sects of men there were?[488]
Independents,[489] Quakers,[490] Presbyterians,[491] Fifth Monarchy Men,[492]
    Episcopalians,[493] Anabaptists,[494]   **1560**

---

[487] *Exodus* 19:18-25.

[488] Hobbes echoes the pamphlet literature of the 1640s, for instance, the anonymous *A Discovery of 29 Sects here in London* (1641), and *Ephraim Pagett's, *Heresiography, or, a Description and History of the Hereticks and Sectaries sprang up in
these latter times* (London, 1645) a treatise of almost 160 pages, the first 55 of
which treat the *Anabaptists, and the rest a plethora of sects, some described in a
few pages, some in a single paragraph.

[489] *Indepententes*, Independents, Members of congregations each of which is
believed to be a church independent of any external authority. Thomas Edwards in
Gangraena (1646) observed of the Independents:

> yet of that Army, called by the sectaries, Independent, and of that part of it
> which truly is so, I do not think there are 50 pure Independents, but higher
> flown, more seraphical (as a chaplain, who knows well the state of that Army,
> expressed it) made up and compounded of Anabaptism, Antinomianism,
> Enthusiasm, Arminianism, Familism; all these errors and more too sometimes
> meeting in the same persons, strange monsters, having their heads of Enthusi-
> asm, their bodies of Antinomianism, their thighs of Familism, their legs and
> feet of Anabaptism, their hands of Arminianism, and Libertinism as the great
> vein going through the whole; in one word, the great religion of that sort of
> men in the Army, is liberty of conscience, and liberty of preaching.

[490] *Tremuli*, *Quakers.

[491] *Presbyteriani*, Presbyterians, i.e. governed by Presbyters, the established
Church of Scotland.

[492] *Quintimonarchiastae*: *Fifth Monarchy Men, a millennarian Puritan sect
which believed that Oliver Cromwell's rise to power was a preparation for the
Second Coming of Christ, and the establishment of the great fifth and last monarchy.

[493] *Praesulici*, from *Praesul -ulis*, bishop, i.e. governed by bishops, *Episcopalian.

[494] *Dibaphi* (Chambers Murray) (from Gr. *dibaphos*), literally twice dipped, an
epithet reminiscent of some of the more scurrilous works on the Anabaptists of

Quàm[a] multo saevum satiabant sanguine Martem.[b]
    Scituri bello judice verba Dei.
Qui cupit in celsum[c] Sinae conscendere montem,
    Antè[d] in Parnasso fabricet ille scalam.[e]
Pr.[f] Tune adeo bonus es, tantorum ut causa malorum
    Visa sit esse tibi Biblia Sacra[g] legi ?
Sederat in Clero[h] veteris[i] faex ambitionis ;
    Non illis nostrae cura salutis erat :[j]
Quis Fidei nostrae,[k] certabant,[l] imperitaret,[m]
    Et caperet lucrum, quod venit inde, sibi.[n]   1570
Nam cum naufragium passa est Romana potestas
    Ad scopulos nostros, juraque perdiderat,
Evasere tamen Praelati,[o] et fragmina pauca
    Antiqui juris salva tulere sui.
Hoc lucrum quam vis non magnum Presbyter illis
    Invidet,[p] et partem clamat habere suam.

---

[a] A B C Quam • [b] A B Martem, • [c] A Celsum • [d] A B C Ante • [e] A B scalam
• [f] uA *Pr.* missing • [g] A C sacra • [h] B C clero • [i] A Veteris • [j] A erat B erat. •
[k] uA B nostrae • [l] uA B certabant • [m] uA imperitaret • [n] A B sibi • [o] uA B
Praelati • [p] uA C Invidet

How they sated savage Mars with much blood,[495] those about to decide the
    words of God with war as their judge.
He who wants to climb Mount Sinai to the summit, should first construct
    a ladder on Parnassus.[496]
Pr. Are you so innocent as to maintain that the cause of so much
    wickedness was reading the Bible?
The dregs of ancient ambition[497] had settled within the clergy; their
    concern was not for our salvation,
They were competing to see who would control our faith and take for
    himself the profit that accrues from it.   **1570**
For when the authority of Rome suffered a shipwreck on our rocks and
    lost its rights,[498]
The prelates nevertheless escaped and carried off a few fragments of their
    ancient rights intact.
But the Presbyterian[499] begrudged them even this rather paltry profit and
    cried out for his own share.

Hobbes's time. See *Daniel Featley, The Dippers dipt or the Anabaplists d'nckt
and plunged over head and ears* (1645). The term Anabaptist means 're-baptizer'
and in the 1640s the Anabaptists were mercilessly attacked for their practices.
Ephraim Pagett in his notorious *Heresiography*, insisting (p. 31) that 'true baptism
to be as well by sprinkling as by dipping', claimed to have observed the Anabaptists (pp. 32-3):

> their manner of rebaptizing, and other rites. They flock in great multitudes to
> their *Jordans,* and both Sexes enter into the River and are dipt after their
> manner with a kind of spell, containing the heads of their erroneous Tenets,
> and their ingaging themselves schismaticall Covenants and combination of
> separation. In the Thames and Rivers, the Baptizer and the party baptized goe
> both into the Rivers, and the parties to be baptized are dipt or plunged under
> water.

[495] Lucan, *Pharsalia,* 7.317: 'satiavit sanguine ferrum'.

[496] *Mount Parnassus was the site of the ancient Greek shrine to Apollo and
sacred to the muses. Hence, the phrase the path to Parnassus means the road to classical learning and artistic accomplishment. *Gradus ad Parnassus* is the traditional
title of primers on Latin verse composition, the first said to have dated from 1687
(*OED*), but perhaps with predecessors.

[497] Hobbes's phraseology, 'Sederat in Clero Veteris faex ambitionis', combines
two ideas: Lucan and Juvenal on the dregs (faex) of humanity, and Lorenzo Valla on
the lust for power. Valla, *The [Supposed] Donation of Constantine*, ed. Coleman,
pp. 30-31, remarked of the Pope: 'Nay, this very ardor and this thirst for wide
dominion is such that whoever is most powerful, him it thus torments and stirs the
most'.

[498] Hobbes is referring to the English Reformation.

[499] Hobbes juxtaposes to the Roman prelates the English Presbyter: see the
1722 paraphrase, which translates the latter as 'the modern Presbyter'.

Dumque illi bello certant de Relligione,
    Ius Regni Populus[a] certat habere sibi.
Non erat in culpa divini lectio Libri,[b]
    Nec vacuum est populo ruris,[c] adesse libris.   1580
Sed redeo Romam[d] quae nil nisi grande sepulchrum est,[e]
    Et Papa[f] ad tumulum Caesaris umbra[g] minax,[h]
Regnans in tenebris[i] quas fecerat,[j] et facit ipse;[k]
    Verborumque dolis regia[l] jura petens.[m]
Nicenae Synodi Patribus concesserat olim
    Rex Constantinus (sed nimium temerè)[n]
Ne[o] Fidei[p] lites alio sub Judice[q] finem
    Acciperent,[r] praeter Spirituale[s] forum.
Pro se,[t] dumque mererentur[u] concesserat ille;[v]
    Hi semper poscunt,[w] et quasi jure suo.   1590
De causis Fidei[x] tantùm[y] concesserat ille;[z]
    Isti personis applicuere suis.
Desiit ex illo jam longo tempore Clerus[aa]
    Formidare minas Caesaris,[ab] atque forum.
Nec de criminibus vult respondere vocatus
    Coram Civili[ac] Judice[ad] Clericulus.[ae]

---

[a] uA B C populus • [b] uA B libri C libri, • [c] uA B C ruris • [d] A Romam, • [e] A
B est • [f] uA papa • [g] A Umbra • [h] uA B minax • [i] A tenebris, • [j] B fecerat •
[k] uA B ipse • [l] A B Regia • [m] A petens • [n] A temere) B temeré) • [o] mv A B
Nec • [p] uA B C fidei • [q] A B C judice • [r] uA B Acciperent C Accipèrent • [s] A
B C spirituale • [t] uA B C se • [u] mv uA B merentur C merentur, • [v] A B ille •
[w] C poscunt • [x] uA B C fidei • [y] A B C tantum • [z] uA B ille • [aa] B clerus •
[ab] A B Caesaris C caesaris • [ac] A B C civili • [ad] A B C judice • [ae] uA B C cler-
iculus.

And while these men were going to war over their religion, the people
were struggling for the right to a kingdom for themselves.[500]

Bible reading was not responsible, nor did people of the countryside have
the leisure to consult books.   **1580**

But I'll get back to Rome, which is nothing but a great sepulchre, and the
Pope a menacing ghost at Caesar's tomb,[501]

Ruling in the shadows which he himself made, and continues to make;
and seeking by verbal trickery, royal rights.

The Emperor Constantine once conceded (but too heedlessly) to the
Fathers of the Nicene Council,[502]

That no legal cases concerning the Faith could come to a decision under
any jurisdiction other than the spiritual court.[503]

Constantine had conceded the rights for himself, and as long as the
Fathers were deserving, but they demand them for ever.[504]   **1590**

Constantine had made concessions only in cases concerning faith; the
clerics applied them to their own persons.

From that point for a long time, the clergy stopped being afraid of the
threats of Caesar or his courts.

And not even a cleric of the lowest rank, when called to answer criminal
charges before a civil magistrate, was willing to do so.

---

[500] Note the language is reminiscent of Polybius and Livy on the political struggles between the Senate and the plebs, which determined the final shape of the Roman Republic.

[501] *Lev.*, xlvii, §21, 387/482-3:
> And if a man consider the original of this great ecclesiasticall dominion, he will easily perceive, that the Papacy, is no other than the ghost of the deceased Roman empire, sitting crowned upon the grave thereof. For so did the Papacy start up on a sudden out of the ruins of that Heathen Power.

[502] Note the error in line numbering in the 1688 edn, where only 8 lines instead of 10 separate line indicators 1580 and 1590; as earlier lines 50 and 60 are separated only by 8 lines instead of 10. Now there is an accumulated difference between A and the 1688 edn of 4 lines; and an accumulated difference of 2 lines between B and the 1688 edn, due to the fact that B does not include lines 1229 and 1230.

[503] i.e., the ecclesiastical court, first introduced at line 770, as having been created by Constantine. Lines 1582 to 1590 reprise lines 550-616.

[504] This was the argument not only of Valla's *De falso credita. . . donatione,* but also the point of Luther's constant references to 'die Constantinheit der Kirche'. See S. I. Camporeale, 'Renaissance Humanism and the Origins of Humanist Theology', in *Humanity and Divinity in Renaissance and Reformation: Essays in Honor of Charles Trinkaus,* ed. John O'Malley, et al. (Leiden, E.J. Brill, 1993), p. 104, and Paganini, 'Thomas Hobbes e Lorenzo Valla', p. 543.

Cur? Quia Paulus ait,[a] Nonne[b] inter vosmet habetis
    Solvere qui justè[c] jurgia vestra sciat?
Sec. Quae Deus indulsit crudeli jura sub hoste,
    Non eadem Sanctis[d] semper habenda dedit.   1600
Vivere vix licuit;[e] licuit jus dicere?[f] Sancte,[g]
    Nunc quoque si placeant accipe utrumque simul.
Pr. Si fur,[h] si latro, si moechus Clericus[i] esset,[j]
    Regum Judiciis[k] eripiendus erat;
Sique suum Regem jugulasset proditor ipsum,
    Aut compilasset delubra sancta[l] Dei;[m]
Tunc moderabatur poenas Ecclesia Judex,[n]
    Non inconsulta commoditate sua.
Sed si quis Laicus,[o] non dico laeserit[p] illos,[q]
    Sed si,[r] quod dicunt,[s] dicere nolit idem;   1610
Ure,[t] Ure,[u] exclamant,[v] et vociferantur ad ignem,
    Mortemve atrocem,[w] siqua sit,[x] igne magis.[y]
O Sancti,[z] soli[aa] qui Sancti vultis haberi,[ab]
    Commendat vobis saevitiemne[ac] Deus?

---

[a] uA ait • [b] A C nonne • [c] A B C juste • [d] B C sanctis • [e] A B licuit, • [f] mv uA B dicere. • [g] A B Sancte C sancte, • [h] A B fur • [i] B C clericus • [j] B esset • [k] A C judiciis • [l] A Sancta • [m] A B Dei • [n] A B judex C judex, • [o] A B Laicus • [p] sc mv uA B laeserit (grammatically necessary to parallel nolit) A C 1688 laeserat • [q] A B illos • [r] uA B si • [s] uA B dicunt • [t] uA B Ure • [u] uA B Ure • [v] uA B C exclamant • [w] uA B atrocem • [x] uA B C sit • [y] C magis; • [z] uA B Sancti C sancti, • [aa] A Soli, C soli, • [ab] A B haberi • [ac] mv A B saevitiemve

[505]Why ? Because Paul said, 'Don't you have among yourselves someone
who knows how to resolve your quarrels justly ?'[506]

Sec. The rights God allowed Church Fathers under a cruel enemy,[507] he
did not give them to be held in perpetuity.   **1600**

It was hardly permitted to live, so was it permitted to give judgement?[508]
Now too holy man, take both of these privileges, if they please you.

Pr. If a cleric was a thief, a bandit, an adulterer, he had to be rescued
from the royal law courts;[509]

And if he was a traitor who had cut the throat of his own king; or had
pillaged the holy sanctuaries of God;

The Church as judge then regulated the punishments, but not without
having consulted its own advantage.

But if any layman didn't want to say the same thing that they say – and I
am not saying he harmed the Fathers –   **1610**

They screamed, 'Burn him, Burn him', and shouted 'to the fire' or
whatever terrible death is worse than death by fire.

O holy men, you who alone wish to be considered holy, does God
commend this savagery to you?

---

[505] Should Secundus begin here?

[506] I Corinthians 6:5. Lorenzo Valla, in *The [Supposed] Donation of Constantine*, ed. Coleman, pp. 24-5, boldly declared, 'perhaps I am not a Paul that I should reprove a Peter', but affirming, 'Yea, I am a Paul because I imitate Paul'.

[507] I Corinthians 6:1, 6:4, 6:7.

[508] See I Corinthians 6:3: where Paul claims that early Christians, although in danger for their lives, were still in a position to judge disputes among themselves. Hobbes turns the argument to claim that the juridical powers exercised by the Church Fathers were in violation of the practice of the early Church and the injunctions of St. Paul. See *Lev.*, xlii, §131, 318/395-6 where, in answer to Belarmine, Hobbes asserts, quoting I Corinthians 6:

It is not, therefore, for want of strength, but for conscience sake, that Christians are to tolerate their heathen princes, or princes (for I cannot call anyone whose doctrine is the public doctrine, an heretic) that authorize the teaching of an error. And whereas for the temporal power of the Pope, he [Bellarmine] allegeth further that St. Paul (1 Cor. 6) appointed judges under the heathen princes of those times, such as were not ordained by those princes, it is not true. For St. Paul does but advise them to take some of their brethren to compound their differences, as arbitrators, rather than to go to law one with another before the heathen judges; which is a wholesome precept, and full of charity, fit to be practiced also in the best Christian commonwealths. And for the danger that may arise to religion by the subjects tolerating of an heathen, or erring prince, it is a point of which a subject is no competent judge; or if he be, the Pope's temporal subjects may judge also of the Pope's doctrine. For every Christian prince, as I have formerly proved, is no less supreme pastor of his own subjects than the Pope of his.

[509] c.f. I Corinthians 6:9-10.

Non tamen ingenii sunt haec,[a] sed facta timentum,[b]
    Quae conabantur[c] ne patefacta forent.
In populum laqueos pluerant, ideoque timendum,[d]
    Si populus sciret, ne plueret lapides.
Crimina criminibus celantur prima secundis;[e]
    Ultima sed tandem non erit unde tegant.   **1620**
Nempe Lutherus erit qui fraudes deteget omnes;[f]
    Et Papas[g] feriet fulmine Saxonico.
Ambitio in longos perrarò[h] prospicit annos,
    Quantumvis,[i] praesens utile,[j] acuta videt.
Nec sua,[k] Philosophi credebant posse refelli
    A Laicis unquam,[l] dogmata docta,[m] viris.
His quia temporibus turbabant Mounothelitae,[n]
    Cum Christi Sanctum distraherentque gregem;[o]
Principis injussu tunc primùm[p] Papa vocavit,[q]
    Ipsius arbitrio,[r] Catholicam Synodum:[s]   **1630**
Coeperunt Reges tunc primum posse[t] putari
    Haeretici,[u] et vinctos legibus esse Scholae.[v]
Sec. Legibus esse Scholae subjectos non puto Reges;[w]
    Subjectos nosti Legibus[x] esse Dei.
Pr. Lex divina nihil de nugis[y] continet istis;[z]
    Nam Lex[aa] haec lux est, recta jubendo docens.
Sed doctrinarum tenebras has, nec videt ipse[ab]
    Umbrarum dominus,[ac] qui sine luce videt.
Mille voluntates[ad] habet unus,[ae] dum modo vult hoc,[af]
    Deinde aliud;[ag] nullam,[ah] si nihil optat,[ai] habet.   **1640**
Christus ait clarè,[aj] Sumus[ak] unus Egoque Paterque;[al]
    Visne Voluntates Unius,[am] esse duas?[an]

---

[a] A B haec • [b] mv uA timendum (miscopied from 2 lines below) B timentum • [c] A conabantur, • [d] A B C timendum • [e] uA B secundis • [f] A B omnes • [g] uA papas • [h] A C perraro • [i] uA B Quantumvis • [j] uA B utile • [k] uA B sua • [l] uA B unquam • [m] A B docta • [n] A Mounothelitae • [o] uA B gregem. • [p] A B C primum • [q] A B vocavit • [r] A B arbitrio • [s] A B Synodum. • [t] B posse mv C esse • [u] uA B Haeretici, C Haeretici • [v] A C scholae. • [w] A B Reges, C reges; • [x] A B C legibus • [y] mv A B legibus (error repeating legibus in the line above) • [z] A B istis • [aa] A B C lex • [ab] A ipse. • [ac] A Dominus, C Dominus • [ad] A voluntates, • [ae] uA unus • [af] uA B C hoc • [ag] uA B aliud, • [ah] A B C nullam • [ai] uA B optat • [aj] uA clare A clare; B claré C clare, • [ak] uA B C sumus • [al] A B Paterque • [am] A B unius C unius, • [an] uA duas,

For these are not acts of intelligence, but of people who are afraid that
    their ventures may be made public.

They rained nooses on the people, and so there was reason to fear that if
    the people knew it would rain stones on them.

Earlier crimes are concealed by later crimes; but ultimately there will be
    nowhere where they can hide their final crimes.[510]   **1620**

Luther will of course be the one who uncovers all these fraudulent deeds
    and who strikes the Pope with a Saxon thunderbolt.

Ambition very seldom looks far into the future, however acutely it sees
    the immediate advantage.

Nor did the philosophers believe that their learned doctrines could ever be
    refuted by laymen.

Because the Monothelites were causing problems during these times, and
    were tearing the flock of Christ apart,

The Pope then for the first time without orders from the Emperor,
    summoned a universal Council by his own decision.[511]   **1630**

Then for the first time it began to be possible for kings to be considered
    heretics and bound by the laws of the School.

Sec. I don't think kings are subject to the laws of the School: you know
    they are subject to the laws of God.

Pr. Divine law contains nothing about these trifles, for this law is the
    light, teaching by ordering right things.

But not even the Lord of the Shades, who sees without light, penetrates
    these dark places of doctrines.

An individual man has a thousand wills; at one time he wants this, and
    then later something else; if he desires nothing, he has no will. **1640**

Christ clearly affirms, 'we are one, the Father and I',
    do you want one person to have two wills?[512]

---

[510] Hobbes is speaking of the ecclesiastical courts and clerical privilege after
Justinian, using the retributive language of the ecclesiastical historians. See Springborg Introduction, chapter 4.3.

[511] The Council of Rome, 649, called by Pope Martin I (reigned 649-55) without
the permission of the Emperor, Constans II, who had the pope arrested and imprisoned.

[512] Hobbes here resumes the debate on the Monothelite heresy from lines
1069ff. and 1528ff. See Ostrogorsky, *History of the Byzantine State*, pp. 152-3, who
recounts the hostility between the Pope and the Armenian Monothelite emperor,
Philippicus-Bardanes (deposed and blinded 713) who, by imperial edict, abrogated
the decrees of the sixth ecumenical council and declared that *Monotheletism alone
was orthodox.

Haec provenerunt ab inani Philosophia
     Temporis illius,[a] quam coluere Patres.
Namque animae lepidam narrabant Oeconomiam[b]
     Illis[c] temporibus,[d] Philosophi veteres :[e]
Quod domus est Animae[f] Corpus,[g] fit quod jubet illa ;[h]
     Non homo,[i] non corpus, non opus ipsa facit :[j]
Sed bene dispositis peraguntur cuncta ministris ;[k]
     Fungitur et promptè[l] munere quisque suo ;[m]   **1650**
Olfacit,[n] et Gustat,[o] Tactu sentit,[p] Videt,[q] Audit,[r]
     Non homo,[s] sed Sensus[t] proprius ista facit.
Nempe suum mittit simulachrum res in ocellos,
     Idque videt Visus ;[u] non videt illud Homo.[v]
Nec sonus auriculas penetrat quin audiat illum
     Auditus ;[w] nihil[x] est ipse quod audit Homo.[y]

---

[a] uA B illius • [b] uA B C oeconomiam • [c] mv uA B His • [d] A B temporibus • [e] A Veteres. B veteres; C veteres. • [f] uA B C animae • [g] uA C corpus • [h] uA B illa A illa, • [i] C homo • [j] A B facit. • [k] A Ministris, B ministris, • [l] B prompte • [m] A B suo. • [n] A B Olfacit • [o] uA B gustat A C gustat, • [p] uA B sentit C sentit, • [q] uA B videt C videt, • [r] uA B Audit C audit, • [s] uA B homo • [t] A C sensus • [u] uA B visus, C visus; • [v] A B C homo. • [w] uA C Auditus B Auditus, • [x] uA B nil • [y] uA B C homo.

These ideas arose from the vacuous philosophy of those times which the
Fathers cultivated.

For the ancient philosophers had in those days spoken of an ingenious
organization of the mind.[513]

Because the body is the house of the mind, it does what the mind
commands; it is not the person, nor the body, nor the mind itself that
executes the work.

But everything is carried out by the proper organization of its servants,
and each readily performs its own function.   **1650**

It is not the person that smells and tastes, touches, sees and hears; but the
particular sense.

It smells and tastes, it feels by touch, it sees, it hears; not the person as
such, but the particular sense does that.

Indeed an object sends its image into the eyes;[514] and the faculty of sight
sees it, the person does not.

---

[513] Hobbes refers in the lines that follow to late medieval scholastic debate
over the nature of perception, which was in terms of objects sending out 'sensible
species', images that strike the senses, a theory affirmed by Pierre Aureole, for
instance, but denied by William of Ockham. See Charles Trinkaus, 'Lorenzo
Valla's Anti-Aristotelian Natural Philosophy', p. 301, citing K. H. Tachau, *Vision
and Certitude in the Age of Ockham*. Hobbes, after earlier entertaining species
theory (as he acknowledges in the 1668 Appendix to *LL*, §93 trans. Wright,
p. 366), explicitly rejects it in *Lev.*, i, §5, 4/7, and at length in the *LL*, xlvi, §21,
322/475 (Curley edn). See Springborg Introduction, chapter 6.2.

[514] Hobbes, probably under the influence of Galileo and Gassendi, embraced
the inertial principle of matter in motion, the constant vibration of which caused
atoms to discharge atomic films (εἴδωλα or *simulachra*) at high speed, similar in
shape to the objects themselves. He revised *species* theory in favour of Lucretian
simulachra which, when received by the eyes produce vision, when by the mind,
produce dreams. *De re. nat.*, 2.167-83, 5.156-234. Gianni Paganini believes,
however, that Hobbes, like Gassendi, has reservations about the concept of simulachra, and 'was much more inclined to a thesis concerning movement's transport
than matter's transport'. Although Epicurean simulachra are very different from
Aristotelian 'species', Paganini points out that 'both concepts rely on the copy-
principle that Hobbes early abandoned. Paganini is also 'convinced that skeptical
influences . . . push[ed] him to give up the thesis of a similitude or likeness
between the known and the empirical representation'. (Communication Paganini
to Springborg, 7/5/2002). See also Paganini, 'Hobbes, Gassendi e la psicologia
del meccanicismo'.

Acceptas species,[a] considerat Intellectus;[b]
    Supputat et Ratio;[c] Visque[d] memor retinet.
Sic quoque Judicium[e] discernit;[f] vultque Voluntas;[g]
    Sic verè[h] dictum est, Est Microcosmus[i] Homo.[j]   **1660**
Sec. Nil facit ad nostram comoedia stulta salutem;[k]
    Nec nos salvabunt Physica,[l] vera licet.[m]
Sunt credenda quidem libris quaecunque leguntur[n]
    Sacris;[o] sed Codex[p] non habet ista,[q] Dei.[r]
Non tollit peccata hominum Sapientia[s] Graeca,[t]
    Nec facta est tardis poena Gehenna[u] animis;[v]

---

[a] uA B C species. • [b] A intellectus B Intellectus C intellectus; • [c] uA ratio, B Ratio, C ratio; • [d] C visque • [e] A B C judicium • [f] uA B discernit A discernit, • [g] uA B voluntas C voluntas; • [h] B C vere • [i] uA C microcosmus • [j] A homo B homo. C homo: • [k] A B salutem • [l] uA B C Physica • [m] mv C licet • [n] B leguntur, • [o] A B Sacris, • [p] C codex • [q] A B C ista • [r] mv A B Dei C DEI: • [s] A C sapientia • [t] uA Graeca, • [u] A C gehenna • [v] A B animis.

And no sound enters the ears, without the faculty of hearing it; there is nothing that the person himself hears.[515]

Once the images have been received, the intellect considers them, Reason evaluates them, and memory retains them.[516]

In this way also the faculty of judgement judges and the faculty of will wills, so it is truly said that man is a microcosm.[517] **1660**

Sec. This foolish comedy does nothing for our salvation;[518] Nor will natural philosophy save us,[519] however true it may be.

Whatever is read in Holy Scripture is to be believed; but God's code does not include *these* things.[520]

Greek wisdom does not take away men's sins,[521] nor has the punishment of Hell[522] been created for the slow witted,

---

[515] Lorenzo Valla, who also rejected the idea that visual objects, colors and shapes are transmitted to the eye by a medium, or sensible species, devoted 5 chapters of the *Repastinatio* (bk 1, chs 18-36, pp. 425-36) to the objects of the individual senses: to the objects of vision, hearing, taste and smell, touch and finally, to senses of one's own bodily state or actions. See Trinkaus, 'Lorenzo Valla's Anti-Aristotelian Natural Philosophy', pp. 300-2. Valla believed, like Hobbes, that objects are perceived directly by the senses, emphasizing the active power of the mind in responding to sensation.

[516] Note that this is Hobbes's theory of memory as the relics of sensation, a retrieval system activated by wave after wave of images or simulachra hitting the sensors of the eye, ear, etc. See *Lev.*, chapter 3, 'Of the Consequence or Train of Imaginations'.

[517] The 'microcosmus' doctrine represents 'man as a small world, and the world as man writ large' (c.f. Macrobius, *in Somm. Scip.* 2.12.11), maintaining that the individual has the same internal organization as the universe, including a guiding power (*hegemonika*): s/he is a 'fragment' of the whole. It was a doctrine shared by the Stoics, by Pico della Mirandola and a number of Renaissance writers.

[518] A return to the topic of the vain philosophy of the Fathers of line 1643ff.

[519] See Thomas's Lexicon of 1584, for the translation of *Physica* as Natural Philosophy.

[520] i.e. the truths of science.

[521] The Latin echoes the Lord's Prayer.

[522] Literally, *Gehenna: A valley near Jerusalem where idolatrous Jews were said to burn their children as offerings to Moloch, Baal, or the sun. See *Luke* 12:5. Wright, '1668 Appendix to Leviathan', pp. 331-2, reproduces a passage from Luther's commentary on *Ecclesiastes* 9:10 which introduces Gehenna, possibly Hobbes's source. Wright, citing Burns, *Christian Mortalism from Tyndale to Milton*, pp. 30-31, notes that, 'In saying that hell is a grave or pit, Luther is referring to the Hebrew word Gehenna, the name of a ravine, the valley of Hinnon, which served as a place of worship of the Semitic god Moloch'.

Sed fastu plenis, mendacibus,[a] atque hypocritis,[b]
   Ingratis, avidis[c] omnibus atque nigris.
Nam bene moratum Physicus si perderet error,[d]
   Quo staret Doctor[e] discipulusque loco?   1670
Pr.[f] Post hanc suppressam,[g] statim venit altera major,
   Quam Reges multi sustinuere diu.
Christicolis dederat primis Ecclesia prima
   Idola (at verso nomine) habere sua.[h]
His populus fudere preces, et honore colebant
   Quem dederat falsis Ethnicus antè[i] Deis.
Id quod Pastores,[j] regnante Leone secundo,[k]
   Innumeri,[l] et docti non potuere pati.
Certatum est centum,[m] scriptoque et voce,[n] per annos,[o]
   An licitè[p] in sacris[q] possit Imago[r] coli.   1680
Sed victi tandem cesserunt Iconomachi,[s]
   Et simul Eoum languiit[t] Imperium.[u]
Nam circa hoc tempus coepit Saracenica Secta
   Fortiter armari,[v] cum Mahomete[w] suo;[x]
Inque dies crescens,[y] Turca duce,[z] tandem Orientis
   Sustulit Imperium,[aa] Catholicamque Fidem.[ab]

---

[a] uA B mendacibus • [b] ~ A hypocritis • [c] A B avidis • [d] A B error • [e] A B doctor, • [f] mv uA B *Pr.* missing • [g] uA B suppressam • [h] A B sua • [i] A C ante • [j] A B Pastores • [k] A Secundo B secundo • [l] uA C Innumeri • [m] uA B centum • [n] uA B voce • [o] A B annos • [p] A C licite B licité • [q] A Sacris • [r] A B C imago • [s] A B Iconomachi • [t] A B languit C languii (error) • [u] A imperium. C imperium • [v] A B armari • [w] A B Mahumete • [x] A B suo. • [y] uA B crescens • [z] uA Turca tandem duce (word order, corrected A) B duce • [aa] uA B C imperium • [ab] uA C fidem.

But for minds filled with pride, liars and hypocrites, for ingrates and all
 that are greedy and black.[523]
If an error in science could ruin a man of sound character, where would
 the Teacher and his disciple stand?[524] **1670**
Pr. After the Monothelite heresy had been suppressed, there came
 immediately another even greater one which many kings supported
 for a long time.
The early Church had allowed the first Christians to keep their own idols
 (but with the names changed).
The people poured forth prayers to these idols and worshipped them with
 a devotion that the pagan had previously given to false gods.
This was a situation that the countless pastors and scholars during the
 reign of Leo II could not allow.[525]
For a hundred years it was disputed, in pamphlets and in public debate,
 whether a statue could be lawfully worshipped in devotions.[526] **1680**
But finally the defeated Iconomachs[527] retreated, and at the same time the
 Eastern empire was a spent force.
For around this time the Saracen sect, under their Muhammad, began to
 be strongly armed.[528]
Increasing in strength by the day, this sect, under the leadership of the Turk,
 finally brought down the Eastern empire and the Catholic Faith.

---

[523] For 'niger' (black) of bad character see *Oxford Latin Dictionary.*
[524] Possible reference to the trial by the Inquisition of *Galileo Galilei in 1633.
Hobbes met Galileo in the spring of 1636 in Florence.
[525] Hobbes confuses the emperor Leo II for Leo III, who reigned 717-741. Leo
III, the founder of the Isaurian dynasty, was the principal iconoclast who promulgated the edict for the destruction of icons in 730. Pope Gregory III condemned
the Byzantine iconoclasts at two synods in Rome (731), but Leo III had Gregory's
legates thrown into prison. See Florovsky, 'Origen, Eusebius, and the Iconoclastic
Controversy', pp. 77ff.
[526] Hobbes resumes from lines 1311-38 and 1375-1408 the subject of iconoclasm, debated at the 7th oecumenical council held at Nicaea in 787 under Pope
Hadrian I in the reign of the Empress Irene, 'which wisely received the former iconoclasts back into the Church after they had abjured their heresy before the assembly'. Iconoclasm was formally declared a heresy and veneration of icons reestab-
lished as part of the doctrine of salvation, in accordance with the teachings of St.
John of Damascus, so that the respect shown the icon is understood as for the holy
person represented and distinguished from the worship owed God (Ostrogorsky,
pp. 178-9).
[527] Synonym for iconoclast.
[528] See Ostrogorsky, *History of the Byzantine State*, p. 182, who notes a series of
Arab incursions beginning in 781.

Haeresis interea longùm[a] lassata quievit
       Partibus Occiduis,[b] pòst[c] valitura tamen.
Sed quantum Papae derasum est partibus illis,
       Partibus his tanto durius incubuit.   1690
Ut ferrum candens subitum si frigus ab una
       Sensit parte, magis fervet ab opposita;[d]
Sic quoque conatus Paparum Oriente repulsi,
       Partibus Occiduis[e] invaluere magis.
Credi namque jubent fieri miracula ab illis[f]
       Quorum sunt usi simplicitate virûm.[g]
Sed non ante obitum,[h] nec post,[i] nisi tempore longo:[j]
       Non[k] patitur praesens ficta valere dies.
Non tot Moeonius narravit monstra Poeta,[l]
       Quot populo Christi Papa Legenda[m] dedit.   1700
Sec. Nicenae Fidei[n] subscripsit Episcopus unus[o]
       Qui, paulò,[p] ut dicunt,[q] mortuus antè[r] fuit.[s]
Namque Patres ipso posuerunt Acta[t] sepulchro,[u]
       Orantes subtùs[v] scribere ut ille velit.

---

[a] A B longum • [b] uA B occiduis, C occiduis • [c] A B post • [d] A B opposita. •
[e] uA B C Occiduis • [f] C illis, • [g] uA B virum. • [h] uA B obitum • [i] uA B post.
• [j] A B longo • [k] mv A B Nec • [l] A C Poëta, B Poéta, • [m] uA B C legenda •
[n] uA C fidei • [o] C unus, • [p] uA paulo A paulo, B paulò C paullo, • [q] uA B
dicunt • [r] A B C ante • [s] A B fuit, • [t] uA C acta • [u] A sepulchro B sépulchro •
[v] uA B C subtus

Meanwhile Heresy, exhausted,[529] rested quietly for a long time in the
    Western parts,[530] only later to regain its former vigour.
To the extent that the Pope's power had been eroded in the Eastern
    provinces, he bore down all the more heavily on the West.[531]   **1690**
Just like a white hot iron, if it suddenly feels cold on one side, it burns
    that much hotter on the other side.
In the same way the efforts of the Popes, repulsed in the East, grew all the
    more strong in the West.
For they ordered it to be believed that miracles were performed by those
    whose simplicity they exploited.
But not before their death, nor indeed till long after: the present does not
    allow falsehoods to prevail.
And the poet Moeonius[532] did not tell so many extravagant tales as the
    legends the Pope gave the people of Christ.   **1700**
Sec. One Bishop signed the Nicene Creed who, so they say, had died a
    little while before,[533]
In fact, the Fathers placed the Articles in his tomb, praying that he would
    sign them below.[534]

---

[529] By the Iconoclast struggle.

[530] See Prudentius' *Psychomachia*.

[531] See Ostrogorsky, *History of the Byzantine State*, pp. 183-4, who notes that
the decisions of the Council of Nicaea were not well received in the East.
> Those clauses in which the Pope claimed the right to censure the uncanonical
> consecration of the Patriarch Tarasius and to protest against the title of 'oecu-
> menical' Patriarch were likewise deleted; and the many passages in the papal
> communication which raised the question of the rights of primacy of Rome, or
> even only of the primacy of St. Peter were carefully suppressed. The Papacy
> was virtually excluded from the East, just as the Byzantine Empire was
> excluded from the West.

[532] *Maeon* is Homer. See Milton, *Paradise Lost* (1667), book 3, line 35: 'Blind
Thamyris and blind Maeonides'.

[533] For the story on the false signing see Gelasius of Cyzicus, *History of the
Nicene Council*, vol. 2 of his 3 vol. *Syntagma*, transmitted through Photius of Constantinople, *PG* CIII, cols 56-292, which according to Hefele, *Histoire des conciles*,
includes both probable and improbable accounts from eye-witnesses.

[534] No source can be found for this particular story in relation to the Nicene
Council, but Hobbes may be conflating a famous story from the fifth session of the
Council of Chalcedon, AD 450, which took place in the *martyrium* of Saint
Euphemia, with a striking parallel in *The [Supposed] Donation of Constantine* (ed.
Coleman pp., 19, 133-4), which includes as a guarantee of its veracity the claim to
have been placed in the tomb of Saint Peter. Lorenzo Valla, in his Treatise exposing
the work as a forgery alights on the outrageous anachronism, observing that the doc-
ument was 'dead and buried before it was born. . . that it was confirmed before it

Discessere boni Patres,[a] Saxoque reposto[b]
    Cauti signa omnes applicuere sua.
Postridiè[c] redeunt, subscriptum[d] nomen et Actis
    Inveniunt,[e] gaudent, magnificantque Deum.
Pr. Audiit hoc etiam Rex Constantinus?[f] An ingens
    Miraclum[g] solus nesciit ille[h] Dei?   1710
Sec.[i] Nescio *Pr.* Ne Credas.[j] Cur[k] non testatus et ipse est
    Rem certam, ut posset certa valere Fides?[l]
Sed nec rem vidit Princeps, nec id audiit unquam:[m]
    Multo posteriùs[n] fabula ficta fuit.
Dein quod Daemoniis infernis imperitarent[o]
    (Nomine nam populus Spectra vocabat eo)[p]
Quodque locis sacris illos expellere Epodis
    Possent,[q] possessis corporibusque hominum[r]
(Cuncta videbatur[s] quia sanctus[t] scire Sacerdos)[u]
    Antiqua didicit credere turba fide.   1720

---

[a] uA B Patres C patres, • [b] C reposto, • [c] A C Postridie B Postridié • [d] A Subscriptum • [e] uA Inveniunt • [f] mv uA Constantinus. • [g] uA B C Miraculum • [h] mv A B esse • [i] mv uA B *Sec.* missing • [j] A credas.C credas; • [k] A cur • [l] sc mv 1688 A C fides. • [m] A B unquam, • [n] A B C posterius • [o] A B C imperitarent, • [p] mv uA B eos. A eo.) • [q] uA B Possent • [r] C hominum, • [s] A B videbatur, • [t] A Sanctus • [u] B C sacerdos)

After the stone had been put back, the good Fathers departed and they all
attached their own seals as a guarantee.

On the next day they returned and discovered the bishop's name had been
signed to the Articles, and they rejoiced and praised God.

Pr.   Did the Emperor Constantine also hear about this? Or was he the
only one who did not know this was a great miracle of God?   **1710**

Sec. I don't know. *Pr.* Don't believe it. Why didn't Constantine testify to it
himself as certain fact, so assured belief could prevail?

But the Emperor didn't see the event, and he didn't even hear about it, the
story was made up much later.

Then that priests controlled the infernal demons (for the people gave that
name to spirits),

And that they could expel them from holy places with incantations,[535] and
even from the bodies of men possessed

(Because the holy priest was believed to know everything), the mob
learned to believe according to the ancient faith.   **1720**

---

had been written, and not with one hand alone at that, but with both of the Caesar's
hands!' He goes on to ask, 'And what was this "confirming"? Was it done with the
signature of the Caesar, or with his signet ring?', answering sarcastically, 'Surely,
hard and fast that, – more so by far than if he had entrusted it to bronze tablets!'. See
The [Supposed] Donation of Constantine, ed. Coleman, pp., 19, 133-4. Coleman
notes (p. 134 n. 2) that 'in the *Liber Pontificalis* (ed. Duchesne, i, 454) the keys of
Ravenna and other cities included in the so-called Donation of Pippin are said to
have been placed in "the confession of St. Peter" (i.e., before his tomb)' and that
'this association seems to have been common in the eighth century'. Hobbes
includes his own story among the 'marvellous legends' which outdo even Homer,
which would fit the case in the *martyrium* of Saint Euphemia from the time of
Council of Chalcedon. When heretic and Catholic bishops were unable to agree
among themselves they decided to place their respective documents in the sealed
and locked tomb of Saint Euphemia to await her judgment overnight. The next
morning the bishops lifted the seal and opened the coffin to find the saint held the
Catholic document in her hand, while the heretic was scornfully thrown at her feet.
In a variant of this story, the Emperor and the Archbishop of Constantinople are
called to witness the wonder, whereupon Euphemia lifts her arm and hands them the
Catholic profession of faith. Saint Euphemia was portrayed as a Sibyl, and became
the patron saint of ecumenical councils. See Hefele, *Histoire des conciles*, 2.2.11,
p. 731. Note also that Quintilian, whose methods Valla used to expose the spurious
Donation of Constantine, includes in his list of false evidence 'any signatory known
to have died shortly beforehand' (aliquis signator dicitur afuisse vel prius esse
defunctus), Quintilian *Institutio oratoria*, 5.5.1., ed. Winterbottom, vol. 1, cited by
Ginsburg in *History, Rhetoric, and Proof*, p. 68n.

[535] *Epodus*, (Cooper), 'a kinde of verses havyng the first verse longer then the
second'. Hobbes refers to the pagan power of poetry to beguile. See 1688 Glossary
(pp. 606-7), and Molesworth note to line 1722, p. 394.

Sec. At Daemon mendax,[a] qui nunc possederat ipsos,[b]
    Si credi cuperent,[c] ejiciendus erat.
Pr.[d] Spiritus (adde) et avaritiae,[e] fastûsque[f] superbi,[g]
    Litis,[h] vindictae, saevitiaeque ferae.
Sed nunc ridiculae miracula mitto Legendae;[i]
    Ut quae jamdudum sunt tibi nota satis.[j]
Hoc aevo terrae spoliavit parte Latinae
    Rex Lombardorum,[k] Pontificem Laicus.
Tum Rex Chilpericus,[l] stupidus cognomine,[m] Regnum
    Gallorum tenuit;[n] fecit at ipse nihil: 1730
Omnia erat Pipinus;[o] opemque oravit ab illo
    Contra Lombardos Papa;[p] nec ille negat.
Armis Italiam petiit,[q] superavit et hostem;[r]
    Pontifici glebam restituitque suam.
Digna rogas[s] operae quae cepit praemia tantae?
    Fit Rex Pipinus;[t] Chilpericus Monachus.[u]
Nec dum finis erat Pipino morte remoto,
    Lombardus victus rursus in arma ruit.
Ablatas iterum Romanas occupat Urbes,[v]
    Quas iterum miles Gallicus eripiet.   1740
Nam Carolus Magnus,[w] Pipini filius,[x] armis,[y]
    Lombardum ereptos reddere cogit agros.

---

[a] uA B mendax • [b] A B ipsos • [c] A B cuperent • [d] mv uA *Pr.* missing • [e] uA B avaritiae • [f] A B C fastusque • [g] uA B C superbi • [h] uA B Litis • [i] uA legendae, A B Legendae, C legendae; • [j] A B satis, • [k] uA B Lombardorum • [l] A B Chilpericus • [m] uA cognomine • [n] uA B tenuit, • [o] uA B Pipinus, • [p] uA B Papa, • [q] uA petiit • [r] uA B hostem, • [s] A Rogas • [t] uA B Pipinus, • [u] ~A Monachus B monachus. • [v] uA urbes, • [w] uA B Magnus • [x] A B filius • [y] A B armis

Sec. But the lying Demon, who had now possessed them ought to have
been cast out, if they wished to be believed.

Pr. Add to that the spirit of greed, of arrogant pride, of contention, of
vengeance and of fierce cruelty.

But I'll now pass over the miracles of absurd legend which are familiar to
you for long enough,

In this period the king of the Lombards, a layman, robbed the Pontiff of
part of his Latin territory.[536]

King Chilperic,[537] as stupid as his name suggests, at that time ruled the
kingdom of the Gauls, but he himself did nothing. **1730**

Pipin was everything, and when the Pope pleaded with him for help
against the Lombards, he did not refuse.

He entered Italy under arms, defeated the enemy, and restored the Papal
lands to the Pope.

You ask what reward did he receive worthy of such great service? Pipin
became a monarch; Chilperic became a monk,[538]

And the matter did not end yet, for when Pipin died the defeated
Lombards rushed to arms again.

They again occupied the Roman cities, which had been taken from them,
and which the Gallic army would again take. **1740**

For Charlemagne, the son of Pipin, compelled the Lombards by force to
return the stolen lands,[539]

---

[536] *Charlemagne conquered peoples with whom the Byzantines had long been
at war, including the Lombards and Avars, restoring them to Papal power and
destroying the power of the Byzantines in Rome. At this point he took the Roman
Imperium, his crown bestowed by a willing Pope. He established his title in the
Libri Carolini on the grounds that the Byzantines had disenfranchised themselves
by heresy. See Ostrogorsky, *History of the Byzantine State*, pp. 182-6.

[537] The co-regency was in fact between *Pepin III, the Short (747-51 and 751-
68) and *Childeric III (743-51), son of Chilperic II.

[538] Note the pun in Latin because the word for monk, *monachus*, is almost identical in sound to *monarchus*, monarch. Hobbes is again mistaken, the king deposed by
Pepin the Short and sent to a monastery was Childeric III, son of Chilperic II, in 751.

[539] See Ostrogorsky, *History of the Byzantine State*, p. 183:
The loss of prestige which Byzantium suffered through developments in the
West was of more importance historically than the military failures in Asia and
the Balkans. It was the tragedy of the old Empire that, at a time when one of
the greatest rulers stood at the head of the Frankish kingdom, its own history
was determined by women and eunuchs. By incorporating Bavaria, Christian-
izing and absorbing Saxony, by expanding his territory at the expense of the
Slavs in the East, destroying the kingdom of the Avars, and by overthrowing
and annexing the Lombard kingdom, Charles the Great had made his realm
the paramount power in the Christian world of his day. In suppressing the

Et veniens Romam turbatis Schismate[a] firmam
    Romanis pacem,[b] Pontificemque dedit.[c]
Sic Papam fecit,[d] victoris[e] jure, Leonem;[f]
    (Tertius ille fuit cui Leo nomen erat.)[g]
Nec fuit ingratus Leo;[h] nam Carolo dedit ille
    Caesaris antiqui nomen et Imperium.[i]
Sec. Talia dona solet producere gratia rarò;[j]
    Contracto potius foedere pacta puto.   **1750**
Italus,[k] aut Gallus quid in Anglos juris habebat?[l]
    Non sua Rex Carolus, non sua Papa dedit.
Pr. Nil refert Quo[m] Jure;[n] sed actum est;[o] et fuit alter
    Terrarum Dominus;[p] Rex Fidei[q] alter erat.[r]
Nec tot ad Imperii[s] potuit tuba[t] signa ciere[u]
    Tela,[v] quot[w] ad Fidei[x] castra venire volunt.

---

[a] B C schismate • [b] uA B pacem • [c] mv uA B reddit. • [d] uA B fecit • [e] A Victoris • [f] uA B Leonem • [g] uA B erat) • [h] uA B Leo, • [i] A imperium, B C imperium. • [j] uA B rarò • [k] uA B C Italus • [l] mv uA B habebat, • [m] A B C quo • [n] uA jure, B C jure; • [o] uA B est, • [p] uA B Dominus, C dominus; • [q] uA B C fidei • [r] mv A B erat, • [s] A C imperii • [t] mv uA B turba • [u] A B ciere, • [v] uA B Tela • [w] mv A C quod • [x] A B C fidei

And, arriving in Rome, he gave to the people troubled by schism a stable peace and a Pontiff.[540]

In this way, according to the right of the victor, he made Leo Pope (he was the third Pope called Leo),[541]

Nor was Leo ungrateful, for he gave Charlemagne the title and power of ancient Caesar.[542]

Sec. It is unusual for gratitude to bring forth such gifts; I rather think it came about by a prearranged treaty.   **1750**

But what right did the Italian or the Gaul have over the English? The Emperor Charles and the Pope gave what was not theirs to give.

Pr. It doesn't matter by what right it was done, it was done nevertheless, and one was lord of the lands and the other was king of the faith.

And the trumpet could not rally as many weapons to the standards of imperial power, as were willing to come to the camp of faith.[543]

Lombards he had succeeded where Byzantium had failed, and this failure destroyed the authority of the Byzantine Empire in Rome. At the same time the Church of Rome strengthened its alliance with the kingdom of the Franks and decisively turned its back on Byzantium.

[540] Note that Ostrogorsky, *History of the Byzantine State* (p. 185), chronicles a divided empire of uncertain structure in which concessions have been made to the Arabs in the East, but where power in the West is not fully established either.

[541] See *Beh.*, *EW* VI, p. 178, where Hobbes once again confuses Chilperic for Childeric III:

In this time it was that the Pope began, by pretence of his power spiritual, to encroach upon the temporal rights of all other princes of the west; and so continued gaining upon them, till his power was at the highest in that three hundred years, or thereabout, which passed between the eighth and eleventh century, that is, between Pope Leo the Third and Pope Innocent the Third. For in this time Pope Zachary the First deposed Chilperic, then King of France, and gave the kingdom to one of his subjects, Pepin; and Pepin took from the Lombards a great part of their territory and gave it to the Church. Shortly after, the Lombards having recovered their estate, Charles the Great retook it, and gave it to the Church again; and Pope Leo the Third made Charles Emperor.

[542] *Pope Leo III made Charlemagne Holy Roman Emperor in a ceremony modeled on the Byzantine coronation (Ostrogorsky, *History of the Byzantine State*, p. 186):

Although the imperial coronation in St. Peter's had been the work of the papacy and not the Frankish king, Charles had to face the momentous consequences of his step; he had to secure that recognition from Byzantium without which his imperial title was legally invalid.

[543] These passages refer precisely to the dispensation of temporal power to the Pope, which Lorenzo Valla considers spurious. With reference to *The [Supposed] Donation of Constantine* as incorporated in Gratian's *Decretum* §3, which confers on the Pope 'the imperial scepters, and at the same time all the standards, and banners, and all the different ornaments, and all the pomp of our imperial eminence, and the glory of our power', Valla comments:

Will now the pontiff carry a sceptre in his hand? Why not give him a sword also, and helmet and javelin? "And at the same time all the standards and

Namque tubae[a] clangor mortales indicat hostes;[b]
    In Sibilo[c] Fidei[d] creditur esse Deus.
Ipse caput Caroli cinxit diademate clarum[e]
    Papa suus (populo conspiciente) Leo.   1760
Nec facile exultans populus sua gaudia texit,[f]
    Corde uno Reges laetus habere duos.
Ut verò[g] capiti Regis Leo Papa coronam
    Imposuit, verbis et benedixit ei;[h]
Unus et alter erat[i] qui clara voce *DEUS DAT*
    Dixit,[j] fortuitus,[k] nescio,[l] an appositus,
Tunc veluti quando nimium ferventia ligna
    Intûs[m] saevo ardent igne, latente tamen;[n]
Admota facula collucent omnia flammis,
    Monstrat et ardorem libera flamma suum;[o]   1770

---

[a] mv uA B turbae (error) • [b] uA B hostes, • [c] A B C sibilo • [d] uA C fidei • [e] A B clarum, • [f] A B texit • [g] A C vero • [h] mv A B ei. • [i] A B erat, • [j] uA C Dixit • [k] A B fortuitus • [l] A B nescio • [m] A Intùs B C Intus • [n] uA B tamen, • [o] A B suum,

For the shrill cry of the trumpet proclaims mortal enemies,[544] and in the
hissing[545] of faith God was believed to be present.
With the people looking on, his own Pope Leo crowned the distinguished
head of Charlemagne with a diadem.[546]   **1760**
And the exultant crowd barely concealed its joy, delighted at having two
rulers of one mind.
In fact, as Pope Leo placed the crown on the head of the King, he also
blessed him with the words of benediction.
And one or two people – by accident or deliberate arrangement, I don't
know which – said in a clear voice, 'God has given'.
Then, as when very hot wood burns with fierce but hidden fire within,
Everything flares up in flames when a torch is brought close, and the
flame is freed and reveals its heat,[547]   **1770**

---

banners." What do you understand by "standards" [signa]? "Signa" are either
statues (hence frequently we read "signa et tabulas" for pieces of sculpture
and paintings; – for the ancients did not paint on walls, but on tablets) or military standards (hence that phrase "Standards matched eagles" [Lucan,
Pharsalia, 1.7]). . . . Now then, did Constantine give Sylvester his statues or
his eagles? What could be more absurd?
See *The [Supposed] Donation of Constantine*, ed. Coleman, pp. 108-10.

[544] See Lucan, *Pharsalia*, 7.475-9 (Joyce edn, p. 184):
Listen! Clarion's blast/ on the screaming air and bugles blaring battle-
signals!/ Listen! Trumpets make bold reply. Listen! The din/ reaches the
ether, shattering the dome of remote Olympus/ where clouds keep their distance, where thunder never rumbles.
See also *Pharsalia*, 7.533 (Joyce edn, p. 185): 'No fight but war waged by an army
of swords on one of throats'.

[545] *sibile*, but should be *sibilo*, a hissing, whistling to show contempt. (Cooper),
'a whistlyng: an hissynge: in Poete the blowyng of wynde (adj.) that hisseth or
whisteleth' (Virgil: *ora sibila*: 'hissyng mouthes'). But scansion is still incorrect.
Possible word play on Sibiline/ sibilant, see Virgil, *Aen*. 2.211: 'sibila lambebant
linguis vibrantibus'.

[546] See Ostrogorsky, *History of the Byzantine State*, p. 185:
Leo III then made a bold and fundamentally revolutionary decision which set
the seal on the admirably purposeful policy of the Roman Church in the eighth
century: he crowned Charles as Emperor at Rome in the Church of St. Peter
on 25 December 800. . . . At that time it was axiomatic that there could only
one Empire as there could only be one Church. The coronation of Charles the
Great violated all traditional ideas and struck a hard blow at Byzantine interests, for hitherto Byzantium, the new Rome, had unquestionably been
regarded as the sole Empire which had taken over the inheritance of the old
Roman *imperium*.

[547] Lucretius discusses the physics of fire, smouldering but concealed, which
then breaks out, in terms of Anaxagoras' theory of immanence, but concludes, *De
rer. nat.*, 1.892-906 (Loeb edn, trans. Rouse, pp. 74-5):
and yet fire is not implanted in the wood, but there are many seeds of heat
which stream together by rubbing and make a conflagration among the

Sic vulgus simul ac sensisset verba DEUS DAT,
    Vocibus extensis,[a] DAT DEUS omne sonat.[b]
Post haec Christicolûm[c] coeperunt regna videri[d]
    Esse data à[e] Papis omnia,[f] Jure[g] Dei.
Sed non prospexit verborum posteritatem,
    Aut parvi fecit Rex generosus eam.[h]
Quae tandem neglecta in Legem[i] transiit Usu,[j]
    Et Regum fecit jura valere parùm:[k]
Quae Caroli soboles conatur reddere firma,[l]
    Frustra; nam Caesar nil nisi nomen erat:[m]   **1780**
Nomen,[n] amicitiis,[o] regnique vigore paterni,[p]
    Egregiis factis,[q] vix tenuere tamen.
Una,[r] Potestatem[s] partam nunc cura manebat,
    Ut,[t] quantis,[u] colerent, artibus esset opus.
Altera,[v] ne possent sua jura reposcere Reges;[w]
    Ne populi saperent,[x] tertia cura fuit.

---

[a] A B extensis • [b] mv A B sonat, • [c] uA C Christicolum B christicolum • [d] A B videri, • [e] A B a • [f] uA B omnia • [g] A C jure • [h] mv B eum. • [i] A C legem • [j] A B C usu, • [k] A B parum. C parum: • [l] mv A firma. • [m] A B erat. • [n] A B Nomen • [o] A B amicitiis • [p] A B Paterni, • [q] A B factis • [r] A B Una • [s] uA B C potestatem • [t] uA B Ut • [u] mv uA B quamvis A quamvis, • [v] uA B Altera • [w] B Réges; C reges; • [x] uA B saperent

So the whole crowd, as soon as it heard the words 'God has given', cried
out with raised voices, 'God has given'.[548]

After these events all the kingdoms of the Christians began to be seen to
have been given by the Pope through Divine Right.

But the generous King[549] did not foresee the future significance of these
words, or else he took little account of it.

And this neglected significance at length passed into law by usage, and
rendered the Rights of Kings of little value.

Charles's children tried to make these rights secure, but in vain. For the
title Caesar was nothing but a name.[550] **1780**

It was a name they just managed to retain, through alliances, by the
vigour of their father's reign, or by outstanding deeds.

The first concern of the Popes now was to cultivate their acquired power,
with all the arts that were necessary.

Their second concern was that kings should not be able to demand their
rights back; and the third concern was that the common people
should not learn wisdom.

---

forests; whereas if the flame were hidden in the forests ready made, the fires
could not be concealed for a moment, they would consume the forests everywhere, burn up the trees.
See also *De rer. nat.*, 6.895-905 (Loeb edn, trans. Rouse, pp. 560-1).

[548] Hobbes himself in the *LL* (*OL*) xlvi, §13, 320/472 (Curley edn), sees the
coronation of Charlemagne as the turning point in church-state relations:

In the meantime, the Roman empire having been torn apart (and already completely obliterated in Italy), the care of the city of Rome (i.e., the royal power
of Rome) was committed to the bishop of Rome. The papacy now seemed to
be a thing worth fighting over. So they did fight over it. In the time when
Charlemagne, king of France, conquered the Lombards, enemies of Rome,
Leo III was driven out of Rome by a schism. But Charlemagne brought Leo
back and confirmed him in the papacy; and Leo made Charlemagne emperor
of the western empire, publicly presenting him, in the name of God, with the
imperial crown, while the people cried out: *God has given it.* From this ceremony the title *by the grace of God, King of France*, became permanent for the
kings of France, as did the dominion of the popes over the kings. To preserve
this dominion of the church, Leo, an old man experienced in worldly affairs,
thought up a remarkable defense: *that all kingdoms of Christians be transferred to him by the arms of the kings themselves.* And he brought this about.

See also *Beh. EW* VI, p. 178 (c.f. note to line 746 above). Note that the election of
the emperor was signaled by public acclamation, which appears to be in the Byzantine tradition. It masks a silent revolution in the case of Charlemagne, for now the
Pope gives the crown. See Ostrogorsky, *History of the Byzantine State*, p. 176.

[549] *Carolus Agnus* (Charles the Lamb) is a sarcastic play on his name, *Carolus
Magnus* (Charles the Great).

[550] Charlemagne's extensive lands did not remain a united kingdom for long, but
were partitioned among his sons at his death.

Ergo Sacerdotum statuerunt[a] ne quis haberet
    Uxorem propriam.[b] (sed statuere senes.)[c]
Sec. A stupro veniens potuit celebrare Sacerdos?
    A propria veniens conjuge non potuit?   **1790**
Pr. Non quo tu reris Legem[d] tinxere Colore,[e]
    Sed qui de Sacro Codice[f] sumptus erat.
In regno,[g] Christus,[h] Coelesti,[i] dicit[j] aperte,[k]
    Conjugium nullum;[l] non Vir[m] et Uxor[n] erit.[o]
Omnibus at[p] Regni,[q] Sanctis Haeredibus,[r] hujus,
    Angelico,[s] vitam vivere,[t] more datur:[u]
Clericus et (docti dicunt) Haeredicus[v] idem est;[w]
    Atque hinc est Clero quod Venus omnis abest.[x]

---

[a] A statuerunt, • [b] uA B propriam • [c] A B C senes) • [d] A C legem • [e] A B C colore, • [f] uA B C codice • [g] uA B regno • [h] uA B Christus • [i] uA B coelesti C coelesti, • [j] mv A B dixit • [k] A B apertè, • [l] uA B nullum, • [m] uA C vir • [n] uA B C uxor • [o] mv A erit, C erat. • [p] mv C ad (error) • [q] uA regni B Regni C regni, • [r] uA B haeredibus C haeredibus, • [s] uA B Angelico • [t] uA B vivere • [u] B datur. • [v] mv A haereticus B haeredicus C Haereticus • [w] ~A est uA est, • [x] ~A abest

So they established the principle that no priest could have his own wife –
(but old men established it).[551]

Sec. So a Priest returning from debauchery could celebrate Mass, but
coming from his own wife, couldn't he?   **1790**

Pr. They did not colour the law with the tint you think, but with one
taken from the scriptures.[552]

Christ said explicitly that in the heavenly kingdom there will be no
marriage, there will be no husband and wife,[553]

But to all the holy heirs of this kingdom it is given to live according to
angelic law:

The cleric[554] and the heir[555] are the same (the learned say), and it for this
reason that all carnal love is distanced from the clergy.

---

[551] Hobbes's satirical point seems to be that preventing priests from marrying prevented their learning from being acquired by wives and children, and that priestly celibacy is ordained by those too old to feel the urge to marry. The subject of priestly marriage was treated in Selden's *Uxor Hebraica*.

[552] *color* in Latin has a rhetorical usage, meaning style, tone, (especially of diction), character, fashion, cast, colouring (Hor. *Ars Poetica* 236); beauty, lustre (Hor. *Carm.* 2.2.1); artful concealment of a fault (pretext, paliation, excuse), colourful excuse (Juven. 6.280. *Cod. The.* 3.6.3). Hobbes uses the term in this way in his 'Answer' to Davenant's *Preface*, see the note 439 to lines 1397-8. Here it means the 'spin' put on the law, the pretext for it. *Sec.* has suggested an immoral reason; *Pr.* alleges the biblical one. The distribution of the speakers is uncertain at this point.

[553] Luke 18:29-30 'And [Peter] said to them, "Truly, I say to you, there is no man who has left house or wife or brothers or parents or children, for the sake of the kingdom of God, who will not receive manifold more in this time, and in the age to come eternal life."'

[554] Hobbes plays perhaps on the false 'kleros'/cleric etymology exposed by Lorenzo Valla in *The [Supposed] Donation of Constantine*, ed. Coleman, pp. 50-1:
   Do we renounce earthly possessions in order to attain them more richly, and
   have we given up our property in order to possess another's and the public's?
   Shall we have cities, tributes, tolls? How then can you call us 'clergy' if we do
   this? Our portion, or our lot, which in Greek is called *kleros*, is not earthly, but
   celestial.

[555] Note that Hobbes's word play on heir/heretic involves signficant variants between A, B, C and 1688. While B and 1688 have *haeredicus* from *haeres*, heir, A and C read *haereticus*, heretic. See the 1688 Glossary (pp. 606-7), and Molesworth, 'Vide Glossarium, p. 397', where he notes of *haeredicus*: 'of the heads of the Lernean Hydra, Ovid, *Met.* 9.74'. But, as Professor Donald Russell notes, Molesworth is mistaken, *haeredicus* is not an attested form from *haeres*, but a coined term modeled on *clericus*, replacing the κλῆρος element (κλῆρος = inheritance) by the stem *haered-*, giving us *haered-icus* meant to sound like *haereticus*. Note that Hobbes does use *haeres* at line 1795 with the intended meaning heir.

Sed Color^a hic falsus,^{b} fugiensque in luce diei;^{c}
   Et nisi sub noctem fallere ineptus erat.   **1800**
Ingeniosa fuit,^{d} meditataque machina,^{e} contra
   Reges,^{f} ne possent Ordinis^g esse Sacri.^{h}
Nam duo conjuncti tituli,^{i} Rex atque Sacerdos,^{j}
   Regnum Civile,^{k} et Spirituale^l dabant.^{m}
Quod ne quando foret, provisum hac lege videre
   Pontifices,^{n} Reges non potuere boni.^{o}
Regibus,^{p} hoc Pacto,^{q} vel Regni^r haerede^s carere,
   Ordinibusve Sacris,^{t} stante,^{u} necesse fuit.
Sec. Nonne sui populi Rex,^{v} Pastor^w summus et idem est?
   Et Sub-Pastores^x nonne creare potest?   **1810**
Ipsa gregis Christi (data sit cuicunque)^y regendi
   Cura,^{z} Sacerdotem solaque (credo) facit.
Pr. Cernere sed Pythico velatas carmine technas,
   Magnanimi Reges quo potuere modo?

---

^{a} A B C color • ^{b} uA falsus • ^{c} uA B diei • ^{d} uA B fuit • ^{e} uA B machina •
^{f} uA Reges C Reges; • ^{g} uA B C ordinis • ^{h} A B C sacri. • ^{i} uA B tituli • ^{j} uA
B Sacerdos C sacerdos. • ^{k} uA B C civile • ^{l} A C spirituale B spiritualé • ^{m} A
dabant, • ^{n} uA Pontifices • ^{o} A boni • ^{p} uA B C Regibus • ^{q} uA B pacto C
pacto, • ^{r} uA C regni • ^{s} B herede • ^{t} uA sacris B C sacris, • ^{u} uA C stante •
^{v} uA B Rex C rex, • ^{w} uA B C pastor • ^{x} A C sub-Pastores B Sub-Pastores, •
^{y} C cuicunque (closing bracket missing) • ^{z} uA Cura

But this tint is false, disappearing in the light of day, and incapable of
    deceiving except under cover of night.[556]   **1800**

In fact it was a clever and well devised stratagem against Kings, to
    prevent them from taking Holy Orders.

For the double title King and Priest, once joined, conferred both the civil
    and religious dominion.

The pontiffs could see that this law ensured this should never happen, the
    innocent kings could not see this.

And so long as this agreement stood, kings had either to be without an
    heir or to refrain from taking holy orders.

Sec. Isn't a king also the supreme shepherd of his people? And can't a
    king create assistant shepherds?[557]   **1810**

Responsibility for guiding the flock of Christ (to whomsoever it is given)
    is itself what makes a priest (in my opinion) and nothing else can.

Pr. But how could noble Kings have discerned the tricks concealed in a
    Delphic oracle?[558]

---

[556] An echo of the parable of the watchful owner and the thief in the night, Matt. 24:42-44. Hobbes several times emphasizes the secrecy with which kings were despoiled of their power by the pope, his language reminiscent of Lorenzo Valla, who points out that the *Donation of Constantine* was never witnessed or properly promulgated: 'I ask whether you can adduce any witnesses of these events, any writers. None, you answer.' 'So! I think all this was done in the nighttime, and no one saw it at all!'. See *The [Supposed] Donation of Constantine*, ed. Coleman, pp. 64-7.

[557] Note the whole question of whether or not the king can ordain, and particularly create bishops, dates to Henry VIII and is raised in Book 3 of *Leviathan*, 'Of Christian Commonwealth'. See at ch. 42, 'Of Power Ecclesiasticall' (*Lev.*, xlii, §68, 296/367): 'Christian Kings are still the supreme pastors of their people, and have power to ordain what pastors they please, to teach the Church (that is, to teach the People committed to their charge)'.

[558] The *Delphic oracle was the most famous of the Greek oracles. But the real comparison is to Rome, where Hobbes continues the *topos* of the Pope as ghost of the Roman Emperor. See H.L. Havell *Republican Rome*, p. 42, on the patrician monopoly on state power in the 5th century BC through control of the mysteries:
    They were masters of the whole mystery of statecraft, acquired by the experience of many generations. . . . Moreover, they controlled the whole machinery of State religion, and their pontiffs and their augurs were trained in the art of working on the superstitious terrors of the multitude.

Nullus erat Princeps, ad sancta oracula Papae,[a]
  Quin stupidus fieret,[b] Chilpericoque magis.
Sec. Sed quare populus non sensit fraudis odorem ?[c]
  Anne illo nasus tempore nullus erat ?[d]
Pr. Nasus erat, toto sed tunc Epidemicus orbe
  Nasorum morbus praevaluit Polypus.[e]   **1820**
Qui ne cessaret,[f] subtilem excogitat artem,[g]
  Callidus ut Vulpes[h] ambitione Leo.
Ingenio,[i] studioque solet sapientia quaeri ;
  Hanc generi humano tollere Papa parat.[j]
Sec. Nescio qui stultus fieri queat ex Sapiente ;[k]
  [l]Ex stulto sapiens erudiendo potest.[m]
Pr. Stultitiam fortasse putas non posse doceri :[n]
  Difficile est durum (credo) docere senem :[o]
Sed teneris annis, ceu mollis cera,[p] figuram
  Quamlibet accipiet, sit bona sitve mala.   **1830**

---

[a] C Papae • [b] C fieret • [c] mv uA B odorem, • [d] mv uA B C erat. • [e] A Polypus
C polypus. • [f] uA B cessaret • [g] uA artem • [h] B Vulpes • [i] A B C Ingenio •
[j] A B parat, • [k] uA sapiente, B Sapiente, C sapiente; • [l] mv uA *Pr.* begins here
(scratched out and moved to line below in A) • [m] C potest: • [n] uA B doceri •
[o] uA B senem. C senem • [p] uA B cera

There wasn't a single Emperor who wasn't stupefied by the sacred oracles
of the Pope,[559] even more stupefied than Chilperic.[560]

Sec. But why didn't people detect the smell of fraud?
Or was there no Nose at that time?[561]

Pr. A nose there was, but at that time an epidemic, polyps, a nose
disease, prevailed throughout the whole world,[562]   **1820**

And Leo, clever as a fox in his ambition,[563] worked out a subtle way of
making sure this disease did not abate.

Wisdom is usually acquired through both ability and application; the
Pope prepared to take this wisdom away from the human race.

Sec. I don't know how a fool can be made out of a wise man, but a wise
man can be made out of a fool through education.

Pr. Perhaps you think that folly can't be taught: it's difficult to teach a
hard old man (in my opinion).

But in his tender years, like soft wax,[564] a man will take any form you
please, whether good or bad.   **1830**

---

[559] Hobbes's account of the struggle between kings and the papacy parallels the
account of Livy, discussing the pressure that wealthy exerted to enforce passage of
the Licinian Law, granting the Consulship and economic reforms to the Plebs,
finally passed in 367 BC. See H.L. Havell *Republican Rome*, pp. 120-1. The crisis
was resolved by the Patrician objection that the plebs would not be able to intercede
with the gods on behalf of the Roman people or interpret auspices, so Licinius added
to his bill that only 5 of the 10 keepers of the Sibiline books would be plebs. See
Hobbes's play on Sibiline/ sibilant at line 1758.

[560] C.f. line 1729 for Chilperic's [Childeric's] stupidity.

[561] Ovidius Publius Naso,* known as the Nose, characterized the Iron Age as full
of conflict based on fraud. Note that Hobbes locates the fraud that no-one smelled, not
with Sylvester's (supposed) Donation to Constantine, but rather with Charlemagne's
deferral to Pope Leo III in AD 800.

[562] 'a polypus in the nose' (Horace, *Sat.* 1.3.40; *Epod.* 12.5). Laurie Nussdorfer,
Civic Politics in the Rome of Urban VIII (Princeton University Press, Princeton,
1992) pp. 145-61, chapter 10, 'Plague', discusses a plague in Rome in 1629 affect-
ing the nose – of which Hobbes may have had first hand knowledge. Possibly a reference also to Hobbes's friend, Sir Thomas Browne's, *Pseudodoxia Epidemica*
(1646; 6th ed., 1672).

[563] The language of Machiavelli's *Prince*, ch. 18: ' Since it is necessary for the
prince to use the ways of beasts, he should imitate the fox and the lion, because the
lion cannot defend himself from snares and the fox cannot defend himself from
wolves. Therefore, it is important to be a fox in order to understand the snares and a
lion in order to terrify the wolves.' Note the parallels between the account of the rise
of Rome in Livy's first pentad, glossed in Machiavelli's *Discourses*, and Hobbes's
account of the rise of the papacy.

[564] See Plato, *Theaetetus* (191c-196d) on the human character as a wax block on
which learning makes an impression. See also the Jesuit maxim: 'Give me the child
until he is seven and I will give you the man'.

Stultior esse potest quisquam,[a] quam qui sapientem,[b]
Et doctum egregiè[c] se putat esse,[d] nec est?
Sec. Certum est. Stultitias in sese possidet omnes,[e]
Qui nimio ingenii est captus amore sui.[f]
Pr. Attamen hic stultus,[g] non Naturalis,[h] at arte[i]
Est factus,[j] gignet persimilesque sui.
Qui bene composito loquitur deliria vultu,
Sermones vacuos fundit et ore gravi,
Anne in Catalogo quaeres hunc classis euntis[k]
Anticyram, an sanis adnumerandus[l] erit?   1840
Nam juvenes etiam deliria discere possunt,
Aut accusandus ludimagister erit.
Sec. Posse quidem stultos fieri concedo docendo,[m]
Verum sic factos nemo fuisse putat.
Dic quare,[n] Quando,[o] quibus artibus, atque Magistris,[p]
Effectum est foedum, pestiferumque scelus.[q]
Pr. Pontificis suasu, Carolus,[r] novus Induperator,
Artibus ingenuis ferre volentis opem,[s]

---

[a] B quisquam • [b] uA B C sapientem • [c] A B egregié C egregie • [d] uA B C esse • [e] A B omnes • [f] A sui • [g] A B stultus • [h] B C naturalis, • [i] mv A B arte. • [j] uA factus • [k] A B euntis, • [l] A annumerandus • [m] A B docendo • [n] A quare; • [o] uA B C quando, • [p] uA B C magistris, • [q] mv C scelus? • [r] A B C Carolus • [s] C opem

Can there be anyone more foolish than the man who thinks himself
    uncommonly wise and learned, but is not?

Sec. That's certainly true. Anyone seiz ɘd with excessive love of his own
    intelligence possesses every folly in himself.

Pr. However, this fool is not born but made by art, and will beget others
    like himself.

Wouldn't the fellow who speaks lunacies with a straight face and pours
    forth empty discourse with a serious expression,

Be the sort you'd look for in the ship list of the deranged going to Anticyra,[565]
    or should he be counted among those of sound mind?[566]   **1840**

For even young men are given the opportunity to learn mad concepts, or
    their Schoolmaster must be reproached.[567]

Sec. I do admit that men can be made foolish through teaching, but surely
    no one thinks that they were created that way.

Tell me how, when, by what methods, and by which teachers, this foul
    and destructive crime was brought about.

Pr. The new emperor Charlemagne, at the instigation of a Pope who
    wanted to help the liberal arts,[568]

---

[565] Anticyra* (Chambers Murray), a town in Phocis, on the Gulf of *Corinth,
now Aspra Spitia; a town in Thessaly, region known for witchcraft; a town in
Locris. All three towns were noted for the production of *Hellebore*, for curing
mental diseases.

[566] See Horace *Sat.* 2.3.82-3 (tr. Fairclough, Loeb, 1929, pp. 160-1, trans.
amended), where according to the Stoic sage Stertinius everyone save the wise man
is mad. 'To the covetous', he says, 'we must give far the largest dose of hellebore:
wisdom, I rather think, would assign them all to Anticyra'.

[567] i.e., the Pope, presented throughout as a Schoolmaster; c.f. *Lev.*, xlii, §83,
301/374 where, speaking of 'the Pope's power without his own dominions', Hobbes
observes: 'for in all other commonwealths his power (if he have any at all) is that of
the Schoolmaster only, and not of the master of the family'.

[568] *Hist. Eccl.*, lines 1847-82, on the creation of the universities at Paris and
Oxford as papal foundations, closely parallels the fuller account in *LL*, xlvi (*OL*),
§14, 320/472 (Curley edn):

> For after a year or two Pope Leo, in his correspondence, exhorted Emperor
> Charlemagne to establish universities throughout his dominions, where all
> letters and sciences would be taught. So he set up, in Paris, the first university;
> and afterwards other kings set up others, each in his own dominion, which,
> once the colleges had been set up and organized for study, were to be governed
> by laws, according to the discretion of the Roman pontiff. Finally, from
> masters such as Peter Lombard, Duns Scotus, and Thomas Aquinas, was born
> the theology which they call scholastic, a hodge-podge of Aristotle's philoso-
> phy and Sacred Scripture....

Behemoth, pp. 40-1, dated about the same time, gives a similar account (see Springborg Introduction chapter 1.4).

Inscius includi curavit moenibus omnes,[a]
    Ut quae cui placita est,[b] inde petenda foret.[c]   **1850**
Et primò[d] foelix studiorum Gallus amator[e]
    Festinat Musis[f] aedificare domum.[g]
Parisiis surgit,[h] quae nunc Sorbona[i] vocatur,
    Theiologûm[j] studiis appropriata Schola.[k]
Hujus ad exemplum,[l] Reges,[m] aliique Potentes[n]
    Christicolûm[o] studiis tecta superba dabant,[p]

---

[a] mv A B omnes. • [b] A B est • [c] A B foret, • [d] A B C primo • [e] A B amator, •
[f] B C musis • [g] A domum • [h] uA B surgit • [i] A Sorbonna • [j] uA B Theologum
A C Theiologum • [k] A C schola. • [l] A B C exemplum • [m] uA B Reges C reges
• [n] uA B potentes, A Potentes, • [o] uA B C Christicolum • [p] C dabant

Unwittingly arranged for them all to be enclosed within walls, so that
whatever arts anyone wanted had to be sought from there.   **1850**
And first that lucky lover of learning, the Gaul,[569] hastened to build a
home for the Muses.
There arose at Paris what is now called the Sorbonne,[570] a School
appropriated for the studies of the theologians.[571]
Following Charlemagne's example, Kings and other powerful men
donated splendid dwellings for the studies of the Christians, [572]

---

[569] Charlemagne, after whom the Carolingian Renaissance is named.

[570] The myth that Charlemagne, by moving the Schola Palatina, founded at Aix
la Chapelle, to Paris, thus founded the Sorbonne, was current in the 17th century, but
it is much earlier. See Hastings Rashdall, *The Universities of Europe in the Middle
Ages* (Oxford, Oxford University Press, 2 vols, c.1895), vol. 1, pp. 271-3. Charlemagne was made patron saint of the Sorbonne in the 17th century. See also François
Rabelais, *Gargantua or Pantagruel* (Paris, 1653, English tr. Thomas Urquhart,
1649), on the Sorbonne and the *Sorbonifers*.

[571] Hobbes, in *Questions Concerning Liberty, Necessity and Chance* (*EW* V,
p. 64), records the censure of Luther by the Sorbonne theologians on April 15, 1521
in a document published as *Determinatio theologorum Parisiensum super doctrina
Lutheriana*, including three articles that Hobbes cites:
> Martin Luther, that was the first beginner of our deliverance from the servi-
> tude of the Romish clergy, had these three articles censured by the University
> of Paris. The first of which was: 'School-theology is a false interpretation of
> the Scripture, and Sacraments, which hath banished from us true and sincere
> theology.' The second is: 'At what time School-theology, that is mock-theol-
> ogy, came up, at the same time the theology of Christ's cross went down.' The
> third is: 'It is now almost three hundred years since the Church has endured
> the licentiousness of the School-Doctors in corrupting of the Scriptures.'
> Moreover, the same Luther in another place of his work saith thus: 'School-
> theology is nothing else but ignorance of the truth and a block to stumble at
> laid before the Scriptures.' And of Thomas Aquinas in particular he saith, that
> 'was he that did set up the kingdom of Aristotle, the destroyer of godly doc-
> trine.' And of the philosophy whereof St. Paul biddeth us beware, he saith it is
> School-theology. And Melancthon, a divine once much esteemed in our
> Church, saith of it thus: 'It is known that that profane scholastic learning,
> which they will have to be called Divinity, began at Paris; which being admit-
> ted, nothing is left sound in the Church, the Gospel is obscured, faith extin-
> guished, the doctrine of works received, and instead of Christs' people, we are
> become not so much the people of the law, but the people of Aristotle's ethics.'

The passage from Melanchthon to which Hobbes refers comes from his apology for
Luther against the Sorbonne theologians, printed together with the text of the condemnation under the title, *Determinatio theologicae facultatis Parisiensis super doctrina
Lutheriana hactenus per eum visa. Apologia pro Luthero aduersus decretum Parisiensum* (Basel, 1521). Noted in Leijenhorst, *Hobbes and the Aristotelians*, pp. 34-5.

[572] See *Beh. EW* VI, p. 184.
> Within the same time, that is, between the time of the Emperor Charles the
> Great and of King Edward the Third of England, began their second polity;
> which was, to bring religion into an art, and thereby to maintain all the decrees
> of the Roman Church by disputation; not only from the Scriptures, but also

Hortosque et libros,[a] et quae tibi singula dici
     Non opus est. Quae sunt, qualia,[b] quotque vides.[c]
Solus Papa tamen Leges dabat[d] atque Magistros.[e]
     Laedere ne posset Philosophia Fidem.[f]   1860
Sec. Non placet hoc. Animis quos non infigere sensus
     Venturi populi, si voluit, potuit?
Nam cum carceribus vinctas concluserat artes,
     Atque Fidem[g] servam fecerat esse sibi,
Quid vetuit,[h] si quas sibi posse nocere putaret,
     Aut prodesse parum, quin jugularet eas?[i]
Pr. Sic fecit. Nam qualis erat doctrina per orbem[j]
     Sparsa,[k] à[l] Lombardo, quae tenebraeque Scoti![m]
Quos Praeceptores habuit Schola Parisiensis
     Primos. Illorum gloria durat adhuc.[n]   1870
Sec.[o] Fama,[p] parum sana es,[q] tantundem dando Sophistis,[r]
     Qui virtute carent,[s] insipidisque viris,
Quantum illis quorum populos sapientia juvit,
     Aut virtus ingens,[t] vel decoravit eos:[u]
Nil tibi Pelides, nil nunc tibi debet Homerus.[v]
     Vilia dona tibi jam periere tua.
Sufficit ergo mihi,[w] si quid bene fecero, vivo
     Aemulus oblatret, laudet amicus homo.
Pr. Hi primi (dicunt) Lombardusque,[x] et Scotus à[y] Duns,
     Cum sociis primae, quos habuere Scholae,[z]   1880

---

[a] uA libros • [b] A B qualia • [c] ~A vides uA B vides, • [d] A dabat, • [e] A B Magistros, C magistros • [f] uA B C fidem. • [g] uA C fidem • [h] uA B vetuit • [i] sc mv A B eas? 1688 C eas. • [j] A B orbem, • [k] uA B Sparsa • [l] A B a • [m] sc mv 1688 Scoti? uA B Scoti, • [n] C adhuc: • [o] mv uA *Sec.* missing • [p] uA B Fama • [q] uA B es • [r] uA B Sophistis • [s] A B carent • [t] uA B C ingens • [u] uA B eos • [v] uA B Homerus, • [w] uA B mihi • [x] mv A B Lombardus C Lombardusque • [y] uA B a • [z] A Scholae B scholae

As well as gardens, books, and other things it is not necessary to itemize for
you. What they were, what type, and how many, you can see for yourself.
But only the Pope could make the laws and appoint the teachers, so that
philosophy could not damage the faith. **1860**
Sec. This was not a good thing. If he wanted to, he could have impressed
any attitudes on the minds of generations to come, couldn't he?
For when he had confined the shackled arts to prisons, and made faith his
slave-girl,[573]
What prevented the Pope, if he thought these arts could harm him or do
him little good, from cutting their throats?
Pr. That's what he did. What doctrines were spread through the world by
Lombard,[574] what darkness did Scotus produce![575]
They were the first instructors the Paris School had. Their reputation
endures to this day. **1870**
Sec. Fame, you are not very sensible in giving to Sophists who lack
virtue, and to worthless men,[576] as much renown
As to those whose wisdom or great virtue helped or honoured their people.
Achilles[577] owes you nothing, Homer[578] owes you nothing. Your worthless
gifts have now perished even for you.
So it is enough for me if I have done some good, that a rival should bark
at me when I'm alive and a friend praise me.
Pr. First (they say), Peter Lombard and Duns Scotus, along with their
associates, whom the first Schools employed, **1880**

---

from the philosophy of Aristotle, both moral and natural. And to that end the
Pope exhorted the said Emperor by letter, to erect schools of all kinds of literature; and from thence began the institution of universities; for not long after,
the universities began in Paris and in Oxford.

[573] Vives, in *Pseudo-dialecticos* of 1519, denounces the scholastic trivium at the
University of Paris, which he refers to as 'Cimmerian darkness'. See Richard Waswo,
'The Reaction of Jean Luis Vives to Valla's Philosophy of Language', *Bibliothèque
d'Humanisme et Renaissance*, vol. 42, no. 3 (1980), pp. 595-609.

[574] Peter Lombard, Theologian, c. 1100-1160, Italian but taught in Paris.

[575] Duns Scotus, (d. 1308), known as the Subtle Doctor (*Doctor Subtilis*), a
Scottish-born Franciscan and theologian, who wrote extensive commentary on the
work of Lombard.

[576] *Fama*, the Roman goddess of fame and the personification of popular rumor.
See Virgil, *Aeneid* IV.173. See also Milton's adaptation of Virgil's Fama in *In
quintum Novembris*.

[577] *Achilles, leader of the Achaeans.

[578] *Homer the famous poet of the 9th or 8th century BC is put in the shade, like
Achilles, because Fame has now honoured the 'sophists' so highly. In lines 1877-8
Hobbes has *Sec.* disclaim any wish for posthumous reputation.

Ex Patribus,[a] Sacris Scripturis,[b] et Stagyrita[c]
    Mixtis,[d] doctrinam composuere novam.[e]
[f]Linguam Romanam vertêre[g] in Gallimatiam.[h]
        Sec.: Sermo quis? *Pr.* Appositè.[i] Ducocalanus erat.[j]
Sec. Quorum hominum sermo?[k] *Pr.* Somnîtum,[l] non procul Umbris.[m]
    Scripsit eo multos Musa Lalia libros.[n]
Quorum doctrinam pleno quicunque bibisset
    Haustu, mutatus,[o] non erat id[p] quod erat.

---

[a] C Patribus • [b] B Scripturis C scripturis • [c] A Stagÿrita • [d] uA B Mixtis • [e] A
B novam, • [f] mv C begins *Sec.* here • [g] A B C vertere • [h] A Gallimatiam • [i] A
Apposite B Apposité C Apposite. • [j] uA B erat C erat; • [k] uA B sermo • [l] uA B
Somnitum, C Somnitum • [m] mv uA B C umbris • [n] mv C libros • [o] uA B
mutatus • [p] C id,

Compounded new doctrine by mixing up the Church Fathers, the Holy
    Scriptures and the Aristotelians,[579]
To turn the Roman tongue into Gallimaufry.[580]
    Sec. What language is that? *Pr.* Appropriately, it was Cock and Bull.[581]
Sec. It was the language of what men? *Pr.* Of sleepites, not far from the
    Shades.[582] The Muse Lalia,[583] wrote many books in that language.
Whoever drank a full measure of the teachings of those books was
    changed, he was not what he was.

---

[579] This is essentially the accusation made against Peter Lombard's *Sentences*
by Joachim of Fiore, who accused him of mixing indiscriminately Biblical and
Patristic sources, giving precedence, if anything to the Church Fathers (c.f.
Catholic Encyclopaedia). Ockham, *Bradwardine and *Suiseth, ridiculed by
Renaissance humanists for their 'barbarous' Latin, meaningless abstractions and
hair-splitting distinctions, became the butt of a later generation of humanists critical of the barbarities of the logicians (Jardine, 'Humanist Logic', p. 177). See
Melanchthon, Gassendi and Chillingworth, especially Gassendi (*Exerc.* 1.1.9,
110b), whose form of words is close to Hobbes: 'Voces commenti sunt barbaras,
phrasesque loquendi ineoptas, quibus intra Scholarum cancellos ita intumescunt,
ut rideant caeteros mortales, quod non assequantur illarum mysteria.'

[580] (*OED*): a word of unknown origin, first found in the 16c.: confused language, meaningless talk, nonsense: 1653: Urquart: *Rabelais*, 1.ii: 'a Galimatia of
extravagant conceits'. The English *Gallimaufry*, from the French *galimafree*, which
might have referred to a kind of sauce or stew, in its earliest English sense meant a
ragout or hash, figuratively a 'hodge-podge': 'So now they have made our English
tongue a gallimaufry, or hodge-podge of all other speeches', Edmund Spenser
lamented in *The Shepherd's Calendar* of 1579. See also *LL* xlvi, §14, 320/472
(Curley trans.), where Hobbes concludes his account of the founding of the universities: 'Finally, from masters such as Peter Lombard, Duns Scotus, and Thomas
Aquinas, was born the theology which they call scholastic, a hodge-podge of Aristotle's philosophy and Sacred Scripture . . . .'

[581] French,'du Coq à l'âne', a completely arbitrary way of proceeding from
one topic to another (Invernizzi, p. 86) See the 1688 Glossary (pp. 606-7):
DUCOCALANUS in gallice du Coq à l'âne. Coq à l'âne.

[582] Gianni Paganini, 'Hobbes, Valla e i problemi filosofici della teologia umanistica', p. 45, notes that Hobbes's description of the scholastics as 'Ducocolanae',
'Somnites', 'sophists', devotees of the 'musa Lalia', and 'lotus eaters', is typical of
humanist theologians in their polemics with the scholastics. These epithets are also
reminiscent of Lucretius' dream demons, *De Rerum Natura*, 1.132-5.

[583] See the 1688 Glossary (pp. 608-9), and Molesworth's note p. 399, 'Vide
Glossarium: Lalia – Infantum balbutientium Dea'. 'Lalia, Goddess of infantile babbling'. 'The name of this "Tenth Muse" introduced by Hobbes, means in Greek,
useless chat, garrulous speech', Invernizzi notes, p. 86. In the 1668 Appendix to the
LL, §56 (tr. Wright, p. 359) Hobbes quotes the Septuagint on '*peri lalias*, concerning the empty talk'.

Potus ut in mensa geminas putat esse lucernas;[a]
Sic Regem ille suum concipit esse duos.   1890
Ut qui veneficae gustarat pocula Circes,[b]
Illic è[c] puero fit lupus,[d] ursus,[e] aper.
Et cicures vigilare jubentur ad atria Circes;[f]
Sic Papis debent advigilare Scholae.
Sicut amor[g] Loti socios mutavit Ulissis,
Ne vellent patriae plus meminisse suae;[h]
Sic Papis cives adjunxit vita Scholaris,[i]
Fecitque aversos regibus[j] esse suis.
Hoc quoque par Ithaci sociis est,[k] atque Scholari,
Mutatus specie[l] ut,[m] se putet esse virum.[n]   1900
Egressusque Scholae tenebris,[o] quos convenit omnes,[p]
Communis vitae nescius ipse,[q] docet.
Exclamat, clamat, declamat fortiter;[r] omnes
Intempestivè[s] corrigit[t] atque docet.[u]
Simpliciter κάτα τί,[v] Typicè,[w] Topicè,[x] Tropicéve[y]
Omnia,[z] quae libitum est dicere,[aa] vera facit.[bb]

---

[a] uA B lucernas, • [b] uA Circes • [c] A B e • [d] uA B lupus • [e] uA B ursus •
[f] uA B Circes, • [g] mv A Amator B amator • [h] uA B suae. • [i] uA B Scholaris •
[j] uA B Regibus • [k] uA B est • [l] C specie, • [m] uA B C ut • [n] mv B virum •
[o] uA B tenebris • [p] uA B omnes • [q] uA B C ipse • [r] uA B fortiter • [s] A B C
Intempestive • [t] C corrigit, • [u] mv C docet • [v] A Κάτά Tί B κατα τί C κατά τί,
• [w] uA C typice, B Typice, • [x] uA C topice, B Topice, • [y] mv uA tropiceque A B
Tropiceque C tropiceve • [z] uA B C Omnia • [aa] uA B dicere • [bb] sc mv 1688 facit
A B C facit.

Just as a drunk man thinks there are two lamps on the table,[584] so that man
imagines his own king to be two men.   **1890**
Like the one who had tasted the potions of the sorceress Circe,[585] from a
boy he straight away becomes a wolf, a bear, a boar.
And as tame beasts are bidden to keep watch over Circe's halls,[586] so the
Schools must keep watch for the Popes.
Just as the love of the Lotus[587] transformed the companions of Ulysses, so
that they would no longer remember their homeland,
So the life of the scholar yoked citizens to the Popes, and made them
hostile to their own kings.[588]
Another equivalence between Ulysses' companions and the scholar is that
the latter has been changed in appearance, thinking he is a man. **1900**
And having emerged from the dark recesses of the School, he teaches all those
whom he meets, even though he knows nothing about ordinary life.
He cries out, he shouts, he vigorously declaims; he teaches and corrects
everyone in an untimely manner.[589]
Literally, relatively, typically, topically, and tropically,[590] he makes true all
the things he likes to say.

---

[584] C.f. Lucretius, *De rer. nat.* 4.448-52 (Loeb edn, pp. 310-11), on seeing double: 'a certain sensation follows which makes it appear that all we look at grows double then and there as we look: two lamps flowering with flames, the furniture all over the house multiplied by two, men with double faces and two bodies each'.

[585] *Circe*, Goddess, famed for her magic, her house was surrounded by men metamorphized as beasts, she changes Odysseus's men into swine; c.f. Homer *Odyssey*. 10.210 ff.; Virg. *Aeneid*, 7.19-20. Hobbes echoes the words of Horace, *Epistles*, 1.2.23-6, who argues Homer is a wiser teacher than all philosophers, and recommends Ulysses refusal of Circe's cup to those tempted by the Schoolmen.

[586] *Odyssey* 10.187ff.

[587] For the *Lotophagi*, see line 1200 and note.

[588] C.f. Lucretius, *De rer. nat.* 5.1120-36, on those whose struggle for honour and reputation, but whose 'wisdom comes from the lips of others', drunk with power, end up regicides.

[589] The irony is that he violates Aristotelian canons of appropriateness.

[590] This is the language of scholastic logic, particularly as applied to forms of preaching in use in the Middle Ages (see Invernizzi p. 87). For the taxonomy of terms, see Beryl Smalley, *The Study of the Bible in the Middle Ages*, 3rd ed. (Oxford, Oxford University Press, 1984), pp. 1-36 ('The Fathers'), and pp. 216, pp. 242-6 on topics; and for typology more generally, Erich Auerbach, 'Figura', in *Scenes from the Drama of European Literature*, trans. Ralph Mannheim (New York, Meridian Books, 1959), pp. 11-76. On the distinction between the literal and tropological interpretation of Scripture, see Smalley's conclusion to *The Gospel in the Schools* (London, Hambledon Press, 1985).

Huic hominum generi mandatum est justificare
    Omnia,[a] quae voluit Papa[b] vocare Fidem;[c]
Obsequiumque Sacrae dare[d] tunc sine limite Sedi,[e]
    Jussaque Pontificis,[f] jussa vocare Dei.   **1910**
Haec omnes sonuere Scholae, docuere Cathedrae,[g]
    A cunis didicit sic puer esse pius;[h]
Contemptus Regum surgit cum Relligione;[i]
    Et plebs civili libera lege furit.
Nempe Deo visum est tunc solvere cingula Regum,[j]
    Qui mox stultitiae verbera digna ferent.
Sec.[k] Non ego Alexandri Magni, nec[l] Caesaris acta
    Amplius admiror, Hannibalisve dolos,[m]
Qui sibi larga quidem,[n] sed sanguine,[o] regna pararunt;[p]
    Parta tenere tamen non potuere diu:[q]   **1920**
Quod potuit subjectus inertibus esse Magistris[r]
    Perdomitus mundus, dum reputo,[s] stupeo.
Castra quidem video;[t] nam sunt Collegia[u] castra,[v]
    Arma tamen desunt, et quibus arma darent.

---

[a] uA B Omnia • [b] uA papa • [c] uA B fidem, A Fidem. • [d] Mv uA B dare sacrae (word order) C sacra dare (error) • [e] A B C sedi, • [f] uA B Pontificis • [g] A C cathedrae, • [h] uA B pius. • [i] uA B Relligione • [j] uA B Regum • [k] mv uA *Sec.* inserted next line, corrected A • [l] mv A B non • [m] uA B dolos • [n] uA B quidem • [o] uA B C sanguine • [p] ~A pararunt uA B pararunt, • [q] A B diu. • [r] uA C magistris • [s] uA B reputo • [t] uA B video, • [u] uA B collegia • [v] uA B castra;

To this sort of man was entrusted the task of justifying everything the
    Pope wanted to call Faith.

And giving the Holy See unconditional obedience, and calling the orders
    of the Pontiff the orders of God.   **1910**

All the Schools repeated these things, all professors' chairs taught them;
    from the cradle a boy learned to be devout in this way.

Contempt for kings developed alongside religion and the common people,
    freed from civil law, went wild.[591]

Indeed God then decided to relieve the kings of their authority,[592] soon to
    bear the blows worthy of their folly.

Sec. No longer have I admiration[593] for the deeds of Alexander the
    Great,[594] or for those of Caesar,[595] or the deceits of Hannibal,[596]

All of whom acquired for themselves vast kingdoms, albeit by bloodshed,
    but could not hold on to their acquisitions for long.[597]   **1920**

When I think it over, I am astounded that the world could be made subject
    and completely tamed by indolent teachers.

In fact I see armed camps, for colleges are camps,[598] but they lack arms,
    and those to whom they might give arms.[599]

---

[591] Echoes of Lucretius, *De rer. nat.*, 5.1120-50, on the overthrow of kings.

[592] 'solvere cingula Regum': 'cingula' are belts, symbolizing the soldiers' duties: so the kings are being retired from duty.

[593] Horace, *Epistles*, 1.6, beginning 'Nil admirari', the famous epistle recommending philosophic calm and avoidance of excess, counseled by both Epicureans and Stoics.

[594] *Alexander the Great (356-323 BC). Note the *Res Gestae Divi Augusti* (c. 14 BC); and the vast medieval literature on the Gests modelled on the deeds of Alexander. See F. P. Magoun, *The Gests of King Alexander of Macedon* (Cambridge: Harvard University Press, 1929).

[595] *Caius Julius Caesar (July 13, 100 – March 15, 44 BC), statesman, general and author, famous for the conquest of Britain and Gaul.

[596] *Hannibal of Carthage (247-183 BC), general extolled in Machiavelli's *Prince*, ch 17, who crossed the Alps with elephants and took his own life, rather than surrender to Rome.

[597] The thesis of Machiavelli's *Prince* and *Discourses*, where the primary distinction is between absolute Princes, who conquer easily but hold their kingdoms with difficulty, and constitutional regimes, which are harder to install but easier to maintain.

[598] This echo Davenant, who in his *Preface to Gondibert*, dedicated to Hobbes, ironically observed (lines 349-52, 368-70, *EW* IV, p. 12):
    Religion is universally rather inherited then taught, and yet the most effectuall Schooles of Morality, are Courts and Camps. . . . Nor are Camps the Schooles of wicked Destroyers, more then the Inns of Court (being the Nursery of Judges) are the Schooles of Murderers. . . .

[599] See Machiavelli's *Prince*, chapter 6, on the Prophet armed and the Prophet unarmed.

Pr. Erras. Pontificum fuit unusquisque satelles,[a]
    Quaeque dabant Reges arma,[b] ferebat eis.
Sec.[c] Heu,[d] Schola[e] qualis erat capiendis Machina Regnis![f]
    [g]Ingenii plusquam Mercurialis opus.
Vincula, quae mollem tenuerunt ferrea Martem,[h]
    Firma fuere minus, crassa fuere magis.   1930
Tanta meâ[i] nunquam sapientia laude carebit,[j]
    Qui sum stultitiae conscius ipse meae.
Pr. Vasa quidem et nummos facile est subducere furto,[k]
    Et sceptrum,[l] si vis, et diadema simul;[m]
Regnum,[n] difficile est;[o] fieri sed tempore longo
    Possibile est. Aetas omnia,[p] longa potest.
Movisset Terrae[q] Siculus mirabilis orbem,
    Si locus esset ubi staret in orbe alius.
Partem operis si dat breve tempus,[r] tempore multo
    Perficiet totum, qui tenet id quod habet.   1940

---

[a] mv ~A Satellet (error) uA Satelles • [b] uA B arma • [c] mv uA *Sec.* missing • [d] uA B Heu • [e] A C schola • [f] uA B Regnis. C regnis • [g] mv the following 2 lines are missing from uA (but present in B C and 1688) rectified in A at the foot of 35[v] and 36[r]. • [h] mv B has Machina Regnis instead of ferrea Martem, copied in error from two lines above. • [i] A B C mea • [j] uA B carebit • [k] uA B furto • [l] uA sceptrum • [m] A B simul. • [n] A B C Regnum • [o] uA B C est, • [p] uA B omnia • [q] A C terrae • [r] A B tempus

Pr. You're mistaken. Every single one was in the service of the Popes
and each brought to them all the arms that the kings handed out.[600]

Sec. Oh, what a machine for capturing kingdoms was the School! A work
of genius that outdoes Mercury.[601]

The iron chains that held the yielding Mars[602] were not as strong, but they
were thicker.   **1930**

Such great wisdom will never lack my praise, I who am conscious of my
own foolishness.[603]

Pr. In fact it's easy enough to secretly make off with dishes and cash, a
sceptre, if you wish, and a Royal diadem at the same time.

It is difficult to steal a kingdom, but it can be done over a long period of
time. A long time-span makes everything possible.[604]

That marvelous Sicilian, Archimedes,[605] would have moved the world if
there had been another place on the globe where he could have stood.

If a little time allows part of the work to be completed, then with a lot of time
the man who conserves what he has will complete the whole task. **1940**

---

[600] The Pontiff is the Prophet Armed. The King is the Prophet Unarmed.

[601] Mercury, a herald, the god of eloquence and of scholars, also presided over
the dealings of traders and thieves, while leading souls to the Underworld. (Lewis &
Short). See Horace, *Satires*, 2.3.25, which refers to a slick businessman as 'Mercu-
riale', like Mercury, or 'Mercury's pet' (ed., Fairclough, Loeb edn, pp, 154, 155).

[602] *Mars the Roman god of war and husbandry, father of Romulus, and thus the
progenitor of the Roman people, was caught in. *corpus delicti* with Venus by
Vulcan, who forged a strong net to trap them and exhibit them in shame before the
assembled gods. See Homer *Odyssey* 8.266ff.

[603] See Horace, *Satires*, 2.3.25, commonly entitled 'The Follies of Mankind',
the inspiration for Erasmus's famous *In Praise of Folly*. (See Loeb edition, ed. Fairclough, p. 149):

> The Satire takes the form of a dialogue between the poet and Damasippus. . . .
> Damasippus, of whom we hear in Cicero's Epistles. . . a bankrupt speculator
> and dealer in works of art, who, having fallen into the depths of despair had
> been rescued by the Stoic sage Stertinius, was converted by him to philosophy,
> and so made into the wise man he has now become.

[604] Herodotus 5.9.3 'I cannot explain this, but anything may happen in the whole
course of time'.

[605] For *Archimedes boast about moving the earth, see *Plutarch, *Life of Marcellus*, (Plutarch, *Makers of Rome*, Harmondsworth, Penguin, p. 99):

> Archimedes in writing to Hiero [the tyrant of Syracuse], who was both a rela-
> tive and a friend of his, asserted that with any given force it was possible to
> move any given weight, and then, carried away with enthusiasm at the power
> of his demonstration, so we are told, went on to enlarge his claim, and
> declared that if he were given another world to stand on, he could move the
> earth.

Unco fur noctu subducit stragula lectis;

     Pastorale pedum,[a] crede,[b] quod uncus erat.

Furtum ne laudes;[c] non est sapientia,[d] sed fraus,[e]

     Quae nunquam magnis insidet ingeniis.

Sec. Sed quid agas? Nolles Collegia habere tot agros,

     Aut tam magnificas,[f] totque habitare domos?[g]

Ergo cave,[h] si vis, ne[i] forte fugâ[j] vitiorum

     In majora ruas, barbariemque meram.

Non Fama pejore videbere Templa deorum,[k]

     Doctrina celebres, quam spoliare Scholas.[l]   1950

Pr.[m] Non illis,[n] studio[o] quibus est sapientia,[p] et artes,

     Tecta superba, libros, invideo nec opes.

Opto sed in primis[q] ut vera scientia crescat,

     Utque[r] sciens omnis sit manus artificis.

Utque omnis Doctor quid justum est norit[s] et aequum,[t]

     Quoque Deum deceat conciliare modo;[u]

Et quae conducunt, quae sunt contraria Paci,[v]

     Quaelibet et virtus unde sit et vitium;

Noverit et factu quid turpe sit,[w] et quid honestum;[x]

     Quosque onerat rerum copia,[y] quosque levat;[z]   1960

Quid sperare facit, quid terret[aa] quidque pudere

     Cogit;[bb] quique humilem noverit erigere.

---

[a] uA B pedum • [b] uA B C crede • [c] uA B laudes, • [d] uA sapientia • [e] uA B fraus • [f] uA B magnificas • [g] mv C domos • [h] uA B cave • [i] mv uA B me (error) • [j] uA B fuga • [k] A B C Deorum, • [l] mv C scholas • [m] mv uA C *Pr.* missing • [n] uA B illis • [o] mv uA B studeo (error) • [p] uA B sapientia • [q] mv A B imprimis (variant) • [r] mv A B Ut C Atque • [s] mv uA B novit • [t] uA B C aequum • [u] uA B modo. • [v] uA C paci, • [w] uA B sit • [x] uA B honestum • [y] uA B copia • [z] A B levat. • [aa] B C terret • [bb] uA C Cogit,

A thief in the night steals the covers from beds with a hook;[606]believe me,
   the shepherd's crook was such a hook.
Don't praise theft; it is not wisdom, but rather fraud, which never resides
   in great intellects.[607]
Sec. But what would you do? Don't you want the colleges to have so
   many lands or to occupy so many magnificent residences?
Then take care, if you please, lest perchance by fleeing some vices you
   rush headlong into greater ones, and even pure barbarism.[608]
To strip the Temples of the gods will not earn you worse repute than
   stripping the famous Schools of their teachings.   **1950**
Pr. I don't begrudge the Schools[609] whose concern is wisdom and the arts
   their magnificent lodgings,[610] their books or their wealth.
But I desire first and foremost that true knowledge increase, and that the
   hand of every artisan be skilled.[611]
And I desire that every Doctor should know what is just and equitable and
   how he ought to reconcile himself to God;
And what promotes peace and what is contrary to peace, and whence
   derives every virtue and vice;[612]
And that he should know what acts are disgraceful and what are
   respectable; whom wealth burdens and whom it comforts.   **1960**
[Every Doctor should know] what gives hope, what fear, what causes
   shame; and he should know how to encourage humble men.

---

[606] 1 Thessalonians 5:2, 'the Lord so cometh as a thief in the night' (Matt. 24.43, Luke 12.39, 2 Peter 3.10). See also Horace, *Epistles*, 1.2.32-3.

[607] Note the ambiguity: *ingeniis*, which can be translated as either natural ability or fraud.

[608] See Horace, *Epistles*, 1.1.41-2 'Virtus est vitium fugere et sapientia prima/ stultitia caruisse'. See also Horace *Ars poetica*, 31, 'In vitium ducet culpae fuga, si caret arte'.

[609] Hobbes appears to be discussing the Oxford and Cambridge Colleges, and for Doctor we may read Don. For his full position on 'The use of Universities', see *Lev.*, xxx, §14, 179-80/225.

[610] 'tecta superbus', Virgil's term for the shrines of the gods, ancestral homes (*Aeneid* books 8 and 12); and here the ivory towers or universities.

[611] Primus's spirited defence of general education, the trades and wage-earners, echoes *Lev.*, xxx, §17, 181/227.

[612] Primus's position seems at odds with that of Hobbes in *Lev.*, vi, §7, 25/28; and *Lev.*, xlvi, §32, 376/464, repeated in lines 235-8 above, that people call good what pleases them and bad what displeases them. But perhaps Hobbes credits people with a simple understanding of good and evil that cuts a swathe through the teachings of the Schoolmen, without sacrificing a theory of truth.

Haec si quis rectè,[a] scierit, poteritque paterno
    Ore,[b] quasi ad natos,[c] cum gravitate loqui ;
Nec propriae suevit contraria dicere voci,[d]
    Nec,[e] quae non quadrant cum ratione,[f] docet ;
Et norit Methodum[g] rectam,[h] qua quaeque docenda[i]
    Ars est ;[j] illius et prima Elementa[k] sciat.
Sec. Verùm[l] quis tam doctus in ipsa est Arte[m] Docendi,[n]
    Omnibus ut mereat scribere jura Scholis ?   1970
Pr. Judicii res est et doctrinae mediocris ;
    Et facere hoc possem forte (vocatus)[o] ego.[p]
Hunc ego quantovis,[q] meritò[r] dignabor honore ;[s]
    Hunc metui,[t] populi postulat utilitas.
Nondum se,[u] Reges satis afflixisse,[v] putabat
    Papa ;[w] fuere amplae[x] quas metuebat opes.
Quas ut pro[y] Christo possent[z] fudisse videri,[aa]
    In bellum Eoum sub Cruce[bb] mittit eos.
Namque armis Asiam Saraceni tunc tenuere[cc]
    Papae subductam, quae repetenda fuit.   1980
Inde mali Martis crudelia verbera passi,[dd]
    Exhausti redeunt,[ee] ad mala multa,[ff] domi.

---

[a] A recte C recte, • [b] uA B Ore • [c] uA B natos • [d] uA B voci • [e] uA B Nec • [f] uA B ratione • [g] uA C methodum • [h] B C rectam • [i] A B docenda, • [j] uA B est, C est • [k] A B C elementa • [l] A B C Verum • [m] uA B C arte • [n] A B docendi, C docendi • [o] mv uA B vocatus • [p] C ego : • [q] A B quantovis • [r] uA B merito • [s] A B honore. • [t] uA B C metui • [u] uA B se • [v] uA B C afflixisse • [w] uA B Papa, • [x] A amplae, • [y] mv A B pro missing • [z] mv uA B posset • [aa] A B videri • [bb] B C cruce • [cc] C tenuere, • [dd] A B passi • [ee] A B C redeunt • [ff] A B C multa

If anyone knows these things correctly, and can speak with gravity in a
fatherly tone, as if to sons,
And is not in the habit of contradicting himself, and doesn't teach things
that don't square with reason;
And if he knows the correct method by which each discipline must be
taught;[613] and if he knows the first principles of that discipline.
Sec.[614]But who is so skilled in the art of teaching, that he deserves to
dictate the rules in all the Schools? 1970
Pr. It's a matter of common sense and moderate learning, and I myself
could probably do it (if called upon).
I shall think this man as deserving of any amount of honour: the public
good demands that he should be respected.[615]
The Pope did not believe he had crushed the Kings sufficiently; their
wealth he feared was very great.[616]
So that they could be seen to pour forth these resources for Christ, the
Pope sent them into the Eastern war, under the sign of the Cross.[617]
For the Saracens at that time occupied Asia with military force, after it
had been wrested from the Pope, and it had to be reconquered. 1980
There the kings suffered the cruel lashes of a disastrous war, and returned
exhausted to many disasters at home.

---

[613] See the *Discourse[s] on Method* of Petrus Ramus and his disciple Jean
Bodin; and Descartes' work of 1637 of that title, to which Hobbes gave careful
attention as attested by his own work on optics of 1641 (See Malcolm, ed., *Thomas
Hobbes, The Correspondence*, vol. 2, p. 825, biography of Descartes).

[614] See the Molesworth note: Hobbes is referring to himself perhaps, as one who
aspired in *Leviathan* to write the curriculum for the universities. As noted in the
Introduction, at this point the distribution of the dialogue between the speakers is
again in doubt. It seems more likely that Secundus should not resume at line 1969,
but that Primus breaks off the long sequence of 'if' – clauses enumerating the qualities of a good teacher, by asking, 'But who is so skilled. . .?' Then at lines 1971-3
Secundus says it is all a trivial act, and Primus denies this by saying (lines 1973-4)
'I shall think this man deserving of any amount of honour: the public good demands
that he should be respected'.

[615] Primus's humanism is reminiscent of Erasmus's *Christian Soldier* and
Luther's promotion of education as the basis for a community of Christian believers.

[616] They had money and armies.

[617] The first crusade took place in 1097-99, following Pope Urban II's declaration of a Holy War in 1095 (Invernizzi note, p. 89).

Mox majora audet, regum feritate subacta,[a]
  (Gesta priora meri gesta fuere hominis.)[b]
Humano majus jus postulat, atque videri[c]
  Posse aliquid,[d] solus quod Deus ipse potest.[e]
In summum commissa Deum peccata remittit
  Maxima, nescio quo Jure Tribunitio;[f]
Quamvis in Sedem[g] sacram commissa remitti
  Aut nunc, aut post haec secula,[h] posse negat.   1990
At peccata idem pretio sine,[i] nulla remittit;[j]
  Sed vult divinas vendere[k] Sector opes.
Ut promus condus Divini,[l] factus,[m] Amoris,[n]
  Distribuit variis fata futura locis.
Egregiè[o] meritos de Sacra[p] Sede[q] locabat
  In summo coeli culmine stelliferi.
Deinde[r] Patres veteres,[s] ut Noen,[t] utque Abrahamum,[u]
  Davidem, Mosen,[v] inferiore loco.
Post hos,[w] Infantes[x] nondum Baptismate[y] lotos,
  Expertes poenae Tertius[z] Orbis[aa] habet.   2000
Perpetuis Quartus[bb] consumit crimina nummis,[cc]
  Et nisi quae non sunt igne levanda,[dd] levat.
Ultimus,[ee] horribilis Serpentibus[ff] atque tenebris,[gg]
  Est datus Haereticis,[hh] Daemonibusque[ii] locus.
Spe summae Sedis[jj] vanos mulcebat amicos,
  Atque hostes Imo[kk] terruit Orbe[ll] leves.
Profuit,[mm] et prodest nunc Purgatorius[nn] ignis
  Pontifici multùm,[oo] Sacrificisque[pp] suis.

[a] A subacta. • [b] A B hominis) • [c] A videri, • [d] uA B aliquid • [e] mv C potest •
[f] A Tribunitio, B Tribunitio • [g] A B C sedem • [h] A B C secula • [i] uA B C sine •
[j] uA B remittit, • [k] A Vendere • [l] uA B C divini, • [m] uA B C factus • [n] uA B
Amoris • [o] uA B C Egregie • [p] A B C sacra • [q] A B C sede • [r] mv uA B
Denique • [s] A Veteres, B veteres C veteres, • [t] A B Noen C Noën • [u] A B Abrahamum mv C Abrahamque • [v] A B C Mosen • [w] uA B C hos • [x] uA B infantes
mv C infants. • [y] uA C baptismate • [z] uA B C tertius • [aa] uA B C orbis • [bb] uA
B C quartus • [cc] B nummis. • [dd] uA B levanda • [ee] uA B Ultimus • [ff] A C serpentibus • [gg] A B tenebris • [hh] uA haereticis B Haereticis C haereticis, • [ii] A C
daemonibusque • [jj] A B C sedis • [kk] A B C imo • [ll] uA B C orbe • [mm] A B C
Profuit • [nn] uA B C purgatorius • [oo] uA B multum A C multum, • [pp] A C sacrificisque

Once the savagery of the kings had been tamed, the Pope soon dared greater
things. (His former achievements were the deeds of a mere mortal.)[618]
He demanded a right greater than that of mortals, and to be considered
capable of something of which only God himself is capable.
He forgives the greatest sins committed against the supreme God, I don't
know by what juridical right,
Even though he denies that sins committed against the Holy See can be
forgiven either now or in the future.   **1990**
Yet the Pope remits no sins without a price; but this profiteer wants to sell
divine bounty.[619]
As steward and store man[620] of Divine Love, he apportioned future
destinies in different places.
He placed those who had deserved particularly well of the Holy See at the
summit of the starry heavens.[621]
Then in a lower place the venerable Patriarchs, like Noah, Abraham,
David and Moses.
After them, the third circle holds infants not yet purified by baptism who
are exempt from punishment.[622]   **2000**
The fourth circle obliterates offences with endless cash, and pays them
off, if they have to be paid off, by fire.[623]
The lowest place, with its terrifying serpents and darkness was set aside
for heretics and devils.
The pope beguiled foolish friends with hope of the highest place; and he
frightened weak enemies with the threat of the lowest.
The fire of Purgatory, greatly benefited, and still benefits, the pope and his
priests.

---

[618] On *monumenta rerum gestarum*, chronicles of the 'great deeds' of kings,
popes, etc., a huge genre, see for instance, the many chronicles comprising the *Monumenta Germaniae Historica*; as well as the *Monumenta patrum* (2. Vol. fol.) mentioned in the Hardwick Hall book list at shelf mark K.3.15. (see Appendix B); the
Gesta pontificum Romanorum, etc.

[619] Lucan 1.178, on a seller of his favour: 'hinc rapti pretio fasces sectorque
favoris ipse sui populus'. Note Hobbes's innuendo: the Papal sale of Indulgences.

[620] Plautus *Pseudolus*, 608.

[621] A benefit for which they have already paid as we have just found out. Dante,
in the *Divine Comedy*, put these popes in the lowest rungs of Hell.

[622] For the fate of the unbaptised in the *limbus infantium*, see the *Oxford Dictionary of the Christian Church (ODCC)*.

[623] Purgatory, whose torments can be remitted by Indulgences, which are sold.

Sec. Sed Patribus quare visum est puerisque seorsim[a]
    Assignare orbes? Nil venit inde boni.[b]   2010
Pr. Non summo hos Patres coelo posuere,[c] quod illi
    De Papa Romae nil meruere boni.[d]
Non imo foedoque loco posuere, quod illi
    De Papa Romae nil meruere mali.[e]
Infantes Limbo[f] neutro posuere,[g] quod illi
    Nil potuere boni, nil potuere mali.[h]
Sed simulatque animas decrerant[i] esse animatas,
    Debebatur eis certus in orbe locus.[j]
Nec dum credebat Reges satis esse subactos,[k]
    Sed Nova[l] Castra[m] parat,[n] Militiamque[o] novam.   2020
Infundit[p] Regum terris examina Fratrum,[q]
    Mendicos sacros,[r] quos aleret populus.
His quoque vermiculis Reges hominesque opulenti
    Magnificas certant aedificare domos.
Unde volant,[s] alis enatis, Templaque bombo
    Implent;[t] nam musca est[u] quae modo vermis erat;[v]
Atque per ora virûm[w] volitans non multa scientum,
    Illorum patulis insidet auriculis;[x]
Corrumpens mores Civiles,[y] nec sinit illos,[z]
    Ut debènt,[aa] fidos Regibus esse suis.   2030
Parendum esse Deo,[bb] potius[cc] quam Regibus,[dd] inquit,[ee]
    Nil dubii est:[ff] Eadem Papa Deusque[gg] jubent.[hh]
Sedulus ad lectum morientibus adstat,[ii] et audit
    Quae sua quisque velit[jj] non benefacta loqui.[kk]

---

[a] A seorsim, • [b] mv A B boni? • [c] uA B posuere • [d] mv A B boni • [e] mv B mali • [f] uA B C limbo • [g] uA B posuere • [h] mv A B mali • [i] mv uA decrant (error) • [j] A locus • [k] A B subactos • [l] uA B C nova • [m] uA B C castra • [n] uA parat • [o] uA B C militiamque • [p] mv A B Infudit (error) • [q] uA C fratrum, • [r] uA B C sacros • [s] uA B volant • [t] uA B Implent • [u] A est, • [v] uA C erat • [w] A B C virum • [x] B auriculis • [y] uA B C civiles, • [z] A B illos • [aa] uA B debent C debent, • [bb] A B C Deo • [cc] C potius, • [dd] A B C Regibus • [ee] A B inquit • [ff] A B est. • [gg] mv A B Deus • [hh] mv uA B jubet. (error) • [ii] A B adstat • [jj] A velit, • [kk] mv A B loqui

Sec. But why did he think it right to assign circles separately to the Patriarchs
and the children? Surely nothing good could come of that.   2010
Pr. They didn't put these Patriarchs in the upper heaven, because they
didn't deserve well of the pope of Rome,
And they didn't place them in the foul depths because they didn't deserve
ill of the Pope of Rome.
They placed the infants in a neutral place, in Limbo, because they could
do nothing good and they could do nothing bad,
But as soon as the Popes had decreed their souls were living, a fixed place
within a sphere had to be given to them.
The Pope did not yet think Kings had been sufficiently tamed, but
prepared a new camp and a new army.   2020
He poured into the lands of kings swarms of Brothers, holy beggars
whom the people had to feed.[624]
Kings and rich men competed to build magnificent houses for these little
grubs too.
From whence, having grown wings, they fly away, filling the Temples
with their buzzing; for each one is now a fly which was a grub but a
moment ago.[625]
And, flying above the mouths of men who don't know much, each settles
on their open ears;[626]
He corrupts the morals of citizens, and he doesn't allow them to be as
loyal to their kings as they should be.[627]   2030
'There's no doubt that a man should obey God rather than kings', he says.
'The Pope and God command the same thing'.
He diligently attends the bed of those dying and listens to the misdeeds
which each wishes to tell;

---

[624] Reference to the diffusion of the Mendicant orders of the 13th century, the
Franciscans, Dominicans, Augustinians and Carmelites. See Daniel-Rops, *The
Church in the Dark Ages* (New York, Dutton, 1959), p. 159 ff. Some idea of the
rapidity with which monasticism spread may be guaged from the Benedictines of
Cluny, founded 910, which by AD 1000 controlled 1000 monasteries. The Cluniac
Reforms and ensuing centralization created 'the first translocal corporation' and
ultimate model for church and empire as a whole, Berman argues in *Law and Revo-
lution*, p. 89.

[625] C.f. Virgil *Georgics*. 3.9.

[626] The point of *per ora virum*, Ennius' epitaph on himself, in Cic. *Tusc.* 1.15.34:
'volito vivu per ora' – 'I fly alive in men's mouths' – is the spread of reputation or
'Fama'.

[627] The sacrament of confession.

Consilioque[a] juvat,[b] pia Testamentaque[c] dictat;[d]
  Daque Deo,[e] dicit, Qui[f] tibi tanta dedit.
Inde tot et tanti sacris Donaria[g] Templis,[h]
  In Reges videas arma parata,[i] Deo.
Explorator erat quoque Confessarius[j] omnis,[k]
  Et confessa Deo dicere doctus erat:[l]   2040
Nam Deus in terris hoc tempore Papa fuisset,[m]
  Si non per Regum jura creandus erat.
Papa Leo Carolusque agnus[n] sibi mutua regna
  Tradiderant pacto,[o] Carnis et Ingenii.[p]
Sed pactum hoc Papae non servavêre[q] sequentes;[r]
  Non aequum est par jus Carnis[s] et Ingenii.[t]
Namque,[u] inconsulto,[v] Papas,[w] Induperatore,[x]
  Est ausus Clerus saepe creare sibi.
Hinc sub Conrado (sed quaere quoto) ferus ille
  Longusque occiduo motus in orbe fuit.   2050

---

[a] mv uA B Consilio • [b] A B C juvat • [c] uA C testamentaque • [d] ~A dictat uA B dictat, • [e] uA B Deo • [f] uA B C qui • [g] uA C donaria • [h] A B Templis C templis, • [i] uA B C parata • [j] uA B C confessarius • [k] uA B C omnis • [l] A B erat. • [m] A B fuisset • [n] mv A Magnus B magnus • [o] C pacto • [p] A B C ingenii. • [q] A B C servavere • [r] A B sequentes • [s] uA C carnis • [t] A B C ingenii. • [u] A B C Namque • [v] A B inconsulto • [w] A B Papas • [x] uA C induperatore A B Induperatore

He gives counsel, he dictates solemn testaments, and he says, 'Give to
God, who has given so much to you.'
That is why you can see so many and such valuable offerings in churches,
arms made ready for God against kings.
Every confessor was also a spy, and was taught to reveal what had been
confessed to God.   **2040**
So the Pope would have been God on earth at this time, if he had not had
to be appointed by the legal right of kings.
The lion Pope and Charles the Lamb[628] handed other to each other by
agreement their respective kingdoms of the Spirit and the Flesh.
But later Popes did not abide by this agreement; it wasn't right to make
the authority of the Flesh and the Spirit equal.[629]
For without consulting the emperor, the clergy often dared to appoint
popes for themselves.
For this reason, under Conrad (query: which Conrad?)[630] there was that
long and savage rebellion in the West.   **2050**

---

[628] *Carlus magnus* rendered *Carlus agnus*, a word play (which A and B miss)
suggesting Isaiah 11:6: the Lion Pope (Leo) and the Charles the Lamb lie down
together.

[629] Hobbes refers to division of the world into temporal and spiritual kingdoms
from the time of Charlemagne and Pope Leo I, playing on the concept of Christ
made flesh, a central and contentious Christian doctrine, addressed again at
lines 2075-8. Tertullian prefers the form of words, *carne est indutus*, to express the
Logos having put on flesh, because he feels *caro factus* suggests transfiguration;
c.f. *homo factus est* of the Nicene Creed as translated by Hilary (Tertullian
Adversus Praxean, PL, II, col. 157, cited Hefele, *Histoire des conciles*, 2.1.9, p. 219
and 1.1.2., p. 446.); Origen sees the union of the two natures as a tissue,
sunuphainesthai, but usually used the word *krasis* to describe this union which corresponds to the Latin *commixtio* (Origen, *Contra Celsum*, bk 3 ch 41, and *De Principiis*, bk 3 ch. 6, in *PG* XI cols 972 and 256). Following this line of reasoning Tertullian saw Christ as *homo Deo mistus* (*Apologeticus*, ch. 21, *PL* I, col. 450), while
Cyprian used the epithet *Deus cum homine miscetur* (*De vanit. idol.*, *PL* IV, col. 585
ff) and Lactantius used the formula *Deus est et homo, ex utroque genere permistus*
(*De div. inst.*, bk 4 ch. 13, *PL* VI, col. 482). They spoke of the life of these two
natures, *sundromei*, as their *copulatio* or *connexio*. Ignatius of Loyola, whom
Hobbes may be satirizing here, preferred to refer to Christ as *sarkophoros*, flesh-
bearer (Ignatius, *Ad Smyrn.*, ch. 5). Citations Hefele, *Histoire des conciles*, 2.1.9,
pp. 219-20.

[630] Hobbes seems to have made an in-text note to check his sources, but does not.
It was Conrad III in fact (r.1138-1152), a German king from the house of Hohen-
staufen, also known by its territorial name, Weiblingen (Ghibelline in Italian), who
fell heir to part of Charlemagne's kingdom. The Gibellines and Venice were on the
side of the German Emperor, while the Welfs (Guelf in Italian) had the hereditary

Pro Papa Guelphi,[a] pro Caesare stant Gibelini,[b]
    (Temporis istius nomina forte ducum)[c]
Exiit hoc bellum Frederico[d] Caesare capto,[e]
    (Illo qui primus nomine Caesar erat.)[f]
Hunc Veneti vicere,[g] Fugatus[h] Papa,[i] triumphat;[j]
    Nomine Alexander Tertius[k] ille fuit;
Qui capta Roma,[l] Veneta[m] latitabat in Urbe,[n]
    Detectusque ipso Caesare major abit.

---

[a] C Guelphi • [b] ~A Gibelini • [c] A B Ducum) • [d] A B C Friderico • [e] A B capto • [f] A B erat) • [g] C vicere • [h] A C fugatus • [i] A B C Papa • [j] mv A B triumphus • [k] B C tertiusHungary and Serbia were on the side of the Pope. Conrad and the Byzantines were[l] A B C Roma • [m] C veneta • [n] A Urbe. B Urbe C urbe,

The Guelphs were on the side of the Pope, the Ghibelines on the side of
the Emperor (these, as it happened, were the names of the leading
men at the time).
This war ended with the defeat of the Emperor Frederick[631] (he was the
first emperor by that name),
The Venetians defeated him, and the exiled Pope triumphed; that Pope's
name was Alexander III;[632]
When Rome was captured, he hid at Venice: when he emerged into the
open, he went away more powerful than the Emperor himself.[633]

---

dukedom of Bavaria from 1170, and with the support of Normandy, France,
Hungary and Serbia were on the side of the Pope. Conrad and the Byzantines were
allies against the Pope and were about to undertake a joint campaign in Italy, but
for the sudden death of Conrad in 1152. See Daniel-Rops, *Cathedral and Crusade*,
2 vols (New York, E. P. Dutton & Co, 1957), vol. 1, pp. 230-1 and Ostrogorsky,
History of the Byzantine State, p. 379-84 for Conrad's manoeuvrings with the
Pope.
    [631] Frederick Barbarossa, German Emperor 1152-90, who was half Guelf, half
Ghibelline and Conrad III's nephew (see Daniel-Rops, *Cathedral and Crusade*,
pp. 236-46). Frederick I, successor to Conrad III, suspicious of the Byzantines and
their competing imperial claims, did not proceed with the campaign and ended up
their enemy, finally defeated in the famous battle of Legano in 1176. See Ostrogorsky, *History of the Byzantine State*, p. 384. Note that John of Salisbury, an eye-
witness, is the most important extant source for Frederick's misadventures in Italy
which Hobbes recounts. See *The Letters of John of Salisbury*, pp. 1-2, cited in
Brooke, 'John of Salisbury and his World', in *The World of John of Salisbury*, ed.
Michael Wilks (Oxford, Oxford University Press, 1994), pp. 1-20, at p. 11. See in
the same volume Timothy Reuter, 'John of Salisbury and the Germans' pp. 415-25.
    [632] Donald M. Nicol, *Byzantium and Venice: A Study in Diplomatic and
Cultural Relations* (Cambridge, Cambridge University Press, 1992), p. 102,
notes that it was
         in July 1177 that Frederick Barbarossa made his truce with the Lombard
         towns and was reconciled with the pope, Alexander III, whom he had refused
         to recognize for seventeen years. The Kingdom of Sicily too was party to the
         treaty of Venice; and the Venetians made sure of their own arrangements with
         Barbarossa by signing a new pact with him in August of the same year. For the
         Doge Sebastiano Ziani it was his finest hour. Never had Venice played host to
         so great a throng of world leaders.
    [633] Alexander III had a history of standing up to Frederick I, and in exile in
Venice in 1167, became a symbol of resistance to German domination. Frederick,
meanwhile, succumbed to the Lombard League, an alliance of the northern cities
of Verona, Vicenza, Padua, Venice, Constantinople, and Sicily and, after numerous attempts to overthrow the League and the Pope, in 1176 surrendered at the
battle of Legnano, recognizing Alexander as Pope at the Treaty of Venice of
1177.

Cujus et in collum steterat, dictisque superbis[a]
Insueto dederat vulnera saeva animo. **2060**
Sec. Crescere plus ultra terrena potentia nescit,[b]
Omnis et ambitio sic satiata perit.
Nil habuere ultra sperandum,[c] nil metuendum
Pontifices;[d] cessit spesque[e] metusque simul.
Ridebat quoties spectabat aruspicem aruspex,[f]
Ingenii[g] miro captus amore sui.
Pr.[h] Quod risere parum est. Humilis sublatus in altum,[i]
Insultans victis ludere saeva solet.
Regibus imponit duram contra Saracenos
Militiam;[j] ipsorum sumptibus atque[k] suis. **2070**

---

[a] mv C superbis. • [b] A B nescit • [c] uA B sperandum • [d] uA B Pontifices •
[e] mv A B spes • [f] A B C aruspex • [g] mv uA B Ingenio • [h] mv uA B *Pr.* missing
• [i] A B altumHungary and Serbia were on the side of the Pope. Conrad and the
Byzantines were[j] uA B Militiam, • [k] sc mv 1688 idque

The pope stood on the emperor's neck,[634] and by his arrogant statements
cruelly wounded him with unusual ferocity. **2060**

Sec. Terrestrial power does not know how to increase further, and all
ambitions, having been sated, perish.[635]

The popes had nothing more to hope for and nothing more to fear; their
hopes and fears died at the same time.

Whenever one soothsayer[636] looked at another he used to smile, seized by
a marvelous love of his own intelligence.[637]

Pr. That they smiled is the least of it. An upstart of humble origin
is apt to play cruel games and insult those he has defeated.

He imposed a tough war against the Saracens on the kings,[638] and in fact at
their own expense and his. **2070**

---

[634] See the formula, *colla ad suescere servitio*, to accustom the necks to slavery
as a symbol of subjection. The reference here is to the encounter in Venice of Frederick Barbarossa and Alexander III of 1177, during which the Emperor kneeled
before the pope in the Piazza San Marco in Venice and the Pope put his foot on the
Emperor's neck, quoting Psalm 91:13: 'thou shall tread upon the lion and the adder,
the young lion and the dragon thou shalt trample under thy feet'. Not coincidentally,
the occasion was the centenary of the humiliation of the Emperor Henry IV by
Hildebrand, Pope Gregory VII, in Canossa in 1077. See Invernizzi note, p. 91, and
Daniel-Rops, *Cathedral and Crusade*, pp. 226-9, and Edwin Curley's commentary
on the parallel passage in *Lev.*, xliv, §20, 343/423 and note.

[635] An ironic portrait of the Pope as Leviathan, so consumed by worldly power
that when all his bodily appetites are sated his power deflates. See the idiom of the
Aesopian fable, 'The Frog Who Wanted to Make Himself as Big as the Bull', e.g.
Phaedrus 1.24, repeated by Jean La Fontaine (1621-95), the great French fabulist
and Hobbes's contemporary: fable 3.1.

[636] Hobbes is quoting Cicero, *De nat. deor.*, 1.71: 'Mirabile videtur, quod non
rideat haruspex, cum haruspicem viderit' (part of an Epicurean statement). In the
same spirit Lorenzo Valla, in response to the *Invectione in Vallam* of his colleague
at the court of Alfonso V, had insisted on using the classical terms *prophetas, arus-
pices, augures,* for the clergy, while nevertheless disdaining to use the term *summus
pontifex* for the pope 'as if I wrote not in my own age but that of Numa Pompilius'.
See Valla's *Recriminationes in Facium* of 1445 (*Opera omnia*, ed. Garin vol. 1,
p. 531), cited in Sarah Gravelle, 'Humanist Attitudes to Convention and Innovation
in the Fifteenth Century', *Journal of Medieval and Renaissance Studies*, vol. 11
(1981), pp. 193-210, at pp. 202-3.

[637] The term *clericus* (cleric) had come to mean simply an educated man. So, for
instance, St Benedict of Aniane (c. 747 – 821), educated at the court of Pippin the
Younger, was concerned about the growth of monastic and cathedral schools
because he believed the emphasis on intellectual pursuits could lead to false pride.
See Daniel-Rops, *The Church in the Dark Ages*, p. 197-8.

[638] Nicol, *Byzantium and Venice*, p. 126, notes that the Third Crusade under
Alexander III was undertaken by kings, whereas no crowned heads participated in
the Fourth Crusade, under taken by Pope Innocent III (elected 1198). 'One lesson of

Deinde animi causa,[a] Reges populique subacti
Experiebatur,[b] quid potuere pati.[c]
Lascivire solet nimiùm[d] secura potestas ;[e]
Regnantumque facit jussa superba quies.
Namque super Panem[f] sanctum si quando Sacerdos[g]
Verba Dei rectè[h] Sacra[i] loquutus[j] erat,
Credi Papa jubet Panem[k] non amplius esse,
Sed veri Carnem,[l] Sanguinem,[m] et Ossa[n] Dei.
Qui non credebat,[o] Christi pellendus ovili[p]
Et vita (nisi se[q] credere juret) erat.   **2080**
Nec tamen hac crevit jam summa Potentia Papae
Lege ;[r] sed ob pulchrè[s] gesta Triumphus[t] erat.
Nam voluit toti manifestum reddere mundo
Obsequium simplex se sibi velle dari,[u]
Nec passurum impunè[v] loqui sua dogmata contra
Quemquam[w] hominem ;[x] Fidei nam dabit ipse modum.[y]
Etsi tu Panem[z] esse putas,[aa] si dixerit ille,[bb]
Caseus est,[cc] dices tu quoque Caseus[dd] est.
Sensit idem tecum ;[ee] non indiget ut doceatur,[ff]
Indiget officiis obsequioque tuo.   **2090**
Post multos cyathos stomachum movet ultimus,[gg] et quod
Antè[hh] erat ebibitum redditur omne simul.

---

[a] C causa • [b] A Experiebatur, • [c] A pati • [d] A B C nimium • [e] uA B potestas • [f] uA B C panem • [g] uA B C sacerdos • [h] A C recte • [i] A B C sacra • [j] A B locutus • [k] uA C panem • [l] uA Carnem C carnem • [m] uA B Sanguinem C sanguinem • [n] uA C ossa • [o] uA B C credebat • [p] C ovili, • [q] mv A se missing • [r] A B Lege, • [s] A B pulchre C pulcre • [t] uA C triumphus • [u] mv A B dari. • [v] uA C impune B impuné • [w] A Quenquam • [x] mv uA B hominum, A hominum; • [y] A B modum • [z] uA B C panem • [aa] uA B putas • [bb] uA B ille • [cc] uA B est • [dd] A B C caseus • [ee] A tecum, B tecum • [ff] A B doceaturHungary and Serbia were on the side of the Pope. Conrad and the Byzantines were[gg] A B C ultimus • [hh] A B C Ante

Then, for amusement, he tested how much kings and their subjugated
peoples could endure.
Too much unconstrained power runs to excess, and the silence of the
reigning kings leads to arrogant proclamations.
In fact, the Pope ordered that when the priest correctly spoke the sacred
words of God over the holy bread,
It should no longer be considered bread, but the flesh, blood and bone of
the true God.[639]
Anyone who did not believe had to be banished from Christ's flock and
from life (unless he swore that he did believe).[640]   2080
Yet the power of the Pope, already supreme, did not increase as a result of
this rule, his triumph was due to his splendid successes.
For the Pope wished to make plain to the whole world that he wanted
unconditional obedience to be given to him.
And that he would allow none to speak with impunity against his dogmas;
for he himself would set the norm of faith,
So even if you think it's bread, if the Pope said, 'It's cheese', you too
should say, 'It's cheese'.[641]
He experienced the same as you did; he doesn't need your teaching, he
needs your respect and obedience.   2090
After many cups the last makes the stomach turn and all the wine that was
drunk before comes back up at the same time.[642]

---

the Third Crusade had been that monarchs in command of their own armies found it
hard to co-operate.' The kings taking part in the Third Crusade, 1189-93, included
Frederick Barbarossa, Philip Augustus of France and Richard the Lion-hearted,
King of England. See Invernizzi, note, p. 91.
   [639] The doctrine of *Transubstantiation, the 13th century dogma of the Church
proclaiming that in Holy Communion, the bread and wine of the host are transformed into the body and blood of Christ.
   [640] Transubstantiation was proclaimed dogma by the Lateran Council of 1215.
   [641] The claim is consistent with Hobbes's view that the sovereign has the power
to proclaim the meaning of words – and at this point the Pope was sovereign. C.f.
Lorenzo Valla's example in the Repastinatio, ed. Zippel, vol. 1, 19.17-20 (cited in
Gravelle, 'A New Theory of Truth', Journal of the History of Ideas, vol. 50 (1989),
pp. 333-4), of the importance of the distinction between 'verbum' and 'res':
      Now false bread and false wine and false prophets are not bread, wine and
      prophets, and true bread, true wine, and true prophets are nothing other than
      bread, wine and prophets as we sense them. Therefore in us, that is, in our
      minds is truth and also falsehood.
   [642] C.f. the proverb about 'the last drink making you bring up the rest'. Hobbes
resumes the idiom of doctrines hard to swallow and regurgitation, last mentioned
with respect to the Eucharist at lines 1091-2.

Moverat haec multos sic Transmutatio[a] Panis,[b]
     Ut scita à[c] Papis plurima rejicerent.
Waldus erat quidam vir Lugdunensis, et idem
     Ingenio atque opibus[d] clarus in urbe[e] sua,[f]
Scripturaeque sciens[g] sacrae Laicus, solitusque
     Non quid sit Dominus quaerere,[h] sed quid ait;
Deque Fide sensit[i] quae nunc Ecclesia sentit
     Nostra ferè;[j] non est nunc nova nostra Fides.[k]   **2100**
Nec sensus narrare suos metuebat amicis,
     Haereticis quanquam tunc grave tempus erat.
Ergo per innumerum populum doctrina volare
     Waldi, et paulatim crescere vera Fides;[l]
Donec ad ingentem strepitum perculsus,[m] in illos,[n]
     Immisit Reges Papa[o] quibusque suos.
Waldenses tandem multi anni, praelia multa
     Extinxere. Dei non sine consilio;[p]
Namque animis hominum tunc semina jacta fuere,[q]
     Quae surgent Papis exitiosa seges.   **2110**
Territus his turbis multo crudelior exit;
     Suspectum Haeretici[r] nomine[s] quemque rapit.
Suspectum abjurare facit (si vult) vel ab igne
     (Si non vult) vivus vertitur in cineres.
Qui falsò[t] abjurat, resipiscere[u] dicitur; at si
     Quem juramenti poenitet,[v] ille perit.
Sec. Nonne quibus vellent potuerunt parcere Reges?
Pr. Non.[w] Non credebant Juris[x] id esse[y] ui.[z]

---

[a] uA B C transmutatio • [b] uA C panis, • [c] A B a • [d] A opibus, • [e] C orbe (error) • [f] mv A B sua. • [g] B Sciens • [h] B quaerere • [i] A sensit, • [j] uA B fere, C fere; • [k] ~A Fides C fides. • [l] uA C fides. • [m] uA B C perculsus • [n] uA B C illos • [o] C Papa, • [p] A B consilio. • [q] ~A fuere • [r] A B C haeretici • [s] mv uA B nomen • [t] A B C falso • [u] uA respicere (misreading) • [v] uA poenitet • [w] uA B Non C Non, • [x] A B C juris • [y] C ipse (misreading) • [z] A B sui C sui.

In fact this transubstantiation of the Bread disturbed many, so that they
rejected a great many of the Popes' decrees.

There was a certain Waldus from Lyons, famous in his own city both for
his intellect and wealth.[643]

He was a layman knowledgeable in the Holy Scriptures, who used to try
to find out not what our Lord might be but what He says.

And on the matter of faith he understood more or less what our Church
now understands by it; because our faith is not a new faith.[644]   **2100**

He was not afraid to share his thoughts with friends, even though it was
then an oppressive time for heretics.

So the doctrines of Waldus quickly spread among countless peoples, and
the true faith gradually grew;

Until the Pope, unnerved by the enormous din, set his own kings against
each group of Waldus's followers.

Many years and many battles finally extinguished the Waldensians, not
without God's help.[645]

For at that time, seeds were sown in the minds of men which were to
come up as a crop ruinous to Popes.[646]   **2110**

Terrified by these disturbances, the Pope proceeded with greater cruelty,
and snatched anyone suspected of being called a heretic.

He made the suspect recant under oath (if he was willing), or (if he was
not willing), the man was turned to ashes by the fire, while still alive.

Anyone who recanted falsely under oath was said to have come to his
senses; but if someone were to repent of his oath, he perished.

Sec. But surely kings could spare those whom they wished?

Pr.   No. They didn't think it was within their jurisdiction.

---

[643] Peter *Waldus (1140-1217). The Waldensian movement spread his doctrines
beyond France to northern Italy and was one of the heresies dealt with by the
Lateran Council of 1215 convened by Pope Innocent III (Invernizzi note, p. 92;
Daniel-Rops, *Cathedral and Crusade*, p. 290ff.). The Waldensians were persecuted
periodically, in particular in 1655.

[644] Hobbes refers to the Anglican Church, indicating that he conforms to the
state religion.

[645] Probably Hobbes confuses the Waldensians with the Albigensians, against
whom the poorer northern French, led by Simon de Montfort, organized a bloody
crusade in rich southern France from 1208-29. (Invernizzi note, p. 92).

[646] Echo of Matthew 13:24-27 again, the parable of the wheat and the tares.

Et mox Concilio[a] Legem tulit in Laterano,
    Ne quis Rex esset mitis in Haereticos;   2120
Qua,[b] nisi post annum,[c] monitus purgaverit omnis
    Haereseos regnum,[d] dejiciendus erat.
Hoc est si Reges Papis parere recusent,[e]
    Civibus obsequii[f] vincula nulla sient.
Quo potuere loco securi vivere Reges,
    Cum percussori Lex[g] daret ista sicam?[h]
Sed solitos repetit securus Papa triumphos
    Ad nomen quamquam[i] palluit Haeretici.
Caetera fortis erat vacuusque superstitione.[j]
    An Romae Clerum spectra timere putas?[k]   2130
Illorum nemo est,[l] etiam sine Aqua[m] Benedicta,[n]
    Qui dubitat noctu[o] solus,[p] et in tenebris;[q]
Ad defunctorum monumenta quiescere sacra;[r]
    Inque adytis Templi;[s] si jubet utilitas.

---

[a] uA C concilio • [b] uA B Qua • [c] uA B annum • [d] C regnum • [e] A B recusent • [f] uA B obsequi (error) • [g] A C lex • [h] A Sicam? • [i] A C quanquam • [j] mv A B superstitione • [k] mv C putas. • [l] uA B est • [m] uA B C aqua • [n] uA B benedicta C benedicta, • [o] A B noctu, • [p] uA B solus • [q] A B C tenebris. • [r] mv A B sacra • [s] uA templi B Templi, C templi;

And soon the Pope proposed a law in the Lateran Council, so that no king
would be soft on heretics;[647]   **2120**
Under this law, any king who, once warned, did not purge his kingdom of
heretics within a year, would have to be overthrown.
That is to say, if kings refused to obey the popes, no chains of obedience
would bind their citizens.[648]
Where could Kings live in safety, when this law handed a dagger to an
assassin?[649]
The Pope on the other hand was secure and enjoyed his usual triumphs,
even though he paled at the mention of a Heretic.
In other respects he was bold and free from superstition – or do you think
the clergy of Rome are afraid of ghosts?[650]   **2130**
None of them had second thoughts about sleeping alone at night, in the
dark, and even without Holy Water;
Among the sacred monuments to the deceased, and inside the temple
sanctuaries, if he judged it expedient.

---

[647] The Lateran Council of 1215, the twelfth ecumenical council, marked the
high point of Pope Innocent III's pontificate. See Daniel-Rops, *Cathedral and
Crusade*, p. 292: 'The Fathers voted with exemplary dispatch, and in accordance
with the Pope's wishes, upon the liberation of the Holy Land, upon the reform of
morals, upon the Albigensian affair, and upon many more thorny questions. . . . The
twelfth oecumenical council, in fact was a striking manifestation of the Church's
unity, and set its seal upon the glory of the papacy.'

[648] 'Chains of obedience' binding citizens to their kings is a metaphor for political obligation, and the Lateran Council absolves citizens from this obligation. See
Lev., xxi, §5, 108/138, where Hobbes refers to the 'artificial man, which we call a
commonwealth', as tied by 'artificial chains, called civil laws, which [citizens]
themselves by mutual covenants have fastened at one end, to the lips of that man or
assembly to whom they have given the sovereign power; and at the other end to
their own ears'. For possible visual references to the Gallic Hercules, see Quentin
Skinner in 'Thomas Hobbes and the Proper Signification of Liberty', *Transactions
of the Royal Historical Society*, vol. 40 (1990), pp. 121-51, and Patricia Springborg,
'Hobbes's Biblical Beasts', pp. 363-9.

[649] *percussor* (Cooper), '(Cicero), a murderer: he that is hyred to kill a man
(Cicero: *deprehensus cum sica percussor Caesaris*)'. Note the analogue between
the killing of Caesar and Charles I.

[650] The 1722 paraphrase words this in terms of the invulnerability of the Pope to
fear of the Roman clergy. But a more likely reading is that the Pope and clergy instill
in their congregations superstitions that they themselves do not share.

Sed metuunt potius[a] ne nos ea non metuamus;[b]
Hoc est,[c] Haereticos, atque patere timent.
Sec. Cur non in Clerum Laicis saevire Latinum
Principibus licuit, parque referre[d] pari?
Pr. Non patiebatur tempus. Papalis arundo
Haesit crudeli[e] non quatienda manu.   **2140**
Post haec Wiccliffus (regeret cum Tertius Anglos
Edwardus)[f] doctus disputat Oxoniae,[g]
Pleraque defuncti defendens dogmata Waldi,[h]
Ingeniis rectis vincere visus erat.
Moxque rei gestae commovit fama Bohemos,[i]
Unde ortum bellum est Haereticale novum.[j]
Perdidit haereticos tandem victoria crebra,[k]
Pontificesque auxit miles utrinque cadens.[l]
Sec. Sed miror potuisse homines tot[m] ad arma vocari[n]
Haereticos.[o] Nemo[p] lege coactus erat.   **2150**
Nec,[q] puto,[r] cura fuit sincerae Relligionis,[s]
De qua securus rusticus[t] esse solet.
Paucis scire datur Verborum[u] sensa Sacrorum;[v]
Uno emptum (sine re) scire,[w] nec asse,[x] velint.

---

[a] uA potius, • [b] A B metuamus • [c] A B C est • [d] mv C referri • [e] A crudeli • [f] uA B Edwardus (closing bracket missing) • [g] mv A B Oxoniae. • [h] A B Waldi • [i] A B Bohoemos • [j] mv A Novum • [k] A B crebra • [l] mv B cadens • [m] mv uA B homines tot potuisse (word order) • [n] A B vocari, • [o] uA B Haereticos, • [p] A B nemo • [q] A B Nec • [r] uA B puto • [s] A B Relligionis C relligionis, • [t] A Rusticus • [u] uA B C verborum • [v] uA B sacrorum C sacrorum; • [w] uA B scire • [x] uA B asse

They feared rather that we should not fear those ghosts: that is to say, they
fear heretics – and being exposed.[651]

Sec. Why couldn't lay emperors attack the Roman clergy and pay back
measure for measure?

Pr. Times didn't allow it. The arrow stuck, not to be shaken out of that
cruel hand.[652]   **2140**

Subsequently the learned Wycliffe debated at Oxford (when Edward III
ruled England),[653]

And defending most of the doctrines of the deceased Waldus, he seemed
to win people over with his honest mind.

And soon the fame of his achievements roused the Bohemians,[654] from
which a new war against heresy began.

Finally, numerous victories defeated the heretics, and the falling soldiers
on both sides increased papal power.

Sec. But I am amazed that so many men could have been called to arms
on the side of heresy. No one was compelled by law.   **2150**

And I don't think their concern was for true religion, about which the
peasant is usually untroubled.

It is given to few men to understand the meaning of the sacred texts, they
wouldn't want knowledge bought for a penny, if there was no material
gain.

---

[651] i.e., because ghosts and spirits are essential to priestcraft, the Roman
clergy fear exposure of their fraud – by 'heretics', among whom Hobbes classes
himself. See *Lev.*, ii, §8, 8/11. C.f., Lucretius *De rer. nat.* 1.100-111 (ed. Smith,
pp. 10-13 and notes). At lines 1.108-11, Lucretius points out that if men did not
fear, 'somehow they would have strength to defy the superstitions and threatening
of the priests (*vatum*); but as it is, there is no way of resistance and no power,
because everlasting punishment is to be feared after death'.

[652] 'papalis harundo' echoes Virgil, *Aen.* 4.73 'letalis harundo': the deer
cannot shake off the fatal arrow; here the pope's arrow sticks in the emperor's
side.

[653] John *Wycliffe (c. 1330-1384) was a professor at the University of
Oxford. His teachings were condemned at the Council of Constance in 1415. (Invernizzi note, p. 93). See also Daniel-Rops, *Cathedral and Crusade*, p. 265, who
presents Wycliffe as one of the theologians who argued against the doctrine of
papal sovereignty and for the independence of territorial kingdoms.

[654] Hobbes is referring to the insurrection of Bohemia, which followed the
execution of John Hus and Jerome of Prague in 1415. The long and bloody war
against the Hussites lasted until 1436. (Invernizzi note, p. 93).

Vulgo[a] nulla mali nota est mensura bonique;[b]
    Juris et Injusti[c] nomina sola tenent.
Justum quisque vocat quicquid tuto facit ipse;[d]
    Quod patitur Nolens, id putat esse Nefas:[e]
Impia sumpserunt in Reges ergo Bohemi[f]
    Arma suos stulti, nec placitura Deo.   2160
Pr. Nec placuere Deo;[g] qui lucem reddere mundo
    Lege parat Justa,[h] non populi facibus.[i]

---

[a] B Vulgò • [b] A B bonique • [c] A B C injusti • [d] A B ipse C ipse, • [e] A B nefas. C nefas: • [f] uA Boehemi • [g] uA Deo B Deo, • [h] uA B justa, C justa • [i] mv uA B fascibus

The crowd has no known measure of good and evil, and regard justice
and injustice as mere words.[655]
Everyone calls 'just' whatever he can get away with; and whatever he
suffers unwillingly, he considers a crime.[656]
So the foolish Bohemians, took up treacherous arms against their own
kings, arms which would not please God either.[657]   **2160**
Pr. Nor did they please the God who intended to restore light to the
world by just law, not by the actions of the mob.[658]

---

[655] Hobbes takes a classic position, reinstated by Lorenzo Valla and Juan Luis
Vives on the relation between signifier and signified. Vives maintained, after
Valla: 'Let us therefore define the signifying word as follows: a public token by
which people among themselves exhibit to others their notions, that is, what they
conceive in their minds: and to usage is the ruler of what is signified'. (Sic ergo
diffiniamus vocem significantem, ut sit: Communis nota, qua inter se aliqui aliis
notiones suas explicant, id est, quae mente concipiunt: itaque usus est dominus
signficantum). Vives, *Opera Omnia*, ed Mayans, vol, 3, p. 143. cited by Richard
Waswo, 'The Reaction of Jean Luis Vives to Valla's Philosophy of Language',
p. 601.

[656] This is an Epicurean principle stated as early as the *Short Tract* (c. 1630) (but
still of doubtful provenance, see Noel Malcolm 'Robert Payne, the Hobbes Manuscripts and the "Short Tract" in *Aspects of Hobbes*): 'Good is to everything, that
which hath active power to attract it locally, *Malum*, therefore, to everything that
which hath active power to repel it'. See, Tönnies, 'A Short Tract on First Principles', pp. 208-9. Hobbes refined the thesis by *De Cive* (1642) and the *Philosophical
Rudiments* (1651) in the light of his own theory of physical inertia, claiming in the
latter (*EW* 2.8): 'For every man is desirous of what is good for him and shuns what
is evil, but chiefly the chiefest of natural evils, which is death; and this he does by a
certain natural impulsion of nature, no less than that whereby a stone moves down-
ward'. The thesis that the names good and evil are simply appellations for the attrac-
tion of pleasure and the avoidance of pain, had been formulated by Valla and Vives,
probable sources for Hobbes. It follows from the separation of 'verbum' from 'res',
and their insistence that language is a common coin. So, for instance, Vives, insisted
of our attribution of qualities to things:

> Therefore we say that such-and-such things exist or do not exist, or are these
> and those, of such or a different kind, we reckon on the basis of our belief, not
> of the things themselves. It is not that they that constitute their measure for us, but
> our mind. For when we call things good, bad, useful, useless, we are not
> speaking according to things, but according to ourselves.

Vives' *De prima philosophia*, in his *Opera*, vol. 1, pp. 532-3, trans. Richard Waswo,
Language and Meaning in the Renaissance (Princeton, Princeton University Press,
1987), pp. 128-9.
[657] Reference to the Hussite war of 1420-34.
[658] Echoes of John 8:12: 'I am the light of the world: he that followeth me shall
avoid . . . darkness, but shall have the light of life', John 9:5, Acts 17:11.

Wiccliffum texit Dux Lancastrensis, et idem
   Insignis fastûs[a] spiritualis osor.[b]
Secta tamen mansit,[c] Lollardorumque[d] vocata est,[e]
   Territa sed duris Legibus[f] obticuit.
Nam Rex Henricus,[g] Rex illo nomine Quartus[h]
   Adjutus populi sceptra favore rapit;[i]
Invidiamque volens Cleri[j] placare, quod hostis
   Verticibus rasis Dux pater[k] ejus erat,[l]   2170
Haereticis nostris Vivi-comburia[m] festum
   Lege dedit primus;[n] expediebat enim.

---

[a] uA B C fastus • [b] mv A B osor • [c] A B mansit • [d] uA B Lollandorumque (error) • [e] ~ A B est • [f] A B C legibus • [g] A B Henricus • [h] A B quartus C quartus, • [i] A B rapit. • [j] uA B cleri • [k] A Pater • [l] A erat. • [m] uA B vivi comburia • [n] A B primus,

The Duke of Lancaster, famous for his hatred of spiritual arrogance,
sheltered Wycliffe,[659]
The sect survived, however, and was called the sect of the Lollards,[660]
although it was silent, terrorized by harsh laws.
For King Henry, the fourth king by that name, seized power, aided by the
support of the people.[661]
He wanted to appease the ill-will of the clergy, because his father the
Duke was hostile to the tonsure. 2170
He was the first to legislate the festival of live-burning for our heretics;[662]
for it was in his interest.[663]

---

[659] *John of Gaunt, Duke of Lancaster, 1340-99, son of Edward III, was for a certain period close to Wycliffe and the Lollards. See V. H. H. Green, *The Later Plantagenets* (London, Edward Arnold, 1955), pp. 193-6.

[660] A name of Dutch origin that from 1387 began to designate the followers of Wycliffe in England (see Invernizzi note, p. 94).

[661] Henry IV of Lancaster (1367-1413), son of John of Gaunt, who came to the throne in 1399.

[662] Note that the 1688 Glossary (pp. 608-9) singles out *Vivi-Comburia*, as of critical importance in the text. See Molesworth's note p. 100. v. 2175: *De Haeretico Comburendo, antea haec in anglia; sed jam Compendio, per Ordinarium quemlibet, sine ambage. Vid. Stat. H. 4.2.15*: 'On the Burning of the Heretic, these things were formerly done in England, but now [i.e. after the statut *De heretico comburendo* = 2 Henry IV c. 15] summarily, by any ordinance [i.e. by any bishop]'. In fact the statute only made more explicit legal procedures already in force. For an English text of the statute see H. Bettenson, *Documents of the Christian Church* (Oxford, Oxford University Press, 1963), p. 251-55, and for a summary of the facts the *ODCC*.

[663] Hobbes in the *Historical Narration* (*EW* IV, 403-4, gives a fuller chronology for the heresy laws in this period:

The first law that was here made for the punishment of heretics, called Lollards and mentioned in the Statutes, was in the fifth year of the reign of Richard the Second, occasioned by the doctrine of John Wicliff and his followers; which Wickliff, because no law was yet ordained for his punishment in parliament, by the favour of John of Gaunt, the King's son, during the reign of Edward the Third, had escaped. But in the fifth year of the next king, which was Richard the Second, there passed an act of parliament to this effect: that sheriffs and some others should have commissions to apprehend such as were certified by the prelates to be preachers of heresy, their fautors, maintainers, and abettors, and to hold them in strong prison, till they should justify themselves, according to the law of holy church. So that hitherto there was no law in England, by which a heretic could be put to death, or otherways punished, than by imprisoning him till he was reconciled to the church. After this, in the next king's reign, which was Henry the Fourth, son of John of Gaunt, by whom Wicliff had been favoured, *and who in his aspiring to the crown had needed the good will of the bishops*, was made a law in the second year of his reign, wherein it was enacted, that every ordinary may convene before him, and imprison any person suspected of heresy; and that an obstinate heretic shall be burnt before the people. In the next king's reign, which was Henry the Fifth, in his second year, was made an act of parliament, wherein it is declared, that the intent of heretics,

Sed post centum annos decimo Papante Leone
    Sub Duce[a] Saxonico Principe legitimo,[b]
Exsurgit damnata Fides,[c] clamante Luthero,[d]
    Qui magno populos permeat ore loquens ;[e]
Disciditque[f] locis plus centum retia Papae,[g]
    Texta à[h] Nobilibus,[i] sed male texta Scholis.[j]
Unde quot elapsi Reges, Urbesque Potentes,[k]
    Papali portant[l] libera colla jugo ;[m]   2180
Quàm[n] sit ubique ferè[o] Papae nunc tonsa Potestas,[p]
    Dicere non opus est pluribus ;[q] ipse vides.
Sec. Quod restat video.[r] Sed[s] te volo pauca rogare,
    Et respondebis tu brevitate tua.[t]
Gloria erat quondam Romani Praesulis ingens,
    Calcavit pedibus Regia colla suis.

---

[a] A C duce • [b] A B legitimo. • [c] uA C fides, • [d] A B Luthero • [e] A B loquens, • [f] mv uA B Discidit • [g] A B Papae • [h] A B a • [i] A B C nobilibus, • [j] A C scholis. B sholis. (error) • [k] A potentes B Potentes C potentes, • [l] A portant, • [m] A B jugo. • [n] A B Quam • [o] A C fere • [p] A B C potestas, • [q] uA B pluribus A pluribus, • [r] A B video • [s] A B sed • [t] A B tua

But a hundred years later, when Leo the Tenth was Pope[664] under the Duke
of Saxony, the legitimate prince,[665]
The persecuted faith recovered strength with the proclamations of Luther
who,[666] speaking with a great voice, reached the people,
And cut the nets of the Pope in more than a hundred places;[667] nets that
had been woven, but badly woven, by the famous Schools.
How many kings and powerful cities slipped out of these nets and held
their heads high, free from the papal yoke,   **2180**
[And] how much the power of the Pope has now been trimmed almost
everywhere, there is no need to tell you at length, you can see for
yourself.[668]
Sec. I see what's still left, but I want to ask you few words, and you will
say in response, with your characteristic brevity,[669]
The glory of the Roman Pontiff was once immense, he trampled Royal
necks with his feet.[670]

---

called Lollards, was to subvert the Christian faith, the law of God, the church,
and the realm: and that an heretic convict should forfeit all his fee-simple
lands, goods, and chattels, besides the punishment of burning.

[664] *Frederick III (1463-1525) elector of Saxony and Luther's supporter.
[665] Pope Leo X, Giovanni de Medici (1475-1521), second son of Lorenzo the
Magnificent (1469-1492).
[666] Martin Luther (1483-1546), Theologian.
[667] Reference to the 95 theses that Luther nailed to the door of the church at Wittenberg on October 31, 1517. The Pope wore on his right hand the Fisherman's
Ring, which featured a stone engraved with the image of St. Peter casting his nets.
See Daniel-Rops, *Cathedral and Crusade*, p. 286.
[668] *Primus* accounts for the decline of the papacy, first, as due to the course of
time, second, to the Turk, and third to Luther.
[669] See Horace, *Ars poetica* 335-7, in praise of brevity.
[670] 'calcavit pedibus Regia colla suis'. There are several precedents for Emperors
treading the necks of humiliated subjects. For example, in the book of Esther (20:3),
when the irate Haman is commanded to lead his arch-enemy Mordecai through the
streets on a royal steed, some rabbinic sources state that Mordecai trod on Haman's
neck as he was mounting the horse. The rabbis' description of Haman's humiliation
bears a resemblance to a story related by Christian writers about the Roman Emperor
Valerian, who, having been captured in battle by the Persian Emperor Shapur I in 260,
was reported to have had his neck used as a stepladder whenever Shapur wished to
mount his horse. (www.ucalgary.ca/~elsegal/ Shokel/060302_StepladdderStabl-
hnd.html - 20k). The more likely example is however, the legend that Pope Alexander III trod upon the neck of Frederick Barbarossa to humiliate him; a story repeated
by John Milton in his *Tetrachordon: Expositions upon the foure chiefl Places in
Scripture which treat of Marriage or Nullities in Marriage* (London, 1645), in the
section of the Tetrachordon on 1-Corinthians. There Milton argues regarding Papal
power over marriage and divorce: 'Yet was not that rigour executed anciently in spiritual Courts untill Alexander the third, who trod upon the neck of Frederic Barbarossa

Illius innumeri Reges mandata manebant,
  Et Regum cicurum bella gerebat ope.
Ut Jovis,[a] illius tremuere ad fulmina gentes,[b]
  Sacro[c] figentes oscula blanda pedi.   **2190**
Divitias omnis cogebat ventus ad illum,[d]
  Frigidus Eurus, Afer, Vesperus, et Boreas.
Ille sedens nutu librabat cuncta verendo.[e]
  Quod curaret erat praeter hiare nihil.

---

[a] uA B C Jovis • [b] A Gentes, • [c] mv A B Sacrae • [d] A B illum • [e] A B C verendo,

Countless kings used to await his commands and he used to wage wars
with the help of these tame kings.[671]
People trembled at his thunderbolts[672] as if they were Jupiter's, planting
fawning kisses on his holy feet.[673]   **2190**
Every wind blew riches to him,[674] the chill East wind, the African wind,
the West wind and the North.[675]
Immovable, he kept everything in balance with a nod that commanded
reverence;[676] he had nothing to bother about except to keep his mouth
open.

---

the Emperor, and summoned our Henry 2 into Normandy about the death of Becket.'
(www.dartmouth.edu/~milton/reading_room/ tetrachordon/corin/text.shtml - 83k.).
    [671] For the account of the Pope that follows, see Valla's *The [Supposed] Dona-*
tion of Constantine, ed. Coleman, p. 179:
    And the Pope himself makes war on peaceable people, and sows discord
    among states and princes. The Pope both thirsts for the goods of others and
    drinks up his own: he is what Achilles calls Agamemnon, Δημοβόρος
    βασιλεῦς, a 'people-devouring king'. The Pope not only enriches himself at
    the expense of the republic, as neither Verres nor Catiline nor any other embez-
    zler dared to do, but he enriches himself at the expense of even the church and
    the Holy Spirit as old Simon Magus himself would abhor doing. And when he
    is reminded of this and is reproved by good people occasionally, he does not
    deny it, but openly admits it, and boasts that he is free to wrest from its occu-
    pants by any means whatever the patrimony given the church by Constantine;
    as though when it was recovered Christianity would be in an ideal state, – and
    not rather the more oppressed by all kinds of crimes, extravagances and lusts;
    if indeed it can be oppressed more, and if there is any crime yet uncommitted !
    [672] '*Fulmen excommunicationis*, (that is the thunderbolt of excommunication)',
Lev., xlii, §31 279/349, see lines 1460-64. Fulmina had a classical usage also, (see
Lewis & Short): destructive power, fiery flashings of the eye (applied to the Scipios
as heros and conquerors of the Carthaginians; see Lucretius, in imitation of Virgil
Aen. 6.843: 'duo fulmina belli Scipiada').
    [673] Audiences with the Pope, for all but sovereign princes, required kissing the
cross on his right shoe – see the reference to kissing the Pope's toe, at line 2224.
    [674] Paolo Sarpi, *The Historie of the Council of Trent Conteining Eight Bookes*,
trans. Nathaniel Brent (1620), 23-4, 28-9, saw Pope and Emperor alike in their posturing for private gain. See Collins, *The Allegiance of Thomas Hobbes*, p. 56.
    [675] Scientific maps of the Renaissance featured personifications in the form of
putti blowing the winds: Euris, the East-wind; Zephyrus, the West-wind; Auster the
South-wind; *Boreas, the North-wind; and Afer, the African wind; as featured in
the maps of Ortelius (1564 world map), and Gerard de Jode (world map 1555). See
Gillies, *Shakespeare and the Geography of Difference* (Cambridge, Cambridge
University Press, 1994), pp. 160-1.
    [676] Reference to Jupiter's nod, which ratifies his decision and makes Olympus
tremble: *Aeneid* 9.106 from *Iliad* 1.528-30. The idea of the Pope balancing the
world with a nod may also refer back Archimedes balancing the globe, Plutarch,
Life of Marcellus, (Plutarch, *Makers of Rome*), p. 99.

Adde quod in tuto fuit illi tanta Potestas ;[a]
Si potes in terris quid reperire ratum.
Stabat namque super populum fundata volentem :[b]
(Quod,[c] non fert populus si bene junctus,[d] onus ?)[e]
At[f] populum sensu varium res unica jungit,
    Jussa sui Regis, jussa putare Dei.   2200
Jussa Dei populis cum solus Papa ferebat,
    Et credebatur vix minor esse Deo ;[g]
Quis tantum imperium,[h] tam fido milite fultum,[i]
    Rupe situm celsa, posse perire putet ?
Verum nunc minus est. Quodcunque attriverit aetas,
    Tandem et conficiet,[j] dente licet tacito.
Magnaque jampridem periit pars ense resecta
    Machummet,[k] quam nunc Turcica Luna[l] regit.
Pars quoque defecit doctis abducta Lutheri
    Scriptis,[m] qui servam noluit esse Fidem.[n]   2210
Longos saepe dies sine Solibus[o] ire videmus,[p]
    Cunctaque perpetua sydera nube tegi ;
Quam Sol[q] mox altus penetrans vibrantibus armis
    Discutit,[r] et varios cogit adire locos ;
Sic nova Saxonici exoriens doctrina Lutheri[s]
    Discussit Papae spirituale jugum.

---

[a] A B potestas, • [b] A B volentem, • [c] A B (Quod • [d] uA B junctus • [e] mv A onus) C onus (closing bracket missing) • [f] mv A B Ad • [g] A B Deo. • [h] A B imperium • [i] A B C fultum. • [j] A B conficiet. • [k] A B Machumet, • [l] A B C luna • [m] A B Scriptis • [n] A C fidem. • [o] A C solibus • [p] A B videmus • [q] A B C sol • [r] A B Discutit • [s] B Lutheri,

Moreover, his immense power was secure – if you can find anything certain on earth.

Indeed, it stood on firm foundations over a willing people (what load cannot a people bear if it is properly united?),

The one and only thing joining those of various opinions together as a people, is that they think the orders of their king are the orders of God. 2200

When the pope alone conveyed to the people the commands of God, and was believed to be barely inferior to God,

Who would think that so great an empire, supported by such loyal soldiers, and situated on so lofty a rock,[677] could perish?

Even so, it has now diminished.[678] Whatever time diminishes it will in the end destroy, though with silent tooth.[679]

And a great part, which the Turkish Crescent now rules, was lost long ago, cut off by Muhammad's sword.

Part also seceded,[680] led away by the learned writings of Luther, who did not want Faith to be a slave. 2210

We often see long days pass without sunshine, the whole sky covered by unbroken cloud;[681]

Which the high sun, as soon as it breaks through, drives away with its gleaming weapons, and forces to disperse in different directions;[682]

So, as it rose, the new doctrine of the Saxon Luther shook off the spiritual yoke of the Pope.

---

[677] A pun on St. Peter, the Rock (John 1:42).

[678] Distribution of speakers in doubt – does Primus return at line 2205?

[679] Horace, *Satires* 2.6.87, 93-7; *Ars poetica* 63-9. Tac. *Agr.* 1, Virgil, *Ecl.* 9.51: 'omnia fert aetas'; Ovid, *Fasti 6.639*: 'omnis aetas currere obviam'.

[680] Note the alternate meaning, 'eclipsed', a word play on *Turcica Luna*, Turkish Crescent.

[681] Luther did not want the faith to be a slave to the Pope and Church Fathers, who in Hobbes's day, at the Council of Trent, insisted on exclusive rights to biblical interpretation in accordance with the principle *unanimen consensum Patrum*. See Springborg Introduction chapter 5.1.

[682] Lines 2211-14 proclaim the victories of Luther against the Pope in the high language of Virgil's depiction of the slaying of Hector by Achilles, *Iliad*, book 22: Hector 'like a soaring eagle . . . swoops down from the clouds', but Achilles, 'with his wondrous shield before his breast, and his gleaming helmet', falls on Hector: 'as the evening star that shines brighter than all others through the stillness of night, even such was the gleam of the spear which Achilles poised in his right hand, fraught with the death of noble Hector'.

Agricolis igitur missis[a] ambos arat Indos,[b]
Hisque novi Imperii semina condit agris;
Tanquam si migrare velit,[c] sedemque locare,[d]
　　Secula post aliquot,[e] fertiliore loco.　　　　　　　　2220
Et Fidei[f] fontem surgentem forte videbunt
　　Monte Potossino[g] secula sera sacrum:[h]
Nos autem Christi populus portabimus istuc
　　Pontificis pedibus basia danda nigri.
Quas habuit tanti causas Ecclesia damni,[i]
　　Tingendique novo[j] retia sicca mari?
Pr. Dicam.[k] Saevitiem,[l] Fastum,[m] gladium Mahometis,[n]
　　Contemptum Regum, Dogmata[o] surda, Typos.
Sec. Scire etiam cupio Christus cui, quae facienti[p]
　　Donat foelices,[q] et sine fine dies.　　　　　　　　2230
Pr. Foelicem[r] fore Christus ait[s] qui non petit alta,
　　Contentus paucis ambitione procul.[t]
Quique sit ingenio mitis[u] nec pronus ad iram;[v]
　　Qui sorti alterius compatiturque malae;[w]
Vivere qui justè[x] toto conamine tendit:[y]
　　Et peccata libens corrigit ipse sua.[z]

---

[a] uA missis missing • [b] A B Indos • [c] uA B velit • [d] A B C locare • [e] A B aliquot • [f] A C fidei • [g] A B Pottosino • [h] A B C sacrum. • [i] A B damni • [j] mv A B novae • [k] A B Dicam • [l] uA saevitiem B Saevitiem • [m] uA Fastum C fastum, • [n] uA B Mahometis • [o] A C dogmata • [p] mv A B faciendi • [q] A felices B foelices C felices, • [r] A B C Felicem • [s] A ait, • [t] uA B C procul • [u] A B mitis, • [v] mv A in iram B in iram. • [w] A malae B malae. • [x] A C juste • [y] A B tendit, • [z] A B sua

And consequently the Pope, having sent his farmers forth, tilled both the
Indies, and buried the seeds of a new Empire in these fields,[683]
As if he wished to move and relocate his seat, some centuries later, to a
more fruitful place.   2220
And perhaps, in some later age, people will see the holy font of faith
rising on Mount Potosi.[684]
Then we, the people of Christ, will carry our kisses there, to be placed at
the feet of a black pope.
[685]What reasons did the Church have for such a great loss and for having
to dip its dry nets in a new sea?
Pr. I'll tell you: cruelty, arrogance, the sword of Muhammad, the
contempt of kings, deaf doctrines, printing.[686]
Sec. I also want to know to whom and for what deeds Christ gives happy
days without end.   2230
Pr. Christ says the happy man is the one who does not seek lofty things;
he is content with little and stays far from ambition.[687]
He is mild by nature, not prone to anger; and he shows compassion for
the misfortune of another.
The one who strives with all his might to live justly, and willingly corrects
his own faults[688]

---

[683] C.f. lines 1272-3, where Hobbes echoes *Pharsalia*, 8.210-395 (Joyce edn,
p. 239), on Magnus [Pompey] having to find a new world in the East in which to till
his fields.

[684] Mount Potosi was the most celebrated of the Spanish colonial silver mines in
the 17c. John Gillies, *Shakespeare and the Geography of Difference*, p. 136, notes
that in Draper's pageants in London and Antwerp, exotic images of wealth were frequent, especially associated with the critiques of the Church. For instance, Rubens
designed a ceremonial arch for the Pageant of the Mint on commission from the
Antwerp mint for the entry of the Cardinal-Infante Ferdinand into Antwerp in 1635,
depicting a quasi-realistic image of Mount Potosi.

[685] Distribution of speakers in doubt – does Secundus return at line 2225?

[686] Among the factors responsible for the break-up of united Christendom,
Hobbes lists the struggle between the Empire and the Papacy; the incursions of
Islam; opaque Scholastic doctrine; and the Protestant Reformation promoted by the
printing press.

[687] See the opening lines of Horace's famous poem, 'Happy is the man',
Epodes, 2; the closing lines of *Satires* 2.6.115-17, and Horace *Satires* 1.6.52-3:
*ambitione procul. Felicem dicere non hoc/ me possim, casu quod te sortitus
amicum*. Echoes also of Christ's Sermon on the Mount and the Beatitudes,
Matt 5:3-12, Luke 6:20-23.

[688] Horace, *Odes* 1.22 'Integer vitae scelerisque puris'.

Cor quibus est mundum, simplexque dolo sine turpi;[a]
    Et qui certantes conciliare studet;
Et[b] qui condonat facilis peccata aliena;[c]
    Atque animo si quis fert sua damna bono.   **2240**
Denique salvus erit[d] quisquis peccata sua odit
    Corditùs;[e] et Christi fixerit illa Cruci.

FINIS[f]

---

[a] A B turpi, • [b] A The last four lines are in the corrector's hand, as if the page had been lost. The catchword *Et* on the previous page is in the first hand (uA). • [c] B aliena • [d] B erit, • [e] B Corditus C Corditus; • [f] B does not conclude with *Finis*, and it is just possible that the poem had not originally ended here, abrupt as the ending is. But note the slight flourish after the final word, *Cruci.*, perhaps an indication of conclusion, however. C ends with Finis.

Has a pure and simple heart, free from evil intent; and he is keen to unite
    those in conflict;
And freely pardons the sins of others and bears his losses in good
    spirit.[689]   **2240**
In short whoever deep in his heart hates his own sins and who nails those
    sins to the cross of Christ will be saved.[690]

FINIS

---

[689] See the old Stoic maxim: to bear both good and evil with an equal mind.

[690] In contrast to those who fasten their kisses to the feet of the Pope for atonement (*Hist. Eccl.*, line 2194). Hobbes uses the same verb in each case, *figo*, which
indicates fixing to, nailing to.

PRAEFATIO

Lectori Salutem.

EN tibi, Lector benevole, *Historiam Ecclesiasticam*;[a] non à Monacho, non à Clerico; sed à Libero,[b] à Philosopho homine, à Thoma Hobbio Malmesburiensi conflatam: qui neque Scholae,[c] neque Sectae, neque Partibus,[d] neque Magistris[e] juravit uspiam; et cui tuto credas decurrenti hunc campum, ubi illi neque [10] seritur neque metitur hilum.

Non haec juvenis lusit; sed bene senex per totam vitam cogitata, jam tandem versibus ligata maluit. Phoebi oracula, primae leges versibus: nec non primus sapiendi Magister[f] Pythagoras nil, nisi carmine sancitum, voluit.

---

[a] C historiam Ecclesiasticam • [b] C libero, • [c] C scholae, • [d] C partibus, • [e] C magistris • [f] C magister

'– there emerged deceits and tricks
and betrayals and violence and wicked lust of ownership'
Ovid. *Met.*[691]

Greeting to the Reader

See here, kind reader, a CHURCH HISTORY, produced not by a monk, or a cleric, but by a free man, a philosophical man, by Thomas Hobbes of Malmesbury. He was a man who swore allegiance neither to School, nor sect, nor party, nor teachers anywhere, and whom you can safely trust in traversing this field where he neither sows [10] nor reaps anything. It was not a juvenile who amused himself with these matters but a really old man, who having reflected on these things throughout his whole life, now finally preferred them fixed in verse.[692] The oracles of Phoebus, the first laws, were in verse. Pythagoras, the first teacher of wisdom, also wanted nothing to be held holy unless it was in verse.[693]

---

[691] The epigram prefacing the 1688 printed edition, 'dolusque insidiaeque et vis et amor sceleratus habendi', a famous line from Ovid's *Metamorphoses* 1.130-1, absent in the manuscripts, may have been selected by Rymer, on the basis of Hobbes's echo of this text at lines 109-10 and lines 805-6 of the poem (*q.v.* and notes).

[692] Lucretius, *De rer. nat.*, lines 1.930-41 (trans. W. H. D. Rouse, pp. 78-9), explains his reasons for writing in verse: 'the subject is so dark and the lines I write so clear, I touch all with the Muses' grace', so that, 'as with children, when physicians try to administer rank wormwood, they first touch the rims about the cups with the sweet yellow fluid of honey, that unthinking childhood be deluded as far as the lips, and meanwhile may drink up the bitter juice' (See *Hist. Eccl.*, lines 1091-2n.).

[693] See Petrarch on the Alexandrian method of concealment under a poetic veil, addressed by Petrarch in *Africa*, 9.100-01: 'sub ignoto tamen ut celentur amictu,/ nuda alibi, et tenui frustrentur lumina velo': ('[Poets may] conceal in an unfamiliar garment things which otherwise are bare, and may baffle our vision with a fine veil'). A method about which Petrarch in his old age expressed doubt in a letter to Federico Aretino on the allegorical interpretation of Virgil, which he is no longer prepared to support. On the subject of 'poetice narrationis archana' of the *Secretum*, he put into the mouth of Augustine the remark that he wonders if Virgil as he was writing was not totally remote from any such consideration: 'sive enim id Virgilius ipse sensit, dum scriberet, sive ab onmi tali consideratione remotissimus'. See Petrarca, *Prose*, ed. Martellotti *et al.*, p. 124. And in the *Senili* 4:5, Petrarch asks: 'Who is there in dealing with such doubtful matters, daring to affirm with assurance that the intention of those authors was absolutely this rather than that, in works which they composed a thousand years ago?' (trans. Thomas M. Greene, 'Petrarch and the Humanist Hermeneutic', p. 222, n. 16).

Limatiori versu Fastorum libros Ovidius; et alii Historias[a]
pompâ[b] [20] quâdam,[c] et Heroico flatu tumentes procuderunt. At quin
liceat, Horatio duce, aliquando dare *Sermoni*[d] *propiora*? et, iisdem
avibus, *Ridentem dicere verum*!

Visum est res Christi, et quae Piscatores[e] docuere tractanti,
humilem Stylum[f] magis idoneum esse et popularem. Et proinde
nudâ[g] indigenáque[h] simplicitate omnia fluunt, sic ut nulla vox[i] [30]
quae non Memoriae[j] praesens paratiórque[k] sit, in versum venit: Ut
pii doctique viri, Alter Enchiridion[l] Fidei,[m] Alter Mnemosynon

---

[a] C historias • [b] C pompa • [c] C quadam, • [d] C sermoni (this and the following
quotations are not italicized in C, although in slightly larger script) • [e] C piscatores
• [f] C stylum • [g] C nuda • [h] C indigenaque • [i] C vox, • [j] C memoriae • [k] C
paratiorque • [l] C enchiridion • [m] C fidei,

Ovid produced the books of the *Fasti*[694] in more polished verse and others, **[20]** puffed up with a certain pomposity and heroic wind, produced histories.[695] But might it not sometimes be permitted, with Horace as our guide, [696] to offer 'everyday language'[697] and, under the same auspices, 'laughing speak the truth'?[698]

It has been thought that a humble style is more suitable for handling the subject of Christ and what the Fishermen taught.[699] And accordingly everything flows with a plain and native simplicity, so that no word **[30]** which is not present and ready to the memory, appears in the verse. So pious and learned men have produced, one a Handbook of Faith,[700] another a Biblical Pledge,[701]

---

[694] A Roman calendar, almanac; especially the *Fasti consulares*, or registers of the higher magistrates according to their years of service; *Fasti*, title of a poem of Ovid on the Roman festivals, the festival-calendar, which, however, he completed for but six months of the year (Lewis & Short).

[695] Valla uses this terminology referring to the author of *The [Supposed] Donation of Constantine* (ed. Coleman, pp. 90-1, 110-11): 'how inflated he is with puffed-up pride (tumida superbia inflatum est)', later quoting Horace, *Ars Poet.*, 97, 'He discards bombast and cubit-long words' ('Proicit ampullas et sesquipedalia verba'), as a recommendation to the Pope.

[696] Rymer uses Horace's form of words in *Epistle* 2.3.466 on poesy as *ut pictura poesis*: Sit ius liceatque perire poetis.

[697] *sermoni propiora* (Horace, also Quint.), everyday language. Sermoni (pl.) the Satires of Horace. (Chambers Murray).

[698] Democritus was known of as the laughing philosopher because of his ethical ideal of cheerfulness. See also Horace, *Satires* 1.4.4, and 1.1.23-7 (for the latter, Fairclough trans, pp. 6-7):

> Furthermore, not to skim over the subject with a laugh like a writer of witticisms – and yet, what is to prevent one from telling the truth as he laughs, even as teachers sometimes give cookies to children to coax them to learn the ABC?.

[699] See Auerbach, *Literary Language and its Public* (Princeton, N.J., Princeton University Press, 1993), especially ch. 1, 'Sermo humilis'. The implicit comparison appears to be to Prudentius' *Psychomachia*, which ironically tells the triumph of primitive Christianity over the excesses of imperial Rome in the Virgilian and Ovidian hyperbolic epic style. To the extent that Prudentius may have been satirizing the Roman classics, Hobbes certainly appears to be satirizing Prudentius' particular church history.

[700] *Encheiridion*, something held in the hand; 15c. handbook. (R. E. Latham, *Revised Medieval Latin Word-list*, London, British Academy, Oxford University Press, 1965). Title of Arrian's 'Manual of Epictetus', Enchiridion; c.f., Augustine's Enchiridion, On Faith, Hope, and Love; and Erasmus, *Enchiridion Militis Christiani*.

[701] *Mnemosynum Biblicum. mnemosynon* (Chambers Murray), a souvenir (Cat.). *mnemosynon*, (Cooper), 'a monument, token, or pledge left with ones friende in remembrance of a thyng'. Several works with this title were published in the 17th century. See John Copinger, *Mnemosynum or memorial* (Tholosa, Brell, 1606); John Willis, *Mnemonica, sive reminiscendi ars* (London, Browne, 1618) Cyriacus Lentulus, *Mnemonicon Sacrae Scripturae tripartitum, librorum, capitum, rerum: in*

Biblicum, Alter Memoriale Biblicum, et id genus Carminice[a] prolata concinnarunt; non alio fine, quam ut memoriae inserviretur. Noster quidem mole rerum mentem occupatus, et materia tutus, flores et pigmenta [40] poetica parvi fecit.[b] Non[c] tamen, quod omnia tam siccè,[d] tam religiosè,[e] quin aliquando incalescat, aliquando illucescat illa *Mens[f] Divinior,[g] atque Os[h] magna sonaturum*.

Quae philosophice scripsit magna in vestibulo ferunt Mersenni et Gassendi nomina; quin et in his poeticis memoretur 'ὁ μακαρίτης Edmundus Waller,[i] nobilissimus poeta[j] Anglus, [50] et apud suos quasi Numerorum[k] pater, qui authori Nostro[l] semper inter amicissi-

---

[a] C carminice • [b] C fecit; • [c] C non • [d] C sicce, • [e] C religiose, • [f] C mens • [g] C divinior, • [h] C os • [i] C Waller • [j] C poëta • [k] C numerorum • [l] C nostro

and yet another a Biblical Book of Remembrance, [702] and that sort of thing in poetry, for no other reason than that the memory might be assisted. Indeed our Hobbes, whose mind was filled with the weight of his subject and who was secure in his material, cared little for ornamentation and poetic colouring. [40] That fact that he expresses everything so soberly and conscientiously does not prevent that 'divine mind' and 'lips that utter great sounds' occasionally displaying their warmth and light. [703]

What he wrote philosophically bears at the very entrance the great names of Mersenne[704] and Gassendi;[705] and in poetical matters the blessed Edmund Waller should also be mentioned, the most famous English poet,[706] [50] and among his own people, almost the father of verse,[707] who was always among the dearest friends to our author; and Waller as a mentor

---

usum pietatis et historiae sacrae candidatorum elaboratum, *Lentulus* (Herbornae Nassoviorum, 1661); and Christian Keimann, *Mnemosyne sacra i.e. Monosticha biblica memorialia* (Leipzig, 1652).

[702] *Memoriale Biblicum. memorialis* (adj.), (Chambers Murray) pertaining to memoranda (libellus, Suet.) (Cooper) 'pertaining to memorie, *Memorialis liber* Suet. A memoriall: a booke of remembrance'. See Petrus de Rosenheim, *Roseum memoriale divinorum eloquiorum* (Nuremberg, Friedrich Creusener, 1493), many editions.

[703] Horace, *Satires* 1.4.39-44:
primum ego me illorum, dederim quibus esse poetas,
excerpam numero: neque enim concludere versum
Dixeris esse satis neque, si qui scribat uti nos
Sermoni propiora, putes hunc esse poetam;
ingenium cui sit, cui mens divinior atque os
magna sonaturum, des nominis huius honorem.

Horace, *Satires* 1.4.39-44 (tr. Fairclough 1929, p. 51-2):
First I will take my own name from the list of such as I would allow to be poets. For you would not call it enough to round off a verse, nor would you count anyone poet who writes, as I do, lines more akin to prose. If one has gifts inborn, if one has a soul divine and tongue of noble utterance, to such give the honour of the name.

[704] *Marin Mersenne (1588-1648), French theologian, philosopher, and mathematician, with whom Hobbes was acquainted in Paris in the 1640s.

[705] Pierre Gassendi (1592-1655), French philosopher and scientist, Epicurean scholar and associate of Hobbes in Paris in the 1640s.

[706] *Edmund Waller (1606-87), poet and statesman was elected to Parliament at the young age of 16, and became a noted orator, said by Aubrey to have possessed 'a great mastership of the English Language'.

[707] Waller, belonging to Hobbes's circle, was not only the author of Divine poems, but also author of an important letter to Hobbes, dated 1657 according to annotations to the Folger Waller (Appendix, *The European Magazine* for 1790), praising *Leviathan* in the context of Cromwell's 'perfect foundation of Government'. This letter is not included in the *Hobbes Correspondence* edited by Malcolm (1994).

mos fuit; et Monitor[a] non defuisset, si Materia[b] Culpam[c] non prote-
lasset.

Praeter paròdias[d] nonnullas,[e] nihil hîc[f] cum Virgilio, Ovidio,
reliquisve poetarum[g] principibus. Noluit de toties recoctis phrasibus,
et de communi penu quicquam apponere. **[60]** Quid Nobis *servum*[h]
pecus Imitatores,[i] cum ipsosmet, quos imitantur,[j] praesentes
habemus? Quis guttam quaerit, cui ad manum est ut *toto se proluat*
auro?[k]

---

[a] C monitor • [b] C materia • [c] C culpam • [d] C parodias • [e] C nonnullas • [f] C
hic • [g] C Poëtarum • [h] C Servum • [i] C imitatores, • [j] C imitantur • [k] mv C
auro.

would not have failed in his duty, if the subject matter had not warded off blame.[708]

Except for some adaptations, there is nothing here in the style of Virgil Ovid, and the remaining leading poets. Hobbes did not want to serve up any of their so frequently rehashed diction or anything from the common stock.[709] What are imitators to us but a 'slavish herd',[710] when we have at hand those very people whom they imitate? Who looks for a drop (of wine) who has the opportunity to 'drench himself out of a full gold cup?'[711]

---

[708] Rymer may be referring to Waller as an arch-royalist close to the Cavendish family, who could protect Hobbes at court. (Rymer himself was William III's historiographer and therefore not of the Stuart camp.)

[709] See Juvenal, e.g., *Satire* 1, (ed. Green, p. 65):
The stale themes are bellowed daily/ in rich patron's colonnades, till their marble pillars/ crack with a surfeit of rhetoric. The plane-trees echo/ every old trope – what the winds are up to, whose ghost/ Iachus has on his hellish rack . . . / . . . . you get the same stuff from them all, established poet/ and raw beginner alike.
The terminology, 'recoctis phrasibus', recooked phrases, and 'de communi penu', from the common stock, which could also mean from the common coin, are also reminiscent of Lorenzo Valla, who took the notion of language as a common currency from Quintilian *Institutio oratoria*, 1.6.3: 'usage is the surest guide in speaking, and language should be used just as a coin with public stamp' ('consuetudo vero certissima loquendi magistra, utendumque plane sermone ut nummo, cui publica forma est'). See Marsh, 'Grammar, Method, and Polemic in Lorenzo Valla's "Elegantiae"', *Rinascimento, Rivista dell'Instituto Nazionale di Studi sul Rinascimento*, vol. 19 (1979), pp. 91-116, at pp. 104-5.

[710] Horace, *Epistle*, 1.19.19 (ed. Fairclough, 1929, pp. 382-3), 'Oh you mimics, you slavish herd!' ('o imitatores, servom pecus'). Petrarch's frequent reflections on imitation,·and particularly the cult of Virgil, include his remark to Boccaccio about his own copyist and aspiring poet, Giovanni Malpaghini, as 'alieni dulcedine raptus ingenii' ('rapt with the sweetness of another's wit'). See Thomas M. Greene, 'Petrarch and the Humanist Hermeneutic', p. 209, citing Petrarch, *Le familiare*, ed. Vittorio Rossi and Umberto Bosco, 4 vols (Florence 1933-42), 23.19. Petrarch goes on to expound on the principles of true imitation:
A proper imitator should take care that what he writes resemble the original without reproducing it. The resemblance should not be that of a portrait to the sitter – in that case the closer the likeness the better – but it should be the resemblance of a son to his father. Therein is often a great divergence in particular features, but there is a certain suggestion, what our painters call an 'air'. . . . Thus we may use another man's conceptions and the color of his style, but not his words. . . . The first procedure makes poets, the second makes apes.

[711] *Aeneid*. 1.739, trans. David West (Harmondsworth, Penguin, 1991) p. 27: 'pleno se proluit auro [ille impiger hausit] spumantem pateram'. 'Nothing loth, he took a great draught from the golden bowl foaming to the brim, and bathed himself in wine'.

Avia Pieridum, ut et ubivis aliquid novum, et minime tritum meditari[a] amavit. Si in Syllabarum[b] Modulo[c] quandoque negligentior sit,
profecto apud veteres poetas (Christianos [70] velim) hoc non
insolens fuit. Fortasse et alia sunt quibus non tanti habuit criticorum
plebi in omnibus abblandiri.

---

[a] C meditari, • [b] C syllabarum • [c] C modulo

Hobbes liked to study the wild country of the Muses,[712] as also wherever there was anything new or original.[713] If he might be sometimes negligent in the measure of syllables, this was actually not unusual among the ancient poets (especially the Christian ones).[714] **[70]** And perhaps there are other ways in which he did not consider it worth the price to flatter the common run of critics in all things.[715]

---

[712] Lucretius 1.926: 'Avia Pieridum peragro loca, nullius ante Trita solo'. *Pieris idis* (f.) Muse; *pieridus* (adj.) of the Muses, poetic. See Horace's reference to the Calabrian muses, *Odes* 4.8.20: 'laudes quam Calabrae Pierides.' The most ancient cults of the Muses were in Pieria and Ascra but smaller cults existed throughout Greece, to which Horace refers in *Odes* 1.12.6, mistakenly associating them with Pindus. Pythagoreans, Plato and Aristotle, organized their Schools as places for Muses, hence *museum* (*mouseion eionis* Gr.), the most famous being that of Alexandria (*OCD*), c.f. *Hist. Eccl.*, line 1852-3, with reference to the Sorbonne. Cooper, *Thesaurus*: gives *Musae*: for humanities. Horace: *amicus Musis*: 'a studient: one geuen to learnyng'; c.f. *Hist Eccl.*, lines 6-7.

[713] The language of Petrarch, who visited Virgilian haunts near Mantua:
> It is in this city [Mantua] that I have composed what you now are reading. It is here that I have found the friendly repose of thy rural fields. I constantly wonder by what path you were wont to seek the unfrequented glades in thy strolls, in what fields were want to roam, what streams to visit, or what recess in the curving shores of the lake, what shady groves and forest fastnesses. Constantly I wonder where it was that you rested upon the sloping sward, or that, reclining in moments of fatigue, you pressed with your elbow the grassy turf or upon the marge of a charming spring. Such thoughts as these bring you back before my eyes.

Petrarch, *Le familiare*, trans. Mario Emilio Cosenza, ed., *Petrarch's Letters to Classical Authors* (Chicago, University of Chicago Press, 1910), pp. 138-9; cited by Thomas M. Greene, 'Petrarch and the Humanist Hermeneutic', pp. 203-4. Petrarch's comments are in imitation of the first lines of Virgil's *Eclogues*, also reprised in the closing lines of his *Georgics* (565-6): 'Tityrus, lying back beneath wide beechen cover,/ you meditate the woodland Muse on slender oat.' Virgil's famous verse has an important echo in lines 11-19 of Hobbes's country house poem, *De mirabilibus pecci carmen.*

[714] Hobbes linguistic construction and versification was sloppy compared with the Continentals, but typical of Anglo Latin poetry; see J. W. Binns, *Intellectual Culture in Elizabethan and Jacobean England: the Latin Writings of the Age* (Leeds, Francis Cairns, Ltd., University of Leeds, 1990), p. 27. The Christian poet Rymer has in mind is likely Prudentius, famous as an imitator (and satirist) of Virgil. Virgil was the ancient poet who set the pattern of the Latin hexameter, while Ovid and Catullus set the form of the elegiac couplet (see Thomas G. Rosenmeyer, *et al.*, *The Meters of Greek and Latin Poetry*, pp. 68, 71-20).

[715] This whole passage is strikingly close in form of words to Davenant's panegyric to Hobbes in his 'Author's Preface to his Much Honor'd Friend, M. Hobbes', lines 821-32 (Molesworth edn, *EW* IV, p. 24), and Rymer, although giving no indication of knowing the work, surely must have:
> who is he so learn'd (how proud so ever with being cherish'd in the bosome of Fame) that can hope (when through the severall ways of Science, he seek

Si quaerant Historici[a] unde ista de Aethiopibus; de Neptuno, de Jove, diísque[b] reliquis convivantibus μετ 'αμύμονας αίφιοπγς; videant Homerum testem satis luculentem. De Rege Ergamene;[c] et famosâ[d] illâ[e] [80] Sacerdotum strage consulant Diodorum Siculum lib. 4. De more isto Aegypti dirimendi lites per *Collare*,[f] et Gemmam,[g] *veri indicem*, eundem habent Diod. Sic. et AElianum, à quibus V.V.C.C. Seldenus, et Marshamus, et plures alii in sua traduxerunt.

---

[a] C historici • [b] C diisque • [c] C Ergamene • [d] C famosa • [e] C illa • [f] C collare, • [g] C gemmam,

If historians should seek the source for those things about the Ethiopians,[716] Neptune, Jove, and the other gods feasting 'with the excellent Ethiopians',[717] they may consider Homer a sufficiently illuminating witness. Concerning King Ergamenes[718] and that famous massacre of the priesthood,[719] **[80]** they should consult Diodorus Siculus, book 4.[720] Concerning the well-known Egyptian[721] custom of settling disputes by means of the 'Collar' and the Gem as the 'touchstone of truth',[722] Diodorus Siculus and Aelianus,[723] from whom the very famous[724] Selden,[725] Marsham[726] and several others have excerpted in their works, have the same.[727]

Nature in her hidden walks) to make his Journy short, unlesse he call you to be his Guide? . . . because you move not by common Mapps, but have painfully made your owne Prospect; and travaile now like the Sun, not to informe your selfe, but enlighten the World.

[716] Hobbes talks about the Egyptian legal practices in both *Hist. Eccl.*, lines 227-76, and *Behemoth (EW* IV, p. 92ff.).

[717] 'met 'amumonas aithiopeias', Homer *Iliad* 1.423 and *Odyssey* 1.22.

[718] *Ergamenes, king of the Ethiopians in the reign of Ptolemy II Philadelphus (BC 285-46), had been educated in Greece. C.f. Diodorus Siculus (1946-52 edn. C. H. Oldfather, tr. Cambridge, Mass.: Harvard University Press. 3 vols.), 3.6.3.

[719] Molesworth notes 'Vide infra, vers. 205-12'.

[720] See Diodorus Siculus (Oldfather, trans.) vol. 1 bk 3, para 6, ff.

[721] Note that the custom was practiced in Meröe in Upper Egypt, sometimes referred to as Ethiopia in the 17c. Hobbes's account, lines 227-76, is based on Diodorus, 1.75.5 (Oldfather, trans. p. 261) and recounted by Hobbes in *Behemoth, EW* IV, p. 92ff.

[722] In fact Diodorus Siculus, vol. 1 bk 3, para 6, ff.

[723] Aelianus Claudius (c. AD 170-235), also known as Aelian Praenestor, where he was pontifex, was a teacher of rhetoric in Rome, known for his Herodotean simplicity but wrote later than Diodorus, whose source was rather *Varia Historia* 14.34 (Loeb edn, ed. N. G. Wilson). Because Aelian wrote of manifestations of providence and divine justice he was widely cited by Christian writers.

[724] Molesworth inserts V.V.C.C.: 'viri clarissimi'.

[725] John Selden was a fellow member of Magdalen Hall with Hobbes, and the two later became close friends (see Aubrey, vol. 1, p. 369). Letter 18 of the Hobbes *Correspondence*, ed. Malcolm, vol. 1, p. 32, records Hobbes as reading Selden's *Mare Clausum* in 1636, soon after it was published. But Selden was also a formidable antiquarian and probable source for Hobbes on a number of matters, including the names of those who attended the Nicene Council. See Selden's *Eutychii Aegyptii*, and *Hist. Eccl.*, lines 561-2 and notes. See also Springborg Introduction, chapter 5.2.

[726] Sir John Marsham, (1602-1685), author of the *Diatriba chronologica*, 1649, and the *Chronicus Canon Ægyptiacus, Ebraicus, Graecus, et disquisitiones*, 1672, accused Eusebius of doctoring the Hebrew chronologies to disguise the importance of ancient Egyptian wisdom, and Hobbes too believed that Egyptian wisdom came first (c.f. *Hist Eccl.*, lines 155-6, 159-60, 167-8, 217-18, 273-6, 335-6).

[727] Molesworth notes, 'Vide infra, vers. 229-42.'

Quoad caetera,[a] neque Chronologos, neque Philosophos moramur [90] multum. Theologis vero[b] ut quodammodo satisfiat[c] nonulla incumbit cura. Non quod Thomistas, Scotistas, aut nescio quos Seraphicos, tanti habeamus; sed Nicaeni Patres, sapientia. Graeca, et magnus ille Athanasius authori[d] nostro horrida bella interminantur. At dicendum est eum in istis mysteriis poeticè[e] aliquando (potius quam Catholicè)[f] delirare. [100]

---

[a] C cetera, • [b] C vero, • [c] C satisfiat, • [d] C autori • [e] C poetice • [f] C catholice)

As far as the rest go, we will not let either the chronologers[728] or the philosophers detain us much.[729] **[90]** The concern to satisfy the theologians in some measure certainly demands some attention. Not because we rate so highly Thomists[730] and Scotists,[731] and certain Seraphists;[732] but because the Nicene Fathers,[733] Greek philosophy,[734] and the great Athanasius,[735] threaten our author with horrid conflicts. But it must be said that the latter sometimes raves on poetically (rather than Catholically) about those mysteries.[736] **[100]**

---

[728] Eusebius's pioneering chronology of church history had been revised by the famous Renaissance philologist, Joseph Scaliger; see Anthony Grafton, 'Joseph Scaliger and Historical Chronology: The Rise and Fall of a Discipline', *History & Theory*, vol. 14 (1975), pp. 156-185'. But the reference could include John Marsham's *Canon Chronicus Aegyptiacus, Ebraicus, Graecus* of 1672. Henry Dodwell's *Quam nupera sit, quamque imperfecta, antiquissima Graecorum historia* (Camden inaugural lecture, Oxford, 25 May 1688 [1692]) pp. 13-14; and his *De veteribus Graecorum Romanorumque cyclis, obiterque de cyclo Judaeorum aetate Christi, dissertationes decem, cum tabulis necessariis* (Oxford, 1701), are too late for Hobbes, but not for Rymer.

[729] Horace, *Odes* 2.17.6: *quid multus moror.*

[730] Followers of St. Thomas Aquinas, known as the angelical doctor, scholastics (*OED*, 1980 edn, 2.329).

[731] Disciples of John Duns Scotus, known as the subtle doctor, Scottish scholastic philosopher and theologian, opposed to Aquinas on the primacy of the undetermined will (*OED*, 1980 edn, 2.250).

[732] St. Francis and St. Bonaventure were known for their ecstatic devotion as the Seraphical Fathers. In the 17c. the term was applied to religious fanatics or passionate speakers; see, for instance, Anthony à Wood, *Ath. Oxon.*, 1691, 2.18, on 'the most florid and seraphical Teacher in the University' (*OED*, 1980 edn. 2.490).

[733] The first *Nicene Council (AD 325) dealt with the Arian controversy concerning the divinity of Christ; the second (AD 787) dealt with the iconoclasts (*OED*, 1980 edn, 1.197). Rymer refers to Eusebius, and the Byzantine trio Socrates of Constantinople, Sozomen and Theodoret.

[734] Rymer refers to the Greek philosophical sects, to which the term heresy refers etymologically, and to whom Hobbes in fact accredits the corruption of primitive Christianity.

[735] Athanasius, c. 295-373, anti-Arian archbishop of Alexandria, famed as the originator of the Athanasian Creed, in the last decade of his life developed the doctrine of the deity and personality of the Holy Spirit. See Athanasius, *Apologia contra arianos*, *PG* XXVI. One of the best accounts of Athanasius and the Arians is to be found in Sozomen's 5th century *Hist Eccl.*, bks 1-6 (ed. J. Bidez, tr. A. J. Festugière, Paris Editions du Cerf, 1983). See also Charles Kannengiesser, ed, *Politique et Théologie chez Athanase d'Alexandrie* (Paris, Beauchesne, 1974). For the Arianleading Athanasius' bitter battles with Constantine, who was exiled thrice, and Eusebius, see the Springborg Introduction, chapter 4.3.

[736] Although Rymer distances himself from Hobbes's hostility to the Fathers and the Scholastics here, he goes on to record how Hobbes's complaints about their doctrinal wranglings echo those of Hilary of Poitiers and Constantine himself.

Sed vero et istius Saeculi[a] Divus ille Hillarius,[b] ad Constantinum Augustum libro, eadem queritur; *Conscii[c] sumus[d] quod post Nicaenam Synodam nihil aliud[e] quam fidem scribimus, dum in verbis pugna est, dum de novitatibus quaestio est, dum de ambiguis occasio est, dum de Autoribus[f] querela est, dum de studiis certamen est, dum in* [110] *consensu difficultas est, dum alter alteri Anathema[g] esse coepit,[h] prope jam nemo Christi est. Incertis enim Doctrinarum[i] verbis vagamur; et aut dum docemus perturbamur,[j] aut dum docemur erramus. Proximi anni fides quid immutationis in se habet? primum quae Homousian[k] decernit taceri, sequens rursus Homousian[l] decernit et praedicat; tertium quae Usiam simpliciter* [120] *à patribus praesumptam per indulgentiam excusat, quartum non*

---

[a] C Seculi • [b] C Hillarius • [c] C conscii (the quotation is not italicized) • [d] C sumus, • [e] C aliud, • [f] C autoribus • [g] C anathema • [h] C coepit • [i] C doctrinarum • [j] mv C perturbamus • [k] C homousian • [l] C homousian

In fact, the Divine Hilary of that era complains about the same things in his book, *Against Constantius Augustus*:[737]

We are aware that after the Nicene Council we do nothing but write the Creed;[738] while the battle is over words, while the issue concerns new heresies, while the occasion is about ambiguities, while the quarrel is about authorities,[739] while the contest is about scholarship, [110] while the difficulty lies in consensus, and one side begins to be anathema to another, at this point almost no-one belongs to Christ. We wander among the uncertain words of doctrines,[740] and either we are confused when we teach, or we lose our way when we are taught. What changes does next year's Creed contain?[741] First, the Creed decrees that consubstantiation[742] be passed over in silence; next, just the opposite,[743] it decrees and publicly proclaims consubstantiation; third, it indulgently excuses the simple understanding of Substance[744] [120] by the Fathers; fourth, the Creed does not absolve it but condemns it. Finally we have

---

[737] Molesworth notes: 'Constantium evidently the son of Constantine the Great, *vide* the Blessed Hilary, *Ad Constantium Augustum liber quem Constantio ipse tradidit*. Hilary, *Opera*, fol. 1570, p. 211' (published only after Constantine's death). See St Hilary, vols. 9 and 10 of the *Patrologia Latina, juxta editionem monachorum ordinis sancti Benedicti* and also Hilary, *Contra Constantium Imperatorem*, PL X, col. 577-606 on the persecutions of Constantius II. The Hardwick Hall book list shows the Latin Hilarii Opera fol. (Paris, 1631?) at shelf mark J.3.4.

[738] Molesworth amends the Latin to read: 'Conscii sumus post Nicaenam Synodum nihil aliud quam fidem scribi [*sic*.]': ' We are mindful of the fact that after the Nicene Council what is to be written is nothing but the Creed'.

[739] Molesworth notes, 'Haec uncis inclusa verba sunt Rymeri, non Hilarii': 'These words enclosed in brackets [i.e. the indented paragraph] are Rymer's, not Hilary's'

[740] Molesworth amends the Latin: 'Incerto enim doctrinarum vento vagamur': 'We wander blown by the shifting wind of doctrine'.

[741] Molesworth amends the Latin to read: 'Jam vero proximi anni fides quid de immutatione in se habet?': 'What does faith already have in itself for change in the next few years?'

[742] Rymer uses the term 'Homousion'. The debate whether Christ the son of God was *homoousios* (ομοούσιον), of the same substance, or consubstantial (Latin *consubstantialis*), with the Father, i.e. sharing an identity of being, or whether rather he was or *homoiousios* ('ομοιούσιον), 'of like substance', consumed the Church Fathers from AD 400 on (see *Hist. Eccl.*, lines 663, 674, etc.).

[743] Molesworth amends the Latin: 'Rursus, *quae*': 'On the contrary, which article of faith'.

[744] Molesworth notes '*Usia*, id est *ousia* [Gr.] sive *substantia*', i.e. 'matter without substance'.

excusat, sed condemnat. Tandem eo processum est, ut neque penes nos, neque penes quenquam ante nos[a] sanctum exinde aliquid aut inviolabile perseveret; annuas atque menstruas de Deo fides decernimus, decretis poenitemus, poenitentes defendimus, defensos Anathematizamus,[b] aut in nostris aliena, aut in alienis nostra damnamus: [130] *et mordentes invicem,[c] jam absumpti sumus[d] ab invicem.* Et ipsemet Constantinus quam dissentiens fuit à sacris hujus temporis rixis, et quam aegre tulit Graeculorum altercandi ingenium, Index[e] sit illa ad Alexandrum,[f] et Epistola apud Eusebium:[g] ubi dolet pro parvis et valde modicis causis, propter leviculam quaestionem, propter parva et [140] vana Sermonum[h] Certamina,[i] inanem verborum strepitum, subtilitates, futilitates, infantum fatuitates, fratres fratribus committi;[j] et ad necessitatem blasphemiae, aut Schismatis[k] impelli.

Ad eadem concinit inter Catholicos istius saeculi[l] Poetas[m] Aurelius Prudentius:

Fidem minutis dissecant ambagibus,   [150]
   Ut[n] quisque lingua est nequior.
Solvunt ligantque quaestionum vincula
   Per[o] Syllogismos[p] plectiles.
Vae Captiosis[q] Sycophantarum strophis,
   Vae[r] versipelli astutiae.
Nodos tenaces recta rumpit regula
   Infesta[s] dissertantibus.
Idcirco Mundi[t] stulta delegit Deus,
   Ut[u] concidant Sophistica.

---

[a] C nos, • [b] C anathematizamus, • [c] C invicem • [d] mv C substitutes absumsimus for absumpti sumus • [e] C index • [f] C Alexandrum • [g] C Eusebium • [h] C sermonum • [i] C certamina • [j] C committi • [k] C schismatis • [l] C Seculi • [m] C poëtas • [n] C ut • [o] C per • [p] C syllogismos • [q] C captiosis • [r] C vae • [s] C infesta • [t] C mundi • [u] C ut

reached the point[745] when it is not in our power, as it was not in the power of anyone before us, that anything sacred or inviolable would thenceforth persist. We decree beliefs about God for a year and for a month, we regret the decree, we protect penitents and we anathematize those protected. We either condemn the doctrines of others in our own, or we condemn our own in those of others, **[130]** and biting one another we are finally mutually consumed.

And that Constantine himself disagreed to the same extent with the holy disputes of this time, and was annoyed with the Greeklings' talent for quarrelling, may be seen from his letter to Alexander where, according to Eusebius,[746] he lamented that brother quarreled with brother, and they were driven to the necessity of blasphemy and schism for trivial and unimportant causes, on account of minute questions, **[140]** petty and pointless semantic struggles, and over the empty clatter of words, the subtleties, futilities and the fatuities of childish people.

Among the Catholic poets of this era, Aurelius Prudentius[747] sings about the same contentions:[748]

> They dissect faith into minute quibbling   **[150]**
> According to the wickedness of each man's tongue.[749]
> They loosen and tighten the chains of Argument with
>   complicated syllogisms.
> Woe to the captious tricks of Cheats!
> Woe to their sly cunning!
> Right rule, dangerous to disputants, breaks
>   obstinate knots.
> For that reason God willed the follies of the world,
>   So that sophistry might perish.

[745] Molesworth notes: 'Et quo tandem processum est': 'And so it has further proceeded.'

[746] Rymer refers to 'Constantine's Letter to Alexander the Bishop, and Arius the Presbyter', AD 324, from Eusebius' *Life of Constantine*. See Molesworth's note, p. 346: '*De vita Constantini*. lib. ii. EUSEBII ECCLES. HIST. fol. 1570. p. 155-7'.

[747] Aurelius Clemens Prudentius (AD 348-c.405), a native of Spain and layman, was the greatest of the Christian Latin poets.

[748] See Molesworth note, [Aurelii Prudentii APOTHEOSIS, *Hymns in Infideles*. 33-34]. But Molesworth is inaccurate, in fact Rymer quotes, Prudentius' *Apotheosis*, lines 21-30. See *Prudentius, Works*, ed. H. J. Thomson, (London, Heinemann, 1949), vol. 1, pp. 118-19.

[749] See *Laurentii Valle Repastinatio dialectice et philosophie*, ed. G. Zippel, vol 1, ch. 6, pp. 41-6, 'De distinguendo forum verborum "essentia" et "substantia" usu, ne ambagibus sermo implicetur'.

Utcunque autem illius saeculi[a] Poetae[b] [160] novum prospicientes campum, in arenam descendunt fervidi: non jam Laestrygonas, Harpiasque premunt, aucupantur; sed Monothelitas, Pneumatomachos, Homuncionistas (nova Monstra)[c] Haereticos toto Marte[d] confodiunt.

Et quàm[e] avide ubique sectantur aenigmata illa Sacra,[f] Oidipodas agere delectati! Nova Mysteriorum [170] segete luxuriantes, et insolito caecuntientes lumine,[g] mirifico alite aethera petunt. Bellè[h] Noster ille Sedulius Presbyter, in uno versiculo totum spirans Athanasium[i]

– *una manens deitatis forma perennis*
Quod[j] simplex triplicet, quodque est triplicabile simplet.
Haec est vera fides –

Nos profectò[k] longe[l] sequimur;[180] entheus[m] ille tandem deferbuit ardor; tali oestro non rapimur; et *Nobis non licet esse tam disertis.*

Maluit hic Noster[n] inter primos et piscatores Apostolos simplicitatem discere Christianam, quam apud Nicaenos patres,[o] et Graeculos Theosophistas cerebellum perdere attonitus.[p] Contentus[q] nomine Philosophi, laïco[r] ingenio, et ultra rationale animal [190] parùm[s] sapientis. Sed nollem te, Lector, ulteriùs[t] detineri. Vale,[u] et fruere.

---

[a] C Seculi • [b] C poëtae • [c] C monstra) • [d] C marte • [e] C quam • [f] C sacra • [g] C lumine • [h] C Belle • [i] C Athanasium. • [j] C quod • [k] C profecto • [l] C longé • [m] C 'entheus • [n] C noster • [o] C Patres • [p] C attonitus • [q] C contentus • [r] C laico • [s] C parum • [t] C ulterius • [u] C Vale

In whatever way the poets of those times, **[160]** on the lookout for a new battle field, rush down hell-bent into the arena, no longer chasing and lying in wait for Homer's Laestrygonians[750] and Virgil's Harpies,[751] instead they demolish Monothelites, Spirit-fighters,[752] heretical *Homuncionites*[753] (new monsters), in all-out war.[754]

And how eagerly they chase the sacred riddles everywhere, delighted to act the Oedipuses.[755] Running riot in a new crop of mysteries **[170]** and blinded by the strange light, they seek heaven on wondrous wings. How nicely our Sedulius the Priest expresses Athanasius completely in one little verse:[756]

> *... One abiding form of perpetual divinity:*
> *Makes threefold what is one, and makes one of what is threefold.*
> *This is the true faith.* ·

We indeed follow a long way behind. **[180]** Inspired ardor has at last ceased raging. We are no longer carried away by such frenzy and 'We are not allowed to be so eloquent'.[757]

Our author preferred on this matter to learn Christian simplicity among the first Apostles and fishermen rather than to lose his little brain, bewildered, among the Nicene Fathers and Greekling Theosophists.[758] He was satisfied with the name of philosopher, with a layman's expertise, **[190]** and with little understanding beyond that of a rational animal. But I do not wish to detain you further, Reader. Farewell and enjoy!

---

[750] *Laestrygones a race of cannibalistic Giants encountered by Odysseus (*Od.* 10.82ff.).

[751] *Harpies, mythical monsters, half woman, half bird (*OCD*). Virgil emphasizes they are birds with women's faces, see *Aen.* 3.210ff.

[752] *pneumatomachos* [Souter] (adj.) resisting the Holy Spirit [Rustic. S.; *cod.* Iust. 1.5.5.]. (Blaise), heretic, adversaries of the Holy Spirit.

[753] *Homuncionistas* (*ODCC*), heretics who see Christ as a man and not a God. *Homuncionitae* (Souter), people who believed Christ was wholly human, i.e. Arians.

[754] This is the language of Prudentius' *Psychomachia*.

[755] See *Hist. Eccl.*, lines 1183-4 and 1421-2, and notes.

[756] *Sedulius *Carmen Paschale* 1.297-9. Sedulius (early 5c. AD), a Christian Latin poet known for the sweetness of his poetry (see *Corp. Scr. Eccl. Lat.* 10). His works include the Paschale Odes, which adapt the Gospel narrative to Christian verse. (*OCD*, 1970 edn, p. 970). A work by Sedulius, appears to be listed in the Hardwick Hall library at shelf mark F.1.23 according to the General List in MS E1A.

[757] Martial, 9.11.15-16 'Arej' Are decet sonare: nobis non licet esse tam disertis qui Musas colimus severiores'.

[758] A pun on Athenaeus's *Deipnosophists*.

[1688 GLOSSARY].

Siquae voces insolentiores sont, habes qualem qualem
Explicationem

Pag. 5. Ver. 89 [lines 87-8][1]. Umbri, *Umbrarum filii*
Somnites, *Somnigenae, à Somno prognati.*
Amenenees, Astheneentes, *invalidi, languescentes,* αμενηνεες,
αςθενεντες
p. 6. v. 103. [line 101] Agyrtis, *Montinbanchis.*   [200]
p. 17. v. 348. [line 346] Alazonibus, *Jactatoribus.*
p. 21. v. 434. [line 430] Tertia verba Dei, *SS. Scriptura. In lib. de
Cive, c. 15. triplex verbum Dei, 1. Rationale. 2. Sensibile.
3. Propheticum.*
p. 22. v. 474. [line 472] Plemmyris, *Mare plenum, seu aestus
maximus.*
p. 26. v. 548. [line 546] Ephorum, *Episcopum.*
p. 27. v. 367. [line 565] Bouleuterion, *Locus ubi patres
considebant.*

---

[1] Line numbers inserted in square brackets (both in the Latin Glossary and in
the English translation), to correct the misnumbering in the 1688 edition.

[1688 GLOSSARY].

If these words seem unusual,[759] at least you have some
explanation.

Page 5, verse 89. [lines 87-8] *Umbri*, sons of shades.[760]
Somnites, race of sleepers, descended from the god of Sleep.
The Amenenees[761] and Asthenentes,[762] i.e.,
the weak and ill, αμενηνεες, αςθενεντες
p. 6. v. 103. [line 101] *Agyrtis*,[763] Mountebanks.   [200]
p. 17. v. 348. [line 346] *Alazonibus*,[764] Braggards.[765]
p. 21. v. 434. [line 430] *Tertia verba Dei, SS.* Sacred Scripture. In the
Book *De Cive*, ch. 15. the Three Words of God, 1. Rational. 2. Sensible. 3. Prophetic.
p. 22. v. 474. [line 472] *Plemmyris*,[766] Flood tide or very great surf.
p. 26. v. 548. [line 546] *Ephorum*,[767] Bishop.[768]
p. 27. v. 367. [line 565] *Bouleuterion*,[769]Place where the Fathers
deliberated.

---

[759] insolentiores *insolentia* [Souter] Gr. *propeteia, aponoia*, madness, (Conc. *S.*)
i.e. *Acta Conciliorum oecumenicorum*, ed. E. Schwarz, Berlin, 1914; (pl.) annoy-
ances (Greg. M. *epist.* 3.56).

[760] See the 1688 Glossary (pp. 604-5), 'the sons of shadows', evocative of
Aeneid 6, where Aeneas sees in the Underworld his progeny that may be the future
race of Rome.

[761] The Amennnees are Homer's νεκύων αμενηνά κάρηνα 'the powerless
heads of the dead', from *Odyssey* 11.49.

[762] Astheneentes, αςθενεντες from *astheneis* (Gr. adj.) weak, feeble; sick; poor,
insignificant = 'invalidi, languescentes'.

[763] *agyrtes -ou* (Gr. m.) beggar, tramp; buffoon; cognate of *aguris* from *ageiro*
[Autenreith], chance gathering, company, host.

[764] *Alazonibus* from (Gr.) *alaomai*, wander, rove, roam, of adventurers, free-
booters, mendicants, and homeless or lost persons.

[765] *Jactatoribus*. See Molesworth's reference to *jactator*, from Gr. *aladzon -onos*,
braggard, swaggerer, imposter; vagabond.

[766] Molesworth's note, to l. 472, p. 362: *pleimmuris, maris aestuans accessus*,
the flood-tide of the surging sea.

[767] See *ephorus -i* (m.) a Spartan magistrate, Gr. *ephoros* probably from *ephoran*
look on, oversee, inspect.

[768] *episcopus -i* (m) overseer, guardian, bishop.

[769] *Bouleuterion* (n.) Gr. council-house, council-board.

p. 37. v. 1239. [line 1237] Cnodula, *Animalia magnitudine, aut* **[210]** *qualitate noxia.*

p. 60. v. 1299. [line 1297] Chronometra, *Horologium.*

p. 68. v. 1475. [line 1473]. Ovescere, *Oves fieri.*

p. 79. v. 1722. [line 1717] Epodis, *Exorcismis, incantationibus.*

p. 82. v. 1779. [line 1775] Verborum posteritatem, *Consequentiam.*

p. 83. v. 1881. [line 1797] Haeredicus, *Haeres.*

p. 87. v. 1975. [line 1883] Gallimatiam, *Inconditam verborum farraginem.*

v. 1976. [line 1884] Ducocalanus. *Fr, du Coq à l'âne.*   **[220]**

p. 37. v. 1239. [line 1237] *Cnodula,*[770] dangerous animal, monster.   **[210]**

p. 60. v. 1299. [line 1297] *Chronometra,*[771] clock. [772]

p. 68. v. 1475. [line 1473] *Ovescere,*[773] to be made sheep.

p. 79. v. 1722. [line 1717] *Epodis,* [774] expelled with incantations.

p. 82. v. 1779. [line 1775] the future significance of these words.

p. 83. v. 1881. [line 1797] *Haeredicus,* sect.[775]

p. 87. v. 1975. [line 1883] *Gallimatiam,*[776] confused speech, *farraginem.*[777]

   v. 1976. [line 1884] Ducocalanus.[778] *Fr, du Coq*[779] *à l'âne.*[780]   **[220]**

---

[770] *Cnodula,* see Gr. *knodalion* (n.) dangerous animal, monster. See *Odyssey,* 17.317. Rymer's Latin *Animalia magnitudine, aut qualitate noxia,* simply translates the Greek.

[771] *Chronometra,* clock.

[772] *horologium -i -ii* (n.) clock.

[773] *Ovescere*: to be made sheep, see *Hist. Eccl.,* line 1473, *et ovescere reges,* making kings into sheep. Note that the language of the wolf among the sheep is the language of the *Patrologia.* See St. Hilary, *Liber Contra Constantium Imperatorem* p. 587, 570.11, in which he speaks of Constans as a false sheep (*falsa ovis*), and at the same time a rapacious wolf (*lupe rapax*).

[774] *Epodis* (see Horace's *Epodes*) is a form of the Latin *epos* (n. nom and acc. only) epic (poem), heroic song, poem, lay.

[775] *Haeredicus* is a late form of *haeres haeres/is -is* (f.) sect.

[776] *Gallimatia,* see Fr. *galimatias* (m.) a discourse, confused writing, mixed up, unintelligible; enters French in 1580, source perhaps being *bas latin, ballimathia*: an obscene song; associated with the 18c. *amphigouri,* burlesque discourse full of *galimatias* [*Petit Robert*]. Note also that French *coq* is derivative of Latin *gallus,* also the name of a Latin poet. (See *Hist. Eccl.,* line 1884n.)

[777] *farrago -inis* (f.) mixed grain for livestock, fodder; (fig.) heterogeneous mixture. This connects to the pastoral themes of sheep, cows, *pastor* and *boukulos.*

[778] *Ducocalanus,* bastard French for 'from the cock to the anus'. Hobbes is here referring to the great hodge-podge of doctrine, earlier referred to as *Gallimatia,* 'fodder' or 'chicken feed', (see *Hist. Eccl.,* lines 1879-88 and notes).

[779] *coq* (m) sea cook, cook on a maritime vessel.

[780] See Molesworth's revision of Rymer's explanatory note: *DUCOCALANUS in gallice du Coq à l'âne. Coq à l'âne* is a genre of poetry exchanged among friends, often featuring animals, e.g. Clement Marot, famous 16c Protestant court poet who ate meat at Lent and maintained that Catholics were cannibals, went to Geneva, was welcomed by Calvin and detested by the Pléiade. Marot wrote Horatian-style epistles, e.g. *Quatriesme epistre du coq a l'asne a Lyon Jamet* [Garnier-Flammarion, 1973 edn, pp. 91-4, 114-18, 136-40]. Marot defined the language of La Fontaine and other authors of animal poetry in French, see especially his poem *A Son Amy Lyon* [Garnier-Flammarion, 1973 edn, pp. 59-61], and translated the first book of Ovid's *Metamorphoses,* as well as writing a poem to Rabelais. See the 'gallinaceum' the chicken house and Hobbes's Scarronesque characters reminiscent of the colloquialism for shooting the bull, 'everything from roosters to donkeys': *DUCOCALANUS in gallice du Coq à l'âne,* preceded by *GALLIMATIAM.*

v. 1979. [line 1886] Lalia, *Infantum balbutientium Dea.*
p. 94. v. 2047. [line 2043] Carolusque agnus, *Carolus magnus.*
p. 100. v. 2175. [line 2171] Vivi Comburia, *De Haeretico Comburendo, antea haec in anglia; sed jam Compendio, per Ordinarium quemlibet, sine ambage. Vid. Stat. H. 4.2.15.*

v. 1979. [line 1886] Lalia,[781] *Infantum balbutientium*[782] *Dea.*
p. 94. v. 2047. [line 2043] Carolusque agnus,[783] *Carolus magnus.*[784]
p. 100. v. 2175. [line 2171] Vivi Comburia,[785] *De Haeretico Comburendo, antea haec in anglia; sed jam Compendio, per Ordinarium quemlibet, sine ambage. Vid. Stat. H. 4.2.15.*[786]

---

[781] *Lalia* the goddess of the babbling stutterers [i.e. cynics], or goddess of the tongue-tied stammerers.

[782] *balbutientium*, pres. part of *balbutio -ire* (v.t., v.i.) stammer, stutter, lisp, speak indistinctly; (fig.) speak obscurely, babble; [Souter] stumbling.

[783] *Carolus agnus* is not only Charlemagne but undoubtedly Charles I, that sacrificial lamb, Royal martyr and author of the *Eikon Basilike.*

[784] Charlemagne, Charles, Lamb of God. See *Hist. Eccl.*, lines 2043-46, to which this refers, where Charlemagne and Pope Leo, who crowned him, created mutually dependent temporal and spiritual realms.

[785] *Vivi Comburia*, burned alive.

[786] *De Haeretico Comburendo, antea haec in anglia; sed jam Compendio, per Ordinarium quemlibet, sine ambage. Vid. Stat. H. 4.2.15*: 'On the Burning of the Heretic, which was formerly done in England, but now by a short cut, through some ordinances as it pleases, without detour'. See the Henrician statutes, 4.2.14. This is apparently a reference to the English Henry IV's decrees on heresy, e.g. Wycliffe and the Waldensiens.

SELECT GLOSSARY
OF PROPER NAMES

A

Alans, nomadic pastoralists living in south-eastern Russian AD 100-200, forced into the Roman Empire by Goths and Huns. Pauly-Wissowa notes that from AD 406 the Vandals, Suevi and Alans moved into the Rhineland and Gaul, where, after an unsuccessful campaign against the Franks, they moved South into Spain and North Africa. The term Alani was also used interchangeably with Albani and Alamanni. Ostrogorsky argues (pp. 60-3), that from 400 on the with the downfall of the Huns, the Germanic Tribes were redispersed anew, the branch of the Alans ruled by Aspar and his line becoming very important in the Byzantine empire by the mid-fifth century (pp. 61-2). Despite anti-German sentiment in Constantinople, Aspar's son Patricius was married to the Emperor's daughter, and notwithstanding being a foreigner and an Arian, was made heir apparent with the title Caesar. But in 471, anti-German sentiment saw a resurgence, Aspar and his son Ardabur were assassinated, while Patricius, who had escaped with severe wounds, was divorced from the Emperor's daughter and deprived of his position as Caesar. (*Pauly-Wissowa*, *OCD*, 1970, p. 33).

Alaric, Visigoth leader, who died AD 410, led his people out of Lower Moesia in 375 to devastate Greece and, in 401, entered Italy. Defeated by the Roman military leader Stilicho at Pollentia in 402, and at Verona in 403, he went on to beseige Rome three times from 408 to 410. In 410 Alaric, an Arian, took Rome, but out of respect for the Apostle Peter, he refused to desecrate the church built over his tomb, a placatory gesture which earned his acceptance. See Sozomen, *Hist. Eccl.* bk 9, ch. 9, and Hobbes's later discussion of Alaric, lines 1010-16. At length he entered and plundered the city, but left its buildings standing. Moving towards Africa, he marched through Rhegium, but ended up ship-wrecked in a storm and, having abandoned that adventure, he died peacefully at Consentia in 410 (*OCD*, 1970, p. 33).

Alexander Bishop of Alexandria. (A.D. 273-326.) Friend and patron of *Athanasius and master-mind of the Council of Nicaea. Alexander was appointed successor to Achillas, as Bishop of Alexandria, about A.D. 312. His virtues, which Eusebius passed over entirely without mention, other ecclesiastical writers greatly extolled. (See Sozomen, *Hist. Eccl.*, bk 1 ch. 15. See also Hefele, *Histoire des conciles*, 1.1. bk 2, p. 352, citing *PG* LXVII, col. 906.) He was the first to condemn Arius, and taking his stand upon passages of Holy Scripture, as Theodoret remarks (*H.E.*, i. 2), he taught that the Son of God was of one and the same with the Father, and had the same substance with the Father who begat Him. Having failed to persuade Arius from his heresy, he assembled a first and then a second synod of the bishops of Egypt to degrade him from the order of the priesthood and cut him off from the communion of the Church. This proving ineffectual, the Council of Nicaea was convened, in which he was finally condemned. Alexander died shortly after the holding of the council. (*Ante-Nicene Fathers*, ed. Alexander Roberts and James Donaldson, 10 vols. Peabody, MA.: Hendrickson Publishers, 1994, vol. 6, introd.).

Ambarvalia (misspelt **Ambervalia**): Probably derived from the Roman *Terminalia* and *Ambarvalia,* which were festivals in honour of the god Terminus, and the goddess Ceres. In England and the Isle of Man, the festival involved a perambulation of the boundaries of the parishes, an ancient custom which took place in the week before Ascension Day. In Catholic times, this perambulation was a matter of great ceremony, and banners, hand bells, and lights enlivened the procession. In Elizabeth I's reign it was ordained that the people should, once in a year, make a circuit of the parish with the curate, who was to admonish the people to give thanks to God, as they beheld his benefits, and for the increase and abundance of the fruits of the earth. (A W. Moore, *Folklore of the Isle of Man*, 1891, facsimile reprint, Llanerch Publishers, 1994, chapter 6).

Anabaptist, a term used to describe various groups throughout 16th century Europe who refused to allow their children to be baptized in the normal way, reinstituting instead 'the baptism of believers'. Although present in England from the 16th century, Anabaptist views were principally confined to refugees from the Low Countries. *Luther and Calvin vigorously denounced the Anabaptists who were severely persecuted by both Roman Catholics and Protestants. (*The Oxford Dictionary of the Christian Church*).

Anastasius I, Emperor (491-518). After the death of the Monophysite Isaurian Emperor Zeno, a barbarian, the people insisted an orthodox Emperor be elected. A high ranking courtier, Anastasius, who had proved a capable administrator in the treasury, was elected emperor. Upon taking the throne, Anastasius formally proclaimed his orthodoxy, despite his monophysite convictions, but as his reign developed his personal inclinations became clear, causing civil unrest and numerous revolts in which even the army participated. Vitalian, for instance, the leader of the army in Thrace from 513 led three major revolts that took the army and fleet to the very walls of Constantinople. Vitalian's near success was because he represented orthodox belief rising against a monophysite emperor.

Anastasius of Sinai (Anastasius Sinaita), Saint, born in Alexandria, was a seventh century Greek ecclesiastical writer and abbot of the monastery of Mt. Sinai. He was known as 'the new Moses' because of his opposition to the Monophysites, Monothelites, and Jews. His principal work, the *Hodegos*, or 'Guide', written in defense of the Catholic Faith, was a popular manual of controversy among the medieval Greeks.
http://en.wikipedia.org/wiki/Anastasius_Sinaita

Arcadius, Emperor of the East, 383-408, the elder son of Theodosius I, was almost as inept as his brother, and his domain was ruled by ministers against whom Claudian inveighed (*OCD*, 1970, p. 94).

Archimedes, c. 240 BC, is famous for the boast: 'Give me place to stand on and I will move the earth' (see Plut. *Marcellus* 14-19). In addition he constructed two *sphaerae*, a planetarium and a star globe, taken to Rome (see Cicero, *Republic* 1.21.2). His tomb was decorated with a cylinder circumscribing a sphere with the ratio 3/2, which he had discovered (Plut. *Marc.* 17; Cicero, *Tusculans*, 5.64-6); for extant works on the sphere and cylinder, see *The Quadrature of the Parabola* and *On the Heptagon in a Circle*.) Archimedes expressed his mathematical genius in every day language promoting the distribution of knowledge in a way that attracted Plato's condemnation – it was put to practical use by Hiero II, the tyrant of Syracuse, in fact, Plato's pupil.
Eudoxus and Archytas, who were the originators of the now celebrated and highly prized art of mechanics, used it with great ingenuity to illustrate geometrical theorems, and to support by means of mechanical demonstrations easily grasped by the senses propositions which are too intricate for proof by word or diagram. Plato was indignant at these developments, and attacked both men for having corrupted and destroyed the ideal purity of geometry. He complained that they had caused her to forsake the realm of disembodied and abstract thought for that of material objects, and to employ instruments which required much base and manual labour.

Arianism. See *Arius.

Aristotle (384-322 BC) born at Stagyra in Chalcidice, was the son of the physician to Philip of Macedon. In 343-342 Philip invited Aristotle to Pella as his son, Alexander's, tutor. In Athens Aristotle taught in the Peripatos, a covered court which lent its name to his school. Renaissance humanist views of Aristotle, which Hobbes tends to echo, distinguished between the authentic Aristotle and the Aristotle of the Schools. For instance, Leonardo Bruni and Guarino Veronese, both teachers of Lorenzo Valla (and the former a translator of Aristotle), believed that Aristotle (in the words of the latter) stripped of his medieval barbarisms, was eloquent, compared with the 'rough, uncouth, shaggy' Aristotle of the Schools. See Sarah Gravelle, 'Lorenzo Valla's Comparison of Latin and Greek' p. 275, citing Guarino, *Epistolario*, vol. I, p. 17. See also Hobbes's Preface to the Reader of his translation of Thucydides (*EW* vol. VIII, p. vii), where he declares: 'It hath been noted by divers, that Homer in poesy, Aristotle in philosophy, Demosthenes in eloquence, and others of the ancients in other knowledge, do still maintain their primacy'.

Arius (AD 260-336), the most important of the early Christian heretics, probably a Libyan by birth and the disciple of Lucian, presbyter of Antioch, became himself presbyter at Alexandria. Somewhere between 319 and 323 he began to promote a 'subordinationist' doctrine of the persons of Christ in the Trinity, a theological position with which Hobbes was associated in the 1660s. Arius, who was condemned at the Council of Nicaea (AD 325), is accused by Hobbes of sedition and insubordination, but not of heresy. He was rehabilitated in 335 by Bishop Eusebius of Nicomedia, sympathetic to his views, but died soon after. Of his extant writings the most important are three letters. In 320 AD, while in Nicomedia in Asia Minor, Arius wrote his *Letter to Alexander of Alexandria* in which he presents a summary of his views. About the same time, Arius wrote *The Banquet* (or the *Thalia*), a popularized version of his theology, only fragments of which now survive, mostly in the form of quotations in the writings of Athanasius (*OCD*. See also Sozomen, *Hist. Eccl.* chs 29-31, ed. Bidet, pp. 363-71.) Arius was also a figure for the rhetoricians. Hilary accused him of mixing true and false, light and shadows (see Hilary, *Ad Constantium Augustum*, *PL* X. col. 558), while Epiphanius, Bishop of Salamis, whom Hobbes cites in the 1688 Appendix to the Latin *Leviathan*, §88, accused the Arians as Neo-aristotelians (*Haeres. PG* XLII, cols 189-202). For a general discussion of Arius in the patristic sources, see Hilary *Contra Arianos Auxentium*, *PG* X, cols 609-618; see also Hefele, *Histoire des conciles*, 1.1.2, pp. 349-363. On the Arian heresy see Manlio Simonetti's definitive, *La crisi ariana nel IV secolo* (Rome, 1975).

Athanasius (c. 295-373), anti-Arian archbishop of Alexandria in the reign of Constantine was famed as the originator of the Athanasian Creed. In the last decade of his life he developed the doctrine of the deity and personality of the Holy Spirit (*OCD*, 1970 edn, pp. 137-8). See Athanasius, *Apologia contra arianos* (*PG* XXVI). One of the best accounts of Athanasius and the Arians is to be found in Sozomen's fifth century *Historia Ecclesiastica*, bks 1-6 (ed. J. Bidez, tr. A. J. Festugiere, Paris Editions du Cerf, 1983). See also Charles Kannengiesser, ed., *Politique et Théologie chez Athanase d'Alexandrie* (Paris, Beauchesne, 1974).

John Aubrey (1626-1697) English antiquary and writer, best known as the author of *Brief Lives*, was born near Malmesbury, Wiltshire, and educated at the Malmesbury grammar school under Robert Latimer, attended also by Hobbes, whom he first met there. He entered Trinity College, Oxford, in 1642, but his studies were interrupted by the English Civil War. In 1646 he became a student of the Middle Temple, but was never called to the bar, and played no active part in politics, but from his description of a meeting of the Rotary Club, founded by James Harrington (author of *Oceana*), he appears to have had republican beliefs. In 1663 Aubrey became a member of the Royal Society, and in 1667 he came to know Anthony Wood at Oxford, assisting him with the collection of materials for his *Athenae Oxonienses*. In 1680 he began to promise the work 'Minutes for Lives', which Wood was to use at his discretion. Collating as much information as he could, hear-say but also material evidence, he left the task of verification largely to Wood. His papers included: *Architectonica Sacra* (notes on ecclesiastical antiquities) and the 'Life of Mr Thomas Hobbes of Malmesbury', which served as the basis for Dr. Blackburn's Latin life, and also for Wood's account. His survey of Surrey was incorporated in R Rawlinson's *Natural History and Antiquities of Surrey* (1719); his antiquarian notes on Wiltshire were printed in Wiltshire: *the Topographical Collections*, corrected and enlarged by J. E. Jackson (Devizes: Henry Bull, 1862); part of another manuscript, on *The Natural History of Wiltshire*, was printed by John Britton in 1847 for the Wiltshire Topographical Society; the *Miscellanies* were edited in 1890 for the Library of Old Authors; the 'Minutes for Lives' were partially edited in

1813. A complete transcript, *Brief Lives chiefly of Contemporaries set down John Aubrey between the Years 1669 and 1696*, was edited for the Clarendon Press in 1898 by the Rev. Andrew Clark from manuscripts in the Bodleian Library, Oxford.

B

Bachanalia was the Latin term for the Greek *orgia*, a festival which had a specific club identity. The *Bacchanales* was a club in Rome, which broke the rule of voluntary membership. In 186 BC the government intervened to control membership of this troublesome club because of a crime wave. Livy 39.8-18 gives an account of the episode (*OCD*, 1965, pp. 157, 255-6).

Becket, Thomas (1118-1170), Saint, Archbishop of Canterbury, Chancellor of Henry II, whose martyrdom, ordered by the king, is celebrated on December 29. The case of Becket was one of three salient cases of Papal intervention in the affairs of England, as listed in the epic and poetic chronicle of Thomas May, Hobbes's contemporary, *The Reigne of King Henry the Second, Written in Seaven Bookes, by his Majesties Command* (1633).

Behemoth. Hobbes refers to the old meaning of the terms, *Leviathan* and *Behemoth*, from the Isaiah and the Book of Job, to connote despotism, in the case of *Leviathan*, his absolutist state, and in the case of *Behemoth*, the anarchy of Babel, or rule by parliament. See Springborg, 'Hobbes' Biblical Beasts: Leviathan and Behemoth', *Political Theory*, XXIII, 2 (1995), 353-75.

Belisarius (AD c. 505-565), one of Justinian's most famous generals, known for his fiery military zeal rather than his skill, was associated with Tacitus' stereotype of the German. Although born in Germania, as his name indicates, he was probably of Slavic origin. He succeeded in battle against the Persians, the Vandals in Africa and drove the Ostrogoths out of Italy in 540. The latter campaign was nevertheless widely condemned as a waste of imperial funds and effort for small reward. Belasarius, after his victory over the Persians, returned to Constantinople in AD 530, marrying Antonina, a scheming friend of the Empress Theodora, the latter advising him on how to handle popes. Whenever Belisarius fell out of favour with the imperial couple, Antonina usually succeeded in extricating him (*Encyclopaedia Britannica*, 11th edn, 1910-11, vol. 3, pp. 682-3; and vol. 26, pp. 764-5).

Bennet, Henry, Lord Arlington (1618-85), English statesman, fought for the royalists in the English civil war and, after going into exile, served as an envoy in Spain for the future Charles II. After the Restoration, Charles made him a secretary of state (1662), and he became one of the king's closest advisers, and a member of the Cabal. Informed of the king's secret agreement with Louis XIV in the Treaty of Dover (1670), he seems also to have encouraged Charles in promulgating the Declaration of Indulgence (1672) and in instigating the third Dutch War. He was made earl of Arlington in 1672. Impeached (1674) for corruption, betrayal of trust, and pro-Catholic activities, he was acquitted, resigned, and became lord chamberlain (1674). (*Columbia Encyclopedia*, 6th edn, 2001, on-line at http://www.bartleby.com/65/ar/ArlingHB.html).

Boreas, One of the four winds: Euris, the East-wind, Zephyrus, the West-wind, Auster, the South-wind, Boreas, the North-wind. Afer, or African wind, might be coming from anywhere between W-SW and E-SE. See *Hist ecc.* line 2196 on 'Frigidus Eurus, Afer, Vesperus, & Boreas'.

Bouleuterion (Gr.) council-house, council-board. The *boule*, council of nobles, later steering committee of the *ecclesia*, selected according to a tribal roster, and without which Athenian democracy could never have functioned, usually met in the *bouleuterion*.

Thomas Bradwardine (c. 1290-1349) Archbishop of Canterbury, theologian, and mathematician. Bradwardine studied at Merton College, Oxford, and became a proctor there. About 1335 he moved to London, and in 1337 he was made chancellor of St. Paul's Cathedral. He became a royal chaplain and confessor to King Edward III. In 1349 he was made archbishop of Canterbury but died soon after of the plague. (*Encyclopedia Britannica*, on-line version).

C

Centaurs and the **Lapiths**: 'Allusion to the conflict that developed between them during the marriage of Peirithous, king of the Lapiths, to which the Centaurs had been invited. See *Il.* 1.263, 2.742, *Od.* 21.295ff.' (Invernizzi note.)

Charlemagne, (Charles the Great, or Charles I), 742?-814, was emperor of the West (800-814), as well as Carolingian king of the Franks (768-814). Elder son of Pepin the Short and Charles Martel, Charlemagne found common cause with the papacy under Adrian I against the Lombards in 773, and in 799 came to the aid of the new pope Leo III, whom the Romans threatened to depose. When on Christmas day 800 Leo crowned Charlemagne Emperor, he sealed the split between the Western (Roman) and Eastern (Byzantine) Empires.

Edward Lord Herbert of Cherbury (1583-1648), who could fairly be said to be the first British Deist, was a friend of Grotius, Casaubon, and Gassendi, and during a long sojourn in France made himself acquainted with the thought of Montaigne, of Bodin, and especially of Charron. He believed in the so-called 'Five Articles' of the English Deists, 1) in the existence of the Deity, (2) the obligation to reverence such a power, (3) the identification of worship with practical morality, (4) the obligation to repent of sin and to abandon it, and, (5) divine recompense in this world and the next. These five essentials were said to constitute the nucleus of all religions and of Christianity in its primitive, uncorrupted form, and clearly Cherbury, Hobbes's friend and mentor, greatly influenced him.

Childeric III, King of the Franks 743-751, was chosen in 743 by the Frankish nobles to act as a Merovingian puppet. But in 750 Pepin III, who was a growing force, sought permission from Pope Zachary to take the Frankish throne, whereupon the Pope deposed Childeric and Pepin II became the first non-Merovingian King of the Franks in 300 years, and founder of the Carolingian dynasty.

Circe (Gr. *Kirkei*) (Homer *Od.* 10.210 ff.; Virg. *Aen*, 7.19-20), goddess of the fabulous island of Aeaea, in Italy later identified with the geographical point of *Circeii* (the southernmost point of Latium). Famed for her magic, her house was surrounded by men metamorphized as beasts. She changes Odysseus's men into swine, but he escapes by consuming the herb *moli*, compelling her to restore his men to human form, upon which he spends an idyllic year with her until he elicits directions home (*OCD*, 1965, p. 242).

(Cooper's *Thesaurus*):

> The daughter of Sol by Persis the daughter of Oceanus: she knewe the mervailous operations of sundry herbes, and howe to cure all poysons. At the laste she slewe hir husbande, kyng of Scythes, with poyson and bered the people with much tyranny: wherefore she was expelled the countrie, and fled into a deserte yle in the Occean sea. Homere nameth hir the sister of Aeta and sheweth how diuers of Ulisses compaignions arryvyng in the yle where Circe diuelled, were by hir transformed into swyne. And after by the intercession of Ulisses, she restored them to their pristinete fourme, more beautiful and yonge in syght than they weare before.

Constans I, Flavius Julius Constans (320-350), Roman Emperor, who ruled from 337-350, was the third and youngest son of Constantine I and Fausta, Constantine's second wife. Emperor of Italy, Africa and Illyricum, he shared the principate of the West with Constantine II, whom he defeated and killed in 340 to become sole ruler of the West. The last Roman Emperor to visit Britain (343), he was overthrown and killed in Gaul by the nominal Christian Magnentius in 350 (*OCD*, 1970, p. 279).

Constans II, (630-668) was Byzantine emperor from 641 to 668. Under Constans, the Byzantines completely withdrew from Egypt in 642, and the Arab Caliphate launched numerous attacks on the islands of the Mediterranean Sea and Aegean Sea. A Byzantine fleet under the admiral Manuel occupied Alexandria again in 645, but after an Arab victory the following year this had to be abandoned. The situation was complicated by the violent opposition to Monothelitism by the clergy in the west, and the related rebellion of the exarch of Carthage, Gregory. The latter fell in battle against the Arabs, but imperial rule was only restored by paying off the invaders. Constans attempted to steer a middle line in the church dispute between Orthodoxy and Monothelitism, by refusing to persecute either and prohibiting further discussion of the natures of Jesus Christ by decree in 648. But Pope Martin I condemned both Monothelitism and Constans' attempt at a compromise, whereupon the emperor ordered his exarch of Ravenna to arrest the pope, who was brought to Constantinople and condemned as a criminal, ultimately being exiled to Cherson, where he died in 655. Although on friendly terms with Pope Vitalian (657-672), Martin's successor, Constans stripped buildings, including the Pantheon, of their ornaments and bronze to be carried back to Constantinople, and declared the Pope of Rome to have no jurisdiction over the Archbishop of Ravenna. Constans, increasingly fearful that his younger brother, Theodosius, could oust him from the throne, had him killed in 660. Constans' sons Constantine, Heraclius, and Tiberius had been associated on the throne since the 650s and, Constans having personally attracted the hatred of citizens of Constantinople, decided to leave the capital to their rule and to move to Syracuse in Sicily. See Charles Pietri, 'La politique de Constance II: Un premier "cesaropapisme" ou l'*imitatio Constantini*?', in *L'Église et l'Empire au IVe siècle*, ed. Albrecht Dihle (Geneva: Fondation Hardt, 1989), pp. 113-172.

Constantine the Great, Roman Emperor c. AD 285-337, was son of Constantius Chlorus, or Constantius I, who became emperor of the West on the abdication of Diocletian in AD 305, and his concubine Helena. Constantine joined his father in the battle against the Picts in Britain in 306 and succeeded to the imperium when Constantius was killed at York. Constantine, who dreamed at the Mulvian Bridge that he would conquer in the sign of the cross, was reponsible for the conversion of the Empire to Christianity in AD 312, concluding victory over the Goths on the Danube in 332 (*OCD*, 1970, pp. 280-1).

Constantine II, Flavius Claudius Constantinus (c. AD 316-340), was the first son of Constantine I and Fausta and, like his brothers, raised as a Christian. He was made a Caesar on 1 March 317 and was involved in military expeditions at an early age. For instance, in 323, he seems to have taken part in Constantine I's campaigns against the Sarmatians. In 326, he was nominally put in command of Gaul at the age of 10. Constantine II's generals apparently won a victory over the Alamanni, since the title *Alamannicus* appears on his inscriptions from the year 330. In 332 he was Constantine I's field commander during the latter's campaign against the Goths. In the years before his father's death in 337, he held court in Gaul, but thereafter Constantine's new realm included Britain, Gaul, and Spain. Upon his accession, he freed the Trinitarian Bishop Athanasius from his exile and allowed him to return to Alexandria. But whether Constantine II was motivated by sincere Trinitarian belief (popular in his realm) or whether he wanted to cause problems for his brother Constantius II is unclear. In 340 Constantine II, in an attempt to seize some of his brother Constans' realm, was killed by him in a battle fought near Aquileia.

Constantius II, Flavius Iulius Constantius (318-361), Roman Emperor, AD 337-61, was the second son of Constantine the Great, ruler of the East. When Constantine died in 337, Constantius II led the massacre of his relatives descended from the second marriage of his grandfather Constantius Chlorus and Theodora, leaving himself, his older brother Constantine II, his younger brother Constans and two cousins (Gallus and his half-brother Julian) as the only surviving males related to Constantine. The three brothers divided the Roman Empire among them, according to their father's will. Constantine II received Britannia, Gaul and Hispania; Constans ruled Italia, Africa, and Illyricum; and Constantius ruled the East. As Eastern Emperor he was sympathetic to the Arian party, whereas Constans I, Western Emperor, was sympathetic to the Nicene party. Constantius died in 361, while moving to suppress the rebellion in Paris of Julian, whose father he had slain (*OCD*, 1970, 282). See Hilary, *Contra Constantium Imperatorem*, PL X, col. 577-606 on the persecutions of Constantius, who was raised and lived in Antioch, the great centre of Arianism. See also W.H.C. Frend, 'The Church in the Reign of Constantius II (337-361)', in *L'Église et l'Empire au IVe siècle*, ed. Albrecht Dihle (Geneva: Fondation Hardt, 1989), pp. 73-111.

Corinth: *Corinthus* (Cooper):
a famous, riche and greate citie in Achaia, sytuated in the narrowe streicte enterynge into Peloponnesus now called Morea. By reason of the commodious sytuation for resorte of marchaundice out of all countreys, it was the greattest marte towne in all the worlde, and thereby rose to so great wealth and power, that the Romaines began to suspecte and scare them. Wherefore, on a tyme when with proude woordes they abused the Romaine ambassadours, or (as Strabo writeth) cast uryne on theyr heades as they passed through the citie, the Romaines takinge therwith greate displeasure, sent theyr capitaine Mummius against them, who besieged the citie, and within shorte space so destroyed it, that scantly any token of so noble a citie, within fewe yeares remayned. In the burnyng of it, so many ryche & costly ymages, of sundry sortes of metall were melted, that thereof, after was founde a kynde of precious brasse called Aes Corinthium, whiche longe tyme after was had in great estimation.

Council of Chalcedon, AD 451, was convoked by Marcian (Emperor, 450-7 AD), by prior agreement with Pope Leo the Great. This council finally settled the doctrine of hypostatic union, maintaining the real and personal unity of Christ as one person with two distinct natures, human and divine, as affirmed at the first Council of Ephesus. The council was assembled to repudiate the ideas of Eutyches on Christ's divine nature subsuming the human; it also rejected the Monophysite doctrine that Christ had only one nature, and repudiated Nestorianism. It reached a compromise definition of the nature of the son of God intended to satisfy all factions: Christ was one person in two natures, united 'unconfusedly, unchangeably, indivisibly, inseparably'.

Council of Constantinople. Convened in 381, this council, the Second General Church Council, was called by Emperor Theodosius to provide for a Catholic succession in the patriarchal See of Constantinople, to confirm the Nicene Faith, to reconcile the semi-Arians with the Church, and to put an end to the Macedonian heresy. Originally it was only a council of the Orient; the arguments of Baronius to prove that it was called by Pope Damasus are invalid (Hefele-Leclercq, *Hist. des Conciles*, Paris, 1908, II, 4). It was attended by 150 Catholic and 36 heretical (Semi-Arian, Macedonian) bishops, and was presided over by

Meletius of Antioch; and after his death, by the successive Patriarchs of Constantinople, St. Gregory Nazianzen and Nectarius.

Council of Ephesus. The third ecumenical council, convened in AD
431, was summoned at the instigation of Nestorius, who had been
condemned in a council at Rome in August 430, and requested
the emperor Theodosius II to summon it. Theodosius, together
with his co-emperor Valentinian III and with the agreement of
Pope Celestine I, in November 430 requested all those who had
been summoned to be present at Ephesus on 7 June 431. On
22 June, however, before the arrival either of the Roman legates
or the eastern bishops led by John of Antioch, Cyril of Alexandria
ordered the council to commence. Nestorius was summoned
three times but did not come. His teaching was examined and
judgment passed upon it, which 197 bishops subscribed at once
and others later accepted. When, shortly afterwards John of
Antioch and the easterners arrived: they refused communion
with Cyril and set up another Council. The Roman legates (the
bishops Arcadius and Projectus and the priest Philip), on arriving, joined Cyril and confirmed the sentence against Nestorius.
Then the council in its fifth session on 17 July excommunicated
John of Antioch and his party.

Council of Nicaea (Nicene Council), convened in AD 325, was the
first general council of the Church Fathers of the Roman World.
(see Hefele, 1.1.2, p. 352, citing Athanasius, *De decretis Nicaenae synodi, PG* XXV, col. 417ff.). Documentation for the Nicene
Council is significantly lacking. All that remains are the Creed,
the twenty canons and the synodal decree, and the narratives that
use eye-witness accounts, notably those of Athanasius (*Epistola
ad Afros, PG* XXVI, cols 452-1045), Socrates of Constantinople
(*Hist. Eccl.* 1. ch. 8, *PG* LXVII, col. 345 ff.), Sozomen (*Hist.
Eccl.* 1.17), and Eusebius of Caesarea (*Vit. Const., PG* XX, col.
1060ff.). Among these eyewitnesses, Eusebius attended as a
bishop, while Athanasius was called before the Council (see
Hefele, ch. 2, pp. 386-94, esp. 392). Hobbes's contemporary and
friend, John Selden, in his *Eutychii Aegyptii, patriarchae orthodoxorum Alexandrini. . . . ecclesiae suae origines* (London,
1642), p. 71, actually gives a list of the attendants at the Nicene

Council translated from a later Arabic commentary (see Hefele, 1.1.2. pp. 409, 449). Invernizzi notes: 'Hobbes's narrative of the Council's deliberations does not depart much from what has been handed down by tradition. That Constantine had spurred the Fathers to find a common accord and that he had burned before the Council the *libelli*, are facts also recorded by Rufinus, *Hist. Eccl.*, *PL*, vol. 21, cols. 468ff. See also the works of Sozomen and Socrates, which derive in large measure from Rufinus.'

Cyril of Alexandria (d. AD 444) engaged in a long struggle with the Nestorians that culminated in the deposition of Nestorius at the Council of Ephesus of 431. The resulting schism between Antioch and Alexandria was only conciliated by Cyril's cautious concessions in AD 433. Thereupon the struggle with the Monophysites began and in their battle with the defenders of 'two-natured' Christology at the Council of Chalecedon of 451, both sides appealed to Cyril's statements, the interpretation of which became an issue for theological debate in Justinian's reign (*OCD*, 1970, 308).

D

Duns Scotus, (d. 1308), known as the Subtle Doctor (*Doctor Subtilis*), a Scottish-born Fransiscan and theologian who taught for some time at Oxford (c. 1300), graduated from the University of Paris (c. 1304) and was Professor at the University of Cologne, where he died. Scotus was the author of many works, a complete edition of which was published in 1639 in 12 folio volumes by Wadding at Lyons; this, however, included the commentaries of the Scotists, Lychetus, Poncius, Cavellus, and Hiquæus. A reprint of Wadding's edition, with the treatise *De perfectione statuum* added, appeared in 1891-95 at Paris (Vives) in 26 vols. The printed writings deal with grammatical and scientific, philosophical and theological subjects. His commentaries and *quæstiones* on various works of Aristotle are of a purely philosophical nature. But the principal work of Scotus is the so-called *Opus Oxoniense*, i.e. the great commentary on the *Sentences* of Peter Lombard, written in Oxford (vols. VIII-XXI). It is primarily a theological work, but contains many digressions, on logical,

metaphysical, grammatical, and scientific topics, so that nearly
his whole system of philosophy can be derived from this work.
(*Catholic Encyclopaedia*).

E

Ephemerides, diaries, a term particularly designating the royal
journal of Alexander the Great kept by Eumenes of Cardia providing information about Alexander's daily life. (*OCD*, 1970 edn,
386-7).

Epicurus (BC 342-270), moral and natural philosopher, born at
Samos, died at Athens. Although a disciple of Aristippus, Epicu-
rus does not appear to have deserved the odium attached to his
name by Jerome and many others. See Zeller's *Socrates and the
Socratic Schools* (Reichel's translation), second edn, p. 337 ff.
The Epicurean school in Athens included a group that lived in
seclusion on Epicurus' property, avoiding politics and following
the simple life. The company included slaves and women.
Although only fragments of Epicurus have survived, Diogenes
Laertius testifies to his being a prolific writer. Cavendish refers to
Gassendi's *Life of Epicurus* and *Animadversions on the Ten
Books of Diogenes Laertius* published in 1649, to which Hobbes
had access in Paris, as they were being written.

Epiphanius, Bishop of Salamis, born c. 310-20 in Eleutheropolis
in Palestine, died 402. He studied in Egypt before joining an
order of monks in the desert devoted to Athanasius and hostile
to Origen, who was seen as a forerunner of Arius. Epiphanius
entered the debate between Theophilus of Alexandria and John
Chrysostom as an opponent of Origenism. He returned to Palestine and founded a monastery, of which he was ordained Presbyter. Around 366 he was elected Bishop of Constantia
(Salamis), possibly because as an ardent supporter of Nicene
doctrine, life would have proved too difficult under the jurisdiction of the *homoiousian* Bishop Eutychius of Eleutheropolis.
Epiphanius is famous for his *Panarion*, or Medicine chest of
antidotes to the poisons of the sects, composed 374-376 at the
request of the Syrian abbots Paul and Acacius. He treats some

80 sects, a term he uses flexibly to cover both formally organized groups like the Manicheans, as well as schools of philosophy, tendencies of thought, or more general religious classifications. See the list, which includes Barbarism (24), Scythism
(26), Hellenism (28), Judaism (30), Stoics (33), Platonists (34),
Pythagoreans (35), Epicureans (36), Samaritans (42), Hemer-
obaptists (53), etc. See the Forward to the *Panarion of St.*
Epiphanius, Bishop of Salamis, Selected Passages, ed. Philip
R. Amidon, S.J. (Oxford 1990). and *The Panarion of Epipha-*
nius of Salamis. (Books 2 & 3, Sects 47-80, *De Fide*), Frank
Williams, ed. (Leiden 1994). Hobbes mentions Epiphanius as
the author of a work *On the Trinity* in the 1668 Appendix to the
Latin *Leviathan*, §88, undoubtedly referring to his earliest work
against heresy, the *Ancoratus*, or *The Well-Anchored*, of AD
374, which defends the dogmas of the Trinity and the Resurrection against the Arians and the Origenists.

Episcopalian. The name of a form of church organization which
means literally, government by an overseer, from the Greek word
episcopos, meaning overseer, bishop. Used of the established
Anglican Church and particularly of its American counterpart.
(OED).

Ergamenes, king of the Ethiopians in the reign of Ptolemy II
Philadelphus (BC 285-46), had been educated in Greece. Diodorus
Siculus tells the story of a Meroïtic ruler named Ergamenes
who was ordered by the priests to kill himself, but broke tradition and had the priests executed instead (c.f. Diodorus, 3.6.3.).
Some historians think Ergamenes refers to Arrakkamani, the first
ruler to be buried at Meroë, in Upper Egypt. However, a more
likely transliteration of Ergamenes is Argamani, a later king.
http://209.85.135.104/search?q = cache:ASKQEAWtX5wJ:en.
wikipedia.org/wiki/Kush+Ergamenes&hl = en&ct = clnk&cd = 1

Ethiopians. People of Ethiopia. When, from 630 to 600 BC, Egypt
began to fall into the hands of Asia, and was conquered first by
the Assyrians and then by the Persians, the Ethiopian kings kept
their independence. Horsiatef (560-525 B.C.) made nine expeditions against the warlike tribes south of Meroë, and his successor,

Nastosenen (525-500 B.C.) repelled Cambyses. He also removed the capital from Nepata to Meröe, although Nepata continued to be the religious capital and the Ethiopian kings were still crowned on its golden throne. From the fifth to the second century B.C. we find Sudanese tribes pressing in from the west and Greek culture penetrating from the east. King Arg-Amen (Ergamenes) showed strong Greek influences and at the same time began to employ Ethiopian speech in writing and used a new Ethiopian alphabet.

Eusebius (AD 260-340), Bishop of Caesarea and a moderate supporter of Arius, was exonerated from heresy at the Council of Nicaea and later signed the Nicene Creed. He attended the Council of Tyre in 335, which condemned Athanasius. A close associate of Constantine, whose *Life* he may have authored, Eusebius belonged to the long line of Christian chronographers, composing an *Historia Ecclesiastica*, which gives an eyewitness account of the proceedings of the Nicene Council that Hobbes probably read. His school was that of Alexandrian Christian scholarship, particularly hostile to the Hellenistic Greek sects, retaining only those elements of classical philosophy compatible with Scripture, a view with which Hobbes concurs. (*OCD*, 1970 edn. pp. 423-4. See also Chestnut, *The First Christian Histories*, chs 3-6, and Trompf, *Early Christian Historiography*, Part 2.)

Eutyches c. 378-c. 452, Archimandrite in Constantinople. The view that Christ has but one nature after the Incarnation, known as Eutychianism, or the *Monophysite heresy, was named after him. Eutyches was a vehement opponent of Nestorianism, a heresy to which Dioscurus, successor to Cyril (d. 444) patriarch of Alexandria, subscribed. The Antiochian party led by Theodoret of Cyrus (Cyrrhus) and John of Antioch had also, for a time, championed the orthodoxy of Nestorius, but had eventually accepted the Council of Ephesus of 431, making peace with Cyril of Alexandria in 434. Whereas Cyril had agreed with the Antiochenes in 433 that Christ had two natures, Eutyches and Dioscurus insisted that Christ's humanity was absorbed in his divinity and that to accept two natures at all was Nestorian. When Theodoret attacked Eutychianism (447), Dioscurus retaliated by anathematizing him, and Emperor Theodosius II, who was friendly to Eutychianism, confined Theodoret to his diocese (448). But Eutyches was accused of heresy and deposed by a local synod called by Flavian, patriarch of Constantinople (448). Eutyches appealed to his friends, and Theodosius called a general council to meet at Ephesus, the famous Robber Synod (Latrocinium) of 449, which was a sham. Dioscurus presided and disenfranchised most of the clergy inimical to Eutyches. The council reinstated Eutyches, declared him orthodox, and deposed Flavian and Eutyches' accuser, Eusebius of Dorylaeum. Flavian denied the council's authority; and the papal legates denounced the council's proceedings. The soldiery, called in by Dioscurus, compelled an affirmative vote; Flavian was severely beaten by members of the so-called synod and died shortly thereafter. The legates barely escaped. Theodoret was deposed. After the death of Theodosius II (450) his orthodox successors convened the Council of Chalcedon to right the wrongs of the Robber Synod, Eutychianism was finished and Eutyches was deposed and exiled.

F

Fifth Monarchy Men. A Puritan sect which believed, on the basis of a prophecy in the Bible (*Daniel* 2), that Oliver Cromwell's rise to power was a preparation for the Second Coming of Christ and the establishment of the great fifth and last monarchy; the previous four being the Assyrian, the Persian, the Greek and the Roman. In disillusionment, they began to turn against Cromwell and, after the Restoration of the monarchy in 1660, tried to raise a rebellion in London. It was quickly suppressed and the leaders were executed. (*The Macmillan Encyclopedia*, 2001).

Figura Galenica, The Galenical figure in logic. See Reid's 1774, *Aristotle's Logics* iii. §2: 'It (the fourth figure of the syllogism) was added by the famous Galen, and is often called the Galenical', after Galen, an Egyptian physician (*OED*). Invernizzi notes of the called *figura galenica* that its legitimacy was often doubted in antiquity and in the modern epoch, and that Hobbes refers to it in *De Corpore, LW* 4.11.

G

Galileo Galilei (1564-1642) born in Pisa, pioneered the experimental scientific method, and was the first to use a refracting telescope to make important astronomical discoveries. In 1604, learning of the invention of the telescope in Holland, and from the barest description of it, he constructed a vastly superior model. With it he made a series of profound discoveries, including the moons of planet Jupiter and the phases of the planet Venus (similar to those of Earth's moon). As a professor of astronomy at University of Pisa, Galileo was required to teach the accepted Ptolemaic theory that the sun and all the planets revolved around the Earth. But later at the University of Padua he was exposed to a new theory, proposed by Nicolaus Copernicus, that the Earth and planets revolved around the sun. Galileo's observations with his new telescope convinced him of the truth of Copernicus's sun-centered or heliocentric theory. Hobbes is reputed to have met Galileo in 1636# and the Hobbes Correspondence# records Hobbes buying telescopes for Cavendish.

Pierre Gassendi (1592-1655) attended school at, and was later Principal of, the Catholic College of Digne from 1612 to 1614, having also studied philosophy and theology at the University of Aix where he later held a professorship (1617 to 1623). In 1645 he was appointed professor of mathematics at the Collège Royale in Paris. Gassendi had first met Mersenne in 1624 when he visited Paris, who tried to persuade him to give up mathematics and theology in favour of philosophy. As an atomist who defended a mechanistic system, Gassendi rejected the philosophy of Descartes, but was close to Hobbes. His first published work was *Exercitationes paradoxicae* (1624), his lecture course at Aix written up for publication. And in 1649 he published *Animadversiones*, a compilation of sources on Epicurus, but his magnum opus, the *Syntagma philosophicum*, was only published 3 years after his death in his *Opera Omnia* (Lyon, 1658). Gassendi made an important concession to Hobbes by including his famous aphorism, 'homo homini lupus' in his comment to Epicurus *Ratae sententiae* 33 late in the *Animadversions* to illustrate human aggressivity in the state of nature. See Gianni Paganini, 'Hobbes, Gassendi e la psicologia del meccanicismo', p. 438; a discovery made simultaneously by

Olivier Bloch in his 'Gassendi et la théorie politique de Hobbes';
in *Thomas Hobbes, Philosophie première, théorie de la science et
politique*, Actes du Colloque de Paris, ed. Yves Charles Zarka and
Jean Bernhardt (Paris 1990), p. 345. See also the seminal piece by
François Tricaud, '"Homo homini Deus", "Homo homini Lupus":
Recherche des Sources des deux formules de Hobbes', in *Hobbes-
Forschungen*, ed. R. Koselleck, and R. Schnur, (Berlin, 1969). In
the ethical part of the *Syntagma*, dating to the years 1645-6, after
the publication of the first edition of Hobbes's *De Cive* in 1642,
and before the second, which Gassendi helped his friend Samuel
Sorbière promote, Gassendi made transparent reference to Hobbes
on freedom in the state of nature (Gassendi, *Syntagma*, p. 755a-b,
cited in Paganini, 'Hobbes, Gassendi and the Tradition of Political
Epicureanism', p. 12).

Gehenna, for the Jews of the Christian era referred to the place of
the damned, hence, hell, in Tertullian, Prudentius, and the
Vulgate. See Parkhurst, *et. al. A Greek and English Lexicon to the
New Testament*, p. 104.

Germanic Tribes: Sporadic incursions by the Northern Germanic
tribes into the Roman Empire became a concerted movement
around AD 400, culminating in the battle of Adrianople, August
9, 378, where Valens, Arian Emperor of the East, fell in the field
and the Roman forces were wiped out (Ostrogorsky pp. 52-8).
The Byzantines negotiated skilfully with the Germans, but also
excluded them and the policy worked. The Germanic tribes were
repulsed by the Byzantine Empire, and floated into the Western
Empire (p. 55). Ostrogorsky notes that the handling of the Germanic tribes presaged future events. By this clever strategy the
eastern empire was soon free of Alaric, who withdrew with his
army to Italy, and after three attempts at investing Rome took the
city by storm in 410. While the east enjoyed its breathing space,
the Germanic tribes went on to France, where Attila and the Huns
were defeated at the battle of Catalaunian Fields in 451 by Aetius,
the Roman General of the West (Ostrogorsky, p. 57), who was
himself murdered in 454 while Valentinian III, the Emperor was
murdered in 455. At that point the Church, under the leadership
of Pope Leo the Great (440-61), provided the only order in the

Western Empire (Ostrogorsky, p. 458). Germanic tribes then went into Italy. See George Ostrogorsky, *History of the Byzantine State* (New Brunswick, N.J., rev. edn, 1969).

Goths, a Germanic people based in southern Scandinavia, who began moving into the Roman Empire at the beginning of the Christian era and were subsequently divided into different branches. Migrating to a region north of the Black Sea in AD 150-200, in 238 they began to raid the Roman Empire itself, by the mid-third century ravaging the provinces of Asia Minor and the Balkans. The Visigoths defeated and killed Valens at Adrianople in 378, while the Ostro-goths invaded Italy under the leadership of Theodoric the Great in 439. Under the leadership of Alaric, they devastated Greece and Italy, sacking Rome in 410, before continuing on to Gaul and Spain. See Ammianus Marcellinus, bk 27, ch 4, bk 31 chs 4-8, 12 and chs 15-16. (*OCD*, 1970, p. 472).

Gratian, Roman Emperor, AD 367-83, son of Valentinian I, spent most of his reign trying to defend Gaul against the Ostrogoths. A devout Catholic much influenced by St. Ambrose, he was the first emperor to omit the term Pontifex Maximus from his title. Over the protests of the eloquently pagan Symmachus, he commanded the removal of the statue of Victory from the Roman senate. In 383 he was overthrown and murdered at Lyons by Magnus Maximus, a Catholic Spaniard who was recognized as Roman Emperor of the West by Theodosius I (*OCD*, 1970 edn, pp. 476-7). Many of Gratian's decretals were incorporated into the canons of the Council of Laodicea, at Antioch AD 341, and the Council of Gangris in the middle of the fourth century (see Hefele, 1.2.6, p. 998 and 1029 ff.)

Gregory VII, Pope (Hildebrand) (c. 1020-1085). Born in Tuscany and educated in Rome, Hildebrand was chaplain to Pope Gregory VI, following him into exile in Germany when Henry III deposed the Pope. Recalled to Rome by Pope Leo IX to serve as treasurer of the Church, Hildebrand served as papal legate in various capacities before being elected pope himself in 1073 as Gregory VII. He immediately began to institute reforms against simony, clerical marriage and lay investiture (the appointment of bishops, abbots, and other church officials by feudal lords and vassals), declaring the papal supremacy in the encyclical *Dicatus papae* of the same year. The focus of Gregory's ecclesiastico-political projects was his relationship with Germany and the Emperor. Since the death of Henry III the strength of the German monarchy had been seriously weakened, and his son Henry IV had to contend with great internal difficulties. This state of affairs was of material assistance to the pope. Gregory's opposition to investiture led to conflict with the Emperor, who deposed Gregory at the Synod of Worms in 1076, to which Gregory retaliated by excommunicating Henry. The two men were reconciled in 1077 at Canossa, but quarrelled again in 1080. When Henry captured Rome in 1084, Robert Guiscard rescued the Pope, who later fled to Monte Cassino to escape a popular rebellion against Guiscard, dying the next year. Gregory VII was canonized in Hobbes's lifetime, by Pope Paul V in 1606.

H

Harpies, Harpyae (from Greek *'arpuiae*), mythical monsters, half woman, half bird; (*OCD*): supernatural winged beings apparently winds in origin, who 'snatch' as the name implies and carry off various persons and things. They have at the same time some characteristics of ghosts, and, as the ideas of wind and spirit are closely allied (c.f.the etymology of the words in Greek, Hebrew, Latin and other tongues), it is perhaps most correct to say that they are spirit-winds. See *Od.* 20.77, *Aen.* 3.210ff. Virgil emphasizes they are birds with women's faces, but classically they are shown as winged women. Autenrieth, see *Il.* 16.150, *Od.* 1.241, 'the horses of Achilles had Zephyrus [the wind] as sire and the Harpy Podarge as dam.'

Haruspex, a soothsayer, or diviner among the Etruscans, who foretold future events from the inspection of the entrails of victims, a practice they introduced to the Romans (Lewis & Short). Divination favoured the livers and gall bladders of sheep, changes in the shape of which were considered to be providential. The *Etrusca disciplina* interpreted three types of phenomena: the *exta* (the sheep innards); the *monstra* (or prodigies); and the *fulgura* (extraordinary meteorological events). Divination in all these cases required quasi-scientific measurement, and particularly in the third, which required measurement of the heavens, divided in 16 different zones. Emperor Claudius [*q.v.*] founded the college of *Haruspices*, who gradually encroached on the field of the augurs. The art was taken seriously up through AD 600 (*OCD*, 1970, 489, 912-13).

Heraclius, Eastern Roman emperor (610-641) who reorganized and strengthened the imperial administration and the imperial armies but who, nevertheless, lost Syria, Palestine, Egypt, and Byzantine Mesopotamia to the Arab Muslims.

Heruli, a Germanic people who in the sixth century still practiced human sacrifice. Expelled from Scandinavia by the Danes, they entered the Rhine and the Black Sea in the later third century, where in 267 they sacked Athens, Corinth, Sparta and Argos. Alaric was an Herule leader (*Pauly-Wissowa*, *OCD*, 1970, p. 510).

Hilary of Poitiers (315-367) participated in the controversy between Athanasius, who supported the doctrine of the identity of the three persons of the Trinity, and Arius, who supported the subordinationist position. As bishop of Poitiers he refused to sign a condemnation of Athanasius, with the consequence that the Arian emperor Constantius II (second son of Constantine) banished him to Phrygia in 357. His exile lasted three years, during which time he wrote several essays, including *On the Trinity*. Finally the Emperor was forced to send him back to Gaul because he was causing such difficulties for the Arians in the East. In 364, he journeyed to Milan, where he engaged in public debate with the Arian bishop Auxentius, converting him to orthodoxy.

Homer, eighth century BC, Ionian poet and reputed author of the *Iliad*, telling of the fall of Troy to an invading Mycenaean army around 1200 BC, and the *Odyssey*, telling of the wandering of Odysseus on the way back to Ithaca. Legend has it that he was blind, and that he visited Egypt to report of Thebes as the twelve gated city. (*OCD*)

Homoousion. In the 1668 Appendix to the Latin *Leviathan* §17 (tr. Wright, pp. 352), interlocutor A remarks: 'there follows then that great article, which brought so many disorders into the ancient church, so many banishments and killings: "of one substance with the Father, by whom all things were made"'. To which a interlocutor B replies (§18, p. 352), 'And utterly true it is, made manifest in St. John's clear words (John 1:1): "in the beginning was the Word, and the Word was with God, and the Word was God"; and, "all things were made through it"'. For the debate of the Nicene Council on *substantia, homoousios* and the *Logos*, in which Eusebius of Caesarea participated on the losing side ('he hoped to avoid the precision of the word *homoousios* and the strict definition of the doctrine of the Logos'), see Hefele, *Histoire des conciles*, 1.1.2, pp. 432-6, 440-1, citing Athanasius *Epist. de decret. syn. Nic., PG* XXV, col. 448; Theodoret, *Historia ecclesiastica* bk 1, ch. 12, *PG* LXXXII, col. 915; and Gelasius of Cyzicus, *Historia Concilii Nicaeni* bk 2, ch. 34, in J.D. Mansi, ed., *Sacrorum conciliorum nova et amplissima collectio*, 31 vols, Florence and Venice, 1759-98.

Homuncionistas, heretics who see Christ as a man and not a God (Blaise).

Honorius, 384-423, Roman Emperor, younger son of Theodosius I, was elevated to the rank of Augustus by his father in 383 and he became sole ruler of the West in 395, upon his father's death. However, Stilicho, Roman general and Theodosius's lieutenant, held effective power until 408, when he was beheaded at Honorius's behest. Under his reign Alaric besieged Rome several times between 408 and 410, while Honorius remained safely at Ravenna. Also on his watch, Spain was occupied by the Vandals and Goths in 409, and Britain was lost to the Empire (*OCD*, 1970, p. 526).

Huns, a nomadic pastoralist people of unknown origin, which appeared in south-eastern Europe around AD 370, moving into the Roman provinces in 376. Beginning in the fifth century they advanced into central Europe and propelled other barbarians into Italy and Gaul, ruled around 430 by Rua, and followed by Attila who ruled 434-53. (*OCD*, 1970, p. 533).

hypostasis (= Gr. *'upostasis*). substance, personality, hypostacy (Cod. Just. 1.1.6; Hier. [Jerome] *Ep. ad Damas*, 15.3.1), [Souter]. Substance, Person of the Trinity (Lewis & Short).

I

Independents. Members of the system of ecclesiastical polity in which each local congregation is believed to be a church independent of any external authority. The term independency prevailed in England in the seventeenth century, but was not favoured in New England, where the term for the same movement was Congregationalism (*OED*, 1989 edn, vol. 7, p. 848).

Innocent I, Pope (reigned 401-17), was appointed successor to Anastasius and his reign saw Alaric's assault on Rome. When in 408 Emperor Honorius had Stilicho, his able general, killed on suspicion of treason, Alaric took his chance and, although failing to take the city, his men blockaded it and ravaged the region, withdrawing to Tuscany only when bribed. Alaric continued to press on demanding from Honorius Dalmatia, Venetia, and Noricum, plus tribute. To save Rome from another attack, Pope Innocent personally went with an embassy from Rome to the imperial court at Ravenna. Honorius, safe himself, treated with Alaric, who once more marched on Rome, and was once more repulsed. But on a third attempt, traitors opened the Salarian gate and the Goths poured into the helpless city. For five days the barbarians burned and plundered. Innocent returned from Ravenna. Honorius, politically intransigent, was more cooperative in ecclesiastical matters. While the Emperor took steps against heretics, the Pope worked hard to maintain discipline. He issued decretals to Bishop Victricius in Gaul and to the Spanish bishops, as well as approving degrees issued by councils in Jerusalem and Africa condemning a new heresy, Pelagianism. He intervened in Constantinople on behalf of the deposed John Chrysostom, whom the patriarch of Alexandria, intriguing with the weak Emperor Arcadius, had driven from his see.

J

Jews. Three expulsions of the Jews from Rome are recorded, in 139 BC, AD 19 and during Claudius' principate. Each time the Jews seem to have been actively proselytizing, although disorders may also have been provoked by the Christians in Claudius' day.

Hadrian banned circumcision. Anti-Semitic literature, focusing on the exclusivity of the Jews as a sect had appeared from the third century BC, but Julius Caesar and Augustus had supported legislation to protect the civil rights of Jews throughout the empire, Judaism being established as a *religio licita* (See H.I. Bell, *Jews and Christians in Egypt*; H.J. Leon, 1960, *The Jews of Ancient Rome*). Hobbes refers to the Roman Emperors who expelled philosophers, especially Jews, implying that although kings drove them out (reading for king, Roman emperor), the people insisted in bringing them back in.

Jovian, AD c. 331-364, Roman Emperor 363-4. Upon elevation to the imperium he negotiated an unpopular peace with the Persians, whereby he surrendered all the territory previously won by Diocletian, as well as the cities of Nisibis and Singara. A devout Catholic, he died before reaching Constantinople (*OCD*, 1970, 565-6).

Julian, Roman Emperor, AD 332-63, termed 'the Apostate', was acclaimed emperor in 360, proclaiming tolerance for all religions, although himself a pagan and a dedicated and ascetic Neoplatonist monotheist. He instituted wide-ranging bureaucratic and economic reforms but died fighting the Persians in 363. Among his surviving works, the *Misopogon* is a satirical defence of his actions in Antioch, preparatory to his final Persian campaign; while the *Convivium* or *Caesares*, was a comic account of Constantine's reception on Olympus (*OCD*, 1970, 567-8).

Justin, Emperor AD 450-527, was born a peasant in Asia, became commander of the imperial guards of Emperor Anastasius, on whose death he assumed the government in AD 518. Known for his religious orthodoxy, his sister was mother of the later Justinian, whose career he promoted, and whom he made co-emperor on April 1, AD 527. Together they are credited with reconciling the Eastern and Western Churches in 519. Beginning a war with the Persians in 522, Justin allied himself with the Arabs, in addition, ceding the right of naming Consuls to Theodoric, the Gothic king of Italy (*The New Schaff-Herzog Encyclopedia of Religious Knowledge*, New York: Funk & Wagnalls, 1908, vol. 6, p. 285).

Justinian (AD 483-565), Byzantine Emperor, famous for the *Codex Justinianus*. Born at Tauresium north of Salonica, he died at Constantinople. Promoted by the general Justin, to the post of consul in 521, and commander of the army of the East, and soon virtual regent, in 527 he became co-regent, and four months later, sole emperor. Justinian's religious policy was driven by a concern for political unity of the Empire. He promulgated two statutes decreeing the total destruction of Hellenism as rank paganism, which resulted in severe persecution of pagan philosophers and sophists at the University of Athens, as well as Jews, Samaritans and Manicheans. Centralizing power, Justinian was deemed despotic for his tight control over religion and law. But he succeeded in ending the schism between Rome and Byzantium dating from 483, conciliating the Monophysites without offending against the Chalcedonian decrees, enacting into law the Nicaeno-Constantinopolitan creed and the canons of the four ecumenical councils. His mission was not accomplished without incurring the wrath of the Byzantine clerics for vesting supreme ecclesiastical authority with Rome, which earned him the virtual status of a Church Father (*The New Schaff-Herzog Encyclopedia of Religious Knowledge*, vol. 6, p. 285).

L

Laestrygones, a race of cannibalistic Giants encountered by Odysseus (*Od.* 10.82ff.). In their country the night is so short that men going out with their flocks to pasture meet those coming back, a vague echo perhaps of some traveler's tale of northern conditions in summer. Their city Laestrygonia is described as the 'lofty town of Lamos'. Thucydides 6.2.1. locates their country in Sicily, Cicero locates it at Formiae (*Att.* 2.13.2).

Lapiths were a mountain warrior tribe in Thessaly, and were involved in a famous fight with the Centaurs who had been invited to the wedding of Pirithous, king of the Lapiths. See Virgil, *Georgics* 2.455-7: 'ille furentis centauros leto domuit, Rhoetumque Pholumque et magno Hylaeum Lapithis cratere minantem'.Ovid, *Met.* 12.261, 536; Horace, *Ode* 1.18.8, 2.12.5; Virgil, *Aeneid* 7.304; Homer *Il.* 1.263, 2.742, *Od.* 21.295ff (Lewis & Short, Invernizzi note).

Leo I, Pope (reigned 440-61), known as Leo the Great, was a native of Tuscany. As a deacon under Pope Celestine I (422-32), he was already known outside Rome and had relations with Gaul. Leo the Great is claimed by some historians to be the first Pope to articulate doctrines of Papal supremacy, although his views are more generally seen as the culmination of a longer development. In 444, Leo began a campaign against the *Manicheans in Rome, which in 445 received the support of the Emperor Valentinian III who, doubtless at the pope's instigation, issued a stern edict in which he established severe punishments against them. Leo was required to deal with the *Monophysite heresy and *Eutyches the Archimandrite. From his first letter on this subject, written to Eutyches on 1 June, 448, to his last letter written to the new orthodox Patriarch of Alexandria, Timotheus Salophaciolus, on 18 August, 460, Leo demonstrated determination to see the dispute resolved in the interests of the primacy of the Holy See. His negotiations with Attila (452) and Genseric the Vandal (455) saved Rome from barbarian invasion.

Leo I, Roman Emperor 457-74, followed Marcian, and was the first emperor to receive his crown from the Patriarch of Constantinople, rather than from a high imperial official or general, and acclamation by the army, the senate and the people in the Roman tradition. This marked the turning point in ecclesiastical control over the imperium and the conversion of coronation into a religious rite. See Ostrogorsky, *History of the Byzantine State*, p. 61.

Leo III, the Isaurian, or the Syrian (c. 685-741) was Byzantine Emperor from 717 until his death in 741. He put an end to a period of instability, successfully defended the empire against the invading Arabs, and adopted the religious policy of Iconoclasm. http://en.wikipedia.org/wiki/Leo_III_the_Isaurian.

Leo III, Pope (795 to 816), a Cardinal and Roman native, was successor to Adrian I, who had tried to keep the papacy independent of the power struggles between the Eastern Empire and the Western kingdoms. But Leo III immediately supported Charlemagne, recognizing the Frankish king as protector of the city by sending him the keys to St Peter's tomb. An opposing faction led by a nephew of Adrian, either out of jealousy or dissatisfaction with Leo's Frankish alliance, brought perjury and adultery charges against him and in April of 799, Leo was physically attacked in the streets of Rome. He escaped, however, and fled to the protection of Charlemagne at Paderborn, returning to Rome under a safe escort. In November 799 a commission controlled by the Frankish king discredited and deported Leo's assailants, but unrest prevailed in Rome until Charlemagne himself came to the city in the fall of 800 to restore order, and on December 23 Leo officially purged himself of the charges against him in the presence of the king. Two days later, at a mass in St. Peter's Basilica, Pope Leo unexpectedly crowned Charlemagne Emperor, the assembly hailing him 'Charles, the most pious Augustus, crowned by God'. The action, which had no foundation in canon law, established the precedent that only the pope could confer the imperial crown, tying the Church to the Carolingian empire, and widening the schism between the Eastern and Western churches.

Leo IX, Pope (1002-1054), Cousin of Emperor Conrad II, Leo commanded troops under the emperor in the invasion of Italy in 1026. While still in the military, he was made bishop of Toul, a position he held for 20 years. Renowned for his discipline, and with Hildebrand, later Pope Gregory VII, as his spiritual adviser, Leo applied the Cluniac reforms to the monasteries, brought discipline to the clergy as a whole, reforming houses and parishes, fighting simony, enforcing clerical celibacy, and encouraging liturgical development. He fought the coming Great Schism between the Eastern and Western churches, added new Italian regions to the papal states and, when Normans invaded these areas in 1053, he personally led an army to throw them out. But his military adventurism was his undoing, drew wide criticism, brought defeat in the field, his capture, imprisonment, and early death.

Peter Lombard, Theologian (c. 1100-1160), born at Novara, Italy, studied at Bologna, Reims, where his mentor was Bernard of Clairvaux, and Paris, where he later taught. John of Cornwall, his pupil, records that he studied the works of Abelard, whose lectures he had probably followed about 1136. Peter Lombard is famous for his *Magister Sententiarum*, known as the *Book of*

Sentences, one of the most important Medieval theological texts. Grouped around topics such as the Trinity (bk 1), the incorporeal powers, angels and demons (bk 2), the Incarnation (bk 3), the sacraments and the Apocalypse, death, Judgement, heaven and hell (bk 4), Lombard combines biblical and patristic sources. Familiar with Gratian's *Decretum* of 1140, and the Latin translation of John Damascene by Burgundio of Pisa, Lombard is an important transmitter of the Latin Fathers, Augustine, Ambrose, Jerome, Hilary; although the Greek Fathers, with the exception of John Damascene, are scarcely represented. The work was criticized for its method, notably by Joachim of Fiore, who questioned its teachings on the Trinity, but upheld as orthodoxy by the Fourth Lateran Council of 1215. (*Catholic Encyclopaedia*).

Lucian of Somosata (born c. AD 120), author of some eighty works, mainly dialogues. Beginning life as a pleader, he practiced the art of rhetoric as far afield as Gaul, returning to Athens where he abandoned rhetoric for philosophy, developing the special form of dialogue for which he is renowned. At one time accepting a post in the Roman administration in Egypt, he died after AD 180. Hobbes makes explicit reference to Lucian in the *Historia Ecclesiastica* as the author of the spurious *Lucius, or the Ass* (lines 437-8), making implicit reference to him, both in the opening of *Leviathan*, for the figure of the *Gallic Hercules*, and in the *Historia Ecclesiastica* – as the quintessential sophist – for his *Philosophers for Sale* and his treatises, *De astrologia*, and *How to Write History*.

Martin Luther (1483-1546), German Protestant Reformer. Born in Eisleben, the son of a mining family of rural origin, he attended the Latin School in Mansfeld from 1488 onwards, continuing his schooling in Magdeburg and later in Eisenach. In 1501 Luther began his studies in Erfurt and intended to become a lawyer, but instead entered the Augustinian monastery there. Luther's negative personal experiences with the ecclesiastical doctrine of grace led to increasing criticism of the church and a fundamental reconsideration of medieval theology. His public criticism of the misuse of letters of indulgence in 1517 did not result in the desired discussion but led to the start of a court of inquisition culminating in Luther's excommunication after the Imperial Diet of

Worms in 1521. Friedrich the Wise protected Luther's life and, while in hiding in that year, he translated the Old and New Testaments into German, a translation published in 1534 as the Wittenberg Bible.

M

Macedonius of Constantinople, around 335 was deposed as an Arian. After his expulsion from the bishopric of Constantinople on the charge of being a Subordinationist, Macedonius, was considered to have blasphemed against the Holy Ghost, whom he relegated to the level of the angels, writing to other deposed prelates to encourage them in their adherence to the Antiochene formula and to the 'Homoiousian' clause as the watchword of their party (Socr. *Hist. Eccl.* bk 2, ch. 45; Soz. *Hist. Eccl.* bk 4, ch. 27). Sozomen assembles formidable testimony excoriating Macedonius as having disturbed the peace, dividing people not only on religious doctrine, but even daring to profane the body of the emperor Constantine, by removing his remains, which caused pitched battle between Arians and Orthodox Christians. See Sozomen, *Hist. Eccl.* bk 4, ch. 21. Hobbes's vilification of Macedonius may be an attempt to deflect criticism of himself as a subordinationist, a view attributed to him by his contemporaries and by modern commentators. See, Matheron, 'Hobbes, la Trinité et les caprices de la réprésentation', pp. 381-90, esp. p. 385. For the heresy of Macedonius, see Sozomen, *Hist. Eccl.*, bk 3, ch. 3, bk 4, chs 21-27, and bk 5, ch. 4.

Mani (c. AD 215-76), the Persian religious leader and founder of the heretical sect of Manichaeism, began in around 245 to preach his doctrine of the double worlds of good and evil at the court of the Persian king Sapro (Shahpur) I. He traveled widely but was eventually crucified by his Zoroastrian enemies (*Chambers Biographical Dictionary*).

Mars, god of war, the father of Romulus. Mars, the chief Italian god, is patron of war and agriculture, originally a chthonian deity, and god of the wild, of death and of fertility. The New Year's rituals in his eponymous month (March) may reasonably be understood as aimed at bringing divine blessings on the upcoming campaigning season, thus the horse rites (*Equirria*), the *Tubilustrium* (trumpet parade). October, a month also sacred to Mars, is devoted to putting away war materiel. It includes the *Armilustrium* and the *Equus October*, a horse race on the *Campus Martius* in which the horse of the winning team is sacrificed and his head competed for by those living near the *Sacra Via* and the *Suburra* (a popular district of Rome). (*OCD*, 1970, 651).

Marsham, Sir John (1602-1685), author of the *Diatriba chronologica*, 1649, and the *Chronicus Canon Ægyptiacus, Ebraicus, Graecus, et disquisitiones*, 1672. In the latter work, having described the heathen sources of Oriental history, he turns to the Christian writers, and, using the history of Egypt to show that the Church authorities were not exact: 'Thus the most interesting antiquities of Egypt have been involved in the deepest obscurity by the very interpreters of her chronology, who have jumbled everything up (qui omnia susque deque permiscuerunt), so as to make them match with their own reckonings of Hebrew chronology. Truly a very bad example, and quite unworthy of religious writers.' Marsham in particular attacked Eusebian history for its distortions of ancient chronology, defending the case for Egyptian wisdom as the most ancient, and is mentioned by Rymer as a possible source for Hobbes.

Maurice, Byzantine emperor (582-602), was a successful general, proclaimed emperor on his deathbed by Tiberius II, his father-in-law and the successor of Justin II. He failed to halt the Lombards in Italy but ended the war with Persia (591), restored Khosru II to the throne, and defeated the Avars. His strict discipline caused mutiny in the Danubian army, and he was obliged to flee. He was killed by order of the usurper *Phocas (q.v), who was deposed (610), in turn, by Heraclius I.

Monophysite (Gr. one nature) A heresy of the fifth to seventh centuries that taught Christ had one nature, in opposition to the orthodox doctrine (laid down at the Council of *Chalcedon 451) that he had two natures, the human and the divine. Monophysitism developed as a reaction to *Nestorianism and led to the formal secession of the Coptic and Armenian churches from the rest of the Christian church. Monophysites survive today in Armenia, Syria, and Egypt.

Monothelite A heresy that arose in the seventh century as an attempt to reconcile orthodox and Monophysite theologies by maintaining that, while Christ possessed two natures, he had only one will. The initiator of this heresy was Sergius, Patriarch of Constantinople from 610 to 638. *Constantius II (318-361), the successor to the *Emperor Heraclius, had issued his infamous 'Typus' Declaration, formally accepting the Monothelite teaching as official dogma, but it was condemned as a heresy by the Third Council of Constantinople in 680. See L. Van Rompay, 'Proclus of Constantinople's, 'Tomus ad Armenios', in the Post-Chalcedonian Tradition', in *After Chalcedon: Studies in Theology and Church History*, pp. 425-449, esp. p. 447. See also Ostrogorsky, p. 127, on Monothelitism as a political strategy to recover the Monophysite provinces for the Byzantine Empire.

Mount Parnassus rises from the Gulf of Corinth above a valley whose sides held the groves, caves, and ravines sacred to the gods of ancient Greece. Parnassus itself was sacred to Apollo, god of the fine arts, and to the muses, the nine daughters of Zeus. The muses were considered demi-gods and were the guardian spirits of writers and artists.

Medieval logic: the *Logica vetus*, comprising the *Isagoge* of Porphyry, Aristotle's *Categories* and *Perihermeneias*, and the commentaries of Boethius on Porphyry and Aristotle; the *Logica nova*, comprising Aristotle's other logical writings: the *Prior* and *Posterior Analytics*, the *Topics* and *De Sophisticis Elenchis*, plus Gilbert de la Porree's *Liber sex principes*. In the course of the twelfth century, there developed a *logica modernorum*, in which Aristotle's *Organon* was extended by the following: *De Suppositionibus, De Fallaciis, de Relativis, De Ampliationibus, De Appellationibus, De Restrictionibus, De Distributionibus*. The authors who are members of the *logica modernorum* movement, to name just a few, are: William of Shyrewood, Petrus Hispanus, Lambert of Auxerre, Abelard, and Ockham.

Mulciber, a surname of Vulcan, the Softener; (fig.) fire (Lewis & Short); Vulcan in a specific mode, meaning fire, which appears to have contaminated Old Germanic literature, with the syncretic interchange of the fourth century BC on. He appears to have come in from the Eastern Mediterranean through Etruria. His shrine stood in the area Volcani in the Roman Forum at the foot of the Capitol. He was worshipped principally to avert fires, thus his title Mulciber (*qui ignem mulcet*), the fire charmer. His title Quietus, means calm or sleeping and he is associated with the Stata Mater, the goddess who makes fires stand still. His unusual and characteristic form of sacrifice required live fish from the Tiber to be thrown into the fire, perhaps to engage his benevolence to protect them from burning in a hot season. (*OCD*, 1970 edn, 1130-1)

N

Nestorius, Christian Syrian ecclesiastic (died c. 451), patriarch of Constantinople 428-431, who maintained Christ had two natures, human and divine. He was banished for maintaining that Mary was the mother of the man Jesus only, and therefore should not be called the mother of God. Nestorius and his followers fled from persecution in the Byzantine Empire after the Council of Ephesus 431, which banned him and his teachings. They migrated to Persia and from there launched significant missionary movements. By the end of the eighth century they had spread to China and from Central Asia through Afghanistan to India, probably becoming the most numerous church in the world by the nincth ccntury.

Nicene Council, see Council of Nicaea.

O

William of Ockham (1280-1349) the Franciscan school man and nominalist, was born at Ockam in England and died in Munich. Schooled at Oxford and Paris, where he taught between 1315 and 1320, tradition has it that he was a pupil of Duns Scotus. His doctrines had taken such hold in Paris by 1339 that the philosophical faculty felt obliged to issue a warning against them. But by that time he himself had left Paris. The question of poverty which so deeply agitated his order determined the later course of his life, in which, defending the ideal of absolute poverty, he became embroiled with the extreme Franciscans, supported by the Emperor Louis the Bavarian, against Pope John XXII. (*Encyclopedia of Philosophy*, on-line version).

Oedipus (Elyot) 'a man, which dissolved subtyll and darke questions'; (Lewis & Short) proverbial for a solver of enigmas, Oedipus was famous for solving the riddle of the Sphinx. (Cooper's *Thesaurus* gives a much longer account.)

P

Pepin III, the Short, King of the Franks 751-768. On the death of his father Charles Martel in 741, Pepin III and his brother Carloman succeeded as joint Mayors of the Palace of Austrasia. In 746, Carloman abdicated and became a monk, leaving Pepin sole rule of Austrasia. Pepin received papal permission from Pope Zachary to take the Frankish crown from King Childeric III in 751, becoming the first Caroliginian king of the Franks. In 753 Pope Stephen went to Gaul to affirm Pepin's crown. In 755, on Stephen's wishes, Pepin attacked the Lombards of Italy who were harassing the Roman See, and went on to conduct a long campaign in Aquitaine, successfully completed only in 766.

Ovid, Publius Ovidius Naso (43 BC to 17 AD), Roman poet, master of the elegiac couplet (the form of Hobbes's *Historia Ecclesiastica*), was exiled in AD 8 to Tomis on the far edge of the Eastern Roman Empire, where he wrote the five books of poems on his journey and arrival, the *Tristia* and the famous four books of lament, *Ex Ponto*. Menaced by attacking tribes and stultifying boredom, he died there unforgiven around AD 17 (*OCD*, 1970 edn, 763).

Philostorgius, the Arian, whose *Historia Ecclesiastica*, is extant only in the extensive *Epitome* of Photius. See the *Epitome of the Historia Ecclesiastica of Philostorgius*, tr. Edward Walford, London, Bohn, 1855, pp. 433-4.

Phocas, Byzantine Emperor (602-10), exacerbated the conflicts begun in 431, when the Council of Ephesus condemned Nestorianism, followed by the Council of Chalcedon's dismissal of Monophysitism in 451. At these councils the chief defenders of these theological positions represented churches in the East, ranging from Assyria and Persia (Nestorians) to North Africa and Armenia (Monophysites). The situation worsened when the Greeks attempted to subjugate the Eastern churches by seizing their monasteries and churches. The theological denunciation of the Eastern churches coincided with ongoing ethnic and geopolitical infighting. The Persians warred with the Aramaeans, Egyptians, Armenians, and Greeks, greatly destabilizing the Christian territories' frontier with the newly Muslim land on the Arabian peninsula. A struggle in the Byzantine capital of Constantinople between Phocas and his general Heraclius instigated a military mutiny. http://66.102.9.104/search?q=cache:il0gcYkyagYJ:www.christianitytoday.com/history/newsletter/2004/oct14.html+Emperor+Phocas+(602-10)&hl=en&ct=clnk&cd=7.

Phoebus, a name of Apollo, the sun-god, who in mythology makes his daily horse-drawn journey across the sky.

Photius I (or **Photios I**) of Constantinople (c. 820 – 893) was Patriarch of Constantinople from 858 to 867 and from 877 to 886. He is widely regarded as the most powerful and influential patriarch of Constantinople since John Chrysostom and recognized as a Saint by the Eastern Orthodox Church and some of the Eastern Catholic Churches of Byzantine tradition. See his *Epitome of the Historia Ecclesiastica of Philostorgius.*

Plato (c. 429-347 BC) philosopher, founder of the Academy, transmitter of the teachings of Socrates.

Plutarch (c. AD 50-120) from Chaeronea, knew Athens well and visited Egypt. For the last 30 years of his life Plutarch was a priest at Delphi; a devout believer in its ancient cults. He emphasized the dual heritage of Greece and Rome, playing an important role in reviving the Delphic shrine under Trajan and Hadrian. His many works include *De Sollertia Animalium*, on whether water animals are more intelligent than land animals; 9 books of *Quaestiones Convivales*, learned table-talk in the tradition of Aulus Gellius' *Attic Nights*; several major Pythian dialogues, including *De sera numinis vindicta* (Of the late Victory of the Gods) that, set in Delphi, have divine providence as their subject; and *De Genio Socrates* (the Genius of Socrates). An antiquarian, Plutarch also wrote on Menander, Aristophanes and the poets (*OCD*, 1965, 848-50).

pneumatomachos (Souter) (adj.) resisting the Holy Spirit [Rustic. S.; *cod.* Iust. 1.5.5.]. (Blaise), heretic, adversaries of the Holy Spirit.

Presbyter, Cooper's *Thesaurus*: antient or father in yeres or dignitie: an elder: a prieste; [Souter], (= Gr. *presbuteros*) (of age, simply = senior (m.) and (f.)), ancestors, the ancients (Homer, Aristotle, Pindar, etc.); older, old, aged (Tert. on); presbyter, elder (pagan refs. to Christian officials) (Hadrian; Amm. 29.3.4, 31.12.8; Tert on. *Presbuterion* (Gr.) the highest council in Jerusalem; a Christian Church Council. See Daniel-Rops, *Cathedral and Crusade*, p. 297, this was the usual term for parochial clergy.

Presbyterianism is a form of ecclesiastical polity wherein the Church is run by presbyters, i.e. ministers and elders. Presbyterian churches are governed by a hierarchy of local and regional courts, the representatives to these courts being popularly elected by the congregations. The supreme legislative and administrative court is known as the General Assembly. The only Presbyterian State-Church is the Church of Scotland. All Presbyterian Churches believe that the supreme standard of faith and practice is contained in the Scriptures, and their doctrine is traditionally Calvinist (*The Oxford Dictionary of the Christian Church*).

Priapus On account of the reproductive function of the virile member, Priapus has been regarded as a promoter of fertility, a protector of domestic animals, and of all garden produce. He has been honoured not only in cities and temples, but also in the countryside, where his statue served as scarecrow, watching over vineyards and gardens and protecting them against theft. See Suetonius, *On Grammarians* XI, Virgil, *Ecl.* 7.33, and Virgil, *Georg.* 4.111. (Parada, *Genealogical Guide to Greek Mythology*).

Proteus, a minor sea god, herdsman of the flocks of the sea (seals). In Homer (*Od.* 4.385 ff.), he is an Egyptian daimon, servant of Poseidon [Osiris], who has the power to take all manner of shapes, but if held till he resumes the true one, will answer questions (*Georg.* 4.387ff.). In Herodotus 2.112 ff. and Euripides *Helena* 4, he is a virtuous king of Egypt, who takes Helen and her wealth from Paris, and keeps them safe until at length Menelaus arrives and claims them (see the *Telemachia, Od.* 4.385 ff.). Menelaus seized him as he tried to find out the whereabouts of Odysseus for Telemachus, his son; the one chance to catch him was when he came out on the beach to count his herd.

Prudentius, Aurelius Clemens (AD 348-c.405), a native of Spain and layman, was the greatest of the Christian Latin poets. He abandoned a successful Roman administrative career for poetry which celebrated the triumphs of the Church in a style that melded the great imperial tradition to the Christian mission and Universal History. See the *Psychomachia* (The Battle of the Soul), the *Cathemerinon* (Hymns for the Day), the *Peristephanon* (Crowns of Martyrdom), the *Apotheosis* (The Divinity of Christ), *Hamartigenia* (The Origin of Sin), and *Contra Symmachum* (Against Symmachus) an attack on the Roman rhetorical tradition (*OCD*, 1970 edn, p. 893). Prudentius is mentioned by Rymer as a source for Hobbes.

Ptolemy, Claudius. Claudius Ptolemeus (fl. AD 127-48), astronomer, mathematician and geographer, his principal works are the *Almagest*, a textbook of astronomy, and the *Tetrabiblos*, which attempted to establish astrology as a science. He also wrote books on the mathematical theory of harmony, optics, epistemology and geography (*OCD*, 1970 edn, 897-8).

Pythagoras, 6c BC, philosopher and mathematician. Pythagoras is especially significant as the first 'philosopher', i.e. the first to call himself a 'lover of wisdom' (*philosophos*), rather than a 'wise man' (*sophos*). There were three major classical sources of Pythagoras stories: Cicero, *De officiis*, 2.2.5-8; and *Tusculanae disputationes*, 5.3.8-11, where he credits Pythagoras with coining the term philosopher; Augustine, *De civitate dei*, 8.2 (Migne

41.225), and *Contra Academicos*, 2.3.5 (Migne 32.936); and Lactantius, *Divinae institutiones*, 2.2. (Migne 6.352-3). See Lisa Jardine, 'Lorenzo Valla and the Intellectual Origins of Humanistic Dialectic', *Journal of the History of Philosophy*, vol. XV (1977), pp. 154-5.

Q

Quakers. A religious sect that first emerged in the seventeenth century in the midlands of England as the Children of the Light. They spread into the north of England where they gained many adherents, and from there to the south and abroad (*OED*).

R

Robber Council of Ephesus (Latrocinium) of 449, so named because of its irregular proceedings. Called to exonerate Eutyches the Archimandrite, accused of the Monophysite heresy, the Acts of the first session of this synod were read at the Council of Chalcedon, 451, which was called to reverse its proceedings, and have thus been preserved for us. The question before the council by order of the emperor was whether Flavian, in a synod held by him at Constantinople in November, 448, had justly deposed and excommunicated the Archimandrite Eutyches for refusing to admit two natures in Christ. Consequently Flavian and six other bishops, who had been present at his synod, were not allowed to sit as judges in the council, the judgement of Pope Leo, written in a letter to Flavian, was not allowed to be read, and Dioscorus was acclaimed as a guardian of the Faith. Eutyches made his defence that he held the Nicene Creed, to which nothing could be added, and from which nothing could be taken away. He had been condemned by Flavian for a mere slip of the tongue, though he had declared that he held the faith of Nicaea and Ephesus, and now asked for judgment against the calumnies which had been brought against him.

Rufinus of Aquileia (c. AD 345-410), a friend and later antagonist of St. Jerome, traveled in Egypt and founded a monastery on the Mt. of Olives. He authored many translations from the Greek including Eusebius's *Historia Ecclesiastica*, to which he added two books (*OCD*).

Thomas Rymer (1641 ?-1713), English literary critic and Historiographer Royal. Educated at Sydney Sussex College, Cambridge and Gray's Inn, he was called to the bar in 1673 but turned his efforts instead to literature, especially drama. He is known to have contributed a poem *Penelope to Ulysses* to Ovid's *Epistles Translated by Several Hands* (1680), with a preface by Dryden and he was one of the authors of the English *Plutarch* of 1683-86, contributing the life of Nicias. He also had Royalist political interests and wrote *A General Draught and Prospect of the Government of Europe* in 1681, reprinted in 1689 and 1714 as *Of the Antiquity, Power, and Decay of Parliament*. Belonging to the literary circle that Hobbes himself frequented, he contributed three pieces to the collection of *Poems to the Memory of Edmund Waller* (1688), afterwards reprinted in Dryden's *Miscellany Poems*, and is said to have written the Latin inscription on Waller's monument in Beaconsfield churchyard. Not only is the preface to Hobbes's posthumous *Historia Ecclesiastica* (1688) attributed to Rymer, but the *Life of Hobbes* of 1681 is also ascribed to him, but wrongly, it was written in fact by Richard Blackburne. He also translated the sixth elegy of the third book of Ovid's *Tristia* for Dryden's *Miscellany Poems* (1692). Upon the death of Thomas Shadwell in 1692 Rymer was made historiographer royal and in that capacity began in 1693 to edit a work bringing together all public documents on relations between England and other nations from 1101 to 1654. This work, called *Foedera* (1704-35), was modeled after Leibniz's *Codex juris gentium diplomaticus*; the last 5 of the 20 volumes being in fact edited posthumously, by Robert Sanderson. (*Columbia Encyclopedia* on-line, based on the 1911 *Encyclopaedia Britannica*).

S

The **Saturnalia** of December 17, was historically associated with a mock king and the overturning of authority by the temporary releasing of slaves. Considered the most propitious and joyous time of the year, presents were exchanged including wax candles and small pottery figurines. The feast among the ancients was associated with Chronos (see Macrobius, *Sat.* 1.7.36-7), but by the fourth century AD most of its elements had been transferred to Christmas and New Year's Day (*OCD*, 1970, pp. 955-6).

Sedulius (early 5c. AD), a Christian Latin poet whose works include the *Paschale Carmen*, which adapts the Gospel narrative to Christian verse, rendered also in prose as the *Paschale Opus* (*OCD*, 1970 edn, p. 970).

Selden, John, 1584-1654, English jurist and scholar, studied at Oxford, was called to the bar in 1612, and was elected to Parliament in 1623. He had already assisted in preparing the protestation of Commons in 1621, asserting to King James I Parliament's rights in the affairs of state, and he had briefly been held in custody as a result. He continued to support the rights of Parliament in its struggle with the crown, was prominent in the trial of George Villiers, first duke of Buckingham, and helped to draw up the Petition of Right in 1628. For his activity in the recalcitrant Parliament of 1629 he was imprisoned and was not released until 1631. He represented Oxford University in the Long Parliament from 1640 to 1649. Selden was highly regarded both as a antiquarian, establishing his name with *England's Epinomis* and *Jani Anglorum* (1610), and as a legal theorist, his reputation established with his edition of the *Fleta* (1647). His career as Orientalist began with his *De Diis Syris* (1617), and he prepared a number of studies of rabbinical law. His *History of Tithes* (1618) brought him into conflict with the clergy, and the work was suppressed. Among his other works *Mare Clausum* (1635), a defense of England's right to sovereignty over the seas between that country and the Continent, was written in response to Hugo Grotius's *Mare Liberum*. Hobbes probably relies on his friend Selden for the list of the attendants at the Nicene Council Selden provides, translated from an Arabic commentary, in his *Eutychii Aegyptii, patriarchae orthodoxorum Alexandrini. . . . ecclesiae suae origines* (London, 1642), p. 71.

Sphinx. Cooper's *Thesaurus:* (Pliny), a beaste like an ape: a monkey or a marmset (Statius: *iniqua sphinx*). (Elyot): a

monster, whiche had the heed and handes of a mayden the body
of a dogge, wynges lyke a byrde, nayles lyke a lyon, a tayle lyke
a dragon, the voyce of a man, which purposed to men subtyl
questions. It is also a beaste lyke an ape, but more rough, & with
a longer tayle, I suppose it to be a munkay or babyon. (Lewis &
Short): Fabulous monster, located at a crossroads [*crux*] near
Thebes that used to pose riddles to travellers and tear in pieces
those that could not solve them. Usually represented with the
head of a woman and the body of a lion, afterwards also with the
wings of a bird. Augustus had the figure of a Sphinx upon his ring
as a figure of silence (Suetonius, *Augustus* 50; Pliny 37.1.4. §10)

Socrates, protagonist in Plato's Socratic dialogues, was an Athenian
philosopher, accused of leading youth astray and introducing
strange gods, for which he was brought to trial before a popular
jury in 399 BC and condemned to death. He was also renowned
for apparitions and following a divine vision (*OCD*, 1972, p. 998).

Socrates 'Scholasticus' (c. 380-c.450), a lawyer and layman from
Constantinople, was the most judicious and objective of the post-
Eusebian church historians, who used authentic source material
to refine Eusebius' account and to correct that of his translator,
Rufinus. (See Chestnut, *The First Christian Histories*, ch. 7 and
Trompf, *Early Christian Historiography*, Part 3.)

Sozomenos, Salaminius Hermias (c. 400-c. 450), a lawyer at Constantinople and church historian, wrote some ten years after
Socrates Scholasticus (c. 447-50) and with the benefit of his
account. Having grown up in Gaza and traveled more widely than
Socrates, Sozomen has a richer collection of miracle stories, is
less judicious in his judgments, and more polemically anti-
Philostorgian. (See Chestnut, *The First Christian Histories*, ch. 7
and Trompf, *Early Christian Historiography*, Part 3.)

Subordinationism. The distinction between 'begotten' and 'proceeded from' lay at the heart of the problem of 'subordinationism', or whether the relationship between the three persons of the
Trinity was one of equality, or whether the Son and the Holy
Ghost proceeded from and were lesser to the God the Father. Sub-

ordinationism proved to be the major stumbling block to unity between the Greek and Latin Churches at the Council of Ferrara/Florence of 1438-9, played out this time with respect to the procession of the Holy Spirit, which the Latins believed to proceed from (and be therefore equal to) the Father *and the Son* (*filioque*), whereas the Greeks maintained the *arche* or primacy of God the Father. To the Latins 'the Greek view, which stressed the "monarchy" of the Father, seemed to subordinate the Son to the Father' See Geanakopolos, *Byzantine East and Latin West*, Chapter 3, 'The Council of Florence (1438-39) and the Problem of Union between the Byzantine and Latin Churches', pp. 99ff. It is important to note that the Orthodox camp, led by Mark, Metropolitan of Ephesus and exarch of the patriarch of Antioch tried to sidestep the issue of the truth of the *filioque* dogma, focusing instead on the legality of changing the creed as established by the Councils of Nicaea and Ephesus; while the Latins, led by the Greek Latinophile Bessarion, Archbishop of Niceae, focused on the truth of the doctrine.

T

Thales, 6c BC founder of the Greek physical sciences.

Theodoret of Cyrrhus (c. 393-c. 458) Syrian theologian and bishop, supporter of Nestorius and leading critic of Cyril, Eutyches the Archimandrite, who began on the side of Cyril against the Nestorians but ended up leader of the Monophysite heresy, and the orthodox Irenaeus (see Hefele pp. 499-554, citing Cyril *Contr. Nest.*, bk 2 ch. 6, *PG* LXXVI, col. 84ff.). Theodoret's *Epist. LXXX, Ad Eutychium* and *Eranistes seu Polymorphus* AD 447 (*PG* LXXXIII, cols 1276 ff and 27ff.), was a series of three philosophical dialogues on the theological significance of these variants of the Arian heresy all of which turned on the issue of Christ being made flesh, which he gives the unexpected title *The Beggar*. In his *Ecclesiastical History*, Theodoret 'wisely excludes all reference to disputes that left him ecclesiastically isolated (from the so-called Robber Synod of 449, which dismissed him, to the Council of Chalcedon in 451, which exculpated and almost vindicated his position)'. (See Trompf, *Early*

Christian Historiography, Part 3, p. 215; Hefele, 2.1.10 pp. 499-503 and Chestnut, *The First Christian Histories*, ch. 7.)

Theodoric the Great, Ostrogoth conqueror and king of the Ostrogoths 475-526. Under Theodoric, the Ostrogoths moved west and he became king of Italy 493-516. He was succeeded by his daughter Amalasuntha, who was murdered in 535 by her husband and co-ruler, Theodahad. Her allies, the Byzantines, soon attacked Italy, but the Ostrogoth forces held out until 553, when the Byzantines, and later the Lombards, took control of Italy.

Theodosius the Great, Roman Emperor, c. 346-95, an Orthodox Christian and rigorous defender of the Nicene Creed. Gratian appointed him *magister militum* on the death of Valens to fight the Goths, proclaiming him Emperor of the East in 379, where he spent years fighting the Visigoths. In AD 381 he ordered all churches to be handed over to bishops who were Catholic by his strict definition. He called a great council at Constantinople which ratified his action, but refused to accept the candidate for the bishopric of Constantinople, Gregory Nazianus. Theodosius issued 18 decretals against heretics and enforced the death penalty for heretical sects, although at first leaving the pagan temples open, and severely discouraged divination. In AD 391, under the influence of Ambrose, Bishop of Milan, he forbad all forms of pagan practice (*OCD*, 1970, pp. 1055-6).

Theodosius II, emperor 401-450, was the son of Arcadius, proclaimed Augustus in 402 and succeeding his father in 408, ruled mainly through regents and eunuchs. Dominated by his pious older sister Pulcheria until the early 440s and also much influenced during that period by his wife Eudoxia, his reign saw successful wars against the Persians, 421-2 and 441, and a series of unsuccessful wars and disastrous tribute negotiations with the Vandals and the Huns. The ecclesiastical crisis that occurred on his watch, and to which Hobbes refers, resulted in the condemnation of *Nestorius, Bishop of Constantinople by the Council of Ephesus in 431, and of Flavian, Bishop of Constantinople, by the second Council of Ephesus in 449. The leaders of these two councils were bishops of Alexandria, Cyril and Dioscorus, respectively. In 429

the famous legal review was undertaken which ultimately produced the Theodosian Code of 438 (*OCD*, 1970, p. 1056).

V

Valla, Lorenzo (1405-57), Roman Humanist and philosopher,
studied Latin under Leonardo Bruni (Aretino) and Greek under
Giovanni Aurispa. Unsuccessful in obtaining a position in the
papal secretariat, he accepted a chair of eloquence in the University of Pavia, where he wrote his treatise *De voluptate* (1431), an
emended edition of which appeared later under the title, *De vero
bono*. His open letter attacking the jurist Bartolo (1433) and ridi-
culing contemporary jurisprudence forced him to leave Pavia for
Milan, Genoa, later Rome, and he finally settled at Naples
(1433), where he became secretary to Alfonso of Aragon, whose
Court, frequented by the most distinguished writers, was a hotbed
of licentiousness. At Naples he wrote *De libero arbitrio, Dialecticae disputationes, Declamazione contro la donazione di Con-
stantino* (1440), and *De professione religiosorum* (1442, not
printed until by Vahlen in 1869). In 1444 a controversy with Fra
Antonio da Bitonto on the question of the composition of the
Apostles' Creed caused him to be tried for heresy by the Curia at
Naples, but the trial was discontinued through the intervention of
King Alfonso. His standard work is *De elegantia linguae latinae*,
which first placed the study of Latin on a scientific basis. Poggio
Bracciolini's invectives against him, and Valla's no less virulent
answers, are collected in his *Invectivarum libri sex*. Hoping still
to obtain a position in the Curia, Valla wrote an *Apologia ad
Eugenio IV*, to clear his name, but it was only after the election of
Nicholas V that he found papal favour, obtaining first the position
of *scriptor* (1448), and later of Apostolic secretary. Callistus III
bestowed on him a canonry in St. John Lateran, which he was
able to hold only for a few years, and by order of Nicholas V he
translated various Greek authors.

Valentinian I, Roman Emperor AD 364-75, a Pannonian elevated
by the army at Nicaea following the death of Jovian. He raised his
brother Valens to the imperium of the East while he ruled the
West, preoccupied with the successful defence of the northern

frontiers against the Germanic tribes. Known for his cruelty and irascibility he was nonetheless respected for his policy of religious tolerance. In 367 he proclaimed his son *Gratian emperor (*OCD*, 1970 edn, p. 1105).

Valentinian II, known as the Younger, Roman Emperor AD 375-92, son of Valentinian I, was elevated by the army without the sanction of Valens or Gratian, who nonetheless accorded him rule over Italy, Africa and Illyricum. He was expelled from Italy by Magnus Maximus, but restored by Theodosius I (*OCD*, 1970 edn, p. 1105).

The **Vandals**, a Germanic people originally based in southern Scandinavia, around AD 200 were organized into the Asdings and the Silings. At a time they were already putting pressure on the Visigoths in Transdanubian Dacia, and soon began to harass the Roman provinces in the third and fourth centuries, crossing the Rhine near Mainz in 406 with the Alans and the Suebi, ravaging Gaul and raiding into Spain in 409. The Silings occupied Baetica, the Alans Lusitania, and the Asdings and the Suebi, Gallaecia. The Visigoths, instigated by the Romans, virtually exterminated the Silings, the Alans, who escaped the Visigoths, joined the Asdings, whose leaders were then called Kings of the Vandals and the Alans. Leaving the Suebi in Gallaecia, where their rule lasted until 585, the Alans and the Asdings moved into southern Spain and North Africa in the fifth century (*OCD*, 1970, p. 1107).

Vaughan, Sir John (1608-1674), entered the Commons at 20, representing Cardiganshire. Samuel Pepys called him 'the Great Vaugan' and suggested he was the best speaker in the Commons. He was appointed Lord Chief Justice of the Court of Common Pleas, and reputed by Aubrey to have been Hobbes's 'greatest acquaintance'. Judge Vaughan is referred to twice by Aubrey in connection with another of Hobbes's works on heresy, the *Dialogue of the Common Laws*, as someone 'who haz read it and much commends it', 'haz perused it and very much commends it, but is afrayd to license for feare of giving displeasure'. For an account of Vaughan's political views, see Richard Tuck, *Natural Rights Theories* (Cambridge: Cambridge University Press, 1979).

Venus. Although of foreign provenance as an Italian garden goddess, Venus was close to *Charis* or the *Charites*, which caused her to be linked to *Aphrodite* (the Greek form of the Egyptian goddess of love and song and dance, Hathor), and hence to take over her Greek metonymies, as goddess of love-making, the highest throw at dice, luck etc. See cognate *venereus* or *venerius* (adj.), of or belonging to Venus; of or belonging to sexual love; (subst.) i.e. *iactus*, the Venus-throw at dice (Cic. *De divinatione*, often).

Vossius, Gerhard Johann, (1577-1649), a German theologian and Classical scholar, was persecuted for his moderate Calvinist views. Voss held chairs in Greek and Rhetoric at the University of Leiden, refusing an offer from Cambridge, but accepted from Archbishop Laud a Prebend in Canterbury Cathedral without residence and came to England in 1629, when he was made LLD at Oxford. His several histories include *De Historicis Graecis* (1624), *De Historicis Latinis* (1627) and *De Theologia Gentili* (1642). The Hardwick Hall catalogue (Part B) lists Vossius de Historicis 2 vol. at shelf mark S.1.1, etc., without further indication. For parallels between Hobbes's *Historia Ecclesiastica* and Voss's History of the Gentiles (*De Theologia Gentili*), see Springborg, 'Hobbes, Heresy and the *Historia Ecclesiastica*'.

W

Waldus, Peter or Peter Waldo, (1140-1217), a merchant of Lyons, founder of the Waldensian movement, around 1170, which spread his doctrines beyond France to northern Italy and was one of the heresies dealt with by the Lateran Council of 1215 convened by Pope Innocent III (see Invernizzi edn, p. 92; Daniel-Rops, *Cathedral and Crusade*, p. 290ff.).

Waller, Edmund, 1606-1687, poet and orator, was an MP who in the 1640s tried to steer a moderate course between the King and his opponent, in 1643 devising a plot to oust the Parliamentary rebels, and secure London for the King. When the plot, known as 'Waller's Plot', was discovered Waller was arrested and brought before the Parliament. He confessed and paid for his freedom in bribes and betrayal of his co-conspirators, was fined heavily and exiled, living in Paris, on the periphery of the Stuart Court where he probably got to know Hobbes, returning to England also in 1652. He regained royal favor at the Restoration and regained his membership of the House of Commons. Waller was a celebrated poet and wit in his lifetime, and many of his poems had long circulated in manuscript before their 1645 publication, the first fully authorized edition appearing only in 1664. In 1655 he wrote a *Panegyrick to my Lord Protector*, celebrating Cromwell and in 1660 a poem *To the King, Upon His Majesty's Happy Return*, celebrating the restoration of Charles II, suggesting that he flirted with the Protectorate after the manner of the author of *Leviathan*. Waller, a member of the Royal Society, was a master of the heroic couplet and it is no surprise that his poetry was highly esteemed in the eighteenth century. Dryden wrote that Waller `first made writing easily an art'. Alexander Pope acknowledged him as a master, and the *Biographia Britannica* (1766) called him 'the most celebrated lyric poet that ever England produced'. Rymer mentions him in his preface in similar terms.

Z

Zeno of Citium (335-263 BC) founder of the Stoic school, converted to cynicism and later turned to Socratic philosophy. Of his writings only fragments remain.

SELECT BIBLIOGRAPHY

BIBLIOGRAPHIC SOURCES, GRAMMARS
AND LEXICONS

Allen and Greenough, see Greenough, J.B. et al., *New Latin Grammar* (New York, Ginn & Co., 1931).

Arndt, William F., and F. Wilbur Gingrich, *A Greek-English Lexicon of the New Testament and Other Early Christian Literature*, 4th rev. edn. (Chicago, University of Chicago Press, 1952).

Autenreith, Georg, *A Homeric Dictionary* (Oxford, 1873).

Beal, Peter, compiler, *Index of English Literary Manuscripts*, vol. 2. part 1, (London & New York, Mansell Publishing, 1987), pp. 576-86.

Brunet, Jacques Charles, *Manuel du Libraire*, Paris, 1st edn of *Biblioteca veterum Patrum et antiquorum scriptorium ecclesiasticorum* in Latin (Paris, Marguerin de la Bigne, 1575), in 8 vols.

Cambridge History of English and American Literature in 18 volumes (1907-21), online: www.bartleby.com/219/1004.html

The Catholic Encyclopedia (online): http://64.233.183.104/ search? q = cache:RyUtCyL0AZMJ:www.newadvent.org/cathen/+The+Catholic+Encyclopedia&hl = en

Chambers Murray, *Latin-English Dictionary*, by Sir William Smith and Sir John Lockwood (London/Edinburgh, 1933, repr. 1988).

Cooper, Thomas and Sir Thomas Elyot, *Thesaurus Linguae Romanae & Britannicae* (London, 1565).

Dictionary of National Biography (Oxford, Oxford University Press, 1995), referred to as (*DNB*). The new *DNB*, now known as the *Oxford Dictionary of National Biography* (Oxford, Oxford University Press, 2004), 60 volumes, referred to as (*ODNB*).

Dictionary of Seventeenth Century British Philosophers, ed. Andrew Pyle (Bristol, Thoemmes Press, 2000), 2 vols.

Elyot, Thomas. *Dictionary* (London, 1538).

Encyclopaedia Britannica, 11th edn (Cambridge, Cambridge University Press, 1910-11).

Encyclopedia of Philosophy (London, Macmillan, 1967) 8 vols.

Estienne, Robert. *Dictionariolum puerorum, Tribus Linguis* (London, 1552).

Follett World-Wide Latin Dictionary (Chicago, Ill., Follett 1967).

Geschichtliche Grundbegriffe: Historisches Lexikon zur politisch-sozialen Sprache in Deutschland, ed. Otto Brunner, Werner Conze, Reinhart Koselleck, (Stuttgart, Ernst Klett Verlag, 1975), 8 vols.

Gildersleeve's Latin Grammar, 3rd edn, revised and enlarged, ed. B.L. Gildersleeve and Gonzalez Lodge (New York, St. Martin's Press, 1867, 1872, 1895, reprinted 1990).

Hamilton, J., 'Hobbes's Study in the Hardwick Hall Library', *Journal of the History of Philosophy,* vol. 16 (1978), pp. 445-53.

Hefele, Charles Joseph von, *Histoire des conciles d'après les documents originaux,* trans. and augmented by Henri Leclercq, 11 vols. (Paris, 1907-49).

Historical Manuscripts Commission, *H.M.C. Thirteenth Report,* Appendix, Part 1 vol. 2, *The Manuscripts of His Grace the Duke of Portland, preserved at Welbeck Abbey,* (London, 1893).

Latham, R. E. *Revised Medieval Latin Word-list,* London, British Academy (Oxford University Press, 1965).

Lewis and Short, *Latin Dictionary* (founded on the Andrew's Edition of Freund's *Latin Dictionary*), by Charlton T. Lewis and Charles Short (Oxford, Oxford University Press, 1966).

Liddell, H. G. and R. Scott, *Greek-English Lexicon,* ninth edition (Oxford, Oxford University Press, 1996).

Macdonald, Hugh and Mary Hargreaves, *Thomas Hobbes: A Bibliography* (London, The Bibliogaphical Society, 1952).

Maltby, Robert T, *A Lexicon of Ancient Latin Etymologies* (Leeds 1991).

Mansi, J.D., ed, *Sacrorum conciliorum nova et amplissima collectio,* (Florence and Venice, 1759-98), 31 vols.

Oxford Classical Dictionary (Oxford, Oxford University Press, 1980). (*OCD*)

Oxford Dictionary of the Christian Church, ed. F.C. Cross (rev. edn, Oxford 1974)

Oxford English Dictionary, John Simpson and Edmund Weiner, eds (2nd edition, Oxford, Clarendon Press, 1989), 20 vols (*OED*).

Oxford Latin Dictionary (Oxford, Clarendon Press, 1968-80), 3 vols.

Palmer, L.R., *The Latin Language* (London, Faber & Faber, 1968).

Parada, Carlos, *Genealogical Guide to Greek Mythology* (Jonsered, Sweden, 1993).

Parkhurst, John, H.J. Rose and J. R. Major, *A Greek and English Lexicon to the New Testament*, (London, 1845).

Patrologiae Graecae Cursus Completus (P.G.), ed. Jacques-Paul Migne (Paris, Garnier Frères), 2 series, the first of which contains only Latin translations of the originals (81 vols, 1856-61). The second series contains the Greek text with a Latin translation (166 vols, 1857-66). To the Greek Patrology there was no index, but a Greek, D. Scholarios, added a list of the authors and subjects, (Athens, 1879), and began a complete table of contents (Athens, 1883). The *Patrologia Graeca* includes the printed works of Greek Christian writers down to the Council of Florence (1438-39).

Patrologiae Latinae Cursus Completus (P.L.), ed. Jacques-Paul Migne (Paris, Garnier Frères), in two series (217 vols. in all, 1844-55), with four volumes of indexes (vols. 218-221, 1862-64), which contains all the extant published writings of Latin ecclesiastical authors from the earliest known to Pope Innocent III (d. 1216).

Pauly-Wissowa, *Paulys Realencyclopädie der Classischen Altertumswissenschaft*, new edition ed. Georg Wissowa, (Stuttgart, Alfred Druckenmüller, 1893).

The New Schaff-Herzog Encyclopedia of Religious Knowledge (New York, Funk & Wagnalls, 1908).

Rosenmeyer, Thomas G., Martin Ostwald and James W. Halporn, *The Meters of Greek and Latin Poetry* (Westport, Conn., Greenwood Press, 1978).

Royal Historical Commission on Historical Manuscripts, 'Report on the MSS and papers of Thomas Hobbes, Philosopher, in the Devonshire Collections, Chatsworth, Bakewell, Derbyshire, Reproduced for the Trustees of the Chatsworth Settlement' (London, 1977).

Souter, Alexander, *A Glossary of Later Latin to 600 AD* (Oxford, Oxford University Press, 1964).

Thomas, Thomas, *A Dictionarium Linguae Latinae et Anglicanae* (Cambridge, 1587).

Wood, Anthony, *Athenae Oxonienses an exact history of all the writers and bishops who have had their education in the most ancient and famous University of Oxford, from . . . 1500 to the edn of the year 1690* (London, 1691), 2 vols.

MANUSCRIPTS

Aubrey, John, *An Essay towards a Description of the North Division of Wiltshire*, under the heading 'Westport juxta Malmesbury', Bodl. Ms. Aubr. 3, f. 28 (Aubrey, *Brief Lives*, I, p. 394).

Bagot Papers, MS.CAT. [Calendar of], Folger Library (Z6621.F61.B4).

Cavendish-Talbot Manuscripts, MS.CAT [Calendar of], Folger Library (Z6621.F61.C3).

Hardwick Hall Booklist, MS E1A, Chatsworth, Derbyshire.

Hobbes, *Behemoth or the Long Parliament*. Copy in the hand of an amanuensis, with Hobbes's autograph corrections, c. 1668, St. John's College, Oxford MS 13 (HbT8, *Index of Literary Manuscripts*, vol. 2, part 1, Peter Beal, ed., p. 577); the basis for Tönnies' edition, London, 1889.

Hobbes, *De cive*. Hobbes's formal presentation copy to the third Earl of Devonshire, Paris 1641, Chatsworth, MSS A3. (HbT18, *Index of Literary Manuscripts*, vol. 2, part 1, Peter Beal, ed., p. 578); the basis for Warrender's *De Cive: Latin*, Oxford, Clarendon Press, 1983.

Hobbes, *De cive*, addressed to the Earl of Newcastle, with Hobbes's autograph corrections, BL Harley MS 4235 (HbT19, *Index of Literary Manuscripts*, vol. 2, part 1, Peter Beal, ed., p. 578); the basis for Tönnies' edition, London, 1889.

Hobbes, *De Mirabilibus Pecci*. Copy in 2 scribal hands, with dedication to the Earl of Devonshire, Chatsworth Hobbes MSS A.1. (HbT1, *Index of Literary Manuscripts*, vol. 2, part 1, Peter Beal, ed., p. 578).

Hobbes, *De Mirabilibus Pecci*. Copy subscribed 'mihi' in a late 17c. miscellany, BL Egerton MS 669 (HbT2, *Index of Literary Manuscripts*, vol. 2, part 1, Peter Beal, ed., p. 576).

Hobbes, *De Mirabilibus Pecci*. Copy entered at the end of a miscellany compiled by Dr Edward Browne (1644-1708), son of Sir Thomas Browne; late 17c. miscellany, BL Sloane MS 1865 (HbT3, *Index of Literary Manuscripts*, vol. 2, part 1, Peter Beal, ed., p. 576).

Hobbes, *Historia Ecclesiastica Carmine Elegiaco* (C), Vienna MS, Stiftung fürst Liechtenstein, Vienna, Österreichische Nationalbibliothek, MS N-7-6.

Hobbes, *Historia Ecclesiastica Romana* (A), BL Harley MS 1844, (HbT5, *Index of Literary Manuscripts*, vol. 2, part 1, Peter Beal, ed., p. 576).

Hobbes, *Historia Ecclesiastica Romana* (B), Royal Copenhagen Library, Thotts Sml., 4o Nr. 213

Hobbes, *Leviathan*. Copy in the hand of an amanuensis, with Hobbes's autograph corrections and marginal annotations, believed to be the author's presentation copy to Charles II, BL Egerton MS 1910 (HbT32, *Index of Literary Manuscripts*, vol. 2, part 1, Peter Beal, ed., p. 579-80).

PRIMARY SOURCES

Abbott, George, *The Whole Booke of Iob Paraphrased, or Made easie for any to understand* (London, Printed by Edward Griffin for Henry Overton, 1640), (STC 41).

Anon, *A Discovery of 29 Sects here in London* (London, 1641).

Ante-Nicene Fathers, ed. Alexander Roberts and James Donaldson, 10 vols (Peabody, MA., Hendrickson Publishers, 1994).

Ascham, Roger, *The Scholemaster* (London, Printed by Iohn Daye, 1570).

Athanasius, *Historia Ecclesiastica*, bks 1-6, ed. J. Bidez, tr. A. J. Festugiere (Paris, 1983).

Aubrey, John, *'Brief Lives', chiefly of Contemporaries, set down by John Aubrey between the Years 1669 & 1696*. Edited from the Authors Mss. by Andrew Clark. 2 vols (Oxford, 1898).

Aubrey, John, *Remaines of Gentilisme and Judaisme*, in *John Aubrey, Three Prose Works*, ed. John Buchanan-Brown (Fontwell, Sussex, Centaur Press, 1972).

Augustine, *The Literal Meaning of Genesis* (*De Genesi ad Litteram*), trans. John Hammond Taylor S.J. (New York, Newman Press, 1982), 2 vols.

Bede, Venerable, *Historia Ecclesiastica Gentis Anglorum*, in *Baedae Opera Historica*. J.E. King, tr, based on the version of Thomas Stapleton, 1565 (London, Heinemann, 1962), Loeb edn, 2 vols.

Beza, Theodore, *Job Expovnded by Theodore Beza, partly in manner of a Commentary, partly in manner of a Paraphrase. Faithfully trans-lated out of Latine into English* (Printed by Iohn Legatt, Printer to the Uniuersity of Cambridge, 1589?), STC 2020.

Bible, Authorized Version, facsimile of 1611 edn (Oxford, 1911).

Bracciolini, Poggio. *Opera omnia*, ed. R. Fubini (Torino 1964).

Bramhall, John, *The Catching of the Leviathan, or the Great Whale* (1658), printed in Brmhall *Castigations of Mr. Hobbes his last animadversions, in the case concerning liberty and universal necessity; With an appendix concerning . . .* (London, 1658).

Brebeuf, Georges de, *L'Aenéide de Virgile en vers burlesques, livre 7ᵉ* (Paris, A. Courbé, 1650).

Brebeuf, Georges de, *Lucain travesty, ou les guerres civiles de Cesar et Pompée en vers enjoüez* (Rouen, A. de Sommaville, 1656).

Broughton, Hugh, *Iob. To the King. A Colon-Agrippina studie of one moneth, for the metricall translation. But of Many Yeres, for Ebrew Difficulties. Part 2 is Iob. Brought on to familiar dialogue and paraphrase for easier entendement* (London, 1610).

Browne, Sir Thomas, *Pseudodoxia Epidemica* (1646; 6th ed., 1672), ed. Robin Robbins, 2 vols (Oxford, Oxford University Press, 1981).

Browne, Sir Thomas, *Religio Medici*, in *The Major Works of Sir Thomas Browne*, ed. C. A. Patrides (Harmondsworth, Penguin, 1977).

Calvin, John, *Sermons of Maister Iohn Calvin, vpon the Booke of Iob*, Arthur Golding, tr (London, George Bishop, 1584), (STC 4447).

Calvin, John, *A Commentary vpon the Prophecie of Isaiah*. Translated ovt of French, by C.C. (London, Printed by Felix Kyngston for William Cotton, 1609), STC 4396.

Carew, Thomas. *The Poems of Thomas Carew with his Masque Coelum Britannicum,* Rhodes Dunlap, ed (Oxford, Clarendon Press, 1949).

Cavendish, William, Marquis of Newcastle's, *The Country Captaine, A comoedye lately presented by his Majesties Servants at the Blackfreyers* (London, printed for Humphrey Moseley, 1649, bound with *The Varietie*).

Cavendish, William, Marquis of Newcastle, *A General System of Horsemanship in all its Branches* (London, Printed for J. Brindley, 1743, 2 vols); first published under the title, *Méthode Nouvelle et Invention Extraordinaire de Dresser les Chevaux* (Antwerp, printed by Jacques Van Meurs, 1657).

Cavendish, William, 1st Duke of Newcastle, *Ideology and Politics on the Eve of Restoration: Newcastle's advice to Charles II,* transcribed and introduced by T.P. Slaughter (Philadelphia, University of Pennsylvania Press, 1984).

Cavendish, William, Marquis of Newcastle, *Letter of Instructions to Prince Charles for his Studies, Conduct and Behaviour*, reprinted as appendix 2 to, Margaret Cavendish, Dutchess of Newcastle, *Life of William Cavendish, Duke of Newcastle*, ed. C. H. Firth (London, Routledge, 1907).

Cavendish, William, Marquis of Newcastle, *The Varietie, A comedy lately presented by his Majesties Servants at the BlackFriers* (London, printed for Humphrey Moseley, 1649).

Cicero, *De divinatione*, ed. A. S. Pease (Urbana, Ill., Illinois Studies in Language and Literature 6, 1920-26), 2 vols.

Cicero, *De natura deorum*, ed. A. S. Pease (Cambridge, Mass., Harvard University Press, 1955), 2 vols.

Clement of Alexandria, *Exhortation to the Greeks,* ch. 5, 'The Witness of Philosophy', ed. G.W. Butterworth, (London, Heinemann 1979), Loeb edn.

Cluverius (Johann Clüver, 1593-1633), *Historiam Totius Mundi Epitome A prima rerum Origine usque ad annum Christi MXDCXXX* (Amsterdam, 1645).

Cluverius (Philip Clüver), *An Introduction to Geography both Ancient and Modern, comprised in Sixe Books* (Oxford, Leonard Lichfield, 1657).

Cocquius, Gisbertus, Hobbesianismi Anatome, Qua innumeris Assertionibus ex Tractatibus de Homine, Cive, Leviathan Juxta seriem locorum Theologiae Christiane Philosophi illius a Religione Christiana Apostasia demonstratur, & refutatur (Utrecht, Franciscum Halma, 1680).

Cotton, Charles Jr., *Burlesque upon Burlesque: Or, the Scoffer Scoft. Being some of Lucians Dialogues Newly put into 'English Fuslian' For the Consolation of those who had rather Laugh and be Merry, then be Merry and Wise.* (London, Printed for Henry Brome at the Sign of the Gun at the West-end of St. Paul's Church-yard, 1675), Folger Library C6380A.

Cotton, Charles Jr., *Poems of Charles Cotton* with an introduction by John Buxton (London, Routledge, 1958).

Cotton, Charles Jr., *Scarronides, or Virgile Travestie: A Mock Poem. Being the First Book of Virgils Aeneis in English, Burlesque* (Imprimatur Roger L'estrange, London, Printed by E. Cotes for Henry Brome at the Sign of the Gun at the West-end of St. Paul's Church-yard, 1664), Folger Library, C6391.

Davenant, William, *A Discourse upon Gondibert. An Heroick Poem . . .With an Answer to it by Mr. Hobbs.* (Paris, Chez Matthiev Gvillemot, 1650 [Hobbes's Answer dated January 10, 1650]).

Davenant, Sir William, *Gondibert: an Heroick Poem* (London, Printed by Theo. Newcomb for John Holden, New Exchange, 1651), (STC D325).

Davenant, Sir William, *A Proposition for Advancement of Moralitie, By a new way of Entertainment of the People*, London, 1653/4 [British Library 527 d. 17; Bodleian Library 8o L82 Med (2)], pp. 1-5. Published as the Appendix to James R. Jacob and Timothy Raylor, 'Opera and Obedience: Thomas Hobbes and A Proposition for Advancement of Moralitie by Sir William Davenant', *The Seventeenth Century*, vol. 6, no. 2 (1991), pp. 205-50.

Davies, John, *Apocalypsis: Or Revelation of Certain Notorious Advancers of Heresie*, bound together with it (London, John Saywell, 1658).

Decembrio, Angelo, *De Politia Litteraria* (Basel, 1562).

Descartes, René, *Meditationes de prima philosophia* (Paris, 1641).

Descartes, René, *Œuvres de Descartes*, ed. by C. Adam and P. Tannery (Paris, Cerf, 1896-1913).

Descartes, René, *The Philosophical Writings of Descartes*, tr. by John Cottingham Robert Stoothoff, and Dugald Murdoch (Cambridge, Cambridge University Press, 1985).

Descartes, René, *The World and Other Writings*, ed. by Stephen Gaukroger (Cambridge, Cambridge University Press, 1998).

Determinatio theologicae facultatis Parisiensis super doctrina Lutheriana hactenus per eum visa. Apologia pro Luthero aduersus decretum Parisiensum (Basel, 1521).

Diodorus Siculus, *Bibliotheikeis Historikeis (Library of History)*, 3 vols, trans. C.H. Oldfather (London, Heinemann, 1946-52), Loeb edn.

Drayton, Michael, *Poly-Olbion, or A chorographicall Description of the Tracts, Riuers, Mountaines, Forests, and other Parts of this renowned Isle of Great Britaine....* London, Mathew Lownes et al., 1613, reprinted in *The Works of Michael Drayton*, William Hebel ed., (Oxford, Basil Blackwell, 1933), vol. 4.

Edwards, Thomas, *Gangraena, Catalogue and discovery of many of the errors, heresies, blasphemies and pernicious practices of the sectaries of this time* (London, 1646).

Epiphanius, *The Panarion of St. Epiphanius, Bishop of Salamis, Selected Passages*, edited by Philip R. Amidon, S.J. (Oxford, Oxford University Press, 1990).

Erasmus, *Enchiridion militis christiani* (1504), William Tyndale, tr., *Handbook of the Christian Soldier* (London, 1520).

Farewell, James, *The Irish Hudibras, or Fingallian Prince, Taken from the Sixth Book of Virgil's Aenaeids, and Adapted to the Present Times* (London, 1689).

Featley, Daniel, *The Dippers dipt or the Anabaplists d'nckt and plunged over head and ears* (London, 1645).

Ficino, Marsilio, *Opera Omnia* (Basle, 1561; reprinted Turin, 1959).

Firth, C.H., and R.S. Rait, *Acts and Ordinances of the Interregnum* (London, 1911) 3 vols.

Frontinus, Sextus, Julius, *Stratagems*, ed. Mary B. McElwain (London, Heinemann, 1925), Loeb edn.

Galileo, Galilei, *Opere di Galileo Galilei*, ed. F. Brunetti (Turin, 1964).

Gassendi, Pierre, *Animadversiones in decimum librum Diogenis Laertii, qui est de vita, moribus, placitisque Epicuri* (Lyon 1649, New York, 1989), 3 vols.

Gassendi, Pierre, *Syntagma philosophicum*, in his *Opera Omnia*, 6 vols (Lyon 1658, Stuttgart-Bad Cannstatt 1964), vol. 1.

Hale, Matthew, *Historia Placitorum Coronae* (London, 1736), 2 vols.

Harvey, Gabriel, *A New letter of Notable Contents with a Strange Sonet Entituled Gorgon or the wonderfull yeare* (London, John Wolfe, 1593).

Herbert, Edward, *De religione gentilium, errorumque apud eos causis* (Amsterdam, 1663), translated as *The Ancient Religion of the Gentiles* (London, 1705). Folger Library: 153296.

Historiae ecclesiasticae scriptores Graeci, ed. John Christopherson, Bp of Chicester (Cologne, 1570).

Hobbes, Thomas, 'Answer' to Davenant's Preface to Gondibert, in William Davenant's *Gondibert: an Heroick Poem* (London, Printed by Theo. Newcomb for John Holden, New Exchange, 1651), STC D325.

Hobbes, Thomas, *Behemoth, or The Long Parliament* [1679], ed. Ferdinand Tönnies (London, 1889, facsimile edn, ed. Stephen Holmes, Chicago 1990).

Hobbes, Thomas, *Behemoth*, ed. Luc Borot, *Thomas Hobbes œuvres complètes* vol. 9 (Paris, Vrin, 1990).

Hobbes, Thomas, *De Cive: the English Version*, Howard Warrender, ed., Oxford, Clarendon Edition of the Works of Thomas Hobbes, vol. 2 (Oxford, Clarendon Press, 1983).

Hobbes, Thomas, *De Cive: the Latin Version*, Howard Warrender, ed. Oxford, Clarendon Edition of the Works of Thomas Hobbes, vol. 1 (Oxford, Clarendon Press, 1983).

Hobbes, Thomas, *De cive, On the Citizen*, ed. and trans. Richard Tuck and Michael Silverthorpe (Cambridge, Cambridge University Press, 1998).

Hobbes, Thomas, *Le Citoyen ou les fondements de la politique*, trans. S. Sorbire, ed. S. Goyard-Fabre (Paris, Garnier-Flammarion, 1982).

Hobbes, Thomas, *De Corpore*, introduction, édition critique latine, annotation par Karl Schuhmann, *Thomas Hobbes œuvres complètes* (Paris, Vrin, 2000).

Hobbes, Thomas, *The Correspondence*, ed Noel Malcolm, 2 vols, Clarendon Edition of the Works of Hobbes, vols. 6 and 7 (Oxford, Clarendon Press, 1994).

Hobbes, Thomas [1642] (1973), *Critique du De Mundo de Thomas White,* ed. Jean Jacquot and H. W. Jones (Paris, Vrin, 1973).

Hobbes, Thomas, *De Mirabilibus Pecci: Being the Wonders of the Peak in Darbyshire* [1627/28]. In English and Latin; the Latin by Hobbes, the English by 'a Person of Quality' (London, Printed for William Crook at the Green Dragon without Temple Bar, 1678). Folger Library, 159640.

Hobbes, Thomas, *Dialogue between a Philosopher and a Student of the Common Laws of England* [1681], ed. Joseph Cropsey (Chicago, University of Chicago Press, 1971).

Hobbes, Thomas. *Eight Bookes of the Peloponnesian Warre Written by Thvcydides the Sonne of Olorvs Interpreted with Faith and Diligence Immediately out of the Greeke* [London, 1629], ed. David Grene (Chicago, University of Chicago Press, 1989).

Hobbes, Thomas, *The Elements of Law Natural and Politic*, ed. Ferdinand Tönnies (1889), reissued with a new Introduction by M. M. Goldsmith (London, Cass, 1969).

Hobbes, Thomas, *The English Works of Thomas Hobbes*, ed. Sir William Molesworth (London, Bohn, 1839-45), 11 vols (referred to as *EW*). Republished with a new Introduction by G.A.J. Rogers, 11 vols (Routledge Thoemmes Press, London 1992).

Hobbes, Thomas, *Hérésie et histoire*, ed. and trans. F. Lessay, Thomas Hobbes, *Œuvres*, vol. 12, part 1 (Paris, Vrin, 1993). Included in this volume are *Relation historique touchant l'hérésie et son châtiment, Sur les lois relatives à l'hérésie, M. Hobbes considéré dans sa loyauté, sa religion, sa réputation et ses m?urs, Préface à la traduction de 'La guerre du Péloponnèse' de Thucydide, Réponse de M. Hobbes à la préface de Sir William Davenant à 'Gondibert', Préface à la traduction de l'"Illiade' et de l'"Odyssée'*.

Hobbes, Thomas, *Historia ecclesiastica carmine elegiaco concinnata*, ed. with a preface by Thomas Rymer (London, Andrew Crooke, 1688). STC H2237.

Hobbes, Thomas, *A True Satirical Ecclesiastical History, from Moses to the time of Martin Luther, in verse.* (London, printed for E. Curll in the Strand, 1722).

Hobbes, Thomas, *Th. Hobbes, Storia Ecclesiastica, narrata in forma di carme elegiaca*, trans, G. Invernizzi and A. Luppoli, in *Th. Hobbes, Scritti teologici*, trans. G. Invernizzi and A. Luppoli (Milan, Franco Angeli, 1988).

Hobbes, Thomas, *An Historical Narration Concerning Heresy* (1668), *EW* IV, pp. 387-408.

Hobbes, Thomas, *Horae Subsecivae* [1620], in *Thomas Hobbes: Three Discourses: A Critical Modern Edition of Newly Identified Work of the Young Thomas Hobbes*, ed. N. B. Reynolds and A. W. Saxonhouse (Chicago, Il., University of Chicago Press, 1995).

Hobbes, Thomas, *The Iliades and Odysses of Homer. Translated out of the Greek into English. With a large Preface concerning the Vertues of an Heroick Poem; written by the Translator: Also the Life of Homer.* The Third Edition (London, for Will Crook, at the green

Dragon without Temple-Bar, next Devereux-Court, 1686) [Folger Library H2552 Homerus], *EW* X.

Hobbes, Thomas, *Leviathan* [1651], with selected variants from the Latin edition of 1668 ed. Edwin Curley (Indianapolis, Ind., Hackett Publishing, 1994).

Hobbes, Thomas, *Leviathan* [1651], a new critical edition by Karl Schuhmann ad G.A.J. Rogers (Bristol, Thoemmes, 2003), 2 vols.

Hobbes, Thomas, *Léviathan Traduit du Latin et annoté*, trans. et ed., François Tricaud et Martine Pécharman (Paris, Vrin, 2004).

Hobbes, Thomas, *Léviathan Traité de la matière, de la forme et du pouvoir de la république ecclésiastique et civile*, ed. François Tricaud (Paris, Sirey, 1971).

Hobbes, Thomas, *De la liberté et de la nécessité et Résponse à la capture de Léviathan*, trans. Franck Lessay, *Thomas Hobbes œuvres complètes*, vol. 11, part 1 (Paris, Vrin, 1993).

Hobbes, Thomas. *Opera Philosophica quae Latine scripsit omnia.* Sir William Molesworth, ed. (London, Bohn, 1839-45), 5 vols (referred to as *OL*). Republished with a new Introduction by G.A.J. Rogers. 5 vols. Thoemmes Press, Bristol, 1999.

Hobbes, Thomas, 'The Prose Life', in Thomas Hobbes, *Human Nature and De Corpore Politico*, edited by J.C.A. Gaskin (Oxford, Oxford University Press, 1994), pp. 245-53.

Hobbes, Thomas, *The Questions concerning Liberty, Necessity and Chance, clearly stated and debated between Dr. Bramhall, Bishop of Derby and Thomas Hobbes of Malmesbury* (1654), *EW* V.

Hobbes, Thomas, *Les Questions concernant la liberté, la nécessité et le hasard*, trans. L. Foisneau et F. Perronin, *Thomas Hobbes œuvres complètes*, vol. 11, part 2 (Paris, Vrin, 1999).

Hobbes, Thomas, *Seven Philosophical Problems* (London, 1682).

Hobbes, Thomas, *A Short Tract on First Principles*, ed. Ferdinand Tönnies (1889), reissued with a new Introduction by M. M. Goldsmith (London, Cass, 1969)

Hobbes, Thomas, *Six Lessons to the Professors of the Mathematiques. One of Geometry, the other of Astronomy: In the Chaires set up by the Noble and Learned Sir Henry Savile, in the University of Oxford* (London, 1656).

Hobbes, Thomas, *Textes sur l'Hérésie et sur l'Histoire*, ed. Franck Lessay, ed. *De la Liberté et de la Nécessité*, (Paris, Vrin, 1993).

Hobbes, Thomas [1642], *Thomas White's 'De Mundo' Examined.* Harold Whitmore Jones, trans. (Bradford, Bradford University Press, 1976).

Hobbes, Thomas, Writings on Common Law and Hereditary Right A dialogue between a philosopher and a student, of the common

Laws of England. Questions relative to Hereditary right, ed. Alan Cromartie and Quentin Skinner (Oxford, Clarendon Press, 2005).

Homer. Homeri Opera, ed T. W. Allen (Oxford, Oxford University Press, 1912).

Homerus, *Achilles Shield. Translated as the other seuen Bookes of Homer out of his eighteenth booke of Iliades* tr. George Chapman (London, Imprinted by Iohn Windet, 1598), Folger 13635 Homerus.

Horace, *The Complete Odes and Epodes with the Centennial Hymn*, tr. W. G. Shepherd (Harmondsworth, Penguin, 1983).

Horace, *Odes and Epodes*, annotated Latin edn, Paul Shorey and Gordon J. Laing, eds (Chicago, Benj. H. Sanborn, 1919).

Horace, *Satires*, tr. Fairclough (London, Heinemann, 1929), Loeb edn.

Horace. *Satires and Epistles of Horace*, Smith Palmer Bovie, tr. (Chicago 1959).

Hyde, Edward, Lord Clarendon, *A Brief View and Survey of the Dangerous and Pernicious Errors to Church and State in Mr. Hobbes's Book entitled Leviathan* (Oxford, 1676).

John of Salisbury, *The Letters of John of Salisbury*, ed. W.J. Millor, H.E. Butler, C.N.L Brooke, (Oxford, Oxford University Press, 1979).

Jonson, Benjamin, *Works*, ed. C.H. Herford, P. and E. Simpson (Oxford, Oxford University Press, 1925-52).

Juvenal, *The Sixteen Satires*, Peter Green tr. introd and notes (Harmondsworth, Penguin, 1974).

Kennett, White, *A Sermon Preach'd at the Funeral of the Right Noble William Duke of Devonshire . . . with some Memoirs of the Family of Cavendish* (London, 1708).

Lucan, *Pharsalia*, Jane Wilson Joyce tr. (Ithaca, NY, Cornell University Press, 1994).

Lucian, *Works*, ed. A. M. Harmon (London, Heinemann, 1959), 6 vols, Loeb edn

Lucretius, *De Rerum Natura*, critical edn, Cyril Bailey ed. (Oxford, Clarendon, 1947).

Lucretius, *De Rerum Natura*, tr. W. H. D. Rouse, commentary by M. F. Smith, (London, Heinemann, 1975), Loeb edn.

Luther, Martin, *The Reformation Writings of Martin Luther*. Translated from the definitive Weimar edition by Bertram Lee Wolf (London, 1956), 2 vols.

Lyly, John, *Euphues: the Anatomy of Wit; Euphues & his England* (1578-80), Morris William Croll and Harry Clemons, eds (New York, Russell & Russell, 1964)

Marsham, John, *Canon Chronicus Aegyptiacus, Ebraicus, Graecus* (Oxford, 1672).

May, Thomas, *The Reigne of King Henry the Second, Written in Seaven Bookes, by his Majesties Command* (London, 1633).

Mersenne, Marin, *Correspondance du P. Marin Mersenne*, Paul Tannery, Cornelis de Waard, and Armand Beaulieu, eds. (Paris, G. Beauchesne, 1932-1986, 16 vols).

Micanzio, Fulgenzio, *Lettere a William Cavendish (1615-1628), nella versione inglese di Thomas Hobbes*, ed. Robero Ferrini and Enrico de Mas (Rome, Instituto Storico O.S.M., 1987).

Milton, John, *The Prose Works of John Milton*, ed. Rufus Wilmot Griswold. 2 vols (Philadelphia: John W. Moore, 1847).

Milton, John, *On the New Forces of Conscience under the Long Parliament*, sonnet (London, 1646).

Milton, John, *Paradise Lost* (London, 1667).

Milton, John, *The Tenure of Kings and Magistrates* (London, 1650).

Milton, John, *Tetrachordon: Expositions upon the foure chief Places in Scripture which treat of Marriage or Nullities in Marriage* (London, 1645).

Milton, John, *A Treatise of Civil Power in Ecclesiastical Causes: shewing that it is not lawfull for any power on earth to compel in matters of Religion* (London, 1659).

Monsey, R. *Scarronides: or Virgile Travestie, A Mock-Poem. Being The Second Book of Virgils Æneis, Translated into English Burlesque* (London, 1665).

More, Henry, 'Animadversions on Hobbs, concerning Thoughts of Man', in *Letters on Several Subjects . . .* (London, 1694).

Nashe, Thomas, *Christ's Teares over Jerusalem*, in J. Payne Collier's handwritten transcription (Folger Shakespeare Library, Y.d.7 54b).

Nedham, Marchamont, *The Case of the Common-wealth of England Stated: the Equity, Utility, and Necessity of a Submission to the Present Government Cleared out of Monuments both Sacred and Civill all the scruples and pretenses of the opposite parties: Royalists, Presbyterians, Scots, Levellers . . .* (London, 1650).

Nedham, Marchamont, *The Excellency of a Free State* (London, 1656).

Negri, Francisco, *Regulae elegantiarum Francisci Negri*, in A. Dati, ed, *Elegantiarum linguae latinae praecepta* (Lugduni 1589).

Oecolampadius, Jean, *Exposition de M. Iean Oecolompade svr le Livre de Iob*. Traduit de Latin en François. Edition premiere. (Geneve, Vincent Bres, 1562). Wing 218-628q.

Ovid, *Metamorphoses*, tr. J. F. Miller (London, Heinemann, 1977), Loeb edn.

Pagett Ephraim, *Heresiography, or, a Description and History of the Hereticks and Sectaries sprang up in these latter times* (London, 1645).

Parsons, Robert, *Elizabethae, Angliae Reginae Haeresin Calvinianam Propvgnantis, Saevissimvm in Catholicos sui regni Edictum. . . .* (London, apud Ioannem Didier, 1592).

Parsons, Robert, *A Conference abovt the Next Svccession to the Crowne of Ingland. . . .* (London, R. Doleman, 1594), Folger Library, 19398.

Parsons, Robert. *A Quiet and Sober Reckonning with M. Thomas Morton* (St. Omer, English College Press, 1609), STC 19412.

Patrizi, Francesco, *Nova de Universis Philosophia* (Rome, 1591).

Peacham, Henry, *Garden of Eloquence* (London, 1593, 2nd edn).

Percy, Thomas, *Reliques of Ancient English Poetry: consisting of Old Heroic Ballads, Songs and other pieces of our earlier Poets* (London, printed for J. Dodsley in Pall Mall, 1765), 3 vols.

Petrarca, Francesco, *Prose*, ed. G. Martellotti *et al.* (Milan, Ricciardi, 1955).

Petrarch, Francesco. *Le familiare*, ed. Vittorio Rossi and Umberto Bosco (Florence, 1933-42), 4 vols.

Petau, Denis (Dionysius Petavius), *Theologicorum Deorum, Prolegomena* (Paris, 1644-).

Petau, Denis (Dionysius Petavius), 'De Trinitate', in *Opus de theologicis dogmatibus auctius in hac nova editione* (Antwerpiae apud G. Gallet, 1700), vol. II, bk. IV, pp. 182 ff.

Photius, *Epitome of the Historia Ecclesiastica of Philostorgius*, tr. Edward Walford (London, 1855).

Plutarch, *Makers of Rome*, tr. with introd by Ian Scott-Kilvert (Harmondsworth, Penguin, 1965).

Plutarch: Selected Essays and Dialogues, ed. Donald Russell (Oxford, Oxford University Press, 1993).

Pontano, Giovanni, *Dialoghi*, ed. C. Previtera (Florence, 1943).

Pope, Walter, The *Life of the Right Reverend Father in God, Seth, Lord Bishop of Salisbury* (London, 1697).

Prudentius, Clemens, Aurelius, ed. H. J. Thomson, *Prudentius, Works* (London, Heinemann, 1949), Loeb edn, 2 vols.

Prudentius, Clemens, Aurelius, *The Latin Glosses on Arator and Prudentius in Cambridge, University Library*, Ms Gg.5.35, Studies and Texts 61 (Toronto, 1983).

Prynne, William, *A Full Reply to Certaine Briefe Observations and anti-Queries. . . . Together with Certaine Breife Animadversions on Mr. John Goodwins Theomachia* (London, 1644), Folger Library, 133114.

Puttenham, Richard, *The Art of English Poesie* (London, 1589).

Quintilian, *Institutio Oratoria*, trans. H. E. Butler (Cambridge, Mass., Harvard University Press, 1953).

Quintilian, *Institutio oratoria*, ed. M. Winterbottom (Oxford, Oxford University Press, 1970).

Rabelais, François, *Gargantua or Pantagruel* (Paris, 1653), English tr., Thomas Urquhart, 1649 (New York, Knopf, 1994).

Rainolds, John, *An Excellent Oration of the Late Famously Learned John Rainolds, DD. . . . very useful for all such as affect the Studies of Logick and Philosophie and admire profane learning*, ed. John Leycester (Oxford, 1637).

Ross, Alexander, *Pansebeia: or A View of All the Religions of the World* (London, John Saywell, 1658).

Sandys, George, *Ovid's Metamorphosis Englished, Mythologized and Presented in Figures* (Oxford, 1632).

Sarpi, Paolo, *Historio del Concilio Tridentino* (Venice, 1619), translated by N. Bent as, *The History of the Council of Trent* (London, 1620).

Scarron, Paul, *Le Virgile Travestie* [1648-52], ed. Jean Serroy (Paris, Garnier, 1988).

Selden, John, *Eutychii Aegyptii, Patriarchae Orthodoxorum Alexandrini, Ecclesiae suae Origines. Ex ejusdem Arabico nunc primum typis editit, ac versione & commentario auxit*, included in Selden's *Opera Omnia* (London, 1626), 6 vols, vol. 3, pp. 410-527 (Also published separately in 1642).

Selden, John. *Jewish Marriage Law*, (*Uxor Hebraica*), tr. Jonathan R. Ziskind (Leiden, E.J. Brill, 1991).

Socrates of Constantinople, *Ecclesiastical History of Socrates Scholasticus in VII Books* (3rd edn London, 1729).

Sozomen, *Historia Ecclesiastica*, bks 1-6, ed. J. Bidez, tr. A. J. Festugiere (Paris Editions du Cerf, 1983).

Spencer, John, *Dissertatio de Urim et Thummim* (London, 1669).

Spenser, Edmund, *The Works of Edmund Spenser: A Variorum Edition*, ed. Edwin Greenlaw, C. G. Osgood, et al. (Baltimore, Johns Hopkins Press, 1932-57), 10 volumes.

Sidney, Sir Philip, *An Apology for Poetry*, in *Elizabethan Critical Essays*, ed. G. G. Smith (Oxford, Oxford University Press, 1904), 2 vols.

Valla, Lorenzo, *De falso credita et ementita constantini donatione*. W. Setz, ed (Weimar 1976, repr. Munich 1986).

Valla, Lorenzo. *Opera omnia*, ed. E. Garin (Torino, 1962).

Valla, Lorenzo, *Oraciones y Prefacios (pro una renovación de los métodos de estudio)*, ed. Francesco Adorno (Santiago, 1955).

Valla, Lorenzo. *Orazione per l'inaugurazione dell'anno accadmico 1455-1456*, ed. S. Rizzo (Rome 1994).

Valla, Lorenzo, *On Pleasure (De Voluptate)*, ed. Maristella de Panizza Lorch, tr. A. Kent Hieatt and Maristella Lorch (New York, Abaris Books, 1977).

Valla, Lorenzo, *Recriminationes in Facium* (1445), in his *Opera omnia*, ed. E. Garin (Torino, 1962), vol. 1.

Valla, Lorenzo, *Laurentii Valle Repastinatio dialectice et philosophie*, ed. G. Zippel 2 vols (Padua, Antenore, 1983).

Lorenzo Vallas Schrift gegen die Konstantinische Schenkung: De falso credita ementita constantini donatione. Zur Interpretation und Wirkungsgeschichte, W. Setz, ed. (Tübingen, 1975).

Valla, Lorenzo, *A treatise of the donation or gyfte and endowment of possessyons gyven and graunted unto Sylvester pope of Rhome by Constantyne emperour of Rome*, Thomas Godfray, ed. (London, 1534, repr. Norwood, N.J., 1979).

Valla, Lorenzo, *The Treatise of Lorenzo Valla on the Donation of Constantine, Text and Translation into English*, ed. Christopher B. Coleman (New York, Russell and Russell, 1922, reprinted Toronto, University of Toronto, 1993).

Virgil. *Aeneid*, ed. David West (Harmondsworth, Penguin, 1991).

Virgil, *Eclogues*, ed. Guy Lee, (Harmondsworth, Penguin, 1984).

Vives, Juan Luis, *Opera*, 2 vols, (Basle 1555).

Vives, Juan Luis, *Opera Omnia*, ed G. Mayans (Valencia, 1782-90), 8 vols.

Vossius, Gerardus, *De Historicis Graecis Libri IV, Editio altera, priori emendatior, & multis partibus auctior, Latinis* (Leiden, Ex Officina Ioannis Maire, 1623, 1627).

Vossius, Gerardus, *De Theologia Gentili et Physiologia Christiana; sive de origine ac progressu idololatriæ, ad veterum gesta, ac rerum naturam, reductæ; deque naturæ mirandis, quibus homo adducitur ad Deum* (Amsterdam, Joannes and Cornelius Blaeu, 1641).

Walton, Izaak and Charles Cotton, *The Compleat Angler* (1653), ed. Jonquil Bevan (London, Everyman edn, 1993).

Webbe, Thomas, *Mr. Edwards Pen no slander, or, The Gangraena once more searched* (London, 1646).

Webbe, William, *Discourse of English Poetry* (London, 1586).

Wilkins, David, *Concilia Magna Britanniae et Hiberniae* (London, 1737), 4 vols.

Wilson, Edmund, *Synodus Anglicana* (London, 1702).

Wood, Anthony, *Athenae Oxonienses: An Exact History Of All The Writers and Bishops Who have had their Education in The most ancient and famous University Of Oxford, From The Fifteenth Year of King Henry the Seventh, Dom. 1500, to the End of the Year 1690* (London, Thomas Bennet, 1691-2), 2 vols.

SECONDARY SOURCES

Ames-Lewis, Francis, ed., *Sir Thomas Gresham and Gresham College: Studies in the Intellectual History of London in the Sixteenth and Seventeenth Centuries* (London, Ashgate, 1999).

Arbusow, Leonid, *Colores rhetorici*, 2nd edn, ed. Helmut Peter (Göttingen, Vandenhoeck & Ruprecht, 1963).

Auerbach, Erich, 'Figura', in *Scenes from the Drama of European Literature*, trans. Ralph Mannheim (New York, Meridian Books, 1959).

Auerbach, Eric, *Literary Language and Its Public in Late Latin Antiquity and in the Middle Ages*, trans. Ralph Manheim (Princeton, Princeton University Press, 1993).

Axtell, J., 'The Mechanics of Opposition: Restoration Cambridge v. Daniel Scargill', *Bulletin of the Institute of Historical Research*, vol. 38 (1965), pp. 102-11.

Bailey, Cyril, *Epicurus, the Extant Remains* (Oxford, Clarendon Press, 1926).

Bailey, Cyril, *The Greek Atomists and Epicurus* (Oxford, Clarendon Press, 1928).

Barraclough, Geoffrey, *The Medieval Papacy* (New York, W. W. Norton, 1968).

Barnes, T. D., 'Christians and Pagans in the Reign of Constantius' and following Discussion, in *L'Église et l'Empire au IVe siècle*, ed. Albrecht Dihle (Geneva, Fondation Hardt, 1989), pp. 301-43.

Barnouw, Geoffrey, 'Le vocabulaire du conatus', in *Hobbes et son vocabulaire: Etudes de lexicographie philosophique*, ed. Yves Charles Zarka and Jean Bernhardt (Paris, Vrin, 1992), pp. 103-124.

Barton, Anne, 'Harking Back to Elizabeth: Ben Jonson and Caroline Nostalgia', *ELH* (*English Literary History*), vol. 48 (1981), pp. 706-31.

Bedford, R. D. *The Defence of Truth: Herbert of Cherbury and the Seventeenth Century* (Princeton, N.J., Princeton University Press, 1987),

Berman, David, 'Deism, Immortality, and the Art of Theological Lying', in J. Leo Lemay, ed. *Deism, Masonry and the Enlightenment* (Newark, N.J., University of Delaware Press, 1987), pp. 61-78.

Berman, David, 'Disclaimers as Offence Mechanisms in Charles Blount and John Toland', in M. Hunter and D. Wootton, *Atheism from the Reformation to the Enlightenment* (Oxford, Clarendon Press, 1992), pp. 255-72.

Berman, Harold, *Law and Revolution, The Formation of the Western Legal Tradition* (Cambridge, Mass., Harvard University Press, 1983).

Berman, Harold J., 'The Papal Revolution', in *The Middle Ages*, Vol. II, *Readings in Medieval History*, ed. Brian Tierney, 4th edn (New York, McGraw Hill, 1992), pp. 217-23.

Bertrand, Dominique, 'The Society of Jesus and the Church Fathers in the Sixteenth and Seventeenth Century', in Irena Backus, ed., *The Reception of the Church Fathers in the West, from the Carolingians to the Maurists* (Leiden, E.J. Brill, 1979), 2 vols, vol. 2, pp. 889-950.

Bettenson, H., *Documents of the Christian Church* (Oxford, Oxford University Press, 1963)

Beyssade, Jean-Marie and Jean-Luc Marion, eds, *Descartes: Objecter et répondre* (Paris, P.U.F., 1994).

Binns, J. W. *Intellectual Culture in Elizabethan and Jacobean England: the Latin Writings of the Age* (Leeds, Francis Cairns, Ltd., University of Leeds, 1990).

Bloch, Olivier René, 'Gassendi et la théorie politique de Hobbes'; in Thomas Hobbes, Philosophie première, théorie de la science et politique, ed. Yves Charles Zarka and Jean Bernhardt (Paris, P.U.F., 1990).

Bloch, Olivier René, *La Philosophie de Gassendi, Nominalisme, Matérialisme et Métaphysique* (The Hague, Martinus Nijhoff, 1971).

Blumenthal, Uta-Renate, *The Investiture Controversy. Church and Monarchy from the Ninth to the Eleventh Century* (Philadelphia, University of Pennsylvania Press, 1988).

Bowersock, Glen W., *Julian the Apostate* (Cambridge, Mass., Harvard University Press, 1978).

Bradley, Robert, 'Blacklo and the Counter-Reformation: An Enquiry into the Strange Death of Catholic England', in Charles Howard Carter, ed., *From Renaissance to the Counter Reformation* (New York, Random House, 1965), pp. 355-8.

Bradner, Leicester, *Musae Anglicanae: A History of Anglo-Latin Poetry 1500-1925* (New York, 1940, repr. 1965).

Bredekamp, Horst, 'From Walter Benjamin to Carl Schmitt, via Thomas Hobbes', *Critical Inquiry*, vol. 25, 1999, pp. 247-266.

Bredekamp, Horst, *Stratégies visuelles de Thomas Hobbes. Le Léviathan, archétype de l'État moderne. Illstrations et portraits* (Paris, Maison des Sciences de l'Homme, 2003, French translation of Thomas Hobbes visuelle Strategien).

Bredekamp, Horst, *Thomas Hobbes der Leviathan. Das Urbild des modernen Staates* (Berlin, Akademie, 2003, 2nd enlarged edn of Bredekamp, Thomas Hobbes visuelle Strategien).

Bredekamp, Horst, *Thomas Hobbes visuelle Strategien: Der Leviathan, Urbild des modernen Staates – Werkillustrationen und Porträts* (Berlin, Akademie, 1999).

Bredekamp, Horst, 'Thomas Hobbes's Visual Strategies', in Patricia Springborg, ed., *Cambridge Companion to Hobbes's Leviathan* (New York, Cambridge University Press, 2007), pp. 29-60.

Brock, S., 'A Monothelete *Florilegium* in Syriac', in C. Laga, J. A. Munitiz and L. Van Rompay, eds, *After Chalcedon: Studies in Theology and Church History* (Leuven, Orientalia Lovaniensia Analecta 18, 1985), pp. 35-45.

Brooke, Christopher, 'John of Salisbury and his World', in *The World of John of Salisbury*, ed. Michael Wilks (Oxford, Oxford University Press, 1994), pp. 1-20.

Brown, Cedric, 'Courtesies of Place and Arts of Diplomacy in Ben Jonson's Last Two Entertainments for Royalty', *The Seventeenth Century*, vol. 9, no. 2 (1994), pp. 147-71.

Brown, Alison, 'Platonism in Fifteenth-Century Florence and its Contribution to Early Modern Political Thought', *Journal of Modern History* vol. 58 (1986), pp. 383-413.

Brown, Keith, 'The Artist of the Leviathan Title Page', *British Library Journal*, vol. 4 (1978), pp. 24-36.

Bryant, Lawrence M., 'Politics, Ceremonies and Embodiments of Majesty in Henry II's France', in Heinz Duchhardt, Richard A. Jackson, and David J. Sturdy, eds, *European Monarchy, its Evolution and Practice from Roman Antiquity to Modern Times* (Stuttgart, Franz Steiner Verlag, 1992), pp. 127-54.

Burns, Norman T., *Christian Mortalism from Tyndale to Milton* (Cambridge, Mass., Harvard University Press, 1972).

Butler, John A. *Lord Herbert of Cherbury 1582-1648: An Intellectual Biography* (Lewiston, NY., Edwin Mellen, 1990).

Butler, Martin, *Theatre and Crisis 1632-1642* (Cambridge, Cambridge University Press, 1984).

Butler, Martin, ed., *Representing Ben Jonson: Text, History, Performance* (London, Palgrave Macmillan, 1999).

Camporeale, S. I. *Lorenzo Valla: filosofia e religione nell 'umanisimo italiano* (Rome, Edizioni di. Storia e Letteratura, 1971).

Camporeale, S. I. *Lorenzo Valla: umanesimo et teologica* (Florence, Istituto Nazionale di Studi sul Rinascimento, 1972).

Camporeale, S. I., 'Lorenzo Valla's *Oratio* on the Pseudo-Donation of Constantine: Dissent and Innovation in Early Renaissance Humanism', *Journal of the History of Ideas,* vol 57 (1996), pp. 9-26.

Camporeale, S. I. 'Renaissance Humanism and the Origins of Humanist Theology', in *Humanity and Divinity in Renaissance and Reformation: Essays in Honor of Charles Trinkaus*, ed. John O'Malley, *et al.* (Leiden, E.J. Brill, 1993).

Champion, J. A. I., *The Pillars of Priestcraft Shaken: the Church of England and its Enemies, 1660-1730* (Cambridge, Cambridge University Press, 1992).

Chestnut, Glenn F., *The First Christian Histories: Eusebius, Socrates, Sozomen, Theodoret and Evagrius* (Paris, Editions Beauchesne, 1986).

Clucas, Stephen, 'The Atomism of the Cavendish Circle: A Reappraisal', *The Seventeenth Century*, vol. 9, no 2 (1994), pp. 247-73.

Clucas, Stephen, 'Samuel Hartlib's Ephemerides, 1635-1659, and the pursuit of scientific and philosophical manuscripts: the religious ethos of an intelligencer', *The Seventeenth Century*, vol. 6 (1991), pp. 33-55.

Cole, Thomas, *Democritus and the Sources of Greek Anthropology* (Cleveland, Ohio, American Philological Association Monographs, 1967; repr. Oxford, Oxford University Press, 1990).

Collins, Jeffrey R., *The Allegiance of Thomas Hobbes* (Oxford, Clarendon Press, 2005).

Collins, Jefffrey R., 'Christian Ecclesiology and the Composition of Leviathan: a Newly Discovered Letter to Thomas Hobbes', *Historical Journal* 43 (2000), pp. 217-31.

Collins, Jeffrey R., 'Silencing Thomas Hobbes: The Presbyterians and Leviathan', in Patricia Springborg, ed., *The Cambridge Companion to Hobbes's Leviathan* (New York, Cambridge University Press, 2007), pp. 478-500.

Collins, Jeffrey R., 'Thomas Hobbes and the Blackloist Conspiracy of 1649', the *Historical Journal*, vol. 45 (2002), pp. 305-331.

Collinson, Patrick, 'Biblical Rhetoric: the English Nation and National Sentiment in the Prophetic Mood', in *Religion and Culture in Renaissance England*, Claire McEachern and Deborah Shuger, eds (Cambridge, Cambridge University Press, 1997), pp. 15-45.

Crist, Timothy, 'Government Control of the Press after the Expiration of the Printing Act in 1679', *Printing History*, vol. 5 (1979), pp. 48-77.

Curley, E., 'Calvin and Hobbes, or Hobbes as an Orthodox Christian', *Journal of the History of Philosophy*, vol 34 (1996), pp. 257-71.

Curley, E., '"I durst not write so boldly", or How to read Hobbes' theological-political Treatise', in E. Giancotti, *Hobbes e Spinoza. Scienza e politica* (Napoli, Bibliopolis, 1992), pp. 497-594.

Curley, E., 'Reply to Professor Martinich', *Journal of the History of Philosophy*, vol. 34 (1996), pp. 285-7.

Daniel-Rops, Henri, *Cathedral and Crusade*, 2 vols (New York, E. P. Dutton & Co, 1957).

Daniel-Rops, Henri, *The Church in the Dark Ages* (New York, Dutton, 1959).

Davis, Paul, 'Thomas Hobbes's Translations of Homer: Epic and Anti-clericalism in Late Seventeenth-Century England', *The Seventeenth Century*, vol. 12 (1997), pp. 231-55.

Davis, Richard B., *George Sandys, Poet Adventurer: A Study in Anglo-American Culture in the Seventeenth Century* (New York, Columbia University Press, 1955).

Diamond, William Craig, *Public Identity in Restoration England: From Prophetic to Economic*, Ph. D. Dissertation, Johns Hopkins University (Ann Arbor Microfilms, 1982).

Dowlin, Cornell, *Sir William Davenant's Gondibert, its Preface, and Hobbes's Answer: A Study in Neoclassicism* (Philadelphia, n.p., 1934).

Duffy, Eamon, '"Whiston's Affair": the Trials of a Primitive Christian 1709-24', *Journal of Ecclesiastical History*, vol. 27 (1976), pp. 129-50.

Edmond, Mary. *Rare Sir William Davenant* (Manchester, University of Manchester Press, 1987)

Erskine-Hill, Howard, *Poetry and the Realm of Politics: Shakespeare to Dryden* (Oxford, Oxford University Press, 1998).

Farneti, Roberto, *Il canone moderno. Filosofia politica e genealogia* (Turin, Bollati Boringhieri, 2002)

Farneti, Roberto, 'The "Mythical Foundation" of the State: Leviathan in Emblematic Context' in *Pacific Philosophical Quarterly*, 82 (2001), pp. 362-382 (a special Issue on Hobbes's *Leviathan*)

Farneti, Roberto',Hobbes on Salvation', in Patricia Springborg, ed., *The Cambridge Companion to Hobbes's Leviathan* (New York, Cambridge University Press, 2007), pp. 291-308.

Firth, Katharine R. *The Apocalyptic Tradition in Reformation Britain, 1530-1645* (Oxford, Oxford University Press, 1979).

Fisher, Alan, 'The Project of Humanism and Valla's Imperial Metaphor', *Journal. of Medieval and Renaissance Studies*, vol. 23 (1993) pp. 301-22.

Fleischmann, W. B., *Lucretius and English Literature* (Paris, A. G. Nizet, 1964).

Florovsky, G., 'Origen, Eusebius, and the Iconoclastic Controversy', *Church History*, vol 19 (1950), pp. 77ff.

Foisneau, Luc, *Politique, droit et théologie chez Bodin, Grotius et Hobbes* (Paris, Kimé, 1997).

Foisneau, Luc, *Hobbes et la toute-puissance de Dieu* (Paris P.U.F., 2000).

Foisneau, Luc, 'Omnipotence, Necessity and Sovereignty: Hobbes and the Absolute and Ordinary Powers of God and King', in Patricia

Springborg, ed., *The Cambridge Companion to Hobbes's Leviathan* (New York, Cambridge University Press, 2007), pp. 271-90.

Frend, W.H.C., 'The Church in the Reign of Constantius II (337-361)', in *L'Église et l'Empire au IVe siècle*, ed. Albrecht Dihle (Geneva, Fondation Hardt, 1989), pp. 73-111.

Gabrieli, Vittorio, 'Bacone, la riforma e Roma nella versione Hobbesiana d'un carteggio di Fulgenzio Micanzio', *The English Miscellany*, vol. 8 (1957), pp. 195-250.

Ganshof, François L., *The Imperial Coronation of Charlemagne* (Glasgow, Jackson, 1949).

Gascoigne, John, '"The Wisdom of the Egyptians" and the Secularisation of History in the Age of Newton'. In Stephen Gaukroger, ed., *The Uses of Antiquity* (Dordrecht, Reidel, 1991), pp. 171-212.

Geanakopolos, Deno J., *Byzantine East and Latin West: Two Worlds of Christendom in Middle Ages and Renaissance* (Oxford, Oxford University Press, 1966).

George, Charles H. and Katherine George, *The Protestant Mind of the English Reformation, 1570-1640* (Princeton, Princeton University Press, 1961).

Gillies, John, *Shakespeare and the Geography of Difference* (Cambridge, Cambridge University Press, 1994).

Ginsburg, Carlo, *History, Rhetoric, and Proof* (Hanover, New Hampshire, Brandeis University Press, 1999).

Gladish, David F., *Sir William Davenant's Gondibert*. (Oxford, Clarendon Press, 1971).

Glaziou, Yves, *Hobbes en France au XVIIIe siècle* (Paris, P.U.F., 1995).

Goldie, Mark, 'The Reception of Hobbes', in J. H. Burns and Mark Goldie, eds, *The Cambridge History of Political Thought, 1450-1700* (Cambridge, Cambridge University Press, 1991), pp. 589-615.

Goldsmith, Maurice, 'Picturing Hobbes's Politics: the Illustrations to the *Philosophicall Rudiments*', *Journal of the Warburg and Courtauld Institutes*, vol. 44 (1981), pp. 231-7.

Goldsmith, Maurice, 'Hobbes's Ambiguous Politics', *History of Political Thought*, vol. 11 (1990), pp. 639-73.

Grabmann, M., 'Aristoteles im 12. Jahrhundert', *Medieval Studies*, vol. 12 (1950), pp. 123-162.

Grafton, Anthony, 'Joseph Scaliger and Historical Chronology: The Rise and Fall of a Discipline' *History & Theory*, vol. 14 (1975), pp. 156-185.

Grafton, Anthony, *Joseph Scaliger: A Study in the History of Classical Scholarship*, I: *Textual Criticism and Exegesis* (Oxford, 1983).

Grafton, Anthony & Lisa Jardine, '"Studied for Action": How Gabriel Harvey read his Livy', *Past and Present*, no 129, (1990), pp. 30-78.

Gravelle, Sarah Stever, 'Humanist Attitudes to Convention and Innovation in the Fifteenth Century', *Journal of Medieval and Renaissance Studies*, vol. 11 (1981), pp. 193-210.

Gravelle, Sarah Stever, 'Lorenzo Valla's Comparison of Latin and Greek and the Humanist Background', *Bibilothèque d'Humanisme et Renaissance*, vol. 44, 2 (1982), pp. 279-80.

Gravelle, Sarah Stever, 'A New Theory of Truth', *Journal of the History of Ideas*, vol. 50 (1989), pp. 333-4.

Greenblatt, Stephen, *Renaissance Self-Fashioning, from More to Shakespeare* (Chicago, University of Chicago Press, 1980).

Green, V. H. H., *The Later Plantagenets* (London: Edward Arnold, 1955).

Greene, Thomas M., 'Petrarch and the Humanist Hermeneutic', in Giose Rimanelli and Kenneth John Atchity, eds, *Italian Literature, Roots and Branches: Essays in Honor of Thomas Goddard Bergin* (New Haven, Yale University Press, 1976), pp. 201-24.

Gregory, Timothy Edmund, *The Urban Crowd in the Religious Controversies of the Fifth Century AD* Ph. D. Thesis, U. of Michigan (Ann Arbor Microfilms, 1971).

Habermas, Jürgen, *The Philosophical Discourse of Modernity* (Camb., Mass., Harvard University Press, 1987).

Hadot, Pierre, *Philosophy as a Way of Life: Spiritual Exercises from Socrates to Foucault* (Oxford, Blackwell, 1995).

Hamburger, Philip, 'The Development of the Law of Seditious Libel and the Control of the Press', *Stanford Law Review*, vol. 37 (1985), pp. 662-765.

Hankins, James, *Plato and the Italian Renaissance*, 2 vols (Leiden, E. J. Brill, 1990).

Harrison, Charles T. 'The Ancient Atomists and English Literature of the Seventeenth Century', *Harvard Studies in Classical Philology*, 45 (1934), pp. 1-79.

Harrison, Charles T. 'Bacon, Hobbes, Boyle, and the Ancient Atomists', in *Harvard Studies and Notes in Philology and Literature*, 15 (1933), pp. 191-218.

Havell, H. L., *Republican Rome* (London, 1914, reprinted 1996).

Helgerson, Richard, *Forms of Nationhood: The Elizabethan Writing of England* (Chicago, Ill., University of Chicago Press, 1992).

Hill, Eurgen D., *Edward, Lord Herbert of Cherbury* (Boston, Mass., Twayne, 1987).

Hoekstra, Kinch, 'The *De Facto* Turn in Hobbes's Political Philosophy', *Leviathan After 350 Years*, ed. Tom Sorell and Luc Foisneau (Oxford University Press, 2004), pp. 34-73

Hoekstra, Kinch, 'Disarming the Prophets: Thomas Hobbes and Predictive Power', commemorative Hobbes volume of *Rivista di storia della filosofia*, vol. 59 (2004), ed. George Wright and Luc Foisneau, pp. 97-153.

Hoekstra, Kinch, 'The End of Philosophy (The Case of Hobbes)', *Proceedings of the Aristotelian Society* 106:1 (2006), pp. 23-60.

Hoekstra, Kinch, 'Hobbes and the Foole', *Political Theory* 25:5 (1997), pp. 620-54

Hoekstra, Kinch, 'Hobbes on Law, Nature, and Reason', *Journal of the History of Philosophy* 41:1 (2003), pp. 111-20.

Hoekstra, Kinch, 'Hobbes on the Natural Condition of Mankind', in Patricia Springborg, ed., *The Cambridge Companion to Hobbes's Leviathan* (New York, Cambridge University Press, 2007), pp. 291-308.

Hoekstra, Kinch, 'A Lion in the House: Hobbes and Democracy', *Rethinking the Foundations of Modern Political Thought*, ed. James Tully and Annabel Brett (Cambridge, Cambridge University Press, 2006), pp. 191-218.

Hoekstra, Kinch, 'Nothing to Declare? Hobbes on the Advocate of Injustice', *Political Theory* 27:2 (1999), pp. 230-35.

Hoekstra, Kinch, 'Tyrannus Rex *vs*. Leviathan', in special issue of *Pacific Philosophical Quarterly* 82:3&4 (2001), 'Recent Work on the Moral and Political Philosophy of Thomas Hobbes', ed. S. A. Lloyd, pp. 420-46.

Holbrook, Peter and David Bevington, eds, *The Politics of the Stuart Court Masque* (Cambridge, Cambridge University Press, 1998).

Hüning, Dieter, *Freiheit und Herrschaft in der Rechtsphilosophie des Thomas Hobbes* (Berlin, Duncker & Humblot Verlag 1998).

Hüning, Dieter, 'From the Virtue of Justice to the Concept of Legal Order – The Signifance of the Suum Cuique Tribuere Formula in Hobbes's Political Philosophy'. In Ian Hunter, David Saunders (eds.), *Natural Law and Civil Sovereignty: Moral Right and State Authority in Early Modern Political Thought*: (Houndsmill, Basingstoke, Palgrave Macmillan Ltd. 2002), pp. 139-152.

Hüning, Dieter, 'Hobbes on the Right to Punish', in Patricia Springborg, ed., *Cambridge Companion to Hobbes's Leviathan* (New York, Cambridge University Press, 2007), pp. 217-41.

Hüning, Dieter, '"*Inter arma silent leges*" – Naturrecht, Staat und Völkerrecht bei Thomas Hobbes'. In Rüdiger Voigt (ed.), *Der Leviathan*, (Baden-Baden, Nomos Verlag 2000), pp. 129-163.

Hüning, Dieter, '"Is not the power to punish essentially a power that pertains to the state?" The Different Foundations of the Right to Punish in Early Modern Natural Law Doctrines'. In *Politisches Denken. Jahrbuch 2004*, edited by Volker Gerhardt, Henning Ottmann und Martyn P. Thompson (Berlin, Duncker & Humblot Verlag 2004), pp. 43-60.

Hüning, Dieter, ed. *Der lange Schatten des Leviathan: Hobbes' politische Philosophie nach 350 Jahren* (Berlin, Duncker & Humblot Verlag 2005).

Hüning, Dieter, 'Naturrecht und Strafgewalt. Die Begründung des Strafrechts in Hobbes' Leviathan'. *In Dieter Hüning (Hrsg.): Der lange Schatten des Leviathan. Vorträge des internationalen Arbeitsgesprächs „350 Jahre Leviathan an der Herzog August Bibliothek in Wolfenbüttel im Oktober 2001* (Berlin, Duncker & Humblot Verlag 2005), pp. 235-276.

Hüning, Dieter, *'Von der Tugend der Gerechtigkeit zum Begriff der Rechtsordnung: Zur rechtsphilosophischen Bedeutung des suum cuique tribuere bei Hobbes und Kant'*. In Dieter Hüning/ Burkhard Tuschling (eds), *Recht, Staat und Völkerrecht bei Immanuel Kant* (Berlin, Duncker & Humblot Verlag 1998), pp. 51-82.

Hughes, Philip Edgcumbe, *Theology of the English Reformers* (Grand Rapids, Michigan, Eerdman's Publishing, 1965).

Hulse, Lynn, 'Apollo's Whirligig: William Cavendish, Duke of Newcastle and his Music Collection', *The Seventeenth Century*, vol. 9, no 2 (1994), pp. 213-46.

Hume, Robert D. *The Development of English Drama in the Late Seventeenth Century* (Oxford, Oxford University Press, 1976).

Hutton, Sarah, 'Plato and the Tudor Academies', in Francis Ames-Lewis, ed., *Sir Thomas Gresham and Gresham College: Studies in the Intellectual History of London in the Sixteenth and Seventeenth Centuries* (London, Ashgate, 1999), pp. 106-24.

Hutton, Sarah, 'Thomas Jackson, Oxford Platonist, and William Twisse, Aristotelian', *Journal of the History of Ideas*, 39 (1978), pp. 635-52.

Jaume, Lucien, 'Autour de Hobbes: représentation et fiction', *Droits*, no. 21, 1995, pp. 95-103.

Jaume, Lucien, 'Hobbes and the Philosophical Sources of Liberalism', in Patricia Springborg, ed., *Cambridge Companion to Hobbes's Leviathan* (New York, Cambridge University Press, 2007), pp. 199-216.

Jaume, Lucien, *Hobbes et l'Etat représentatif moderne*, (Paris, P.U.F., 1986).

Jaume, Lucien, 'Hobbes ou l'Etat représentatif', in *Les philosophes de Platon à Sartre*, L.-L. Grateloup, ed. (Paris, Hachette, 1985), pp. 157-168. (Reprinted as Livre de Poche, 1996, 2 vols).

Jaume, Lucien, 'Peuple et individu dans le débat Hobbes-Rousseau: d'une représentation qui n'est pas celle du peuple, à un peuple qui n'est pas représentable', in *La Représentation*, F. d'Arcy, Paris, ed. *Economica*, 1985, pp. 39-53.

Jaume, Lucien, 'La théorie de la "personne fictive" dans le *Léviathan* de Hobbes', *Revue française de science politique*, vol. 33, 1983, pp. 1009-10035.

Jaume, Lucien',Le vocabulaire de la représentation politique de Hobbes à Kant', in *Hobbes et son vocabulaire*, Y.-C. Zarka, ed. (Paris, Vrin, 1992), pp. 231-257.

Jacob, James R. and Timothy Raylor, 'Opera and Obedience: Thomas Hobbes and *A Proposition for Advancement of Moralitie* by Sir William Davenant', *The Seventeenth Century*, vol. 6 (1991), pp. 205-50.

Jardine, Lisa, 'Humanist Logic'. In Charles B. Schmitt, Eckhard Kessler and Quentin Skinner, eds., *The Cambridge History of Renaissance Philosophy* (Cambridge, Cambridge University Press, 1988), pp. 173-198.

Jardine, Lisa, 'Lorenzo Valla and the Intellectual Origins of Humanistic Dialectic', *Journal of the History of Philosophy*, vol. 15 (1977), pp. 143-64

Jayne, Sear, *John Colet and Marsilio Ficino* (London, 1963).

Johnston, David, *The Rhetoric of Leviathan* (Princeton, Princeton University Press, 1986).

Joseph, H. W. B., *An Introduction to Logic*, 2nd edn (Oxford, Oxford University Press, 1916).

Joy, L. S., *Gassendi the Atomist: Advocate of History in an Age of Science* (Cambridge, Cambridge University Press, 1987).

Kannengiesser, Charles, ed., *Politique et Théologie chez Athanase d'Alexandrie* (Paris, Beauchesne, 1974).

Kantorowicz, Ernst, *The King's Two Bodies: A Study in Medieval Political Theology* (Princeton, Princeton University Press, 1957).

Kargon, Robert, *Atomism in England from Hariot to Newton* (Oxford, Clarendon Press, 1966).

Kargon, Robert, 'Robert Boyle and the Acceptance of Epicurean Atomism in England', *Isis*, vol 45 (1964), pp. 184-92.

Keen, Maurice *The Pelican History of Medieval Europe* (Harmonsworth, Penguin, 1968).

Kennedy, George A., *The Art of Persuasion in Greece* (Princeton, 1963).

Kennedy, George A., *Classical Rhetoric and its Christian and Secular Tradition from Ancient to Modern Times* (Chapel Hill, University of North Carolina Press, 1980).

Kenyon, J., *The History Men: The Historical Profession in England since the Renaissance* (London, Weidenfeld and Nicolson, 1983).

Kors, A.C., *Atheism in France, 1650-1729* (Princeton, Princeton University Press, 1990).

Koselleck, Reinhart, 'Historia Magistra Vitae: The Dissolution of the Topos into the Perspective of a Modernized Historical Process', and 'Perspective and Temporality: A Contribution to the Historiographical Exposure of the Historical Word', in *Futures Past: On the Semantics of Historical Time*, tr. Keith Tribe (Cambridge, Mass., MIT Press, 1985), pp. 21-38 and 130-55.

Knight, G. Wilson, *The Imperial Theme. Further Interpretations of Shakespeare's Tragedies* (London, Methuen, 1961).

Knight, L. C. *Drama and Society in the Age of Jonson* (London, Chatto and Windus, 1937).

Kristeller, Paul O, *Studies in Renaissance Thought and Letters* (Rome, Edizioni di Storia e Letteratura, 1969).

Kroll, R, Ríchard Ashcraft, and Perez Zagorin, eds, *Philosophy, Science and Religion in England, 1640-1700* (Cambridge, Cambridge University Press, 1992).

Lamont, William M., *Godly Rule: Politics and Religion, 1603-60* (London, Macmillan, 1969).

Lees-Milne, James. *The Age of Inigo Jones* (London, B.T. Batsford, 1953).

Leijenhorst, C.H., 'Hobbes and Fracastoro', *Hobbes Studies* vol. 9 (1996), pp. 98-128.

Leijenhorst, C.H., 'Hobbes's Theory of Causality and its Aristotelian Background', *The Monist*, vol. 79 (1996), pp. 426-47.

Leijenhorst, C.H., 'Jesuit Conceptions of *Spatium Imaginarium* and Hobbes's Doctrine of Space', *Early Science and Medicine*, 1 (1996), pp. 355-80.

Leijenhorst, C.H., 'Motion, Monks and Golden Mountains: Campanella and Hobbes on Perception and Cognition', *Bruniana e Campanelliana*, vol. 3 (1997), pp. 93-121.

Leijenhorst, C.H., *Hobbes and the Aristotelians: The Aristotelian Setting of Thomas Hobbes's Natural Philosophy* (Utrecht, Zeno Institute for Philosophy, 1998).

Leijenhorst, C.H., 'Sense and Nonsense about Sense', in Patricia Springborg, ed., *Cambridge Companion to Hobbes's Leviathan* (New York, Cambridge University Press, 2007), pp. 82-108.

Leon, H.J., *The Jews of Ancient Rome* (Philadelphia, The Jewish Publication Society of America, 1960).

Lessay, Franck, 'L'état de nature selon Hobbes, point de départ ou point de dépassement de l'histoire', *Actes du colloque (octobre 1983) de la*

Société d'Études Anglo-Américaines des XVIIᵉ et XVIIIᵉ siècles (Saint-Étienne, Publications de l'Université de Saint-Étienne, 1984, pp. 3-14.

Lessay, Franck, 'La figure cachée du tyran dans le *Léviathan* de Thomas Hobbes', *Bulletin de la Société d'Études Anglo-Américaines des XVIIᵉ et XVIIIᵉ siècles*, vol. 16, June 1983, pp. 7-19.

Lessay, Franck, 'Filmer, Hobbes et Locke: les cassures dans l'espace de la théorie politique', *Archives de Philosophie*, 55 (1992), pp. 645-660.

Lessay, Franck, 'Hobbes and Sacred History', in G. A. J. Rogers and Tom Sorell, eds., *Hobbes and History* (London, Routledge, 2000), pp. 147-59.

Lessay, Franck, 'Hobbes's Covenant Theology and its Political Implications', in Patricia Springborg, ed., *Cambridge Companion to Hobbes's Leviathan* (New York, Cambridge University Press, 2007), pp. 243-70.

Lessay, Franck, 'La loi, le temps et la raison chez Hobbes', in L. Roux and F. Tricaud, eds, *Le pouvoir et le droit* (Saint-Etienne, Publications de l'Université de Saint-Etienne, 1992), pp. 141-153.

Lessay, Franck, 'Souveraineté absolue, souveraineté légitime', in Y. C. Zarka and J. Bernhartd, eds, *Thomas Hobbes: philosophie première, théorie de la science et politique* (Paris, P.U.F, 1990), pp. 275-287.

Lessay, Franck. *Souveraineté et légitimité chez Hobbes* (Paris, P.U.F., 1988).

Lessay, Franck, 'Le vocabulaire de la personne', in Y. C. Zarka, ed, *Hobbes et son vocabulaire: études de lexicographie philosophique* (Paris, Vrin, 1992), pp. 155-186.

Lloyd, S. A., *Ideals and Interests in Hobbes's Leviathan* (Cambridge, Cambridge University Press, 1992).

Lloyd S. A., ed., 'Recent Work on the Moral and Political Philosophy of Thomas Hobbes', *Pacific Philosophical Quarterly* 82:3&4 (2001) entire issue.

Love, Harold, *Scribal Publication in Seventeenth-century England* (Oxford, Clarendon Press, 1993; repr. 1997).

Maine, Henry Sumner, *Ancient Law: Its Connection With the Early History of Society, and Its Relation to Modern Ideas* (London, John Murray, 1861).

Malcolm, Noel, *Aspects of Hobbes* (Oxford, Clarendon Press, 2002).

Malcolm, Noel, 'Behemoth Latinus: Adam Ebert, Tacitism and Hobbes', *Filozofski vestnik*, vol. 24 (2003), pp. 85-120.

Malcolm, Noel, 'Charles Cotton, 'Translator of Hobbes's *De cive*', *Huntington Library Quarterly*, vol. 61 (1998), pp. 259-87, reprinted in *Aspects of Hobbes*, pp. 234-58.

Malcolm, Noel, 'Hobbes and the European Republic of Letters', in *Aspects of Hobbes*, pp. 457-546.

Malcolm, Noel, 'The Printing and Editing of Hobbes's *De Corpore*: A Review of Karl Schuhmann's Edition', *Rivista di storia della filosofia*, vol. 59 (2004), pp. 329-57.

McGee, J. Sears, *The Godly Man in Stuart England; Anglicans, Puritans, and the Two Tables, 1620-1670* (New Haven, Yale University Press, 1976).

McGrath, Elizabeth, 'Rubens's *Arch of the Mint*', *Journal of the Warburg and Courtauld Institutes*, 37 (1974), pp. 191-217.

McIlwain, Charles, ed. The Political Works of James I, Cambridge, Mass., Reprinted from the Edition of 1616. Harvard University Press, 1918.

MacIntosh, J. J., 'The Intellectual Resources of Robert Boyle's Philosophy of Nature: Gassendi's Voluntarism, and Boyles's Physico-Theological Project', in R. Kroll, Richard Ashcraft, and Perez Zagorin, eds, *Philosophy, Science and Religion in England, 1640-1700* (Cambridge, Cambridge University Press, 1992), pp. 178-98.

McManaway, J. G., 'The "lost" Canto of Gondibert', *Modern Language Quarterly*, vol. 1 (1940), pp. 63-78

Magoun, F. B., *The Gests of King Alexander of Macedon* (Cambridge, Cambridge University Press, 1929).

Maguire, Nancy Klein, *Regicide and Restoration: English Tragicomedy*, 1660-1671 (Cambridge, Cambridge University Press, 1992).

Malcolm, Noel, *Aspects of Hobbes* (Oxford, Clarendon Press, 2002).

Malcolm, Noel, 'Charles Cotton, Translator of Hobbes's *De cive*', *Huntington Library Quarterly*, vol 61 for 1998 (2000), pp. 259-87, reprinted in *Aspects of Hobbes*, pp. 234-258

Malcolm, Noel, 'Hobbes, Sandys, and the Virginia Company', *The Historical Journal*, vol. 24 (1981), pp. 297-321; reprinted in Malcolm, *Aspects of Hobbes*, pp. 53-79.

Manselli, Raoul, 'Giovanni de Salisbury e l'Italia del suo Tempo', in *The World of John of Salisbury*, ed. Michael Wilks (Oxford, Clarendon Press, 1994), pp. 401-14.

Marsh, David, 'Grammar, Method, and Polemic in Lorenzo Valla's "Elegantiae"', *Rinascimento, Rivista dell'Instituto Nazionale di Studi sul Rinascimento*, vol. 19 (1979), pp. 91-116.

Martinich, A. P., 'The Bible and Protestantism in *Leviathan*', in Patricia Springborg, ed., *Cambridge Companion to Hobbes's Leviathan* (New York, Cambridge University Press, 2007), pp. 375-391.

Martinich, A. P., *Hobbes*, Routledge Philosophers Series (London, Routledge, 2005).

Martinich, A. P., *Hobbes: A Biography* (New York, Cambridge University Press, 1999).

Martinich, A. P., *A Hobbes Dictionary* (Oxford, Blackwell Publishers, 1995). (NetLibrary, 2000).

Martinich, A. P., 'Hobbes's Reply to Republicanism', *New Critical Perspectives on Hobbes's Leviathan*, ed. Luc Foisneau and George Wright, *Rivista di storia della filosophia, vol. 59* (2004), 227-39 (Milano, FrancoAngeli, 2004), pp. 227-40.

Martinich, A. P., 'Hobbes's Translations of Homer and Anticlericalism', *The Seventeenth Century* 16 (2001), pp. 47-57.

Martinich, A. P., 'Interpretation and Hobbes's Political Philosophy', *Pacific Philosophical Quarterly* 82 (2001), pp. 309-331.

Martinich, A. P., 'The Interpretation of Covenants in Leviathan', in Tom Sorell and Luc Foisneau, eds, *Leviathan after 350 Years* (Oxford, Clarendon Press, 2004), pp. 17-40.

Martinich, A. P., 'Presbyterians in Behemoth', in *Filozofski vestnik/Acta philosophica*, ed. Tomaz Mastnak (Ljubljana, Slovenia, 2003), pp. 121-38.

Martinich, A. P., 'On the Proper Interpretation of Hobbes's Philosophy', *Journal of the History of Philosophy*, 34 (1996), pp. 273-83.

Martinich, A. P., *Thomas Hobbes: Perspectives on British History* (London, Macmillan, 1997); (New York, St. Martin's Press, 1997).

Martinich, A. P., *The Two Gods of Leviathan* (Cambridge, Cambridge University Press, 1992).

Matheron, Alexandre, 'Hobbes, la Trinité et les caprices de la répresentation', in *Thomas Hobbes, Philosophie première, théorie de la science et politique*, Actes du Colloque de Paris, ed Yves Charles Zarka and Jean Bernhardt (Paris, P.U.F., 1990), pp. 381-90.

Milton, P., 'Hobbes, Heresy and Lord Arlington', *History of Political Thought*, 14, 4 (1993), pp. 501-46.

Mintz, Samuel, 'Hobbes on the Law of Heresy: A New Manuscript', *Journal of the History of Ideas*, vol. 29, no 3 (1968), pp. 409-14.

Mintz, Samuel, *The Hunting of Leviathan: Seventeenth-Century Reactions to the Materialism and Moral Philosophy of Thomas Hobbes* (Cambridge, Cambridge University Press, 1969).

Momigliano, Arnaldo, *The Conflict Between Paganism and Christianity in the Fourth Century* (Oxford, Clarendon Press, 1963).

Monfasani, John, 'The Theology of Lorenzo Valla', in Jill Kraye and M. W. F. Stone, *Humanism and Early Modern Philosophy* (London, Routledge, 2000), pp. 1-23.

Monfasani, John, 'Was Lorenzo Valla an Ordinary Language Philosopher?', *Journal of the History of Ideas*, vol. 50 (1989), pp. 309-23.

Moreau, Joseph, 'Epicure et la Physique des Dieux', *Revue des Études Anciennes*, vol. 70 (1968), pp. 286-94.

Morris, Colin, *The Papal Monarchy: The Western Church from 1050-1250* (Oxford, Clarendon Press, 1989).

Mortley, Raoul, *The Idea of Universal History from Hellenistic Philosophy to Early Christian Historiography* (Lewiston, New York, Edwin Mellen Press, 1996).

Neill, Michael, *Issues of Death: Mortality and Identity in English Renaissance Tragedy* (Oxford, Oxford University Press, 1997).

Nethercot, A. H., *Sir William D'Avenant, Poet Laureate and Playwright-Manager* (Chicago, University of Chicago Press, 1938).

New, John F. H., *Anglican and Puritan; the Basis of Their Opposition, 1558-1640* (Stanford, Stanford University Press, 1964).

Newdigate, Bernard, *Michael Drayton and his Circle* (Oxford, Oxford University Press, 1941).

Nicol, Donald M., *Byzantium and Venice: A Study in Diplomatic and Cultural Relations* (Cambridge, Cambridge University Press, 1992).

Norbrook, David, *Poetry and Politics in the English Renaissance* (London, Routledge, 1984).

Norbrook, David, 'Lucan, May and Republican Literary Culture', in Kevin Sharpe *et al.*, *Culture and Politics in Early Stuart England* (Stanford, Stanford University Press, 1993).

Norbrook, David, *Writing the English Republic: Poetry, Rhetoric and Politics, 1627-1660* (Cambridge, Cambridge University Press, 1999).

Nussdorfer, Laurie, *Civic Politics in the Rome of Urban VIII* (Princeton, Princeton University Press, 1992).

Ostogorsky, George, *History of the Byzantine State* (New Brunswick, N.J., rev. edn, 1969).

Pacchi, Arrigho, 'Una "biblioteca ideale" di Thomas Hobbes: il MS E2 dell'archivio di Chatsworth', *Acme, Annali della Facoltà di Lettere e Filosofia dell' Università degli Studi di Milano*, vol. 21, no. 1, 1968, pp. 5-42.

Pacchi, Arrigho, 'Hobbes e l'epicureismo', *Rivista Critica di Storia dell Filosophia*, vol. 33 (1975), pp. 54-71.

Packer, John W., *The transformation of Anglicanism 1643-1660 with special reference to Henry Hammond* (Manchester, Manchester University Press, 1969).

Paganini, Gianni, 'Alle Origini del "Mortal God": Hobbes, Lipsius e il *Corpus Hermeticum*', presented to the National Institution of Studies on the Renaissance at its Conference on Neoplatonism, 25-30 October 2001

Paganini, Gianni, 'Hobbes among ancient and modern sceptics: phenomena and bodies', in Paganini, ed., *The Return of Scepticism. From Hobbes and Descartes to Bayle* (Dordrecht, Kluwer 2003), pp. 3-35.

Paganini, Gianni, 'Hobbes and the "Continental" Tradition of Scepticism', in Paganini, *Skepticism in Renaissance and Post-Renaissance Thought. New Interpretations*, ed. by J. R. Maia Neto and Richard H. Popkin (Amherst, Mass., Humanity Books 2004), pp. 65-105.

Paganini, Gianni, 'Hobbes face à l'héritage érasmien: philologie humaniste et philosophie nouvelle', *Institut d'Histoire de la Réformation. Bulletin annuel*, Genève, vol. 24 (2002-2003), pp. 33-51.

Paganini, Gianni, 'Hobbes, Gassendi e la psicologia del meccanicismo', in *Hobbes Oggi*, Actes du Colloque de Milan (18-21 May, 1988), ed. Arrigo Pacchi (Milan, Franco Angeli, 1990), pp. 351-446.

Paganini, Gianni, 'Hobbes, Gassendi e la psychologie dans le project mécaniste', *Kriterion. Rivista de Filosofia*, vol. 43, 106, 2002, pp. 20-41 (fascicolo monografico su "Filosofia do século XVII", a cura di J. R. Maia Neto).

Paganini, Gianni, 'Hobbes, Gassendi and the Tradition of Political Epicureanism', *Hobbes Studies*, vol 14, 2001, pp. 3-24 (reprinted in *Der Garten und die Moderne. Epikureische Moral und Politik vom Humanismus bis zur Aufklärung.* (Stuttgart, Frommann-Holzboog 2004, pp. 113-137).

Paganini, Gianni, 'Hobbes, Gassendi et le *De Cive*', in *Materia Actuosa: Antiquité, Âge Classique, Lumières; Mélanges en 'honneur d'Olivier Bloch*, ed. Miguel Benitez, Antony McKenna, Gianni Paganini, Jean Salem (Paris, Champion, 2000), pp. 183-206.

Paganini, Gianni, 'Hobbes, Gassendi und die Hypothese der Weltvernichtung', in *Die Konstellationsforschung*, hrsg. von Martin Mulsow und Marcelo Stamm (Frankfurt a. M., Suhrkamp, 2005), pp. 258-339.

Paganini, Gianni, 'Hobbes, Valla e i problemi filosofici della teologia umanistica: la riforma "dilettica" della Trinità', in L. Simonutti, ed. *Dal necessario al possibile. Determinismo e libertà nel pensiero anglo-olandese del XVII secolo* (Milan, FrancoAngeli, 2001), pp. 11-45.

Paganini, Gianni, 'Hobbes, Valla and the Trinity', *British Journal for the History of Philosophy*, vol. 40, no. 2 (2003), pp. 183-218.

Paganini, Gianni, 'Hobbes's Critique of the Doctrine of Essences and its Sources', in Patricia Springborg, ed., *Cambridge Companion to Hobbes's Leviathan* (New York, Cambridge University Press, 2007), pp. 337-57.

Paganini, Gianni, 'Montaigne, Sanches et la Connaissance par Phénomènes: Les Usages Modernes d'un Paradigme Ancien', in

Montaigne, Scepticisme, Métaphysique, Théologie, ed. Vincent Carraud and Jean-Luc Marion (Paris, P.U.F., 2004), pp. 107-35

Paganini, Gianni, 'Thomas Hobbes e Lorenzo Valla. Critica umansitica e filosofia moderna', *Rinscimento, Rivista dell' Instituto Nazionale di Studi sul Rinascimento*, 2nd series, vol. 39, 1999, pp. 515-68.

Parkin, Jon, 'Hobbism in the Later 1660s: Daniel Scargill and Samuel Parker', *The Historical Journal*, vol 42, 1 (1999), pp. 85-108.

Parkin, Jon, 'The Reception of Hobbes's *Leviathan*', in Patricia Springborg, ed., *Cambridge Companion to Hobbes's Leviathan* (New York, Cambridge University Press, 2007), pp. 441-59.

Parry, Graham, 'Cavendish Memorials', *The Seventeenth Century*, vol. 9, no. 2 (1994), pp. 275-87.

Patterson, Annabel, 'The Egalitarian Giant', in *Reading Between the Lines* (Madison, Wisc., University of Wisconsin Press, 1993).

Pearcy, Lee T., *The Meditated Muse: English Translations of Ovid 1560-1700* (Hamden, Conn., Archon Books, 1984).

Peck, Linda Levy, 'Constructing A New Context for Hobbes Studies', in *Politics and the Political Imagination in Later Stuart Britain, Essays Presented to Lois Green Schwoerer*, Howard Nenner, ed. (Rochester, New York, University of Rochester Press, 1998), pp. 161-79.

Perrine, Galand-Hallyn, *Le Reflet des Fleurs: Description et Metalangage Poetique d'Homère à la Renaissance* (Geneva, Droz, 1994).

Phillipson, Nicholas and Quentin Skinner, *Political Discourse in Early Modern Britain* (Cambridge, Cambridge University Press, 1993).

Pietri, Charles, 'La politique de Constance II: Un premier "cesaropapisme" ou l'*imitatio Constantini?*', in *L'Église et l'Empire au IVe siècle*, ed. Albrecht Dihle (Geneva, Fondation Hardt, 1989), pp. 113-172.

Pocock, J.G.A., *The Ancient Constitution and the Feudal Law* (Cambridge, Cambridge University Press, 1957).

Pocock, J.G.A., 'The Concept of Language', in Anthony Pagden (ed.), *The Languages of Political Theory in Early Modern Europe* (Cambridge, Cambridge University Press, 1987), pp. 19-38.

Pocock, J.G.A., *The Machiavellian Moment: Florentine Political Thought and the Atlantic Republican Tradition* (Princeton, N.J., Princeton University Press, 1975).

Pocock, J.G.A., 'Time, History and Eschatology in the Thought of Thomas Hobbes', in *Politics, Language and Time: Essays on Political Thought* (New York, 1971), pp. 148-201.

Pocock, J.G.A., et al., 1993. *The Varieties of British Political Thought 1500-1800* (Cambridge, Cambridge University Press, 1993).

Polin, Raymond, *Politique et philosophie chez Thomas Hobbes*, 2e édition augmentée (Paris, Vrin, 1977).

Potter, David, *Prophets and Emperors: Human and Divine Authority from Augustus to Theodosius* (Cambridge, Mass., Harvard University Press, 1994).

Potter, Lois, *Secret Rites and Secret Writing: Royalist Literature, 1641-1660* (Cambridge, Cambridge University Press, 1989).

Quantin, Jean-Louis, 'The Fathers in Seventeenth Century Roman Catholic Theology', in *The Reception of the Church Fathers in the West, from the Carolingians to the Maurists,* Irena Backus, ed. (Leiden, E.J. Brill, 1997), 2 vols, vol. 2, pp. 953-76.

Rashdall, Hastings, *The Universities of Europe in the Middle Ages,* 2 vols (Oxford, Oxford University Press, c.1895).

Raylor, Timothy, *Cavaliers, Clubs and Literary Culture: Sir John Mennes, James Smith and the Order of the Fancy* (Wilmington, Del., University of Delaware Press, 1994).

Raylor, Timothy, '"Pleasure Reconciled to Virtue": William Cavendish, Ben Jonson and the Decorative Scheme of Bolsover Castle', *Renaissance Quarterly,* vol. 52, no. 2 (1999), pp. 402-39.

Reik, Miriam, *The Golden Lands of Thomas Hobbes* (Detroit, Wayne State University Press, 1977).

Reuter, Timothy, 'John of Salisbury and the Germans', in *The World of John of Salisbury,* ed. Michael Wilks (Oxford, Oxford University Press, 1994), pp. 415-25.

Rigg, David, *Ben Jonson: A Life* (Cambridge Mass., Harvard University Press, 1989).

Rogers, G. A. J., 'Hobbes and His Contemporaries', in Patricia Springborg, ed., *Cambridge Companion to Hobbes's Leviathan* (New York, Cambridge University Press, 2007), pp. 413-40.

Rogers, G. A. J.,and Tom Sorell, *Hobbes and History* (London, Routledge, 2000).

Rogow, Arnold A. *Thomas Hobbes: Radical in the Service of Reaction* (New York, W. W. Norton, 1986).

Rompay, L. Van, 'Proclus of Constantinople's, "Tomus ad Armenios", in the Post-Chalcedonian Tradition', in C. Laga, J. A. Munitiz and L. Van Rompay, eds, *After Chalcedon: Studies in Theology and Church History* (Leuven, Orientalia Lovaniensia Analecta 18, 1985), pp. 425-449.

Rossi, Paolo, *The Dark Abyss of Time,* Lydia G. Cochrane, trans. (Chicago, University of Chicago Press, 1984).

Russell, Donald, *Plutarch* (Oxford, Oxford University Press, 1st edn 1972, 2nd edn 2001).

Ryan, Alan, 'Hobbes, toleration and the inner life', in *The Nature of Political Theory,* ed. by David Miller and Larry Seidentop (Oxford, Clarendon Press, 1983),

Ryan, Alan, 'A more tolerant Hobbes', in Susan Mendus, ed., *Justifying Toleration* (Cambridge, Cambridge University Press, 1988).

Salem, Jean, *Tel un dieu parmi les hommes : l'ethique d'Epicurus* (Paris, Vrin, 1989).

Sarasohn, Lisa T., 'The Ethical and Political Philosophy of Pierre Gassendi, *Journal of the History of Philosophy*, vol. 20, no. 3 (1982), pp. 239-60.

Scheffer-Boichorst, Paul, 'Neue Forschungen über die Konstantinische Schenkung', in the *Mittheilungen des Instituts für österreiches Geschichtsforschung*, vol. 10 (1889), pp. 325ff., vol. 11 (1890), pp. 128ff.

Schmitt, Carl, *Der Leviathan in der Staatslehre des Thomas Hobbes. Sinn und Fehlschlag eines politischen Symbols* (1938). (Köln-Lövenich, Günter Maschke, 1982).

Schmitt, Carl, *The Leviathan in the State Theory of Thomas Hobbes* (1938). Translation of *Der Leviathan in der Staatslehre des Thomas Hobbes*, by. George Schwab. Westport, Connecticut, Greenwood Press, 1996).

Schmitt, Charles B., *John Case and Aristotelianism in Renaissance England* (Kingston and Montreal, McGill-Queen's University Press, 1983).

Schochet, Gordon, 'John Locke and Religious Toleration', in Lois G. Schwoerer, ed., *The Revolution of 1688-1689, Changing Perspectives* (Cambridge, Cambridge University Press, 1992), pp. 147-164.

Schuhmann, Karl, 'Hobbes and Aristotle's Politics', in *Thomas Hobbes. Le Ragioni del Moderno tra Teologia e Politica*, ed. G. Borrelli (Napoli, Morano, 1990), pp. 97-127.

Schuhmann, Karl, 'Hobbes and Renaissance Philosophy', in *Hobbes Oggi*, Actes du Colloque de Milan (18-21 May, 1988), ed. Arrigo Pacchi (Milan, Franco Angeli, 1990), pp. 331-49.

Schuhmann, Karl, 'Hobbes and Telesio', *Hobbes Studies*, vol. 1 (1988), pp. 109-33.

Schuhmann, Karl, *Hobbes. Une chronique* (Paris, Vrin, 1998).

Schuhmann, Karl, 'Phantasms and Idols : True Philosophy and Wrong Religion in Hobbes', *Rivista di Storia della Filosofia*, vol. 59, 1, 2004, pp. 15-31

Schuhmann, Karl, 'Rapidità el pensiero e ascensione al cielo : alcuni motivi ermetici in Hobbes', *Rivista di Storia della Filosofia*, vol. 40 (1985), pp. 203-27.

Schuhmann, Karl, 'Le Short Tract, première œuvre philosophique du Hobbes', *Hobbes Studies*, vol. 8 (1995), pp. 3-36.

Schuhmann, Karl, 'Thomas Hobbes und Francesco Patrizi', *Archiv für Geschichte der Philosophie*, vol. 68 (1986), pp. 253-79.

Schuhmann, Karl, 'Zur Entstehung des neuzeitlichen Zeitbegriffs: Telesio, Patrizi, Gassendi', *Philosophia Naturalis,* vol. 25 (1988), pp. 37-64

Schwoerer, Lois G., 'Liberty of the Press and Public Opinion 1660-95', in J. R. Jones, *Liberty Secured: Britain Before and After 1688* (Stanford, Ca., Stanford University Press, 1992), pp. 199-231.

Shagan, Ethan H., *Popular Politics and the English Reformation* (Cambridge, Cambridge University Press, 2002).

Shapin, Steven and Simon Schaffer, *Leviathan and the Air-Pump* (Princeton, Princeton University Press, 1985).

Sharpe, Kevin *et al., Culture and Politics in Early Stuart England* (Stanford, Ca., Stanford University Press, 1993).

Shuger, Deborah Kuller, *Habits of Thought in the English Renaissance: Religion, Politics, and the Dominant Culture* (Berkeley, Ca., University of California Press, 1991).

Shuger, Deborah Kuller, *The Renaissance Bible: Scholarship, Sacrifice, and Subjectivity* (Berkeley, Ca., University of California Press, 1994).

Shuger, Deborah Kuller, *The Roman and Protestant Churches in English Protestant Thought, 1600-1640* (Cambridge, Cambridge University Press, 1995).

Simonetti, Manlio, *La crisi ariana nel IV secolo* (Rome, Augustianum, 1975).

Skinner, Quentin, *Foundations of Modern Political Thought* (Cambridge, Cambridge University Press, 1978), 2 vols.

Skinner, Quentin, 'Interpretation and the Understanding of Speech Acts', in *Visions of Politics* (3 vols, Cambridge, Cambridge University Press, 2002), vol. 1, pp. 117-20.

Skinner, Quentin, *Liberty Before Liberalism* (Cambridge, Cambridge University Press. 1998).

Skinner, Quentin, 'Hobbes on Persons, Authors and Representatives', in Patricia Springborg, ed., *Cambridge Companion to Hobbes's Leviathan* (New York, Cambridge University Press, 2007), pp. 157-80.

Skinner, Quentin, 'Hobbes on Representation', *European Journal of Philosophy* 13 (2005), pp. 155-84.

Skinner, Quentin, *Reason and Rhetoric in the Philosophy of Hobbes.* (Cambridge, Cambridge University Press, 1996).

Skinner, Quentin. 1993b. *'Scientia civilis* in Classical Rhetoric and in the Early Hobbes', in Nicholas Phillipson and Quentin Skinner, eds. *Political Discourse in Early Modern Europe.* Cambridge, Cambridge University Press, 67-93.

Skinner, 'Thomas Hobbes and the Renaissance *studia humanitatis',* in *Writing and Political Engagement in Seventeenth Century England,* ed. Derek Hirst and Richard Strier (Cambridge, Cambridge University Press, 1999), pp. 69-88.

Skinner, Quentin, 'Thomas Hobbes on the Proper Signification of Liberty', *Transactions of the Royal Historical Society*, vol. 40 (1990), pp. 121-51.

Skinner, Quentin. 'Thomas Hobbes: Rhetoric and the Construction of Morality'. *Proceedings of the British Academy*, vol. 76 (1990), 1-61.

Skinner, Quentin, *Visions of Politics* (Cambridge, Cambridge University Press, 2002), 3 vols.

Slomp, Gabriella, 'From Genus to Species: The Unravelling of Hobbesian Glory', *History of Political Thought*, vol. 19 (4), Winter 1998, pp. 552-569.

Slomp, Gabriella, 'Hobbes and the Equality of Women', *Political Studies*, vol. 42(3), Sept 1994, pp. 441-452.

Slomp, Gabriella, 'Hobbes on Glory and Civil Strife', in Patricia Springborg, ed., *Cambridge Companion to Hobbes's Leviathan* (New York, Cambridge University Press, 2007), pp. 181-98.

Slomp, Gabriella, 'Hobbes, Thucydides and the Three Greatest Things', *History of Political Thought*, vol. 11, Winter 1990, pp. 565-586.

Slomp, Gabriella, 'Hobbes's *Behemoth* on Ambition, Greed, and Fear', *Filozofski Vestnik (Acta Philosophica)*, special issue on Hobbes's *Behemoth*, ed. Tomaz Mastnak, vol. 24, no. 2 (2003), pp. 189-204.

Slomp, Gabriella, 'Leviathan: Revenue-Maximizer or Glory-Seeker' (joint with M. La Manna), *Constitutional Political Economy*, vol. 92, 1994, pp. 159-172.

Slomp, Gabriella, *Thomas Hobbes and the Political Philosophy of Glory* (London, Macmillan/New York, St Martin's Press, 2000).

Smalley, Beryl, *The Gospels in the Schools c. 1100-c. 1280* (London, Hambledon Press, 1985).

Smalley, Beryl *The Study of the Bible in the Middle Ages*, 3rd edn (Oxford, Oxford University Press, 1984).

Sommerville, Johann P., 'Conscience, Law, and Things Indifferent: Arguments on Toleration from the Vestiarian Controversy to Hobbes and Locke', in Harald Braun and Edward Vallance, eds., *Contexts of Conscience in Early Modern Europe, 1500-1700*, Houndmills, Palgrave Macmillan, 2004, pp. 166-79.

Sommerville, Johann P., 'Lofty science and local politics', in Tom Sorell, ed., *The Cambridge Companion to Hobbes,* Cambridge University Press, 1996, pp. 246-73.

Sommerville, Johann P., 'Hobbes and Independency', in *Rivista di storia della filosofia*, vol. 59 (2004), pp. 155-73.

Sommerville, Johann P., 'Hobbes, Selden, Erastianism, and the History of the Jews', in G.A.J. Rogers and Tom Sorell, eds, *Hobbes and History* (London, Routledge, 2000), pp. 160-187.

Sommerville, Johann P., '*Leviathan* and its Anglican Context', in Patricia Springborg, ed., *Cambridge Companion to Hobbes's Leviathan* (New York, Cambridge University Press, 2007), pp. 358-74.

Sommerville, Johann P., *Thomas Hobbes: Political Ideas in Historical Context* (London, Palgrave Macmillan, 1992).

Sorell, Tom, 'Le Dieu de la Philosophie et le Dieu de la Religion chez Hobbes' in L Foisneau, ed. *Politique, Droit et Theologie chez Bodin, Grotius et Hobbes* (Paris. Editions KIME, 1997), pp. 243-264.

Sorell, Tom, *Hobbes. Arguments of the Philosophers* (London, Routledge, 1986 and 1994).

Sorell, Tom, 'Hobbes and Aristotle', in C. Blackwell and S Kusekawa, *Philosophy in the Sixteenth and Seventeenth Centuries* (New York, Scholar Press, 2000) 364-380.

Sorell, Tom, Hobbes and Gassendi' in GHR Parkinson, ed. *Routledge History of Philosophy* vol. 4 (London, Routledge, 1993), pp. 235-272.

Sorell, Tom, 'Hobbes and the Morality beyond Justice' *Pacific Philosophical Quarterly* 82 (2001), 2 pp. 27-242.

Sorell, Tom, 'Hobbes on the History of Philosophy' in GAJ Rogers and T Sorell, *Hobbes and History* (London, Routledge, 2000), pp. 82-96.

Sorell, Tom, 'Hobbes Overcontextualised?' *The Seventeenth Century* 16 (2001), pp. 123-146.

Sorell, Tom, 'Hobbes without Doubt' *History of Philosophy Quarterly* (1993) 121-36.

Sorell, Tom, 'Hobbes's Moral Philosophy', in Patricia Springborg, ed., *Cambridge Companion to Hobbes's Leviathan* (New York, Cambridge University Press, 2007), pp. 128-155.

Sorell, Tom 'Hobbes's Objections and Hobbes's System' in R Ariew and M Grene, eds., *Descartes and his Contemporaries.* (Chicago, University of Chicago Press, 1995), pp. 83-96.

Sorell, Tom, 'Hobbes's Scheme of the Sciences' in Sorell, ed. *Cambridge Companion to Hobbes* (Cambridge, Cambridge University Press, 1996), pp. 45-61.

Sorell, Tom, ed. *The Cambridge Companion to Hobbes* (Cambridge, Cambridge University Press 1996. Third Printing).

Sorell, Tom, and John Rogers, eds. *Hobbes and History* (London, Routledge. 2000).

Sorell, Tom, and L. Foisneau, eds. *Leviathan After 350 Years.* (Oxford, Clarendon Press, 2004).

Sorell, Tom, L. Foisneau, J-C Merle and Tom Sorell, eds. *Hobbes and 20th century Political Philosophy* (Berlin, Perterlang, 2004)

Southgate, Beverly, *Covetous of Truth: the Life and Works of Thomas White, 1593-1676* (Dordrecht, Reidel, 1993).

Southgate, Beverly, "'A Medley of Both'": Old and new in the Thought of Thomas White', *History of European Ideas*, vol. 18 (1994), pp. 53-9.

Southgate, Beverly, "'To Speak the Truth'": Blackloism, Scepticism and Language', *Seventeenth Century*, vol. 10 (1995), pp. 237-54.

Springborg, Patricia, *'Behemoth* and Hobbes's "Science of *Just* and *Unjust*"', *Filozofski vestnik*, special issue on Hobbes's *Behemoth*, ed. Tomaz Mastnak, vol. 24, no. 2 (2003), pp. 267-89.

Springborg, Patricia, 'Classical Modeling and the Circulation of Concepts in Early Modern Britain', *Contributions*, vol 1, no 2, 2005, pp. 223-44.

Springborg, Patricia, 'Classical Translation and Political Surrogacy: English Renaissance Classical Translations and Imitations as Politically Coded Texts', *Finnish Yearbook of Political Thought*, vol. 5 (2001), pp. 11-33.

Springborg, Patricia, 'The Duck/Rabbit Hobbes: Review Essay on Jeffrey Collins, *The Allegiance of Thomas Hobbes*', *British Journal for the History of Philosophy*, 14, 4 (2006): 765-71.

Springborg, Patricia, 'The Enlightenment of Thomas Hobbes: Review Essay on Noel Malcolm's, *Aspects of Hobbes'*, *British Journal for the History of Philosophy*, vol. 12 no. 3 (2004), pp. 513-34.

Springborg, Patricia, 'Hobbes and Epicurean Religion', in *Der Garten und die Moderne: Epikureische Moral und Politik vom Humanismus bis zur Aufklarung*, ed. by Gianni Paganini and Edoardo Tortarolo (Stuttgart-Bad Cannstatt, Rommann-holzboog Verlag 2004), pp. 161-214.

Springborg, Patricia, 'Hobbes and Historiography, Why the Future, he says, does not Exist', in *Hobbes and History*, ed. G.A.J. Rogers and Tom Sorell (London, Routledge, 2000), pp. 44-72.

Springborg, Patricia, 'Hobbes, Heresy and the *Historia Ecclesiastica*', *Journal of the History of Ideas*, vol. 55, 4 (1994), pp. 553-571 (Reprinted in *Great Political Thinkers,* ed. John Dunn and Ian Harris, Cheltenham, Elgar, 1997, vol. 3, pp. 599-61)

Springborg, Patricia, 'Hobbes on Religion', in *The Cambridge Companion to Hobbes*, ed. Tom Sorrell (Cambridge, Cambridge University Press, 1995) pp. 346-80.

Springborg, Patricia, 'Hobbes's Biblical Beasts: Leviathan and Behemoth', *Political Theory*, vol. 23, 2 (1995), pp. 353-75.

Springborg, Patricia, 'Hobbes's Theory of Civil Religion: the *Historia Ecclesiastica*', in *Pluralismo e religione civile:* Una prospettiva filosofica, ed. Gianni Paganini and Edoardo Tortarolo (Milano, Bruno Mondadori, 2004), pp. 61-98.

Springborg, Patricia, *'Leviathan*, Mythic History and National Historiography', in David Harris Sacks and Donald Kelley, eds., *The*

Historical Imagination in Early Modern Britain (Cambridge, Cambridge University Press/Washington, DC, Woodrow Wilson Center Press, 1997), pp. 267-297.

Springborg, Patricia, 'Republicanism, Freedom from Domination and the Cambridge Contextual Historians', *Political Studies,* vol. 49, no 5 (2001), 851-76.

Springborg, Patricia, 'Review Article: The View from the "Divell's Mountain"': Review of Quentin Skinner, *Reason and Rhetoric in the Philosophy of Hobbes', History of Political Thought,* vol. 17, 4 (Winter 1996), pp. 615-22.

Springborg, Patricia, 'Thomas Hobbes and Cardinal Bellarmine: Leviathan and the Ghost of the Roman Empire', *History of Political Thought,* vol. 16, 4, (1995), pp. 503-31.

Springborg, Patricia, 'What can we say about History? Reinhart Koselleck and *Begriffsgeschichte',* in *Zeit, Geschichte und Politik: zum achtzigsten Geburtstag von Reinhart Koselleck,* ed. Jussi Kurunmäki and Kari Palonen (Jyväskylä, Finland, Jyväskylä University of Press, 2003), pp. 55-84.

Springborg, Patricia, 'Writing to Redundancy: Hobbes and Cluverius', *The Historical Journal,* 39, 4 (December 1996), 1075-78.

Springborg, Patricia, ed., *Cambridge Companion to Hobbes's Leviathan* (New York, Cambridge University Press, 2007).

Spurr, John, '"Latitudinarianism" and the Restoration Church', *The Historical Journal,* vol. 31, no. 1, (1988), pp. 61-82.

Spurr, John, '"Rational Religion" in Restoration England', *Journal of the History of Ideas,* vol. 49, no. 4 (1988), pp. 563-85.

Spurr, John, 'The Church of England, Comprehension and the Toleration Act of 1689, *English Historical Review,* vol. 104 (1989), pp. 927-46.

Stead, G. Christopher, '"Homoousios" dans la Pensée de Saint Athanase', in Charles Kannengiesser, ed., *Politique et Théologie chez Athanase d'Alexandrie* (Paris, Beauchesme, 1974).

Strong, Roy and Stephen Orgel, *Inigo Jones, The Theatre of the Stuart Court,* eds (Berkeley Ca., University of California Press, 1973), 2 vols.

Strong, Tracy, 'How to Write Scripture: Words, Authority, and Politics in Thomas Hobbes', *Critical Inquiry* vol. 20 (Autumn 1993), pp. 128-59.

Tachau, K. H. *Vision and Certitude in the Age of Ockham: Optics, Epistemology and the Foundations of Semantics 1250-1345* (Leiden, E.J. Brill, 1988).

Thierry, Am., *Nestorius et Eutychès* (Paris, 1878).

Tierney, Brian, *Foundations of Conciliar Theory* (Cambridge, Cambridge University Press, 1955).

Tierney, Brian, *Origins of Papal Infallibility, 1150-1350* (Leiden, E.J. Brill, 1972).

Tillich, Paul, *Christianity and the Encounter of the World Religions* (New York, Columbia University Press, 1963).

Toohey, Peter, 'Epic and Rhetoric: Speech-making and Persuasion in Homer and Apollonius', University of New England, Armidale, Australia(*http://www.cisi.unito.it/arachne/num1/toohey.html*).

Tralau, Johan, 'Leviathan the Beast of Myth: Medusa, Dionysos, and the Riddle of Hobbes's Sovereign Monster', in Patricia Springborg, ed., *Cambridge Companion to Hobbes's Leviathan* (New York, Cambridge University Press, 2007), pp. 460-77.

Tricaud, François, '"Homo homini Deus", "Homo homini Lupus": Recherche des Sources des deux formules de Hobbes', in *Hobbes-Forschungen*, ed. R. Koselleck, and R. Schnur, (Berlin, Duncker & Humblot, 1969), pp. 61-70.

Tricaud, François, 'Le vocabulaire de la passion', in *Hobbes et son vocabulaire: Etudes de lexicographie philosophique*, Yves Charles Zarka and Jean Bernhardt eds (Paris, Vrin, 1992), pp. 139-154.

Trinkaus, Charles, 'Lorenzo Valla's Anti-Aristotelian Natural Philosophy', *I Tati Studies*, 5 (1993), pp. 279-325.

Trompf, Garry W., *Early Christian Historiography: Narratives of Retributive Historiography* (London, Continuum, 2000).

Trompf, Garry W., 'On Newtonian History', in Stephen Gaukroger, ed., *The Uses of Antiquity* (Dordrecht, 1992), pp. 213-249.

Tuck, Richard, 'The Civil Religion of Thomas Hobbes', in Nicholas Phillipson and Quentin Skinner, eds, *Political Discourse in Early Modern Europe* (Cambridge, Cambridge University Press, 1993), pp. 120-38.

Tuck, Richard, *Hobbes* (Oxford, Oxford University Press, 1989).

Tuck, Richard, 'Hobbes and Locke on Toleration', in *Thomas Hobbes and Political Theory*, ed. Mary G. Dietz (Lawrence, KA, University of Kanzas Press, 1990), pp. 153-71

Tuck, Richard, *Natural Rights Theories* (Cambridge, Cambridge University Press, 1979).

Tuck, Richard, *Philosophy and Government 1572-1651* (Cambridge, Cambridge University Press, 1993).

Ullmann, Walter, *The Growth of Papal Government in the Middle Ages* (3rd ed. Cambridge, Cambridge University Press, 1970).

Ullmann, Walter, *Medieval Papalism: The Political Theories of the Medieval Canonists* (London, 1949).

Ullmann, Walter, *The Origins of the Great Schism* (London, 1948).

Vessey, Mark, 'English Translations of the Latin Fathers, 1517-1611', in
    Irena Backus, ed., *The Reception of the Church Fathers in the West,
    from the Carolingians to the Maurists* (Leiden, E.J. Brill, 1979), 2
    vols, vol. 2, pp. 775-838.
Vivanti, Corrado, 'Henry VI, the Gallic Hercules', *Journal of the
    Warburg and Courtauld Institutes*, vol. 30 (1967).
Walker, David P., *Spiritual and Demonic Magic from Ficino to Cam-
    panella* (London, Warburg Institute, 1958).
Waswo, Richard, *Language and Meaning in the Renaissance* (Princeton,
    Princeton University Press, 1987).
Waswo, Richard, 'The Reaction of Jean Luis Vives to Valla's Philosophy
    of Language', *Bibliothèque d'Humanisme et Renaissance*, vol. 42,
    no. 3 (1980), pp. 595-609.
Wilcox, Joel F., 'Ficino's Commentary on Plato's *Ion* and Chapman's
    Inspired Poet in the *Odyssey*', *Philological Quarterly*, vol. 64 (1985),
    pp. 195-209.
Willman, Robert, 'Hobbes on the Law of Heresy', *Journal of the History
    of Ideas,* vol. 31 (1970), pp. 607-13.
Wilks, Michael, 'John of Salisbury and the Tyranny of Nonsense' in
    Wilks, ed., *The World of John of Salisbury*, (Oxford, Oxford Univer-
    sity Press, 1994), pp. 263-86.
Winterbottom, M. 'Fifteenth-Century Manuscripts of Quintilian', *Clas-
    sical Quarterly*, vol. 17 (1967), pp. 339-69.
Wright, George, *Religion, Politics and Thomas Hobbes* (Dordrecht,
    Springer, 2006).
Wright, George, 'Authority and Theodicy in Hobbes's *Leviathan*: "We
    are God's Slaves"', *Rivista di storia della filosofia*, vol. 59 (2004),
    pp. 175-204.
Wright, George, 'Curley and Martinich in Dubious Battle', *Journal of
    the History of Philosophy* 40 (2002), pp. 461-76.
Wright, George, 'Hobbes and the Economic Trinity', *British Journal for
    the History of Philosophy* 7 (1999), pp. 397-428.
Wright, George, *Nuove prospettive critiche sul Leviatano di Hobbes nel
    350° anniversario di pubblicazione* (*New Critical Perspectives on
    Hobbes's* Leviathan *upon the 350th Anniversary of its Publication*),
    co-editor with Luc Foisneau; *Rivista di storia della filosofia*, vol. 59
    (2004), and published separately in Europe, Collana di filosofia
    (Milan, FrancoAngeli, 2004).
Wright, George, 'Thomas Hobbes: 1668 Appendix to *Leviathan*', *Inter-
    pretation*, vol. 18, 3 (1991), pp. 324-413.
Wright, George, 'The 1668 Appendix and Hobbes's Theological
    Project', *Cambridge Companion to Hobbes's Leviathan*, ed. Patricia

Springborg (New York, Cambridge University Press, 2007), pp. 392-411.

Yates, Frances A., *Giordano Bruno and the Hermetic Tradition* (London, Kegan Paul, 1964).

Yates, Frances A., *The Occult Philosophy in the Elizabethan Age* (London, Routledge and Kegan Paul, 1970).

Yoch, James J., 'Architecture as Virtue', *Studies in Philology*, vol. 75 (1978), pp. 422-3.

Zagorin, Perez, 'Clarendon against *Leviathan*', in Patricia Springborg, ed., *Cambridge Companion to Hobbes's Leviathan* (New York, Cambridge University Press, 2007), pp. 460-77.

Zagorin, Perez, 'Clarendon and Hobbes', *Journal of Modern History*, vol. LVII, no. 4 (1985), 593-616.

Zagorin, Perez, 'Cudworth and Hobbes on Is and Ought', *Philosophy, Science, and Religion in England 1640-1700*, ed. Richard Ashcraft, Richard Kroll, Perez Zagorin (Cambridge, Cambridge University Press, 1992).

Zagorin, Perez, 'Hobbes on Our Mind', *Journal of The History of Ideas*, vol. LI, no. 2 (1990), 317-35.

Zagorin, Perez, 'Hobbes Without Grotius', *History of Political Thought*, vol. XXI, no. 1 (2000), 16-40.

Zagorin, Perez, 'Hobbes's Early Philosophical Development', *Journal of The History of Ideas*, vol. LIV, no. 34 (1993), 505-18.

Zagorin, Perez, 'Thomas Hobbes's Departure from England in 1640: An Unpublished Letter', *Historical Journal*, vol. 21 (1978), 157-60.

Zagorin, Perez, 'Two Books on Thomas Hobbes', *Journal, of The History of Ideas*, vol. 60, no. 2 (1999), 361-71.

Zarka, Yves Charles, *La Décision métaphysique de Hobbes, Conditions de la politique* (Paris, Vrin, 1987);

Zarka, Yves Charles, 'Liberty, Necessity and Chance: Hobbes's General Theory of Events', in *British Journal for the History of Philosophy*, vol. 9, 3, 2001, pp. 425-37.

Zarka, Yves Charles, *Philosophie et politique à l'âge classique* (Paris, P.U.F., 1998).

Zarka, Yves Charles, 'Le Vocabulaire de l'apparaitre: champ sémantique de la notion de *phantasma*', in Yves Charles Zarka and Jean Bernhardt, eds, *Hobbes et son vocabulaire: Etudes de lexicographie philosophique* (Paris, Vrin, 1992), pp. 13-29.

Zarka, Yves-Charles and Jean Bernhardt, eds, *Thomas Hobbes Philosophie première, théorie de la science et politique* (Paris, P.U.F., 1990).

Zarka, Yves-Charles and Quentin Skinner, 'Actualité de Hobbes', *Le Débat*, vol. 96 (1997), pp. 108-120.

Zarka, Yves-Charles and Quentin Skinner, 'Deux interprétations de Hobbes', *Le Débat*, vol. 96 (1997), pp. 92-107.

Zwicker, Steven, *Lines of Authority: Politics and English Literary Culture 1649-1698* (Ithaca, N.Y., Cornell University Press, 1993).

INDEX OF PROPER NAMES

712

INDEX

Gregory of Nazianzus (c. 330-390), 169

Magna Biblioteca Patrum, 169

Gregory of Nyssa, Cappadocian Father, mid 3rd century, 169, 186, 373n170

Gregory II, Pope (d. 731), 170

Gregory VII, Pope 1073 to 1085 (Hildebrand), 128, 137-8, 559n634, 631-2, 639

Dicatus papae, 632

Gresham College, 58-9, 188n2

Gresham, Sir Thomas (1519-1579), London merchant, 59, 115

Gretzer, Jacob (1562-1625) Patristic scholar, 169

Grosseteste (c. 1170-1253), Bishop of Lincoln, philosopher, 232

Grotius, Hugo (1583-1645), 62, 64, 70, 102n2, 122, 171, 441, 617, 651

De Imperio Summarum Potestatum Circa (c. 1648)

Grund, Georg (fl. 1680s), Danish Diplomat, 78, 82-3, 98-9, 271-9, 293-9, 457

Guelphs, 12th century pro-papal faction in Italy, 557

Habington, William (1605-1654), poet and historian, 244

Hadot, Philip, 185

Haeresis (hairesis) sect, see heresy

Hale, Metthew (1609-1676), Lord Chief Justice of England, 111n2

Hall, John (of Durham), 67

Confusion confounded (1654)

Grounds and Reasons for Monarchy (1650)

Hannibal of Carthage (247-183 BC), 543n596

Hardwick Hall book list, 14, 81, 102n2, 117, 149, 171, 177, 186, 431n313, 551n618, 597n737

Hargreaves, see Macdonald and Hargreaves, 15, 88n1, 269-70

Harley, Robert, 1st Earl of Oxford (1661-1724)

Harpyae, Harpies, 601n751, 632*

Harrington, James (1611-77), 614

Commonwealth of Oceana 614

Prerogative of Popular Government

Hartlib, Samuel (?1600-1662), English intelligencer, 243n2, 339n82, 407n244, 483n453

Haruspex, soothsayer, 339n83, 559n636, 632*

Henrietta, Maria, Queen (1609-69) Charles I's consort, 32, 51, 243, 253n3

Henry I Duke of Swabia (= Henry III of Saxony, *q.v.*), 137

Henry II, King of England (1154-1189), 240, 483n454, 615

Henry III, King of France (1551-89), 447n353

Henry III of Saxony (1017-1056), 137, 631-2

Holy Roman Emperor (from 1046-56), 137, 521n542

Henry IV, Duke of Bavaria (= Henry III of Saxony, *q.v.*), 137-8, 559n634, 632

Henry IV, Duke of Lancaster, 112, 571nn661-2

Henry IV, King of France (1553-1610), 225n3, 447n353

Henry VIII, King of England (1491-1547), 45, 111, 117n1, 263, 529n557

Henri De Valois = Henry III of France (*q.v.*), 156n2

Hephaestos, god of fire

Heracles (Hercules), 145, 353n121

Heraclius, (610-41), monothelite Byzantine emperor, 492-3, 619, 633*, 642-3, 646

Herbert, Edward, Lord Cherbury (1582/3-1648), 70, 73-5, 93, 128, 140, 241, 243, 247, 617*

De religione gentilium, 140

TABLE OF CONTENTS

HOBBES'S HISTORIA ECCLESIASTICA: INTRODUCTION
HOBBES, HISTORY, HERESY AND THE UNIVERSITIES
(by Patricia Spingborg)

CHAPTER 1

TEXT AND CONTEXT, TEXT AND RECEPTION

CHAPTER 2

TEXT AND TIMEFRAME: MATERIAL EVIDENCE

CHAPTER 3

HOBBES AND HERESY

THE *HISTORIA ECCLESIASTICA*

Achevé d'imprimer en 2008
à Genève (Suisse)